Radical Platonism in Byzantium

Byzantium has recently attracted much attention, but principally among cultural, social and economic historians. This book shifts the focus to philosophy and intellectual history, exploring the thought-world of visionary reformer Gemistos Plethon (c. 1355–1452). It argues that Plethon brought to their fulfilment latent tendencies among Byzantine humanists towards a distinctive anti-Christian and pagan outlook. His *magnum opus*, the pagan *Nomoi*, was meant to provide an alternative to and escape route from the disputes over the Orthodoxy of Gregory Palamas and Thomism. It was also a groundbreaking reaction to the bankruptcy of a pre-existing humanist agenda and to aborted attempts at the secularisation of the State, whose cause Plethon had himself championed in his two utopian *Memoranda*. Inspired by Plato, Plethon's secular utopianism and paganism emerge as the two sides of a single coin. On another level, the book challenges anti-essentialist scholarship that views paganism and Christianity as social and cultural constructions.

NIKETAS SINIOSSOGLOU is a British Academy Post-doctoral Fellow in the Faculty of Classics and Junior Research Fellow of Wolfson College, University of Cambridge. He is the author of *Plato and Theodoret: the Christian Appropriation of Platonic Philosophy and the Hellenic Intellectual Resistance* (Cambridge, 2008).

CAMBRIDGE CLASSICAL STUDIES

General editors

R. L. HUNTER, R. G. OSBORNE, M. MILLETT, D. N. SEDLEY,
G. C. HORROCKS, S. P. OAKLEY, W. M. BEARD

RADICAL PLATONISM IN BYZANTIUM

Illumination and Utopia in Gemistos Plethon

NIKETAS SINIOSSOGLOU

CAMBRIDGE
UNIVERSITY PRESS

CAMBRIDGE
UNIVERSITY PRESS

University Printing House, Cambridge CB2 8BS, United Kingdom

Cambridge University Press is part of the University of Cambridge.

It furthers the University's mission by disseminating knowledge in the pursuit of education, learning and research at the highest international levels of excellence.

www.cambridge.org
Information on this title: www.cambridge.org/9781316629598

© Faculty of Classics, University of Cambridge 2011

First published 2011
First paperback edition 2016

A catalogue record for this publication is available from the British Library

Library of Congress Cataloguing in Publication data
Siniossoglou, Niketas.
Radical platonism in Byzantium : illumination and utopia in Gemistos Plethon / Niketas Siniossoglou.
p.   cm. – (Cambridge classical studies)
Includes bibliographical references and index.
ISBN 978-1-107-01303-2
1. Gemistus Plethon, George, 15th cent.   2. Gemistus Plethon, George, 15th cent. Nomon syngraphes ta sozomena.   I. Title.
B785.P564S56   2011
186′.4 – dc23   2011025237

ISBN 978-1-107-01303-2 Hardback
ISBN 978-1-316-62959-8 Paperback

CONTENTS

CONTENTS

Part IV: The path of Ulysses and the path of Abraham

PREFACE

The conventional way of interpreting philosophical texts and ideas is within heuristic frameworks defined by the well-established criterion of periodisation. Ancient philosophy is considered within the borders of its own context and so are medieval, modern and contemporary philosophy. But there is another way *to do* history of philosophy: explore the development of notions and conceptual shifts spanning particular time periods and socio-cultural contexts. This means to focus on the recurrent manifestation and transformation of key ideas within shifting networks of meaning, rather than the more restricted study of individual authors and texts.

Two opposed ideas, or rather existential positions, run through the history of Western thought and resurface in various forms and manifestations. One is that man may apprehend god/truth by means of his own natural disposition and faculties. This is the belief that social and epistemic truths are cognisable, that man may access the ultimate foundation of reality by utilising inherent intellectual gifts. This entails man's being actually or potentially capable of attaining godlikeness or moral perfection, and of realising or approximating a perfectly just *politeia*. This conviction about human perfectibility has its roots in one interpretation of Plato's epistemology and political philosophy (see for example *Republic* 532a–b; *Timaeus* 90b–d) and became the hallmark of the philosophy of the Enlightenment and the project of modernity.

There is a contrary position, which appears in various guises: any philosophical, religious or political project claiming to access truth by investing unlimited confidence in human powers is destined to degenerate into either intellectual hubris/sin, or totalitarianism, or both. This persuasion is commonly associated with the Judaeo-Christian world-view that acknowledges the limitations of human nature and prioritises divine revelation. Godlikeness becomes an issue of spiritual illumination, grace and experiential, rather than cognitive, contact with god/truth. Consequently, it is not the reification within history of any secular utopia but the return to a spiritual homeland that emerges as the desired and feasible end. There is a caveat. Often the polarity between these existential positions can be nuanced or even diminished; for example, Friedrich Nietzsche attacked Platonic optimism and utopianism, while also hammering Judaeo-Christian aspirations. As he saw it, both are offspring of a single error, namely man's fallacious tendency to idolise or make an absolute of concepts, be it the Idea of the Good or god. This said, a case can be made that from the viewpoint of the history of ideas the tension between a primarily pagan/modern and a Judaeo-Christian position refers to antagonistic ideal-types or paradigms and, moreover, that this tension broadly construed signifies an unresolved schism deep within Western intellectual identity.

This book explores the clash between these two blueprint ideas of thinking about man, god, the world and *politeia* in a crucial, albeit under-studied, period: the late Byzantine fourteenth and fifteenth centuries. It focuses on an unconventional man whose enduring legacy appears to have developed underground: Georgios Gemistos Plethon. Often considered among the founders of modern esotericism, Plethon continuously stimulated the interest of uneasy spirits ranging from Marsilio Ficino, Thomas More and John Dee to Giacomo Leopardi and Ezra Pound. This book argues that Plethon's radical Platonism exemplifies the pagan origins of modern epistemological optimism and utopianism. But it also deals with the process that led into Plethon's philosophical and political radicalism. Part of the background is the intellectual civil war that erupted between the Roman Orthodox theology of Gregory Palamas and Byzantine humanism in the fourteenth century, though the beginnings of the confrontation were much earlier. (In this book the term 'Roman Orthodox' is used more or less interchangeably with the anachronistic modern coinage 'Byzantine'. The Byzantines defined themselves as Romans of the Eastern Empire. See p. 4, n. 8.)

My primary interest has been to bring to light two alternative intellectual constellations, two competing world-views that transcend conventional periodisation in the history of philosophy. To be sure, the pagan Platonic paradigm represented by Plethon clashed with Christianity (Hesychast and Thomist) in a particular historical context. Still, the philosophical hallmarks of each have deep roots in the pagan–Christian confrontation in late antiquity and extensions into modernity. Plethon's pagan Platonism and the Christian Orthodoxy of his time are manifestations of trans-historical paradigms, which issue in philosophically irreconcilable intellectual and spiritual identities assumed by different agents throughout the history of ideas.

In this regard, I believe that it is time to abandon the anti-essentialist or anti-foundationalist (in reality relativist) methodological approaches that blur the boundaries between Hellenism and Christianity, and to return to a realist perspective.

This does not necessarily amount to the hypostatisation or reification of Hellenism and Christianity. Max Weber warned against the danger of seeing ideas as a 'true' reality, which ostensibly operates outside history. The 'pagan' Platonic ideal-type is a mental construct that embraces a set of metaphysical, theological, moral and hermeneutical views, inclinations and contentions, some of which may be absent from Proclus, while present in Plethon – or vice versa. Historical descriptions and ideal-types such as Platonism and Christianity do not strictly or necessarily contain the same conceptual contents in all their manifestations. They are causal schemata referring to existential positions. Thus, I do not contend that pagan or Christian ideal-types are ahistorical. However, they can, and in my view should, be seen as referring to real modes of being, even if they are never fully exemplified or exhausted within social and cultural phenomena.

Christian theologians, philosophers and intellectuals in late antiquity and Byzantium certainly thought about Christianity and Hellenism in realist terms: as possessing an essential core or inalienable meaning. To study these essentialist world-views and the texts in which they are contained by adopting a relativist non-essentialist standpoint, as is commonly done in recent scholarship, means never to take Christian intellectuals, philosophical pagans and other intellectuals at their word, to assume, in effect, that they were not the persons they thought themselves to be. The intellectual and religious identities which Christians such as Gregory of Nyssa and Gregory Palamas or pagans such as Proclus and Plethon gave themselves should not be thought of as unreal and should not be dissolved into constantly shifting, impersonal collective discourses.

This book was written in Cambridge. I am grateful to the British Academy for the award of a post-doctoral fellowship and to the Faculty of Classics, University of Cambridge, for hosting this project. I am indebted in many different ways to Malcolm Schofield and David Sedley for their encouragement and feedback. Anthony Kaldellis read an early draft of this book and made incisive comments of rare acuteness. Dr Constantin Macris provided excellent feedback at the closing stages. Thanks are due to Michael Sharp and Jan Chapman for expert advice and valuable assistance in preparing this manuscript for publication. Finally, I am grateful to Peter Garnsey for initially encouraging me to work on Plethon and for his intellectual and personal support over the years.

This book is for my friends.

ABBREVIATIONS

The abbreviations used for ancient and late antique sources conform to those in LSJ, the *OCD* and Lampe, *PGL*. Abbreviations of journal titles correspond to those used in *L'Année Philologique*. Other abbreviations used are listed below. Full bibliographical details are given only for those editions of texts and reference works not listed in the bibliography of primary sources.

Alexandre	C. Alexandre (ed.), *Pléthon: Traité des lois*, French trans. A. Pellissier, Paris 1858 (reprinted Amsterdam 1966)
Apomn.	V. Laurent (ed.), *Les 'Mémoires' du grand ecclésiarque de l'Église de Constantinople Sylvestre Syropoulos sur le concile de Florence (1438–1439)*, Rome 1971
Basilica	H. J. Scheltema and N. van der Wal (eds.), *Basilicorum libri LX*, 8 vols., Groningen 1955–88
BG	J.-A. Fabricius (ed.), *Bibliotheca Graeca*, vol. XII, Hamburg 1809
CAG	*Commentaria in Aristotelem Graeca*, Berlin 1882–1909
CHC	M. Angold (ed.), *The Cambridge History of Christianity*, vol. v: *Eastern Christianity*, Cambridge 2006
CJ	*Codex Justinianus*
DHGE	M. Baudrillart *et al.* (eds.), *Dictionnaire d'histoire et de géographie ecclésiastiques*, Paris 1912–
DK	H. Diels and W. Kranz (eds.), *Die Fragmente der Vorsokratiker*, 3 vols., 6th edn, Berlin 1951–2

DOP	*Dumbarton Oaks Papers*, Washington, DC 1941–
HAB	S. S. Horujy (ed.), *Hesychasm: an Annotated Bibliography*, Moscow 2004
Lampe, *PGL*	G. W. H. Lampe (ed.), *A Patristic Greek Lexicon*, Oxford 1961–8
Lampros, *PP*	Sp. Lampros (ed.), Παλαιολόγεια καὶ Πελοποννησιακά, 4 vols., Athens 1912–30
LS	A. A. Long and D. N. Sedley (eds.), *The Hellenistic Philosophers*, vol. I, Cambridge 1987
LSJ	H. G. Liddell, R. Scott, H. S. Jones *et al.*, *A Greek–English Lexicon*, 9th edn, Oxford 1996
MB	K. N. Sathas (ed.), Μεσαιωνικὴ Βιβλιοθήκη, 7 vols., Venice 1872–94
Mohler III	L. Mohler, *Aus Bessarions Gelehrtenkreis: Abhandlungen, Reden, Briefe von Bessarion, Theodoros Gazes, Michael Apostolios, Andronikos Kallistos, Georgios Trapezuntios, Niccolò Perotti, Niccolò Capranica*, Paderborn 1942
Notizie	G. Mercati (ed.), *Notizie di Procoro e Demetrio Cidone, Manuele Caleca e Teodoro Meliteniota: ed altri appunti per la storia della teologia e della letteratura bizantina del secolo XIV*, Rome 1931
OC	L. Petit, X. Siderides and M. Jugie (eds.), *Œuvres complètes de George Scholarios*, 8 vols., Paris 1928–36
OCD	S. Hornblower and A. Spawforth (eds.), *The Oxford Classical Dictionary*, 3rd rev. edition, Oxford 2003
ODB	A. Kazhdan *et al.* (ed.), *Oxford Dictionary of Byzantium*, Oxford 1991
Petit, *Documents*	L. Petit (ed.), *Documents relatifs au concile de Florence*, vol. II: *Œuvres*

	anticonciliaires de Marc d'Éphèse, PO
	17.2, Paris 1923
PG	J. P. Migne (ed.), *Patrologiae Cursus*
	Completus: Series Graeca, Paris 1857–66
PLP	E. Trapp *et al.*, *Prosopographisches*
	Lexikon der Palaiologenzeit, 15 vols.,
	Vienna 1976–96
PO	R. Graffin and F. Nau (eds.), *Patrologia*
	Orientalis, Paris, Turnhout 1903–
PS	P. Chrestou *et al.* (eds.), *Γρηγορίου τοῦ*
	Παλαμᾶ, Συγγράμματα, Thessaloniki
	1962–
Synodicon	J. Gouillard (ed.), 'Le Synodicon de
	l'Orthodoxie. Éd. et commentaire',
	T&MByz 2 (1967): 1–316
TBT	C. G. Conticello and V. Conticello (eds.),
	La théologie byzantine et sa tradition, vol.
	II: *XIIIe–XIXe s.*, Turnhout 2002
TLG	*Thesaurus Linguae Graecae*
Tomus I, II, III	*Tomi synodici tres in causa Palamitarum*
	(*Tomus I: Contra Barlaam et Acindynum*;
	Tomus II: Contra Prochorum Cydonium;
	Tomus III: Contra Barlaamitas et
	Acindynianos) *PG* 151.679–774

Works by Plethon are abbreviated as follows:

Contra Lat.	*Contra De dogmate Latino librum*
Contra Schol.	*Contra Scholarii pro Aristotele obiectiones*
Diff.	*De differentiis* (*Περὶ ὧν Ἀριστοτέλης πρὸς*
	Πλάτωνα διαφέρεται)
Mem. I	*Consilium ad despotam Theodorum de*
	Peloponneso
Mem. II	*Oratio ad Manuelem Palaeologum de rebus*
	in Peloponneso
Nomoi	*Book of Laws* (*Νόμων Συγγραφή*)
Orac.	*Commentary on the Chaldean Oracles*
	(*Μαγικὰ λόγια τῶν ἀπὸ Ζωροάστρου*
	μάγων)

Recapitulation	Recapitulation of Zoroastrian and Platonic Doctrines (Ζωροαστρείων τε καὶ Πλατωνικῶν δογμάτων συγκεφαλαίωσις)
Reply	Reply to Certain Questions (Πρὸς ἠρωτημένα ἄττα ἀπόκρισις)

Works by Scholarios are abbreviated as follows:

Ad Pleth.	Ad Gemistum Plethonem de libro suo contra Latinos (OC 4.118–51)
Contra Pleth.	Contra Plethonis ignorationem de Aristotele (OC 4.1–116)
Ad exarchum Josephum	Ad exarchum Josephum de Gemisti Plethonis libro et contra multorum deorum cultum (OC 4.155–72)
Ad principessam Pelop.	Ad principessam Peloponnesi de Gemisti Plethonis Tractatu de legibus (OC 4.151–5)
Against Polytheists	Tractatus de uno deo et contra quos qui deum esse negant et multos deos colunt (OC 4.172–89)

Translations of Platonic passages are from *Plato: Complete Works*, ed. J. M. Cooper and D. S. Hutchinson (Indianapolis 1997). Individual translators are acknowledged in the notes. Occasionally I have made use of and modified the English translations of Plethon's texts by Charles Woodhouse and George Finley.

INTRODUCTION

Plethon and the notion of paganism

Plato's escape from Athos

In November 1382 the maverick Manuel Palaiologos (1350–1425), future emperor of the Byzantine Empire, defied the policy of his father, Emperor John V, and devoted all his energy to the cause of defending Thessaloniki against the Turks. The young Manuel waged war and defended the city for no less than four and a half years. His mentor at the time was Demetrios Kydones (c. 1323–1397/8), translator of Aquinas, statesman and diplomat, Platonising philosopher and critic of the Orthodox establishment, a key man in late Byzantine intellectual history and among the first to sound the alarm when the Ottoman forces occupied Gallipoli (Kallipolis), their first city in Europe. In the middle of these dramatic circumstances Manuel and Kydones exchanged letters, one of which concerned an intriguing topic: the need to bring Plato back to life.

Kydones persistently asked Manuel to send him a manuscript held in Mount Athos. In Manuel's witty letter from Thessaloniki a *Plato redivivus* appears grateful finally to flee from Athos to Constantinople. Among the monks Plato was like a corpse, says Manuel. Kydones is the man who will redeem the philosopher from the hands of these monks to whom he does not belong (ἀνάρμοστος):

What you were so fondly requesting you have, your Plato. But we like to think that there is nothing strange in presenting the man as a gift to you. Actually, he has just as much reason to express his gratitude to us as you do on receiving him, that is, if one subscribes to his teaching that a living thing is better than a non-living thing. Now, something which does not move or act or speak could never be properly called alive in any sense at all. This, in fact, has been his condition for many years, since he did not fit in with the monks, who have long ago renounced worldly wisdom. But you now bring him to life and make him active again, and it is I who am the cause of this. (Manuel Pal. *Ep.* 3.1–9; trans. Dennis)

Oddly then, amidst military turmoil and eschatological scenarios regarding the collapse of an empire, the future emperor is concerned with the revival of Plato. But Kydones' reply is even more intriguing. That letter, he writes, was like a dream in which he met a Plato brought back to life, moving and talking, in fact resurrected through Manuel's words.[1] Kydones has no trust in the monks either. Here they are compared to the tyrant Dionysius of Syracuse, the man who sold off Plato, and Manuel is urged to redeem the son of Ariston. Kydones concludes with a significant sentence: apparently there *are* people ready to welcome a revived Plato and to listen attentively to what he would have to say:

By god, translate words into deeds and hasten to liberate the son of Ariston [Plato] from many Dionysiuses. *For Athos is certainly not treating him more gently now than did Sicily, and perhaps they intend to sell him twice as the tyrant did* ... Now, if you approach them [the monks] in a mild manner, they will call the transaction a sacrilege and will feign indignation. But if it is the emperor who demands it, and they realize there is no refusing, then you will see these men, who are now intransigent, giving in and thanking you for having asked. Only be insistent with these men, and you will soon have us see this old man [Plato] crossing not only Charybdis, but also the Aegean, and easily return to Athens, *among men who are his friends and are in a position to understand what he is saying.* (Dem. Kyd. *Ep.* 276.19–31)[2]

Kydones is precise. The time is ripe for Plato's voice to be heard again. To this end, political authority should be used in order to liberate Plato from certain men who are unfit to understand philosophy, unfriendly towards imperial sovereignty and who obviously do not think much of ancient philosophy. Kydones finally received his Plato. Regretfully the manuscript was in a horrible state.[3] This truly shocked him and brought tears to his eyes. And

---

[1] Dem. Kyd. *Ep.* 276.5–15 Loenertz: καὶ σὺ τὸν πάλαι κείμενον τοῖς λόγοις ἀνέστησας.

[2] Trans. Dennis in n. 2 to Manuel Pal. *Ep.* 3, with modifications. For the background to these letters see also Tinnefeld (2005)182–3.

[3] The book arrived 'all soaked through, all torn, the outside in disarray, the inside shrunk, dark stains all over, and in such a state that you would never have recognised it' (Dem. Kyd. *Ep.* 259.1–8).

yet Kydones was deeply appreciative of the efforts of his student. Apparently Manuel 'promised his friendship if they [the monks] gave it to him and threatened with his enmity if they refused; finally, just to do me a favour, he endured dangers'.[4] It is thus how the son of Ariston was saved 'for us' and escaped 'prison and fetters and tyrants (εἱρκτὴν καὶ δεσμὰ καὶ τυράννους)', albeit bearing clear marks of his misadventures.

One wonders: how could some monks be so powerful as to cause such trouble to a future emperor and to a star of the Byzantine intellectual firmament? Chapter 2 deals with the intellectual and religious identity of these people. Here it is sufficient to recall Sathas. Writing of Psellos' unhappy sojourn in a monastery in Bithynia, Sathas observes that the son of Ariston was occasionally seen as the 'Greek Satan', whose name was enough to make monks spit on the ground and recite averting prayers.[5] Significantly, Kydones' epistle to Manuel affirms that not only in Psellos' time, but in late Byzantium too, there were *others*, eager to listen attentively to Plato's voice.

At the same time as Manuel agreed with Kydones that Plato deserved better than being left in the company of the monks of Mount Athos, Georgios Gemistos, the man who would soon achieve notoriety under the cognomen Plethon, was in his late twenties. Perhaps Kydones had already made the acquaintance of the young philosopher, or he was just about to. Either way, he could hardly imagine how far that young man would go in the direction of bringing Plato back to life. Plethon is the man who actually took the endeavour of resurrecting Platonic philosophy to its extreme consequences.

It appears that Demetrios Kydones was one of Plethon's early instructors in the study of Platonism. In an epistle to Bessarion, Plethon mentions the 'wise Kydones' as the man who showed him sometime in the past the complexity of Plato's mathematics in Book 8 of the *Republic*.[6] Plethon's knowledge of Aquinas

---

[4] Dem. Kyd. *Ep.* 293.58–60.   [5] *MB* vol. IV, lxviii.

[6] Cf. Pleth *Ep. Bess.* 2, Mohler III 467.15–22; *Resp.* 546b–c; Woodhouse (1986) 22; Baloglou (1998: 25) suggests that around 1390 Plethon was a student of Kydones.

strengthens the assumption of an early association with Kydones and his circle.[7] Further, we shall see that Demetrios' political views anticipate Plethon's model of sovereignty. One may reasonably infer that the young Plethon studied by the side of the established famous teacher of philosophy, though we do not know for how long and under what circumstances.

Plethon's relation to Manuel is clearer. Plethon was one of the chief intellectuals and advisors appointed to Manuel's court in Mistra from early on and enjoyed the full support of the future Roman Orthodox emperor.[8] Plethon was aware of Manuel's philosophical and political merits. He might have been aware too that Kydones had already discerned in that charismatic young man the personification of Plato's philosopher-king.[9]

A few decades after the incident involving the manuscript of Plato, Plethon repeated Kydones' advice and asked Manuel to impose his authority upon 'these men'. This time there was more at stake than a nice Plato manuscript to be enjoyed by elitist circles: the salvation of the Peloponnese from Ottoman occupation. Still, here too Plato is at the centre. In two *Memoranda* addressed respectively to Despot Theodore (*Consilium ad despotam Theodorum*, c. 1416) and Manuel (*Oratio ad Manuelem Palaeologum, c.* 1418) Plethon conveyed a radical socio-political reformist plan, one that was largely inspired by Plato and is suggestive of modern utopianism.

Manuel does not appear to have considered implementing his advisor's ideas. Plethon was not disillusioned. He continued to experiment with the spirit of Platonism, though in other ways. Since the publication of the seminal book on Plethon, François Masai's *Pléthon et le Platonisme de Mistra*, the predominant opinion is that Plethon was the founder of a pagan cell or

---

[7] On Demetrios Kydones see Ryder (2010) 5–128; Tinnefeld (1981) 4–74. On Plethon and Thomism see Demetracopoulos (2004); (2006) 276–341.

[8] In this book the term 'Roman Orthodox' is used interchangeably with the established yet misleading term 'Byzantine'. The terms 'Byzantium' and 'Byzantine' would be meaningless to 'Byzantines'. The latter were the Romans of the Eastern Empire and they defined themselves as such. The modern coinage 'Byzantium' retrospectively designates *Romania*. See here Kaldellis (2007a) 47. Current scholarship is slowly moving towards a terminological revision. See, for example, Bryer (2009) on the 'Roman Orthodox world (1393–1492)'.

[9] On the personality and life of Manuel see the classic study by Barker (1969).

brotherhood (φρατρία) operating in Mistra.[10] Plethon's magnum opus, the *Nomoi*, inspired by Plato's *Laws*, contains the constitution for a utopian pagan city-state.[11] The surviving fragments do not contain any appeal to imperial authorities, as do the two *Memoranda*. Nor do civil structures assume any role in the realisation of this new reformist programme. Instead, Plethon appears to have gone underground, turning to sectarianism as the proper vehicle for the spiritual and political regeneration of mankind. The *Nomoi* suggests that metaphysical as well as social-political truths are the business of an enlightened pagan cell or brotherhood rather than of established institutions. The *Nomoi* was cast into the fire and partially destroyed by Plethon's dogged adversary, Georgios Gennadios Scholarios, the first Roman Orthodox patriarch under Ottoman rule. It has been argued that one version of another key work by Plethon, the idiosyncratic recension of and commentary on the Platonising *Chaldean Oracles*, was also part of the notorious manuscript, and that so was the short treatise *Recapitulation of Zoroastrian and Platonic Doctrines*.[12]

Explaining his decision to destroy the *Nomoi* Scholarios observes that Plethon is an *apostate* who departed 'from all Christians' in extending his study of Hellenism beyond the level of *lexis* and *phone*, in effect seeking in Hellenism much more than the

---

[10] The term *phratria* was used by Plethon's opponent Scholarios. However, in *Nomoi* Plethon refers to his 'brothers' (*phratores*). See below, p. 390. Masai (1956: 300–14) considers John Argyropoulos, Bessarion, Michael Apostoles, Raoul Kabakes and other *literati* who later took up important roles in Italy as members of Plethon's sect. A pioneer scholar of Plethon, Fritz Schultze, was one of the first to have made a strong case for a pagan 'Sekt' and 'Bund' led by Plethon. See here Schultze (1874) 53–5.

[11] The *Nomoi* originally comprised three books and 101 chapters. According to the table of contents Book 1 contained 31 chapters, Book 2 had 27 chapters and Book 3 had 43 chapters. The last chapter is entitled 'Epinomis' after the work attributed to Plato. Chapter 6 from Book 2 on the notion of *heimarmene* was circulated independently during Plethon's lifetime (*De fato*). Of the original 101 chapters only 21 survive. They extend to 130 pages in the edition of Charles Alexandre. Scholarios wrote that it took him four hours to go through the whole book (Schol. *Ad exarchum Josephum, OC* 4.160.4–5: ἐν ὥραις τέτταρσιν ὅλαις, ἐλαχίστῳ μιᾶς ἡμέρας μορίῳ, τὸ βιβλίον ἅπαν ἐπήλθομεν). On what this information might mean with regard to the original extent of the book and some speculations regarding the relation between the surviving Greek text and the original, see Monfasani (1992) 49–51.

[12] See the introduction by Tambrun to her edition of the *Oracles chaldaïques*, xiii; Tardieu (1980) 54. On the destruction of the *Nomoi* see below, Ch. 3.

aesthetic beauty of words: that is to say, spiritual guidance.[13] Other powerful Orthodox rhetors and intellectuals also wrote invectives against Plethon. But Scholarios remains his first and philosophically as well as theologically better-equipped enemy.[14]

The *Nomoi* affair was not the first clash between Scholarios and Plethon; rather, that took place following Plethon's seminal lectures *On the Differences between Plato and Aristotle* delivered in Florence in 1439. The call for a new reading of Plato and the attack on Aristotle in the *Differences* initiated a lively and long-standing debate regarding the relation between Plato's and Aristotle's philosophy that has been seen as announcing the end of the medieval theologico-philosophical epoch and the rise of a new way to do philosophy.[15] This has numerous phases. The first involves Plethon's work of 1439, Scholarios' reply *Against Plethon* compiled in or before 1444/5 and Plethon's counter-attack *Against Scholarios* of around 1449.[16] Italian Renaissance philosophers and Greeks in exile took up the task of continuing the debate on the merits and shortcomings of Platonism and Aristotelianism. The stars of this second phase are Plethon's most illustrious student, Cardinal Bessarion, arguing against the 'calumniators' of Plato, and George of Trebizond arguing for Aristotle, against Plethon, and generally against all φιλοζοφοῦντες or *philotenebrae*

---

[13] Cf. Schol. *Ad principessam Pelop.*, *OC* 4.152.30–2; *Ad exarchum Josephum*, *OC* 4.160.25–35, 162.30. Matthew Kamariotes, *Contra Pleth.* 2 Reimarus also considers Plethon as an *apostate*. For the meaning of this accusation and the 'Plethon affair' in general see below, pp. 141, 146.

[14] The most detailed and nuanced study on Scholarios is by Blanchet (2008). Good recent scholarly work on his life and times include Tinnefeld (2002) 477–541 (with extensive bibliography on pages 536–41) and Livanos (2006) 9–69; Zeses (1988) provides a zealotic and enthusiastic portrait of Scholarios from the viewpoint of Eastern Orthodoxy.

[15] Couloubaritsis (2006) 143. In the epilogue to this book I argue that this interpretation is only partly correct: the Renaissance philosophers did not really follow up Plethon's call to liberate Plato and Aristotle from the clerical hegemony of discourse. This move took place only during the early modern reaction to Renaissance theology. The *Differences* attracted from early on the interest of scholars; cf. Gass (1844) and J. W. Taylor (1921). Important studies on this text include Lagarde (1976) and Bargeliotes (1980).

[16] Scholarios wrote his reply after Constantine Palaiologos, at the time despot of Mistra, urged him to respond to the *Differences*. But Scholarios did not address the work to Plethon but rather to the latter's student, the major Orthodox theologian and fervent anti-unionist Mark Eugenikos. In his turn, Plethon addressed his reply to Constantine and not to Scholarios. For the dating see Tinnefeld (2002) 482 n. 37, 484, 488. Woodhouse (1986: 283–307) provides a good summary of Plethon's *Against Scholarios* in English.

Platonists.[17] One of Plethon's later adversaries, Theodore of Gaza, Plethon's student Michael Apostoles and Andronikos Kallistos participated in another heated debate stirred by the criticism of Aristotle's notion of substance in the *Differences* and Bessarion's inflammatory remarks.[18] Apparently Plethon's version of Platonism earned him fervent enemies. But Plethon was also fortunate to have dear friends. Inspired by the epitaph Speusippus devoted to Plato ('the earth holds in its bosom this, the body of Plato, but his soul is equal in rank to the blessed gods'),[19] the following *distichon* written by Cardinal Bessarion to honour his teacher encapsulates the admiration and respect that Plethon stirred among many of his contemporaries and students:

Γαῖαν σώματι, ψυχῇ δ' ἄστρα Γεώργιος ἴσχει
Παντοίης σοφίης σεμνότατον τέμενος.

Georgios holds fast the earth with his body, the stars with his soul,
Most venerable temple of all kinds of wisdom.[20]

Bessarion's verses intend to convey a sense of stability, firmness and steadiness. This sharply contrasts with the hazy image of Plethon in modern bibliography. According to the latter, almost everything about Plethon is either arbitrary or elusive: the exact date and place of Georgios Gemistos' birth;[21] his formative years and especially the purported sojourn in the Ottoman court, for some a peculiar place to study, for others an excellent choice for cutting-edge studies in the occult, interfaith discourse, medicine and philosophy; the role of a mysterious instructor, Elissaios, described by Scholarios as an Aristotelian Jew of Zoroastrian

---

[17] See here Hankins (1990) 193–263; Monfasani (1976) 201–29; Todt (2006) 149–68; Schulz (1999) 22–32. But see Mohler's note ad loc. on Bessarion's eclectic tendencies in the short treatise *Adversus Plethonem de Substantia* (Mohler III 148–50). See also Monfasani (2002) on the background of the Plato–Aristotle controversy and the role of Ficino.

[18] Mohler III 148–203.

[19] Speus. fr. 87b Tarán; *Anth. Pal.* 16.31 (trans. Paton); see Irmscher (1994) 188.

[20] Mohler III 469; Fabricius, *BG* 102; Schultze (1874) 108.

[21] Plethon was born between 1355 and 1360; on Plethon's life and times see the good recent account by Neri (2010) 15–196; Woodhouse (1986); W. Blum (1988) 1–6; Tambrun (2006a) 35–51. For Plethon's works see Neri (2010) 196–225.

background and polytheist inclinations;[22] the possibility that
Plethon echoes the philosophy of the Persian mystic Suhrawardi[23]
and that he was acquainted with Ottoman mystics and reformers such as al-Bistami and Sheikh Bedreddin; the real meaning
of the cognomen 'Plethon';[24] the evidence that Gemistos served
as a judge;[25] the nature of his notorious paganism; the date and
the circumstances under which Gennadios Scholarios committed
Plethon's manuscript to the flames.[26]

Mystery also surrounds Plethon's reasons for opposing the union
of the Churches in the Ferrara/Florence Council of 1438/9; his
influence upon Greek and Italian contemporaries and his role as
mentor of Greek émigré intellectuals such as Demetrios Raoul
Kabakes and Cardinal Bessarion; the transmission of his Platonism among Renaissance intellectuals such as Ficino and Pico della
Mirandola;[27] the likely 'cultural translation' of his paganism into

---

[22] On Plethon's sojourn in Ottoman territory, the identity of Elissaios, and the analogies
between his reformism and the radical Islamic mystical and revolutionary movement of
Sheikh Bedreddin, cf. Siniossoglou (2012); Gardette (2007c).

[23] For a concise statement of the alleged link between the *Oracles*, Zoroaster, Suhrawardi
and the Persian Magi see Tambrun (2006b). The thesis has been criticised by Hladký
(2009) and (forthcoming). See also Siniossoglou (2012).

[24] Scholarios (*Ad exarchum Josephum, OC* 4.160.25–32) notes the shift from 'Gemistos'
to 'Plethon'. According to Matthew Kamariotes (*Contra Pleth.* 2 Reimarus), Plethon's
intention to purify Hellenism is already evident in this metonymy: 'Plethon' is the purist
version of the demotic 'Gemistos' (ἑλληνικώτερον δῆθεν). See also Ellissen (1860) 2–
3. On the other hand, Plethon's follower Michael Apostoles hints at the resemblance
between 'Plethon' and 'Plato' (see here Masai 1956: 384): αὐτός . . . ἑταῖρος Πλάτωνι
καὶ ὁμώνυμος. Manuel Corinthios, Bessarion, George of Trebizond and Marsilio Ficino
popularised the idea that 'Plethon' is a symbolic reference to Plato. See Fabricius, *BG*
85–6 for an early treatment of this issue, and Zakythinos (1975) 322 n. 2.

[25] The evidence comes from the monody composed by the monk Gregory (Μονῳδία τῷ
σοφῷ διδασκάλῳ Γεμιστῷ, *PG* 160.817), where Plethon is called 'protector of the
laws of our fathers' and 'protector of the court of the Hellenes' (*PG* 160.817). See also
Hieronymos Charitonymos, *Encomium Plethonis, PG* 160.807c.

[26] On the latter issue see Monfasani (2005).

[27] The recurring story (for others just a Ficinean legend) has it that the 1439 Plethonean
lectures on the differences between Plato and Aristotle at the house of Cardinal Cesarini
inspired Cosimo de Medici to create the Florentine Academy and focus on a long-term
Hermetico-Platonic project. The evidence is contained in Ficino's preface complementing his 1492 translation of Plotinus (Neri 2010: 255–61; P. R. Blum 2010: 96, 106–7;
Monfasani 2002: 197). Its interpretation has caused fierce debates among scholars. For
the traditional view that Plethon might have inspired Cosimo de Medici's foundation of
the Academy of Florence see e.g. *ODB* III s.v. 'Plethon'; Masai (1956) 327ff.; Irmscher
(1994) 190. But see also the criticism of Maillard (2008: 68–85) and Monfasani (2002:
184–5), who notes that 'Ficino was harshly critical of Plethon.' See also Pagani (2008)
4 n. 1, 11 n. 15. On Plethon and the Italian humanists see P. R. Blum (2010) 107–8 and

the anti-feudal and anti-papal outlook of Sigismondo Malatesta, the pagan tendencies of Cyriaco d'Ancona and the pagan hymns of Marullus Tarcaniota; the influence exercised upon the *Utopia* of Thomas More.[28] One cannot even be absolutely certain whether or not we have a portrait of Plethon, though scholars believe they have identified him in different paintings.[29] Even his tomb is full of ambiguity. As Johannes Irmscher noted, the intellectual 'bipolarity' of Plethon's life is symbolically represented in the peculiar pagan-Christian icons and ornaments of the Tempio Malatestiano in Rimini, where Sigismundo Malatesta, another man accused of paganism, transferred Plethon's remains from Sparta in 1465. As for these remains, it seems that they were wrapped in a piece of red barathea that immediately dissolved when, in 1756, the sarcophagus was opened.[30]

To all appearances it is difficult to grasp Plethon, either as a subject for biography, or from the viewpoint of intellectual history. As time goes by more questions than answers are added to an already long list. Contrary to ordinary expectations, the rise in scholarly interest has proved unable conclusively to dissolve the

(2004) 162–72; Gentile (1994) 813–32. Recently, Tambrun (2010: 642–7) connected Plethon's attribution of the *Chaldean Oracles* to the Magi with the *Compagnia de' Magi*, the fraternity maintained by the Medicis, and Cosimo's decision to have Plato translated. According to this view, Cosimo saw the translation of Plato as the vehicle to get to the most ancient wisdom of the Magi. On Plethon and Renaissance philosophy cf. Tambrun (2006a); P. R. Blum (2004); Couloubaritsis (2006) 143. Perhaps the first to comment on Plethon's impact on the Latins is Hieronymos Charitonymos in his *Encomium Plethonis*, PG 160.807C–D: τούτου τὴν σοφίαν Ἕλληνες ὁμοῦ τε καὶ βάρβαροι διὰ θαύματος ἦγον. Another view is that Plethon influenced the occult interests of Ficino – a theory taken up by G. R. S. Mead and Ezra Pound (see here Tryphonopoulos 1992: 138–42). It has been argued that Plethon is the man who essentially introduced Strabo to the West. See Hunger (1978) 511 and Anastos (1952) 1–18.

28 On the links between Cyriaco, Malatesta and Plethon see Neri (2010) 126–8, 226–41 and Ronchey (2003). Raoul Kabakes ended up in Italy and his son, Manilius Cabacius Rhallis, might well have influenced the paganism of Marullus Tarcaniota. See Zakythinos (1975) 376: 'Michel Marulle Tarchaniote est en effet le dernier et le plus brillant représentant du mouvement païen qui rattache à Mistra, non par Pléthon, mais par Démétrius Raoul Kavakès.' On the question of neopaganism in the hymns of Marullus see Kidwell (1989) 199–200. On Plethon and Thomas More see Ch. 7, pp. 335–8, 386. On various aspects of the reception of Plethon's ideas and work cf. W. Blum (2005); Baloglou (1998) 78, 89–114; Knös (1950); Argyropoulos (1982); Neri (2010) 226–91.

29 See here Neri (2010) 256; Seitter (2005) 131–42; Berger (2006) 85; Ronchey (2006) and the introduction by Moreno Neri to his edition of the *Differences*, 10–12.

30 See Berger (2006: 89), who refers to Ricci (1924) 291–2. Berger notes that according to one account the skull was unusually big – indeed a strange parallel to the names 'Plethon' and 'Gemistos'.

smokescreen covering the life and times of Plethon and establish the *Sitz im Leben* of his work.[31] Plethon seems to become more and more elusive.

For example, recently doubts were expressed whether Plethon really died in 1452, that is to say, whether he was fortunate enough to have been spared witnessing the fall of Constantinople in 1453, as the 'apocryphal' tradition has it and as is commonly held.[32] What is more, the apparent conflict between Plethon's self-professed Orthodoxy, openly propagated in the Synod of Ferrara/Florence, and the explicit paganism of the *Nomoi*, which appears to be corroborated by what his enemies reported about him, presents us with a riddle. Recently, this led to renewed doubts

[31] The revival of international scholarly interest in Plethon is in itself an interesting phenomenon. It is reflected in a series of recently completed and ongoing research projects and in publications in diverse languages: Smarnakis (forthcoming); Hladký (forthcoming); Raszewsky (forthcoming); Neri (2010); Garnsey (2009); Hanegraaff (2009); Pagani (2006); (2008); (2009); Tambrun (2006a); Matula (2008); W. Blum and Seitter (2005). New editions and translations of Plethon's works are in preparation.

[32] Some problems with the 'apocryphal' tradition regarding Plethon's death were first noted by Ellissen (1860: 3 and 16). As Dain (1942: 8) observes, the main evidence seems to come from a note by an anonymous hand on the last folio of a fifteenth-century manuscript of Thucydides, according to which ἐτελεύτησεν ὁ ἀγαθός διδάσκαλος ὁ Γέμιστος (*sic*) on the first hour of Monday, 26 June in the fifteenth Indiction. This corresponds to the year 1452. Dain (1942: 10) did not rule out Bessarion or Kabakes as possible authors of this note. A second note written in the margin below the epitaph of Gregory of Nazianzus (some might see the irony in this) in *Monacensis gr.* 495, fol. 50v appears to have been modelled on the first note (Dain 1942: 11), thus reproducing the same 'apocryphal' version regarding the death of ὁ διδάσκαλος Γόμοστος (*sic*) (Hardt 1812: 155; Alexandre 1858: xliii n. 2). Monfasani attributed this second note to Raoul Kabakes and certainly the orthography speaks for Raoul's eccentricities (Monfasani 2005: 459 n. 3). Drawing on George of Trebizond, who in his *Comparatio* (1457) considers Plethon to have been dead for three years, Niccolo Perotti's preface to his *De generibus metrorum* and a change of tenses in Matthew Kamariotes' refutation of Plethon's *De fato*, Monfasani (2005: 461) argues that Plethon died in mid-1454 and that the tantalising note might have been partly wrong: it is possible that Plethon died on Wednesday, 26 June 1454. Still, as Blanchet (2008: 178 n. 44) points out, 'ces divers arguments peuvent difficilement aller contre une datation aussi précise et cohérente que celle de la note du *Monacensis gr.* 495'. The reservations of Blanchet are corroborated in so far as Monfasani too attributes the second note to Kabakes: how plausible is it to assume that such a devoted and enthusiast follower of Plethon as Kabakes (and also the man who probably saved for posterity what was left of the *Nomoi*) committed himself to an error as grave as that of placing the death of his beloved mentor *before* the fall of Constantinople? The year 1453 was long associated with all sorts of apocalyptic and eschatological scenarios and effectively marked the end of a world and the birth of another. It is unlikely that Kabakes completely lost touch with the *Zeitgeist* – and it is even less plausible to assume that he was unaware whether his mentor died before or after the event that changed the fate of Hellenism and, as Kabakes and his contemporaries believed, the world.

about the intention and nature of the *Nomoi*. Modern research doubted the links between Plethon and the secret fraternity of Mistra.[33] It then went even further by re-calibrating a hypothesis made by E. Wind and O. Kristeller that casts doubts on whether Plethon really intended his *Nomoi* as a manifesto for a return to paganism.[34] Plethon's direct or indirect 'rehabilitation' to Christianity appears to be under way. Seen in this light, Scholarios might have preserved and manipulated pagan parts of the *Nomoi* with the intention of framing his adversary. And yet, palaeographical evidence from Plethon's recension of Platonic works suggests that the *Nomoi* represents a partial but representative body of evidence with regard to Plethon's conviction.[35]

The only scholarly consensus seems to be that Plethon stood at the crossroad between the disintegrating Byzantium and the emerging Italian Renaissance, thus producing philosophical and religious ideas that announce the end of the medieval world and the rise of the modern one. In this process the spirit or *nous* of Plato's philosophy, rather than his word, readily identified by Scholarios and conservative clerical authorities as potentially threatening Christianity, appears to have played a pivotal role.

Against this background, I take as my starting point two questions: what, according to Plethon's reception and interpretation of Platonic philosophy, is 'pagan' or 'Hellenic' in Platonism? How could it be, in the first place, that salient components of a pagan Platonic world-view survived until the eve of modernity? The first question is relevant to the essence of Plethon's Platonism. The second concerns its roots.

The argument

Fourteenth- and fifteenth-century Byzantium, observed Igor Medvedev, anticipates *en miniature* the whole history of Europe in successive centuries. Its intellectual history includes a *humanism* that asked for the liberation of the study of ancient philosophy from

---

[33] Monfasani (1992).   [34] Hladký (forthcoming). Cf. Wind (1968) 244–58.
[35] Pagani (2008) 45. For a detailed discussion of different approaches to this problem see below, Ch. 3, pp. 148–60.

clerical control; attempts at a *Reformation* of the Church at the doctrinal level; a *Counter-Reformation* represented by Gregory Palamas and the Hesychasts, which identified humanism with paganism and reclaimed the control of political, cultural and intellectual resources; and in its final days Byzantium offered an *Enlightenment*: Plethon's cult of Reason and quest for a philosophical-religious brotherhood, one that, as Masai and Medvedev correctly noted, anticipated experimentations with 'rational religion' by European secret orders such as the Illuminati.[36] Still, late Byzantium is commonly, if not exclusively, approached from the viewpoints of either theology or cultural and socio-economic history. This book proposes a philosophical approach to this period by doing three things.

The first is to define the constitutive philosophical elements of a particularly radical version of Platonism expounded by Plethon and explain its relation to the pre-existing reception of Platonic philosophy in Byzantium. Departing from existing accounts of Plethon's philosophy such as the masterful and seminal book by Masai and the recent studies by Tambrun and Hladký, I aim to recover the intention, contents and significance of Plethon's religious, philosophical and political reformism by devising a contextual intellectual framework. This is derived not only from Plethon's works and their ties to late antique Platonism, but primarily from the intellectual civil war that took place in the fourteenth-century Roman Orthodox world. This strife is most commonly known as the Hesychast controversy.

I argue that the impulse behind Plethon's quest for a new ontology was provided by the need to address the same unresolved core intellectual issues that fuelled the Hesychast controversy: (a) the relation between the One and the Many, (b) the nature of illumination, (c) the possibility of philosophical and political reformism by means of an experimental reception of ancient philosophy.

---

[36] Medvedev (1981) 547–8; Masai (1956) 300. For a different view on the significance of Plethon for esotericism see Hanegraaff (2009). In my view, three texts testify to the great importance of Plethon in the history of experimentations with natural religion and rational religion: Book 1 of the *Nomoi*; the description of an unnamed, universal religion in the *Memorandum to Theodore*; and its resonances in the *Monody for the Empress Helen*. I discuss all three below on pp. 179, 302 and 377.

My thesis is that the fourteenth-century Hesychast controversy was neither a domestic 'Byzantine' phenomenon, nor a manifestation of a Latin–Greek conflict over the definition of Christianity, as is often assumed. Rather, it was an epiphany of a latent Hellenic–Christian clash of intellectual paradigms that ultimately provided the fermentive elements for Plethon's reformation of Hellenism. Further, against the scholarly consensus that sees in Plethon a forerunner of Renaissance Platonism, I argue that the radicalism of Plethonean Platonism is intrinsically incompatible with the conformism of Renaissance Platonists who sought to maintain the agreement between Platonism and Christianity along with that between Plato and Aristotle. Thus, this is a book about Plethon, but also about fourteenth- and fifteenth-century Byzantine intellectual/philosophical history with extensions to late antiquity and early modern European thought.

In the second place, this book offers a new conceptual definition of paganism as philosophical Hellenism. The two recent in-depth studies of Plethon by Hladký and Tambrun have either cast doubts on his paganism or cautiously explored the roots of his philosophy in late antique Platonism while refraining from expressly identifying and insisting on Plethon's relapse to religious paganism. Similarly, in the most recent book-length study Moreno Neri underlined the prevalent view that Plethon's paganism is the surface expression of an esoterical perennial philosophy (*prisca philosophia* of the Renaissance type).[37] In a sense, the latter approach is a prudent and safe choice. The term 'paganism' is problematic and ideologically as well as rhetorically loaded. In the Byzantine context, the word 'Hellene' has been taken to mean a pagan in the sense of either a 'polytheist' or, more broadly speaking, a 'worshipper of a false god'.[38] In modern scholarship the term 'paganism' is usually connected to a Hellenic religious/cultural tradition and heritage that went under by the end of the sixth century CE.

And yet the 'Plethon affair' possesses inextricable ideological and politico-religious dimensions. After all, this is why Scholarios cast the *Nomoi* into the flames. These ideological, religious and

---

[37] Hladký (forthcoming); Tambrun (2006a); Neri (2010) 12, 146, 287–8.
[38] Livanos (2010) 106.

even rhetorical clashes are at the heart of this book. My contention is that Plethon was a pagan. I do not use the term with reference to any particular manifestations of ritual paganism in history and cult, and I do not intend to elaborate on Masai's thesis regarding the pagan fraternity of Mistra. Rather, I use the term 'paganism' heuristically to designate the intellectual and moral contents of a particular philosophical constellation that transcends the historical borders of late antiquity.

This redefinition of paganism as philosophical Hellenism calls for a revisionist approach to the intellectual identity of dissenting Byzantine theologians and philosophers before Plethon. Consciously or not, thinkers such as Psellos, Theodore Metochites, Barlaam of Calabria, Nikephoros Gregoras and Demetrios Kydones became carriers of conceptual elements of an essentially 'Hellenic' world-view that eventually resurfaces with Plethon. Intentionally or not, these intellectuals cleared the way for more radical experimentations with Platonism.

One might object that the people who the Orthodox establishment designated as 'Hellenes', that is to say 'pagan', were not *really* pagan. Rhetoric played an important role in Byzantium and it is customary to note that charges of paganism were often the means to frame a political opponent.[39] To be sure, one should not conclude that someone was a pagan just because he was accused of being one. On the other hand, it is an equally misleading and precipitous conclusion that a Byzantine was not pagan *because* he was accused of being one. I would like to examine the possibility that often in late Byzantium there was more in the accusation of paganism than rhetoric or insult. Part II of this book corroborates the Hesychast accusations that philosophical Hellenism did shape the way in which Byzantine intellectual dissenters thought of the relation between multiplicity in universe and singularity in god; the means by which one may achieve illumination and godlikeness; and *a fortiori* their views on clericalism and education.

Thirdly, this book is about intellectual history and its methodology in general, inasmuch as it challenges the dominating anti-essentialist and relativist trends in current scholarship. These

[39] Livanos (2010) 103.

effectively liquidate the difference between Hellenism and Christianity by describing either or both (usually both) as culturally constructed, shifting and contingent phenomena, rather than as essentially opposed philosophical world-views. In contrast, this book joins Plethon as well as his Christian opponent, Gennadios Scholarios, and the pillar of Orthodoxy, Gregory Palamas, in a search for the philosophical substances of paganism and/or Orthodox Christianity. It thus argues in favour of the intrinsic incompatibility between two conflicting existential positions or modes of thinking about man, the world, and god.

In the remainder of this introduction I will provide an extended account of each of these three main claims. I will do so by defining four key terms involved in my argument: 'paganism', 'utopianism', 'humanism', and 'idolatry'.

Defining key terms, 1: paganism

Peter Gay traced the rise of modern paganism to the Enlightenment reprise of the classical intellectual and cultural ideal: 'the Enlightenment was a volatile mixture of classicism, impiety, and science; the *philosophes*, in a phrase, were modern pagans'.[40] This type of modern paganism spurred, among other things, experimentations with natural religion and various philosophically substantiated cults after 1789, of which Plethon's secret society in Mistra provides an early model. Still, the notion of modern paganism begs the question regarding the common conceptual substratum shared by modern as well as ancient paganism. In its ancient and modern manifestations paganism as philosophical Hellenism presupposes an underlying intellectual set of ideas antagonistic to the Judaeo-Christian one, which managed to transcend the defeat of cultic paganism in late antiquity.

Nowadays scholarship is sceptical about essentialist approaches to paganism and Christianity. It appears sensible to argue that the phenomenology of what counts as Platonic, Hellenic, pagan or Christian shifts through time. Anti-essentialist positions involve minimal risk. After all, today few people would agree with

---

[40] Gay (1966) 8.

Plethon that there are any 'true doctrines' about possessing a trans-historical and immutable essence, as he was arguing.[41] Similarly, cultural historians are highly critical of polarising conceptions. Nuanced approaches that blur the borders between world-views and relativise the boundaries between opposed philosophical identities are in vogue. One often encounters a vocabulary that describes the clash between Hellenism and Judaeo-Christianity in terms of varying 'narratives' or 'master-narratives'.[42]

The problem is that this approach would hardly make sense to Christian intellectuals from late antiquity to late Byzantium. These people opposed paganism not only as ritual and cultic veneration of non-Christian deities but also as a distinctive 'Hellenic' philosophical thought-world. As a rule, this thought-world was related to Platonism and seen as possessing the ability to resurface parasitically and regenerate itself by means of heresy.[43] From Epiphanius and Hippolytus to Scholarios and the critics of Spinoza's pantheism in the seventeenth century, there is a persisting suspicion that Platonism *qua* philosophical paganism is the mother of all Christian, Gnostic and even modern philosophical heresies.[44] Heresy becomes the vehicle of pagan doctrines and Platonism is rendered the proprium of heresy. The best example of the latter phenomenon in late antiquity is Eunomianism, still remembered in fourteenth-century sources and related to the contemporary humanist experimentations with Platonic philosophy.[45]

---

[41] For this Plethonean position and its Neoplatonic and Kabbalist parallels see below, pp. 179, 289–90.

[42] In a post-modern age, this seems an appropriate and politically correct way to write history. For its deficiencies and shortcomings see Siniossoglou (2010b).

[43] The classic account of Hellenism as a mother of heresy is in Epiphanius, *Panarion* 157.3–8. Two examples are pertinent here. Socrates Scholasticos (*Hist. eccl.* 1.22.34–5) brings the point home when arguing that Hellenism (and this primarily means Platonism) was parasitically surviving within Christianity by using Christian heresy as its vehicle and as its means of expression. The books of the heretics, we read, are Christianising in form but Hellenic in their doctrinal core. According to Socrates (*Hist. eccl.* 1.22.3–6) 'Hellenising Christianity' developed by clinging to pre-Constantine Christianity 'in the same sense that pseudo-prophets are attached to prophets and pseudo-apostles to apostles'. Photius too (*Ep.* 288, 145) sincerely believed that some sort of Ἑλληνόφρων λογισμός seduced Origen and Didymus the Blind into the 'ultimate depths of godlessness'.

[44] Epiphan. *Pan.* 185.13–25; Hipp. *Haer.* 1.prol.1.1–9; 1.19.1ff. For Spinoza and Platonism see the epilogue to this book.

[45] An explanation is provided by Gregory of Nyssa. The Eunomian claim that the names attributed to god possess an absolute and independent truth-value accessible to the

In Scholarios' *Epitome* of Aquinas' *Summa contra Gentiles* Plato and the Platonists poisoned Christianity, leading notorious heretics, namely Arius and Eunomius, to Hellenism.[46] Scholarios' theologically elaborate response to Plethon's *Differences* betrays a transparent anxiety that the real danger concerned the revival of a pagan Platonic intellectual paradigm, rather than any revival of pagan rituals. Scholarios makes this clear in the accompanying epistle he sent to Mark Eugenikos: *this was no encyclopaedic show-off.*[47] The controversy was not really academic. Scholarios even added an appropriate subtitle: 'against the Hellenes'. In the same vein as Aquinas, Palamas and Scholarios, George of Trebizond in his *Comparatio philosophorum Aristotelis et Platonis* expressly connected Plato to Origenes, Arius, Gregory Palamas and Plethon's paganism.[48] The point recurs in Plethon's student, Mark Eugenikos.[49] In late antiquity Christian intellectuals recaptured Platonic notions by adapting them at will. But then a deep and persisting anxiety grew that tenets of a deeply 'Hellenic' version of Platonism managed to pervade mainstream Christianity.

Admittedly, postulating the existence of a pagan core latently present throughout the history of Christian heresy requires clarification. What could possibly be really *pagan* within Platonism in

---

human intellect is tantamount to a relapse to the realism of the *Cratylus*. See Gr. Nyss. *Contra Eun.* 2.1.403–4. Thus late Byzantine humanist philosophical endeavours were repeatedly reproached for reviving Eunomius' attempt to comprehend divine essence. Palamas closes *The One Hundred and Fifty Chapters* (*Capita CL*) with a call to avoid Akindynos and his followers for 'in agreement with Eunomius, they heretically say that the substance of god is visible through the study of created beings (διὰ τῶν κτισμάτων ἡ οὐσία τοῦ θεοῦ ὁρᾶται). So the harvest of their impiety is abundant.' Cf. Gr. Pal. *Capita CL* 8–10; *Triads* 3.2.24.

46 Arius and Eunomius are considered to be Platonists to the extent that they allowed for 'some sort of supreme *nous*', who emanates from the godhead to contain all Forms and initiate a hierarchical procession of beings – a description that recalls Palamas' similar condemnation of what 'the Hellenes' say and that comes strikingly close to Plethon's henotheistic onto-theology in the *Nomoi* and the *Differences*. Cf. Schol. *Epitome Summae contra Gentiles, OC* 5.4.6.44–8. Cf. Ch. 6, pp. 292–3.

47 Schol. *Ad Marc. Eug., OC* 4.116.36: Οὔτε δὲ σοφίας ἐπίδειξις ἦν.

48 See Todt (2006) 157.

49 Mark notes that there is a single principle of Logos – not a first cause, a second cause, and a third cause, as think Plato, the Gnostics, Arius and Eunomius. See Mark Eug. *Testimonia spiritum sanctum* 49.1–5.

such a way as effectively to survive the prevalence of Christianity from late antiquity and continuously challenge its dominance at the philosophical level?

Plethon provides a starting point. His reception of Plato is conducive to a self-sufficient philosophical paradigm that may be more closely defined as Hellenic or pagan Platonic owing to its merging of four salient and intertwined philosophical components: (a) epistemic optimism, that is, the persuasion that man may by virtue of his own powers apprehend truth, and that illumination is the product of intellectual ascent; (b) a pagan ontology that promises to depose a transcendent and ineffable Judaeo-Christian God in favour of a unified and humanly cognisable notion of One/The Good *qua* Being; (c) a multi-causalist or 'polytheist' metaphysical model that eliminates contingency and substitutes the determinist notion of *heimarmene* or fate for Christian free will; and (d) political utopianism, the persuasion that an ideally just society is realisable by approximation. I will argue in Parts II and III of this book that all four philosophical elements of Plethon's philosophical paganism are traceable either directly to Plato, or to an ancient interpretation of Plato, which, as it happens, has very good chances of being a legitimate one.

Plethon was a pagan in so far as the existential position resulting from maintaining these doctrines was radically incompatible with Christian Orthodoxy as understood from late antiquity until his time. His reception of Platonism meant replacing Orthodox theology with Platonic ontology, that is, a supra-essential godhead with a cognisable Being; substituting *heimarmene* for Christian providence; utopianism for millenarianism and apocalypticism; the ideal of the *polis* for that of a religious ecumene. Eventually, the reintroduction of these philosophical positions provided Plethon with the opening to address the theme of salvation (σωτηρία) according to Plato's original conception of the philosopher's 'salvation' as concomitant with the preservation of the terrestrial *polis*.[50] Plethon's plan was to displace Christianity by supplanting it with what he viewed as Platonism in its purest

---

[50] *Resp.* 494a11–12.

and most radical form, even if this meant parting from late antique Neoplatonism.

For heuristic reasons I use the terms 'pagan Platonism', 'philosophical paganism' and 'philosophical Hellenism' interchangeably to describe a paradigm or ideal-type composed either of all or of some of these intellectual components. This is a mental construct and system of meaning that does not exist within history in any pure form but is variously exemplified through different agents and carriers. It was customary among the Fathers of the Church to look upon the terms 'Hellenism' and 'paganism' as negative in themselves. I consider both to be more or less neutral.

However, in agreement with both Plethon and Gregory Palamas I understand philosophical Hellenism/paganism and Orthodox Christianity as essentially conflicting *modes of existence*, that is to say, distinct modes of thinking and perceiving one's place and role in this world. Underneath the manifold historical transformations persists an essential or ideal intellectual paradigm that is, as Plethon hoped, philosophically retrievable. Thus, I do not mean to deal with paganism and Christian Orthodoxy as historically and culturally constructed phenomena. My interest is not in what appears to connect or disconnect Hellenism and Christianity at any given time but in what ideally and philosophically sets them apart as conflicting ideal-types and fields of meaning. This irreducible philosophical difference transcends the successive Hellenic Christian experimentations that took place on the surface of intellectual history.

I combine Weberian ideal-types with *Konstellationsforschung*, for this allows for different agents to manage diversely the same intellectual capital: not all elements of the Platonic ideal-type described above are present in any particular Platonising intellectual. There are not only similarities but also differences between the versions of pagan Platonism maintained by Proclus and Plethon. Still, in contrast to contemporary anti-essentialism, the driving methodological conviction informing this book is that all phenomena are phenomena *of* something; all nuances and variations are nuances and variations *of* something. The conception of ideal-type as causal schema addresses and solves a crucial point with regard to concept formation and historical descriptions: that ideas 'may be more or less present in different actors' minds, i.e., some may be consciously aware of them, others not, some may be exclusively guided by them, some may entertain additional consideration, etc.'[51] In the late Byzantine context, humanists such as Nikephoros Gregoras and Demetrios Kydones were carriers of characteristics of the Hellenic world-view in different degrees and possibly less consciously than Plethon. Still, they were drawing on the same paradigm, existential position, or *Gedankenbild*. As Weber has it,

An ideal type is formed by the one-sided accentuation of one or more points of view and by the synthesis of a great many diffuse, discrete, more or less present and occasionally absent concrete individual phenomena, which are arranged according to those one-sidedly emphasised viewpoints into a unified analytical construct. *In its conceptual purity, this mental construct (Gedankenbild) cannot be found anywhere in reality. It is a utopia.* Historical research faces the task of determining in each individual case, the extent to which this ideal-construct approximates to or diverges from reality . . . [52]

Failure to appreciate this rupture between the Hellenic and the Judaeo-Christian world-views at the philosophical level renders deficient any attempt at understanding the intention of men like Plethon but also runs counter to the self-understanding of men like Gregory Palamas and Scholarios. These latter Christians unhesitatingly did everything, from compiling masterpieces of theological and mystical speculation such as the *Triads* to casting Plethon's *Nomoi* into the flames in order to stop the spread of ideas distinctively felt to be Hellenic, rather than merely in order to rebut individuals like Plethon.

Seen in this light, the fundamental difficulty with the recent trend in modern scholarship to 'rehabilitate' Byzantine and Renaissance religious dissenters such as Psellos, John Italos and Plethon to Christianity is that it eradicates the essential philosophical distinction between paganism and Christianity by, intentionally or

---

[51] Burger (1987) 116. Cf. Mulsow and Stamm (2005) on constellation analysis.
[52] Weber (1949) 90; my emphasis.

not, merging conflicting intellectual paradigms into a generic and unqualified type of supposedly Christian discourse.

In this regard, the synodical triumph of Gregory Palamas in the fourteenth century and the clash between Scholarios and Plethon in the fifteenth have a significant, if unnoticed, hermeneutical dimension. For the first time since late antiquity, the 'negotiation' of Hellenism is openly dismissed as having relied upon mere linguistic community. For Palamas, Platonism agrees with Christianity only on a surface level of common signifiers, that is to say, in the *lexis* but not the *nous* of words. No real synthesis between Hellenic philosophy and Christianity ever took place. Arguing against Barlaam and the anti-Hesychasts, Gregory Palamas is adamant that:

if one of the Fathers appears to say the same things as those 'beyond the gates' do, he does so only in what concerns the linguistic surface; for when it comes to the meaning, there is a huge distance between them. For the Fathers have the '*nous* of Christ', according to Paul, whereas the Hellenes speak through human mind (διάνοια) – that is if we are not to say anything worse. 'How great is the distance between heaven and earth, so great is the distance between my mind (διάνοια) and your mind' says the Lord. (Gr. Pal. *Triads* 1.1.11.9–14)

Plethon and Palamas are in agreement. As they see it, the distance between *lexis* and *nous* calls for a hermeneutical enterprise that gets things straight and shows the inner incompatibility of Hellenism and Christianity. Contrary to the anti-foundationalist maxims of modern cultural historians, who might be tempted to see Hellenism and Christianity as liquid narratives vying for rhetorical power, Palamas and Plethon have no difficulty in seeking an intellectual substance of Christianity and one of Hellenism. What Palamas did for his version of Orthodoxy in the fourteenth century, Plethon did for his version of Hellenism in the fifteenth.

Defining key terms, 2: utopianism

A case has been made that the socio-economic reform proposed in the *Memoranda* qualifies as 'utopian' in so far as it was unworkable.[53] The *Nomoi* accentuates this impression of Plethon as a 'dreamer of dreams'.[54] But what counts, after all, as 'utopian'? The term was applied in the philosophical context of Plato's *Republic* in order to signify 'a description of an imagined society put forward by its author as better than any existing society, past or present'.[55] In this book the term 'utopian' is used according to the classic definition by Karl Mannheim: 'A state of mind is utopian when it is incongruous with the state of reality within which it occurs.' Mannheim then adds a significant qualification, which is, I believe, especially applicable to Plethon's case: 'Only those orientations transcending reality will be referred to by us as utopian which, when they pass over into conduct, tend to shatter, either partially or wholly, the order of things prevailing at the time.'[56] Plethon is a utopian thinker in so far as his Platonic reformist ideal shatters the established socio-political order of late Byzantium.

Contextualisation is crucial. Mannheim observed that '[t]he representatives of a given order will label as utopian all conceptions of existence which *from their point of view* can in principle never be realised. According to this usage, the contemporary connotation of the term "utopian" is predominantly that of an idea which is in principle unrealisable.'[57] Plethon considered his plan to be viable, yet his contemporaries do not appear to have either attempted or even considered its implementation. They must have thought and felt that Plethon was a utopian thinker – even if they lacked the word 'utopian'.

Few have discussed the issue of Plethon's influence on Thomas More's *Utopia*. It appears that More was familiar with Plethon's ideas, possibly through the channel of mediators such as Pico

---

[53] See the interesting discussion in W. Blum (1988) 77–80. One of the first to note the utopian character of Plethon's radicalism is George Finley (1877) 241–2. On the other hand, van Dieten (1979: 9–11) moved the spotlight from Plethon's utopianism to his realism. Spentzas (1996: 47, 73) argued that Plethon was not a utopian thinker and that his measures were in principle applicable and viable. In his preface to Spentzas' book, Woodhouse (Spentzas 1996: 8) seems to agree, noting that Plethon's 'fiscal programme was sufficiently realistic' to attract the interest of modern economic historians. On utopianism in Byzantium see the remarks of Irmscher (1985) and van Dieten (1979); see also Matschke and Tinnefeld (2001): 365.

[54] Nicol (1993) 344–5. As Laiou (2007: 229) notes, Plethon's plan was coherent but 'negated all contemporary realities.'

[55] Morrison (2007) 232.   [56] Mannheim (1997) 173.   [57] Mannheim (1997) 177.

della Mirandola, Erasmus and Theodore of Gaza. In a pioneering article, Derrett argued that More was influenced by Plethon's *Memoranda*.[58] The thesis was expanded by Blum but criticised by Maltese.[59] More recently, Garnsey noted that 'the extent of More's borrowings is surprising, especially in the sphere of religion' and suggested that Plethon's *Memoranda* might well have also influenced the Utopian measures relating to the abandonment of private property and the cultivation of land.[60] Further, both More and Plethon studied Plato's political philosophy. Chapter 7 focuses on Plethon's reformism as a variant of Platonic utopianism and advances a comparison with the spiritual utopianism of Gregory Palamas and Gennadios Scholarios.

Defining key terms, 3: humanism

One of those very few modern scholars to have felt the tension between the clerical establishment and intellectual dissenters in Byzantium with regard to the relation between the *lexis* and *nous* of Greek philosophy, Arnold Toynbee, is unpopular among contemporary Byzantinists (understandably perhaps, given the rift between his harsh criticism of Byzantium and the nowadays *en vogue* tendency to 'rehabilitate' Byzantium), but also surprisingly ignored by specialists on Plethon:

For an educated Graecophone Eastern Orthodox Christian, it was obligatory to ape the classical Hellenic Greek writers' language and style, but it was no less obligatory to ignore the ideas and beliefs that were conveyed in classical Hellenic Greek literature . . . In other words, the correct Byzantine Greek attitude towards Hellenic Greek literature was to draw a rigid distinction between its verbal form and its intellectual substance. This distinction is absurd, but, by Scholarios' time, it had been in vogue continuously for about eighteen centuries. . . . This is one of the maladies that killed the Hellenic Greek culture and blighted its Byzantine Greek successor. The absurdity was extreme, but the punishment for taking seriously the matter of Hellenism, as well as its form, was condign. Photios in the ninth century, Psellos in the eleventh century and Plethon in the fifteenth century all came under suspicion and all suffered in various degrees for their intellectual honesty.[61]

---

[58] Derrett (1965).
[59] Cf. W. Blum (1988) 39 n. 36; Dedes (1985); Maltese (1990) 151.
[60] Garnsey (2009) 339.   [61] Toynbee (1981) 305–6.

Toynbee's perceptive approach to the distinction between the 'verbal form' and the 'intellectual substance' of Hellenism raises a set of questions regarding the actual interpretative tools, strategies and tropes by which Plethon attempted to re-merge the *lexis* and *nous* of philosophical vocabulary – an endeavour that was, I shall argue, not at all unrelated to his political agenda of approximating the nearly perfectly just *polis*. But one also wonders about the formative context and the immediate intellectual roots of Plethon's return to Plato.

A major contention in this book is that fourteenth-century Byzantine humanism is the barren midwife (*Tht.* 148e–149c) of the conceptual or philosophical paganism recovered and systematised by Plethon in the fifteenth century. Plethon is the direct intellectual heir of Byzantine intellectuals of humanist inclinations in so far as he restates their demand for a reappraisal of ancient philosophy even if in a manner that is far more extreme. Plethon's philosophical Hellenism is the radicalisation of latent Platonic tendencies vitalising those Byzantine humanists and dissenters who have challenged, undermined and occasionally endeavoured to overthrow the Judaeo-Christian establishment since late antiquity. His Platonism is the radicalised cumulative effect of repeated yet failed attempts at reforming the religious establishment that were still going on at his time.

According to the developmentalist thesis I present here, Plethon attempted a radical response to the ultimate defeat of Byzantine humanism and to the concomitant triumph of Orthodox mysticism represented by Gregory Palamas. The doctrinal triumph of Gregory Palamas and the Hesychast hegemony of discourse aborted the evolution of emerging Platonising tendencies towards a natural and secular-political religion as well as in epistemology and ontology. Plethon radicalised the rehabilitation of Platonism that was interrupted, anathematised and repeatedly condemned in the late fourteenth century, by bringing the intellectual and hermeneutical tendencies initiated by Byzantine humanists such as Theodore Metochites, Nikephoros Gregoras and the Kydones brothers to their extreme conclusion: philosophical paganism.

Seen in this light, Plethon's radicalism was provoked by the failure of moderate Platonist humanists such as Demetrios Kydones to complete the intellectual rebellion against Palamas' spiritualism and prevent the upsurge of religious ecumenism and the monastic takeover of the State, in brief, by their failure to offer a remedy to the malaise they diagnosed. At a time when the Ottoman siege guns approached Constantinople, the pagan Platonism of Plethon stands out as the most extreme and uncompromising offshoot of Byzantine humanism, a late response to an old call for reform.

Applied to the late Byzantine context the term 'humanism' carries different associations from those commonly known from the Italian Renaissance humanists. Byzantine humanism does not primarily or merely signify the love for classical literature. Already during the intellectual movement often referred to as the 'First Byzantine humanism' of the ninth and tenth centuries, Hellenism provided the material for a court ideology that challenged the dominion of clericalism. This opposed political and secular institutions to the Church and sought to liberate the interpretation of religious and philosophical texts from clerical indoctrination. Similarly, in the fourteenth century Byzantine humanists reverted to and experimented with philosophical, hermeneutical, moral and political tenets of ancient philosophy that directly or indirectly clashed with the contemporary Orthodox clerical-monastic establishment.

The intellectuals who attacked religious Orthodoxy in the fourteenth century were not united by any shared fondness for Thomas Aquinas, as is commonly but erroneously assumed.[62] Rather, what connects these intellectuals while separating them from Palamas and Scholarios is their association with an intellectual movement inspired by the spirit of ancient philosophy and in particular Platonism that is sometimes identified as part of 'the Palaiologean Renaissance', 'the last Byzantine Renaissance' and which may more adequately be characterised as a pre-Renaissance.[63] In both

---

[62] For example, the humanist anti-Palamite, Nikephoros Gregoras severely attacked another major anti-Palamite, Barlaam of Calabria. The latter is sometimes presented by Orthodox theologians as a Latin agent, despite the fact that Barlaam was critical of Latin dogma. Besides, Scholarios too was a Thomist, but this was hardly enough to make him critical of Palamism.

[63] Medvedev (1984) 117, 126, 129. See Ševčenko (1984: 144–71) for the definition of the terms 'Palaiologan', taken to mean the period from 1261 to 1453, and 'Renaissance'. As Masai (1965: 141) observes, the term 'Renaissance' initially did not refer to a

the 'first' and 'second' Byzantine Renaissances, Byzantine humanists were stigmatised as 'Hellenising' or paganising intellectuals.
There is much more than rhetoric in this accusation. One of
the common characteristics shared by almost all major Byzantine
dissenters, from Psellos and Theodore Metochites to Gregoras,
Plethon and Bessarion, is their sympathy for Plato. Byzantine
humanists were Hellenes, not because they revived the religion
of the ancients, but because they deviated from Orthodoxy by
experimenting in varying degrees with 'pagan' philosophy and
especially Platonism. In the twelfth century Nicholas of Methone
provided a succinct definition of the Hellenic core of the Byzantine
humanist project. In the course of a severe attack on the contemporary revival of interest in Proclan philosophy, Nicholas reverted
to Paul's description of the Hellenes as 'those who are after the
human wisdom (ἀνθρωπίνη σοφία) that is demolished in Christ'.[64]
Faced with a similar revival of Hellenic studies in the fourteenth
century, Gregory Palamas too reverted to Paul and repeated that
'wisdom beyond the gates' is nothing but *carnal wisdom* (σαρκικὴ
σοφία) incapable of advancing beyond nature.[65]

In this book the term 'humanism' is used in precisely this sense.
It stands for an intense preoccupation and experimentation with
'human' or 'carnal' wisdom, that is, with ancient philosophy and
rational discourse, which extends to a direct or indirect opposition
to the world-view and policy advocated by the Byzantine Orthodox
establishment.[66]

Salient motives of Byzantine humanism that (re)surfaced during the strife of the Hesychast controversy include a preference
for a contemplative life (θεωρητικὸς βίος) that focuses on an
autonomous διάνοια rather than on divine grace; a firm belief

---

particular historical period but to a *réalité d'ordre éthique*: 'La notion est apparue
d'abord au service d'un idéal d'action; c'était, en quelque sorte, le programme d'un
mouvement...' Elsewhere, Masai (1958: 55) called for a redefinition of the term
'Renaissance'.

[64] Nicholas of Methone, *Refutatio* proem. 1–2: οἱ τὴν ἀνθρωπίνην καὶ καταργουμένην ἐν
Χριστῷ σοφίαν ζητοῦντες.

[65] Gr. Pal. *Triads* 1.1.2.22–4.

[66] See here also the brief but interesting remarks by Meyendorff (1963: 329–30) on the
notion and evolution of Byzantine humanism: '[L]es triomphes palamites de 1341,
1347, 1351 et 1368 ferment, dans une large mesure, la porte au développement d'une
philosophie et d'une civilisation vraiment profanes dans les cadres de l'État byzantin.'

in hidden intellectual recesses potentially enabling man to acquire true knowledge and attain godlikeness; also, a preference for what is sometimes called 'cosmic' piety, that is, the Hellenic tendency to make the universe 'an object of a religious attitude';[67] and the intentional or unintentional promotion of an elitist and anthropocentric perception that ran counter to the ecclesiastical and theocentric perception of Orthodoxy.

Further, we shall see that fourteenth-century Byzantine humanist reformism resulted in successive re-conceptualisations of polytheism and monotheism and daring theological experimentations. To these aspects of Byzantine humanism I will be adding the rise of anti-clericalism and anti-monasticism in the fourteenth century, the advancement of an 'un-orthodox' open-ended hermeneutical model conducive to proto-deist natural theology, as well as an intriguing persistence of orality and dissimulation that challenges institutionalised education – one identified by Gregory Palamas with the evil channel (κακομήχανος μηχανή) by which the pagan world-view of the ancient 'Illuminati' (πεφωτισμένοι) was successfully transmitted to Byzantium.[68]

The main intellectuals and philosophers who are considered in this book to be exponents of Byzantine humanism and are treated as providing the raw material for Plethon's reformism are Psellos, John Italos, Theodore Metochites, Barlaam, Nikephoros Gregoras, Demetrios and Prochoros Kydones. These men claimed that it is possible to divorce Platonic philosophy from its ritualistic aspect. Whereas in late antiquity Proclus attributed to Platonism a religious and ritualistic dimension, these Byzantine intellectuals experimented with the substance of Platonic philosophy while discarding ritual paganism. The explicit inclusion of most members of this group in the list of heretics anathematised in the *Synodicon of Orthodoxy* shows that, at least from the viewpoint of Orthodox theology, they were unsuccessful.

Palamas responded that pagan philosophy cannot be *really* separated from pagan religion. He recognised in Byzantine humanism the possibility of a philosophical cult, of a 'hidden, unconscious cult without hieratic rites', to apply here an expression by

---

[67] For this definition of cosmic piety see Pépin (1986) 408.   [68] Gr. Pal. *Ep.* 3.36.11–16.

27

Emmanuel Lévinas that, intentionally or not, challenged Christianity by reverting to ancient philosophy.

It might be objected, as is sometimes argued, that the term 'humanism' is not applicable to the Byzantine context. Psellos and Theodore Metochites, among others, notes John Meyendorff, were not really 'humanists', for they remained faithful to the dogma of the Church.[69] We read similar things about John Italos, Psellos' notorious student. The accusations included in the *Synodicon of Orthodoxy* do not really apply for Italos, who repeatedly stressed that he followed the Christian rather than the Hellenic worldview.[70] Ostensibly there were political, rather than religious reasons that led to his trial. Even his bad Greek is brought into the discussion to explain away his anathematisation as some sort of theological misunderstanding.[71] Both Psellos and Italos are rehabilitated as pious Christians misunderstood by opportunistic contemporaries, on the grounds that they repeatedly claimed to be Orthodox, regardless of what their insights meant philosophically. No surprise here: we shall see that this is how the 'paganism' of earlier Byzantine dissenters is explained away and how Plethon's support for Eastern Orthodoxy in the Council of Ferrara/Florence can be used to the same end.

H. G. Beck argued that the late Byzantine controversy was not necessarily one between Palamites and humanists or one between paganising tendencies and Christian spirituality, but one among Christians.[72] Further, scholars sympathetic to Hesychasm object that 'the division between Hesychasts and anti-Hesychasts does not coincide with that between humanists and anti-humanists', that Palamism was not by definition anti-humanist.[73] As a consequence, in the past scholars were too quick to dismiss

---

[69] Meyendorff (1971) 54.   [70] Joannou (1956) 7, 27.

[71] See Podskalsky (2003) 72–3 and bibliography in n. 342.

[72] Beck (1963) 75: '[D]er Streit zwischen Palamiten und Antipalamiten [ist] nicht aus dem Gegensatz zwischen paganisierendem oder neutralistischem Humanismus und Theologie entstanden, sondern zwischen zwei theologischen Richtungen, die sich beide auf die παράδοσις berufen.' Part II of this book argues in the opposite direction that the clash between Palamism and humanism reflects an ancient clash of world-views.

[73] Tsirpanlis (1993) 14–15. If this is taken to mean that Hesychasts did not include any 'systematic struggle against the Hellenic heritage', then one might only reluctantly agree – since successive anathematisations make sufficiently clear that the tension between two opposed notions of illumination remained unresolved.

the possibility of any link between Plethon's project and the fourteenth-century anti-Hesychast movement. Barlaam did not abandon Christianity for the sake of paganism, we read – he became a bishop in Calabria and was devoted to the mission of uniting the Greek and the Latin Churches. On the contrary, Plethon opposed such efforts and offered a totally new direction that departs from those of both Barlaam and, for example, Scholarios.[74] More recently though, Couloubaritsis has sensed that 'perhaps Plethon's thought is the fruit of a complex history of debates between Platonists and Aristotelians' and ventured the assumption of a link between Plethon's Platonism and the progressive triumph of Aristotelianism in the fourteenth century.[75]

But to my knowledge Igor Medvedev is the only scholar to have seen behind appearances and to have moved *grosso modo* in the right direction, when observing against Beck that Byzantine humanism unveiled certain Platonic modes of thought that potentially enabled the emergence of Plethon's neopaganism.[76] A complementary point of departure can be found in the thesis of John Meyendorff that Palamism brought to a halt pagan philosophical tendencies such that their carriers were forced to turn to Thomism.[77] Latin theology and scholasticism eventually attracted the majority of late Byzantine dissenters. But was there no alternative? The circle of Mistra, consisting of philhellenes such as George the Philosopher makes sufficiently clear that at least some tried to pave a third way other than the ostensible polarity of Orthodoxy and Thomism. Plethon pushed the boundaries of their endeavour to a new level.

Undoubtedly, the intellectuals who unearthed and brought Platonism to the foreground in the fourteenth century considered themselves pious Christians. Still, intentionally or unintentionally, these men planted the seed for Plethon's turn to a type of philosophical paganism that latently persisted in their own preoccupation with an ancient Platonic paradigm.

---

74 Nikolaou (2004b) 108–9; Baloglou (2002) in his introduction to the *Memoranda*.
75 Couloubaristis (2006) 153.
76 Medvedev (1981) 537, 541–3; (1984) 136; (1997) 66–126.
77 See Meyendorff (1955) 47; H. G. Beck (1963) 71–2.

It is likely that some or even all the members of this movement were unconscious of the fact that the unarticulated yet natural conclusion of their resuscitation of the philosophy of ancient Illuminati (πεφωτισμένοι), as Barlaam of Calabria called Plato and the Platonists, extended to much more than the reformism of Palamite Orthodoxy that they were propagating. In the fifteenth century Byzantine Thomism put an end to their quest for an alternative to Orthodox notions. Plethon's Platonism shared with Byzantine humanism the same starting point but offered a solution different from Thomism. His philosophical Hellenism is a reaction to both Palamism and Thomism, though philosophically an upshot of fourteenth-century humanism.

The Palamite Orthodox establishment was right in discerning in its contemporary rediscovery of Plato the revival or epiphany of philosophical institutions of an ancient world-view that was irreducibly Hellenic, that is, pagan. Palamas acutely realised that the intellectual substance of pagan philosophy did not allow for experimentations without irrevocably corroding the Orthodox understanding of the essence of Judaeo-Christianity. In this Palamas is in accord with Plethon: a 'secular' Plato is impossible. Or rather, a secular Plato is ultimately a pagan Plato, for Platonising versions of natural religion are compatible with the pagan Platonic world-view while being irredeemably incompatible with Roman Orthodoxy.

Plethon distilled the secular Platonist paradigm that resurfaced during the Hesychast controversy, stripped it of its Christian points of reference and replied to the major metaphysical queries of fourteenth-century theological discourse regarding multi-causalism and monotheism in exclusively pagan terms. He radicalised, affirmed and codified a version of pagan Platonism that was, until then, denounced in horror one way or another by all parties, even though it was persistently present all along.

It follows that Plethon is not an 'extreme case' in the sense in which this is normally argued – namely an 'odd man out', an exceptional, bizarre or quixotic *begabter Einzelgänger*.[78] His

---

[78] Nicol (1993) 345: 'He was not really even a man before his time. As a Byzantine he was an odd man out.' van Dieten (1979) 31 and 10: 'Plethon ist aber ein Extremfall, und seine

project is *extrem* but Plethon is no *Extremfall*. Masai too thought that Plethon's polytheism was a 'révolution religieuse' and an innovation.[79] This is formally speaking correct. And yet philosophically Plethon's endeavour is the radical outgrowth of previous moderate experimentations with secular and humanist thought. Similarly, the utopia of the *Nomoi* is not irrelevant to those contemporary religious and social needs predominantly addressed by apocalyptic visions and superstition, as Podskalsky assumed.[80] To a large extent the *Nomoi* was a reaction to contemporary spirituality and messianic beliefs just as the two *Memoranda* were a reaction to established conceptions of sovereignty. These works are sites of intersection and continuation of previous quests for religious and philosophical reform that applied Platonism as their common point of reference.

Defining key terms, 4: conceptual idolatry

Modern scholarship is right to cast doubts on Plethon's paganism albeit for the wrong reasons. In the context of late antique and Byzantine Orthodox theology Plethon's philosophy means more than a reversion to paganism. It stands for idolatry.

The Orthodox Fathers of the Church identified a particular type of idolatry that does not refer to material but to mental simulacra. The human intellect may be idolised as easily as any object: philosophical notions are products of human faculties just as material images are. Gregory of Nyssa provides us with a concise definition of conceptual idolatry. Any meaning stemming from inherent intellectual faculties and attributed to the divine produces an idol of God.[81] Evoking Isaiah 40:25; 46:5 (τίνι με ὁμοιώσατε;) and Ecclesiastes 5:1, Gregory of Nyssa introduces God reproaching

mit der byzantinischen politischen Ideologie unvereinbare Preisgabe des Christentums blieb auf einen kleinen Kreis von eingeweihten Schülern beschränkt.'
79 Masai (1958) 59.   80 Podskalsky (1975) 81–2.
81 Gr. Nyss. *V. Mos.* 2.165.4–8: Ἀπαγορεύει γὰρ ἐν πρώτοις ὁ θεῖος λόγος πρὸς μηδὲν τῶν γιγνωσκομένων ὁμοιοῦσθαι παρὰ τῶν ἀνθρώπων τὸ Θεῖον, ὡς παντὸς νοήματος, τοῦ κατά τινα περιληπτικὴν φαντασίαν ἐν περινοίᾳ τινὶ καὶ στοχασμῷ τῆς θείας φύσεως γινομένου, εἴδωλον Θεοῦ πλάσσοντος καὶ οὐ Θεὸν καταγγέλλοντος. For notions as idols according to Gregory of Nyssa see the excellent analysis by Skaltsas (1998) 92–120.

31

the application of thoughts (στοχασμοί) to depict divine essence.[82] The divine law given to Moses prohibits the assimilation of the divine to any cognisable thing and this includes material as well as conceptual avatars. Man cannot equate his comprehensive power (καταληπτικὴ δύναμις) to God.[83] It is possible to know that God *is*, but no knowledge of divine quality, quantity, modality and origin is at all possible.[84] As John of Damascus has it, the divine is uncircumscribed (ἀπερίγραπτον) and incomprehensible (ἀκατάληπτον).[85]

In Plethon's intellectual context this was succinctly put forward in Gregory Palamas' rejection of the autonomy of Hellenic philosophy on the grounds that it generated an intellectual simulacrum, a 'deceiving idol of true wisdom' (σοφίας ἀληθινῆς ἀπατηλὸν εἴδωλον).[86] One might be tempted to take this as part of some abstract exercise in theology. But Palamas is not theorising. Rather, he inveighs against those fourteenth-century philosophers whose 'object, desire and zeal' is 'to find the knowledge of beings' at the cost of having thus 'deprived God of his sovereignty', in other words, those people who attempt to replace theology with ontology.[87] As Neilos said of Barlaam of Calabria, the future acquaintance of Petrarch and Boccacio, the philosopher claimed to 'ascend to the point of knowing the causes of being'.[88] Philosophically this means more or less an endorsement of the Platonic doctrine in the *Republic* that illumination consists in the γνῶσις τῶν ὄντων and blindness to a privation of intellectual knowledge.[89] Conversely, the Hesychast notion of illumination championed by Palamas depends upon psychophysical *askesis* culminating in an experiential, rather than intellectual, ascent and assimilation to the

---

[82] Gr. Nyss. *Orationes viii de beatitudinibus,* PG 44.1280.15–24. In this book I occasionally use the form 'God' to denote the Christian belief in god as a personal agent beyond human notions of Being, non-Being and knowledge, as opposed to Hellenic philosophical conceptualisations of god.

[83] Gr. Nyss. *Contra Eun.* 2.1.94: Τίς γὰρ ἐν νεφέλαις ἰσωθήσεται τῷ κυρίῳ; φησὶν ὁ Δαβίδ.

[84] Gr. Nyss. *V. Mos.* 1.22.   [85] Joh. Dam. *Expositio fidei* 13.42–6.

[86] Gr. Pal. *Triads* 1.1.17.   [87] Gr. Pal. *Triads* 1.1.18.

[88] Neilos, *Enc. Gr. Pal.,* PG 151.664A–C. For Neilos' *Encomium of Palamas* see Ch. 2, p. 100.

[89] Plato, *Resp.* 484c–d.

divine. Viewed from this angle, any claim that the divine is cognisable by the human intellect and that god is apprehensible *qua* Being corresponds to a particular species of idolatry that extends to self-idolatry.

In the *Magnus Canon* of Andreas the insistence on human intellectual credit is taken to mean that man passionately shapes and venerates an idol of himself (αὐτοείδωλον).[90] This rejection of human αὐτοείδωλον contrasts with the Plotinean motto according to which man is a sculptor who must create and shape his own image: 'never cease working at thy statue'. As Plotinus puts it, 'there is no reason why we should not, *by virtues peculiar to our state*, attain Likeness to a model in which virtue has no place'.[91] Pico della Mirandola fully grasped the essence of Platonic humanism and epistemic optimism in his conception of human *dignitas* as depicted in *Oration on the Dignity of Man*.[92] Man may shape his own image (*sui ipsius quasi arbitrarius honorariusque plastes et fictor*), just as the ideal ruler should base his sovereignty upon his own qualities and ability to ensure the safety and prosperity of his people. Like Plethon before him, Pico only spells out what is already present in the opening sections of Plato's *Republic* Book 6 and Plotinus' *Enneads* 1.2.1.

Palamas and the Hesychasts locate the 'idols of God' not only in pagan thought but also in Latin scholasticism. Their point is that the Thomist quest for a *sacra scientia* substitutes a perverted type of Aristotelian logic for experiential knowledge of god thus leading to sterile 'pagano-Latin' intellectual constructions, as Palamas said of Barlaam.[93] The Greek East appears to have remained faithful to the principle that the essence of god cannot be the subject of any *scientia*.[94]

---

[90] Andreas of Crete, *Magnus Canon, PG* 97.1352C.   [91] *Enn.* 1.2.1.

[92] This notion is already prefigured, we shall see, in Demetrios Kydones' demystification of sovereignty and its reconfiguration in terms of the ruler's own *schema*.

[93] Marion (1991: 121–2) observed that when Thomas Aquinas applies the notion and name of *ens* to god, he escapes the suspicion of idolatry only with difficulty. Of course, the presuppositions of Marion's argument are very different from those of Orthodox theologians, though pointing in the same direction concerning the human capacity of intellection to claim its autonomy.

[94] See below, Ch. 4, pp. 208–10.

In classifying products of human cognitive faculties within the same category as handmade idols, Palamas was in step with Basil, Gregory of Nazianzus and Gregory of Nyssa. The Cappadoceans elaborated on the idea that mental simulacra claim to comprehend and comprise divinity just as material idols and temples do. Like pagan *sancti loci*, notions about God are by default limited – not by geographic or material restrictions but by those of human intellection. The difference between geographical, material or intellectual attempts to circumscribe divinity is secondary. As Gregory of Nazianzus put it, intellectual comprehension is a species of circumscription (ἐν γὰρ περιγραφῆς εἶδος καὶ ἡ κατάληψις).[95] Comprehension equals seizure.[96] The theologian should always acknowledge that he can provide nothing but an 'image of truth' (τὸ τῆς ἀληθείας ἴνδαλμα) or a shadow (ἀποσκίασμα).[97] Otherwise, theology degenerates into idolatry. Just as Samaritans were condemned by Christ for localising god, in the same manner, says Gregory of Nyssa, 'new Samaritans' (in this case the followers of Eunomius) hope to circumscribe the divine essence in words as if in some locus (οἷόν τινι τόπῳ).[98]

In the course of Byzantine history, Eunomianism, iconoclasm and Byzantine humanism are three instances where Orthodox theology is thought to have uncovered mutations of conceptual idolatry surviving within Christianity by means of heresy. Maintaining false views about god is tantamount to 'intellectual idolatry (νοητὴ εἰδωλολατρεία)', we read in a treatise attributed to Basil of Caesaria. The curse of Deuteronomy (27:15) regarding humanly constructed 'abominations' (βδελύγματα) is extended to cover conceptual abominations as well.[99] Already Maximus of Tyre had noted the tendency of human intellect to deteriorate towards the production of material and intellectual idols owing to its inability to comprehend the essence of god.[100] But whereas in pagan Platonism this was seen as a natural condition, Basil

---

[95] Gr. Naz. *De theologia* 10.15–18.
[96] Thus Prochoros Kydones was anathematised for his alleged belief in the possibility of seizing god (κατάληψις) by apprehending divine wisdom. See below, pp. 204–10.
[97] Gr. Naz. *De filio* 17.11–14. [98] Gr. Nyss. *Contra Eun.* 3.1.110.5–15.
[99] Basil, *Enarratio in Prophetam Isaiam*, 2.96.43–8. [100] Max. Tyr. 2.10a5–10.

sees 'conceptual idolatry' arising through the susceptibility of intellect to daemonic attacks. *Nous* potentially deviates to idolatry (ὁ νοῦς . . . εἰδωλολατρήσει) and leads man to a fall from the proper existential condition of piety.[101] The autonomy of philosophy is demonised and taken to mean an objectification of concepts that is as questionable as is the creation of material idols (εἰδωλοποιία). The application of metaphors in theology is treated with circumspection too. Metaphors are images that bring man to a state of vertigo (ἰλιγγιάσωμεν).[102] When Paul said that we see god 'through a mirror and an enigma', notes Gregory, he meant that the ensuing meaning (τὸ ἐγγινόμενον νόημα) is but a simulacrum (ὁμοίωμα) that does not really reflect the object of desire. The mirror reproduces a misdirecting image (εἰκασμός) and not the true species of god (τὸ εἶδος).[103] Conversely, the metaphor of the mirror enjoys a prominent place in Plethon. One of the analogies used in the *Nomoi* to explain the emanation of a self-sufficient symbolic *systema* involves 'gods' produced like idols in a natural process of mirroring. The Plethonean 'gods' are interchangeable with Platonic *Ideas* but also affirmed and conceptually apprehended as *idols* mirroring aspects of Being.

Consequently, in the context of the Orthodox establishment that he wished to subvert, Plethon counts as an idolater in two ways. First, because of his central position that man may cognise 'Zeus' through his own intellectual resources (Ch. 4). This rendered Plethon susceptible to the accusation of making an Absolute of the human intellect by confuting notions of god with God as a personal Being. On a second level, Plethon claimed to encode and decode the blueprint of all that is into the symbolic philosophico-religious *systema* of the *Nomoi*. The 'gods' in this system represent Platonic Ideas and Aristotelian categories. For Basil, Gregory of Nyssa, and Palamas, these are nothing but conceptual avatars and mental simulacra, as empty of real Being as was any material

---

[101] Basil, *Ep.* 233.2.18–20.
[102] Cf. Basil, *Ep.* 38.5; Gr. Nyss. *De virgin.* 10.2: εἰς τὸ δυσθεώρητον ἐμπεσόντες.
[103] Gr. Nyss. *In Cant. Canticorum* 6.86.12–18 Langerbeck.

idol. Or, as Scholarios puts it, they are nothing but 'myths and dreams'.[104]

Why Plethon matters: pagan ontology versus Judaeo-Christian theology

In *Twilight of the Idols* Nietzsche applied the idol as a root metaphor for the – Platonist – philosophical tendency to idolise or make an absolute of concepts by substituting one or the other philosophical 'system' for God.[105] By liquidating the difference between Judaeo-Christianity and Platonism, Nietzsche anticipates anti-essentialist trends in post-modern intellectual history. Nietzsche thought that 'the Christian belief, which was Plato's belief, is that god is the truth, that the truth is divine'.[106] And yet a significant conflict that took place in the context of twentieth-century continental philosophy highlights the inner incompatibility between two fundamentally different world-views and provides a good starting point for understanding why Plethon matters.

In the aftermath of World War II Hans Jonas and Emmanuel Lévinas approached philosophical paganism as an intellectual paradigm rather than as a historically contingent phenomenon. According to Jonas, the essence of philosophical paganism is exemplified in Martin Heidegger's supplanting of the Judaeo-Christian generosity of God with the generosity of Being, namely in the supplanting of theology with ontology. Beneath 'the seeming, false humility of Heidegger's shifting the initiative to Being', objected Jonas, hides 'the most enormous hubris in the whole history of thought'. This is that man may ever be the 'shepherd of Being', when, says Jonas, he has failed to be his brother's keeper.[107] Emmanuel Lévinas captured the ancestry of the issue when commenting on idolatry in the Torah: 'The problem is an important one. Is idolatry excluded from the *logos*? Is Greek intelligibility sufficient for the human?' Rather, for Lévinas' understanding of

---

[104] Schol. *Ad exarchum Josephum, OC* 4.169.35: ἀλλ᾽ ὡς ἄν τις ἀκούσειέ του μύθους ἢ ὀνείρους διηγουμένου.
[105] Nietzsche (2005) 155.   [106] Nietzsche (2001) 201.
[107] Jonas quoted in Cohen (1994) 302.

idolatry according to the Torah, a 'pure logos' presents a definite danger.[108] Drawing on the Talmud, Lévinas approached idolatries either as cults 'properly so called', or as 'hidden, unconscious cults without hieratic rites'. These evolve around possible symbols and representations taken for concepts and thus displacing God.[109] At one with Lévinas, Jonas sees any 'claims of having "grasped" not only God but also our neighbour "or the world as it really is" as idolatrous, for we in effect claim to take the place that can be filled only by One'.[110] This paganism 'without rites' establishes what Jonas calls an *immediacy* between human intellect and divine intellect. The essence of paganism, then, concerns the claim 'that in principle the basic human condition, that of being at a distance of things... can be remitted, avoided, overcome. The claim, that is, to a possible immediacy...'[111] In this sense Heidegger is a pagan. For the paramount effect of pagan mysticism is that it necessarily cancels out the theistic distinction between god the Creator and man as a created being, or, in terms taken from Orthodox theology, the distinction between imparticipable, unqualified essence (god) and participable qualified substance (creation).

In Part II of this book I will try to show in detail why and how, for the first time since late antiquity, Plethon's Platonic ontology purports to diminish this distinction. The claim to a 'possible immediacy' between man and the divine constitutes the nerve centre of his reception of Plato. Plethon believed that man may be redeemed only by a relapse to what Heidegger called the 'Greek dawn'. Heidegger sought this pagan ontology in the Presocratics and Plato's *Parmenides*, Plethon in Plato and in social as well as metaphysical truths allegedly beyond history. The impetus behind both projects is a deep conviction that truth has been obstructed by a theological tradition that separates and alienates man from his genuine position. In Plethon's case, Hellenism spurs on a sort of ontological *nostos* that emerges in a historical moment critical for the survival of an empire.

---

[108] Lévinas (1994) 70.   [109] Lévinas (1994) 57.   [110] Benson (2002) 10.
[111] Cf. Jonas (1966) 257–8; Cohen (1994) 303.

As Plethon saw it, the recovery of Being leads to a philosophy of action and radicalism within history – an antidote to the Judaeo-Christian transposition of hope to the world beyond. Platonism carries a political message based on the assumption that salvation lies in retrieving and grasping Being, not in god's grace. Affirming the deeper unity between humanity and divinity, Plethon proceeded to demolish the unknowability and transcendence of divine essence and reconnect man to history and philosophy. Long before Heidegger, Plethon seeks in the *Nomoi* and the *Differences* a genuine understanding of Being, while in the *Memoranda* he advances a pre-modern notion of proto-nationalism. By contrast, his arch-enemy Scholarios welcomed the end of history and the collapse of terrestrial national and political entities as a prerequisite for achieving redemption in an 'eternal home country' beyond history and temporality.

'Only in some corner and in darkness' are polytheist doctrines still discussed, triumphs Scholarios, for everybody believes in a single god.[112] This attempt to marginalize Plethon's ideas rests on a false basis: that Plethon's paganism consisted in belief in many gods or in ritual paganism. Plethon matters because he was the first to define the philosophical properties of a pre-existing Platonic ideal-type that was momentarily defeated by Roman Orthodoxy as expressed by Palamism but ultimately evolved within modernity and early Enlightenment into the autonomous outlook defined by Peter Gay as modern paganism – and later diversified into the ontological and epistemological ramifications that triggered the awareness of Jonas and Lévinas.

Philosophically the real dawn of modern paganism did not take place during the Enlightenment. It happened in late Byzantium within a disintegrating and falling empire.

Structure and outline of the book

Part I comprises three chapters that focus on Plethon's intellectual context. These explore how secular and paganising philosophical tendencies in Byzantium evolved out of Neoplatonism and argue

---

[112] Schol. *Against Polytheists, OC* 4.181.5–10.

that Plethon's world-view descends through a long ancestry of intellectual dissenters. It thus seeks to recover the lost rings in a Platonist golden chain from late antiquity to late Byzantium in order to argue that Plethon's support for Roman Orthodoxy in the Council of Ferrara/Florence in 1438/9 was not the product of Christian sympathies but of intellectual expediency. Plethon opted for the Greek Church because of an inner persuasion that the pagan reform of the *Nomoi* was possible only within the intellectual context of the East. The union of the Churches required the submission of Orthodoxy to Latin Christianity and cancelled out any alternative. Conversely, Plethonean reformism echoed a long Platonic tradition that survived in the East even if in constant tension with Christian Orthodoxy.

For heuristic reasons I distinguish three phases in the Byzantine reception of pagan Platonism from late antiquity to Plethon. The first phase concerns *the archetypical Plato* and deals with the immediate competition between pagan Platonism and Christian revelation in late antiquity. The second phase concerns *the occult Plato* and deals with the period from the seventh century to the ninth century. Phase three focuses on *the secular Plato* and examines the processes by which pagan Platonism resurfaces as a secular political religion. This division is primarily a phenomenological rather than a historical one: the emphasis is not on the philosophical elements of conceptual idolatry (see Part II for those) but rather on the modalities and tropes through which a Platonist world-view antagonistic to Christianity was preserved, appropriated, re-calibrated and continuously juxtaposed to Christian monastic and clerical hegemony. The focus is on intellectual connections and patterns of resistance.

The mechanics by virtue of which pagan Hellenism was transmitted from late antiquity to Plethon are set out by enlarging on two intertwined motifs: (a) the conflict between a 'lived' versus an 'intellectual' ideology, that is to say, between social identity and intellectual identity in Byzantium; and (b) the opposition between, on the one hand, the occult, humanism and secular Platonism, and, on the other hand, clerical/political authority. These are not irrelevant to what has been called 'la tragédie de la pensée byzantine', a profound schism in Byzantine intellectual history that often assumes, as Zakythinos notes, the phenomenology of an opposition between rationalism and mysticism, Hellenism and Orthodoxy, Psellos and Symeon the New Theologian.[113]

Chapter 2 concludes that Plethon's endeavour is not as ahistorical and cut off from his immediate context as it may appear and as his arch-enemy Scholarios would have us believe. Rather, the intellectual context that shaped Plethon's philosophical, political and social position continuously pressed in the direction of a Platonist turn that was partly realised before Plethon.

The decay of central political authority in fourteenth-century Byzantium is conversely analogous to the rise of Palamism. This fuelled the monastic takeover of secular and political institutions. Palamas triumphed – but it was a Pyrrhic victory. The Hesychast controversy brought to the surface intellectual resources that had their roots in an underground 'Hellenic' philosophical tradition as old as Byzantium and that ultimately provided the seedbed for the Plethonean project. The Hesychast controversy shaped the intellectual circumstances that made Plethon's philosophical activity possible in the first place. In the process of their 'pagano-Latin' opposition to Orthodoxy, to apply Palamas' expression, Byzantine humanists of Platonising tendencies unearthed a *hereditas damnosa*, a Platonic conception of illumination antagonistic to the Palamite one that had definite repercussions in epistemology, ontology and late attempts at political reformism.

In this context Platonism and Aristotelianism acquired peculiar associations that instigated Plethon's famous *Differences between Plato and Aristotle* and his clash with Scholarios. Crucially, an understanding of this background is necessary to approach the question of Plethon's relation to Christianity and the puzzle presented by the *Nomoi*, a work here seen as a manifesto of pagan philosophy. Available approaches to the *Nomoi* and the story of the 'Plethon affair' are presented in Chapter 3.

Part II is entitled 'The elements of pagan Platonism'. I argue that the actual foundations of Plethon's pagan Platonism are present in works purportedly addressed to a Christian audience, namely in the *Differences between Plato and Aristotle* and in the *Monody*

---

[113] Zakythinos (1975) 364.

for the Empress Helen, as well as in Plethon's commentary on the *Chaldean Oracles*. The core of these works is no less suffused with philosophical paganism than is the *Nomoi* project. This begs the question of defining in what sense Plethon's philosophy is a pagan one and establishing what exactly, according to Plethon, renders Plato incompatible with Christianity.

Chapter 4 deals with competing versions of illumination presented by Hesychast *theoptia* and humanist *theoria* in order to trace the origins of Plethon's epistemic optimism. The revival of Plato's epistemology in the fourteenth century challenged the Christian desacralisation of the human intellect and led to an intellectual civil war between Byzantine humanism and Palamite Orthodoxy. The Palamite doctrine of supernatural illumination was confronted by the philosophical conception of illumination that Byzantine humanists and anti-Palamites supported with arms taken from the arsenal of ancient philosophy. Theodore Metochites was among the first to revert to a profane tradition of 'the old sages' (παλαιοὶ σοφοί) who, like some 'modern sages' (νέοι σοφοί), employ reason, study nature and depend upon their intellectual faculties to achieve wisdom and enlightenment. Similarly, Barlaam of Calabria considered pagan philosophers to be Illuminati, 'Enlightened-ones', who acquired knowledge in ways alien to experiential mysticism. Godlikeness is occasionally seen as a contemplative ascent unaided by external ritualistic aids that revives the intellectualist approach to *eudaimonia* in the *Timaeus*, the *mathemata* and *epitedeumata* leading to the vision of a 'wide ocean of intellectual beauty' in the *Symposium* (210d), the process towards the *megiston mathema* in *Republic* Book 6 and the role of dialectic in the *Sophist*. Conversely, Gregory Palamas drew from the tradition of Eastern Greek mysticism in order to relate illumination to psychophysical practices and fiercely attacked the claim of humanist circles that Platonic philosophy may provide access to the divine.

Like Barlaam's Illuminati and Metochites' 'old sages', the chain of archetypical wise men in the *Nomoi* that managed to persist and challenge clerical and monastic exclusivity relies upon the Platonic model of 'true philosophers' (πεφιλοσοφηκότες ὀρθῶς). Plethon sidesteps theurgic Platonism and reverts to Plato's original notion of intellectual-moral godlikeness, extracting the doctrinal essence out of a Platonic tradition that believed in the divine origin of mankind and its ability to comprehend god *qua* Being by the operation of faculties inherent in man and moral self-improvement. The first part of the *Nomoi* presents one of the most emphatic defences of rational discourse and epistemic optimism in the history of philosophy, resoundingly reappearing in Plethon's suggestion of a universal philosophical religion derived from common notions peculiar to humanity. Plethon departs not only from Palamite apophaticism, but also from any variant of Platonism that potentially served Christian anti-intellectualism and experiential mysticism.

Chapter 5 focuses on the formation of a distinctively pagan ontology. Plethon collided with a dubious interpretation of Plato initiated by Plotinus that put forward a thesis of obvious use to Christian theology: that god or the One is really *beyond* Being. But Plethon also clashed with another Plotinus-inspired position that enjoyed popularity in Byzantium, that Platonic Forms are not independent entities but the 'thoughts of god'. In the light of modern scholarship Plethon may well have been right to criticise both points. Plato's Idea of the Good is not truly beyond Being, and the identification of Forms with the thoughts of god finds little support in Plato – even though it obviously has a long history within Neoplatonism.

Plethon revives pagan ontological monism by abandoning the theistic notion of God as an unqualified transcendent personal being for one of Being as a universal and supreme genus. In the *Differences* he dechristianises Platonic ontology and advances three revolutionary positions that offer the presuppositions of philosophical paganism in the *Nomoi*. First, Plethon claims against the Byzantine appropriation of Aristotle that the postulation of a plurality of productive causes between the first principle and the world of becoming is metaphysically and logically necessary. As he sees things, god is the 'creator of creators' and the 'originator of originators'. Second, he affirms the possibility of achieving a firm knowledge even of what comes about by accident, thus excluding the contingent basis of creationism; third, he challenges Aristotle's and Aquinas' position that Being *cannot* be a *genus*.

Aquinas' insistence that god cannot be a *genus* meant that god is ultimately indemonstrable. Plethon challenges and subverts this thesis. God as a knowable and comprehensible principle is identifiable with Being *qua genus*. According to Plethon's commentary on the *Chaldean Oracles*, man may achieve cognitive contact not only with the intelligible Forms, namely the gods in the *Nomoi*, but also with their summit. Consequently, Plethon's use of the adjective 'supra-essential' (ὑπερούσιος) for god in the *Differences* should be read with the same caution with which one approaches Plato's notorious assertion that the Idea of the Good is 'beyond being' in *Republic* 509b. Plethon's interpretation of Platonic ontology departs from the ambiguities of later Neoplatonism and anticipates recent scholarship in postulating that Plato's Idea of the Good/One/god is not really beyond Being. Thus Plethon's understanding of 'Zeus' as extreme Being marks a departure from medieval scholasticism and Eastern Greek mystical theology.

Chapter 6 charts Plethon's polytheist, or rather henotheist symbolic theology and traces its philosophical roots in the Hesychast controversy. The relentless strife between Palamites and anti-Palamites was the progenitor of a long discussion on the nature of polytheism. Were Palamas' 'uncreated energies' equivalent to 'gods', as his opponents claimed? Or is it rather the case that experimental notions like those of 'created gods' put forward by the anti-Hesychast humanist party lead to polytheism and Hellenism, as Palamas argued? Chapter 6 concludes that, contrary to Scholarios' view, the polytheism of the *Nomoi* is an offspring of its age, part of an extended debate on gods and god, polytheism and monotheism, Hellenism and Judaeo-Christianity.

Part III puts the spotlight on Plethon's call to socio-political reformism. The effort to overthrow Palamas' and Scholarios' Judaeo-Christian transcendent God by identifying the One with Being is mirrored on the political level in the substitution of a secular (in the *Memoranda*) and alternatively a pagan (in the *Nomoi*) utopia for Christian millenarianism. The Platonic ideal of a *polis* that achieves a state of self-reliance and self-preservation offered the ideal alternative to the threat presented by Christian ecumenism and especially Palamite trans-nationalism. Palamas' and Scholarios' anticipation of the 'eternal home country' is a manifestation of

Judaeo-Christian spiritual utopianism that privileged ecumenism even under Ottoman rule at the expense of any attempt to conserve or reform Byzantium as a *civitas terrena*. In the *Memoranda* Plethon substituted the perseverance of a single political community for the universality of trans-national Orthodox faith. With these two addresses he not only daringly parted from all stereotypes of Byzantine 'mirrors for princes' but also demanded a shift from religious ecumenism to state formation. In the fourteenth-century context of an empire falling apart the old rift between political utopianism and spiritual utopianism acquired an urgent ideological resonance.

Plethon's reformism in the *Memoranda* is an evolution of previous inconclusive and aborted attempts at secularisation. In the light of Nicholas Kabasilas' *Discourse* and Kydones' epistles Plethon ceases to appear as a quixotic reformer. The concept of sovereignty in the *Memoranda* takes a step further the desacralisation of imperial authority exemplified in Demetrios Kydones' epistles to Manuel II. With Kydones and Plethon a secular and classical notion of kingship is openly and persistently reinvigorated for the first time since late antiquity as an alternative and proper substitute for Christian millenarianism, at the same time that powerful lay circles presented in Kabasilas' *Discourse* openly demanded the replacement of Christianity with a new political theology. Thus, I argue that the proto-nationalism of the *Memoranda* evolves as a new ideological framework intended to overcome the legal and political obstacles that blocked large-scale attempts at secularisation in the fourteenth century. The *Memoranda* offered a total plan intended to succeed where partial secularisation measures could not.

Seen in this light, the *Memorandum to Manuel* was the last secular attempt to achieve the demystification of the Byzantine State. The introvert paganism of the *Nomoi* is the outcome of the ultimate failure of secular lay circles and possibly of Manuel personally to disentangle the State from the control of a Church still conditioned by Hesychasm and Palamism. The *Memoranda* envisage a *secular* utopia; the *Nomoi* stands for a *pagan* utopia presumably capable of succeeding where the secular circles described in Nicholas Kabasilas' *Discourse* and Plethon's *Memoranda* failed: in radical reform. But in the *Nomoi* utopianism assumes a totalitarian form. Religion is not an abstract framework for appeasing people, as in *Memorandum to Manuel*; religion is now used to ensure obeisance and conformity and to define the identity of the citizenship.

Chapter 8 sums up the main points of this book. The *epilogue* investigates one further issue: the complex relation between Plethon and modernity. Plethon has been misleadingly seen as a forerunner of Renaissance Platonism. In reality, Plethon anticipates the early modern reception of ancient philosophy that was effectively a reaction to Renaissance Platonism. Furthermore, from a philosophical viewpoint Plethon anticipates Spinoza rather than the Christian Platonism of Ficino. His case confirms the now forgotten thesis of pioneer textual critics and intellectuals such as Gundling and Bayle regarding the pagan Platonic origins of that particular early modern outlook aptly christened *Spinozismus ante Spinozam*.

PART I

LOST RINGS OF THE PLATONIST GOLDEN CHAIN

UNDERGROUND PLATONISM IN BYZANTIUM

Towards a reformulation of K. N. Sathas' thesis

The scholarly *communis opinio* is that Hellenic resistance to Christianity ended around the sixth century. Proclus, Damascius and Olympiodorus appear to have been the last rings in the Platonist 'golden chain' envisaged by Hierocles. This seemingly leaves us with two options: either agree with Scholarios and consider the author of the *Nomoi* a quixotic neopagan; or doubt the seriousness of Plethon's purported paganism. After all, we shall see presently that according to one account Plethon ostensibly posed as a devout servant of the Orthodox Church on at least one occasion.

Part I of this book introduces a third alternative. It challenges the prevalent view in regard to the purported obsolence of philosophical paganism in Byzantium (Chs. 1–2) as well as the possibility of an ultimately Christian Plethon (Ch. 3). Instead, it documents the survival of the Hellenic philosophical outlook from late antiquity to Plethon and seeks to uncover the channels through which it evolved. This part does not expressly deal with the contents or philosophical institutions of this pagan paradigm; these are laid out in detail in Part II. Rather, what is in the spotlight here is the historical phenomenology of Hellenism within the Byzantine context. The objective is to reclaim from the margins of Byzantine history the necessary intellectual context within which it was possible for Hellenic/pagan ideas to survive.

More rings should be added to Hierocles' *golden chain* of Hellenes than Scholarios would have liked us to believe. Plethon's pagan existential position did not miraculously resurface *ex nihilo* in the fifteenth century after ten centuries of obsolence. It is part of an intellectual tradition which utilised calculated dissimulation, occultism, humanism and secular education, and last but not least, Christian heresy, as its vehicles in order to pass on the torch of a world-view that remained essentially incompatible with Judaeo-Christianity. Plethon should be acknowledged as an expert in religious and ideological dissimulation.

My second interest in this part of the book is to use the intellectual history of pagan Platonism within Byzantium as a framework to provide an answer to that tantalising question regarding Plethon's support for the Orthodox Church in 1438/9 and his anti-unionist position. Plethon's presence in the Ferrara/Florence Council and his advocacy of Orthodoxy against Latin theology has been taken to indicate that he was not so 'pagan' after all. Possible approaches to Plethon's advocacy of Orthodoxy in the Synod are presented in Chapter 3. Here it suffices to say that the ultimate motivation behind Plethon's support for Orthodoxy is related to the long history and deep roots of Hellenic tendencies within Eastern Christianity that resurfaced during the fourteenth-century Hesychast controversy. These rendered Plethon's reformist project meaningful only within the Eastern intellectual framework.

It is worth evoking here the pioneering theory of Konstantinos Sathas regarding the survival of pagan Hellenism within Byzantium. Sathas did not maintain that paganism ultimately shaped the Christian mysteries from the inside, as Protestant and deist philosophers had done.[1] Rather, Sathas, nowadays considered eccentric and very rarely (if at all) remembered by modern Byzantinists, argued in favour of a covert pagan movement operating within the Christian Empire and bowing to clerical hegemony while maintaining its own distinct identity.[2] Masai noted the fundamental difficulty with Sathas' theory. Even if one goes along with the hypothesis that Hellenism was an option available to certain Byzantine intellectuals, there is no conclusive proof that these apostates were members of anything like a secret society with the aim of transmitting pagan faith.[3] To put it bluntly, Sathas' hypothesis is not falsifiable. There is a rather unsatisfactory reply already anticipated by Sathas: the successful survival of pagan Hellenism within Byzantium depended upon the elimination of any abundance of evidence

---

[1] See for example Toland (1997) 93–4.
[2] The fullest exposition of Sathas' thesis is in his extensive introduction to volume VI of *MB*.
[3] Masai (1956) 283.

that might provoke the authorities. Besides, Byzantine historiography is largely the product of ideological manipulation. The evidence is there, argued Sathas, provided one can read between the lines. There were 'Hellenes' before Plethon, some of whom were in high positions in the clerical and political hierarchy. Much of the material presented by Sathas points to behaviours unusual and bizarre, to say the least, even if this may not be sufficient to fully validate his theory.

Yet the great contribution of Sathas lies elsewhere. Long before theorists of power and authority relations, Sathas was among the first to note the clash between what we would now be inclined to see as philosophical discourse and clerical/monastic hegemony. Acquiescence in Christian religious hegemony and compliance with an establishment of ideological indoctrination may manifestly lead to outward conformity, which, nonetheless, may well hide within it a burning esoteric disquietude that fertilises ideological dissent. Sathas daringly applied this model to the case of Byzantium. He thus acutely understood something that still escapes his (post)modern colleagues: that it is imperative to distinguish between the perseverance of pagan Platonic ideas and the professional or social identity of those men possibly responsible for their intellectual diffusion.

The social and philosophical identity of Plethon will remain a paradox unless the problems and complexities involved in the impact of authority on social and intellectual discourse in Byzantium are taken into account. Contemporary social psychology has identified a particular kind of ideological conflict described in terms of disjunctions between 'lived' and 'intellectual' ideologies. An intellectual may firmly believe in the possibility of achieving a perfectly just society and may hold particular ideas on how such a society should be ultimately organised; yet he may also conform to the laws of the present society and be fully adjusted to its social or religious normativity.[4] Religious and ideological dissimulation is not confined by culture or epoch.[5] It is unwise to insist

---

4 Billig *et al.* (1988) 33. For example, Marx and Engels disagreed with the bourgeois establishment, even if they conformed to bourgeois lives themselves.
5 On dissimulation see Zagorin (1990). Its use in the sixteenth and seventeenth centuries by dissident religious leaders and intellectuals in Western Europe may serve as an

that Orthodox Byzantium was an exception and that anyone who waved his certificates of Orthodoxy was really deaf to the sirens of Hellenism. Rather, religious and ideological dissimulation had a long history in the East before Plethon's time.[6] Some of the most interesting Byzantine intellectuals faced conflicts between 'lived' and 'intellectual' ideologies, conflicts accentuated by the absence of any sufficient climate of intellectual and religious freedom.

To the extent that philosophical dissension meant religious dissension (and this is certainly a premise respected throughout Byzantine history by pillars of Orthodoxy from the early Christian apologists to the Palamites) it is a Hellenic philosophical paradigm, rather than ritualistic paganism, that adapted to and survived Christian inculcation and indoctrination. Fourteenth-century humanists and Plethon resuscitated the philosophical cult of the ancient *pephotismenoi*, the Hellenic sages combated by Palamas, one that potentially threatened religious Orthodoxy all along. In terms of the internal distinction within Neoplatonism, Hellenes in Byzantium form a chain of *philosophoi* rather than of *hieratikoi* that managed to resurface at critical points within the Byzantine clerical framework. As Damascius noted, the philosophical and hieratic aspects of Neoplatonism are, according to Plato's conception of a philosopher-Bacchus, nothing but two faces of the same coin.[7] Like Damascius, Sathas does not explicitly distinguish between pagan ritualistic paganism and pagan philosophy. Rather, he often focuses on an elusive pagan sentiment, which, like other nineteenth-century thinkers and intellectuals,[8] he deeply suspected and related to Platonism but could not philosophically define.

Intriguingly, Masai prepared the ground for such a revision of Sathas' hypothesis. Masai noted the presence of a Byzantine *élite laïque* in conflict with the Byzantine hierocratic establishment.

---

example. Protestants only apparently conformed to Catholic worship, and so did Jewish communities in Spain. The same is true of ideological dissenters in Soviet Union: dissimulation is a common phenomenon in history from Europe to China.

[6] See Kaldellis (forthcoming); (2004); (2005); (2003); (1999b); (2007b); (1999a); (2007a) on the dissimulation of Procopius of Caesaria, John Lydus, Agathias, Attaleiates and Psellos. On Leon Choirosphaktes see Magdalino (1997) and below, pp. 66ff. On Italos and Psellos see below, pp. 82ff.

[7] Dam. *In Phaedonem* 1.172.

[8] I have in mind Walter Pater and Swinburne, often considered to be forerunners of neopaganism. See Pearson (2006) 829.

This secular elite consisted of patricians and intellectuals who reverted to antiquity, developed a humanist world-view, claimed their independence and occasionally collided with clericalism. Masai mentions Psellos and Italos. The implication here is that the policy of complaisance with the clerical hegemony was one potential channel through which Byzantium managed to transmit to the Renaissance what Masai called *conceptions des modalités plus laïques de civilisation*.[9]

Seen in this light, secularism has its origins in the evolution of a Hellenic philosophical tradition striving to survive in a Christian world. This insight is signalled in a neglected paper delivered to the Brussels *Société de philosophie* in 1958. Masai argues that the 'caractère libertine, incrédule, anti-chrétien du platonisme byzantin' was due not only to historical contingencies, but to the very *principles* of Platonic philosophy: 'c'est en approfondissant leurs principes que les platoniciens byzantins devinrent incrédules, ou le demeurèrent, malgré toutes les pressions du totalitarisme orthodoxe'.[10] The nature of Platonism was in itself profoundly anti-Christian – which is to say, it was Hellenic/pagan. Thus in *Pléthon* Masai argues that the cases of Psellos and John Italos oblige us to make at least one capital concession to Sathas, namely that long before Plethon certain Byzantine intellectuals consciously chose to bow to authority and carry the mask of the pious Christian instead of that of a Pythagorean-Platonist pagan philosopher.[11]

This begs the question why Platonism in itself is necessarily incompatible with Christianity, in other words, Hellenic/pagan. I deal with this in Part II. Here it suffices to note that intellectual connections often transcend temporal distance, and it is such connections that ensured the viability of Hellenic tendencies in the Byzantine Empire. The metaphor of a wave that constantly changes shape is an apt one for describing Platonism in Byzantium.[12] From late antiquity to Plethon philosophical Hellenism constantly changes shape – and so it does within the corpus of Plethon's works: Hellenism may appear to be a world-view explicitly opposed to the

---

[9] Masai (1956) 297.   [10] Masai (1957/8) 400.   [11] Masai (1956) 294.
[12] The metaphor of the *Wellenlinie* was proposed by Darko (1930) 17.

Christian establishment, as heresy, or a form of proto-secularism and humanism. The first type is exemplified by late antique Neoplatonism; the second and third are appropriate to recalcitrant Byzantine intellectuals from Psellos and Theodore Metochites to the anti-Hesychast dissenters of the fourteenth century. All three eventually provide the presuppositions for the resurfacing of pagan metaphysical notions.

Divine Plato: pagan Platonic dissonance in late antiquity

Late antique anti-Christian discourse has been almost exhaustively researched. Celsus, Porphyry, Hierocles and Julian attacked Christian intellectual imperialism both at the philosophical and at the rhetorical level. Yet beside anti-Christian polemics and explicit conflict there were further, alternative channels, by means of which philosophers 'beyond the gates (θύραθεν)' could exercise their criticism and implicitly distinguish themselves from Christian Orthodoxy. Pagans put to new use literary forms commonly used by Christians, such as the 'gospel' or the epistle for spiritual guidance. But similitude of medium and likeness of the form does not presuppose doctrinal community. Lucien Jerphagnon viewed Porphyry's *Life of Plotinus* as a response to Christian gospels, that is to say, as 'l'Évangile de Plotin selon saint Porphyre, le disciple que Plotin aimait, son saint Jean'.[13] John Dillon and Peter Garnsey note that in Iamblichus' *On the Pythagorean Way of Life* Pythagoras 'is to be seen as a pagan holy man and rival of Jesus of Nazareth, with parallels to be drawn to the Gospels'.[14] And Raffaele Sodano noted that Porphyry's *Letter to Marcella* may be read as another 'pagan gospel'.[15] Porphyry's insistence on the importance of reason in order to perform the return to god, the constant references to intellectual catharsis, the tacit attacks on *amathia* (Iamblichus used the same word to allude to the Christians) and to the *sophists* (Plethon used the same word to designate the Christians), leave little doubt as to the anti-Christian function of the epistle. The author of another pagan gospel after Porphyry's example, Marinus,

---

[13] Jerphagnon (1990) 43.   [14] Dillon (2002); Garnsey (2005) 77.
[15] See the introduction by Raffaele Sodano to his edition of *Ad Marcellam*, 9.

provides us with a concise account of a shift that made it necessary for pagans to develop new tactics of survival in a Christian world. In just one paragraph Marinus describes the passage from Proclus' initial policy of 'Herculean courage' to his adoption of the now understandably more prudent motto 'live unnoticed':

For he [Proclus] managed to save his life in the midst of the greatest perils, when he had to weather terrible tempests, when all the unleashed typhoons were shaking his so well regulated life, without letting himself be frightened or discouraged. One day, indeed, when he found himself the object of the suspicions and vexations of a sort of vultures (γυποψίγαντες) that surrounded him [i.e. certain Christians], obeying that [divine] Power which starts revolutions in this world, he left Athens and made a journey to Asia, where his residence became most profitable to him. For his guardian spirit furnished him the occasion of this departure in order that he might not remain ignorant of the ancient religious institutions which had been there preserved. Indeed, among the Lydians, he succeeded in gaining a clear conception of these doctrines, while they through long vicissitudes had come to neglect certain liturgical operations, received from him a more complete doctrine, because the philosopher more perfectly conceived what relates to the divinities. By doing this and in thus ordering his conduct, he succeeded in achieving oblivion, even better than the Pythagoreans observed the inviolate command of their master, to 'live unnoticed'. (Marinus, *Procl.* 15; trans. K. S. Guthrie)

The implication is that opposition to Christianity had to go underground and inevitably appear muted. In Simplicius' terms, one has two options under oppressive regimes: either to leave and seek one's fortune elsewhere, for example in Persia; or to lead a low-profile life as a scholar. When forthright polemic was no longer wise, Plato's text was put to new uses.[16] From the fifth century onwards *thurathen* thought was progressively excluded from institutionalised education and Platonist philosophers temporarily found a safe haven in philosophical commentary. Assuming the *personae* of commentators rather than of pagan gurus, Proclus, Simplicius and Olympiodorus avoided direct conflict with the Christian authorities and hoped to preserve for posterity the Platonist world-view. Allusions to the Christians did find their way into their commentaries with relative safety.

In terms of social identity theory, these code phrases testify to a pagan self-perception that sharply distinguishes between a

---

[16] Siniossoglou (2008a) 43–7.

Hellenic ingroup and a Christian outgroup linked by a power relationship: the Christians are not only 'alien to our world (ἐκτετοπισμένοι τῆς καθ᾿ ἡμᾶς οἰκουμένης)' but they also are 'those in power (οἱ κρατοῦντες)', or, according to Marinus, the 'giant vultures (γυπογίγαντες)' and the *Typhonean spirits* (τὰ τυφώνεια πνεύματα) that have subverted the 'lawful life' establishing what is, *mutatis mutandis*, a lawless state. At least three Neoplatonists, namely Iamblichus, Proclus and Simplicius clearly suggest what is a form of *Machtpolitik*. Against a stronger opponent it is better to remain unnoticed than to provoke.

The best formulation of this idea is contained in Proclus' Scholia to Hesiod's *Works and Days*. This unnoticed little gem shows that what appeared to be the commentary of an academic classicist might actually have concealed a political statement and even programme. The Hesiodean myth concerns a hawk that gripped a nightingale fast and carried it high up among the clouds; the nightingale, pierced by his crooked talons, cried pitifully. The hawk responded to her with much disdain:

'Miserable thing, why do you cry out? One far stronger than you now holds you fast, and you must go wherever I take you, songstress as you are. And if I please I will make my meal of you, or let you go. He is a fool who tries to withstand the stronger, for he does not get the mastery and suffers pain besides his shame.' So said the swiftly flying hawk, the long-winged bird.

This 'you must go wherever I take you', comments Proclus, implies that whoever exercises more violence (ὁ βιαιότερος) leads and that the weaker (ὁ ἀσθενέστερος) is led according to the former's wishes. Hesiod had no option but to conform to the wishes of unjust kings, for it was in their power to make a nice dinner out of him (ἐπ᾿ ἐκείνοις γὰρ εἶναι καὶ δεῖπνον αὐτὸν ποιήσασθαι: this is an attempt at Neoplatonic humour), just as the hawk can make a meal out of the nightingale. Once in the iron grip of a powerful ideological mechanism, only an imprudent man would not succumb to acquiescence and conformity. There is a double loss to be suffered by going against authority: shame, which comes from defeat; and pain for having been beaten: ἐπὶ τῷ κρατηθῆναι λύπην.[17] One recalls Damascius' stereotypical expression for the

---

[17] Procl. *Sch. ad Hes. Op.* 208 (78.1–15 Marzillo).

Christians: οἱ κρατοῦντες. Hesiod, who is here used as an example of maintaining apparent conformity to the demands of political authority in order to avoid the worst consequences, was actually counted among the fountainheads of pagan theology.

Yet the necessary background in order to discern the intention behind Proclus' commentary is contained in a previous remark in the same context of Hesiodean myths: 'it is possible that people suffer violence (βιασθῆναι μὲν δυνάμενοι), even if they are more pious (ἱεροπρεπέστεροι ὄντες)'.[18] The example of Hesiod offers the right guidance for minimising the repercussions of colliding with those in power, albeit in direct contravention to the classical ideal of *parrhesia*. For by now it was crystal clear that concessions to authority and complaisance might be the only ways to ensure freedom of thought.

Pagan dissimulation in a Christian world could extend beyond the sphere of current literary forms into real life. Julian pretended to be Christian for years. In the fifth century Eunapius of Sardis, using historiography as a weapon of intellectual resistance, described how at some point between 379 and 383 CE Goths crossed the Danube and entered the empire pretending to be Christians. Eunapius used a Greek proverb to describe the subterfuge: pagan Goths 'wore a large fox-skin' and passed like Christians, though remaining secretly faithful to their religion.[19] Eunapius did not merely insinuate 'that Christianity could, albeit unwittingly, endanger the security of the Empire', as Blockley correctly noted.[20] His intent goes much further. Eunapius' text 'more likely reveals a sense of irony that paganism could succeed by assuming the pose of Christianity'.[21] This reading fully explains why Eunapius does not confine himself to describing the effects of barbarian trickery but insists further on the 'noble intent' with which those barbarians remained faithful to their ancestral religion, as well as on how easy it was for them to pass as Christians under the cover of 'deep and impenetrable silence' and 'secrecy' surrounding 'their mysteries'. What is actually in the foreground here is not

[18] Procl. *Sch. ad Hes. Op.* 202.11–12 (76.9–10 Marzillo).
[19] Eunapius fr. 48.2 (pp. 74–7, Blockley 1983). On the chronology of the incident see Paschoud (2006) 488.
[20] Blockley (1981) 18.   [21] Sacks (1986) 55.

the accusation that Theodosius was so *stupidement chrétien* that he was fooled by a bunch of barbarians[22] but, rather, the realisation that one did not have to be Christian, but merely to look like one. To be sure, the Goths were not Hellenists and it is not their beliefs that Eunapius is interested in but their profession of dissimulation. A variety of sixth-century sources, including imperial legislation, attests that many Romans did not hesitate to pretend to be Christians for worldly advantage.[23] At even later times, in the eighth century, John of Damascus testifies that groups of pagans still used misdirection as a refuge, feigning their Christian identity. He calls them ἐθνόφρονες: 'those who follow the customs of the gentiles', introducing beliefs on *tyche* and *heimarmene* (as Plethon would do in the *Nomoi*), studying pagan astronomy and astrology (as Byzantine humanists would do), professing every kind of *manteia* and apotropaic rituals, sharing with the gentiles a belief in impious myths and honouring the Hellenic festivities by observing the pagan calendar.[24] As Andrew Louth observes, the decrees of the Quinisext Synod of 691/2 affirm that there must have been plenty of these ἐθνόφρονες around.[25]

Like Gregory Palamas much later in *Capita CL*, John of Damascus does not distinguish philosophical paganism from ritualistic paganism. Both are versions of Hellenism, which evolved, as it were, from idolatry, assuming the form of various philosophical sects. Platonism in particular was correlated by John with polytheism: Plato's doctrine is that many gods emanate from one god.[26] Writing in the thirteenth century, Niketas Choniates copies John's description of the *ethnophrones* into his *Thesaurus Orthodoxae Fidei* and proceeds to provide refutations of the Hellenic views on fate and necessity, divination, cledonomancy and other forms of pagan superstition described by John. Even if Niketas does not have in mind contemporary *ethnophrones* (though this is the impression he conveys),[27] he is certainly at one with John in

---

[22] This is how Paschoud (2006: 488) reads the passage.
[23] For references, see Kaldellis (2004) 168–71.
[24] *Haer.* 94.1–8: ταῖς συνηθείαις τῶν ἐθνῶν ἐπακολουθοῦντες, χριστιανοὶ τἆλλα ὑπάρχοντες.
[25] Louth (2002) 60.   [26] *Haer.* 3–8.
[27] See Rochow (1991: 138), who nevertheless insists on the political usages of the accusation of Hellenism.

leaving open the possibility of Hellenes falling back on religious dissimulation in order to hold on to their religious, intellectual and cultural identity.[28] Eunapius thought that it was 'neither laborious nor difficult' to forge a Christian identity while holding secret pagan rites, and John of Damascus seems to affirm that *ethnophrones* pretending to be Christians were operating in the eighth century. One may then plausibly infer that it must have been even less difficult to hold on to a Platonist philosophical cult that did not presuppose a ritualistic aspect but consisted of multiple philosophical *haireseis*. On the other hand, one may reasonably wonder whether and how far a philosophical and religious constellation may preserve its doctrinal essence under an exclusivist intellectual and religious hegemony, without having its *dianoia* corroded and its *lexis* assimilated by means of unceasing rhetoric, apologetics and institutionalised education. This is a fascinating issue.

Two developments within late antique hermeneutics explain how the presumed core of the Platonist ideal-type could survive even though threatened by an antagonistic world-view that claimed exclusivity. The first concerns the resurgence of a type of esoteric Platonism claiming to preserve the 'hidden' meaning of Plato's philosophy; the second concerns the multi-levelled hermeneutical model devised by the last Neoplatonist commentators. Both factors ensured that a Platonic system of meaning persevered and was rendered a permanent possibility in Byzantium.

The assumption of an esoteric core that was retrievable only with much labour and effort beyond established institutions refined a pre-existing hermeneutical model that (a) stressed the openendedness of the Platonic text, thus enhancing its flexibility and adaptability, (b) prepared the ground for valuing an oral tradition of esoteric instruction and interpretation that went beyond the mainstream exegesis of ancient philosophy, and (c) disengaged paganism from ritual ensuring its self-sufficiency, so that even if the rites became obsolete the pagan world-view would be rescued. Porphyry is illuminating in *Letter to Marcella*: it does no harm to profess ritual paganism; but this is neither a necessary nor

---

[28] *PG* 139.1343B–C, 1352C–1355B.

sufficient condition of philosophical illumination. Esoteric Platonist instruction essentially liberated Plato from the way he was officially read, taught and commented on in Christianised institutions, as well as from pagan ritual. The golden chain could thus continue its tradition outside the confinement of institutionalised education and cultic paganism. Synesius best exemplifies this development:

It is an old tradition, I think, and quite in the manner of Plato, to conceal the profound thoughts of philosophy behind the mask of some lighter treatment, that thereby whatsoever has been acquired with difficulty shall not be again lost to men, nor shall such matters be contaminated by lying exposed to the approach of the profane. The end accordingly has been most zealously pursued in the present work, and whether it attains this end, and whether in other respects it is wrought with distinction after the manner of the ancients, let those decide who shall approach it in a spirit of loving labour. (Synesius, *On Dreams*, prol.; trans. Fitzgerald)

Synesius probably did not believe in any personal deity transcending the universe both causally and in time; and he certainly did not believe in the end of history and the world. His disbelief he communicated to his brother – albeit in a private letter, not in a public sermon. There are 'certain doctrines', he said, which he would never give up; still, he could operate as a bishop in a Christianised society, but pursue philosophy 'at home'. One can assume that this activity includes the study of a 'hidden' Plato too. In his commentary Nikephoros Gregoras sides with Synesius in an interesting reversal of Euripides' saying: apparently there are cases when wisdom is shown in obscurity, not in clarity.[29]

Esoteric Platonism did not imply anything close to an 'orthodox' Platonism, in so far as orthodoxy means exclusivity. On the contrary, the summit of Neoplatonist interpretation was the realisation that the Platonic text functions on many levels – be it moral, theological, physical, mathematical and even literal. A pupil of Hierocles reported that, according to his mentor, Socrates' words are like dice: 'however they fall, they fall rightly'.[30] This is no concession to hermeneutical relativism. According to Proclus' commentary on the *Timaeus*, the most profound reading of Plato's

---

[29] Cf. Syn. *Ep.* 105.82–8; Nik. Greg. *Expl. in Syn.* 3.5–9 Pietrosanti; Eur. *Or.* 397.

[30] Dam. *Philosophical History* 45B Athanassiadi (fr. 106 Zintzen): ἔλεγε δὲ ὁ αὐτὸς Θεοσέβιος ἐξηγούμενον φάναι ποτὲ τὸν Ἱεροκλέα, κύβοις ἐοικέναι τοὺς Σωκράτους λόγους· ἀπτῶτας γὰρ εἶναι πανταχοῦ, ὅπῃ ἂν πέσωσι.

description of the battle between the Atlantines and the Athenians is not one that invalidates all previous ones but rather one that includes and at the same time surpasses all. Proclus discusses previous approaches to the story, presenting his own view on the matter, one that distinguishes between levels of interpretation. We see the same methodology at work in the beginning of Proclus' commentary on the *Parmenides*. But the passage best exemplifying this direction of Neoplatonist hermeneutics is provided by Olympiodorus:

Shortly before he died, Plato dreamt that he had become a swan which flew from tree to tree thereby causing the utmost trouble to the archers who wanted to shoot him down. Simmias the Socratic interpreted the dream as meaning that Plato would elude all the efforts of his interpreters. For to archers the interpreters are similar who try to hunt out the hidden meanings of the ancients, but elusive is Plato because his writings, like those of Homer, must be understood in many senses, both physically, and ethically, and theologically, and literally. (Olymp. *In Alc.* 2.156–62 Westerink)

This interpretation of Plato's dream also figures in the anonymous *Prolegomena to Plato's Philosophy*, where hermeneutical pluralism does not present any danger to Neoplatonist exegesis. Rather, it functions as a very intelligent cover intended to appease a Christian audience with little understanding of Neoplatonist exegesis.[31] Multi-levelled hermeneutics did not conflict with esoteric Platonism; on the contrary, it actually rendered esoteric Platonism invulnerable: giving away layers of interpretation that were compatible with institutionalised education, the author of *Anonymous Prolegomena* could hold on to (and thus rescue) the belief in Plato's *agraphai synousiai*. Purportedly Pythagoras, Socrates and Plato left behind them students as 'ensouled works' (ἔμψυχα συγγράμματα) of theirs.[32]

By ensuring the adaptability of Platonism to different contexts and the transferability of its doctrines this Neoplatonic strategy

---

[31] See also *Anon. Proleg.* 1.29–38: ταὐτὸν γὰρ ἑκάτερος, Ὅμηρός τε καὶ Πλάτων, πεπόνθασιν· διὰ τὸ ἐναρμόνιον αὐτῶν τῆς φράσεως ἑκάστῳ βάσιμοι γίνονται, ὅπως ἂν βούληται ἐπιχειρεῖν τις.

[32] Cf. *Anon. Proleg.* 13.10–27; Arist. fr. 1.2 (Philop. *In De an., CAG* 15, 75.34–5): τὰ περὶ τἀγαθοῦ ἐπιγραφόμενα περὶ φιλοσοφίας λέγει. ἐν ἐκείνοις δὲ τὰς ἀγράφους συνουσίας τοῦ Πλάτωνος ἱστορεῖ ὁ Ἀριστοτέλης. But cf. Arist. *Ph.* 209b14–15: ἐν τοῖς λεγομένοις ἀγράφοις δόγμασιν.

provided the perfect alibi to anyone wishing to look for what Psellos labelled 'the golden streams'. Multi-layered interpretation provided Psellos too with his defence when arguing apologetically that he studied Plato for the sake of Christianity – that is, after the example of the Fathers. Plato could be invoked to this end too, namely to support aspects of Christian dogma. Plethon made a similar claim in the beginning of the *Differences*: ostensibly Plethon is a Platonist in so far as he is a good and pious Orthodox Christian too. But was this the only end to which intellectuals such as Psellos and Plethon studied pagan philosophy and edited the *Chaldean Oracles*?

Occult Plato: Hellenism and the first Byzantine humanism

Sometime in the middle of the ninth century an order was placed for the copying of texts among which stand out Proclus' commentaries on the *Republic* and the *Timaeus*, Damascius' commentary on the *Parmenides*, Olympiodorus' commentaries on the *Gorgias*, *Alcibiades I*, *Phaedo* and *Philebus*, and the works of Albinus and Maximus of Tyre. It has been admitted that 'this group of texts is a remarkable phenomenon' given the occasional dangers associated with approaching Plato from a philosophical point of view.[33] This is a mild formulation. The texts are tantamount to the heavy arsenal of an advanced pagan Platonist, with only Proclus' *Platonic Theology* missing from the assembly. The patron(s) who commissioned the production of these books invested considerable amounts of time, effort and money, while running a considerable risk of attracting the accusation of Hellenism.

L. G. Westerink noted the puzzle posed for scholars of Platonism by the 'first Byzantine humanism'. The transmission of Neoplatonic texts seems to have continued uninterrupted; yet there is no evidence of active philosophical interest with regard to the contents of the books copied.[34] In theory the possibility of some bizarre antiquarian's taking up the risky reproduction of texts containing pagan wisdom to satisfy his hobby cannot be ruled out.

---

[33] Wilson (1983) 87.   [34] Westerink (1990) 105.

But this does not necessarily mean that the philosophical ideas contained in these same texts were uninspiring and unappealing to their collectors owing to their unconditional, unshakeable and unnegotiable faith in Roman Orthodoxy. For what it is worth, Scholarios would not be easily persuaded: his portrait of Plethon suggests that the wrong type of books have the potential to stimulate pagan relapses.[35] We have seen that mechanisms suitable for covering up the study of Platonic philosophy were available from the sixth century – mechanisms that did not necessarily lead to an 'unsociable' philosophy of which Plato would disapprove, but to intellectual elitism and esoteric philosophy.

On the other hand, Westerink rejected the possibility of any 'widespread study of Neoplatonic texts, covered by any intentional mantle of silence'. His reasonable argument is that even if names and sources were kept secret, nevertheless the Platonist terminology and world-view (*Gedankenwelt*) should have left their traces at least on some of the ninth-century intellectuals.[36] Yet this means projecting onto the period from the ninth to the eleventh century what we know about the modes of the philosophical reception of Plato in late antiquity. It may well be that shifting circumstances resulted in ancient philosophy's being put to new uses. These were not exhausted in extracting Platonist technical terms and explicitly pagan notions, though, as we shall see presently, this too was occasionally the case. Rather, Hellenism provided points of reference for the construction of a novel court ideology that competed with the clerical establishment by enhancing political and secular institutions. This challenged the clerical hermeneutical hegemony by promoting philosophical and scientific inquiry. This ideology may be defined as a humanist one and its opponents were right in identifying philosophical paganism as its ultimate source.

The transmission of Platonist texts in the ninth century coincides with the beginning of the intellectual movement known as 'the first Byzantine humanism', the foundation of an important institution,

---

[35] Scholarios blamed Plethon's preoccupation with volumes of Neoplatonic lore, primarily those of Proclus, for his conversion to paganism. Schol. *Ad principessam Pelop.*, *OC* 4.153.25–34; *Ad exarchum Josephum*, *OC* 4.162.20–5.

[36] Westerink (1990) 121.

the Magnaura School of Philosophy, and the significant reappearance of the accusation of 'Hellenism'. This emerging humanist movement provided political support for the preservation of two vital channels transmitting pagan lore: for astrology and the occult sciences; further, for the continuation of hermeneutical approaches to Platonism that appear to have been non-conformable to the mainstream of that clerical 'school philosophy' that demonised any excursus from Plato's *lexis*.

In the ninth century the School of Philosophy of Magnaura represents a major breach in the established clerical hegemony. To begin with, the school was secular, largely owing its existence to the emperor Bardas' love for the 'wisdom beyond the gates'. Bardas organised its operation around 855/6. The key man involved in teaching there was Leon the Philosopher or the Mathematician, a man who, according to his own wish, was 'also known as *the Hellene*'.[37] The school was a place where transmission of knowledge and ancient lore could be performed in relative safety. This hardly means that the Orthodox establishment did not react to the activities of the important figures associated with the school. Theodore Stoudites attacked John the Grammarian on the grounds that he rewrote the doctrines of the Holy Fathers according to his 'illegal religion (κατὰ τὴν σὴν θρησκείαν παράνομον)'. One wonders what was John's religion according to Theodore. This is clarified to some extent by the note that John is worthy of the names of Pythagoras, Kronos or Apollo or of any other god whose lives he envies, rather than the name 'John'.[38] Divine grace has put out the fire of heresy 'burning those who think like the Chaldeans and refreshing the pious advocates of the Trinity'.[39] Leon the Hellene too was attacked as a pagan, this time by one of his own students, the philosopher and grammarian Constantine from

---

[37] Lemerle (1971: 148, 175) called Leon the Mathematician the first true 'homme de la Renaissance'. Leon had a strong interest in Plato and he is responsible for the first *diorthosis* of Plato's text – though for some inexplicable reason he stopped at *Laws* book 5, 743b. Leon also exemplified a very strong interest in astrology and divination. Hence he corrected Porphyry on the calculation of the *horimaia* and the establishment of the horoscope as well as being the author of a series of interesting treatises on the art of predicting the future, including that relating to the reign of emperors and princes (Lemerle 1971: 171–2).

[38] Thdr. Stud. *PG* 99.1773D; 1776C.   [39] Thdr. Stud. *PG* 99.1776A.

Sicily. Lemerle assumed that this Constantine was 'converted' by the patriarch Photius,[40] whose Aristotelianism and erudition made him the right person to discern possible cases of dissent.[41]

It is tempting to dismiss all accusations of paganism against John the Grammarian and Leon the Mathematician as one rhetorical aspect of the conflict between iconodules and iconoclasts. In so far as Stoudites is concerned, it is true that his attacks are accompanied by a condemnation of John's position on the subject. Yet curiously enough, nothing in the pamphlets of Constantine hints at the significance of this conflict. Even when accused of ingratitude and compelled to write a sequel to his first libel, Constantine did not claim that the accusation of paganism had anything to do with Leon's alleged iconoclasm. Constantine did not even qualify his position by claiming that Leon was a heretic rather than a pagan. He stood firm in his verdict. Constantine accused Leon the Mathematician of losing his soul in a sea of impiety represented by *thyrathen* wisdom. Leon is an apostate from the Christian faith, guilty of polytheism, venerating Zeus as his god. He may burn in Tartarus with Chrysippus, Socrates, Proclus, Plato, Aristotle, Epicurus, Eucleides and Ptolemy – not to mention Homer, Hesiod and Aratus. Constantine concludes his reply by extending his curses to cover 'those who venerate the gods of the Hellenes', speaking of Hellenism and polytheism as a contemporary heresy, rather than as a metaphor for iconoclasm.[42] Was he just a 'hysterical' student?[43] Possibly. After all, every single occurrence of the accusation of Hellenism can be conveniently dismissed as little more than a malicious attempt at despoiling political or theological opponents, rather than as testifying to the genuine survival of paganism.[44]

But this seems to ignore the fact that those Orthodox Christians who reacted against 'Hellenism' did so with reference to a

---

[40] Lemerle (1971) 172.

[41] See also Photius' reservations in regard to the orthodoxy of John Lydos (*Bibl.* 180). It may well be that intelligent Christians like Photius were keener to search beyond appearances than are many modern scholars.

[42] Lemerle (1971) 173.   [43] Constantine as hysterical: Kaldellis (2007a) 182.

[44] See Rochow (1991) 137–52. The same argument is often used to explain the accusation of 'Hellenism' in later periods, most patently in the case against Psellos and Italos, but also in regard to the confinement of Nikephoros Gregoras in the fourteenth century. This is a handy explanation and partly true. On paganism in Byzantium see also Livanos (2010).

particular mindset and outlook. The accusation of Hellenism was meant to provide a bulwark against the emergence of a humanist spirit.[45] Hellenism *qua* philosophical paganism stands here for a way to enquire about the world, theology and the interpretation of texts that is recognisably un-Orthodox, rather than ritual paganism.

In this context the case of Leon Choirosphaktes (*c.* 840–919) sheds light on the real meaning of the accusation of 'paganism' or Hellenism as well as on the spirit of Byzantine humanism. A disciple of Leon the Hellene, Leon Choirosphaktes also appears to have presented a direct challenge to the educational indoctrination of the Church. As is usually the case with religious dissenters in Byzantium, scholarship is quick to assume that 'paganism' was little more than a handy accusation and that Choirosphaktes was attacked for political rather than ideological reasons.[46] Convenient as this approach may be, it merits to be reconsidered from a philosophical point of view. How far were his opponents really making things up? The only way to deal with this question is to present the accusations made against Leon and then turn to his own work.

Three people attacked Choirosphaktes on religious grounds and contributed to his exile: Arethas, Constantine the Rhodian (a capable libellist), and a court eunuch. Constantine's libel is a collection of calumnious verses of ingenuity. An example of the man's literary skills will suffice. Leon is condemned as ὀλεθροβιβλοφαλσογραμματοφθόρος, ψευδομυθοσαθροπλασματοπλόκος and finally Ἑλληνοθρησκοχριστοβλασφημοτρόπος.[47] I single out the accusations of falsifying books, devising myths and 'tending to profess the Greek religion while blasphemising Christ' because they also turn up in Arethas' text, albeit in more appropriate form. Still, Arethas is at one with Constantine in holding that Leon should already be burning in hell. The title of the libel *Misogoes* is a clear allusion to Julian's *Misopogon*.

Arethas' main point is not only that Leon is a pagan (this seems to him to be evident), but that he pretends to be Christian; further,

---

[45] H. G. Beck (1952) 67.

[46] See the introduction by Vassis to his edition of Leon's *Chiliostichos theologia*, 10.

[47] *Anecdota Graeca* 2.624 (Matanga).

that he elevates himself to the position of approaching the Fathers independently of the Church – that is to say, of initiating some sort of secular approach to the teaching of the Fathers. Arethas makes clear that Choirosphaktes was not alone in this endeavour. There are others 'like him' and – what makes him even more dangerous – 'his insanities buzz in pious ears'.[48] Leon's tactic is to 'simulate piety and make himself a reputation for virtue'. Interestingly enough for potential followers of Sathas' theory, the possibility that a secret society could succeed in worshipping Bacchus in ninth-century Constantinople does not appear to shock Arethas at all. For his part, he does not seem to have had any major difficulty with this eventuality:

Go revel with the worshippers of Bacchus with sileni and satyrs and maenads and Bacchants . . . Yes truly, and boast of some antique Hecabe who has initiated to her nasty secrets many godless like you. Strive with her in worthy emulation, in your labours of smallness and ignorance. In these domains prosper, in these succeed, O disgusting monster of flattery. In them you can gain a reputation and arouse no envy, or a poor one, and incur no reproach.

What really annoys Arethas is that Leon has made his aim 'to compete with the Holy Fathers'. It is not for everyone to teach about God, Arethas corrects the intellectual layman, 'at least they must be Christians, not pagans, let alone a godless wretch like you'. Leon had 'unlearned and forsworn the Christian faith' he received from his parents; he 'relearned instead the marvels of paganism, even if now he has cunningly pretended to forsake it.' To be sure, Choirosphaktes was writing panegyrics of holy men! He, who had this 'plot' against the Fathers, to 'show that they have no advantage' over himself (Arethas, *Scripta minora* 1.21.205–10 Westerink)! We may further infer from Arethas' libel that Leon's attempt at a secular approach to patristics was occasioned by the study of a particular branch of specifically pagan Platonist philosophy. His heroes are Porphyry and Julian:

Now may Christ be of no avail to you. Flee from piety. Trouble us no more with this great shamelessness of yours. Go your own way, wiped out with the

---

[48] Cf. *Arethae Scripta minora* 1.21.212 (Westerink); Karlin-Hayter (1965) 455–81.

Tyrian of old [Porphyry], with the impious Julian, whose works you admire and emulate, already enrolled among them and participant with them in Acherousia and Cocytos and Tartaros and Acheron and Pyriphlegethon whither your sage Plato dismissed those who strive to live like you. I say this not in jest but in earnest. What room is there for joking when the unholy hatred towards God of the contriver of this business has provoked against him the just enmity of the defenders of piety? (Arethas, *Scripta minora* 1.21.212.14–26 Westerink; trans. Karlin-Hayter)

This is how Arethas' libel ends. Beyond the level of rhetoric and polemic, the background of the conflict between Leon and Arethas concerns the reception and interpretation of Plato. Leon's challenge to the authority of the Fathers comes down to how one reads Plato. According to Arethas, Leon falsified not only the Fathers, but Plato too: it is Leon's own 'sage', namely Plato, who should send him straight to hell. The remark 'I say this not in jest but in earnest (σπουδάζοντος ἀλλ'οὐ παίζοντος)' is a nice allusion to Plato's typical ambivalence between earnestness and playfulness.[49] Arethas is an austere man who does not like duplicity and maintains little sympathy for Neoplatonic hermeneutical pluralism.

One wonders how Leon's Platonism differs from Arethas', in other words, what is peculiar to Leon's world-view that renders him susceptible to the charge of 'paganism' and Julianic Platonism. Leon's *Chiliostichos theologia* or *Thousand-Line Theology* provides the answer. This is supposedly a didactic poem on Christian theology that condemned 'the Hellenic mob' and pagan doctrines. Yet it does so in an odd way.

Thousand-Line Theology promotes a form of mysticism and negative theology reminiscent of Pseudo-Dionysius Areopagita. And yet, a lot is scandalously absent from this work, beginning with Pseudo-Dionysius' respect for the clerical hierarchy.[50] More substantively, not a sentence is spared for Christian soteriology, and no value is attributed to the Incarnation or the doctrine of the Fall. On the contrary, illumination seems to be a philosophical endeavour to be pursued by the philosopher outside or independently of the Church. There is no professed need for the soul to be saved and redeemed by divine grace; rather, the individual should utilise

---

[49] Cf. for example *Phdr.* 476e; *Resp.* 536c.   [50] *Chil. theol.* 74–93.

reason and employ the soul's inherent rational faculty to achieve godlikeness. The divine 'unlimited nature' draws certain people, here called 'ennobled through Reason (οἱ λόγῳ τιμώμενοι)' to the heavens and reveals to them certain 'intellectual substances (νοητὰς οὐσίας)'.[51] Moreover, as Magdalino put it, Leon promotes a 'court ideology that marginalises the Church'. The message of Choirosphaktes' *Thousand-Line Theology* is that 'mere faith is not enough; only those with logos can rise toward God, and logos is the science of reading the codes which God has written into the book of creation'.[52] It was observed that Leon dealt with pagan theology as if this was still an available option.[53] Magdalino saw correctly that the deeper intention of Leon's reference to paganism exceeds that of performing a rhetorical exercise: it was to condemn pagan doctrines in order thus to devise 'a smokescreen to obscure the controversial nature of the author's own propositions'.[54] In this he was followed by others, most notably Psellos and Plethon in the *Differences*.

Leon heralds a tenet of Plethon's public references to theology. This is an abstract and generic type of philosophical monotheism provocatively disconnected from the scriptural literary context and liberated from any references to exclusively Judaeo-Christian origins.[55] To be sure, Leon was an advocate of monotheism; but was he an advocate of *Christian* monotheism? As if this ambiguity were not enough, a very unorthodox explanation is offered with regard to prophecies and theology. Owing to god's being ineffable and beyond knowledge, says Leon, prophets and theologians use symbolic and metaphorical language.[56] Leon's mysticism culminates in a form of fideistic agnosticism that will find its most powerful exposition in members of the anti-Hesychast party of the fourteenth century such as Barlaam of Calabria. This new

---

[51] *Chil. theol.* 125.21–2; 148.10–11. On these points see also the comments by Vassis in his introduction to *Chil. theol.* 33–4; Vassis explains this divergence from Church doctrine in terms of a 'philosophische Mystik'.

[52] Magdalino (1997) 160, 157.   [53] Vassis, introduction to *Chil. theol.* 32.

[54] Magdalino (1997) 151.

[55] See below, pp. 300 and 377 for Plethon's monotheism in the *Monody for the Empress Helen* and *Memorandum to Theodore*.

[56] *Chil. theol.* 130–3.

69

epistemology does not cancel out philosophical enquiry; instead, it liberates philosophy from the status of an *ancilla theologiae*. If god cannot be known, then philosophy and science should be pursued as the next best thing to absolute knowledge.

It is remarkable that a text as suspect as the *Thousand-Line Theology* was put forward as a confession of Christian Orthodox faith. If this was Leon's best shot at compiling an ostensible declaration of religious orthodoxy, one may reasonably assume that the reasons for the initial accusations of paganism against him were not only political but also philosophical. The real problem concerned Leon's secularism; the reluctance to admit the non-negotiable priority of the Fathers and doctrinal Orthodoxy; his interest in astrology; the application of symbolic and allegorical hermeneutics to Christian sacred texts; the emphasis on *logos* and science as prerequisites to attain godlikeness; the decrease of emphasis on Christian revelation; the *ex silentio* anti-clericalism expressed by his disregard for the role of the Church. For these reasons, the accusation of Hellenism involved much more than politics and rhetoric.

The parallel reading of Arethas' attack and Leon's *Chiliostichos theologia* suggests, first, that Leon's reception of Plato did not conform to the dominant clerical (i.e. linguistic) one, thus challenging the officially approved hermeneutical approach that valued the *lexis* but not the *nous* of Platonist texts. Second, Leon's reading relates to a philosophical theology that progressively leads from rational discourse to divine illumination with no intervention of clerical hierarchy. This is an essentially Platonist theology of the Proclan rather than the Pseudo-Dionysian type that resurfaces in later thinkers such as Psellos and Plethon. Third, here philosophy carries a definite political dimension, to the extent that it is the business of a secular elite consisting of courtiers and politicians. Leon was more than an able diplomat and politician enjoying the favour of the emperor and the titles of *anthypatos, patrikios, magistros* and *mystikos:* Leon Choirosphaktes 'was in effect advocating a monopoly of power and learning by the emperor and a small secular elite of court philosophers'.[57] So did Plethon.

---

[57] Magdalino (1997) 160.

Leon exemplifies a rising tension between elite secular court philosophers and the clergy that culminates in Plethon's *Memoranda*. Last but not least, Leon's philosophical theology was compatible with astrology, a channel that, as the Church knew well, transmitted a reformed version of polytheism.[58] It has been noted that Leon's rationalism, his critical approach to the *vitae* of the saints and the mysteries of the Church, as well as his obvious contempt for asceticism fully qualified him for the death penalty. Leon got away with exile, probably because he was related to the emperor.[59]

Byzantine humanism maintained the core of a die-hard Hellenic naturalistic paradigm that persistently challenged Christian exclusivity, revelation and soteriology and whose exponents in the ninth century are to be found among high-profile advocates of secular education with excellent connections in the court. Leon Choirosphaktes and Leon the Mathematician were motivated by an emerging secular version of Hellenism hidden under the veil of a supposedly innocent antiquarian interest in the occult, divination and Platonism. The link between Hellenising secularism (θύραθεν παιδεία) and divergent forms of Christianity ensured the adaptability of the former while nourishing the latter. The great service of the School of Magnaura to Platonism is that it prepared the intellectual ground for those later humanists who, including Psellos and Theodore Metochites, would more openly adopt the Platonist *theoretikos bios*.

Secular Plato: Psellos and the art of dissimulation

Psellos is fascinating for his incorporation of many of the themes and motives already described. A layman with expert knowledge of how to present his love for Platonism and the occult as actually beneficial for the Church and Orthodoxy under the cloak of *polymatheia*, Psellos may (like Plethon) be read in at least

---

[58] *Chil. theol.* 106–8. As Cumont argued (1911: 162ff.), astrology reformulated polytheism on an abstact level while preserving the connection to pagan oriental lore; it was a scientific religion promoting the idea of sympathy and universal solidarity.

[59] Kolias (1939) 56.

two ways. The first sees in Psellos a Neoplatonist paying lip service to Christian hegemony in order to maintain intellectual freedom through unfriendly times; the other takes at face value his many declarations that he is no crypto-pagan but a pious Christian and sees nothing but a passionate teacher unjustly accused of paganism.[60]

Psellos' moderate Platonism anticipates Plethon's radical Platonism in four ways: (a) at a surface level Psellos successfully conceals, like Plethon, the conflict between his social identity as a Christian intellectual and his philosophical identity as a Platonist; (b) at the philological level Psellos is the man responsible for the transmission of the *Chaldean Oracles*, which Plethon dechristianised and attributed to Zoroaster;[61] (c) at the hermeneutical level Psellos foreshadows the political dimension of anti-Aristotelianism that acquired a vital role in Plethonean hermeneutics; (d) at the purely philosophical level, Psellos is the mediator of the pagan belief in fate in Byzantium, Platonist epistemology, as well as of the allegorical/symbolical use of mythology. Moreover, occasional anti-monasticism and anti-clericalism and the firm persuasion that the contemplative life should be combined with political virtue also connect Psellos to Plethon.

Psellos' importance lies in anticipating a major development that became explicit only much later, during the Hesychast controversy, and which attributes a new role to pagan Platonism. This concerns the recalibration of pagan Platonism in order to put to the test the world-view of intellectual (and ultimately religious) opponents. A most characteristic case is Psellos' attack on the zealotic Nazireans. Psellos integrates Proclan conceptions of moral virtue in order to counter those monks who behaved like 'demigods' and disrupted the harmony between man's soul and the divine.[62] Contrary to Nikephoros Gregoras, who later openly

---

[60] Zervos (1973: 195) argued that Psellos was interested in the study of Neoplatonist philosophy for its own sake. For a different view see Joannou (1956) 7. Psellos' dissimilation has been noted by Wilson (1983) 157–60 and Kaldellis (2007a); (1999b).

[61] The large number of Psellos manuscripts dating from the fourteenth century testifies to his popularity. Psellos probably influenced Nikephoros Gregoras, thus occasioning the latter's interest in the *Chaldean Oracles* and Palamas' attack on theurgy in the *Capita CL*. See the introduction by Sinkewicz to the latter work, 6 and Gr. Pal. *Capita CL* 28.

[62] *Chronographia* 2.80–1 (Renauld).

applied Proclus against the Hesychasts, Psellos does not admit the pagan Platonic origin of the intellectual paradigm against which he measures that of his opponents. But it is Psellos, long before the anti-Palamites and Plethon, who first reactivates the philosophical rather than rhetorical uses of Platonic tenets, re-ascribing to pagan philosophy a semi-autonomous intellectual significance and contemporary value. Proclus is tacitly employed not only to refute the Nazirean world-view but to bring to the foreground an alternative perception of moral conduct: how well do the Christian monks meet the challenge of comparing with this Hellenic alternative?[63]

Conscious or not, arguing this way plants the seed for a potential resurgence of pagan Platonism. At least in theory, the option of a Platonist perception of virtue stands on its own right and Christian alternatives have to compete with it. This is the cornerstone of the philhellenism and anti-clericalism of fourteenth-century Byzantine humanists, and it is here that ultimately Plethon's essay on the self-sufficiency of Greek virtue (*De virtutibus*) as a way of life has its genuine origins.[64] So does Plethon's anti-Aristotelianism. Psellos was one of the first to note the disastrous (mis)appropriation of Aristotle by the educational and presumably clerical and political Byzantine establishment. In the defence of his disciple John Italos he attributes the following thoughts to him:

There has been such a reversal of roles that Hellenes are now barbarians and the barbarians Hellenes ... [I]f a pretentious barbarian visited us and talked to people in Hellas or any part of our continent, he would treat the majority of men not as asses but as of mulish stupidity. The greater part of the population know nothing of the world of nature or of what lies beyond it, *the remainder think that they know everything but do not in fact even know the route towards knowledge.* Some claim to be philosophers and a great many more are anxious to learn. But the teachers sit with smug faces and long beards, looking pale and grim, with a frown, shabbily dressed. *They dig up Aristotle from the underworld, from the depths of Hades, and give the impression of passing judgment on everything that he covered in a cloud of obscurity.* When they ought to be expounding at length his confusing brevity, they give instead many brief explanations of the broad range of his researches. Our barbarian visitor is convinced that this is a

63 On Psellos and the Nazireans see Lauritzen (2006/7) 361.
64 On *De virtutibus* see the introductions to the editions by Neri (2010) 295–419, and Tambrun.

childish game, gloats over our incompetence, and departs, with no addition to his knowledge but reduced to a state worse than ignorance (Psell. *Oratoria minora* 19.35–55; Eng. trans. in Wilson 1983: 155–6; my emphasis).

This grotesque description of frowning teachers of philosophy with long beards, pale and grim, 'digging up Aristotle' to the point of nausea amply shows why an *esprit inquiet* was more than likely to abandon institutionalised Aristotelianism and venture on an intellectual expedition to the seductive but forbidden philosophical constellation of Platonism.

The reference to the reversal of roles between Hellenes and barbarians is equally significant. Plato needed new allies. Aristotle was an old ally too alienated by the accumulation of successive Christian interpretations. Conversely, the so-called 'Chaldean oracles' carried a powerful arcane pagan symbolism as well as the allure of an uncorrupted barbarian or 'alien wisdom'. With Psellos' edition of the *Chaldean Oracles* presumably intended to serve Christianity, another potential *symphonia* comes to the foreground: that between Platonism and the surviving 'oracles', which, as Plethon later put it in tacit agreement with Proclus and Psellos, are 'clearly consistent with the doctrines of Plato, totally and in every respect'.[65]

In comparison with Aristotle's works the *Chaldean Oracles* could be far more easily re-paganised and aligned with Plethon's understanding of genuine Platonism. Plethon's re-attribution of the oracles to the archetypical figure of Zoroaster and Psellos' more moderate and diplomatic preoccupation with this obscure collection of texts are reactions to the same hermeneutical *status quo* imposed by religious Orthodoxy and academic Aristotelianism.

Psellos provides ideal material for a case study of how contextual restraints affect self-presentation; further, of the strategies by means of which a conflict between a lived and an intellectual ideology may escape the notice of the authorities. This strategy follows the same pattern as modern disclaimers of the following type: 'I am not a racist (sexist etc.), *but*...' In the cases of Psellos and Italos their confession of faith takes the following form: 'I am not a pagan, *but* it is useful to know *what pagans think* in order to avoid

---

[65] Pleth. *Contra Schol.* 5.32–4.

their traps.' Predictably, if we isolate such disclaimers from their context, Psellos does fully conform to the conditions set by the Orthodox situational environment he moved in. Still, disclaimers do not merely transmit one's thoughts but adapt what one says to the expectations and beliefs presumably shared by one's recipients. They are a form of 'impression management'.[66] In this sense Psellos' self-presentation is conditioned by his assumed role as a teacher of Christian theology. Underlying ideologies produce context restraints to which one may (or has to) conform. The position one holds determines to some extent one's self-presentation – and so does the perceived world-view or ideology of one's audience.[67]

From a sociolinguistic perspective Psellos' warnings and disclaimers are very similar to today's parental advice stickers and television messages: they *have* to be there – hence making legitimate and enabling the circulation of ideas or images that would otherwise face censorship. The warnings are there for protection but also so that the contents may be freely and safely distributed.

Let us examine a few of Psellos' disclaimers, supposedly meant to warn his pious audience of the presence of *aporrete* Hellenic philosophy. Psellos disapproves of the 'Platonist lies' (Πλατωνικῶν ψευδολογιῶν)'.[68] He is even more precise in condemning Porphyry as a 'lunatic' when it comes to his criticism of Christianity, though fairly representing his argument;[69] he also condemns the 'teratologos' Proclus, though he expertly summarizes the Neoplatonic discussion on the modes and aids by which the divine may be said to be visible to human eyes. Elsewhere, he has different things to say.[70] He concludes an *opusculum* supposedly explaining Acts 2:4 and Gregory of Nazianzus' commentary to his disciples thus:

---

[66] Van Dijk (2008) 183–4.
[67] Modern examples include the use of politically correct language in specific circumstances, e.g. a job interview.
[68] Psell. *Theolog.* 1, 90.54.   [69] Psell. *Theolog.* 1, 75.106; 97.20; cf. 32.124–5.
[70] While condemning Porphyry, Iamblichus and Proclus in some of his theological treatises, in others Psellos refers to the μέγας Iamblichus (Psell. *Theolog.* 1, 97.30); similarly, to the μέγας Porphyry, who followed Plato in distinguishing between *nous* and *dianoia* (*dianoia* taking its name from ὁδὸν διά τι διανύουσα, that is, because it apprehends things by constantly moving). See Psell. *Theolog.* 1, 12.115. As for Proclus, we learn that he is a 'truly divine man'. Like Iamblichus, Proclus is one of a group of philosophers here called – perhaps after Procopius' expression – οἱ καθ' ἡμᾶς "Ελληνες, 'our Hellenes', who came to 'venerate and love' the wisdom of the *Chaldean Oracles* (Psell. *Theolog.* 1, 23.46–55. On the use of this expression by Procopius see the comment of des Places

These are the hallucinations of Porphyry and Iamblichus and that creator of monstrosities Proclus; let me say here that nothing of these is true. But for our part we ought to know not only of healing herbs, but also of those that are poisonous, in order that we get well with the former, while we avoid the latter and we do not fall into the trap of alien [doctrines] as if they were our own. (Psell. *Theologica* 1, 74.145–9 Gautier)

Here Psellos appears to be conforming to the advice of Gregory of Nazianzus. One has to acquire some knowledge of the Hellenes in order to avoid giving the impression that one has no idea what one is condemning.[71] Indeed, it is the authority of Gregory that he fell back on when attacked as a crypto-pagan by Ioannes Xiphilinos: if Psellos is following Gregory and Basil, then why is he to be presumed less orthodox than they were? An excellent argument, it seems. However, there is a key difference between Gregory and Psellos. The former was concerned with pagan ideas in the fourth century, at a time when pagan Platonism was still an option: at that time Christian authors truly had to 'negotiate' Platonic philosophy. But was there such a need in the eleventh century?

Psellos essentially preserved philosophical Hellenism in so far as he made it available to his students. Like Proclus and Marinus, Psellos applies code phrases to distinguish between an ingroup and an outgroup. To be sure, the valorisation of these groups has been reversed. Now the Christians form an ingroup and the Hellenes are the outgroup. Still, in Psellos we constantly stumble upon two intellectual camps fighting over the question of *how* truth is attainable, thus ensuring the continuation of an intellectual confrontation that was purportedly resolved in late antiquity. This never arises in Christian theologians such as Symeon the New Theologian. Obviously, for Symeon there was no reason whatsoever to reconstruct at the intellectual level a conflict already settled with a clear winner at the historical level.

---

in his edition of the *Oracles* (*Oracula Chaldaica*, 154)). Of course, Psellos explains to his 'dear children', his pupils, that Gregory distinguishes between the concept of metaphysical monarchy according to the theologians of the Hellenes and 'our' Trinitarian doctrine. Thus his audience enjoys the rare privilege of acquiring an in-depth knowledge of both Hellenic and Christian theology – presumably in order for it to opt for the latter, since it is superior.

[71] Gr. Naz. *Or.* 21, *PG* 35.1088.15–18.

Xiphilinos thought that Psellos was an 'apostate' from Christ, seduced by Plato, eroding Orthodoxy from the inside by devising a convenient smokescreen to preserve and perpetuate the pagan world-view.[72] His case against Psellos essentially repeats a great truth that has been put nicely into words in a Nietzschean aphorism: if you look into the abyss for too long, the abyss starts to look back at you. Psellos' experimentations with Hellenic philosophy go far beyond any 'hellenising' Christian philosophy of the Fathers he claimed to follow. Once we begin to scratch a little around the ground, interesting things come to the surface. Psellos talks of *streams* (φλέβες) *of the past*, that is of golden, silver and other streams of metal 'more worthless still' that were in his time dammed up. Unable to reach the 'living sources', Psellos was forced by the circumstances to study the images of these streams and 'devoured' in his soul 'idols of the second order' (εἴδωλα ἄττα καὶ αὐτὰ δεύτερα).[73] No matter how inadequate then, sometimes idols ensure the preservation of a message that would otherwise be lost. Psellos' metaphor stresses the ability of Hellenism to transcend historical conditions by generating *idols* of what lies in its depths and inspiring individuals to look for them. *A stream of the past* may be blocked for a substantial period of time before it is rediscovered, revealed and allowed to flow again. Platonist philosophers such as Psellos and Plethon apply 'idols of the second order' as well as the intellect as an 'idol of god' in order to ascend to truth by virtue of individual effort.

In reality, Psellos was making a choice between the two schools of pagan Platonism, famously described by Damascius. Using Keroularios as a straw man and explicitly condemning Hellenism in the form of occult divinatory practices, Psellos allowed Hellenism to slip in by the back door in the form of speculative philosophical theology.[74] It is Porphyry's 'philosophical and logical

---

[72] Psell. *Ep. Xiphilin.* 230.   [73] Psell. *Chronog.* 6.43.

[74] Psellos is the man who in his *Oration against Keroularios* appears to expose the Platonic roots of divination harshly condemning occult practices. Patriarch Keroularios became fascinated by the claims of a woman called Dosithea, who claimed to profess divination and was accused of Hellenism, that is, paganism. Psellos convincingly shows that Plato in the *Phaedrus* allows for a divine *mania* inspiring the priestesses of Dodone and the oracle

(φιλοσόφως μᾶλλον καὶ λογικῶς)' approach to divinity, according to Iamblichus, and not the 'hieratic school' that Psellos – and Plethon too – is struggling to preserve.[75] By getting rid of Hellenism as occultism, Psellos was rescuing Hellenism as discursive philosophy and Platonist intellectual mysticism. Hence in a hagiographical oration Psellos denounces the divination and ritual practices (κενόσπουδος περὶ τὰ μαντεία καταφυγὴ καὶ ἡ τελεστικὴ τούτων παρασκευή) of the Hellenes. 'I would be ashamed', he contends, 'to compare the follies of the Hellenes to our superior doctrines.' But then after a few pages he comes up with a summary of the Neoplatonist view on the principle of sympathy upon which the entire practice of Proclan *hieratike techne* relies. Psellos is silent about his pagan source, merely noting that he draws from the 'most secret philosophy (ἀπορρητοτέρα φιλοσοφία)' – without seeing anything here that deserves to be denounced as folly.[76] Doctrinal Neoplatonism is separated from its ritualistic aspect. This is more than a façade for studying Plato at his leisure: it is an intellectual strategy. Psellos condemned Hellenic theurgy but preserved Hellenic philosophical paganism.

To put it in another way, Psellos openly disapproved of the contents of *Phaedrus* 244a–e regarding divination; but was he ever ready to denounce *Republic* Book 6, for example? Reading his commentary on Gregory of Nazianzus' reference to a λόγῳ καὶ θεωρίᾳ assimilation to God,[77] one gets the impression that Psellos does not opt to comment on it because of what is Christian in it, but because of what is Platonic. Gregory used Plato to elucidate the Christian perception of godlikeness; now Psellos uses Gregory to elucidate the Neoplatonist perception of godlikeness. Indeed, Psellos goes beyond Gregory and certainly far beyond Symeon the

of Delphi. 'I even suspect that Dosithea coined this name from the expression δόσει θείᾳ in Plato's text (244a)', he says. Disapproving of τὰ τῶν Ἑλλήνων Psellos emerges as the humble servant of the Church who usefully employs his secular knowledge to identify and condemn revivals of paganism to the best interest of Orthodoxy. Here Psellos expertly implements his favourite argument, namely that the study of Plato, suggested by the Cappadocean Fathers themselves, is profitable to the identification and combating of heresy. See Psell. *Ep. Xiphilin.* 5–10.
[75] Cf. Iamb. *Myst.* 2.11.5–13.
[76] Compare Psell. *Orationes hagiographicae* 4.387–90, 417–19 to 4.673–85.
[77] Gr. Naz. *Or.* 21, *PG* 35.1084.31–5.

New Theologian or any Byzantine theologian at seeing *logos* and *theoria* as superior means than grace, experiential illumination or asceticism to *approach* god. Psellos' aim is to approach the divine immediately by means of firm knowledge.[78] The intention behind Psellos' *opusculum* is not to comment on Gregory's oration – this merely provides him with a safe framework. The patterns by which Psellos manipulated Gregory of Nazianzus to expand his observations on the Platonist philosophical world-view merit a separate study.

Psellos' Neoplatonist reading of Gregory defines *psychanodia* as a task for the soul's inherent faculties: it is not a gift of divine grace, but a philosophical quest initiated by a discursive λόγος τῆς ἐπιστήμης and a θεωρία that reproduces in one's soul an image of the paradigm. The example used by Psellos is that of the painter: our soul is a drawing board; virtues are colours; the mixing of colours is 'the power of the science of painting'; and God is the paradigm. The science of virtue (τὴν τῆς ἀρετῆς ἐπιστήμην) leads to godlikeness. There are no references to either prophets or the Fathers here. Nothing reminds us of Justin's famous 'interpretation' of Platonic virtue as standing for Christian divine grace.[79] On the contrary, Psellos is the man who most fully anticipates Plethon's epistemic optimism.

The epistle to Xiphilinos concisely exemplifies Psellos' masterful dissimulations and the epistemological core of his philosophical Hellenism. It is a strange irony, deliberate or not, that, like Leon's *Theologia*, this epistle purports to testify to Psellos' orthodoxy. And yet it culminates in a manifesto in favour of the epistemic foundations of pagan Platonic philosophical theology. In this epistle one encounters the main ingredients of Platonist natural theology that resurface in Plethon's œuvre. The 'hater of reason', 'hater of Plato' and 'hater of philosophy' Xiphilinos fails to see that Plato ascended to the edge of *nous*, saw what is beyond *nous* and reached the One (*Ep. Xiphilin.* 40–2).

Statements like these revive a type of philosophical paganism much more dangerous to Byzantine Orthodox Christianity than

---

[78] Psell. *Theolog.* 1, 104.17–25.
[79] Cf. Ps.-Justin, *Cohortatio ad gentiles* 30B–D; Plato, *Meno* 99e–100a.

was Keroularios' fascination with divination and theurgy condemned by Psellos. The confession of what exactly Psellos was seeking in the 'meadows of secular literature' is illuminating. Once in these meadows, Psellos makes use of syllogisms and tunes himself to 'natural doctrines'; he looks for the reasons behind phenomena and occupies himself with *nous* and with what is beyond *nous* (= the One). Eventually he looks for the gate to ascend to a superior level. 'This is how I purify my intellect from any association to matter, ascending as far as I can.'[80] This is a startling confession.

Psellos' 'natural doctrines' effectively stand for Plethon's trans-historical and universal 'true doctrines'.[81] Both are versions of a secular/pagan natural religion. In both cases the absence of any reference to divine grace and an exclusively Christian way of achieving godlikeness says more than do the hidden references to the Platonic-Plotinean tradition of intellectual purification and assimilation to the divine. Psellos' concluding declaration, 'I consider the Hellenic wisdom of old – and I include in this the wisdom of the Chaldeans and the Egyptians and any other secret (ἀπόρρητος) knowledge – as inferior in all respects to that of a monk' is pure sarcasm. Psellos did not last long as a monk himself: upon his departure from Mount Olympus in Bithynia a monk wrote comic verses about his 'polytheism' and Psellos responded with a poetic sketch of subtle irony.[82] Besides, it appears that elsewhere Psellos offers a very wide (Platonist, we may add) and handy definition of 'monk' extended to cover anybody practising an 'internal *anachoresis*'.[83] Psellos could conveniently advertise his respect for monks by applying the word 'monk' homonymously. What he really thought about their methods of achieving godlikeness is less clear.

One wonders whether this epistle, laying the potential foundations of natural religion based on Platonism, was ever really intended to persuade Xiphilinos to change his mind about Plato. We may surmise that Xiphilinos disapproved of Psellos' Platonist experimentations precisely because they led to the Hellenic

---

[80] Psell. *Ep. Xiphilin.* 214–25.   [81] See Ch. 4, p. 179.   [82] *Poemata* 21 (Westerink).
[83] Gouillard (1965) 323.

notion that godlikeness is the outcome of an internalised cognitive process. Conversely, Christians like Xiphilinos (and later Gregory Palamas and Scholarios) preferred Aristotle to Plato because to their eyes Aristotle did not compete with Orthodoxy on the level of theology and seemingly authorised the experiential basis of Christian godlikeness.

Psellos' use of allegory is another vehicle of dissimulation. The ascent of Moses to Mount Sinai is not to be taken literally, argues Psellos in a letter purportedly intended to showcase his orthodoxy. It stands for the soul's effort to transcend matter. So far one might observe that Maximus Confessor can be interpreted as making more or less the same statement.[84] The difference is that Psellos extends his allegorical readings beyond the sources of Christian mysticism. He finds such 'hidden meanings' in Hellenic myths too. This time his excuse is that 'to allegorise the Hellenic myths in a non-Hellenic way, this is all I want, and also to render transferable their secret lore to our doctrines'.[85] But this is not all. Psellos allegorised myths in *too* Hellenic a way. His comments on Homer's description of the cave of the myths (*Od.* 13.102) are lifted from Porphyry's brilliant essay on the topic.[86] As for the explanation of the Homeric 'golden chain' and Hellenic myths, Psellos ends up expounding the symbolic meaning of Zeus and his connections to the other gods along exactly the same lines as Plethon would do in his *Nomoi*: Zeus is the principle of Life, also called by the best theologians of the Hellenes *The One*;[87] as for the gods connected by means of the 'golden chain', these are 'Cherubim *or* powers *or* rulers *or* authorities *or* liturgical spirits sent to serve'.[88] This convertibility and transferability of a common doctrinal core from pagan myths to Orthodoxy is a very perilous move: for it admits that the Hellenic myths possess an arcane religious value, an internal significance of such a superior quality as to integrate and assimilate Christianity.

---

[84] Max. Conf. *Ambigua PG* 91.1117B–C.
[85] Psell. *Philosophica minora* 1, 46.8–10 Duffy: οὐχ ἥκιστα δὲ ὅτι μὴ Ἑλληνικῶς τὰ Ἑλλη-νικὰ ἀλληγορέειν ἐμὲ βούλεσθαι μόνον, ἀλλὰ καὶ πρὸς τὰς ἡμετέρας δόξας μεταβιβάζειν τὰ παρ' ἐκείνοις ἀπόρρητα.
[86] Psell. *Phil. minora* 1, 45.   [87] Psell. *Phil. minora* 1, 43.110–11; 46.30–8.
[88] Psell. *Phil. minora* 1, 42.48–56.

John Italos is the man who followed Psellos' strategy to the extreme, challenging the limits of freedom allowed to any Byzantine intellectual. Predictably he was condemned and anathematised. Even if Italos was not guilty of really believing in the eternity of the world or the reality of the Platonist ideas, he nevertheless was responsible, as was Psellos, for making possible the circulation of pagan philosophical doctrines, for passing them on, preserving them, interpreting and seriously considering them. Here is a masterpiece of circumlocution:

> According to the wise men of the Hellenes, the World-soul acts by imitating what comes before her (of course it is an impious doctrine to think that the world is ensouled, *but nothing prevents us from interpreting it*). Hence it is obvious that partial souls should necessarily imitate the soul that comes before them; for the ratio between the World-soul and what is before her is the same ratio as the individual souls share in regard to her. Indeed they imitate the World-soul accordingly and this is the cause of their illumination; for it is by means of likeness that emanations and illuminations occur. Further, the ratio between the World-soul and the body of the world is the same ratio as between the other souls in respect to each of their bodies; and just as the Soul governs and moves the body of the World, so do the other souls govern and move their respective bodies. And just as a multitude of souls comes from one soul, as the Hellenes think (*but of course we do not hold this view either*), similarly out of one world come worlds analogous to the souls, and out of one ensouled sphere a multitude of ensouled spheres and everything else that is part of the universe, the suns and the moons and the sum of stars; and if something is present in All, then one should reasonably assume that it is also present in the parts. (Joh. Ital. *Quaest.* 68.138–50; my emphasis)

This recalls Psellos' strategy of claiming to explain pagan beliefs in order to interpret rather than endorse them. It is here used to present two Platonist doctrines of great importance. The first is that of sympathy, concordance or proportionality – an all-time favourite of occultists, mystics and Platonists, which, we shall see, Plethon also shared. The second is that of the interrelation between the whole *as cause* of its parts and the whole consisting *in* its parts articulated by Proclus in the *Elements of Theology*.[89] Italos might have been the actual initiator of the Proclan Renaissance that developed even after his condemnation: when Nicholas of Methone attempted to

---

[89] Procl. *ET* 66–9.

refute the Proclan propositions which introduced a plurality of 'wholes-before-the-parts' and 'wholes-within-the-parts', he was well aware that he was battling against the actual philosophical qualifications of Neoplatonist polytheism.[90] In what concerns emulation of the prevalent version of Orthodoxy Italos is as interesting as Psellos, though not as good with words. In a striking passage he admits that the 'mystagogues' are from time to time forced by circumstances to modify their teaching. After all, what was beneficial in the past may well appear harmful later.[91] In the context of a theological discussion the message is clear: to a large extent replies to doctrinal questions depend upon circumstances. This is a revolutionary implication especially in conjunction with Italos' use of the hermeneutical strategies of his mentor Psellos. But what is intriguing in Italos is that he goes beyond Psellos in an effort to liberate Platonic philosophy from the Christian intellectual context and (re-)ascribe to this philosophy its lost autonomy.

As in Plethon, the alibi for this act of hermeneutical subversion concerns the comparison between Plato and Aristotle. It makes sense to solve queries in regard to Plato *ex Platone* and others in regard to Aristotle *ex Aristotele*: πλατωνικῶς τὰ Πλάτωνος λυτέον, ἀριστοτελικῶς δὲ τὰ τοῖς περιπατητικοῖς δοκοῦντα.[92] In other words, the issue is no longer to what extent Plato and Aristotle agree with Orthodoxy as prescribed by the doctrines of the Ecumenical Synods; rather, that one should aim for the internal agreement of Plato's or Aristotle's philosophy. A basic Neoplatonist hermeneutical principle is revived[93] – even if the *symphonia* within Plato's corpus does not preclude that with Aristotle's philosophy as well. Italos exempts logic from the domain of philosophy. This particularly bold and straightforward attack on Aristotelianism is justified with a nice aphorism: 'Logic is just a tool for philosophy, but in no way is it a part of it.'[94] Italos is clearly trying to reclaim Plato and in this he is following Psellos. Plethon will later walk along the same path.

90 Nicholas of Methone, *Anaptyxis* 66.1–5.   91 Joh. Ital., *Quaest.* 50.1–9.
92 Joh. Ital., *Quaest.* 3.13–15.   93 See for example *Anon. Proleg.* 22.35–8.
94 Joh. Ital., *Quaest.* 16.41: Διὰ ταῦτα ἄρα ὄργανον μὲν τῆς φιλοσοφίας ἡ λογικὴ εἰκότως λεχθείη, μέρος δὲ οὐδαμῶς.

Clerical authorities deemed it necessary to provide a bulwark for such secular-Platonist reactions to the prevalent religious-Aristotelean paradigm. To this effect they added to the *Synodicon of Orthodoxy* the notorious anathemas against Hellenic paideia. Modern scholarship has focused on the Hellenic doctrines condemned by this series of eleven anathemas (including the belief in the eternity of the world, in the Platonic Ideas and in the pre-existence of the souls) rather than on how, according to the *Synodicon*, the circulation and discussion of these doctrines was possible in the first place. According to the second anathema, it is emulation of Christian piety that enables the reintroduction of ungodly doctrines:

Anathema on those who claim to be pious but shamelessly or rather impiously introduce the ungodly doctrines of the Hellenes into the Orthodox Catholic Church. (*Synodicon* 190–1)

The third anathema affirms that certain people 'prefer the so-called wisdom of the philosophers outside the Church and follow its teachers'.[95] According to the seventh anathema, teaching is used as an alibi:

Anathema on those who go through a course of Hellenic studies and are taught not simply for the sake of education but follow these notions and believe in them as the truth, upholding them as a firm foundation to such an extent that they lead others to them, sometimes secretly, sometimes openly, and teach them without hesitation. (*Synodicon* 214–18)

As for the eighth anathema, this is sometimes quoted for its condemnation of the belief in the reality of the Platonic Ideas and the doctrine of principles intermediate between the creator-god and his creation. The very first line suits well Psellos' experiment with allegory and the *Chaldean Oracles*: 'Anathema on those who of their own accord invent an account of our creation along with other myths, who accept the Platonic forms as true, etc.'[96]

The *Synodicon* affirms that philosophical paganism was no longer a latent or theoretical possibility. It was an option seriously considered for its own sake, which means that it was present

---

[95] *Synodicon* 193–4.   [96] *Synodicon* 219–24 (trans. in Wilson 1983: 154).

in Byzantine intellectual life. Even if we cannot be sure of the exact extent of belief that Italos and Psellos put in particular Platonist doctrines, they nevertheless did think that godlikeness is a question of philosophy rather than revelation; they did use allegory to reformulate pagan theology; they did experiment in regard to its compatibility with Christianity, which means they studied Hellenic doctrines to establish whether truth is contained in them rather than being a 'handmaiden' of theology.

Thus the seventh anathema really finds its target. This concerns the intention behind Italos' (and Psellos') approach to pagan philosophy. The person(s) who compiled this was fully aware that it is only a small step from assuming that there might be some qualifiable truth in Hellenic doctrines after all, as Psellos and Italos did, to actually luring students to these doctrines, as Plethon did later. The conceptual apparatus needed for the Plethonian reformulation of pagan Platonism was not only preserved but commented upon and even refined by laymen such as Psellos and Italos. Plethon applied it in order to advance a pagan Platonic theological paradigm capable of enticing those intellectuals disappointed by both Orthodoxy and Thomism.

The twelfth-century *Proklosrenaissance* and Theodore Metochites

The first chapter in the *Doctrinal Armoury* of Euthymios Zigabenos begins with an attack on philosophical polytheism represented by a potential 'hellenising' interlocutor. This Hellene might not doubt that divinity (τὸ θεῖον) exists, yet rather argue that divine existence is brought out in many gods (πλῆθος θεῶν).[97] The articulation of a pagan theology is a theoretical possibility for which Christian intellectuals should be well prepared and adequately armed.

Occasionally this possibility appears to have become an actuality. In *Refutatio institutionis theologicae Procli* Nicholas of

---

[97] *Panoplia dogmatike*, PG 130.33C–36B.

Methone attacked the old Proclan view regarding the perpetuity of the world in an attempt to obstruct what Podskalsky called a 'Proklosrenaissance in Byzanz'.[98] Nikephoros Choumnos too deemed it necessary to condemn the Hellenic doctrine regarding the perpetuity of matter and the eternity of the Platonic Ideas. In these cases Hellenism is not tantamount to ritual paganism. Rather, as Nicholas affirms, his contemporary Hellenes count among their ranks people *from within our own court* – people who have in the past enjoyed the divine grace and tasted divine mysteries, but now place alien doctrines and 'human wisdom' before Christ. According to Nicholas it is their participation in paideia 'beyond the gates' that led to their Hellenism.[99] In order to protect those who consider Proclus' *Institutio* a worthy object of study from intentional or unintentional commitment to blasphemous heresy, namely Hellenism, Nicholas goes on to show in what respect the Proclan work runs contrary to the 'divine faith'. He does a good job in exposing how Proclan and Platonic multi-causalism offers the pretext (πρόφασις) for polytheism.

Manuel of Corinth (c. 1483/1530), one of those people who took up the tedious task of refuting Plethon long after the latter's death, copied extensively from Nicholas of Methone's refutation of Proclus. Nicholas of Methone was a professional plagiarist in his own right, as Petit observes.[100] And yet it is intriguing to highlight this connection between late antiquity (Proclus), the Byzantine *Proklosrenaissance* (Nicholas of Methone) and the attacks on Plethon long after the fall of Constantinople (Manuel of Corinth). To Christian eyes pagan Platonism possesses an almost ahistorical, foundationalist dimension: it possesses its own essence transcending modern periodisation. How else to explain the urge driving Nicholas of Methone in the twelfth century to refute a pagan philosopher of the fifth century and Manuel's urge to copy Nicholas' arguments in order to recontextualise them against a deceased philosopher of the fifteenth? This is not all. Intermediate

---

[98] Podskalsky (1976) 509–23.
[99] Nicholas of Methone, *Anaptyxis*, prol. 1–26 and *Anaptyxis* 58.
[100] See the introduction by Petit, *Documents*, 332.

between Nicholas and Manuel, in the fourteenth century, Palamas fiercely attacked Neoplatonic cosmology of the Proclan type in the first chapters of his *Capita CL*.

Another source, Michael Italikos, testifies that the choice of Proclan philosophy rather than Proclan theurgy was always available to Byzantine intellectuals. The iatrophilosopher Pantechnes not only believed that one has to study philosophy in order to claim the title of the philosopher but also admired Proclus' exegesis of Plato while dismissing his 'Chaldean monstrosities'.[101] This, we have seen, was Psellos' method: to dismiss Proclan theurgy but study Proclan Platonism. The possibility of a Neoplatonist revival is affirmed by George Tornikes in his praise of Anna Comnene: the empress acknowledged as her initiators in divine mysteries authorities like Dionysius Areopagita, *unlike some other people*, who followed Πρόκλους καὶ Ἰαμβλίχους.[102] Is this just a rhetorical trope? Perhaps. On the other hand, there is evidence that it was possible for individuals to pursue an isolated private study of Proclan theurgy, including its practical aspects, without maintaining any connection to institutionalised education.[103]

George Akropolites too proves himself to be a direct heir of the tradition inaugurated by Psellos when admitting in a remarkable passage that his study of Plato, the μουσόληπτος Proclus, the ἐνθεαστικώτατοι ἄνδρες Iamblichus, Plotinus 'and the rest, whom it is not the appropriate time to name now', leads him by the hand finally to understand what Gregory of Nazianzus meant by a *rheton* with regard to the relation between unity and multiplicity.[104] One really wonders who are the 'others' associated with the Neoplatonists here mentioned by George; and when exactly is the right time

101 Michael Italikos, *Or.* 9, 112.3–8, 113.15–20.   102 Tornikes, *Or.* 299.24–30.

103 An epistle by Michael Italikos shows that knowledge even of practical aspects of paganism, that is, Proclan theurgy, could be acquired behind the back of the authorities. See *Ep.* 31 (202.2–14). Michael might have studied the *Chaldean Oracles* in the collection of Psellos, as did later Nikephoros Gregoras. If that is the case, then Psellos' attempt to 'Christianise' the *Oracles* was less than successful, since here the *Oracles* appear in very dubious company.

104 Georg. Akropol. *In Gregorii Nazianzeni sententias* 2.15–20; Gr. Naz. *Or.* 29.2.7–8: ἔστι γὰρ καὶ τὸ ἓν στασιάζον πρὸς ἑαυτὸ πολλὰ καθίστασθαι.

for their enumeration. But above all one cannot help wondering what Gregory of Nazianzus would have thought about Iamblichan and Proclan philosophy's determining the meaning of his sentence. Obviously, such an application of Neoplatonist philosophy serves the elucidation of Christian Trinitarian doctrine and the perpetuation of the Neoplatonist polytheist/henotheistic model equally well. Psellos' crypto-pagan hermeneutics found their way into mainstream theology.

Whether a real *Proklosrenaissance* took place in Byzantium, as Podskalsky postulated, enabling the emergence of a pagan Platonic paradigm, may appear in the light of modern scholarship to be debatable. There is a common trend to dismiss references to Proclan and Iamblichan philosophy (together with anything threatening the narrative regarding the obsolence of paganism in Byzantium) as little more than rhetorical tropes. Still, things appear differently once we take into account the developments in theological and philosophical discourse. Podskalsky is particularly insightful when concluding that the twelfth-century experiments with the pagan concepts of unity, multiplicity and participation herald the conflict between Palamas and Barlaam in the fourteenth century as well as Plethon's polytheism in the fifteenth.[105] This partial injection of Orthodox theology with typically 'Hellenic' concerns signifies at the philosophical level a noticeable challenge to the hegemony of the Roman Orthodox clerical establishment.

The *Ethicus* by Theodore Metochites is one of the most important manifestations of this breach. Like his teacher Joseph the Philosopher and his pupil Nikephoros Gregoras, Metochites was a layman of Platonising tendencies. Both Metochites and Gregoras considered the return of the ancient intellectual and cultural paradigm an ἀναβίωσις: a Renaissance.[106] Plethon has been called 'in many ways the intellectual successor and heir of Metochites'.[107] It was suggested that the two men shared a common political attitude towards monarchy and democracy.[108] What is certain is that Plethon held Metochites in particularly high esteem. In a

---

[105] Podskalsky (1976) 522–3.   [106] Medvedev (1984) 116; (1997) *passim*.
[107] Nicol (1993) 342.   [108] Baloglou (1998) 53–4.

manuscript Plethon's loyal disciple Raoul Kabakes quotes his mentor as contending that Metochites remained unrivalled.[109] Interestingly, Kabakes' family appears to have claimed Theodore Metochites as its ancestor.[110]

The *Ethicus* effectively inaugurates the final and most fierce phase of the conflict between, on the one hand, a secular or humanist Hellenic philosophical and political world-view, and, on the other hand, Byzantine clericalism and monasticism. On the level of social interaction this emerging Byzantine Renaissance managed to establish channels beyond clerical control. Such were the informal literary associations called θέατρα in which Theodore Metochites, Nikephoros Gregoras, Demetrios Kydones and other intellectuals discussed philosophy, astronomy and rhetoric. The select few participants humorously described these 'theatres of the wise' (θέατρα σοφῶν) as 'Bacchic orgies' and 'orgies of Kouretes and Korybantes', illustrating the underlying tendency of elite circles to separate themselves from the established Christian institutions and pursue nonconformist ideological and aesthetic projects.[111] The *Ethicus* is at once a disguised ode to Platonist *theoria* and an indirect criticism of Christian experiential mysticism. It promotes a secular ideal of *vita intellectualis* completely disengaged from any concern for the ritual aspect of religion, recalling the pattern already heralded in Leon Choirosphaktes' *Chiliostichos theologia* and Psellos' philosophy and later applied by Plethon in his 'exoteric' writings. In the *Ethicus* the outlook of certain 'sages of old' resurfaces with unprecedented immediacy. These sages reclaim their status as guarantors of a *medicina mentis* and as proper guides to illumination. According to Metochites it is neither revelation nor any kind of experiential knowledge nor prayer nor grace that leads to god. Rather, the main thing is the study of *mathemata*. Esoteric Platonism sets the tone in an extended manifesto in favour of secular wisdom, which challenges Christian eschatology and messianism. Metochites' affirmation of worldly wisdom is ultimately a celebration of this world rather than an

---

[109] For this note see Shawcross (2008) 116.   [110] Zakythinos (1975) 375.

[111] On the phenomenon of *theatra* see Medvedev (1993) 233, who considers these associations to be precursors of those 'academies with amusing and burlesque self-given names ... that later spread all over Italy'.

anticipation of the life beyond, cleverly undermining the Judaeo-Christian messianic model by keeping silent about any salvation through faith or the Second Judgement.

Here too dissimulation is present. Metochites testifies to the presence of informants ready to report any suspicious intellectual activity to the clerical authorities. He calls these people 'leeches': βδέλλαι. In this respect the vulgar and insensible *hoi polloi* are stronger than the rational – Proclus and Simplicius would undoubtedly have seconded this.[112] We shall see that Scholarios relied on similar methods to collect his evidence against Plethon. In the *Ethicus* Metochites is clearly taking precautions when, at the beginning of his exposition, he awkwardly admits the priority of Orthodoxy and advises his readers to avoid risky positions in theology and keep silent about them: 'for you are unaware of what you might thus achieve, but you do know that if you fail and commit a tiny error, even in one word or one notion, you will be immediately destroyed!'[113]

There is something odd at work here. Metochites never returns to the significance of Orthodoxy, nor mentions piety and Christian salvation in the course of no fewer than sixty-two chapters celebrating 'wisdom beyond the gates'. As a matter of fact, he never draws any distinction between 'our wisdom' and 'the wisdom of the Hellenes', nor does he presuppose such a distinction. Neither does he denounce Hellenism as a philosophical outlook, nor does he fall back on the Christian *locus* that one should be eclectic and selective when approaching the wisdom of the Hellenes. Instead, he reminds us of a Pythagorean *symbolon*: one should not walk on crowded streets but opt for the path most people frequent the least. The meaning is, according to Metochites, that we should not linger on popular doctrines – nor penalise knowledge.[114]

Profound meditations follow on the links between philosophy and godlikeness. These affirm the typically pagan Platonic belief that *nous* may exit the body and achieve godlikeness by means of scientific and philosophical discourse. Medvedev corrected Beck and Hunger by showing that Metochites' ideal is not that of a

---

[112] Thdr. Met. *Ethicus* 8.   [113] Thdr. Met. *Ethicus* 9.
[114] Thdr. Met. *Ethicus* 8.

contemplative life in the monastic sense, but of an intellectual life anticipating the *otium intellectuale* prominent among Italian humanists.[115] Metochites endorses a type of intellectual hedonism stemming from cosmic piety and the celebration of intellectual faculties, praising rational thought as the sole medicine against confusion, while condemning *amathia* and those attacking secular knowledge.[116] He unabashedly confesses that he has come to think that rational thought is the best thing in the world.[117] Rationality is the teacher and keeper of genuine happiness and prudence.[118] But he is silent in regard to other, more revered and popular routes of securing divine illumination, for example divine grace. Instead, he notes that the *amatheis* shall never be happier than the man who follows reason and 'king *nous*'; otherwise, a pig would be happier than all men.[119] In some one hundred and forty pages Metochites presents the most extensive manifesto in favour of 'a life according to *nous* (κατὰ νοῦν ζωήν)', reason and philosophical contemplation (θεωρία). The hasty declaration of Christian faith at the very beginning only accentuates the contrast with what follows. Syllogisms are the slaves of King Nous, and thought (*dianoia*) constructs everything under the guidance of *nous*.[120] Thus,

If god mixed the most wise with the most pleasing life, as, I think, was the opinion of the majority *of the ancient and modern wise men*, then this would truly be the best end and I would be very satisfied if I ever experienced this coincidence. (Thdr. Met. *Ethicus* 60)

These are very bold statements at an age when intellectuals could still be persecuted and condemned for deviating from religious Orthodoxy. Metochites is not only anticipating the conflict between his student Nikephoros Gregoras and Gregory Palamas; he is redefining 'paideia' as a means to attain divinity. He is also reactivating a secular religious paradigm. Seen in this light, the conflict with the Aristotelean philosopher Nikephoros Choumnos in regard to the priority of astronomy or physics is significant: like Gregoras

---

[115] Medvedev (1981) 538.   [116] Thdr. Met. *Ethicus* 53, 58; 44.
[117] Thdr. Met. *Ethicus* 61.   [118] Thdr. Met. *Ethicus* 61.
[119] In late antiquity *amathia* was employed to describe the Christian inability to understand pagan theology. See Porph. *Peri agalmaton*: τοὺς ἀμαθεστάτους. Cf. Procl. *In Alc.* 264.10: ἄγνοια, *In Alc.* 364.6: ἀνεπιστημοσύνη.
[120] Thdr. Met. *Ethicus* 61.

and Plethon, Metochites sees in astronomy a mathematical science that is fully compatible with Platonic idealism and rationalism. This leads away from the experiential, that is to say, non-rational knowledge of the divine advocated by Hesychasts and Christian mystics from Dionysius Areopagita to Palamas.

2

THE RISE OF THE BYZANTINE ILLUMINATI

How to see god: the quest for the Thabor light

The fourteenth-century Hesychast controversy is crucial for any attempt to understand Plethon's reformism in the *Memoranda* and the *Nomoi*, for two reasons. First, because the discursive context of these works is still conditioned by the triumph of Gregory Palamas and the establishment of his version of Orthodox Christianity. Second, because the humanist opposition to Gregory Palamas unleashed secular and Hellenising tendencies that effectively paved the way for a more extreme response: Plethon's radical rehabilitation of Plato. These were readily identified by Palamas and the religious establishment as 'pagan'. To be sure, Barlaam, Nikephoros Gregoras and Demetrios Kydones returned the accusation and made it abundantly clear that they considered themselves to be more Christian than Palamas. Still, the Hesychast controversy opened Pandora's box.

For around thirty years, from the 1340s to the end of the 1360s, as the empire was disintegrating and the Turks were at the gates, all intellectual resources were committed to a fierce conflict seemingly concerning the psychophysical practices by means of which man could (or could not, depending on one's perspective) relive the experience of spiritual illumination that Jesus' three apostles had on Mount Thabor: that of a divine light provided by grace and visually apprehended through one's transformed physical eyes.[1]

Gregory Palamas (1296/7–1359) came to be the main spokesman of Hesychasm, the mystical tradition of the Greek

---

[1] Matt. 17:1–3: 'After six days Jesus took with him Peter, James and John the brother of James, and led them up a high mountain by themselves. There he was transfigured before them. His face shone like the sun, and his clothes became as white as the light. Just then there appeared before them Moses and Elijah, talking with Jesus.'

East.[2] The Hesychasts (from ἡσυχία: stillness) maintained their stronghold on Mount Athos. They were monks and ascetics who applied methods sometimes compared to those of the *yogi* and *sufi*.[3] These mainly consisted of respiration control and concentration techniques (primarily navel-gazing) accompanied by the continuous vocal invocation of the name of Jesus (cf. Acts 4:12, 'there is no other name under heaven given to men by which they are to be saved') in the formula of a simple prayer. The Hesychasts considered indefinitely uninterrupted prayer (1 Thess. 5:17: ἀδιαλείπτως προσεύχεσθαι) to be the primary medium for attaining a transcendent state of the soul analogous to the Evagrian 'primeval state' (ἀρχικὴ κατάστασις), which included visions of light (θεοπτία).[4] In the Hesychast tradition the intellect (νοῦς) is thought to be as located in the heart, which also assumes the role of the primary respiratory organ. Identified with the spirit (πνεῦμα), *nous* is distinguished from rational discourse (διάνοια) and viewed as the means for incessant prayer that leads up to the vision of the uncreated energy of god. The aim is to see with the eyes and understand with the heart (cf. John 12:40), that is to say to really 'come and see' (John 1:45).[5] In a sense this is the Christian version of experiential mysticism popularised in the pagan world by the motto associated with the mysteries of Eleusis: ὅστις δὲ εἶδεν, οἶδεν ὃ λέγω.[6]

---

[2] On Hesychasm see the massive bibliography in *HAB* that includes sections on Scholarios, Mark Eugenikos, Bessarion and other figures related to Plethon. A good starting point on the life and times of Palamas is Sinkewicz (2002) 131–73; 173–82 (Bibliogr.). Extensive specialised bibliography on Palamas in *HAB* 376–410.

[3] For example, Gardette (2002: 130) draws attention to the similarity between the 'Jesus prayer', *dhikr* and god-given prayer in Sufism, and the evocation of god (*memrare*) in Ramon Lull. See below, Ch. 4, p. 171 for further parallels between the mystical philosophy of Suhrawardi and Palamism. Given the opposition between Palamism and Plethon's epistemology, I take these as indirect but firm proofs that Plethon could not possibly have been influenced by Suhrawardi.

[4] The classic description of the Hesychast technique is contained in a short treatise by the monk Nikephoros (*PG* 147.963–4), sometimes described in the sources and bibliography as a thirteenth-century Italian who converted from the *kakodoxia* of the Latins to Greek Orthodoxy. On the background of the 'Jesus prayer' see especially Hausherr (1927) 100–42; (1978) 309–24; Meyendorff (1982) 168–87; Krausmüller (2006) 102–8.

[5] Further scriptural passages point to this capacity of human regeneration to uncover true sight and reactivate the heart. See for example Matt. 13:13–15; Rom. 11:8–10.

[6] Paus. *Gr. Descr.* 1.37.4.12–13; Plot. *Enn.* 6.9.9.46–7. The analogies and/or differences between ancient epiphany (or theophany) and Palamite experiential mysticism have not,

The recitation of the Jesus prayer in the Hesychast's heart is allegedly occasioned and carried on by the Holy Spirit – it is no longer the Hesychast who says the prayer but the prayer that is saying itself in his heart.[7] The Hesychast pays attention to and attunes to this recitation with the aim of experiencing a spiritual illumination and achieving deification (θέωσις). This end coincides with entering within the uncreated light, seeing light and becoming light by divine grace: ἐν τῷ φωτί σου ὀψόμεθα φῶς (Ps. 35:10). Not only physical eyes but the whole human body participates in the final stage of glorification. Job 42:5 provides an insight into the antiquity of this Jewish tradition: '... but now my eyes have seen You'. The Hesychast mystical ideal is utterly opposed to the (Neo)Platonic end of intellectual union with the divine, that is to say, the ecstatic ascent of the intellectual part of man alone, a process coinciding with the separation of soul and body (*psychanodia*). Obviously, what Hesychasm has on offer sounds more attractive: full communion with god in body and spirit.

The first openly to challenge the Hesychast claim of witnessing the Thaborine light with physical eyes is the Greek monk Barlaam of Calabria, a man famous for his knowledge of Plato, Aristotle and Eucleides, who later became the teacher of Petrarch. According to Nikephoros Gregoras, Barlaam came from Italy to Greece in order to discover the genuine Aristotle and converse directly with the philosopher's *dianoia* without the filters of Latin scholasticism.[8] Posing as a novice, Barlaam entered a Hesychast circle. 'Upon hearing the claim of seeing the (Thaborine) light with physical eyes he could not rest', says the Hesychast emperor John Kantakuzenos. Barlaam is thought to have exposed the Hesychasts as 'impostors and liars', heretics (in particular Messalians, namely *euchetai*, 'the praying ones')[9] and ὀμφαλόψυχοι:

<hr>

to my knowledge, been studied to date. A good starting point for ancient epiphany is Versnel (1987) 42–55.

7 See also Gal. 4:6: 'Because you are sons, God sent the Spirit of his Son into our hearts, the Spirit who calls out: Abba, Father.'

8 Nik. Greg. *Florentios*, lines 350–65. On Barlaam, see Jugie (1912) cols. 817–34; Krausmüller (2006) 110–13; Sinkewicz (1982) 196–222.

9 The Messalians, the 'praying ones' whom Barlaam linked to the Hesychasts, appear to have read John 6:27 literally, 'Do not labour for bread that perishes.' They thus denounced labour on the gounds that they were seeking eternity, not worldly values associated with it. See here Hausherr (1978) 126.

95

'people-having-their-soul-in-their-navel', for Hesychasts focus on prayer by lowering their heads towards the centre of human body.[10] Initially closer to fideism, Barlaam then praised ancient Greek sages including Plato and Pythagoras as Illuminati (πεφωτισμένοι) and saw in Hesychasm a phenomenon of obscurantism, irrationality and – literally – omphaloscopy. Like Barlaam, later leaders of the anti-Palamite and anti-Hesychast party, in particular Akindynos, Nikephoros Gregoras and the brothers Kydones, were carriers of reformative humanist and secular tendencies that revived a very different notion of illumination – one that relied heavily on Platonist intellectualism.[11] One cannot see god with one's own eyes, they said, echoing Leon Choirosphaktes, Psellos and Theodore Metochites: illumination passes through philosophy, not through psychophysical experiences.

This is a peculiar debate. From the very start there was no possibility for Hesychasts and anti-Hesychasts to reach any kind of agreement. Consider the sarcasm of Nikephoros Gregoras when talking of Palamas. The latter claims that piety does not derive from names or letters, but from the things themselves – alas! – Palamas is λασιόκωφος and hence his want of knowledge regarding names suits him well.[12] Λασιόκωφος is a man deaf owing to hair growing in his ears. The inspiration behind this word coinage is Plato's *Phaedrus* 253e: περὶ ὦτα λάσιος, 'shaggy-eared'. In his reply Palamas recognised the allusion to Plato and returned the compliment: it is Gregoras who resembles that deaf horse described by Plato, for he thinks that 'the divine nature is identical with the divine energies' and fails to grasp the distinction

---

[10] Joh. Cant. *Hist.* 1.548–9. According to the description of the Hesychast breathing discipline by the monk named Nikephoros: 'You know that we breathe our breath in and out only because of our heart ... so, as I have said, sit down, recollect your mind, draw it – I am speaking of your mind – in your nostrils; that is the path the breath takes to reach the heart. Drive it, force it to go down to your heart with the air you are breathing in. When it is there, you will see the joy that follows: you will have nothing to regret.' Quoted in Meyendorff (1982) 185.

[11] On Gregoras see Moschos (1998); Beyer (1976) 17–118; Couloubaritsis (2006) 151–3; *ODB* II s.v. 'Gregoras'; *HAB* 369–76 (Bibliogr.). On Akindynos see Cañellas (2002) 189–256; *ODB* I s.v. 'Akindynos'. But note that according to one view (Ryder 2010: 224–8) anti-Palamism did not necessarily imply anti-Hesychasm and opposition to Orthodoxy, and that Hesychasm did not necessarily imply Palamism.

[12] Nik. Greg. *Hist. Rom.* 3.313.3–11.

in god between the uncreated essence (which is unknowable) and the divine energies (which are knowable and participable).[13] As we shall see, Gregoras was reiterating the classic pagan Platonic position, which Plethon revives once again in the *Nomoi*, identified already by Justin as pagan *par excellence*, that the energy of god cannot differ from his essence.[14] In any case, it is apparent that a debate between people mutually described as deaf owing to an excessive growth of hair is more than likely to be sterile. Demetrios Kydones might say that both Palamas and Gregoras were deaf: the culmination of the clash between Hesychasts and anti-Hesychasts occurs around the time the Turks set foot in Europe. But few were then paying any attention to the conquerors.

One easily misses how much was at stake behind this apparently bizarre and marginal story about visions of light, prayers continuing *ad infinitum* and uncreated energies. In reality Hesychasm is the most idiosyncratic element of Eastern Christianity. P. François Richard tells of a seventeenth-century Jesuit mission in Santorini. The Jesuits were hampered in their attempt to convert the Greeks because of the legacy of 'Palamas et ses Sectateurs'. To Catholic eyes, Palamas was nothing but a 'méchant héresiarque'. According to Richard's account the Greeks had a different view on the matter. They replied with 'a million anathemas against our Fathers, saying that we wished to uproot their faith and abolish their rites'. The Jesuits were quick to appropriate and reiterate the arguments of Nikephoros Gregoras and Demetrios Kydones: Palamas, says Richard, believes that this uncreated light is 'une divinité par dessus la divinité', that it is distinct from the essence of god and that it can be seen with corporeal eyes – these are most shocking claims to any Christian in the West.[15] But the Greeks obstinately refused to see in Palamas a heresiarch – they saw him as a saint. There was a yawning chasm between Eastern mysticism and Western theology. Looking ahead four centuries, it is rumoured that when the *Philokalia* was published in Venice in 1782, all copies were transferred to the East, presumably because the Eastern mystical tradition was felt to be incongruous with that

---

[13] Gr. Pal. *Adv. Greg.* 1.33 (*PS* 4.256.13–23).   [14] See below, p. 266.
[15] Hausheer (1927) 104–5.

97

of Catholics and Protestants. The Hesychast 'Jesus prayer' and the *Philokalia* had no place in the West.[16]

To return to the fourteenth-century controversy, it soon became abundantly clear that the Palamites were on strong ground. The roots of Orthodox mystical practices were shown to stem from an ancient Christian tradition ultimately going back to Paul. Hesychasm was not a 'Byzantine' phenomenon.[17] Palamas defended the supra-rational and experiential contemplation of his contemporary Hesychasts by elaborating the distinction between essence and energy in god that was first developed by the Cappadoceans, Dionysius Areopagita and the early Fathers of the Church. The essence of god is inaccessible and transcendent; the energies are not and may be reached by means of divine illumination, grace and Hesychast practices. Creation is vivified through divine energies ensuring the presence and immanence of god in all things, while supposedly not threatening the radical, as we shall see, ontological difference between the uncreated and unqualified divine essence and temporal or created substance. In Palamas' interpretation, the transfiguration of Christ did not reveal god's unknowable essence but was a manifestation of that essence as an uncreated divine energy. Mystics who reached the highest level of illumination and perfection were able to experience this energy through physical eyes. Moses' visual experience of the burning bush and the fiery ascension of Prophet Elija are two such instances.[18]

---

[16] Hausheer (1927) 101.

[17] See for example 1 Cor. 14:15: προσεύξομαι τῷ πνεύματι, προσεύξομαι δὲ καὶ τῷ νοΐ. Palamas' main thesis can be shown to be as 'orthodox' as is Basil's distinction between a multitude of energies that communicate knowledge of god to man and the 'simple divine essence' which remains forever unknowable: 'on the one hand the energies of god come down to us; on the other hand his essence stays unapproachable'. Some might say that 'if you do not know the essence you do not know him', says Basil. But this should be reversed: in reality, 'if you claim to see god's essence, then you do not know him' (Basil, *Ep.* 234.1.27–2.3). A mystic often associated with Hesychasm, Symeon the New Theologian, in a treatise on 'how one sees god', pointed to another passage, John. 14:9: 'He who has seen me has seen the Father.' Does not Paul say that 'all of you who were baptised into Christ have clothed yourselves with Christ'? Hence how could one think that he who has clothed himself with god, will not know god *noeros* – how can we assume that one who has clothed himself in god has no sense perception (οὐκ αἰσθάνεται) of what he is wearing? (Symeon, *Orationes ethicae.* 5.1.55–74).

[18] Exodus 3:2–5; Kings 2:11–12.

The anti-Palamite party was defeated in successive synods (1341, condemnation of Barlaam; 1347, condemnation of Akindynos; 1351, condemnation of Gregoras; 1368, condemnation of Prochoros Kydones) not least thanks to the support of their chief political supporter John Kantakouzenos, who prevailed in the civil war of 1341–7. Demetrios Kydones gained first-hand experience of the most turbulent phase of the Hesychast controversy. His brother Prochoros reinvigorated the anti-Hesychast argument against the Palamites.[19] The latter mitigated to some extent the harshness of Palamas' original position.[20] Still, the patriarch Philotheos Kokkinos tells us that while on Mount Athos Prochoros Kydones was the 'first and foremost' to 'devote himself maniacally to the vanity of Hellenic studies' and to have 'drunk copiously of their fallacies'.[21] Similarly, in his rebuttal of Nikephoros Gregoras, Philotheos sees the rejection of the Orthodox distinction between the essence and the energies of god as philosophically opening the gates to the pagan view that divinity and the universe are contemporaneous. Justin is thus juxtaposed to the theology contained in Julian's *Hymn to the King Helios*.[22]

'Hellenic' and secular tendencies were immediately recognised as the most serious threat to Orthodoxy, though Thomistic influences gradually became discernible. Prochoros was anathematised in 1368, described in Palamite sources as a 'fake monk' and blasphemous 'enemy of god'. He died two years later. Demetrios Kydones, though a student of the renowned Palamite Neilos Kabasilas and future patriarch Isidore,[23] sided with his brother and turned against Philotheos, supporter of the anathematisation against Prochoros and prominent follower of Palamas.[24] From this point the controversy acquired serious political and ideological dimensions. Gradually, anti-Palamism became synonymous with

---

[19] On Prochoros see Russell (2006) 75–91.
[20] Like humanism, Palamism was not a rigidly static movement. Neo-Palamites elaborated on the basic premises of Palamas' legacy.
[21] *Tomus II* 694B; cf. Russell (2006) 77.   [22] Phil. Cocc. *Contra Greg.* 5.1048–67.
[23] Tinnefeld (1981) 6.
[24] In an invective against Philotheos, Demetrios uses the same accusation that an anonymous student of Plethon would later formulate against Scholarios: that of persecuting a dead man (πῶς οὐ φρίττεις τὸν Πρόχορον καὶ μετὰ τὸν τάφον ἐλαύνων...;) and grave-robbing. Apparently Philotheos sent people to obstruct the burial of Prochoros. See *Notizie* 53 n. 1.

the intrusion of Thomism into Byzantium and 'Latinising' voices advocating the union of the Churches. Its original humanist or 'Hellenic' roots were progressively forgotten. To this day, these roots remain unexplored. So does their conceptual connection to Plethon's Platonic epistemology and ontology.

The 'Enlightened-ones': anti-Hesychast discourse according to Palamite sources

The fourteenth-century Hesychast controversy emerged as a revival of the late antique clash between philosophical Hellenism and Christianity. Palamite sources imply an intriguing phenomenon: that the distance in time between late antiquity and late Byzantium was conversely analogous to their intellectual proximity. In both cases the actual clash between 'Hellenes' and Christians concerns competing definitions of *enlightenment*. The following abstract is from Patriarch Neilos Kerameus' encomium of Gregory Palamas and deals with the first leader of the anti-Palamite party, Barlaam of Calabria:

Hence he [Barlaam of Calabria] thought that nothing exists superior and higher to Hellenic wisdom and the necessity of its syllogisms that lead to the conquest of a presumed truth – and that nothing else exists capable of ensuring man's ascension *to the point of knowing the causes of being*. But there is a claim even more stupid, which we could really consider to be the most grave mistake: namely that one cannot approach and know God-in-Himself unless one has chosen that path (of Hellenic wisdom) and ascends to the conquest of truth *by virtue of becoming familiar with Pythagoras and Aristotle and Plato*, thus learning from them the laws governing nature by necessity and the sequence of the generation and corruption of Being. For, he [Barlaam] was arguing, that if God is Truth and this is what He is called, then to be ignorant of truth is to be ignorant of God, and anybody who is not educated according to the 'wisdom from the outside', that is to say, is ignorant of the movement of the heavenly bodies and physical nature as studied by the Hellenes, is completely ignorant of truth. And he also said that ignorance is nothing but the darkness of the soul; just as *illumination* of the soul is to know all these things. *Hence if this is necessarily how things are, nobody has a right to claim that he is an 'Enlightened one', unless he is trained in this wisdom, that is to say, the 'wisdom beyond the gates'*. (Neilos, *Enc. Pal.*, *PG* 151.664A–C)

Neilos describes here what is effectively a revival of Platonic epistemology in the fourteenth century. In Constantinople, he writes, 'there were many who participated in Hellenic paideia' and the Calabrian counted upon their support.[25] In Palamas' response to Barlaam the latter emerges as a Λατινέλλην, that is, a 'Pagano-Latin' cunningly (δολίως) confounding the Scriptures with the 'Hellenic lessons' as if their end was one and the same.[26] Barlaam would do well to focus on the *idioteia* of the Fathers, rather than on the *nous* of Plato and Nicomachus' son.[27] We may recall that Leon Choirosphaktes, Psellos and Italos were accused of similar experiments. Apparently Barlaam was fully aware of the fact that Palamas' attacks created the impression that 'he was only pretending to follow the Christian world-view, whereas in reality he was an unequivocal pagan (ἕλλην δ' ὢν καθαρῶς)'.[28] In fourteenth-century sources one constantly encounters this deep disquietude that Byzantine humanists were only pretending to be Orthodox in order to undermine, mislead and corrupt the pious Christians.[29] According to John Kantakouzenos, Barlaam's hypocrisy (ὑποκρινόμενος) went as far as compiling anti-Latin treatises in order to win over the Orthodox and avoid raising suspicions.[30] Manuel of Corinth later made the same point explaining why a pagan such as Plethon wrote a bizarre treatise against

---

[25] Neilos, *Enc. Pal.*, *PG* 151.668A.
[26] Gr. Pal. *Triads* 3.3.10.30; 3.3.16.5; 2.1.17.33–4. On Palamas' opposition to Barlaam see Sinkewicz (2002) 164–71.
[27] Gr. Pal. *Ep.* 3.30.20. [28] Meyendorff (1953) 116 n. 2.
[29] The case of Akindynos, another leader of the anti-Palamite faction, is characteristic. Palamas accuses Akindynos (ἄνευ κινδύνου = *harmless*) of assuming this name, rather than his Christian baptismal name, which he carefully concealed, for two reasons: first, in order to purposefully mislead the gullible by exploiting the associations between the illusory safety implied by his cognomen and Orthodoxy; second, because he had developed a fixed idea about putting as much distance as possible between his 'harmless' doctrines and the monastic tradition. In reality, Akindynos has nothing but contempt for the latter, for he does not even want to carry a name common among the Hesychasts. In reality he is *polykindynos* (very dangerous, dangerous in many ways) rather than akindynos (harmless). See Gr. Pal. *Adv. Akind.* 3.23.106 (*PS* 3.238.13–239.10). Akindynos often wrote his name with a small *a* thus making of it an adjective, e.g. ἡ τοῦ ἀκινδύνου διάνοια meant both 'a safe (harmless) thought' and 'Akindynos' thought', but people unaware of his treacherous games, as Palamas viewed them, would spontaneously opt for the former reading.
[30] Joh. Cant. *Hist.* 1.543.10–18.

Latin theology, namely *The Reply to the Treatise in Support of the Latin Doctrine*.

Eventually Barlaam was condemned in the *Synodicon of Orthodoxy* for reviving Plato's Forms, those Forms that Plethon later identified with pagan gods. His religious dissimulation was exposed by another prominent Hesychast, Philotheos Kokkinos. Barlaam is wearing the mask of a pious Christian, we read; in reality, he is an agent of the Latins mocking 'our sacred doctrines'. Once uncovered, Barlaam returned to Italy 'disgraced, having suffered what he hoped to do to others'.[31] In Italy Barlaam became the teacher of Petrarch.[32]

Anti-Palamite and anti-Hesychast discourse is often associated with 'Byzantine Thomism'. But fourteenth-century Byzantine humanism was no uniform phenomenon. During the first phases of the Hesychast controversy its aims and development were not yet conditioned by Thomism and scholasticism.[33] Palamites were initially concerned with combating Platonising, heretical and 'paganising' tendencies that had not as yet found a common medium of expression and political agenda in Byzantine Thomism. It was only after the formal end of the controversy that anti-Palamism really merged with unionist and pro-Latin policy through men such as Kydones' student John Kyparissiotes, Manuel Kalekas, Manuel Chrysoloras and Plethon's student Bessarion.

Even the late *tomus* of 1368 dealing with the doctrinal errors of the anti-Hesychast party conveys the impression that the Latin conception of Christianity was but one possible threat among others. For that matter, it was *not* the most dangerous one. What the *tomus* affirms is that early anti-Palamites, namely Barlaam, Akindynos and Gregoras, as well as the brothers Kydones, advanced a novel, raw intellectual world-view that claimed to be still Christian

---

[31] Phil. Cocc. *Contra Greg.* 12.28.30.

[32] It is telling of the links between moderate Platonist tendencies and Plethonean Platonism that in the 1370 *De sui ipsius multorumque ignorantia* Petrarch praised those Italian humanists upon whose request Plethon appears to have compiled the *Differences* in Florence – those that were, according to the sarcasms of Scholarios 'as much competent in philosophy as is Plethon in dancing'. Cf. Schol. *Contra Pleth.*, *OC* 4.4.2–8. For the similarities between Petrarch's and Plethon's defense of the Platonic theory of the Forms against Aristotle's criticism see Beyer (1994) 1–4.

[33] H. G. Beck (1963) 67, 70.

yet facilitated the potential emergence of intellectual converts to a paganising 'Hellenic' understanding of god, knowledge and illumination. Thus, when Demetrios Kydones supported the anti-Palamism of his brother Prochoros, he was condemned on the grounds of attacking the Fathers and undermining the Palamite distinction between divine essence and divine operation by reverting to pagan philosophy: τὴν τῶν Ἑλλήνων μυθοποιΐαν.[34] Is this just rhetoric aiming to stigmatise the anti-Palamite faction by utilising the horrible accusation of paganism? Convenient though this interpretation might be, Palamas' *Capita CL*, one of the most important works of this period, written in 1349/50 during the second phase of the Palamite controversy, conveys the opposite impression.

The *Capita* testifies to a contemporary revival of interest in the pagan belief in the perpetually renewed sempiternity and sanctity of the *cosmos*; in Hellenic naturalism and intellectualism, that is a devotion to intellectual pursuits and 'human wisdom', as well as to renewed interest in theurgy and pagan rites.[35] As in his other major work, the *Triads*, Palamas hardly conceals his anxiety to provide a bulwark to the unqualified study of those ancient 'Hellenic sages' who 'worshipped and served the creature rather than the creator'.[36] It is paganism – what Palamas calls 'a soul-destroying, many headed serpent (πολυκέφαλος ὕδρα)' – not Thomism, that is in the foreground here.[37] The Hellenic sacralisation of the universe and, significantly, late antique Eunomianism, are explicitly identified as two heads of this monster – but Latin theology is not.

In *Capita CL* Palamas attacks the revival of interest in Proclan theurgy, quoting from Marinus' *Life of Proclus*. Sinkewicz suggested that Palamas had Gregoras' preoccupation with the *Chaldean Oracles* in mind and notes that Gregoras' interest 'was probably not unique'.[38] The passage is interesting, linking the *en*

---

34 *Synodicon* 666–71. For the condemnation of Prochoros Kydones see *Notizie* 55–61.
35 Gr. Pal. *Capita CL* 19–20; 28.
36 Gr. Nyss. *De creatione hominis* 1.3.8–9; Gr. Pal. *Capita CL* 26.10–15.
37 Gr. Pal. *Capita. CL* 11–12.
38 The opening for Gregoras to disclose his preoccupation with the pagan *Chaldean Oracles* was provided by Synesius' *On Dreams*. See the introduction to *Capita CL* by Sinkewicz, 15 and Appendix 1 in Pietrosanti's edition of Gregoras' commentary, 109–16.

vogue humanist study of the ancient Illuminati, natural science and astronomy to the worship of the devil, polytheism and theurgy:

> But natural scientists, astronomers, and those who boast of knowing everything have been unable to understand any of the things just mentioned on the basis of their philosophy and have considered the ruler of the intelligible darkness and all the rebellious powers under him not only superior to themselves but even gods and they honoured them with temples, offered them sacrifices, and submitted themselves to their most destructive oracles by which they were fittingly much deluded through unholy things and defiling purifications, through those who inspire abominable presumption and through prophets and prophetesses who lead them very far astray from the real truth. (Gr. Pal. *Capita CL* 28; trans. Sinkewicz)

All prominent members of the anti-Palamite party were associated with this complex revival of Hellenism and late antique heresy regardless of the fact that some of them were also sympathetic to Thomism and others were not. Neilos Kerameus, Philotheos Kokkinos and Gregory Palamas had no doubt that the humanist outlook of Barlaam, Gregoras, Akindynos and others was heretical because of its Hellenic starting point.

It may appear perilous to rely on Hesychast sources to reconstruct the philosophy of anti-Hesychast philosophers. Part II of this book shows in what sense the epistemology and ontology of the Byzantine humanists was, indeed, infiltrated by philosophical paganism. For the time being it is imperative to note that at least a generation before Plethon the use of Hellenic philosophy to reach divine illumination was considered by the religious establishment to be a dangerous possibility, and, what is more, as a real and sufficiently plausible threat. Resembling a self-fulfilling prophecy, this threat progressively acquired flesh and blood.

This becomes apparent in the case against Nikephoros Gregoras. The leader of the anti-Palamite party, Gregoras was a prominent Platonising humanist, layman and student of Theodore Metochites. Though a fervent opponent of Barlaam and an anti-unionist, Gregoras too was repeatedly accused of being a *philosopher* in an unacceptable sense of the word. His error was to contradict Paul's famous motto regarding 'wisdom made foolish'. This means he failed to separate 'drinkable' discourses from 'salty' ones – a clear reference to a distinction also applied by Gregory of Nazianzus –

and refrained from classing the wisdom of this world as enslaved to a 'superior wisdom' of the Church philosophers, as he should have done. Instead, continues Philotheos, he made an alliance with the ancient philosophers and had *them* guide him, rather than the prophets, apostles and the Fathers of the Church. But that is not all. Gregoras is faking his concern for Orthodoxy. In reality he is a man misled into blasphemy, calumny and heresy.

As in the case of Barlaam, this accusation does not appear to be rhetorical in nature. Rather, it concerns specific positions in metaphysics and epistemology considered as incompatible with Orthodox Christianity. As Couloubaritsis and Medvedev observed, in Gregoras' *Florentios* (1337) Plato as a philosopher, mathematician and astronomer becomes the hallmark of science and free thought and is opposed not only to Aristotelianism but also to Roman Catholicism and unionist politics. In this sense Gregoras anticipates Plethon's anti-Aristotelianism.[39]

In the end Gregoras paid the price for his attack on the clerical establishment: four years of confinement and continuous pressure to give in to Palamite Orthodoxy. He could not claim not to have been warned. As Philotheos put it, by obstinately refusing to follow the example of the 'philosophers of the Church' and to acknowledge that secular wisdom is the slave (δούλη) and handmaid (θεράπαιναν) of theology – alas! – he now lost both.[40] Gregoras was condemned by the Synod of 1351. Preparing himself for the Synod, Gregoras addressed his pupils outside his house. He drew parallels with Leonidas and his three hundred Spartans. One should deal with the Palamite party, he says, in the manner that Leonidas dealt with the invading Persian army in Greece: by straightforward heroism. *Tonight we dine in Hades*, says Gregoras, or, he quickly corrects himself, we should better say *tonight we dine in Paradise*.[41] Those eager to compare Byzantium with the glory of ancient Greece to the detriment of the former might find in Gregoras' self-portrayal as a modern Leonidas a tragelaphic mixture of Byzantine rhetorical exaggeration and unintentional

---

[39] Cf. Couloubaritsis (2006) 152; Medvedev (1984) 130–1 on Gregoras' Neoplatonic theology.
[40] Phil. Cocc. *Contra Greg.* 4.376–80. Cf. Medvedev (1981) 534.
[41] Nik. Greg. *Hist. Rom.* 2.895.10–896.2.

self-parody. The Turks were soon expected outside the gates of Constantinople, yet the spirit of Leonidas was remembered in the context of an obscure theological controversy regarding the nature of the Thaborine light.

On the other hand, we should not lose sight of the bizarre fact that questions of theology and mysticism were now affairs of the State. The emperor John Kantakouzenos was called to preside over Synods. The issue was not only theological, but also political. For all its pomposity, Gregoras' appeal to ancient history involves a clear subtext: Palamas was an internal enemy. He was felt to be as alien to and destructive of Gregoras' philosophical and religious identity as was the advance of Xerxes' Persian army to Greece. He was seen as the leader of a type of intellectual and religious imperialism eroding Byzantium from within. Plethon's references to Lycurgus and Sparta are more delicate than is Gregoras' appeal to Leonidas, yet the point in *Memorandum to Manuel* remains the same. A monastic movement effectively works against the 'common salvation'; an internal conquest is in full progress and it is time (καιρός) for a heroic ideological and philosophical response.[42]

Demetrios Kabasilas visited Gregoras during his imprisonment.[43] Gregoras witnessed his old and dear friend, now converted to the Palamite party, enter a bizarre state of stillness and spiritual introspection, speechlessly looking at the ground. Gregoras imagines that his friend might well be lamenting the degeneration of scientific study into *silence* – in any case, he tells us that this is what he was doing. The passage uniquely captures the violent defeat of secular paideia by Palamite authority:

He greeted me in an ordinary way and sat down turning his head towards the earth. He somehow gave me the impression of being moved by seeing the disaster that had befallen my home and this new tragedy, and that it was for this reason that he went within himself and sat there in this state, in pure stillness of all passions (turning his senses towards the inmost part of the soul) and bringing to his mind the changes of fortune: how could it be that this house, which was so full of voices, was suddenly made voiceless? And how could it be that the continuous gatherings of wise men and competitions in logic, in which participated many and different men, disappeared at such short notice? And how did the streams flowing from the unexhaustible fountains of Mathematics turn into a desert of silence in this

---

[42] See Ch. 7, pp. 342ff.   [43] On Demetrios Kabasilas and Gregoras see Beyer (1989).

conclusive manner? And how could it be that the channels of manifold questions and solutions of astronomical wisdom had to hide in the tombs of oblivion? This is what my friend's position gave me to think about – as well as what follows from this. (Nik. Greg. *Hist. Rom.* 2.1050.21–1051.14)

Gregoras argued that his students were threatened and that his circle was dissolved by violence exercised by the clerical authorities.[44] It is difficult to know whether he is exaggerating or not. Still, he asks a question that evokes the world of late antiquity: is there a reason for religion to separate friends? 'For Libanius', he says, 'though he was a follower of the Hellenic religion, was a friend of Basil the Great.' The implicit point is that the times of Gregoras and Demetrios Kabasilas are very different to those of Libanius and Basil. In contrast with late antiquity, a world-view different from the prevalent one was now held to entail dissent and conflict with an established intellectual hegemony that used indoctrination, anathematisation and imprisonment as means to preserve its orthodoxy.

Gregoras was not a Hellene in the sense that Libanius was. But he was a philhellene and the Palamites rightly recognised that philhellenism in Byzantium could mean much more than a fondness for encyclopaedic secular learning in the Photian sense. In the course of his clash with Palamism, Gregoras redeployed intellectual weapons that had not been put to use in this way for centuries. Like Barlaam, he used pagan philosophy and appealed to the authority of pagan philosophers in order to put Palamite Orthodoxy to the test. The collateral consequence is that, perhaps for the first time since late antiquity, Neoplatonic arguments were openly re-calibrated and consistently employed against Orthodoxy, while their Hellenic origin was explicitly recognised.

In the case of Gregoras, Hellenism and in particular Platonism is too often seen as the measure by which to define and understand Orthodoxy. As Gregoras saw it, Palamas imitated Proclus in the worst possible way, corrupted his *lexis* (διέφθαρκε τὴν λέξιν) and proceeded into a fatal error, which no Hellene, or at least no wise Hellene, ever committed: for neither Plato, nor Proclus ever postulated any series of uncreated divinities, as the Palamites

---

[44] Nik. Greg. *Hist. Rom.* 2.1012.

do when distinguishing between the divine essence and 'uncreated' divine energies.[45] A close study of Plotinus and Aristotle, argues Gregoras, reveals that truth is very different from Palamas' perverted doctrines: for according to the Hellenes, there is no difference between divine essence and energy.[46] Here Palamas is refuted with reference to a Hellenic-Christian *symphonia* regarding the impossibility of distinguishing between essence and energy, one 'confirmed' by an appeal to Plotinus and Proclus.[47] Pythagoras, Numa and Plutarch are three further authorities evoked by Gregoras to show the superiority of Hellenic theology over its corrupt form favoured by Palamas.[48] Thus Palamas is shown to be polytheist in a way far worse than the Hellenes were, one that is unacceptable from a Hellenic viewpoint.

With Gregoras the spirit of Neoplatonic philosophy, rather than its *lexis*, is made relevant again and is now applied to strengthen the intellectual resistance to established clerical authorities. People have no respect for innovators, says Gregoras, repeating an argument as old as Celsus' *Alethes Logos*. Palamas is incapable not only of appreciating 'the Hellenic Muse and any scientific teaching' used by the Fathers but also of ascending to the meaning (διάνοια) carried by the *lexis* of texts – though he wishes to.[49] Palamas misuses Proclus, appropriating the worst parts, while leaving out things well said.[50]

Out of Gregoras' intention to combat Palamas' version of Christianity evolves the need for a new reception of Hellenism. By reactivating Proclan theology and accusing Palamas of misusing

---

[45] Nik. Greg. *Hist. Rom.* 2.1103.

[46] Nik. Greg. *Hist. Rom.* 2.1088.1ff.; Plot. *Enn.* 6.8.13.33–40. For the identification of Plotinean passages used by Gregoras see the remarks by van Dieten in vol. IV of his translation of Gregoras' *History*, 331 n. 558.

[47] Nik. Greg. *Hist. Rom.* 2.1092.6 –1094.6.   [48] Nik. Greg. *Hist. Rom.* 2.1108.12–17.

[49] Nik. Greg. *Hist. Rom.* 2.1080.5–1081.9. Demetrios Kydones made a similar criticism. What is intriguing here is the view that ancient philosophy was not properly studied but utilised for reasons of clerical and ideological expediency. The conservative Orthodox party, he says, considers its theology to be identical to that of the earliest Fathers of the Church, while also pretending to have the highest esteem for Plato and Aristotle. The problem, he says, is that its members then recite the Hellenic doctrines without actually having read them. They also think that all Latins are barbarians and that it is only through the Orthodox Greeks that the latter acquired some knowledge of Plato and Aristotle. See *Notizie* 354.83–93.

[50] Nik. Greg. *Hist. Rom.* 2.1109.11–15.

Proclus and Plato, Gregoras makes Hellenic philosophy pertinent again – not as a dialectical and rhetorical weapon, but rather as a paradigm to be reclaimed from the Palamites, reappraised and reinterpreted.

This is a move of tremendous importance. The Palamite doctrine concerning the distinction between divine energies and essence contradicts Christian Orthodoxy *because* it contradicts Hellenic philosophy. As occasionally in Psellos, it is the Fathers who appear to be in agreement with the Hellenes, rather than Hellenic philosophers who foreshadow the Fathers. Platonism is made the measure for interpreting Christian doctrine. In other words, Gregoras (consciously or not) promoted a version of Orthodoxy that ceased to be exclusive. Even if there was no intention to subvert but rather to reform Christianity, ancient philosophy was now set out as a weapon of discourse and an instrument capable of effecting change to the existing hegemony of spiritualism and monasticism. This weapon would soon fall into Plethon's hands. In the *Nomoi* Pythagoras, Numa, Plutarch and Plotinus are counted among the transmitters of universal truths without any reference to Christianity.[51]

One example is particularly apt here. Gregoras explained the *symphonia* between Hellenes and Christians in terms of common rules of scientific discourse, which god purportedly gave to all, 'those of the same and those of another race', just as the rules of haunting and cultivating the earth are the same, or even earth and heaven, air and rain, sun and the moon are common to all.[52] Similarly, in the *Encomium* of Palamas, Neilos Kerameus testifies that according to Barlaam too 'one should not be ignorant of anything discovered by the wise men of old'; instead, one should be taught by them 'regardless of whether they were Hellenes, Barbarians or Scythians, that is, if one wishes to have his intellect illumined and acquire knowledge of the divine and humane things'. Barlaam 'did not only teach this to his immature pupils but was also writing speeches'.[53] These pioneering efforts at a universally valid natural religion or *réligion cosmique* (to apply here a term of

---

[51] *Nomoi* 30, 32 (1.2.45; 1.2.76–9). See below, Ch. 4, p. 179.
[52] Nik. Greg. *Hist. Rom.* 2.1099.6–15.   [53] Neilos, *Enc. Pal.*, PG 151.665A–B.

Festugière) have their roots in the Platonist intellectual paradigm mediating between late antique pagan Platonism and Plethon's reformation of paganism. They are ultimately founded upon the Neoplatonic and Stoic belief in *common notions* and so is Plethon's belief in universal 'true doctrines'. Of course, Plethon went on to exclude Christians from this *symphonia*. But the application of philosophical Hellenism in fourteenth-century Orthodox theology had already compromised the centuries-old Christian privilege of claiming exclusivity in accessing truth.

The conflict between the Palamite establishment and Byzantine humanism is sometimes presented as one between monks and intellectuals or high members of the clergy favoured by the court. In this sense the conflict represents an 'internal drama of Byzantine civilisation', as Meyendorff put it, one that 'revived a long-standing intellectual and spiritual incompatibility between the monks and the admirers of Ancient Greek philosophy' that has its roots in the ninth century.[54] We shall see that the philosophical roots of this civil war go much deeper. Be that as it may, fourteenth-century humanist and anti-Hesychast discourse profoundly shocked the Byzantine intellectual world by undermining, for the first time since late antiquity, the commonly assumed relation between *lexis* and *nous* in theology and philosophy: in other words, what people took for granted.

This became fully apparent in 1351 when John VI Kantakouzenos, the emperor who became a Hesychast monk, asked Byzantine theologians to address the *real* issue: is this a war (πόλε-μος) regarding the letter of theological vocabulary (λέξεις) or is it about the actual essence of religious doctrine? In the latter case 'we have to examine the naked things and seek the truth in them'. The anti-Hesychasts, we read in the synodical tome of that year, 'are clearly waging a war not against the names (λέξεις) but against the corresponding truths (πράγματα) and doctrines (δόγματα)'.[55] Christianity was under attack.

Neither Barlaam nor Gregoras, nor later the Kydones brothers were really 'pagans' or Hellenes in Sathas' meaning of the word.

---

[54] Meyendorff (1953) 88; cf. the introduction in Meyendorff (1974) §4.
[55] *Tomus III* 725A–726C.

It is likely that, as current scholarship assumes, Barlaam represented 'a genuinely monastic tradition, which he felt threatened by the Hesychasts',[56] at least in the initial phase of the debate. It is also likely that the Kydones brothers were moved by Latinophile tendencies and that a complex agenda underlies the secularist tendencies of Nikephoros Gregoras. Still, anti-Palamite discourse created and subsequently left open the possibility of an agent more radical than they were to take their philhellenic and philosophical argumentation back to its Platonic roots. Palamas was right that Byzantine Thomism and humanism, whether consciously or not, provided for a pagan Platonic philosophical paradigm antagonistic to the Roman Orthodox intellectual hegemony and educational indoctrination. Tellingly, when faced with the Byzantine Illuminati, Palamas adopts the same position towards secular wisdom as Basil and apologists including Eusebius and Theodoret advised when dealing with philosophical Hellenes in late antiquity:

In the case of secular wisdom, you must first kill the serpent, in other words, overcome the pride that arises from this philosophy. How difficult that is! 'The arrogance of philosophy has nothing in common with humility', as the saying goes. Having overcome it, then, you must separate and cast away the head and tail, for these things are evil in the highest degree. By the head, I mean manifestly wrong opinions concerning things intelligible and divine and primordial; and by the tail, the fabulous stories concerning created things. As to what lies in between the head and tail, that is, discourses on nature, you must separate out useless ideas by means of the faculties of examination and inspection possessed by the soul, just as pharmacists purify the flesh of serpents with fire and water. Even if you do all this, and make good use of what has been properly set aside, how much trouble and circumspection will be required for the task! (Gr. Pal. *Triads* 1.1.21; trans. Gendle).

Obviously not much remains of the original snake after such a cooking process, but then again this is precisely the point Gregory is trying to make. Philotheos tells us that Palamas was trained in *thyrathen* paideia in order to appropriate 'missiles (βέλη) and weapons (ὅπλα)'.[57] The contrast between this instrumental eclecticism and the hermeneutics of Gregoras, who looked at Plato and the Greek wise men as 'mystagogues' (μυσταγωγοί)[58] is

---

[56] Krausmüller (2006) 113.   [57] Phil. Cocc. *Enc. Greg. Pal.* 10.2–3.
[58] Phil. Cocc. *Contra Greg.* 1.415–19.

sufficiently pronounced. The argument is that 'We are in full possession of your armoury and we could use your weapons against you, but we prefer to rely on something better – the illumination of the Spirit.'[59] Palamas was perfectly aware of what precisely rendered Hellenism threatening to his world-view –metaphysics, theology, mathematics combined with the 'arrogance' of secular wisdom – and he saw this threat as directly relevant to contemporary attacks on Hesychasm.

The political dimension of this Byzantine 'internal drama' is exemplified in Demetrios Kydones' complaint, a few years after the formal end of the Hesychast controversy, that in the eyes of Orthodox Christians his consideration of Latin theology rendered him guilty of attempting to 'shift the established order of things': ὡς καὶ τὰ καθεστῶτα ἐπιχειροίην κινεῖν. As in the case of Martin Luther, translation stimulated theological discussions that necessarily carried with them a socio-political aspect. Kydones' note has been rightly read as meaning that the assault on Orthodoxy and Hesychasm was tantamount to political dissent.[60] Like earlier Byzantine humanists, Kydones attempted to reform an ideological and religious hegemony *from within*.[61] At the time this was the only available option. As Scholarios puts it: 'in our times', he says, 'it is dangerous (ἐπικίνδυνον) to experiment with the discovery of new things'.[62] Instead, one should focus on preserving the 'ancestral' tradition of the Fathers of the Church.

Kydones admits that 'perhaps' his critics were not entirely mistaken – the difference being that they thought he was undermining the Orthodox Church on purpose, 'though I had no such intention'.[63] There is no reason to doubt Kydones' statement. Still, this hardly means that the Palamites were wrong in their judgement. Perhaps unintentionally, Kydones and the Byzantine humanists set in motion a mechanism supporting disestablishment (τὰ καθεστῶτα κινεῖν). The Hesychast controversy incited an almost

---

[59] Quoted in Ware (1995) 12.   [60] Moschos (1998) 131.
[61] On the political aspect of the Kydones affair see Ryder (2010) 148–68.
[62] Schol. *Dialogi de processu spiritus sancti* 2, *OC* 3.33.20–2: καὶ ἐν τοιούτοις καιροῖς, ἐν οἷς ἐπικίνδυνόν ἐστιν ἐξευρίσκειν πειρᾶσθαι, ἀλλὰ μὴ τοῖς ὑπὸ τῶν πρεσβυτέρων ἐξευρημένοις ἕπεσθαι.
[63] *Notizie* 365.69–76.

existential worry about the relation between words and things, the essence of things, the meaning of religious authority, the relation between Orthodoxy and antiquity, East and West – about Byzantine identity as such.

The cases against Barlaam, Akindynos, Gregoras and the brothers Prochoros and Demetrios Kydones show that each revival of the Hesychast controversy was felt to be more intense than the last: Akindynos is said to have introduced more novel and subversive ideas than Barlaam, and Gregoras is said to have developed a theology more monstrous and innovative than any of his predecessors. We read the same thing about Prochoros Kydones. Even though Palamite Orthodoxy managed to prevail against successive assaults, and presumably preserve a unified 'Orthodox' doctrinal core, its humanist opponents kept diversifying and shifting their philosophical outlook. The Palamites saw nothing but an escalating series of abominable heresies. But this continuation and intensification of philosophical experimentations with religion prepared the ground for further novel approaches to the Platonic heritage.

One may thus sympathise with Philotheos Kokkinos when he describes Gregoras as a 'philosopher' issuing 'laws in rivalry with' those of the Church (ἀντινομοθετεῖν), 'restoring human wisdom' and elevating himself to the status of 'a self-elected interpreter and teacher of divine and sacred things'.[64] What was at stake was the autonomy of philosophy, the rift between established 'legislation' and an intruding 'rival legislation' based on profane wisdom. With Barlaam, Gregoras and other fourteenth-century humanists, a self-confident philosophical paradigm that was only latently present in Metochites' *Ethicus* begins to emerge, fully supported by the authorities of Plato, Plotinus, Pythagoras and Proclus. The intellectual paradigm of these ancient Illuminati was still perfectly capable of leading to serious assaults not only on the Hesychasts but on Christianity as such.

Plethon's *Nomoi* is a militant version of the secular/pagan project of *antinomothetein*: an introduction of unauthorised legislation antagonistic to that sanctified by Roman Orthodoxy.

---

[64] Phil. Cocc. *Contra Greg.* 1.454–6; 482–4.

Plethon and the twilight of Palamism

Plethon first saw the light of the sun at more or less the time that Palamas departed from this world. Still, the world he came to know was infused in both the theological and the political arenas by Palamas' doctrinal triumph. Plethon witnessed the intellectual and political collapse of the anti-Palamite humanist party; the eventual sway of Palamism over secular tendencies well into the fifteenth century; the failure and horrors of anarchic political reformism (the 'Zealots' reform') in Thessaloniki; but also the last efforts of secular circles and his teacher Kydones to promote a return to ancient philosophy. When in 1382/3 Kydones was asking Manuel to obtain from the monks at Athos that precious Plato manuscript, Palamism was at the height of its glory, having recently emerged victorious from a long intellectual civil war. Palamism now played a major role influencing and to a large degree determining Orthodox theology as well as the Byzantine position towards the Ottomans and the Latin West.

Owing to repeated synodical acknowledgements that 'Palamism' was, after all, the real essence of Roman Orthodoxy, the Church was by the end of the fourteenth century effectively controlled by bishops trained in the Hesychast tradition. The following remarks by an authority sympathetic to Palamism, John Meyendorff, aptly illustrate the political and intellectual repercussions of this 'monastic takeover' that defined Plethon's world:

While the empire in the fourteenth century was reduced to only a shadow of itself, the Church, as an institution, had never exercised so much influence both inside and outside the imperial frontiers. This was particularly true of monasticism. Mount Athos, traditionally endowed and administered by the emperors, was now placed in the patriarchal jurisdiction by a chrysobull of Andronicus II (1312). The exact significance of this measure is difficult to evaluate, but it may have contributed to the alliance between monastic circles and the church hierarchy – rather unusual in previous centuries – and, in fact, *to a takeover, after 1347, of the high church administration by an entirely monastic personnel, with disciples of Palamas on the patriarchal throne* (Isidore, 1347–1349; Callistus I, 1350–1354, 1355–1363; Philotheos, 1354–1355, 1364–1376; Macarius, 1376–1379, Neilos, 1380–1388, etc.). With *the further disintegration of the state, this monastic takeover will have even greater significance* because of the relative growth of the patriarchate's importance . . . *Geographically and morally, the patriarchate had certainly a greater impact on society than the imperial throne, and this impact inevitably carried with it economic and political consequences.*

Meyendorff puts in a nutshell these fourteenth-century 'economic and political consequences' of the Palamite takeover when talking of

[a] new power acquired by the Church, now ruled mainly by the monastic party, *a power that the emperors were too weak to challenge seriously . . . The empire had practically ceased to exist. But the Church was keeping its influence on the people* – in Constantinople, in much of Eastern Europe and the remaining imperial territories, and also in occupied Asia Minor.[65]

Meyendorff's thesis is corroborated by recent research. In the words of a modern scholar, the monks threatened to turn Byzantium into a 'monastic economy of almost Tibetan proportions'.[66] This included making deals with the Ottomans. It appears, for example, that in the second half of the fourteenth century Athonite monasteries made prudent and profitable arrangements with the Ottoman ruler Orkhan.[67] The latter ensured protection against naval raids and secured the prosperity of the monasteries in exchange for collaboration. The great probability that the man who served as mediator between the Ottomans and the Athonites was none other than the Byzantine emperor John VI Kantakouzenos says a lot about the disintegration of the State and the rising power of the monastic establishment. While the State was fading away, the Church continued to pursue contact with the Ottomans in the fifteenth century.[68]

Hesychasm was a world-view particularly expedient to the Ottomans owing to the importance of 'holy men' in Islam and, perhaps more significantly, the defeatist politics it entailed. But the monasteries also attracted donors and prospered economically: extensive donations of land and sums of money guaranteed an

---

[65] Meyendorff (1982) 129–33; my emphasis.   [66] Bryer (2009) 862.
[67] Zachariadou (2006) 158–9.
[68] See Balivet (2007) 72–3 on the case of the monks of the monastery of Saint-John Prodromus in Serres, who avoided taxation by the Turks by collaborating with Osman before the conquest of the Balkan peninsula. No wonder then that in 1553 the French voyager Pierre Belon tells of the Turkish veneration for Mount Athos that extended to their giving alms to the Athonites (Balivet 2007: 78 n. 82).

annual income to the Byzantines, not to mention the various banking, maritime and business activities of the Athonites, and, predictably, the possibility of salting away money.[69] Behind the façade of Hesychast tranquillity, spirituality and utopian communality, Mount Athos was in a much better position to attract investors and guarantee the economic safety of Byzantines than was the State.

As Byzantine humanism proved its impotence to reform Orthodox Christianity from within and provide an ideological alternative, Orthodox ecumenism replaced geographical and national conceptions of identity with a spiritual one. Plethon witnessed Palamite supra-rational mysticism take over the Church and the State before expanding through the whole Balkan Peninsula. Variations of Byzantine Neo-Hesychasm were spreading fast in Bulgaria, Serbia and Russia. For decades Palamite Orthodoxy successfully propagated and represented a religious ecumenism and Graeco-Slav cosmopolitanism unrestrained by traditional notions of imperial borders and secular political ideals. The Hesychasts formed a supra-national community, aptly termed 'The Hesychast International', while maintaining 'a common loyalty to a spiritual *alma mater*, such as Mount Athos'.[70] The followers of Palamas had little interest in national and political freedom. What mattered to them was spiritual illumination and salvation, they claimed – and the expansion of a trans-national movement. At the same time, almost nothing was left of the empire, as Plethon affirms in that urgent *Memorandum* to Theodore, but a couple of cities in Thrace, parts of the Peloponnese 'and perhaps some of the smallest islands, if any at all were left'.[71]

The Hesychast takeover put in motion the realisation of Julian's nightmare: imperial and political institutions were dying away, as a gargantuan Christian monastic/clerical authority was rising by appropriating their essence. What did not happen in late antiquity finally took place in late Byzantium: the growth of the Church brought about the collapse of the State. One might be tempted to claim that Theodore and Manuel ignored the measures proposed

---

[69] Zachariadou (2006) 160–5.   [70] Obolensky (2007) 495–6.
[71] *Mem. I* 129.14–17.

by Plethon in his two *Memoranda*. More than that, they did not have the power to enforce them.

All three major theologians of the era associated with the Byzantine courts, Joseph Bryennios, Mark Eugenikos and Gennadios Scholarios, were spiritually, intellectually and even politically formed within a Palamite context, continuing into the fifteenth century the legacy of the three champions of Hesychasm, Palamas, Philotheos Kokkinos, and Neilos Kabasilas. Manuel, the man on whom Plethon invested his hopes for the regeneration of Hellenism, was not only a philosopher but also a theologian skilled in the mystical tradition of the East. Thus when Plethon submitted the two *Memoranda*, theological discourse in Constantinople was about to pass into the hands of Mark Eugenikos, Plethon's student who was arguably the best Greek theologian of his time,[72] and Scholarios; another significant Palamite, Symeon, became bishop of Thessaloniki (1414–29); and Demetrios Chrysoloras, a member of Manuel Palaiologos' close circle, supported the Orthodoxy of Palamism against Demetrios Kydones,[73] while Plethon's student Bessarion attacked Palamas and Mark Eugenikos.[74] Plethon was surrounded by Palamites and their defeated opponents. From the 'wise Kydones' and Manuel II to his own students, Mark Eugenikos and Bessarion, everyone was involved in one way or another.

At times even Scholarios was forced to suppress his Thomist sympathies in favour of Palamite Orthodoxy. This might appear odd. Still, in the concluding sentence of a rarely cited 1976 article, Masai insightfully suggested that the urgent need to oppose the resurgence of Platonism in Mistra might well explain why Scholarios reverted to theological notions that might be incompatible with Thomism yet were more effective against the philosophical paganism of the Plethonean type.[75] Though Byzantine Thomism was in the ascendance, Palamism still provided the theological arsenal for fighting Plethon's Platonic epistemology and ontology.

---

[72] On Mark Eugenikos see Constas (2002) 411–61, 461–4 (Bibliogr.); *HAB* 472–7 (Bibliogr.).
[73] On Chrysoloras see *PLP* 31156.
[74] See *PLP* 1439. On Bessarion versus Palamas see Mohler (1923) 213–18.
[75] Masai (1976) 38.

The impact and significance of Palamism in Plethon's world becomes fully apparent if we consider the theological position of the Greek representatives in the Synod of Ferrara/Florence in 1438/9. The received opinion is that Plethon made his name there as the most confident supporter of Eastern Orthodox dogma alongside his former pupil Mark Eugenikos. The Orthodox position was to a large extent based upon the work of the Palamite Neilos Kabasilas. The union of the Churches, with all the political implications it entailed, depended upon doctrinal issues defined in the East by Palamism. During the preparatory phase for the Synod, Scholarios and Mark Eugenikos were given the task of studying Neilos' work in order to turn it against the Latins. It was thus that, according to Syropoulos, they ἐσκέπτοντο καὶ ἐγύμναζον τὰ ζητήματα in the emperor's presence.[76]

Although Greek delegates appear to have done their best to avoid mentioning the name of Palamas in the Ferrara/Florence Synod, their theological gymnastics in Palamite theology proved useful. The Greeks were repeatedly challenged by the Latins to clarify their position with regard to fundamental issues of Eastern Orthodox dogma that concerned, intriguingly, the outcome of the Hesychast controversy in the second half of the fourteenth century. How does divine essence relate to divine operations? What are these energies? And how does *theoria* of god relate to the presumed unknowability of god? Do not the saints witness god's essence? Apparently the Latins had done their homework too. At one point, Mark Eugenikos had to provide explanations regarding the αἴγλη (*fulgor*), which, according to the Greeks, the saints are said to enjoy. His sibylline reply that 'we neither wish to nor can discuss what is invisible and unknowable' comes backed up by a neat reference to John of Climacus' definition of illumination (ἔλλαμψις) as an 'ineffable energy invisibly made visible and unknowingly knowable', and it shows how the spirit of Palamism was still alive and kicking, undermining any rapprochement between the Eastern Church and Western scholasticism, even if by now Palamism had lost its initial thrust and, it goes without saying, was not

---

[76] *Apomn.* 170.15–20.

unanimously held by Orthodox delegates.[77] Only ten days before the end of the Synod in June 1439, pressed by the circumstances and obviously with no alternative left, the Orthodox delegation retreated from the distinction between a fully inaccessible divine essence and 'certain rays', as Cesarini put it, that were actually accessible to the souls of the saints.[78]

By that time Plethon, who had earlier appeared so confident of the correctness of Greek Orthodox theology, had found new company: the Florentine intellectuals. An eyewitness at the Synod, George of Trebizond, alarmed and horrified, quoted him as claiming that the rise of a new religion no different from paganism was only a question of time.[79]

Apart from this episode, Plethon appears to have thought inexpedient (in the tradition of Proclus) any direct clash with an opponent far stronger than he was. Instead, he performed covert anti-Palamite moves in the course of his commentary on the *Chaldean Oracles*.[80] This veiled criticism of Orthodoxy should not be treated independently of the Platonist anti-monastic measures in the *Memoranda*.[81] Combined with an extensive plan of social engineering, the explicit attack on monasticism makes sufficiently clear that Plethon's reasons for disapproving of Hesychasm were not only philosophical, as one might infer from his commentary on the *Chaldean Oracles*, but also political.

The last ring of the Platonist golden chain: the Platonic fraternity of Mistra

Scholarios' *Refutatio erroris Judaeorum* is dated to around 1464, fourteen years after Plethon's death. This is long after Scholarios confronted Plethon's paganism and physically destroyed the *Nomoi*. But most significantly, it is long after the rupture with the past signified by the Turkish occupation and the election of

---

77 Mark Eug. *Responsio ad Quaestiones Latinorum* 161.18–162.2; cf. Joh. Clim. *Scala Paradisi* 7 (*PG* 88.813): Ἔλλαμψίς ἐστιν ἐνέργεια ἄρρητος ὁρωμένη ἀοράτως καὶ νοουμένη ἀγνώστως. For a discussion of Palamite theology in the framework of the Ferrara/Florence Synod and Markos' replies see Kuhlmann (1968) 115.
78 Cesarini quotes in Kuhlmann (1968) 116.   79 See below, p. 128.
80 These are noted and discussed by Tambrun (1992) 168–79.   81 See below, p. 341.

Scholarios to the patriarchy. In a note in passing Scholarios recalls his old enemy and considers whether pagans will still carry on his legacy. There are no Hellenes around, says Scholarios, with the possible exception of any decaying cell (πλὴν εἰ μὴ διεφθορότες τινές) credulously following Plethon's nonsense and the deceiving fame of his wisdom. Owing to ignorance, these people may resurrect in their souls the Hellenic error, continues Scholarios, the one extinguished by divine epiphany.[82] This is intriguing. By now more powerful than any other living Greek in the Ottoman Empire, Scholarios is still concerned with the impact that Plethon's personality and fame had on people many years before. Apparently the marginal group of extravagant pagans that operated in Mistra under the auspices of Plethon was not as yet delivered to the *damnatio memoriae* normally reserved for religious apostates in Byzantium.

Since the publication of Masai's *Pléthon* in 1956 the idea of a pagan ritualistic fraternity operating in the fifteenth century during the last years of Plethon's life has understandably captivated modern researchers. Its influence may be traced beyond the late Byzantine context in the paganism of the 'soldier of the Renaissance' Marullus Tarcaniota and of Cyriaco d'Ancona.[83] John Monfasani has argued that such a brotherhood may well never have existed. His argument is that the people usually associated with the much-debated fraternity that Scholarios hunted down cannot be conclusively shown to have had any substantial connection to the presumed Plethonean project of reinstituting ancient gods. For example, the pagan most famously associated with Plethon, Raoul Kabakes, 'may have been merely a Christian with some bizarre paganising ideas. But whatever the extent of his paganism, it was sui generis, and to a substantial degree independent of Pletho.'[84] Kabakes is credited with collecting the remnants of

---

[82] Schol. *Ref. erroris Judaeor.*, OC 3.287.2–6.

[83] For the question of Marullus' paganism see Kidwell (1989) 199–200; Masai (1956) 343 leaves the possibility open for a link between the pagan *phratria* of Mistra and the Academia Romana. Pope Paul II considered the members of the Academia to be crypto-pagans, and it is possible that Sigismondo Malatesta, great admirer of Plethon, expressly condemned for paganism (among other things), was in contact with them. See also Neri (2010) 126.

[84] Monfasani (1992) 58.

Plethon's *Nomoi* after Scholarios destroyed the manuscript.[85] He was one of the people closest to Plethon, shared Plethon's proto-nationalism, and described himself as a 'Hellene Lacedaemonean'. This man, who studied Julian's *Hymn to King Helios*, making notes in the margins like: 'Julian: Iamblichus: Sallust: divine men' and who confessed that at the age of seventy-four, when copying Julian, his *pothos* for the Sun god was even greater than when he first began to revere the sun at the age of seventeen,[86] can hardly be rehabilitated as a Christian with some bizarre paganising ideas. Yet I do not intend to defend Masai's thesis at this point, the core of which seems to me to be able to withstand attacks.

Gregory Palamas, Patriarch Neilos, Philotheos Kokkinos and Scholarios were worried about paganism as a philosophical paradigm rather than about its ritual and sectarian aspects possibly pursued by marginal intellectuals. Neilos concluded that according to Barlaam 'there was nothing superior to Hellenic wisdom', and we have seen that here 'Hellenic' encompasses both the late antique sense of 'pagan' philosophical notions and the Byzantine meaning of 'secular' wisdom. The Palamites would have had little understanding of modern periodisation, as well as of our heuristic application of terms such as 'paganism', 'secularism' and 'humanism'. They saw Hellenism and Christianity as intellectual camps vying for hegemony. In this they certainly were at one with Plethon. It might well be that the real members of the pagan fraternity of Mistra were not ritual pagans like Kabakes, but philosophical pagans of a quite different order.

Since 1348 Mistra was the heart of a despotate, a semi-autonomous state ruled by younger members of the Palaiologean imperial family.[87] When Plethon appeared in Mistra around 1409 he found it to be an intellectual outpost nourished by philhellenic theological and philosophical concerns. In the words of Donald Nicol, the 'intellectuals of Mistra were without a doubt a tiny minority, living on an island of culture in what they themselves

---

[85] See n. 1 by Alexandre to *Nomoi* 2, and n. 4 to *Nomoi* 136. See also Bidez (1929) 76. But see Tardieu (1980: 55) for a different scenario regarding Scholarios' copy.

[86] For Kabakes' notes see Bidez (1929) 76–9 and Grégoire (1929/30) 733–4.

[87] On the historical context see Necipoğlu (2009) 259–89. On the Despotate of Mistra the study of Zakythinos (1975) remains classic.

described as a sea of barbarism and ignorance'.[88] For present purposes it is worth delving into the history of this circle. This constitutes the last ring in the Platonist golden chain linking Proclus to Plethon.

The intellectual circle of Mistra was largely formed as a collateral result of the hegemony of Palamism in the main theological and political centres. Mistra provided shelter to intellectuals and *literati* forced by circumstances to leave Constantinople and Thessaloniki. Unable to cope any longer with the new Palamite establishment in Constantinople and Thessaloniki, renegade philosophers and humanists arrived in the Despotate of Mistra first under the reign of Despot Manuel Kantakouzenos and after 1383 under the reign of the Palaiologues.[89] There they formed a circle of little known intellectuals who escaped the *status quo* of the Palamite Counter-Reformation. The two most prominent intellectuals active in Mistra before Plethon, George Gavrielopoulos, known as George the Philosopher, and Manuel Raoul Metochites, appear to have found refuge in Mistra.[90] The activity of copyists in Morea in the second half of the fourteenth century is witness to the profound influence exercised by the Hesychast controversy. The contemporary authors copied are mainly Prochoros Kydones, Demetrios Kydones, John Kantakouzenos and, later, Nikephoros Gregoras.[91] It appears that during this period the Peloponnese witnessed a revival of ancient themes in visual art.[92] This created the ideal framework for Plethon's project.

George the Philosopher and Manuel Raoul Metochites were confessed Platonists, anti-Palamites and well acquainted with Demetrios Kydones, though favouring Plato over Aquinas. George's extreme enthusiasm for Plato and his eagerness 'to listen to Lycurgus' laws' out of 'an extreme philhellenism (τὸ λίαν εἶναι φιλέλλην)', as Kydones said of him, have been perceptively seen

---

[88] Nicol (1993) 342.

[89] On Mistra as the refuge 'of all those who are unable to stay in the capital due to their political, theological and philosophical beliefs both in this period as well as in the next century' see the illuminating article by Mergiale-Falaga (1991) 241–60 that makes good use of Demetrios Kydones' epistles to George the Philosopher, Raoul Metochites, John Laskaris and others. See also Matschke and Tinnefeld (2001) 324–5.

[90] *PLP* 3433; 17984.   [91] Zakythinos (1952) 348.   [92] Livanos (2010) 110.

as anticipating Plethon's Platonism and enthusiasm for Sparta in the next century.[93] George's criticism of Kydones' fondness of Aquinas highlights the fact that not all anti-Palamites were eventually absorbed by late Byzantine Thomism and that philhellenism presented an alternative even if that meant 'parting from one's friends'.[94] Another good friend of Kydones with philosophical interests who appears to have arrived in Morea in 1381/2 is the adventurer John Laskaris Kalopheros. The monk Agathias also abandoned Constantinople for Mistra under mysterious circumstances and emerges in Kydones' epistles as fully mesmerised by Hellenism.[95] We may surmise that the inclusiveness of the Mistra intellectual circle grew in significance in the aftermath of the final defeat of the mainstream humanist movement. It appears that Kydones maintained contact with this circle of secular intellectuals, functioning as the link between Constantinople and an amalgam of anti-Palamites, philhellenes and anti-Thomists who opted for a very different path from his. It has been plausibly argued that Plethon may well have known through Kydones about this marginal and remote close-knit group of Hellenising intellectual fugitives who shared a common interest in Greek antiquity, one occasionally bordering on romantic nostalgia. This information might have led Plethon to discover in Mistra the ideal framework for setting up a Hellenic cell beyond the reach of central imperial institutions.[96]

Two factors make this a particularly appealing and plausible theory. First, it has been recently shown that in the fifteenth century the Peloponnese was a site of ongoing political and ideological experimentation. Only faint echoes of the anaemic central authority of Constantinople reached the borderland of the Peloponnese, a country 'under construction', as a modern scholar put it, marred by the mortal conflict between local landowners and the political representatives of Constantinople, that is to say the despots of Mistra and their counsellors – Plethon included.[97] Secondly, we may

---

93 Mergiale-Falaga (1991) 248; Dem. Kyd. *Ep.* 32.16–22.
94 See below, Ch. 8, p. 402 on George's reluctance to follow Kydones' Thomism.
95 Mergiale-Falaga (1991) 250.   96 Baloglou (2002) 37–9 and 87 n. 121.
97 Smarnakis (2007) 108.

recall that Kydones turned to Thomism long before his death in 1397 and that George the Philosopher, who had been the mentor of the Platonist Raoul Metochites as early as 1362/5 would not take up the task of instructing a new generation into the mysteries of Platonism.[98] Plethon was the only intellectual at the time capable of offering an ideological direction to anyone not sharing Palamite mysticism, Kydones' Thomism or Scholarios' millenarianism – but also to advise the despots on political matters.

It is plausible that around 1409 Plethon was more than happy to leave behind a philosophically and theologically exhausted Constantinople, to discover a safe haven for his private immersion into Platonist philosophy and to pursue the application of radical reformist measures in a newly established court whose viability required extensive socio-economic experimentation. Beyond the reach of central clerical authorities, Plethon was free to take Platonism to its extreme conclusion, transforming the pre-existing philhellenic ambience of Mistra (one that nevertheless lacked proper spiritual guidance) into philosophical paganism, able to articulate an alternative to both Palamite Orthodoxy and Thomism.

---

[98] See Dem. Kyd. *Ep.* 30.28–31, where Kydones describes George as an excellent teacher and friend.

3

THE PLETHON AFFAIR

George of Trebizond and Scholarios against Plethon

Provided one trusts appearances Plethon supported Eastern Christianity against the Latins on two occasions: in the Council of Ferrara/Florence in 1438/9 and by writing a notorious treatise against Latin theology.[1] The historian Syropoulos informs us that Plethon was so highly regarded as a theologian that the patriarch privately asked for his advice regarding the *filioque*. Could it be that the Greeks were in error? Ostensibly Plethon was adamant that 'no member of our Church should have any doubts regarding the correctness of our doctrine, when not even the dissidents could honestly claim this'.[2] According to Syropoulos' account Plethon seems to have maintained reservations regarding the Synod all along. Around 1426/7 he appears to have advised the emperor John VIII Palaiologos that if the Greeks went to Italy, they would be a minority and potentially intimidated by a majority of Latin theologians. If the whole dispute came down to a vote, 'you will not have come to a synod, but to a jury (οὐκ ἀπελεύσεσθε εἰς σύνοδον, ἀλλ᾽ εἰς κατάκρισιν)'. Thus, as he put it, 'I do not think it is a good idea that you go to Italy, nor do I think that anything will result to our advantage.' But then again, if the Greeks decide to go, they should then see if there is anything to be gained by the whole enterprise. In any case, they should make sure that Greek

---

[1] On the Ferrara/Florence Synod see Angold (2006) 73–8, esp. 75–6 for Plethon as a representative of the Orthodox delegation. On the different positions followed by unionists and anti-unionists before and mainly after 5 July 1439, when the union of the Churches was finally signed, see Blanchet (2007). The classic history of the Synod of Florence by Gill (1961) remains a good starting point. For bibliography on the Council see Constas (2002) 468–75. For Plethon's 'anti-Latin' treatise see the discussion in Woodhouse (1986) 136–87.

[2] *Apomn.* 368.2–3.

and Latin votes are equivalent, regardless of which party forms the majority.[3] All this was excellent advice.

According to Syropoulos, Plethon continued to advise the Greek delegation during the Synod. At times he appears to have been passionately concerned: 'this day shall bring us life or death', he is reported to have said at one point.[4] His skills must have made an impression. He crossed swords with Cardinal Cesarini over the Latin insertion (προσθήκη) of *filioque* in the Acts of the Seventh Ecumenical Council in Nicea (787).[5] As the Synod was progressing, Plethon began to distrust the abilities of certain Greek delegates – and he objected to a declaration written by Scholarios regarding the procession of the Holy Spirit.[6]

Syropoulos' account portrays Plethon as a pious defender of Orthodoxy. According to a widespread view, Plethon's presence in the Council may be taken as strengthening the opinion that he was not that 'pagan' after all. However, it was recently argued that the account of Syropoulos is not by itself sufficient to prove Plethon's allegiance to Christianity. The work was compiled years after the Synod took place. It relies heavily on testimonies of numerous participants in the Synod, it is often unsystematic in its use of sources and, most importantly, it is the product of Greek resentment concerning the decision to sign the union of the Churches. The aim of the work is political and apologetical. Syropoulos may well have credited Plethon and other members of the Greek delegation with views and a role expedient to his own cause.[7] Crucially, it has also been noted that two important contemporary chronicles, those of Chalkokondyles and Sphrantzes, do not record Plethon's role as a defender of Orthodoxy. This is a bizarre fact, since both were acquainted with Plethon. Sphrantzes became governor of Mistra in 1446 and Chalkokondyles was a disciple of Plethon. This leaves Doukas as the only chronicler to record *en passant* the participation of a certain 'Gemistos from Lacedaemonia' in the Synod,

---

[3] *Apomn.* 312.5–17.   [4] *Apomn.* 366.15–20; 370.24.
[5] *Apomn.* 330.26–332.9.   [6] *Apomn.* 380.25; 426.15.
[7] Pagani (2008) 14–16. On the other hand, Hieronymos Charitonymos too noted in his *Encomium Plethonis* (PG 160.807C–D) that Plethon impressed his contemporaries during the 'most significant struggle' that took place during the Council.

without emphasising his role as Syropoulos does, or in any other way.[8] It is sometimes assumed that Plethon really turned to paganism only after experiencing the Council of Ferrara/Florence.[9] Yet even if we suppose that Syropoulos' portrait of Plethon is accurate to some extent, there may be more to Plethon's attitude than his social identity as an Orthodox allows us to see. First, Plethon might have purposefully misdirected Scholarios and possibly other clerical authorities away from his as yet not fully developed pagan beliefs.[10] Further, it may well be that at the time Plethon was already an unequivocal pagan, concerned that a united Christendom would undercut his pagan reform.[11] A third, albeit more farfetched explanation, is that Plethon boycotted the union in order to accelerate the collapse of Christianity *in toto* and the ascendance of a new world order.[12] And another possibility is that, regardless of his apparent religious ideas, Plethon acted out of patriotism, namely out of a serious concern for keeping not only the Turks, but also the Latins/Franks out of Greece.[13]

The attempt here to recover lost rings in the Platonic golden chain from late antiquity to late Byzantium sheds a different light on this issue. Owing to its complex relation with a long tradition of subterranean philosophical Hellenism, the Roman Orthodox intellectual context was capable of serving as host and carrier of a new Platonising religion 'not different from paganism', according to George of Trebizond's account of Plethon's vision. Conversely, Latin Christianity was a dangerous competitor not only to Palamas' Orthodox theology as represented in the Synod by Mark Eugenikos but also to Plethon's plans for a regeneration of pagan Platonism. Plethon did not side with his old pupil Mark Eugenikos against the Latins because he shared his faith in Orthodoxy but, rather, because the Roman East provided a live tradition of intellectual

---

8 Dabrowska (1991) 165; Doukas, *Hist.* 31.3.8.
9 See for example Constantelos (1998) 71.
10 Dabrowska (1991) 163.   11 See Berger (2006) 81, 83.
12 See Schultze (1874) 59: 'Beide [Kirchen] waren seine Gegner, die er sich so schwach wie möglich wünschen musste, um desto leichter zum Sieg zu gelangen.'
13 That patriotism was the main motive force of otherwise divided Greek delegates is noted by Bryer (2009) 860ff.

and linguistic connections to the pagan thought-world that were inactive in Latin Christendom. The East provided fertile ground for Plethon's project.

This was obvious to George of Trebizond, one of the first to accuse Plethon openly of paganism.[14] In step with Gennadios Scholarios, George was an Aristotelian who suspected that Platonism provided the platform for philosophical paganism. 'I have hated Plato since I was a young man', wrote George in his *Comparatio*.[15] Like the Athonite monks carrying on the legacy of Gregory Palamas, George too was harshly disposed towards Plato. Oddly though, one of the main reasons why George of Trebizond disliked Platonism was his opposition to Palamism. In the same vein as other Byzantine intellectuals sympathetic to Thomism, George was persuaded of the pagan Platonic origins of Palamism and blamed a Platonic undercurrent for corrupting the theology of the Orthodox Church and sabotaging the Unity of the Churches.

It has become customary to quote George on his notorious encounter with Plethon at the Council of Ferrara/Florence. The circumstances are unclear. It is likely, as Berger notes, that the immediate recognition of Plethon's philosophical authority by the Florentine intellectuals might well have unleashed in Plethon a certain euphoric sentiment that led to an unwise exposition of very personal considerations regarding religion. These finally resulted in the incident reported by the austere George of Trebizond:

I heard him myself in Florence (he was there at the Council with the Greeks) asserting that within a few years the entire world, with one mind and one preaching, would adopt the same religion. I asked him, 'Christ's or Mohammed's?' 'Neither', he replied, 'but one that does not differ from paganism (*gentilitas*).' I was shocked by these words, and have hated and feared him ever after as a poisonous viper.[16]

One might be tempted to discredit George's account as pure calumny, perhaps owing to academic jealousy. How probable is it that the man who so firmly supported the Greek East in the Council

---

[14] On the turbulent life and times of George of Trebizond see Monfasani (1976) 3–237.

[15] Cf. Geo. Treb. *Comparatio* 3.7; Hankins (1990) 168.

[16] Geo. Treb. *Comparatio* 3.21, quoted and translated in Hankins (1990) 172. Cf. Berger (2006) 85; Pagani (2008) 8; Monfasani (1976) 39.

of 1438/9 openly predicted at more or less the same time the end of monotheism? This is a crucial question, for if George is being honest here, we may plausibly surmise that the *Nomoi* project was intended already before 1439 for that new order of things expected to emerge 'within a few years'. In that case Scholarios and his associates were not making things up when later claiming that Plethon was surreptitiously working for the disestablishment of Orthodoxy even before the Synod.

A near contemporary source, Nicholas Kabasilas' 'Anti-Zealot Discourse', makes abundantly clear that Plethon would not have been either unique in openly testifying to the exhaustion of Christianity or the only intellectual publicly anticipating and welcoming the collapse of religious establishments. Plethon's audacious reply to George comes markedly close to the views of secular and lay circles around Manuel II. These openly claimed that Christianity had fulfilled its historical cycle and pressed for an immediate groundbreaking ideological and socio-political reform.[17] Nicholas Kabasilas (1319/23–post 1391), mystic and able theologian,[18] took up the task of rebutting them. But voices announcing the coming of a new religious, intellectual and political order were not limited to within the Byzantine framework. They also arose, almost simultaneously, in the Ottoman Empire. Using not paganism, but Islamic mysticism as the proper vehicle, Plethon's contemporary Sheikh Bedreddin (1358/9–1419) attempted to persuade both Muslim and Christian populations that the time was ripe for a new religion to emerge and challenge the foundations of the Ottoman State. Contemporaneously Plethon and Bedreddin respectively opposed the Byzantine Palamite establishment and the Sunnite Ottoman one, using sectarianism in order to instigate a religious reform allegedly meant to issue in political change.[19]

Kabasilas' unnamed secular opponents in the 'anti-Zealot' treatise, Plethon and Bedreddin, provide strong evidence that the time

---

[17] For a full discussion of the 'Anti-Zealot Discourse', or *Discourse Concerning Illegal Acts*, see Ch. 5, pp. 359ff.

[18] On Kabasilas see *HAB* 442–53 (Bibliogr.); Spiteris and Conticello (2002) 389–95 (Bibliogr.).

[19] On Plethon, Bedreddin and the question of the influence of radical Islamic sects, see Siniossoglou (2012).

span from the end of the fourteenth century to the first decades of the fifteenth was one in which the radicalisation of Christian and Muslim religious 'orthodoxy' combined with economic and socio-political shifts in both the Byzantine Empire and the Ottoman periphery (in particular Thrace). In this context heresy, mystical societies and religious dissent acquired an enhanced political role. Drawing on Islamic mysticism, paganism and large-scale secularisation respectively, Bedreddin, Plethon and the anonymous laymen in Kabasilas' treatise present three different reactions to the same situation: the economic, political and spiritual shifts in empires ruled by religious hegemonies that, it was felt, had irreversibly fulfilled their historical cycle.

The pagan conspiracy theory seems to have haunted George, who converted to Catholicism and aspired to proselytise Sultan Mehmed II. As he saw it, the best way to prevent pagans from besieging Rome was to turn the Turks from imminent conquerors of the West into able Christian persecutors of paganism. Perhaps unintentionally, George of Trebizond too was ultimately involved in this bizarre mosaic of utopian-universalist tendencies. His address to Mehmed II carried the implication of a new ecumenical religion, even if George opted for Catholicism, rather than for Islamic mysticism, paganism or secularism.[20]

For his part Scholarios had no real difficulty in explaining away the weird case of a major Byzantine intellectual propagating Hellenism while representing the Orthodox Church at the Council of Ferrara/Florence. Plethon employed religious dissimulation as his cover already in Constantinople, though he had, according to Scholarios, already been converted to paganism by a shadowy Jewish master called Elissaios.[21] 'Dissimulation' is the modern equivalent for Scholarios' λανθάνειν, a term repeatedly used by Plethon's enemies to describe his attitude to Christianity, just as it was used by late antique Christians to describe Julian's private study of pagan philosophy.[22] Apparently, Plethon's lip service to

---

[20] See Balivet (1999d: 188–9 and 1997) for the echoes and origins of these Islamo-Christian mystical-apocalyptical universalist plans.

[21] On the possible intellectual identity of Elissaios, see Siniossoglou (2012); Gardette (2007c).

[22] See Socrates Scholasticos *Hist. eccl.* 3.1.59: καὶ λεληθότως μὲν ἠσκεῖτο τὰ φιλόσοφα.

Christian hegemony was not persuasive enough (ἀλλ᾽ οὐκ ἠδύ-
νατο) and since he was purportedly corrupting students (προαγό-
μενος τοῖς ὁμιληταῖς τὰς δόξας ἐνσπείρειν), Emperor Manuel sent
Plethon to some sort of intellectual exile in the far-flung outpost
of Mistra sometime between 1405 and 1410.[23] This seems to be
Scholarios' version of what happened. But it might well be that
Manuel invited Plethon to leave Constantinople in order to satisfy
clerical authorities or to protect him. Another explanation is that,
as Zakythinos notes, Plethon was not 'exiled' to Mistra but was
only assigned a post there, in order to advise Theodore II, despot
of Mistra and son of Manuel. After all, Theodore affirms as much
in an official document of 1433.[24] What is certain is that, as we
have seen, Mistra suited Plethon's interests and possibly his plans
very well.

Scholarios claimed that he was aware of Plethon's pagan magnum opus, the *Nomoi*, long before the Council of Ferrara/Florence
(1439). 'It was apparent to *us* for a long time what sort of man
he really was', he wrote in the *Epistle to Exarch Joseph regarding Gemistos' Book* (*c*. 1457), one of the main sources for the
Plethon affair, 'and *we* were also aware of his working on such a
book at diverse times; for trustworthy witnesses had given *us* their
accounts of it, and *we* obtained much and undisputed evidence, first
when *we* were in the Peloponnese, and then in Italy.'[25] It has been
suggested that Scholarios refers to the year 1428, when he accompanied the Emperor John VIII Palaiologos in the Peloponnese.[26]
However, Lampros considered it probable that Scholarios studied
in Mistra. His evidence comes from a piece attributed to Scholarios
that mentions an unnamed ὑφηγητὴς ἀρετῆς, παράδειγμα βίου,
who may possibly be identified with Plethon.[27] Zakythinos provided stronger grounds for considering a link between Scholarios
and Mistra: Scholarios is the author of the epitaph of Demetrios
Laskaris Leontarios, an important personality in the despotate who

---

[23] Schol. *Ad principessam Pelop.*, *OC* 4.153.10–11. Cf. Matschke and Tinnefeld (2001)
357.
[24] Zakythinos (1975) 325.   [25] Schol. *Ad exarchum Josephum, OC* 4.155.30–156.1.
[26] Tozer (1886) 359, probably following Alexandre's hypothesis (1858: xiv).
[27] This is the Ἐγκώμιον τοῦ ὁσίου Λεοντίου τοῦ ἐν Ἀχαΐᾳ (Lampros, *PP* 2.161–8).
Tinnefeld (2002: 520) considers the work spurious 'aus inneren Gründen'. For the
likelihood that Scholarios was a student of Plethon, see Zeses (1988) 83–4.

died in 1431.[28] In that case Scholarios' testimony implies that he first had contact with Plethon's ideas before that date.

Scholarios also deals with Plethon and paganism in the *Epistle to the Empress Theodora regarding the Book of Laws by Gemistos Plethon* (1453/4) and in the short treatise *Against Atheists and Polytheists* of 1457/8.[29] *Against Plethon*, Scholarios' attempt to counter Plethon's attack on Aristotle, was ostensibly meant and is unfortunately still read as a philosophical apology for Aristotelianism. We will see that its intention goes much deeper. Scholarios directly addressed Plethon in a 1450 epistle on the occasion of the latter's advocacy of Orthodox and anti-Latin beliefs. Significantly, this epistle also targets the 'Hellenes' and is often read as an implicit warning to Plethon.[30] Furthermore, a florilegium against the pagan notion of fate, probably targeting *De fato*, a chapter from the *Nomoi* that was circulated independently during Plethon's lifetime, was recently attributed to Scholarios.[31] But there is another epistle by Scholarios that stirred much debate and which, I will presently argue, contrary to what has been recently maintained, is in effect directly related to the Plethon affair. This is the epistle to Manuel Raoul Oises (1451/2) regarding the pagan Juvenalios.[32] The following pages discuss the evidence from these sources.

In *Against Plethon* Scholarios makes abundantly clear that by that time (1444/5) parts of the *Nomoi* full of τῆς παλαιᾶς τῶν Ἑλλήνων φλυαρίας were in circulation.[33] By 1450 Scholarios still did not possess a full copy of the book, though he was aware of its

---

[28] Zakythinos (1975) 331–2; Lampros, *PP* 2.172; Schol. *Carmina diversa, OC* 4.377–8.

[29] Schol. *Ad principessam Pelop., OC* 4.151–5; *Against Polytheists* (*Tractatus de uno deo et contra quos qui deum esse negant et multos deos colunt*), *OC* 4.172–89. The epistle to Theodora is often dated to 1453. Tinnefeld (2002: 503–4) dates the epistle to 1454–6; Monfasani (2005: 463), following his revision of the date of Plethon's death suggests the year of composition as 1460, 'just before Scholarios wrote to Exarch Joseph'. For the dating of Scholarios' works I am following Blanchet (2008) 485 and Tinnefeld (2002) 502–4.

[30] As Masai (1976: 26) observes, Scholarios' epistle to Plethon regarding his refutation of Argyropoulos' pro-Latin sentiments (Schol. *Ad Pleth., OC* 4.118–51) has the apparently paradoxical aspect of focusing less on showing the procession of the Holy Spirit *a solo Patre* than the inanity of polytheism.

[31] For the edition, attribution and contents of this florilegium see Demetracopoulos (2007) 301–76.

[32] Schol. *Ad Raulem Oesem, OC* 4.476–89.   [33] Schol. *Contra Pleth., OC* 4.114.17–27.

contents, presumably through the channel of his informants. This may be inferred from the epistle 'congratulating' Plethon on his anti-Latin treatise. There, Scholarios finds the perfect opening to condemn those who resuscitate 'Plato, Zoroaster and the Stoics' (the three sources acknowledged in the introduction of the *Nomoi*) and promises to write a full refutation once their writings fall to his hands (εἰ συμβαίη μοι ἐς χεῖρας πάντα ἐλθεῖν) – 'and others will do so, too'.[34] Indeed they did.[35]

The later critics of Plethon are Matthew Kamariotes, Theodore of Gaza and Manuel Corinthios.[36] A few years after Plethon's death (1452), Scholarios' student Matthew Kamariotes rebutted chapter 6 from the second book of the *Nomoi*, namely Plethon's *De fato* and compiled a philosophically intelligent refutation in the form of two orations *Contra Plethonem*.[37] Theodore of Gaza too targeted Plethon's notion of *heimarmene* as presented in Plethon's correspondance with Bessarion.[38] Manuel Corinthios (*c.* 1483–1530) attacked Plethon in two treatises. The former was aimed at Plethon's anti-Latin treatise (κατὰ τοῦ Πληθωνικοῦ συγγράμματος, οὗ ἡ ἀρχὴ Τὸ ὑπὲρ Λατίνων βιβλίον), while the second (*Against Gemistos and Bessarion*) attacked both Plethon and Bessarion's philosophical paganism.[39]

In the *Epistle to the Empress Theodora* (*c.* 1454/6) Scholarios appears to have eventually changed his mind. It was not enough to rely on refuting Plethon. In Plethon's hands, he writes, words

34 Cf. Schol. *Ad Pleth., OC* 4.125.20–9; *Nomoi* 2 (proem. 1.1–7).
35 For a Latin protest against the *Nomoi* from as late as the sixteenth century, see Woodhouse (1986) 364; for a Greek one from as late as the twentieth century, see Zeses (1988) 222–4.
36 For Christian reactions to Plethon see Mamone (1990) 209–24. Cf. *PLP* 10776 (Matthew); *PLP* 3450 (Theodore).
37 See P. H. Beck (1937) 108–11; Demetracopoulos (2007) 338.
38 Thdr. Gaz., *De fato* (Mohler III 239–46; cf. Taylor (1925)). Theodore also targeted Plethon's notion of substance in *Adversus Plethonem pro Aristotele de substantia* (Mohler III 153–8) that caused a heated debate between Plethon's devoted student Michael Apostoles (*Ad Theodori Gazae pro Aristotele de substantia adversus Plethonem obiectiones*, Mohler III 161–9) and Andronikos Kallistos, who defended Theodore (*Defensio Theodori Gazae adversus Michaelem Apostolium*, Mohler III 170–203).
39 The latter treatise was edited by Petit, *Documents*. Cf. the remarks of Petit, *Documents* 332–3 and *PLP* 16712. On Plethon's anti-Latin treatise and Manuel's response see Woodhouse (1986) 273–7.

were like a sword in the hands of a madman (μάχαιρα ἐν χερσὶ μαινομένου). Thus, instead of rebutting Plethon, he would rather cast his work into the flames.[40] Plethon was no longer around to protest. The Byzantine State had already collapsed. Still, anti-pagan legislation was recently put into effect in the case against the pagan Juvenalios.

Juvenalios

In the 1451/2 epistle to Oises concerning Juvenalios, Scholarios describes a pagan cell operating in the Peloponnese, a place deemed most suitable for such endeavours because of its 'poisoned seeds' – undoubtedly an allusion to Plethon's presence and possibly to that of earlier humanists like George the Philosopher, who shared an extreme interest in antiquity.[41] Scholarios narrates that his spies intercepted the correspondence between a pagan propagandist, Juvenalios, and other 'co-apostates' (συναποστάται) from Christianity. Juvenalios, an odd case of a Christian monk who converted to ritual paganism, was not, as Scholarios affirms, as low-profile as his shadowy mentors were. He was tortured to death. His hand, tongue and ears were cut off and he was then sentenced to death by drowning in the sea. In his epistle Scholarios makes sure that the authorities responsible are not as naive as to have any feelings of remorse or humanitarian concerns. By getting rid of the pagan Juvenalios, the officer Oises, this soldier of Christ, made god happy.[42] Thus Scholarios' decision to take radical measures against the spread of paganism dates to around 1450/2.

Plethon is not mentioned by name in the epistle. This has recently led scholars to doubt his involvement in the Juvenalios affair. Arguing that Plethon had no significant impact among either his Italian or his Byzantine contemporaries, Monfasani doubted that Scholarios had any real evidence linking Juvenalios with

---

[40] Schol. *Ad exarchum Josephum, OC* 4.4.155.6–11.
[41] Schol. *Ad Raulem Oesem, OC* 4.479.16–19.
[42] Schol. *Ad Raulem Oesem, OC* 4.485.1–2: Καὶ τῷ μὲν ἐξελεῖν ἐκ μέσου τὸν ἀσεβῆ εὔφρανας τὸν Θεόν, εἰς ὃν ἐκεῖνος ἠσέβει.

Plethon.[43] Still, there is no doubt that Plethon is here in the foreground, even if Scholarios could not persecute him or did not want him persecuted at this stage. Masai observed that Scholarios' description of the activities of this pagan cell incorporates two elements that are clearly lifted from the introductory sketch of the *Nomoi*.[44] Juvenalios and his teachers are said to revive 'appellations of gods that were not corrupted by the poets' and to perform 'the proper rites' (ἁγιστείας εὐσταλεῖς), since this is what 'they claim':

> They defend Hellenism by oral teaching and written works, trying to bring back to life genealogies of gods and divine appellations that have not been corrupted by the poets, and the right doctrines, as they say, and constitutions, everything that has justly been left to rot and die away. And they have not dared to say or write anything publicly against the sayings, doctrines and deeds of Christ, as Juvenalios did, though they conspire towards the abolition of holy religion...
> (Schol. *Ad Raulem Oesem, OC* 4.479.21–2)[45]

One may add a third reference to the *Nomoi*: Scholarios mentions pagan experiments with 'constitutions' (*politeiai*). This echoes Plethon's reference to the Spartan *politeia* in the same introductory note. But this is not all.

Medvedev proved the link between the accusations against Juvenalios and Plethon's *Nomoi* in a 1991 article that specifically deals with the Juvenalios affair from the viewpoint of Byzantine law. Of all crimes punished by mutilation of the hand in late Byzantium, only one accords with any of the accusations mentioned by Scholarios in the epistle to Oises. This concerns the opening of graves and sacrilege. Scholarios mentions that Juvenalios performed sacrilege and exhumed the relics of the dead with the aim of burning or dispersing them. As Medvedev notes, the only possible explanation is that Juvenalios put into action Plethon's call in the *Nomoi* to

---

[43] Monfasani (1992) 59, followed by Hladký (forthcoming). By contrast, Tinnefeld (2002: 488) agrees with Masai that Juvenalios was 'zweifellos von Plethon beeinflusst'. This is also the view of Constantelos (1998) 70 and Neri (2010) 180–2.

[44] *Nomoi* 2–4 (proem. 1.1–20).

[45] See Masai (1956) 304 and Woodhouse (1986: 272), who notes that 'the implied connection between Juvenal and Plethon evidently became known before long, for a manuscript in the Patriarchal Library at Jerusalem contains a clear reference to the letter, describing it as 'from Gennadios of Constantinople to the Peloponnesians against the polytheism of Gemistos while Manuel Rales was despot'.

purify sacred *loci* and empty the graves – an issue that has disrupted relations between Christians and pagans since late antiquity.[46] A second accusation against Juvenalios seems connected with the former and also speaks for an attempt to implement Plethon's plan for resurrecting paganism. This concerns the performance of rituals without proper licence. According to the *Nomoi*, any adult may address hymns to the gods in the open air without participating in a clerical hierarchy for as long as the *locus* is properly purified.[47]

Moreover, Scholarios credits Juvenalios with preaching the doctrine of automatism (αὐτοματισμός), that is to say, the denial of divine providence and belief in *heimarmene* featured in Plethon's *De fato*, as well as with fierce attacks on monasticism that recall Plethon's anti-monastic tendencies openly expressed in the *Memoranda*. As Medvedev showed, Scholarios quoted legislative citations of the *Procheiros Nomos* (missed by the editors of Scholarios' epistle) regarding apostasy and the disavowal of the sacred baptism that authorised the death penalty for Juvenalios. Still, the precise manner of carrying out the death penalty was often left to the authorities to define. In the case of Juvenalios, death by drowning may have been selected either in an effort to deliver Juvenalios to absolute *damnatio memoriae*, divesting him even of burial, or in accordance with a belief in the purifying force of water.

On the other hand, it is clear that Scholarios did not want Plethon tortured or executed. This was not necessarily because of any difficulty of obtaining hard evidence or to any high esteem for Plethon. Rather, at that time waging a vendetta with Plethon's friends in high positions had few chances of success and was a potentially imprudent move on the part of the career-oriented Scholarios. In contrast with Juvenalios, who was an easy target, Plethon earned the reverence of significant personalities, both in Byzantium and Italy, who testified to his erudition and learning – from Bessarion to Cyriaco d'Ancona. The 'philosopher-king' Manuel, for all his expertise and training in Palamite theology, maintained ties with Plethon. Scholarios would think twice before asking Manuel to

---

[46] Medvedev (1991) 162–3; *Nomoi* 230 (3.36.11–13).
[47] Medvedev (1991) 161; *Nomoi* 230 (3.36.11–13).

serve as the hand holding Christ's sword (μάχαιρα), as he actually did in the epistle to Oises. As Garnsey notes, this is the only way to explain how Plethon managed to avoid exposure and persecution even though Scholarios had his eye on him for decades: 'One can only suppose that people in high places turned a blind eye to his religious views, while appreciating his talents as a politician, diplomat, cultural magnet and guru.'[48]

That this is indeed the case may be inferred from reviewing the dates corresponding to imperial edicts that certified concessions of land to Plethon: 1427, 1428, 1433 and, significantly, 1450.[49] These testify to continuous support on the part of political authorities, even at a time when Scholarios' eavesdroppers were spreading the word regarding the man's apostasy. Plethon's *Against Scholarios* is dated to around 1449.[50] By 1450, only two years before Plethon's death, Scholarios and his able informants looked askance at Plethon's moves – and yet they witnessed his properties being confirmed and enlarged by the highest political powers. Plethon was beyond Scholarios' reach.[51]

The Juvenalios affair might have been intended to send Plethon a clear message that the net was slowly closing around him. And yet there is strong evidence that in late Byzantium religious dissenters could ask for and successfully acquire the patronage of collapsing political authorities. Barlaam headed the Byzantine embassy to Avignon in 1339 and had been sent to negotiate with Dominican theologians in 1333. It has been correctly noted that he could not have overcome the objections of monastic zealots without serious support from high up in the political establishment.[52] An even more interesting parallel is the case of Prochoros Kydones and Plethon's early mentor, Demetrios Kydones. Demetrios' strong social connections and role as a statesman, advisor to the emperor and politician prevented a condemnation as harsh as that imposed on his brother Prochoros. The political role of intellectuals within the imperial court of the Palaiologues made it almost impossible for people like Philotheos Kokkinos and Scholarios to have

---

[48] Garnsey (2009) 330.   [49] These are collected in Lampros, *PP* 4.104–9, 192.
[50] Tinnefeld (2002) 488.   [51] This is also the view of Berger (2006) 87.
[52] Meyendorff (1982) 131.

Demetrios and Plethon condemned while still alive and operative within powerful lay circles – to which we shall return.[53]

The political establishment may not have had the means to clash with the Palamite monastic party and its clerical representatives, nor to enforce progressive reformatory plans. But the Palaiologues were still in a position to protect advisors and intellectuals who either openly or covertly worked on alternative plans.

The *Nomoi* in flames

The real opportunity for Scholarios to take care of his unfinished business with Plethon appeared after Plethon's death, when the manuscript came into the possession of the despot Demetrios and his wife Theodora.[54] Naturally, the despots were shocked by the contents and refused to pass on the manuscript to 'many people who asked for it in order to make copies'. Instead, they decided to send it to Scholarios. The latter did not destroy the work on the spot. He sent the manuscript back with the meaningful remark that god would recompense the princess for its destruction. Perhaps Scholarios thought that the blow to the Plethonean circle would be greater if the highest political authorities of Mistra destroyed the manuscript.[55] Another explanation is that political as well as clerical authorities were in agreement that they should get rid of the work, yet neither showed the willingness to take responsibility, which indicates that Plethon's legacy was still alive.[56]

But the explanation of Scholarios' movements might lie in the argument developed in the epistle to Oises. There, Scholarios suggests that the Church should pass on to secular authorities the responsibility for the penalties inflicted upon religious apostates, including mutilation or execution (by *anascolopismos*).[57] In the case of Plethon's manuscript Scholarios followed the same tactic as when authorising theologically the torture and death of Juvenalios,

---

[53] See below, pp. 359–81.   [54] See here Woodhouse (1986) 357–61.
[55] P. H. Beck (1937) 108.   [56] Livanos (2003) 29.
[57] Schol. *Ad Raulem Oesem, OC* 4.486.30–6; 487.1–18; see Medvedev (1991: 168), who notes that Scholarios' suggestion runs counter to the principle regarding the non-participation of the Church in the *potestas gladii.*

while expertly transferring the responsibility for the execution of the penalty to politicians.

According to most scholars Scholarios finally committed Plethon's manuscript to the flames between 1460 and 1465 during a supposed second or third term of serving as patriarch. Recently Marie-Hélène Blanchet made a good case for 1455 or early 1456 at the latest during a single term in that office.[58] Scholarios publicly refuted the contents of the book and proceeded to its destruction in ceremonial manner,[59] showing lack of respect for the dead philosopher, as one of Plethon's followers protested, and performing 'sacrilege' by burning a dead man's manuscript.[60] We may notice a similar accusation of 'grave-robbery' and the same disapproval for the continuing persecution of religious dissenters after their death in Demetrios Kydones' apology for his brother Prochoros, who was *post mortem* mercilessly attacked by Philotheos Kokkinos. Still, Scholarios' decision to destroy Plethon's manuscript was fully legitimate on the basis of both clerical canons and civic legislation and conformed to a long tradition of casting heretical books into the fire, which went back to Justinian's time. *Basilica*, the ninth-century Byzantine legal code that drew heavily on Justinian's Codex and was completed during the reign of Leo VI the Wise, prescribed the scrupulous search for heretical books and authorised their destruction by fire while prohibiting their possession, study and reproduction.[61] Similarly, the seventh ecumenical synod in 787CE ordered the destruction of all products of heretical 'pseudology'.[62] Hence, when Scholarios requires of anyone who might come across any surviving copy of the *Nomoi* to follow his example, he does not necessarily do so as a religious fanatic but in accordance with what was expected

---

[58] Blanchet (2008) 177; 185–7; Monfasani (2005: 463) argued for 1460. Much depends on the chronology of Scholarios' epistle to the Exarch Joseph. See Zakythinos (1975) 366–7 n. 1 for a brief presentation of the problem.

[59] Schol. *Against Polytheists*, OC 4.180.30–181.2.

[60] On the anonymous reply to Scholarios see below, p. 147.

[61] *Basilica* 1.1.23: Καὶ μὴ ἐχέτω τις ἢ ἀναγινωσκέτω ἢ μεταγραφέτω τὰ κατὰ τῶν ὀρθῶν δογμάτων αὐτοῦ συγγράμματα, ἀλλ' ἐπιμελῶς ζητήσας καιέτω.

[62] For a full discussion see here Yiannakopoulos (1990: 352–4), who examines Scholarios' decision in the light of Roman and Byzantine law and clerical sources.

from civic and clerical authorities by both Church and Byzantine law.[63]

One argument that may be used to justify Scholarios' behaviour on moral grounds is that in the *Nomoi* Plethon suggests the death penalty for dissent, and on this account the 'sophists' (namely the Christians) would be the first to be persecuted in Plethon's utopia.[64] Scholarios did not fail to take note of the passage and condemn Plethon's intention for new persecutions of Christians.[65] But perhaps his own words in the short treatise against polytheism around 1456 shed more light on his mentality. As he puts it, the decision to destroy Plethon's project was ultimately dictated by his 'love and fear of the perfect law of the Son of God'.[66] Scholarios was a genuine 'soldier of Christ'.

It is usually assumed that the target of Scholarios' wrath was only the *Nomoi*. Yet apparently Scholarios cast into the flames more than this. The Arabic transmission of Plethon's collection of the *Chaldean Oracles* shows that the manuscript of Plethon delivered to the flames also included the *Recapitulation of Zoroastrian and Platonic Doctrines* and Plethon's version of the *Chaldean Oracles*, accompanied by at least a brief version of his commentary.[67] This seems to corroborate Ellissen's assumption that not only *De fato* but also the *Recapitulation of Zoroastrian and Platonic Doctrines* formed parts of a single project that circulated independently in Plethon's lifetime.[68]

---

[63] As Alexandre (1858: l), put it: 'à mes yeux, Gennadius fit son devoir'.

[64] For a sympathetic approach to Scholarios, see Constantelos (1998) 67–73 and Zeses (1988: 222), who thinks that Plethonean scholarship is *parti pris*: Scholarios is accused for burning the *Nomoi*, but scholars are silent in regard to Plethon's wish to establish a 'tyrannical dictatorship'. Zeses is right that modern scholarship is unfair: a really fair comparison would be between Plethon's totalitarian tendencies and the urge of Scholarios to put to death all 'Hellenists': according to Scholarios, the executions of the 'shameless apostates from the true piety' should be carried on 'by fire and sword and water and every means' (Schol. *Ad Raulem Oesem, OC* 4.476.15–17). This urge was partly realised with the torture and death of Juvenalios. This is not to say that Plethon is a model of tolerance; for a discussion of Plethon's totalitarianism see Ch. 7.

[65] Schol. *Ad exarchum Josephum, OC* 4.170.30–3.

[66] Schol. *Against Polytheists, OC* 4.181.1–4: ὁ πόθος καὶ ὁ φόβος τῆς ἀρίστης νομοθεσίας τοῦ Ὑιοῦ τοῦ Θεοῦ.

[67] Tardieu (1980) 35–57; cf. the introduction by B. Tambrun to her edition of Plethon's *Chaldean Oracles*, xiii.

[68] Ellissen (1860) 16.

Scholarios thought that his decision was not only dictated by the need to protect others from a dangerous book but also meant as 'punishment' for Plethon's apostasy.[69] The choice of words is significant. Scholarios understood apostasy from Christianity as related to *apistia* (infidelity), which qualifies in itself as a form of paganism. Scholarios preserved the table of contents and selected chapters containing the hymns as proofs of Plethon's paganism and firmly asked for anybody who came across any surviving copies to burn them – otherwise, there would be repercussions.[70] Turkish authorities and intellectuals seeking to better understand the culture and achievements of conquered Byzantines translated excerpts into Arabic.[71]

The accusation of dissimulation

In the *Epistle to the Exarch Joseph* Scholarios portrays Plethon as a delirious polytheist. The paganism of the *Nomoi* belongs to the realm of 'myths and dreams'.[72] Fascinated by his 'Greek books', that is to say Plutarch, Porphyry and Iamblichus, and above all Proclus, Plethon reverts to doctrines refuted many times in the past, doctrines which, so thinks Scholarios, had no power any more over the souls of his contemporaries.

Undoubtedly Scholarios would approve of the dominant scholarly trend that takes late Byzantine references to Proclus or Iamblichus to be little more than rhetorical tropes. After all, elsewhere Scholarios takes it for granted that 'idolatry' and 'polytheism' ended with Constantine, who inaugurated an era of universal monotheism.[73] After more than a thousand years of Christian hegemony, one gathers from Scholarios' epistles to public authorities,

---

[69] Schol. *Ad exarchum Josephum, OC* 4.171.8–11.
[70] Schol. *Ad exarchum Josephum, OC* 4.171.34–172.11.   [71] See here Akasoy (2008).
[72] Schol. *Ad exarchum Josephum, OC* 4.169.35: ἀλλ' ὡς ἄν τις ἀκούσειέ του μύθους ἢ ὀνείρους διηγουμένου.
[73] Schol. *Ad principessam Pelop., OC* 4.153.16–34; *Ad exarchum Josephum, OC* 4.162.17–29. Cf. *Ref. erroris Judaeor., OC* 3.297.17–21: Τοῦτ' ἀληθές ἐστι καὶ οὐδεμίαν ἔχον ἀντίρρησιν, ὅτι ἀπὸ τῶν Αὐγούστου χρόνων ἀρξαμένη ἡ εἰδωλολατρεία καὶ πολυθεΐα ἐνδιδόναι, ἐπὶ Κωνσταντίνου τελείως ἔσβεσται, καὶ ὁ εἷς Θεὸς ἐντεῦθεν πιστεύεται πανταχοῦ, πάντων, εἰ καὶ ὑπὸ διαφόροις, ὡς ἔλεγες, νομοθέταις, τῇ ἑνότητι τοῦ Θεοῦ βεβαίως προστεθειμένων.

Plethon was suddenly inspired by the insane vision of worshipping many gods. Plethon was a ridiculous old man led astray by daemons, one who lost his mind and introduced *innovations*. The late antique pagan accusation against Christianity, that of *kainotomia*, is here recharged and thrown back in order to designate neopaganism.[74] Certainly a deranged man is less of a problem to the clerical establishment than would be a respectable philosopher holding key positions in the imperial court.

And yet Scholarios' epistles betray a deeper anxiety regarding Hellenism as an ideological and philosophical paradigm that sought to overthrow Orthodoxy in the Peloponnese. Addressing Oises, Scholarios describes the situation as follows:

There is contempt for the faith; strong infidelity everywhere; *for some it is called Hellenism*; for others mere fatalism and atheism. Others are indifferent and weak about the faith. Thus they abandon the doctrines of the Fathers (ἀποστασία) and frenzy in impieties taking advantage of the present ecclesiastical confusion. (Schol. *Ad Raulem Oesem, OC* 4.480.7–13; trans. in Constantelos 1998: 69)

The real problem here does not seem to be any crude worship of idols, but rather the quest for ideological and philosophical/religious alternatives to Roman Orthodoxy. Writing on the destruction of the *Nomoi*, Scholarios becomes more specific. Plethon did not stay with the letter of Platonic philosophy but attempted to proceed to its heart and seize its spirit: that is to say, its *pagan* spirit. This is corroborated by his suspicions regarding the real motivation behind Plethon's assault on Aristotle in the *Differences*, which testify to his persuasion that Plethon was attempting to reconnect the aforementioned mythical, dream-like version of paganism of the *Nomoi* with Platonic philosophy. Plethon might really be a follower of Christ's legislation and not seeking to introduce new laws in its stand, he says – but it is clear that this possibility is discarded as wishful thinking. Scholarios links the intention of the *Differences* with that of the *Nomoi* project.[75] Do

---

[74] Schol. *Ad exarchum Josephum, OC* 4.160.7–24. See also the more general condemnation of innovations in theology in *OC* 4.144.5–6.
[75] Schol. *Contra Pleth., OC* 4.114.8–115.30.

not assume, he avers in his defence of Aristotle (*Against Plethon*), that Plethon slanders Aristotle owing to any sudden inspiration that made of him such a fervent advocate of Plato.[76] A marginal note in Scholarios' hand on one manuscript is telling. Next to the title *Againt Plethon's Questions concerning Aristotle* we read the following: Καὶ κατὰ Ἑλλήνων ἤτοι πολυθέων: *And Against the Hellenes, namely Polytheists*.[77] A note in passing early on in this treatise corroborates the suspicion that at the time Scholarios was not only aware of the *Nomoi* project but had successfully accessed its key doctrines. Scholarios refers to 'some other work' by Plethon (ἐν τινι ἑτέρῳ αὐτοῦ συγγράμματι) where his adversary declares revelation to be deception and glorifies discursive reason. This description fully accords with the doctrinal core of Book I of the *Nomoi*.[78]

Further evidence that Scholarios acknowledged a clash between paganism and Christianity behind Plethon's alibi of an academic comparison between Plato and Aristotle is contained in the epistle to the exarch Joseph. There, Scholarios admits that his rebuttal of the *Differences* was written in a condition of religious zeal: ζήλῳ τῆς πίστεως. Scholarios was alarmed by information concerning the *Nomoi* project and he was profoundly disquieted by Plethon's 'objective' in the *Differences*.[79] George of Trebizond also explicitly connected the controversy over Plato and Aristotle with an underlying religious agenda: his *Comparatio philosophorum Aristotelis et Platonis* (1458) was written as a warning to the Latins against Plato's and Plethon's paganism.[80]

---

76 Schol. *Contra Pleth.*, *OC* 4.8.2–3: μηδὲ πιστεύειν Πλήθωνι, ὅτι Πλάτωνι σύμμαχος γινόμενος Ἀριστοτέλη διαβάλλει· οὐδὲ γὰρ Πλάτωνα αὐτὸν οἶδε καλῶς. Rather, Plethon's aim is to attack 'our faith'; cf. *Contra Pleth.*, *OC* 4.114.17–21: Ἔπειτα καὶ τῇ ἡμετέρᾳ περὶ τοῦ θείου πίστει ἀμύνειν καὶ τοῖς ταύτῃ ἀνθισταμένοις ἀπεχθῶς ἔχειν ἱεροὶ νόμοι κελεύουσιν· αὐτὸς δὲ τοιαύτην τινὰ ἐδέξατο διαβολὴν ὑπὸ πλείστων, οἳ πιθανοὶ δοκοῦσιν, καὶ συγγράμματι αὐτοῦ ἐντυχεῖν τῷ ἰσχυριζόμενοι, νομοθεσίαν ἀρίστην ἐπαγγελλομένῳ· οὗ καὶ ἐκγράψαντες μέρη τινὰ δεικνύουσιν τῆς παλαιᾶς τῶν Ἑλλήνων ἀνάπλεω φλυαρίας. See also *Contra Pleth.*, *OC* 4.114.28–30: Τοιαῦτά τινα περὶ τοῦ ἀνδρὸς πολλοὶ λέγουσιν, οἷς οὐ ῥάδιον ἀπιστεῖν, καὶ τούτων μάλιστα ἢ τῆς πρὸς Ἀριστοτέλη εὐνοίας ἕνεκα ἐπαχθέστερον αὐτῷ ἐν τῷδε τῷ συγγράμματι χρῆσθαι προήχθην.
77 See Schol. *Contra Pleth.*, *OC* 4.4.1, note ad loc.
78 Schol. *Contra Pleth.*, *OC* 4.16.31–5; I discuss this passage below, p. 166.
79 Schol. *Ad exarchum Josephum*, *OC* 4.155.30–156.10.   80 Todt (2006) 156.

If Scholarios and George are right in suspecting a pagan dimension behind Plethon's Platonism in the *Differences*, then Plethon emerges as the master of dissimulation. The crypto-pagan *Differences* were first presented to an Italian audience at more or less the same time as its author made his name in the Synod of Ferrara/Florence as a traditionalist with full confidence and non-negotiable faith in the Orthodox dogma.

Besides Scholarios, all four Christian adversaries of Plethon's ideas draw attention to his ideological dissimulation: Matthew Kamariotes, George of Trebizond, Theodore of Gaza and Manuel of Corinth. Plethon's epistles to Bessarion aroused the awareness of Manuel, who went even further than Theodore of Gaza in observing that something was seriously wrong with Plethon's *Reply to the Treatise in Support of the Latin Doctrine.* This is a work purportedly advocating Christian Orthodoxy against John Argyropoulos' justification of the position agreed in the Council of Ferrara/Florence.[81] On a first reading it might be taken as supporting the thesis of a Christian Orthodox Plethon opposing his unionist student. Like Scholarios in the epistle to Oises, Manuel applies the verb λανθάνειν to describe Plethon's tactic: he is said to have 'escaped notice' by writing against the Latin position, while in reality he was disseminating pagan beliefs.[82] The alternative title ἢ κατὰ Ἑλλήνων in Scholarios' 1450 epistle purportedly congratulating Plethon for his Orthodox position against the Latins makes abundantly clear that Scholarios was the first to cast serious doubts on the intention of Plethon's treatise.[83] As Woodhouse notes, Manuel 'supports the view of Scholarios that to an Orthodox theologian Plethon's treatise should have been suspect from the first'.[84]

Interestingly, Manuel extended the accusation to include Bessarion too. Both 'feigned their participation in divine grace'. Plethon

---

[81] On Argyropoulos and his treatise *De processione Spiritus Sancti* (ed. Sp. Lampros, Ἀργυροπούλεια, Athens 1910: 107–28) see Masai (1976) 33. Plethon's treatise was edited by Alexandre (pp. 300–11).

[82] *PG* 160.791–2.

[83] Schol. *Ad Pleth., OC* 4.118: Σχολαρίου τοῦ ὕστερον Γενναδίου πρὸς Πλήθωνα ἐπὶ τῇ πρὸς τὸ ὑπὲρ Λατίνων βιβλίον αὐτοῦ ἀπαντήσει ἢ κατὰ Ἑλλήνων. Cf. Woodhouse (1986) 271, 278ff.; Tinnefeld (2002) 488, 503.

[84] Woodhouse (1986) 363, 273.

'escaped notice' but in reality he compiled this treatise in a cunning manner (ὑπούλως συντεταχώς) 'against us'.[85] Manuel was an acute reader. Modern research on Plethon has noted that with the anti-Latin treatise Plethon did not specifically target the Latins but, rather, Trinitarian theology as such: Plethon attacked not only the *filioque* but the doctrinal foundations of Christianity.[86] While ostensibly criticising Latin Christianity, Plethon cast doubts on the *homousion* of the Trinity and allowed the Neoplatonic hierarchical structure of essence to enter the debate through the back door. The intention behind the treatise was not to condemn admirers of Latin theology such as Kydones and Argyropoulos, but to make abundantly clear to those considering whether it was time for a radical intellectual regeneration that Christianity was incapable of instigating one in either its Orthodox or its Latin version of Trinitarian theology. As Masai perceptively argued, Plethon used the professed 'anti-Latin' aims of his treatise in order to pose to a broad audience as a defender of Orthodoxy and to divert suspicion, while fully aware that his own students (including John Argyropoulos) would acknowledge the real subtext, namely that the sole escape route lay in the Platonism of Mistra.[87] Plethon was following the old method of waving certificates of Orthodoxy in order securely to invite comparisons with Hellenism. On the pretext of attacking the Latins, Plethon found a first-rate opportunity to note that different faculties (δυνάμεις) correspond to different substances (οὐσίαι).

Plethon did add that this is an idea with which 'our Church' disagrees. Still, by implication it can be inferred that according to this principle nothing like a creation of the world according to God's free will (κατὰ βούλησιν) is at all possible: for the modality

---

[85] Cf. Manuel Corinthios, *PG* 160.791–2; Manuel Cor., *Adversus Gemistum et Bessarionem, impiorumque eorum librorum refutatatio* 355.37: αἱρετικοὶ [Πλήθων καὶ Βησσαρίων] ὑπούλως. Cf. *BG* 100.

[86] Cf. Blanchet (2008) 179; Monfasani (1994) 833; Woodhouse (1986) 273.

[87] Masai (1976) 25–6, and especially 34–5 for the theological 'vice originel' that, to Plethon's eyes, neither the Eastern nor the Western Church managed to overcome. This concerns the inability of any Trinitarian theology to accommodate the 'fundamental principle of reason', as Masai has it, according to which 'different powers' signify 'different substances'. This principle is attested in both Plethon's alleged 'anti-Latin' treatise and the *Nomoi* and squares well with the subordinationism of pagan theology of the Julianic-Plethonean type. See below, pp. 252 and 279.

of generation that controls the corruptible physical world cannot be analogous to the eternal essence of the first principle. A variant of precisely this 'pagan' thesis is affirmed and applied in the *Nomoi* in order to bring the point home that the physical world cannot immediately proceed from 'Zeus'. If essence is always analogous to the modality of generation, then the eternal essence congenial to 'Zeus' cannot be the cause of the world of generation and corruption.[88] Whether or not Manuel was aware of the connection between the opening statement in the *Reply* and the pagan axiom in the *Nomoi*, he corroborates Scholarios' suspicions regarding Plethon's Orthodoxy.

To the list of crypto-paganising works we should reserve a special place for *De fato*, the chapter on fate from the *Nomoi* that was circulated to a wide audience. The work was immediately recognised as transmitting a distinctively pagan outlook binding the divine to a world run by inexorable laws of necessity and abolishing the Judaeo-Christian notion of God as a free agent creating the world *ex nihilo*. Yet the culmination of Plethon's religious and philosophical dissimulation is the use of natural theology as cover for the transmission of hallmarks of pagan philosophy. This method is applied twice.

First, in the *Memorandum to Theodore*, an unnamed religion is provocatively recognised as universally valid without any reference to Judaeo-Christianity. Second, in the *Monody for the Empress Helen* the principal positions of the pagan epistemology and ontology of the *Nomoi* are summarised in two carefully crafted paragraphs, once again under the cover of natural religion.[89] Plethon's silence concerning Orthodox doctrines should not be taken lightly. In the epistle to Oises, Scholarios conjoins apostasy from Christianity with 'indifference for the faith' (ἀδιαφορία περὶ τὴν πίστιν).[90] Given the gravity of the crime of apostasy, it becomes apparent that whereas today a Christian is not obliged to state his religious affiliation in every discourse on metaphysics or political theology, things were rather different in

---

[88] *Nomoi* 96 (3.15.63–74).

[89] See below, pp. 234–5, 377–9 on religion in the *Memorandum to Theodore* and p. 302 on the *Monody*.

[90] Schol. *Ad Raulem Oesem* 4.480.9–12.

the fifteenth century. At a time when ethics, political philosophy and imperial theory were inextricably bound to the post-Palamite Eastern Orthodox version of Christianity, the mere attempt at a dechristianisation and secularisation of religion in these two texts was scandalous enough.

Plethon ventured beyond that. The tenets of religion that he proposes in the *Monody* are incompatible with Christianity, though perfectly compatible with those of the pagan religion in the *Nomoi* and the Platonism of the *Differences*; they are constitutive and structural elements of an essentially Hellenic world-view.[91] Plethon was not advocating a *prisca philosophia* as Ficino did, namely one that culminates in Judaeo-Christianity, but a distinctively pagan reformation of Platonism that excludes Christology and fundamental Christian notions regarding creation, salvation and knowledge. The Orthodox theologians, convinced that Plethon was a crypto-pagan who λαγὼ βίον ἔζη, as Matthew Kamariotes put it, had excellent reasons for thinking so.[92] Plethon drew not only on the dusty volumes mentioned by Scholarios, but on a persistent pagan intellectual paradigm that managed to survive until his time.

Suppose Plethon could speak his mind about all this. What would he say? An imaginary response is provided by an anonymous disciple, possibly Kabakes or Apostoles, who has nothing but contempt for the 'superstitious man', Demetrios Palaiologos, his 'harem' (γυναικωνίτης), namely Princess Theodora, and above all for Scholarios, for whom he reserves a list of unflattering adjectives (φθονερός, ἀπαίδευτος, δημώδης, ἀλιτήριος, βάσκανος, κακοήθης, ἀμαθής, μοχθηρός: Anon. *Πρὸς Πλήθωνα, ἢ περὶ τῆς βίβλου* 409–10 Alexandre). In the mind of this anonymous disciple late Byzantium merges with late antiquity: Plethon, he says, would not fail to notice the similarities with the pattern followed 'by those who opposed Porphyry and Julian'. Unable to refute the *Nomoi* in writing, Scholarios was possessed by envy and found just the right occasion to release the venom 'he has always cultivated against me'. Yet 'I know well', continues this imaginary Plethon

---

[91] For detailed discussions of these passages see below, Ch. 5, pp. 302–3.
[92] Kamariotes, *Contra Pleth.*, 218 Reimarus.

after asserting the immortality of the soul, that 'those men who are well educated will judge by what remains of that book whether there was anything useful in it after all'. As for Scholarios, he is said to have reserved his place in history as despoiling the memory of a man who attained goodness and for hindering wise men from accessing wisdom. Of course, it may be that in the future wise men will find ways to knowledge superior to that contained in the *Nomoi*; for a delivery (ἐπίδοσις) of useful and really great things will take place.[93] I shall argue elsewhere that the man who fell back on this doctrine regarding the persistence of truth in history on the aftermath of the destruction of the *Nomoi* was intimately familiar with and transmits a salient component of Plethon's outlook. He was an initiated member of the latter's *phratria*.[94] Now, however, it is time to turn to what seems to have been the cause of discord: the *Nomoi*.

The puzzle of the *Nomoi*

The recent trend to 'rehabilitate' those Byzantine humanists previously considered to have suspiciously paganising tendencies (Italos, Psellos) and those Renaissance thinkers who experimented with Platonism after Plethon, most notably Marsilio Ficino, has inevitably led to doubts regarding the impact and even the nature of Plethon's paganism.[95] According to the formulation of James

---

[93] Anon. Πρὸς Πλήθωνα, ἢ περὶ τῆς βίβλου (Alexandre 409–10).

[94] See below, Ch. 4, p. 180.

[95] See Hankins (1990) 197 n. 75 and Pagani (2008) 6 n. 4 for the authorities who have doubted Plethon's paganism. These include E. Wind, C. H. Lohr, N. G. Wilson, and, most notably, P. O. Kristeller, (1972: 96–8). For recent advocacies of a Plethon who was more Christian than pagan, or who may have been Christian rather than pagan, see the introduction by Chatzimichael to his Modern Greek translation of *Nomoi*, 34 n. 58 and Hladký (forthcoming). Still, it appears that Masai's thesis persists. The majority of scholars working on Plethon, Scholarios, late Byzantine history and the question of Plethon's esotericism consider *Nomoi* a reflection of Plethon's very real and conscious conversion from Christianity to paganism, or at any rate to a non-Christian and potentially anti-Christian world-view; cf. Alexandre (1858) lxxxi; Anastos (1948) 189; Masai (1958) 59: 'La renaissance du polythéisme est donc très réelle dans le platonisme de Mistra'; Bargeliotes (1974) 127 n. 8; Toynbee (1981) 312–14; Dedes (1985) 356; Woodhouse (1986) 320–1, 378; Berger (2006) 83; Livanos (2006) 81–2 and (2010) 110; Blanchet (2008) 182; Pagani (2008) 44–5; Garnsey (2009) 328; Hanegraaff (2009) 40; Neri (2010) 105–12; Smarnakis (forthcoming).

Hankins, Plethon might have 'thought himself a better Christian'.[96] Monfasani, while considering Plethon an 'unequivocal pagan' and elsewhere criticising the attempts to see Plethon as 'essentially an unconventional Christian', summarises the popular notion that only the *Nomoi* testifies to Plethon's paganism and shows why one might be tempted to reconsider Plethon's paganism too:

[I]f one looks at the works Pletho published in his own lifetime, one finds that Pletho never explicitly embraced paganism nor pretended to do any more than explain the ideas of Plato, Zoroaster and other ancient sages. Furthermore, in his eulogy of the princess Cleopa, he spoke of her taking the 'bread of the most holy of our mysteries', in an obvious reference to the Eucharist; in his treatise on the Filioque Pletho defended the Byzantine position as the one we hold; and at the Council of Ferrara-Florence he clearly argued for the maintenance of traditional Greek positions against the Latins. Consequently, any belief in Pletho's paganism must depend on his posthumously published *Treatise on the Laws*. There, and only there, did Plethon prescribe in his own person a polytheistic creed and religious practices based on a Neoplatonist hierarchy of gods.[97]

Obviously, if the *Nomoi* is shown not to be intended as a pagan manifesto, then Plethon is not a pagan – hence, he may be Christian. I suspect that such an interpretation of the *Nomoi* might have come as a great surprise to Plethon himself. After all, does his book not prescribe that 'sophists' should be burned in graveyards?[98] Still, one of the first to move in this direction of a 'Christian Plethon', Edgar Wind, ventured the suggestion that in its original form the *Nomoi* might have been closer to More's *Utopia* than to any genuine plan for a pagan reformation. Consequently, Plethon's polytheism should not be taken at face value anymore than More's philosophical religion and the *Nomoi* might be a *Staatsroman* rather than a pagan manifesto.[99] In the same vein, Kristeller

---

[96] Hankins (1990) 202.

[97] Quotation from Monfasani (1992) 48–9; cf. (1994) 833; (2002) 183 n. 19.

[98] *Nomoi* 126 (3.31.83–5); see below, Ch. 7, p. 387.

[99] Wind (1968) 244–8. The argument was repeated by Antony Kenny in a review of Woodhouse's book. See Kenny (1989) 727: 'If *Utopia* had never been published in its author's lifetime one can well imagine how Thomas Cromwell might have released fragments of it after his death to prove that, so far from being a Catholic martyr, Thomas More was not even a believing Christian. Can we be sure that nothing similar happened in the case of Scholarios' posthumous treatment of Gemistos' text?' The classification of *Nomoi* in the genre of *Staatsromanen* next to works by More, Valentin Andreae and Campanella is left open by Yiannakopoulos (1990) 355.

assumed that those parts of the *Nomoi* that have not been preserved would mitigate the paganism of those that have. Scholarios might have framed Plethon by preserving what is 'pagan' and destroying what is not.[100] The most extensive arguments casting doubts upon Plethon's paganism were recently presented by Hladký, who considers the possibility that the *Nomoi* project might be closer to a scrapbook, thought experiment and *sui generis* type of discourse rather than a genuine confession of pagan faith.[101]

According to this view, Scholarios must have suffered from either uncontrolled religious fanaticism or academic jealousy extending to the point of torching a book that was in reality a literary experiment and not a pagan manifesto. In that case, Scholarios should not be accused of naiveté but rather of consciously framing Plethon. For in *Against Plethon* he did recognise the possibility of Plethon's having written the *Differences* as an exercise (γυμνασίου χάριν καὶ λόγου ἕνεκα).[102] This means that Scholarios was perfectly capable of asking the same question with regard to the *Nomoi*: could this be some sort of experiment, rather than serious in intent? I will be arguing that Scholarios had good reasons, other than academic rivalry, for not asking this question in the case of the *Nomoi*. However, given the fascination that the puzzle of the *Nomoi* exercises on scholars, it is worth listing all approaches that one might possibly take in regard to the nature and aims of this obscure work. It appears that they come down to seven:

(a) According to the oldest interpretation of Plethon's *Nomoi* this is an esoteric handbook intended for a pagan brotherhood and private cult operating in Mistra, which contains the outline of a distinctively pagan political theology and philosophical religion.[103] Masai and Medvedev drew the attractive parallel between Plethon's circle and 'occult esoterical forms of organisation' such as the Rosicrucians

---

[100] For a response to Kristeller's argument see Livanos (2006) 80–1 and Pagani (2009). Kristeller's hypothesis is as unhelpful as is that of E. Garin, who saw in the *Nomoi* nothing but a work related to Plethon's purported Platonising solar cult on the grounds that George of Trebizond mentions certain hymns to the sun that are not preserved (for these see below, Ch. 5, p. 238, n. 60). In both cases the verdict on what we have depends upon assumptions on what is lost.

[101] Hladký (forthcoming).   [102] Schol. *Contra Pleth., OC* 4.116.15–25.

[103] Alexandre (1858) lxxxiv; Schultze (1874) 54.

and the Illuminati. Others considered Plethon's *phratria* to be modelled upon the Islamic Darkih orders or radical sects that he might have encountered while on Ottoman territory.[104] Two elements in the *Nomoi* strengthen the view that Plethon's pagan religion had a practical aspect: the inclusion of a carefully worked out calendar and liturgy.[105]

The liturgical significance of the *Nomoi* is first attested by Scholarios, who implies in his epistle to Oises that Plethon was the patron and mentor of a pagan cell in the Peloponnese. Scholarios described a vulnerable Eastern Orthodox minority in the Peloponnese that witnessed the rise and suffered under the spread of a pagan plague. Deliverance from paganism will be brought about 'as the Lord sees fit', which obviously does not exclude but contrariwise enhances the possibility of god's sending in the Turks. It is hard to resist the temptation to quote the first Greek patriarch under Turkish rule lamenting the fall of the Peloponnese in the hands of the pagan brotherhood of Mistra:

Ἵλεως γενοῦ, Κύριε, τῷ λειψάνῳ τούτῳ τῶν ὀρθοδόξων χριστιανῶν. Μὴ ἐγκαταλίπῃς, ἀλλὰ διόρθωσαι ὡς οἶδας αὐτός, καὶ ἐμὲ τὸν ἁμαρτωλὸν καὶ ἀχρεῖόν σου δοῦλον ἐλέησον.

Lord be gracious to this piece left of Orthodox Christians [i.e. the Peloponnese]. Do not forsake but correct [us] as You think fit, and have mercy on me, your sinful and foolish slave. (Schol. *Ad Raulem Oesem, OC* 4.481.20–3)

Here the pagan threat might be hyperbolically employed as a rhetorical device. Still, the impression that Plethon was not alone in his project is corroborated by the information of Matthew Kamariotes years after the end of the Plethon affair: 'certainly the worst thing is that others too shared his [Plethon's] beliefs'.[106]

(b) The *Nomoi* was not intended for any pagan brotherhood, but to prepare 'the intellectual foundations of the coming new world order'. It is a gospel intended for a future 'Restitutio Hellenismi' and

---

[104] Medvedev (1981) 548; Masai (1956) 300. For the the analogies between Plethon's scheme, the religious-political programme of Sheikh Bedreddin and the esoteric philosophy of al-Bistami, see Siniossoglou (2012). On al-Bistami see Fleischer (2010); on Bedreddin see Balivet (1995). Plethon was familiar with aspects of the military and fiscal organisation of the Ottomans; see *Mem. I* 118.10–12; *Oratio ad Manuelem*, Lampros, *PP* 3.310.7–10. On Plethon, Ottoman military and fiscal principles and Islam see Necipoğlu (2009) 275; Akasoy (2008); Täschner (1929); Klein-Franke (1972) 3.

[105] Medvedev (1984) 132.

[106] Kamariotes, *Contra Pleth.* 3.7–8 (Astruc): Τὸ δὲ καὶ ἄλλους τὰ ἐκείνου ἀσπάσασθαι, τοῦτοδὴ καὶ παγχάλεπον.

'Restitutio rerum Graecarum'.[107] If scholarship has yet to discover any real follower of Plethon's pagan sect, as Monfasani argued,[108] we are left with a manifesto without addressees – a work that was not intended for use by any existing pagan circle in Mistra but was meant to fulfil its mission in due time.

(c) The *Nomoi* did not lay down any theoretical ideal but aimed to effect an immediate religious as well as socio-political reform. Its model is the 'second best polity' in Plato's *Laws*, rather than the utopian and ahistorical constitution of the *Republic*. The *Nomoi* is a 'complete code for a social, political, moral and religious reform', intended as an immediate remedy for a decadent and decaying world on the verge of extinction.[109]

(d) The *Nomoi* is part of a rationalist reaction to the political and religious hegemony of Christianity without really implying the need for a reversion to pagan Hellenism. Plethon's religion is new, though its disguise appears to be ancient. This view was recently defended by P. R. Blum, who argues that Plethon advances a rational religion that is, as Toynbee observed, comparable to Comte's 'religion of Humanity'.[110] In the same vein, Codoñer considers the possibility of an exclusively rationalistic reading of the *Nomoi* that restricts its reformatory scope to the socio-political level, while downplaying any alleged need for a complementary pagan-religious reform.[111] Codoñer argues that the word *religion* in Plethon's case should be put within quotation marks and explains away Plethon's use of and preoccupation with pagan symbolism and allegory as 'eine kulturelle Notwendigkeit'.[112] In an interesting argument, he sees pure rationalism at work in Plethon's introduction of a new calendar, eventually making Plethon an apt forerunner of the revolutionary calendar of the French Revolution.

A more mild and evasive variant of this thesis is that the Plethonean project is ultimately not philosophical, but political. According to this approach, shared by Zakythinos, the driving force of Plethon's inspiration is not to be found in the misleading religious surface of the work, but rather in its political aspects. Seen in this light, the *Nomoi* may be read as a political allegory utilising a polytheistic Pantheon as its vehicle.[113] Tambrun has provided the most valuable insights in the direction of a political reading of the *Nomoi*.[114]

(e) The *Nomoi* is the work of a mind weakened and deeply affected by advancing age and acutely fearful for the continuation of Hellenism.

---

[107] Monfasani (1992) 61.   [108] Monfasani (1992) 59.

[109] Webb (1989) 218; this possibility is also discussed by Alexandre (1858) lvi, and Zakythinos (1975) 367.

[110] P. R. Blum (2010) 104.   [111] Codoñer (2005) 94.   [112] Codoñer (2005) 91.

[113] Zakythinos (1975) 372–3.   [114] Tambrun (2006a) 197–220.

Plethon was suffering from a 'deep internal pain in regard to the fall of Greece'. The work is worth studying for historical and psychological reasons, rather than owing to any absolute merits of its own.[115] A variant of this thesis sees in the *Nomoi* the product of a moral crisis afflicting Plethon after 1439. While others ran off to the Latin Church, Plethon found refuge in an imaginary pagan religion. This purportedly explains the 'psychological problem' posed by Plethon's attitude. Plethon was an Orthodox intellectual who happened to go through an intense crisis resulting in messianic tendencies.[116]

(f) The *Nomoi* is some sort of literary exercise, a paper scheme or thought experiment, which does not prove that Plethon was a pagan. This theory has an interesting prehistory. Zakythinos writes that the appreciation of the *Nomoi* as 'un jeu d'imagination' and 'une fantaisie allégorique' has its roots in the years immediately following Plethon's death. No reference is given. One may plausibly assume that this interpretation suits well former students and acquaintances of Plethon who may have wished to protect the memory of their teacher from abuse and *hoi polloi* by downplaying one way or another the paganism of the *Nomoi*. For example, Andronikos Kallistos credited Michael Apostoles with misappropriating and misunderstanding Plethon's works.[117] In any case, Zakythinos sees affinities with the view of Knös and other modern scholars, who considered it a mistake to read the *Nomoi* 'as the gospel of a new religion that Plethon wished to found'. According to their view, Plethon 'was not a prophet, he was an eruditor' and the *Nomoi* 'is not the product of either faith or sentiment, but of thought'.[118]

(g) The *Nomoi* is part of an attempt to transcend both paganism and Christianity by means of a synthetical religion that presents itself as a revival of Hellenism. In this sense, the *Nomoi* may be read as comprehending aspects of the Christian religion too, though it cannot be reduced to the exclusive categories of either 'Christian' or 'pagan'.[119]

---

[115] This is Wilson's (1983: 270) and Ellissen's (1860: 17) verdict: 'wir haben danach den Verlust des Ganzen weniger wegen des ewigen absoluten Werthes als nur in Hinblick auf das historische und besonders auch das subjektiv psychologische Interesse des Buches zu bedauern'.

[116] The view is reported by Zakythinos (1975: 371) who easily refutes it.

[117] Andr. Call. *Defensio Theodori Gazae*, Mohler III 178.35–9.

[118] Zakythinos (1975) 369–70; Knös (1950) 128.

[119] For variants of this interpretation see Stausberg (1998) 81–2; P. R. Blum (2005) 126; Hankins (1990) 200; Couloubaritsis (2005) 76; Constantelos (1998) 71. According to Hankins (1990: 204–5), Plethon was opposed to the clerical hegemony of his day, but not necessarily to Christianity as such. See also Codoñer (2005: 96–7), who notes that Plethon made 'concessions' to Christianity and Woodhouse (1986: 361–2), who thinks that 'try as he might, Plethon could not entirely repudiate Christianity'. However,

Advocates of this thesis do not appear to have made use of important evidence in this direction that provides useful ammunition for their argument. Fifteenth-century mystics and reformers such as al-Bistami and Bedreddin, with whose thought Plethon might well have been acquainted during his sojourn in Adrianople or Bursa, exemplify a simultaneous insistence upon the accessibility of supraconfessional truth. Thus, there is a shared attitude regarding society, religion and political action that both Plethon and Bedreddin may have absorbed by virtue of having studied, perhaps, in the same city and moved in the same esoteric circles. Like Plethon, Bedreddin opts for sectarianism as the vehicle for construing a novel religious identity and for recovering a universal religious law. This indicates the probability of a common nexus between Rumelia and the Western Aegean spanning confessional lines and using sect as a vehicle for attaining utopian religious and socio-political ends.[120]

To a different extent some of these readings tend to see in Plethon's recurrent deference to pagan mythology little more than a classical ornament or to open up the possibility of moderating the clash between the paganism of the *Nomoi* and his social identity as a Christian. I suspect that one or the other version of the last interpretation (g) has better chances of eventually prevailing in the scholarly debate regarding the *Nomoi*. By avoiding the polarisation between Christianity and paganism, this thesis partially satisfies more people than it completely disappoints. To begin with, it is consistent with the popular position that Plethon had a non-Christian starting point or impetus, as well as with the less popular one that Plethon was after all Christian in some generic meaning of the word defined by his social identity. Moreover, this thesis partially satisfies the assumption that Plethon was in equal measure anti-Christian and anti-pagan. But above all, it is compatible with the popular trend in Renaissance and Byzantine cultural and social history of rehabilitating all ideological dissenters into a vague, potentially all-inclusive Christianity: which

---

the evidence provided for this claim is weak. More interestingly, Wokart (1986: 184) stresses the originality rather than the convertibility of the *Nomoi*: 'denn Plethon erweist sich also so anti-christlich wie anti-pagan, oder vielmehr als gleichgültig gegen beides'. This is also the view of Couloubaritsis (2006) 155.

[120] Siniossoglou (2012).

is, ultimately, none other than Ficino's reading of Plethon and the pagan sages.[121]

In reality though, Ficino and Plethon stand at opposite ends of the spectrum. Plethon is not the originator of either the Renaissance *prisca theologia* or *philosophia perennis*.[122] For Ficino's *prisca theologia* is a Christian *prisca theologia*, not a generic one. The Renaissance version of a universal religious philosophy was not compatible with Plethon's 'true doctrines' in so far as the former was primarily and ultimately a Christian philosophy and only secondarily a perennial one. Ficino's *philosophia* does not include Christianity but serves Christianity; it does not accord with Christianity, it is superseded by Christianity. Contrary to those Plethonean 'true doctrines' allegedly coeval with man and the universe, Ficino's *prisca philosophia* prioritises Judaeo-Christian revelation. It is not indifferent to Christian doctrines but culminates in them. Ultimately, this *prisca theologia* is a *pia philosophia* in the Christian exclusive sense of these words.[123] It cannot stand without Christianity.

By contrast, Plethon's notion of 'true doctrines' is non-conformable to Judaeo-Christianity, in so far as Plethon never gives way to that particular and exclusive kind of Christian 'perennial philosophy' contained within and fully revealed only by the Judaeo-Christian Scriptures and the incarnation of Christ. Tellingly Moses and Jesus are excluded from the list of sages in the first book of the *Nomoi*, contrary to the ideal of inclusive pagan monotheism expounded by, for example, Porphyry. Plethon's philosophy became exclusive in order to avoid being eroded from within by a prophetical tradition that claimed exclusivity on its own right.

---

[121] In the introduction to his translation of Plotinus, Ficino surprisingly goes so far as to add Plethon to a series of Aristotelians who purified philosophy from the dangers of Averroism. See P. R. Blum (2005) 126; (2010) 96.

[122] For this widespread view see Hanegraaff (2006b) 1127; Masai (1957/8) 408 applies the term *philosophia perennis* to describe the Plethonean belief in the ahistorical and essential quality of real philosophy. The term is also used by Hladký (forthcoming), *passim*.

[123] See Saffrey (1996) 498.

In addition to the incompatibility between Judaeo-Christian revelation and the Plethonean notion of archetypical doctrines in the *Nomoi*, several considerations present us with insuperable objections to any attempt at either rehabilitating Plethon to Christianity or qualifying the pagan philosophical core of his thought:

(a) To begin with, Plethon's paganism is not confined to the *Nomoi*. One of the truly great merits of Masai's work is that he grasped, as Scholarios did, the interplay between Platonic metaphysics in the *Differences* and Plethon's 'polytheism' in the *Nomoi*.[124] By the time that Plethon revised the *Differences* he had a clear view of his philosophical paganism. The *Nomoi* project was already in progress. As Scholarios acknowledged, the *Differences* is much more than a university lecture. This is a work no less pagan than the *Nomoi*, providing a version of Plethon's polytheist and henotheist model in technical and academic language.[125] For all their calculated obscurity, the correspondences between the mythical framework of the *Nomoi* and Platonist ontology in the *Differences* make abundantly clear that these are contemporaneous literary vehicles for a single genuinely pagan world-view that, we shall see, Plethon expertly summarised in the *Monody for the Empress Helen*.[126]

Part II of this book shows that the correspondences between the *Nomoi*, the *Differences*, the commentary on the *Chaldean Oracles*, the short but valuable *Recapitulation of Zoroastrian and Platonic Doctrines* and the *Monody for the Empress Helen* point to a consistently non-Christian and paganising philosophical thought-world that is incompatible with fundamental Christian beliefs. These works convey a single pagan epistemology (Chapter 4) and ontology (Chapter 5) that stem from a distinctive and radical interpretation

---

[124] Masai (1956) 210; Schultze (1874) 55–6; Couloubaritsis (1997) 118; Bargeliotes (1980) provides the fullest parallel discussion of the two works. Still, the pagan intention of Plethon's argumentation in the *Differences* is either missed or ignored by a number of scholars, e.g. Tavardon (1977) 268–78 and Karamanolis (2002) 268.

[125] See for example *Diff.* 336.20–337.23, where Plethon replaces the Christian appropriation of Aristotelian philosophy with a Neoplatonist hierarchy involving the extreme One, the Intellect, and Forms that clearly correspond to 'Zeus', 'Poseidon' and the other gods of the *Nomoi*. See below, Ch. 5.

[126] In the same vein Hankins (1990: 199 n. 79) acknowledges the principal problem with Wind's hypothesis by bringing attention to the fact that passages in the *Nomoi* have parallels in other works of Plethon that 'could only have been seriously intended, for instance, the *Summary of Platonic and Zoroastrian Doctrines* and the *Reply to the Treatise in Support of the Latin Doctrine*'. See also Stausberg (1998) 81: 'Zu konsistent ist Plethons 'neozoroastrisch'-platonisierendes Selbstverständnis in den verschiedensten Schriften artikuliert, um sich am Ende wieder mit dem Bild eines elitären Reformchristentums in Wohlgefallen auflösen zu lassen.'

of Plato by utilising diverse literary forms. Consequently, far from implying that *Nomoi* is not a vehicle of pagan Platonism but a mere paper scheme, the internal accord between Plethon's works makes abundantly clear that *Nomoi* cannot be anything but such a vehicle. Epistemological optimism (Chapter 4), multi-causalism, determinism and a monistic ontology that abolishes the distinction between unqualified essence and created substance (Chapter 5) combine with the absence of any reference to grace, to the Incarnation of Christ, creationism, eschatology, or to any other specifically Christian doctrine in forming an unequivocally non-Christian philosophy. Further, a number of issues discussed in the *Differences* and *Against Scholarios* in allegedly academic terms recur as key conceptual components of the pagan world-view in the *Nomoi*. Among them are the perpetuity of the world, *heimarmene*, a distinctively pagan ontology, and even the name of Zoroaster. The reiteration of these motifs should not be taken lightly. In the light of Byzantine law, heresy was not limited to any statement of sincere belief in non-Orthodox doctrines but was extended to cover teaching and learning of 'unholy' ideas.[127]

(b) That the *Nomoi* is connected with Plethon's philosophical and theological convictions is corroborated by the results of recent palaeographical research. Fabio Pagani argued that the Platonic manuscripts annotated by Plethon are part of a systematic and original exegetical enterprise that daringly 'corrects' the Platonic text in order to bring it into agreement with Plethon's own version of philosophical paganism. Plethon's intention was to construct an ideal text of Plato that is cleansed of occasional or potential errors in theology owing to Plato's concessions to Homer, Hesiod and morally condemnable myths. Plethon's textual corrections, emendations and obliterations are part of the hermeneutical project of an 'apologetical' recension of Plato in internal agreement with the Plethonean theology of the *Nomoi*. This means that Scholarios was not intending to frame Plethon when arguing that he preserved the surviving fragments from the *Nomoi* in order to justify his actions. As Pagani concludes, Plethon's rewriting of Plato is in step with the spirit of the *Nomoi* and provides evidence of his philosophical Hellenism.[128]

(c) Yet even on the basis of internal criteria alone Plethon leaves us little doubt as to his intentions when compiling the *Nomoi*. There is no reason to suppose that Plethon is not speaking in *propria persona*.

---

[127] *Basilica* 1.1.18: καὶ μηδεὶς τὰ βέβηλα διδασκέτω ἢ μανθανέτω. Cf. *CJ* 1.11.10: πᾶν δὲ μάθημα παρὰ τῶν νοσούντων τὴν τῶν ἀνοσίων Ἑλλήνων μανίαν διδάσκεσθαι κωλύομεν.

[128] Pagani (2008) 40–5.

The ideas and notions developed are presented as reflecting their author's actual religious and philosophical world-view, a set of 'true doctrines' subsequently distorted by old and modern 'sophists'. The use of the first-person plural continuously applied in the discussion of ethical and religious questions throughout a work that has the form of a treatise, rather than of a novel like More's *Utopia*, does not authorise any doubts regarding the author's intention. This is stated by none other than Plethon. The *skopos* is to discuss how 'we' might choose the right *hairesis biou*, to state what 'we postulate' and, conversely, to explain what 'we will not say'.[129]

Throughout the *Nomoi* there is a clear division between 'what we believe' and what is held by 'some among the sophists', accentuated by tacit anti-Christian allusions. These 'sophists', for example, 'enjoy a high appeal among people' by promising to their following greater goods 'than what *we* bring to the human race', that is to say, they offer 'a genuine immortality forever unmixed with anything mortal'.[130] This is a clear allusion to contemporary 'sophistry' and especially to Christian eschatology that was, as we shall see in Chapter 6, dominant in Plethon's time. There is a difference between Plethon's 'wise men' and these contemporary 'sophists': the former are not misled into thinking that truth could be posterior to 'what has been falsely said or what is falsely attested [today]'. Truth comes before error. If an error is now identified, then one should turn back in order to recover truth. This statement targets Judaeo-Christian revelation. Again, Plethon opts for the present tense and one may discern behind this scorn for the sophists' 'innovations' an anti-Christian topos as old as Celsus' *Alethes Logos*: that of καινοποιεῖν.[131] Plethon follows the tradition of Neoplatonic covert references to Christians

---

[129] *Nomoi* 20 (1.1.66–7): εἰ μέλλοιμέν ποτε ἀσφαλῶς τὸν ἄριστον αἱρήσεσθαι βίον. Cf. *Nomoi* 30 (1.2.35): ἡμεῖς μέν . . . ; 128 (3.31.102): ἀξιοῦμεν δ' ἡμεῖς . . . ; 248 (3.43.85): ἀποφαίνομεν . . . Cf. 252 (3.43.111, 3.43.153–4): οὐ . . . φήσομεν; 258 (3.43.213): οἱ ἡμέτεροι λόγοι.

[130] *Nomoi* 258 (3.43.208–12). See also the description of Christian cosmology in *Nomoi* 24 (1.1.114–16) and its distinction from the pagan Neoplatonic one in *Nomoi* 24 (1.1.120–6); the reference to the (Christian) educational establishment that 'holds people captivated from an early age onwards' at *Nomoi* 36 (1.2.120–5); the remark that the prudent man should not follow 'those who promise the most' at 258 (3.43.216–18); the use of the present tense when refuting typically Christian ideas on time and creationism at 258–60 (3.43.228–45); the opposition of the 'right reasoning' (ὀρθοὶ λογισμοί) to the 'irrationalities' (παραλογισμοί) and supernatural accomplishments with which the sophists deceive the uneducated masses – a direct anti-palamite allusion (*Nomoi* 34–6, 1.2.110–19); and the attack on celibacy and sexual abstinence (see below, Ch. 4, p. 185). For Neoplatonic allusions to Christians in late antiquity see Siniossoglou (2008a) 43–7.

[131] *Nomoi* 34 (1.2.85–91).

by turning Proclus' κρατοῦντες into 'sophists'.[132] Nothing authorises us to disregard these allusions and blur the distinction between that notorious 'but we . . . ' with which ends the manuscript of the *Nomoi* and the Christian social identity that any intellectual was expected to assume in the late Byzantine context.

(d) There is a fourth point that needs to be taken into account: the independent circulation of a chapter from the *Nomoi* on fate. Plethon's reintroduction of *heimarmene* in the late Byzantine context was an un-Orthodox and shocking move. From a Greek Orthodox perspective, Plethon's *De fato* compromised the unconditional freedom of God as personal agent. The probability that a man as well-versed in Greek patristics as Plethon circulated a text propagating Stoic-Platonic fatalism would mean that he was testing the waters. In that case, the *Nomoi*, of which *De fato* is but one part, was not really intended as an esoteric work. Rather, Plethon intended to disclose its contents when the time came. As with the *Monody for the Empress Helen* the wide circulation of *De fato* implies that he did not necessarily have only a small circle in mind.

The liquidating strategies of contemporary social and cultural history would be incomprehensible, to say the least, to either advocates of Orthodoxy, such as Gregory Palamas, or dissenters such as Plethon. Plethon's near contemporaries remind us that Hellenism and Judaeo-Christianity are separate intellectual ideal-types and existential positions, that they were felt, and appreciated as such by the actual protagonists of fourteenth- and fifteenth-century conflicts. Refuting Plethon's conception of *heimarmene* contained in *De fato*, Matthew Kamariotes repeated a significant caveat: 'there is nothing in common between Plethon and us' (*Contra Pleth.* 86: οὐδὲν ἔχει κοινὸν ἡμῖν τε καὶ Πλήθωνι). Though according to appearances this is a rather uninspired punch line, its meaning is more significant than George of Trebizond's fear of an underground pagan religion's threatening Rome or Scholarios' reports to the authorities regarding the spread of 'polytheism' in the Peloponnese. Matthew makes clear that he combats *philosophical* rather than ritual paganism – and so did Scholarios, when replying to Plethon's *Differences*. It is the philosophical core of

---

[132] P. R. Blum (2010: 102), suggests that the 'sophists' that Plethon has in mind might have been Aristotelian philosophers. However, there are passages in the *Nomoi* that credit the 'sophists' with views typical of Christian apologetics and rhetoric. See for example *Nomoi* 18 (1.1.28–31) on the futility of reason and learning. Cf. n. 130 above.

the *Nomoi* that matters, and that was both non-negotiable and incompatible with Christianity. The attack of Gregory Palamas on Byzantine humanism shows that Plethon's contemporary Orthodoxy was no religion to be squared within synthetical projects of a 'perennial philosophy', or, for that matter, 'negotiations' of any sort.

PART II

THE ELEMENTS OF PAGAN PLATONISM

4

EPISTEMIC OPTIMISM

Intellectual versus spiritual illumination

The main tenet of Plethon's philosophy is also the cornerstone of Platonic conceptual paganism: epistemic optimism. This is the view than man may, by means of his own intellectual faculties and temporal awareness, rise to the level of godlikeness and achieve happiness. Epistemic optimism is rooted in the belief that the human intellect is ultimately divine – and that living according to *nous* will render god apprehensible and accessible, thus elevating humanity to *eudaimonia*. Karl Popper discerned the Platonic roots of epistemic optimism and, significantly for the argument of this book, its persistence in European intellectual history:

Admittedly Plato's belief in a world we can never learn to know could perhaps be called 'epistemological pessimism'. And it has spread far beyond Europe. But Plato supplemented it, quite in the spirit of the old Ionian critical and rationalist tradition, with an unequalled epistemological optimism. And this epistemological optimism has remained part of our Western civilisation. It is the optimistic theory that science, that is, real knowledge about the hidden real world, though certainly very difficult, is nevertheless attainable, at least for some of us. Man, according to Plato, can discover the reality hidden behind the world of phenomena, and he can discover it by the power of his own critical reason, without the aid of divine revelation.

This is the almost unbelievable optimism of Greek rationalism: of the rationalism of the Renaissance – of European rationalism.[1]

Popper links three 'characteristically European subjects', freedom, industrialism and science, to this 'highly characteristic European theory of knowledge or epistemology'. In one form or another, all three are present in Plethon. The core of the two *Memoranda* is

[1] Popper (1996) 192.

the firm belief that the Peloponnese may by means of the right *politeia* remain free and immune to the Turkish attempts at invasion. The *Nomoi* affirms the ability of man to compensate for the deficiencies and limitations of his mortal body by means of *technai*, technological progress and the manipulation of the power of animals according to human will (ἐς ὃ βουλοίμεθα αὐτοί).[2] As for the 'theory that science, that is, real knowledge about the hidden real world. . . . is attainable', this is a tenet of Plethon's project. Ultimately, the aim of his endeavour is the foundation of ideology and utopianism upon a recovery of the laws underlying and regulating the universe: more than a political ideology, the *Nomoi* purports to convey the science of decoding and understanding the system (σύστημα) of the world.[3] Rational discourse promises to reveal metaphysical and social truths (τὰ ἀληθῆ) and – in a typically Platonic way – leads to genuine and first-hand (οἰκείαν), rather than borrowed (οὐκ ἀλλοτρίαν) *episteme*.[4]

This is the crux of the matter in Plato's *Theaetetus* as well as a main element in the whole Platonic tradition. In this regard, Plethon anticipates what Popper brands as 'the rationalism of the Renaissance'. The *Oratio de dignitate homini* of Pico della Mirandola provides a starting point for elaborating on this aspect of Platonism:

[T]hat other aphorism γνῶθι σεαυτόν, that is, 'Know thyself', invites and exhorts us to the study of the whole of which the nature of man is the connecting link and the 'mixed portion' [2]; for he who knows himself knows all things in himself [3], as Zoroaster first and after him Plato [1], in the *Alcibiades*, wrote. Finally, enlightened by this knowledge, through the aid of natural philosophy [4], being already close to God, employing the theological salutation εἶ, that is, 'Thou art' [5], we shall blissfully address the true Apollo on intimate terms. (Pico della Mirandola, *Oratio* 46 Garin; Eng. trans. Capogrini).

This passage reiterates five ideas prominent in the *Nomoi*. The first in importance is the appeal to the anteriority of Zoroaster and Plato [1]. The second is Plethon's doctrine of man as 'forming a boundary' (μεθόριον), that is, Plato's idea of the human capacity to ascend to godlikeness or descend towards the basest form of mortality: man is on the boundary between the divine realm and

---

[2] *Nomoi* 192 (3.34, 5.102–9).   [3] See Ch. 6, p. 289.   [4] *Nomoi* 36 (1.2.125–33).

the world [2].[5] The third element in Pico that conforms to Plethon's Platonism is the Plotinean and ultimately Platonic idea of man as a sculptor of himself [3]: 'never cease chiselling your statue', writes Plotinus, 'until there will shine out on you from it the godlike splendour of virtue, until you will see the perfect goodness surely established in the stainless shrine'.[6]

Pico did his very best to integrate these ideas into the Judaeo-Christian outlook by putting a biblical plot at the service of pagan Platonic epistemological optimism. Still, the priority of natural philosophy [4] signals the Platonic and Plethonean belief that illumination is attainable without supernatural revelation by acquiring a cognitive knowledge of the divine through a humanly initiated process. It is a fifth doctrinal element in Pico's *Oration* that enables this process, one that is even harder to align with Judaeo-Christianity and which, as it happens, is one of the most interesting aspects of Plethon's philosophy: the interpretation of Plato according to which god *is not* beyond Being, but *is* Being – as Pico argues by drawing from Plutarch, one of Plethon's favourite sources [5].[7]

Plethon departs from both Roman Orthodox apophaticism and negative theology of the Neoplatonic type. The first modern scholar to note this divergence from Neoplatonic 'orthodoxy' was Thomas Taylor, in the course of attacking Plethon from a Proclan viewpoint.[8] But Scholarios was the first, in the course of his fierce assault on the *Differences* from an Orthodox perspective, to acutely suspect that the Plethonean departure from the

---

5 On Plethon's doctrine of man as *methorion* see the detailed discussion below, p. 183.

6 Plot. *Enn* 1.6.9.11–14.

7 This shift of focus from a theology involving a transcendent personal god to ontology will be discussed at length in the next chapter.

8 T. Taylor (2004 [1812]): 225–6) discovered in Plethon a straightforward Platonic heresy. He finds fault with three aspects of his philosophy: first, the abandonment of the *symphonia* between Plato and Aristotle, second, the doctrine that the cause of all is knowable, and third, the confounding of Zeus with the 'highest god', namely the One. Recent scholarship has reached the same conclusion through different routes. See Medvedev (1984) 131: '[P]lethon c'est beaucoup éloigné de l'apophaticisme non seulement des Pères de l'Église mais aussi des néoplatoniciens, en particuliers de Plotin.' On Plethon's breach with Plotinean and Neoplatonic negative theology as well as with Byzantine theology see Tambrun (2006a) *passim* and (2003) 67–93. Bargeliotes (1974: 136) also brings to the foreground Plethon's belief in the power of man to become cognitively aware of divinity. For a different view see Hladký (forthcoming; 2009), who attempts to qualify Plethon's departure from apophaticism. See below, Ch. 5, p. 243.

Neoplatonic theurgic notion of illumination also implied a collateral one from Roman Orthodoxy:

Plethon is reputed to deprecate all talk of 'inspirations' (ἐνθουσιασμούς) and 'revelations' (ἀποκαλύψεις) and to have declared them a deception (πλάνη) – further, to have proved in another work of his that truth can be found only by human discursive reason (ὑπὸ τοῦ ἀνθρωπίνου λόγου) by means of philosophy (διὰ φιλοσοφίας). (Schol. *Contra Pleth.*, OC 4.16.31–4; trans. Woodhouse)

We shall see presently that the 'other work' implied in this passage from *Against Plethon* is the first book of the *Nomoi*. Clearly, by the time that Scholarios attempted to refute the *Differences* he had access to the contents of the *Nomoi*. Aristotle, he avers, agrees that 'sacred truth' transcends reason.[9] Conversely, Plato's purported obscurantism appears to have led Plethon to doubt that inspiration should necessarily be 'godsent', that is, to reinterpret *epipnoia* along rational lines. Nevertheless, Scholarios postpones his reply for a later time – for the time being, he says, his only concern is to expose Plethon's calumnies against Aristotle.[10]

Scholarios openly attacked Plethon on the grounds of introducing a pagan 'religion'. But here he appears to credit Plethon with something different: the attempt to make of philosophy an Absolute. This was the cause of the fierce intellectual civil war in fourteenth-century Byzantium that led to the defeat of humanist Platonism and the victory of the Palamite version of Christian Orthodoxy. Forced to conform to the maxims of Palamism for all his sympathy for Thomism, Scholarios could hardly have missed Plethon's glorification of the philosophy of those pagan Illuminati who caused the outrage of Palamas. 'Indeed,' replied Plethon in an ambiguous note in *Against Scholarios*, 'I do know of both inspirations and human doctrines that one should accept, as well as of inspirations and human doctrines that one should *not* accept.' He then changes the subject without more ado. The real issue is not what he knows, but rather what Scholarios does: nothing but slander and insult.[11] This rare autobiographical reference could

---

[9] Schol. *Contra Pleth.*, OC 4.16.19–26. See below, p. 412, n. 33 for Plethon's reaction to Scholarios' misappropriation of Aristotle on this point.

[10] Schol. *Contra Pleth.*, OC 4.17.6–21. On Plato's purported obscurantism see also Schol. *Contra Pleth.*, OC 4.108.20–6.

[11] Pleth. *Contra Schol.* 9.1–3.

well mean that at some point of his religious and philosophical formation Plethon became familiar with empirical approaches to illumination. These could include theurgy and the philosophy of illumination nurtured in the milieu of Islamic sectarianism, even if eventually Plethon responded differently to the question of godlikeness.

Reflecting on the Plethon affair, Scholarios notes that one of the sources of Plethon's apostasy, as well as of Julian's and a great many other people's, is the absence of the grace of god – the other reasons being the proximity to the daemons, and, significantly, that idiosyncratic study of Hellenic literature and philosophy that persistently departs from linguistic surface.[12] It is worth pausing for a moment to enquire what Scholarios really means when accusing Julian and Plethon of pursuing truth without the grace of god. This is more than a rhetorical trope or theological topos.

According to Basil, apostasy (ἀποστασία) from god is due to the rebellion of one of two faculties inherent in man. This is the intellectual one, which constantly runs the danger of generating bizarre phantasies (φαντασίαις ἀλλοκότοις) and confuses what is not-god with god. In the Greek patristic tradition represented by Athanasius the irrationality of human imaginative faculty (ἄλογος φαντασία) is held responsible for the generic notion of idolatry.[13] Imagination allows for an *ex nihilo* creation of conceptual constructions that simulate and compete with the genuine act of creation that belongs to god alone. Conversely, according to Basil, there is another faculty that really uplifts man to godlikeness: the inherent capacity to receive the Holy Spirit and apprehend 'the most divine matters' as far as possible.[14] This faculty is conducive to spiritual and psychosomatic illumination (ἔλλαμψις). To think that it is possible to uncover the essence of god, says Basil against the Platonising heretic Eunomius, equals vainglory of the utmost kind.[15]

12 Schol. *Ad principessam Pelop.*, OC 4.152.30–7: ὃ καὶ Ἰουλιανῷ καὶ πολλοῖς ἄλλοις ἀποστάταις συνέβη.
13 See for example Ath. *Gent.* 1.28, 12.9, 45.39.   14 Basil, *Ep.* 233.1.1–25.
15 Basil, *Eun.*, PG 29.540.4–6. As so often, Gregory of Nyssa (*Eun.* 3.8.11.16–19) has his ways of making the same point in more elaborate and subtle terms: τὰς δὲ οὐσίας διὰ τῶν ὀνομάτων ἑρμηνεύοντες οἱ ὑπὲρ τὴν ἀνθρωπίνην φύσιν ὀξυωποῦντες, οἱ τὸ μὲν ἀκατάληπτον βλέποντες, τὸ δὲ καταληπτὸν παραβλέποντες...

Seen through this prism Scholarios' reference to Plethon's apostasy has not only a legalistic but also a philosophical dimension. There can be no position more virulently opposed to Orthodox theology than the 'idolatrous' persuasion that godlikeness is tantamount to a cognitive process initiated and completed by man's natural faculties. And yet in Plethon the firm belief in man's capacity to achieve the intellection of 'Zeus' is sufficiently pronounced free of either the formal Renaissance concern to subjugate Platonism to Judaeo-Christianity or the biblical disguise employed by Pico. Plethon is an 'apostate' in so far as he pledges allegiance to the credo that man may comprehend god, undermines apophaticism and substitutes human notions about god for God, that is, revives conceptual idolatry.

To appreciate the radicalism of the Plethonean notion of intellectual illumination and epistemic optimism, due weight has to be given to its deep roots in Plato; further, to the resurgence of a distinctively Hellenic notion of illumination in the fourteenth century. In this chapter I argue that Plethon's reception of Platonic epistemology becomes meaningful only within the context of and against the background of the antagonism between the Palamite experiential notion of illumination and humanist Platonising intellectualism initiated by the Hesychast controversy.

But first, it is imperative to reconstruct Plethon's position on the human capacity to apprehend divinity. It will emerge that both the *Differences* and the *Nomoi* are ultimately pagan in one and the same way. This is by promoting a Platonic ideal of godlikeness, realisable through intellectual ascent alone. The core of Plethon's idolatry is not ritualistic – it is Platonic in the sense of replacing experiential *theoptia* with a purely contemplative type of *theoria*. Further, it will be shown that this type of conceptual paganism is present in Plethon's commentary on the *Chaldean Oracles* and in the *Monody for the Empress Helen*. Plethon made the same point in four works that belong to utterly different literary genres: in an academic treatise full of technical philosophical jargon (*Differences*); in a bizarre miscellany that uses mythology and pagan hymns as a means of conveying its symbolic theology (*Nomoi*); in the radical reinterpretation of a pagan sacred text (*Chaldean*

168

Oracles); and in an ostensible 'Trostschrift', the *Monody for the Empress Helen.*

The intellection of 'Zeus'

In Book I of the *Nomoi* Plethon advances a proto-deistic natural religion based on discursive reason:

Even if we admit that divine nature is far superior to our human nature, this hardly means that divine nature is for that reason unknowable (ἄγνωστον) – for we are rational beings and our nature is in no way utterly alien to divine nature. After all, the divine has rendered us capable of investigating its nature for precisely this reason, namely to investigate, and thus while investigating to learn about the divine, and while learning about the divine to profit as much as possible. In fact, by postulating as principles the common notions and revelations that gods have given to all people, or at least to the majority and the superior kind of men, we should hold firm on them – then we may by rigorous reasoning retrieve from those principles the propositions introduced by the wise men and –with the cooperation of the gods– we shall not fail to opt for what is best concerning all subjects. (*Nomoi* 42 (1.3.63–76)).

Here philosophy is liberated from the imperative of an exclusive religious revelation and attached to rational discourse. This is not the only place where Plethon prioritises rationality. Standing up for the Platonic world-view in the *Differences*, Plethon obliquely refers to a 'rational nature as a whole' that defines human conduct: 'We argue that god does not ordain human nature as a whole for the sake of any individual but individuals for the sake of human nature as a whole, and human nature itself for the benefit of rational nature as a whole.'[16] In the *Nomoi* he explicitly spells out the implications at the religious level. By conjoining the persuasion that god is knowable through 'common notions' shared by all men,[17] Plethon inevitably breaks at once with the monopoly of Christian religious exclusivism as well as with those versions of Platonism that prioritise the ineffability of the divine. But he

---

[16] Pleth. *Diff.* 325.11–16.

[17] The term 'common notions' (κοιναὶ ἔννοιαι) is characteristic of the philosophy of Chrysippus. Nikolaou (2004c: 31–4) plausibly argues that there are two possible sources for Plethon's reception of this doctrine: Plutarch's treatise Περὶ τῶν κοινῶν ἐννοιῶν πρὸς τοὺς Στωικούς and Proclus (see for example *In Ti.* 1.191.22ff.; 168.25ff.). The latter source is, according to Nikolaou, more probable.

goes further. Men and gods, he says, are after the same thing: a communal intellection of Zeus:

We would not say that gods have any task that is more important than the contemplation of beings (τῆς τῶν ὄντων θεωρίας), of which the summit is the intellection of Zeus (Διὸς ἔννοια). Clearly, man enjoys his communion in the contemplation of all other beings, while equally participating in the intellection of Zeus, until the furthest limit that gods themselves can reach. Hence, man is in need of an essence similar to that of gods, which will perform a similar task and which will be immortal too, since the essence of gods is immortal. (*Nomoi* 246 (3.43.70–8))

In a hymn to 'Zeus' Plethon presents another version of the leading idea of gods and men potentially participating in a communal contemplation of Being. Here, the human epistemological potential is explained in terms of a biological kinship with the divine. 'We' were born (γεγάαμεν) from the intellect (νοῦς) of 'Zeus', thus participating in those goods (τὰ καλά) enjoyed by the gods.[18] That this optimism was crucial to the Plethonean world-view may be confirmed by turning to a text that appears to be unrelated to the *Nomoi* project – though we shall see that upon closer scrutiny it is transmitting the same philosophical message: this is the *Monody for the Empress Helen*. There Plethon advances the view that man participates in the selfsame contemplation (θεωρία) of beings and intellection (ἔννοια) of 'the creator and producer of all' that determines the deeds and function of 'another nature' in between man and god. In other words, man and gods (here covertly present as *physeis* and *genera*) share the same aim: to comprehend the divine by virtue of contemplation.[19]

Θεωρία acquires a moral significance. In his treatise on virtues, Plethon defines *wisdom* (φρόνησις) as the contemplative *habitus* (ἕξις) discerning the proper essence of beings.[20] The point recurs in *Against Scholarios*. Contemplation as a form of cognitive speculation on the divine initiated by wisdom is expressly recognised as the most subtle of Plato's doctrines. Plato, we read, believed that without wisdom there cannot be any of the other virtues present.

---

[18] *Nomoi* 220 (3.35, 21.1–5).
[19] *Lampe, PP* 4.276.6–277.1; see below, Ch 6, p. 300 for a more detailed approach to the covert paganism of the *Monodia* and its analogies to the *Nomoi*.
[20] Pleth. *De virt.* a2.52: ἕξις ψυχῆς θεωρητικὴ τῶν ὄντων, ἥπέρ ἐστιν ἕκαστα.

Further, that 'the highest instance of wisdom is *theoria* and intellection (νόησις) of the supreme god'.[21]

The expression θεωρία τῶν ὄντων has a long history in the context of Orthodox mysticism and theology as a technical term to describe the immediate vision of reality. In *Capita CL* Palamas opposed the spiritual and supra-rational *theoria* to the contemporary revival of interest in matters such as the Hellenic belief in the eternity of the world, the notion of the World-soul and natural science.[22] Conversely, Plethon's application of the expression θεωρία τῶν ὄντων strips off its 'orthodox' significance. Rather than supra-rational, contemplation is rendered purely intellectual.

As it happens, *theoria* in Plethon provides one excellent reason to doubt the influential theory of Henry Corbin according to which Plethon was influenced by the illuminationist mystical philosophy of Shihab al-Din al-Suhrawardi (1154–91) preserved on Ottoman territory among Sufi circles.[23] The diametrical opposition between knowledge of god in Sufism and epistemology in Plethon finds corroboration in the fascinating similarities between Sufism and Palamas.[24] This is complemented by Plethon's attack on the Palamite notion of illumination in his commentary on the *Chaldean Oracles*.[25]

Where does Plethon get his notion of *theoria* from? A clue is provided in the passage quoted above concerning the collapse of

---

[21] Pleth. *Contra Schol.* 28.63–70.   [22] Gr. Pal. *Capita CL* 19–29.

[23] I deal with this possibility in Siniossoglou (2012).

[24] The crucial role of 'inner vision', 'existential receptivity', the heart as receptacle and psychophysical prayer point to a possible common source underlying Orthodox and Islamic mysticism: 'the locus of profound comprehension', writes Abu Hafs Umar as-Suhrawardi (539/1145–632/1234) (trans. in Renard 2004: 343–4) in tacit accord with Orthodox Hesychasm, 'is where conversation and mutual communication occur, namely, in the heart's hearing; and contemplative witnessing occurs in the heart's vision'. In Hesychasm incessant prayer aims to reach a point where the prayer is recited within the Hesychast's heart independently of his will through the mediation of the Holy Spirit. Suhrawardi draws from a homologous Sufi tradition: 'Ja 'far fell into a swoon while performing the ritual prayer. Someone asked him about that, and he answered, "I continued repeating the verse until I heard it from the One who spoke it" ' (trans. in Renard 2004: 351). In Suhrawardi 'knowledge is an integral reality granted by God to hearts'. The heart is 'like an ocean', a 'receptacle of being' used in 'experiential knowledge and contemplative vision' (trans. in Renard 2004: 337, 338, 334, 367–8). The Sufis renounce the world and 'the pores of their inner selves are opened and the ears of their hearts hear'. The 'hearts of the Sufis are attentive, for they discipline themselves in this world after becoming firmly grounded in reverential fear'.

[25] See below, p. 212.

the category distinction between human beings and gods at the epistemological level. This recalls Plato's myth in the *Phaedrus* and so does the wish to reach the absolute summit of intellection. In the *Phaedrus* the souls participate together with the gods in a struggle to acquire a vision of reality, namely to acquire knowledge of the Ideas. The gods 'climb the steep ascent even *unto the summit of the arch that supports the heaven*' (247b–c), for it is in that place beyond the heavens 'that true being dwells' and so do the souls. Both the human soul and the minds of gods are nourished by *reason* and *knowledge:*

> Now a god's mind is nourished by intelligence and pure knowledge, as is the mind of any soul that is concerned to take in what is appropriate to it, and so it is delighted at last to be seeing what is real and watching what is true, feeding on all this and feeling wonderful, until the circular motion brings it back to where it started. On the way around it has a view of Justice as it is; it has a view of Self-Control; it has a view of Knowledge . . . One [soul] that follows a god most closely, making itself most like that god, raises the head of its charioteer up to the place outside and is carried around in the circular motion with the others. Although distracted by the horses, this soul does have a view of Reality, just barely. (*Phdr.* 247d–248a; trans. Nehamas and Woodruff)

Plethon demythologises the *Phaedrus* myth and distils its doctrinal core. Psellos and Theodore Metochites had already moved in this direction. It is significant that in the *Phaedrus* myth the soul that has seen the most of Being 'shall not be planted in any brute beast' but shall dwell in a *philosopher*, while the soul that comes fifth in the race will lead the life of a *priest* or *prophet*.[26] This recalls Plethon's and Pico's belief that man as *methorion* is free and able to develop his bestial or divine inclination. According to the *Phaedrus*, philosophy takes up the highest place whereas hieratic art occupies one towards the end of the spectrum – only the Poet, the Artisan/farmer and the Sophist/demagogue separate the Priest from the absolute bottom: the Tyrant. Hieratical religion only mirrors philosophy. How could it be otherwise, since, according to the *Phaedrus*, the realm of true Being ('the place beyond heaven') is superior to the sphere of the gods and 'visible only to intelligence, the soul's steersman'.[27]

---

[26] *Phdr.* 248d–e.   [27] *Phdr.* 247 b–c.

The 'intellection of Zeus' in the *Nomoi*, the 'intellection of the creator of all' in the *Monody for the Empress Helen* and the 'intellection of the supreme god' in Plethon's *Against Scholarios* stand for the same notion: the apprehension of *theoria* as contemplation by means of wisdom and discursive faculties. Plethon was making the same point all along, that is, that the divine is knowable, thus not really beyond Being. We shall see that in recontextualising the 'Chaldean' oracles Plethon is faithful to this principle, also launching an attack on advocates of theurgy and experiential mysticism.

However, Plato's famous caveat in *Theaetetus* 176b, according to which godlikeness extends only as far as is possible to man, provides a cause for concern. How far can man know 'Zeus'/god, in other words, what are the limits of Platonic epistemology according to Plethon? There are good reasons to suspect that Plethon's reply to this question would be as 'unorthodox' for most Platonists as shocking to Orthodox theologians of his time. In the *Differences* he performs a movement that ensures an unlimited potential for pagan Platonic epistemology and underscores the radicalism of his Platonism. Plethon daringly questions Aristotle's persuasion that a science of the accidental is by default impossible. This move merits special attention.

In the *Metaphysics* Aristotle defines the accidental as 'whatever is neither *always* nor *usually* so' as it appears at a given instance. Hence cold during the summer may be called an accident. According to Aristotle there can be no science of the accidental. This is evident, he argues, because all scientific knowledge is of that which is *always* or *usually* so: 'how else indeed can one learn it or teach it to another?'[28] Plethon stretches the determinism and multi-causalism implied by the Platonic theory of the Ideas to the point of liberating the human capacity of comprehension from any need to compromise. According to his argument the manifestation of accidents is reducible to concurring causes. But then all causes can be shown to relate to the world of the Ideas. Given that the soul is illumined (ἐλλαμπομένην) by participation in the intelligible paradigm of the Ideas, it naturally follows that man

---

[28] *Metaph.* 1027a20–4.

is capable of comprehending even what appears to be occurring 'accidentally'. Crucially, illumination (ἔλλαμψις) does not come from without, but through the soul's natural kinship with the noetic paradigm:

As for the question whether accidental occurrences can be objects of knowledge, the answer is that such things arise from the conjunction of multiple causes, each of which can be referred to the other world, and from thence the soul can derive enlightenment (ἐλλαμπομένη) and so acquire knowledge about them too. This is what the Platonists would say in reply to the argument from the principles of knowledge. (*Diff.* 338.10–14)

Certain 'Platonists' would not disagree here. In Proclus' words, *episteme* is the 'illumination (ἔλλαμψις) of *nous*'.[29] As so often in the *Differences*, this attack on Aristotle is a covert anti-Christian statement. By arguing that there can be a science of accidents just as of what 'always or usually is as it is', Plethon challenged the veracity of supernatural experience. The Hesychast practices were purportedly empirically verifiable. The vision of the light of Thabor was the object of experience and not of scientific or abstract logical discourse. In this sense the empirical basis of Aristotelianism was a convenient point of reference that only the latent Platonic tendencies of anti-Hesychasts such as Barlaam and Gregoras and their explicit transformation in Plethon managed to shake off. Plethon's Platonism ruled out appeals to supra-rational illumination of the Hesychast type and *a fortiori* undermined the belief in miracles and the eventuality of a creation *ex nihilo*. Theodore of Gaza perceptively grasped the anti-Christian subtext in Plethon's departure from Aristotle. Plethon's position not only leads to determinism, he protests – it also excludes prayers and worship:

Yet he [Plethon] also leaves no room for accident, since the accident is the beginning and cause of existence, that is, the existence of things not by necessity nor always nor in general but as one of two possible results. Prayers too are at the same time ruled out and supplications and every kind of divine worship; for why should God be called merciful and saviour and protector and averter of evil if all things happen of necessity? (Thdr. Gaz. *De fato* 27.20–7 Taylor)

An excellent question indeed. Theodore's position is that what is likely or intended by God is not identical with what will actually

---

[29] Procl. *In Alc.* 274.21: εἰ τοίνυν ἐπιστήμη νοῦ ἔλλαμψίς ἐστιν.

be. Prayers and offerings, he says, influence the shift from what is intended to what will be. Which means that God listens to prayers. Things may change owing to 'all the customary works of a pious mind'.[30]

This is typical of how Aristotle was misread as supporting Christian theism. For Gaza does not address Aristotle's remark that the cause of things that come to be by accident is also accidental.[31]

Hairesis biou

In Book I of the *Nomoi* the query regarding 'the nature of everything (ἡ τῶν ὅλων φύσις)' leads to the more specific question regarding the nature of man (ὅτι ποτε ἐστιν ἄνθρωπος), which in its turn provides the answer to the question 'what is *eudaimonia*', which then supposedly reveals the right *hairesis biou* (way of life).[32] Epistemology leads to philosophical anthropology, which then leads to ethics and moral choice. Plethon catalogues possible and contradictory positions in regard to (a) moral conduct and virtue, (b) the question of whether there is one god or many gods, and (c) human nature. The Christian views on these topics are presented among others, though not identified as specifically Christian. Instead, they are attributed to 'certain sophists', who persuade people accordingly.[33]

This recalls the habit of late antique apologists of beginning their refutation of Hellenism by exposing the differences and conflicts among philosophers.[34] But Plethon does so in an odd way. Christianity is implied in the list of available choices, as one among others. Conversely, Christian authors from Justin to Palamas presupposed that Christianity was by default the *right* and exclusive choice, hence not to be listed among alternative philosophies and

---

[30] Thdr. Gaz. *De fato* 28.1–7.

[31] *Metaph.* 1027a9–10. As J. W. Taylor notes in the introduction to his edition of *De fato*, 10: Plethon 'at the very least did something to deliver philosophy from the obligation of reaching conclusions agreed to in advance'.

[32] *Nomoi* 20–2 (1.1.64–72; 1.1.80–93).

[33] For the use of the word 'sophists' here and Plethon's possible sources of inspiration see below, pp. 181, 387 and above, pp. 158–9.

[34] For the parallels between Christian apologetics and Plethon's advocacy of Hellenism see Tambrun (2006a) 60–3; Hanegraaff (2009) 40.

haireseis. Plethon thinks that 'there are some who think that reason and learning are unnecessary to acquire virtue', just as there are others who 'pursue a virtuous life not in order to get some prize but for the sake of virtue in itself'.[35] The plurality of available options accentuates the need to discern the right *hairesis biou*, namely to opt for the best way of life – not randomly, but after a careful study of ontology and human nature.

The advocacy of moral and epistemological realism is combined with an attack on hermeneutical and doctrinal relativism. Some doctrines are closer to truth than others, which means that truth *is* there, regardless of how many people endorse it at one point or another. Man should carefully examine and judge all options available until recovering 'the true doctrines, wherever they might be'.[36] It is only in this way, that man may approximate and assimilate true doctrines to the point of consciously, rather than randomly, directing his life and making choices accordingly:

> Along with other important teachers we assert that man's happiness (εὐδαιμονία) depends upon the accomplishment of actions that accord with his kinship (συγγένεια) with the gods. Accordingly, the aim of this book is to render those who listen to our words as happy as (εὐδαιμονεστάτους) a human being can be. (*Nomoi* 248 (3.43.82–8)).

Metaphysical and moral realism emerge as the upshot of the consistent effort to find the way between the Scylla of doctrinal exclusivity and the Charybdis of moral relativism. Admittedly, says Plethon, there is great confusion with regard to important questions. Still, one may 'carefully examine' each available option, thus judging which one truly reflects 'the optimal doctrines' (οἱ βέλτιστοι λόγοι). Firmly holding on to these 'optimal doctrines' man is able to resist the games of chance and randomness, avoid dilemmas and achieve *eudaimonia*.[37] This human capacity of recovering the 'optimal doctrines' as an antidote to agnosticism, fideism and scepticism is debated by Simmias in Plato's *Phaedo*, Plethon's source for the expression *hoi beltistoi logoi* in *Nomoi*:

> I believe, as perhaps you do, that precise knowledge on that subject is impossible or extremely difficult in our present life, but that it surely shows a very poor

---

[35] *Nomoi* 18 (1.1.28–31); 20 (1.1.60–1).   [36] *Nomoi* 26 (1.1.138): ὅπη ποτ' ἔχει.
[37] *Nomoi* 26 (1.1.135–43).

spirit not to examine thoroughly what is said about it, and to desist before one is exhausted by an all-round investigation. One should achieve one of these things: learn the truth about these things or find it for oneself, or, if that is impossible, *adopt the best and most irrefutable of men's theories, and, borne upon this, sail through the dangers of life as upon a raft, unless someone should make that journey safer and less risky upon a firmer vessel of some divine revelation. (Phd.* 85c–d; trans. Grube; my emphasis)[38]

Simmias seems to have a preference for divine revelation, this 'stronger vessel', as he puts it. Yet was this Plato's position? Simmias does not echo either Socrates or Plato. This is the man who argued that if the body is destroyed, then the soul cannot survive. For his part, Plethon opts for the second of the available positions: that man 'must take whatever human doctrine is best and hardest to disprove and, embarking upon it as upon a raft, sail upon it through life in the midst of dangers'. In so doing, Plethon interprets Plato. To the extent that the philosophy of the *Nomoi* is meant to conform to Platonic philosophy, as is programmatically stated, Plethon correctly acknowledges in Simmias a straw man: the stronger vessel is not divine revelation, but human reason. It is discursive reason, which Simmias does not deem to be trustworthy, that Plato employs by means of dialectic in order to uncover truth. Plethon sides with that school of interpretation according to which Plato sincerely believed in man's ability to know truth through the optimal teachings (οἱ βέλτιστοι λόγοι) and dialectical elenchos.[39]

Conversely Scholarios reads Plato as agreeing with Aristotle 'in many places in his dialogues' that man's intellectual resources are not sufficient to know 'the divine and lofty things' but require 'some sort of inspiration (ἐπίπνοια) that will illumine him and uplift him to that high level'.[40] After all, according to Scholarios'

---

[38] On Plethon's dependency on Plato on this point see also Demetracopoulos (2004) 87–8. Cf. *Crito* 46b, where Socrates explains his principle 'never to take advice unless rational examination shows that it is the best course that reason offers': μηδενὶ ἄλλῳ πείθεσθαι ἢ τῷ λόγῳ ὃς ἄν μοι λογιζομένῳ βέλτιστος φαίνηται. Cf. the relation of 'reason' and 'right opinion' to those few who are 'best by nature' and 'best educated' in *Resp.* 431c7: τοῖς βέλτιστα μὲν φῦσιν, βέλτιστα δὲ παιδευθεῖσιν.

[39] Cf. *Resp.* 604c–d, where reflection comes to the aid of man and 'as it were in the fall of the dice' helps us determine 'the movements of our affairs with reference to the numbers that turn up, in the way that reason indicates would be the best'. Hence the 'best part of us is willing to conform to the precepts of reason (λογισμός)'. See also Bargeliotes (1990).

[40] Schol. *Contra Pleth.*, OC 4.21.9–15.

interpretation, Plato agrees with Moses that mortal life is 'base' and 'full of passions', which is some sort of penalty for a 'passionate' form of lust.[41] Presumably this means that from a nature as corrupted as is the human one, we should not expect much.

The position that resurfaces with Plethon is that the real divine gift is no such *epipnoia* but rather the inherent ability to reason. Palamas, we have seen, attempted to turn away from precisely this conclusion when clashing with Byzantine humanists. How can one mistake anything innate in man as a spiritual and divine gift?[42] Palamas' theological triumph made abundantly clear that the true incomprehensible and dazzling divine inspiration was different to the 'daemonic inspiration' dear to pagan philosophers.[43] Now Plethon launches a counter-attack, reclaiming inspiration (ἐπί-πνοια) along the lines of a discursive endeavour rather than transcendental experience. In a passage reminiscent of the myth in the *Statesman*, mortality is seen as drawing man away from gods to wrong assumptions, which account for our tendency towards vice and error. The inspiration of 'reckonings of reason' bring man to the right track, either immediately, or after one suffers the consequences of wrongdoing:

> But on each occasion you [the gods] immediately lift us up and put us on the right track again (ἐπανορθώσαντες), either by means of an immediate inspiration (ἐπιπνοίᾳ) of the optimal reckonings of reason (ἀμείνονες λογισμοί) or by means of some sort of chastisements (δίκαι), in case a corrupted disposition inhibits us from immediately receiving the best reckonings of reason – it is thus that, one way or another, you dispense to us what is good, both in this world and in that beyond. (*Nomoi* 194 (3.34.5.139–46))

At the outset Plethon allows for an inspiration that is sent from the gods. Yet beyond the surface of the language of popular religion and ritual, inspiration is equated with cognition and, specifically, with the 'best reckonings of reason' (ἀμείνονες λογισμοί). Gods strengthen that most divine and kindred element in us: understanding (τὸ φρονοῦν).[44] But what are these optimal reckonings? Here, too, the ultimate source is Plato. In *Laws* book 10, a favourite

---

[41] Schol. *Contra Pleth., OC* 4.21.25–30.   [42] Gr. Pal. *Triads* 1.1.prol.6; 1.1.21.19–21.

[43] Palamas put it somewhat bluntly in *Triads* 1.1.15: Ἡ δὲ τοῖς δαίμοσι φίλη φιλοσοφία, πῶς ἂν εἴη Θεοῦ τε καὶ ἐκ Θεοῦ; Cf. *Triads* 1.3.18.

[44] *Nomoi* 148 (3.34,1.195–8).

source for Plethon, 'the motion and revolution and reckonings (λογισμοί) of reason (νοῦς)' are seen as homologous to the course and motion of heaven. From this, the Athenian stranger concludes that 'the best soul regulates the whole cosmos and drives it on its course'.[45] Plethon views gods as maintaining and regulating a metaphysical and moral order by realigning accordingly and restoring (ἐπανορθώσαντες) human conduct through reason. In the *Memoranda* too, the task is to achieve a restoration (ἐπανόρθωσις) of the *politeia* to its proper, most-virtuous, original condition.[46] Individual souls are readjusted to their proper configuration and the universe once guided by certain 'true doctrines' (τἀληθῆ δόγματα). These are not peculiar to particular people or conditioned by historical contingencies, but universally and eternally valid. The notion of 'true' opinions (τἀληθῆ δόγματα) itself is modelled upon Plato's discussion of *episteme* in the *Theaetetus*, where 'to hold true opinions' (τἀληθὲς δοξάζειν) is acknowledged as a good thing (καλόν) and deception as disgrace.[47] It also recalls Plato's 'true thoughts' in *Timaeus* 90b7–8 (ἀληθεῖς φρονήσεις). Plethon traces these precious doctrines to Zoroaster, Pythagoras, Plato and their successors. But there is a significant caveat: Zoroaster is not the initiator of these doctrines but their ancient and most prominent mediator.[48] Though obfuscated by irrationality and sophistry, truth resides in a permanent state of potential recovery and accessibility through philosophical discourse and rational inquiry:

True doctrines are coeval (συναΐδια) with the universe and mankind, even if they prevail at times over many people and at times over few. (*Nomoi* 252 (3.43.143–6)).

One encounters a tantalisingly similar formulation of this core doctrine in the *Philosophy of Illumination* by Suhrawardi, who is often seen as an indirect influence on Plethon. After praising Plato, Pythagoras and the Persian philosophers, Suhrawardi advises his disciples thus:

45 *Laws* 897c.
46 See below, Ch. 7. The term ἐπανόρθωσις is common in late antique Neoplatonism. See for example Iamb. *VP*. 6.30.19; 12.59.13.
47 *Tht.* 194c1–2. 48 *Nomoi* 252 (3.43.140–3).

Do not imagine that philosophy has existed only in these recent times. The world has never been without philosophy or without a person possessing proofs and clear evidences to champion it . . . Thus shall it be so long as the heavens and the earth endure. (Suhrawardi, *Phil. Illum.* 2.28–30)[49]

The *non velat umbra diem* principle is reflected in a source directly related to the 'Plethon affair'. On the aftermath of the destruction of the *Nomoi*, an anonymous follower of Plethon, of the likes of Kabakes or Apostoles, responded with an outrage targeting Scholarios and the political authorities.[50] The single sober observation in this bizarre text is that Scholarios' destruction of the *Nomoi* cannot prevent the survival of its doctrines. The man who wrote this note was not merely a loyal follower and admirer of Plethon, but a carrier of a significant element of Plethon's esoteric outlook as presented in the *Nomoi*. This is the optimistic view that man naturally tends to knowledge and science and that, as the anonymous Plethonist has it, 'the delivery of what is useful' can be only temporarily obstructed.[51] Contingent obstacles, such as the 'superstition', 'want of knowledge' and 'hatred' personified by Scholarios, according to Plethon's disciple, stop certain messengers, yet the message will eventually come through owing to its natural connection with what is good in human soul. The origins of this belief are Platonic and Aristotelian; strong parallels exist in theosophic Kabbalah.[52]

Plethon's predilection for Plato and Zoroaster may misleadingly appear as an appeal to authority. In reality, it is the result of transferring to epistemology a principle of Platonic ontology, namely that phenomena are preceded by their essence, imperfection by perfection, error by truth.[53] Plethon does not opt for a regression in time and an older paradigm *because* of its purported antiquity but because he reasons, as Plato does in the *Philebus*, that this

---

[49] For an extended discussion see here Siniossoglou (2012).   [50] See above, p. 147.

[51] Anon. Πρὸς Πλήθωνα, ἢ περὶ τῆς βίβλου 409–10 Alexandre.

[52] See below, Ch. 6, p. 290.

[53] For how could one argue, says Proclus, that Nature produced what is less perfect but did not provide the essence of what *is* perfect?; Procl. *Scholia in Euc.* 140.10. The same argument resurfaces in a deist such as Cudworth: observing imperfection, so familiar to us, we understand that perfection exists: 'So that perfection is first conceivable, in order of nature, as light before darkness, a positive before the privative or defect' (Copleston (1999) 58).

should be in closer proximity to the original truth progressively corrupted by an accretion of successive errors.[54] Plethon's epistemic optimism attempts an approximate recovery of archetypical and thus communal rational apprehensions of the divine, world and man ('true doctrines'), which recalls the approximate realisability of his political utopianism. This accounts for a type of Platonist metaphysical and moral realism. But it also calls for serious work on ancient philososophy, to the extent that 'true doctrines' are retrievable through a combination of rational enquiry and hermeneutics:

We shall follow the beliefs and sayings of the most ancient times and of the wisest men of all, and using rational discourse (λογισμός), which is the most powerful and divine of our means for judging (κριτήρια), we shall determine, as far as possible, on the basis of precise comparisons the best (τὸ βέλτιστον) in each case. (*Nomoi* 34 (1.2.93–8))

Plethon addresses the eventuality of someone's finding truth by accident. Some sort of 'divine chance' might help one stumble upon truth, thus setting aside the necessity of utilising one's cognitive apparatus. Yet by no means is such a man *really* happy. Recovered truth matters only in so far as it constitutes *episteme*:

For it is not enough to think that we are happy, which is sometimes the case with lunatics too, if we do not possess firm knowledge of how happiness does occur; further, what is good and bad for man and why this is so. (*Nomoi* 40–2 (1.3.56–9))

The attempt to establish a science of moral behaviour echoes the Stoic distinction between κατορθώματα and καθήκοντα. The former correspond to actions that are not merely right, but right for the correct reason. In *Memorandum to Theodore* this contention is applicable in politics. The situation in a *politeia* may be good owing to a coincidence of contingent factors – yet its future will be uncertain, for circumstances shift.[55] Obviously then, the 'wicked sophists' attacked in the *Nomoi* are not the proper guides, either in regard to how one should live his life or in politics. They are innovators, who 'never give any worthwhile explanation for the

---

54 *Phlb.* 16c: 'the ancients, who were better than we and lived nearer the gods . . .'
55 *Mem. I* 116.20–4.

things they keep on saying but pretend to possess firm knowledge obtained from some prophetic power, which supposedly descends to them from the gods'.[56] There is an anti-Palamite pun at work here: the 'sophists' failed to establish the route to happiness and to *aristos bios*.

Enlightenment by divine revelation is one of two targets in Book I of the *Nomoi*. The other target is moral and metaphysical relativism. Plethon's devastating criticism of Pyrrhonian scepticism as well as of Protagoras is meant to combat its two main variations: the belief that truth is by default inaccessible and that man is the measure of all things. Since late antiquity the disbelief in the human capacity to know god famously pronounced by Xenophanes (DK B34) found its way into Christian apologetics. The appeal to agnosticism purportedly discredited 'Hellenic' optimism and rationalism and by implication strengthened unconditional belief in divine revelation. Plethon defends his realism by launching a preliminary attack on what is, to all appearances, a contemporary application of ancient agnosticism:

We should not pay attention to what some say, namely that we cannot get a firm hold of truth in regard to anything and that it is not appropriate to speculate about divine nature owing to our human nature, that is, because we are supposedly incapable of learning anything certain about the divine nature. [They claim that this is so] because the divine nature is superior to ours and because gods are supposedly displeased with our inquiring about and interfering in their affairs. (*Nomoi* 40 (1.3.34–40))

'That it is not appropriate to speculate about divine nature given our human nature' was a claim made in the framework of the Hesychast controversy. Barlaam initially argued that there is no definition, axiom or syllogistic method applicable to the question of the divine. Proof may be provided for what is within the grasp of intellectual faculties, not for what is outside. Gregory Palamas saw here an obvious danger for doctrinal Orthodoxy. Barlaam rendered theological discourse obsolete. Like the 'pagan' Hellenes, he downgraded theology to a πιθανολογία.[57] If anything appertaining to god is fundamentally mysterious, as certain anti-Hesychasts

---

[56] *Nomoi* 34 (1.2.98–102).

[57] See Sinkewicz (1980) and (1982: 197) for Palamas' accusations and a criticism of his reading of Barlaam. On Plethon's anti-scepticism see also Matula (2008) 60–4.

claimed, then the exclusivity claimed by monastic and clerical indoctrination is seriously compromised. The claim that god was ultimately unknown provided the perfect alibi for deviating from Orthodoxy and the officially certified tradition of the Fathers. Plethon had other reasons to agree with Palamas that agnostic and sceptical tendencies should be eradicated. When carried too far, the humanist experiments potentially threatened the certainties of his pagan theology no less than they threatened those of Palamism. If one cannot speculate about the birth of Jesus, the Holy Spirit or god, as Barlaam and the anti-Hesychasts argued, then why should one speculate about 'Zeus', 'Poseidon' or Zoroaster? As in the case of his support for the Greeks in the Synod of Ferrara/Florence in 1438/9, the real concern was not to safeguard Roman Orthodoxy, but to defend the presuppositions necessary for reviving a purely pagan Platonic world-view.

Methorion

What renders Plethon's optimism possible in the first place? In direct contravention to Palamite apophaticism, which made of God an impenetrable, incomprehensible and radically transcendent divine darkness, Plethon argued that the divine is knowable owing to an immortal essence in man. This is the doctrine of man as μεθόριον that Plethon had fully developed by 1440/3. Plethon openly presented his ideas in Constantinople in the *Reply to Certain Questions*, a short treatise meant to clarify certain points in the *Differences* that attracted the attention of political authorities and intellectuals.[58] In the *Reply* Plethon attacked Alexander of Aphrodisias and distinguished between the mortal aspect of man and his rational part (λογικόν).[59] For the first time Plethon advanced the idea featured in the *Nomoi* that the mixture of mortality and immortality in man serves universal harmony and accounts for man's participation in All.[60] The term μεθόριον used by Plethon is

---

[58] For the dating and background see Benakis (1974) 332–3.   [59] Benakis (1986) 62–3.
[60] See Benakis (1986) 63: σύνθετόν τι χρῆμα ὁ ἄνθρωπος ὑπὲρ τῆς τοῦ παντὸς ἁρμονίας καὶ ἀθανάτου τε καὶ θνητῆς ἐν ἡμῖν μίξεως τῷ θεῷ μεμηχανημένον τῆς τῶν ὅλων ἕνεκα ἐν ἡμῖν κοινωνίας τὸ θνητὸν τόδε ἐνδεδήκαμεν. On the doctrine of *methorion* in the *Nomoi* see Nikolaou (1982), Matula (2003) and Bargeliotes (1979).

Plotinean. In Plotinus the soul is in a borderline situation: μεθόριον οὖσα.[61] It is *amphibious*, for it never wholly participates in the world of matter; it lives partly in the intelligible life and partly in the life in this world.[62] The term *methorion* applied to the human soul is also used by Philo and Plutarch as well as by the fourth-century iatro-philosopher Nemesius, who disconnects *reason* (τὸ λογικόν) from human mortality, seeing it as the divine link to the intelligible realm.[63]

The Platonic origin of this notion is to be found in *Timaeus* 90c where the rational soul-part is recognised as 'the divine element in us'. Similar formulations regarding man's intermediate position are common to Neoplatonists,[64] echoing *Philebus'* account (26b) of the mixture of opposites in man and the universe, as well as the mixed nature of love in the *Symposium*.[65] In the late Byzantine context Demetrios Kydones is the carrier of a variant of this thesis that might have inspired Plethon's radical return to its Platonic origin. Kydones rated man's cognitive faculties as intermediate between the purely intellectual and the sensible realm, thus enabling man to achieve a knowledge of the archetypical Forms by means of rational discourse.[66] In Renaissance philosophy Plethon's *methorion* found its possibly better-known equivalent in the conception of a *copula mundi* developed by Pico, Ficino and Pomponazzi.[67]

The moral and psychological implications of the *methorion* doctrine are spelled out in detail only in the *Nomoi*. Contrary to those who elevate the human soul to divine nature 'according to their wishful thinking', Plethon affirms that the human soul occupies an intermediate position between mortality and divinity and consists of irreducible brutal or animal-like elements combined with

---

[61] *Enn.* 4.4.3.10–12.   [62] *Enn.* 4.8.4.31–5; 4.8.8.1–3; 4.8.7.1–8.

[63] Plut. *De defectu oraculorum* 416c; Philo, *De opificio mundi* 135.10–11: διὸ καὶ κυρίως ἄν τις εἴποι τὸν ἄνθρωπον θνητῆς καὶ ἀθανάτου φύσεως εἶναι μεθόριον. See here the note by Paul Kalligas to Plot. *Enn.* 4.4.3.10–12 in his translation of Plotinus (p. 434). The affinity with Nemesius has been noted by Benakis (1986) 63; Nem. *De natura hominis* 1.51–5; 1.127.

[64] Ammon. *In Cat.*, CAG 4.4, 37.17: μέσην γὰρ ἔχει τάξιν. Plot. *Enn.* 4.8.7.5: μέσην τάξιν. Plot. *Enn.* 3.2.8: ἄνθρωποι δὲ ἐν μέσῳ καὶ κάτω.

[65] It is noteworthy that Gregory of Nazianzus developed a similar theory of man as a mixture of mundane and heavenly qualities (κρᾶμα ἀμφοτέρων). Gr. Naz. *In theophania* (*orat.* 38), PG 36.321–324.17.

[66] Medvedev (1981) 536.   [67] Medvedev (1981) 546.

elements that are immortal and akin to gods.[68] By affirming the reciprocal metaphysical and social function of these elements, Plethon breaks, on one level, with the allegedly Plotinean (according to Porphyry) distaste for bodily constitution, descent (γένος) and homeland (πατρίς).[69]

On a second level, Plethon reverses current monastic views on sexuality. The reason, he says, why gods planted in human beings a sexual drive that is so strong is precisely in order to avoid the error of sexual abstinence and thus remove an obstacle to the communion (κοινωνία) of mortal and immortal elements regulated by 'Zeus'. Owing to divine providence, says Plethon, human sexuality naturally overpowers the opinion (δόξα) that advocates total abstinence from sexual activity. That here Plethon is targeting the monasticism of his time is apparent from the note: 'as is nowadays too the case with certain people'.[70] Gods ensure that the opinion of these people is doomed to exercise a limited appeal and inflict minimal damage on human society – 'that is to say, if man is to be above all a citizen (πολίτης) and not an isolated being (μονώτης)'.[71] Owing to his dual nature, man may potentially degrade himself to the level of a beast, or, thanks to his kinship with gods, elevate himself to the point of complementing the universal harmony, which he is predisposed to serve:

the human soul is sent from the gods to unite with the mortal body on a regular basis, each time with another body, in order to serve the harmony of the universe, so that the communion and union of mortal nature and immortal nature in us contributes to the binding together of the All. (*Recapitulation* 266)

In the *Nomoi* the potential capacity of the human soul to energise itself is contrasted with the permanent actuality of the divine. Divine essence is identifiable with divine energy: 'Zeus' is incessantly in a state of constant actuality. His power is invariable and never stripped bare of its effectiveness. By contrast, the essence of the human soul is distinct from its energy, which remains idle and falls to an inactive state.[72] Plethon is repeating a *topos* in Proclus, namely that divine essence and activity are indistinguishable. As

---

[68] *Nomoi* 246 (3.43.61–4).   [69] Porph. *Plot.* 1.1–3.
[70] *Nomoi* 122 (3.31.40–41): οἷα καὶ νῦν συμβαίνει ἐνίοις.
[71] *Nomoi* 122–4 (3.31.39–56).   [72] *Nomoi* 54 (1.5.133–6).

one 'Chaldean' *logion*, has it, the essence of god is interchangeable with god's thoughts (ὄντως οὐσίαι καὶ ὄντως νοήσεις, καὶ ὁμοῦ ἄμφω).[73] This is the exact opposite of Palamas' famous distinction between essence and energies in god. Prochoros Kydones, we shall see, was anathematised for reverting to this Platonising claim.

The thesis concerning the possibility of a 'communion and union of mortal nature and immortal nature' that results in cosmic harmony echoes the Platonic blueprint of all versions of epistemic optimism. I mean *Timaeus* 90b–d. Plato and Plethon share a belief in man's capacity to choose between developing the mortal or the immortal aspect of his soul [1]. The Platonic description of 'the divine part within us' [2] is mirrored in the Plethonean doctrine of inner kinship with the gods. More substantively, Plato approaches godlikeness in terms of aligning the right motion of man's soul with the intellections of the Universe [3]. Equally noteworthy are the priority of intellectual contemplation [4] with regard to both godlikeness and *eudaimonia*, and the linguistic affinity between Plethon's 'true doctrines' (τἀληθῆ δόγματα) in the *Nomoi* and the Platonic 'true wisdom' (ἀληθεῖς φρονήσεις) [5]:

So if a man has become absorbed in his appetites or his ambitions and takes great pains to further them, all his thoughts are bound to become merely mortal. And so far as it is at all possible for a man to become thoroughly mortal, he cannot help but fully succeed in this, seeing that he has cultivated his mortality all along.

On the other hand [1], if a man has seriously devoted himself to *the love of learning* and to *true wisdom* (ἀληθεῖς φρονήσεις) [5], if he has exercised these aspects of himself above all, then there is absolutely no way that his thoughts can fail to be *immortal* and *divine*, should truth come within his grasp. And to the extent *that human nature can partake of immortality*, he can in no way fail to achieve this: constantly *caring for his divine part* as he does [2], keeping well-ordered the guiding spirit that lives within him, he must indeed be *supremely happy*. Now there is but one way to care for anything, and that is to provide for it the nourishment and the motions that are proper to it. And the motions that have an affinity to the divine part within us are the thoughts and revolutions of the universe [3]. These, surely, are the ones which each of us should follow. We should redirect the revolutions in our heads that were thrown off course at our birth, by coming to learn the harmonies and revolutions of the universe, and so bring into conformity with its objects *our faculty of understanding*, as it was in its original condition [4]. And when this conformity is complete, we shall have

---

[73] Procl. *In Prm.* 895.15–6; *Orac. Chald.* 38 des Places.

achieved our goal: *that most excellent life* offered to human kind by the gods, both now and forevermore. (*Timaeus.* 90b–d; trans. Zeyl)

David Sedley observed that in this passage Plato conveys 'the physics of happiness, with regard to our own psychological constitution and to the structure of the cosmos'. It is safe to equate the 'godlike contemplator envisaged in the *Timaeus* with the prisoner who, having escaped from the Cave, is free to survey the hierarchy of the Forms'.[74] In both cases, epistemic optimism is well founded on the belief that the philosopher's intellect (διάνοια) may by means of its own native disposition (φύσει) find its way to the 'ideal reality in all things'.[75] In the *Timaeus* the study of astronomy and mathematics leads the way to the realignment of the intellect's circular motions according to the paradigm of the World-soul.[76]

The Platonic and Plethonean notion of a temporal alignment between man and the divine is best exemplified in *Laws* Book 10: 'for the whole is not brought into being for your sake, but you are for its sake'.[77] It is also announced in Plotinus, according to whom the descent of the soul in this world occurs for the sake of the perfection (τελείωσις) of the universe.[78] Against the background of centuries of Christian apologetics and theology, Plethon's revival of this model acquires a revolutionary dimension. In the late Byzantine context this was tantamount to a metaphysical *mundus inversus*, in so far as man is taken to exist for the sake of universal harmony – rather than the universe for the benefit of man.[79]

This is commonly felt to be an expressly anti-Christian and typically pagan philosophical position which, as Zizioulas notes, 'contrasts sharply with the Biblical and Patristic view that man was created *after* the world was brought into being and indeed *for his sake*'.[80] In Maximus Confessor we find its full Christian reversal. Quoting Gregory of Nazianzus, Maximus asserts that the physical world is a *microcosm* – and that man is the *macrocosm*.

---

74 Sedley (1999) 327.   75 *Resp.* 486d.   76 See also *Phlb.* 67c–d; *Laws* 818c.
77 *Laws* 903c–d.   78 *Enn.* 4.8.5.2
79 See also Pleth. *Diff.* 325.11–16 on the primacy of the rational nature of man and of the whole over the part, and the opposed Judaeo-Christian view shared by e.g. Nemesius, *De nat. hom.* 8–9.
80 Zizioulas (1985) 32 n. 17a.

Covered by sin, nature is inferior to humanity.[81] It appears that already before Plethon, Byzantine humanists were slowly moving towards a re-examination of the relation between man and nature. Palamas' *Capita CL* testifies to a fourteenth-century revival of profane naturalism that concurs with the increased popularity of texts such as Aristotle's *De mundo*,[82] a text that serves, we shall see, as a hallmark of the pagan sacralisation of the physical world. In an attempt to obstruct the humanist project, Palamas charged the Hellenic sages with 'dishonouring our own nature and acting impiously towards God', for missing the crucial point: that man alone was created in the image of his Maker, which means, among other things, that man 'might know that all things which this heaven and earth bear are inferior to himself and completely devoid of intelligence'.[83]

Jean Baudrillard saw in this tenet of Christian theology the perfect alibi and metaphysical justification for man's conquest of the physical world and the manipulation of the physical resources.[84] Taking a step further and assuming the viewpoint of philosophical paganism, Alain de Benoist criticised the Christian desacralisation of the physical world, with all that this entails.[85] On the other hand, Orthodox Christians readily condemned in Platonism a deterministic model that reduced any notion of man as a free person (πρόσω-πον) to that of an actor carrying a mask in a tragedy (προσωπεῖον) of cosmic proportions. The pagan ideal of unity between man and the world oppressed man by introducing a type of rational and moral necessity.[86] Against such a philosophical and theological clash of world-views, it is a correct assumption that Plethon was effectively reacting to the Christian demystification of the physical world.[87] Besides, his return to the pagan understanding

---

[81] Max. Conf. *Ambigua*, PG 91.1096A; 1104A–B.
[82] See the introduction by Sinkewicz to *Capita CL*, 7–8, 13.
[83] Gr. Pal. *Capita CL* 26.8–12.   [84] Baudrillard (1975) 43–5.
[85] For the pagan criticism on the Christian desacralisation of the physical universe, see de Benoist (1990).
[86] See the stimulating remarks by Zizioulas (1985) 32 and Sherrard (1974: 121), who reads Plethon against the background of the theological clash between the Hellenic notion of god as identifiable 'with an intelligible cosmic order' and the Christian one that transfers the accent 'from the world without to the world within'.
[87] Sherrard (1974) 122. See below, Ch. 5, for Plethon's re-sacralisation of the physical universe.

of the relation between microcosm and macrocosm is intertwined with the typically pagan belief in predestination and *heimarmene* that caused the angry reaction of Matthew Kamariotes in his rebuttal of *De fato*. Nature was created for man's sake, objects Matthew, man is the ruler of nature and the whole creation pays tribute to man as if man were king. Conversely, Plethon allows for the natural bodies to influence human conduct.[88]

In the *Differences* Plethon provocatively implied that nature (φύσις) reveals the reality of the intelligible realm more fully than do human arts: 'For if art imitates nature, as Aristotle himself holds, then nature cannot be inferior to art: on the contrary, *nature must long beforehand possess that which constitutes art in an even higher degree.*'[89] Still, nature reflects and stems from the same source as human art does. This is the divine intellect. Nature is an institution of god (θεοῦ θεσμός) that is necessarily rational, since 'no institution of god could possibly be irrational'.[90] But everything in nature is *also* the product of a divine *art*. Plethon adds this theological dimension and notes its absence from Aristotle:

Of Aristotle's predecessors, it seems to me that it is Anaxagoras whom he mainly admires, to go by his writings. For Anaxagoras began by making the intellect (νοῦς) preside over all things but went on to pursue his argument without reference to the intellect, thus inclining to atheism. Similarly Aristotle makes various gods preside over our universe, and yet in most of his writings he seems to make no mention of the divine, but rather inclines as near as he can to atheism. This is not the case with Plato, either in the context we are now discussing or anywhere else. *On the contrary, he discusses the two arts of god and man, both of which require intellect* (νοῦς). *To the human art he attributes every artefact, to the divine art everything that occurs naturally.* In Pindar's felicitous phrase, god may be described as the supreme artist.[91] (*Diff.* 332.10–23)

[88] Matt. Kamariotes, *Contra Pleth.* 146–8: καὶ γὰρ ἡ πᾶσα κτίσις ὡς βασιλεῖ τῷ ἀνθρώπῳ δωροφορεῖ.

[89] *Diff.* 332.2–6.   [90] *Diff.* 332.9–10.

[91] For a discussion of the *physis/techne* relation in Plethon see Couloubaritsis (1986) 333–40 and Bargeliotes (1980) 198–201. Couloubaritsis sees in Plethon's account of man and god as productive agents the fundamentally modern claim for a 'philosophie par excellence du Sujet' – in this sense the *Differences* is 'un texte essentiel et fondateur de notre modernité'. On Plethon and modernity see Ch. 9, pp. 418ff. Plethon returns to Aristotle's presumed inclination to atheism, as well as to polyarchy in *Against Scholarios*.

Plethon's attribution of rationality to the art of nature draws on Plato's attribution of rationality to any *techne* in the *Gorgias* (Socrates: 'I refuse to give the name of art to anything that is irrational'). There, *techne* is differentiated from habitude (ἐμπειρία) on the grounds that empirical practice 'has no account to give of the real nature of the things it applies, and so cannot tell the cause of any of them'.[92] This recognition of *physis* as a *techne* establishes a firm connection between rationality in nature, man as a rational creator of artefacts, and the divine intellect responsible for both.

Plethon's Plato

From where Plethon was standing, Proclus' philosophical speculations were not that far removed from Palamas' doctrine that 'certain aspects of god are knowable and may be proven', namely the 'divine energies', whereas 'others are unknowable and unprovable', namely divine essence.[93] In fact, Proclus' commentary on the *Parmenides* ends with a concession to *silence*. This would surely ring a bell in the context of the fourteenth- and fifteenth-century intellectual civil war regarding Hesychasm. Late antique Neoplatonism made too many concessions to theurgy and thus to apophaticism and the empirical approach to godlikeness.

Proclus thought that the One, properly speaking, excludes, among other things, the various *genera* of Being; *a fortiori*, the One excludes any notion of 'participation in substance; being existence itself; being participable by existence; expressibleness; knowableness'.[94] Palamas and Scholarios would undoubtedly second this enthusiastically. Proclan apophaticism could be appropriated at any time in order to make Hesychasm philosophically sustainable. It serves well the Orthodox pivotal position that god is unqualifiable in regard to essence but knowable in his energies. In order to combine the type of 'negative theology', with which the first hypothesis of Plato's *Parmenides* ends, with Parmenides' notion of One Being, Proclus drew an analogous distinction. The

---

[92] *Gorg.* 465a.   [93] Gr. Pal. *Ep.* 4.11.13–14.
[94] Procl. *In Prm.* 66κ (Dillon and Morrow p. 598); *De providentia et fato* 4.172.

One itself is 'unparticipable' (ἀμέθεκτος) as a 'whole-before-the-parts', whereas as a 'whole-of-parts' it *is* 'participable' (μεθεκτός) by all beings: 'that which is participated by the many beings is not the only Being, but prior to it is the unparticipated'.[95] This may well mean that the real essence of god is superior to its qualifiable manifestations or 'energies', as Palamas has it.

Proclus' massive commentary of hundreds of pages ends with a sentence that is bound to please mystics and may be read as announcing the Palamite notion of *hesychia*. Aristoteles, we read, follows Parmenides in passing from the nature of Being to the inexpressible itself: 'It is with *hesychia*, then, that he brings to completion the study of the One.'[96] It is *stillness* that has the last word. Platonic philosophy ends in mysticism and apophaticism. Proclus concurs with Pseudo-Dionysius, a source most dear to Palamas.[97] Proclus would thus agree that the Palamites are more faithful to Neoplatonic spirit than are Thomists: it is apophaticism that follows on from where he left off, not scholasticism.

Clearly then, for all its discursive merits Proclan Neoplatonism could neither challenge Hesychasm nor offer a philosophical alternative able to challenge political authority by provoking the religious *status quo*. Barlaam and Nikephoros Gregoras were not far from the truth when accusing Palamas of Proclan Neoplatonism. Orthodox mystical theology successfully put Neoplatonism to its service. In order to battle against the mysticism of his age, Plethon needed to leave behind the burden of an introvert, defeatist and passive late antique Neoplatonism bordering on obscurantism and incapable of inspiring belief in the feasibility of knowing god, grasping Being, reforming society. To provide an escape route from Palamite *hesychia* Plethon first needed to provide one out of Proclus' embarassing *hesychia*.

This was a good incentive to part from established interpretations of Platonic epistemology. After all, Plato had not always

95 Procl. *ET* 67; *In Prm.* 710.1–12.
96 This last part of the commentary is preserved in Latin translation (*In Prm.* 76K; trans. by Morrow and Dillon, p. 603). Wittgenstein provides the most famous modern version of this thesis: 'Whereof one cannot speak, thereof one must be silent.'
97 Dion. Ar. *DN* 218.7–9.

been read that way. Plotinus, Celsus and Porphyry did not necessarily make concessions to ritualism. It was Iamblichus who,
not least in order to compete with the hieratic aspect of Christianity, developed an antagonistic ritualistic system that abandoned
Plotinean intellectual mysticism and prioritised divine grace over
contemplation.[98] Damascius sums up the difference between the
two main streams of Platonism:

> To some philosophy is primary, as to Porphyry and Plotinus and a great many other
> philosophers; to others hieratic practice, as to Iamblichus, Syrianus, Proclus, and
> the hieratic school generally. Plato, however, recognizing that strong arguments
> can be advanced from both sides, has united the two into one single truth by
> calling the philosopher a 'Bacchus'; for by using the notion of a man who has
> detached himself from genesis as an intermediate term, we can identify the one
> with the other. Still, it remains evident that he intends to honour the philosopher
> by the title of Bacchus, as we honour the Intelligence by calling it God, or profane
> light by giving it the same name as mystic light. (Dam. *In Phaedonem* 1.172;
> trans. Westerink).

Notwithstanding Damascius' integrity and sincere efforts to
achieve a *symphonia* between the ends of philosophy and theurgy
(that is to say *theokrasia*, a 'fusion with the divine'), a case
can be made that Plethon's revival of a contemplative or intellectual route to godlikeness is more faithful to Plato's original
epistemology than was Neoplatonic theurgy – further, that it
cannot be absorbed and dissolved within the dominant Judaeo-
Christian ritualistic framework, as was the case with Neoplatonic
theurgy.

According to the pre-Plotinean approach to Plato's epistemology the Idea of the Good is not beyond knowledge and hence
not beyond Being.[99] The Good is *an idea* and *paradeigma* apprehensible by thought. But no idea and *paradeigma* can absolutely
transcend Being and still be an *idea* and *paradeigma*: if the Idea
of the Good is intelligible (νοητόν) then it also possesses being

---

[98] To my knowledge, Zintzen (1983: 328) is one of the few scholars to have noted the
implicit anti-Christian motivation in Iamblichus' advocy of theurgy. On Neoplatonic
intellectual mysticism see Siniossoglou (forthcoming).

[99] See *Resp.* 508e: 'and though it [the Idea of the Good] is the cause of knowledge and
truth, it is also an object of knowledge'. Cf. *Resp.* 517a–b, where the man who exits the
darkness of the cave 'is able to *to see the sun, not images of it in water* or some alien
place, *but the sun itself*, in its own place, and be able to study it'.

(ὄν).[100] In the light of pre-Plotinean interpretation, 'beyond Being' in *Republic* 509b does not imply any radical ontological alterity and hence real super-essentiality of the Good. Rather, the Idea of the Good is beyond the essence of beings in so far it is Being in its extremity; still, it *is* Being. *Mutatis mutandis*, the same applies to the Plethonean 'Zeus'. If the intellection of the primary principle is possible by means of cognitive faculties, then 'Zeus' is not really super-essential, but only relatively so, namely in so far as Zeus is the cause of the essence of the intelligibles.[101]

Scholarios appears to have been unsure whether Plethon's persuasion that reason may ascend to truth was Platonic, as he is claiming, rather than Aristotelian.[102] He was right. Aristotle is also a representative of the view that truth is an achievement of the human capacity to comprehend.[103] But a distinction should be made. Aristotle's optimism concerns the knowledge of particulars; it does not promise access to any realm of eternal Forms. This potentially leaves the supernatural to the monopoly of the Church. As Pierre Aubenque has shown, Aristotelian logic and metaphysics share an apophatic or negative dimension that underscores the non-applicability of human categories in theology.[104] By contrast, Platonism claims a knowledge that transcends

---

[100] See Baltes (1997) 5, 11 and n. 27 for references to *Resp.* 505a, 508e, 517b, 534b and 540a.

[101] Cf. Alcinous/Albinus *Didaskalikos* 10 and Celsus *ap.* Orig. 7.45; Dörrie and Baltes (1996) 107.2, 107.3: God is different from the act of cognition but comprehensible, in the same manner as the sun is different from sight, but can be seen. Celsus in particular seems to anticipate Plethon's epistemology in two ways: first in considering the Idea of the Good as intelligible, and second by distinguishing a particular power, the 'eye of the soul', which can access god by the intellectual faculties of *synthesis*, *analysis* and *analogia*. See Orig. *Cels.* 7.42. Hence arguments used to show why the Idea of the Good cannot be beyond being in *Resp.* 509b are perfectly applicable in the case of Plethon's use of *hyperousios* for the first principle in both the *Nomoi* and the *Differences*. For a full discussion see below, Ch. 5, pp. 243–50.

[102] Schol. *Contra Pleth.*, *OC* 4.16.31–9.

[103] See *Rh.* 1355a14–18 (my emphasis): 'to see both the truth and what is similar to it belongs *to one and the same capacity*, and at the same time people have *a sufficient natural disposition towards truth*, and in most cases they reach it; that is why someone likely to hit on reputable opinions is also someone likely to hit on the truth'. Note that the human capacity to reach truth is innate and sufficient.

[104] Aubenque (1962) 288–9, 362–3, 376–80 and *passim*. To the extent that according to Aristotle (and Solon) no man can be said to have been happy during his lifetime, Aubenque (1962: 468) traces the consequences of Aristotelean apophaticism for moral philosophy.

experience, thus functioning as an antagonist to any religion's claiming exclusivity. Platonic epistemic optimism as conceived by Plethon attributes to the human condition possibilities that both Neoplatonic theurgy and the medieval reception of Aristotle denied.

John of Damascus is particularly instructive on why and how the Middle Platonic as well as the Plethonean version of Platonism could seriously threaten to demolish the very essence of Christian Orthodoxy: 'knowledge is appropriate to beings; it follows that what is beyond knowledge (τὸ ὑπὲρ γνῶσιν) in all respects is also beyond essence (τὸ ὑπὲρ οὐσίαν), and, *mutatis mutandis*, what is beyond essence is also beyond knowledge'.[105] God did not transmit to man his essence – by implication, he did not transmit knowledge of his essence either.[106] Let us not 'shift eternal boundaries, nor go beyond the divine tradition (μὴ μεταίροντες ὅρια αἰώνια μηδὲ ὑπερβαίνοντες τὴν θείαν παράδοσιν)', says John.[107] By contrast, the knowability of divinity compromises the radical transcendence, ontological alterity and freedom of God as a personal agent. This is the culmination of pagan epistemology, one which Christian authors opposed or avoided for hundreds of years. Roman Orthodox apophaticism is predicated on this assumption of a personal God who is beyond both Being *and* non-Being and whose complete ineffability is beyond the grasp of human faculties.

One of Plethon's sources, Plutarch, offers in his *Life of Numa* a fine example of these deep roots of intellectual optimism. According to the Pythagorean tradition associated with Numa the *sole* way to 'touch' god is through the intellect: οὔτε ἐφάπτεσθαι θεοῦ δυνατὸν ἄλλως ἢ νοήσει.[108] Plethon studied the Pseudo-Pythagorean *Golden Verses*, according to which the human

---

[105] Joh. Dam. *Expositio fidei* 1.26–8.

[106] Joh. Dam. *Exp. fidei* 12b.5–6: ὥσπερ οὐ τῆς οὐσίας αὐτοῦ μετέδωκεν, οὕτως οὐδὲ τῆς γνώσεως τῆς οὐσίας αὐτοῦ. On the patristic background of John's views on human knowledge of God see Louth (2002) 90–5.

[107] Cf. Joh. Dam. *Exp. fidei* 4.29–31; 1.1–10, where John quotes John 1:18, 'No one has ever seen God, but the only begotten Son who is at the Father's side, has made him known', Matt. 11:27, 'No one knows the Son except the Father, and no one knows the Father except the Son', and 1 Cor. 2:11, 'For what man knoweth the things of a man, save the spirit of man which is in him? Even so the things of God knoweth no man, but the Spirit of God.'

[108] Plut. *Numa* 7–8.

epistemic capacity naturally extends to the realm of the sacred: 'But take courage, for mortals have a divine origin (θεῖον γένος) | To whom Nature displays and shows each sacred object.'[109] In the same vein, Porphyry in the *Letter to Marcella* offers guidelines on how 'the right philosophy' (ἡ ὀρθὴ φιλοσοφία) leads to assimilation to god. Godlikeness is conditioned upon philosophy and virtue, that is, upon *theoretikos bios*: 'God gives the authority of a god to the wise man' and 'man is purified by the intellection of god' (καθαίρεται μὲν ἄνθρωπος ἐννοίᾳ θεοῦ).[110] But most importantly, 'a man who was worthy of god would be himself a god. You will best honour god by making your mind (διάνοια) like unto Him, and this you can do by virtue alone.'[111] The Porphyrean 'right philosophy' is an early antecedent of Plethon's 'true doctrines'. Both are an upshot of Plato's quest for the βέλτιστος λόγος and φιλοσοφεῖν ὀρθῶς.[112] Nowhere is epistemic optimism better expressed than in Plato.

One of the first to discern the rift between pre-Plotinean Platonic illumination and Christianity was an ex-Platonist, Justin. As a young philosopher, Justin thought that a 'contemplation of beings' (θεωρία τῶν ὄντων) 'gives wings' to his high-mindedness leading to wisdom and to the hope of rendering god visible (κατόψεσθαι τὸν θεόν). For, he adds, 'this is precisely the end of Plato's philosophy'.[113] Horribly shocked by *Timaeus* 28c3–5 ('to discover the Maker and Father of this Universe *would be a task indeed*; and having discovered Him, to declare Him unto all men would be a thing impossible'), Origenes and Gregory of Nazianzus tackled the problem in more theological terms. Plato thinks it is an arduous thing to know god; he thus implies, says the acute but clearly scandalised and appalled Origenes, that it is *not* impossible. Indeed, Plato

does not say that god is indescribable and nameless, but that *although he can be described it is only possible to declare him to a few.* (Orig. *Cels.* 7.42.20–4, 43.1–4)

The same passage scandalised Palamas. Barlaam of Calabria, we shall see, dared to follow the 'sages made stupid' who submit god

---

[109] *Golden Verses* 63–4. [110] Porph. *Ad Marcellam* 11.11–13.
[111] Porph. *Ad Marcellam* 15.12–16.3. [112] *Resp.* 607a6–8; *Phd.* 69d2.
[113] Justin, *Dial. cum Trypho* 2.6. 4–10.

to their intellect on the grounds 'that it is difficult to know god, but not impossible'.[114] Neither Origenes nor Palamas misread the *Timaeus*. The same idea recurs in the *Sophist*. At the heights of reason the light that the philosopher sees is so brilliant that the 'eyes of the soul' may get dizzy.[115] And yet Plato does not say that god is indescribable and nameless by nature; god is apprehensible and nameable only to a few, whom we may safely identify with the πεφιλοσοφηκότες ὀρθῶς praised in the *Phaedo*. This is the Platonic prototype of the fourteenth-century humanist ideal of the 'Enlightened-ones (πεφωτισμένοι)' revived by Barlaam and fiercely combated by Palamas and the Hesychast party.

The *Laws* and Plethon's *Nomoi* understandably call for a comparison owing to the association implied by their titles and legalist content. To some extent such a comparison may prove fruitful.[116] But in others it is misleading. The epistemological core of Plethon's *Nomoi* accords with that of the *Republic* rather than with the *Laws*. The *Laws* puts considerable emphasis on the irrational aspects of the human soul that hinder access to truth. Conversely, the *Republic* assumes that the difference between human and divine intellect may be overcome by means of a cognitive potential innate in man. The mission of 'true philosophy', of the 'perfect philosopher' or 'genuine philosopher' in the *Republic* is to 'touch the nature of being *qua* being' by cultivating a natural disposition.[117] The philosopher ascends by developing his intellectual faculties to the point of comprehending 'the nature of what really is'. The philosopher-king is the carrier of knowledge.[118] The road Socrates has always loved and of which there is no better 'nor can there ever be', we read in the *Philebus*, is that of dialectic. Dialectic has often deserted Socrates, leaving him lonely and forlorn. Nevertheless, this is the gift 'that was tossed down from some divine source through the agency of a Prometheus'.[119] Being, reality, and eternal immutability are the truest kind of knowledge and the best of all the arts, dialectic, is the art of acquiring it.[120] In the *Sophist* dialectic is acknowledged as the greatest and most

---

[114] Gr. Pal. *Ep.* 3.35.1–14; 4.25.11–12; 3.55.4–7. See below, p. 207.   [115] *Soph.* 254a–b.
[116] See for example Webb (1989).   [117] *Resp.* 490a–d, 491b.
[118] See also *Politicus* 292c.   [119] *Phlb.* 16b–c.   [120] *Phlb.* 58a–b.

important form of purification; further, as the path to genuine happiness.[121] There is no question of divine inspiration here.

The *megiston mathema* of *Republic* Book 6 and the 'wide ocean of intellectual beauty' of the *Symposium* (also considered as a *mathesis* and *episteme* at the end of an intellectual ascent) are conditional upon *nous*, embracing dialectic and discursive reasoning of the *dianoia* as well as spiritual exercises and detachment (in the *Phaedo*), astronomy and mathematics (in the *Timaeus* but also in the *Laws*) and moral considerations (in the *Republic* and the *Phaedrus* myth).[122] The philosopher's assimilation to god is an accomplishment of *theoria*, not a product of divine grace. It is developed by means of philosophical exercise initiated by the divine rational part of the soul.[123] It is not conditioned by Christian soteriology:

> when anyone by dialectic attempts through *discourse of reason* and apart from all perceptions of sense to find *his way to the very essence of each thing* and does not desist until he apprehends *by thought itself the nature of the good in itself*, he arrives at the limit of the intelligible. (*Resp.* 532a–b)

Plato's ideal of illumination primarily corresponds to an intellectual and contemplative ascent of the soul (*psychanodia*). In the *Timaeus* the challenge is to tune the natural rotations of the rational soul-part (*Ti.* 90c: 'the divine element in us') to the revolutions of the World-soul, a process consisting in the study of mathematics and astronomy.[124] This psychic and mathematical synchronisation is predicated on the basis that 'we are not an earthly but a heavenly plant' and naturally inclined to achieve *eudaimonia*.[125] According to Plato, those who are 'deprived of the knowledge of the veritable being of things' are *blind* – as opposed to the philosopher-guardians of the State who maintain a 'vivid pattern' (παράδειγμα) in their souls and may fix their eyes on truth, ever 'enamoured of the kind of knowledge which reveals to them something of that essence which is eternal'.[126] The philosopher ascends from awareness of sensible objects (εἰκασία) to a perception of

---

[121] *Sophist* 230d–e.   [122] Cf. *Symp.* 210d, 211c; *Laws* 817e; Sedley (1999).

[123] *Ti.* 90c; *Resp.* 603a4: 'that [part] which puts its trust in measurement and reflection (*logismos*) must be the best part of the soul'.

[124] See here Sedley (1999) 316–23.   [125] *Ti.* 90a–d.   [126] *Resp.* 484c–d, 485a–b.

the Ideas (νόησις) by means of discursive reason (διάνοια). Man prepares his soul for godlikeness by means of a speculative and discursive exercise of which he is the author – salvation comes from within rather than from without.

Significantly, Plethon follows Byzantine humanists such as Theodore Metochites, Barlaam and Nikephoros Gregoras in reverting to astronomy.[127] In doing so, fourteenth-century humanists departed from dominant Aristotelian empiricism that had been put to the service of the Hesychasts' appeal to supernatural experience. Those who have found god, argued Philotheos and Palamas, did so by means of experience (πεῖρα) and a habit of mind (ἕξις), not merely by means of words (λόγοι) and conjectures (στοχασμοί).[128] Conversely, the shared insistence on astronomy revived the Platonic persuasion that knowledge of god is retrievable by recovering the mathematical patterns and correspondences underlying cosmic order and governing the movement of natural bodies. Palamas had his reasons when listing in the *Capita CL* 'those who boast of knowing everything' in the company of natural scientists and astronomers.

The *Timaeus'* belief that godlikeness is attainable by means of profane philosophy, at least for a few, not only opposed Christian mysticism but also affirmed by analogy the emperor's presence in and active connection with the social body. Tambrun observes that like 'Zeus', Plethon's *basileus* is neither inaccessible nor withdrawn but presides over a hierarchically ordered political structure.[129] There are pagan Platonic antecedents of precisely this metaphysical but also political notion in Julian and the anonymous interlocutor of Macarius Magnes.[130] The kinship of mankind with god in epistemology mirrors that between the citizen and the king in politics: if the divine is accessible to human intellect, so is the king sensitive to the needs of his citizens. A

---

[127] Plethon's astronomical manual has been edited by A. Tihon and R. Mercier. See above, p. 91 for Metochites' clash with Choumnos over the priority of astronomy or physics; Barlaam's astronomical work has been edited by J. Mogenet and A. Tihon (Louvain 1977) and Gregoras' treatise by J. Mogenet (Amsterdam, 1983).

[128] Phil. Cocc. *Contra Greg.* 8.723–9, 3.381–3, 6.830–1; 10.459–60. Cf. Palamas' advocacy of *empeiria* as essential part of his criticism of Barlaam, *Ep.* 4.14.10–22.

[129] See the introduction by Tambrun to her edition of Plethon's *Oracles*, xii.

[130] Siniossoglou (2010a) 137–8.

new epistemology potentially leads to a reclaiming of the social solidarity lost at the expense of Christian mysticism that sought salvation in monasticism and prayer. In a genuinely Platonic way Plethon pairs epistemic optimism with political reformism. If the divine is apprehensible by human faculties, then so is the ideal *polis* realisable through those same faculties – at least by approximation.

The Byzantine civil war on illumination

The turn to Platonic epistemological optimism performed by Plethon was not exactly new. This was the latest episode in a long-standing intellectual conflict on the nature of illumination. The iconoclastic dispute in the eighth and ninth centuries was a major turning point. Theodore Stoudites and John of Damascus virulently argued against the claim that intellectual contemplation was sufficient to worship god. In their eyes, a *religio mentis* was tantamount to a relapse to non-Christian religiosity and justified the charge of Hellenism. For Theodore, no one could claim to be an iconoclast and a Christian at the same time.[131] John argued that it was impossible to ascend to what is spiritual without the bodily dimension: it is not by eliminating the senses but through the senses that one reaches the divine.[132] Andrew Louth observed that 'ultimately, for both John and Theodore, defence of icons entailed an acknowledgement of the integrity of embodied human nature'.[133]

The second major attempt to prioritise the intellect over the body took place in a different theological context in the fourteenth century. As we shall see presently, its philosophical points of reference were explicitly identified as 'Hellenic'. By the turn of the century the anti-Hesychast party was formally defeated and the revival of 'Hellenic' epistemology suppressed. But the humanist

---

[131] Cholij (2002) 60. Stoudites notes that the 'Hellenioi' iconoclasts' aim was to throw back to the Orthodox party the accusation of 'Hellenism', that is to say, equate iconodules with idolaters; *Ep.* 546.39–42.

[132] Joh. Dam. *Imag.* 3.12.23–6; *Dialect.* 1.70–5. Cf. Louth (2002) 46, 217, 193–208, for John's arguments against the iconoclasts.

[133] Louth (2002) 218.

project was not really abandoned. The Byzantine Illuminati left for any potential successor an ample fund of thoughts and experimentations upon which to draw. Plethon carried on from where they left off and pushed the boundaries of humanism.

When forced to combat Plethon's epistemic optimism, Scholarios reverted to Orthodox apophaticism, highlighting the principal Palamite thesis that god's individuality was infinitely beyond 'any *nous* and *logos*'.[134] Plethon's wish to find truth was legitimate, one reads, but the methodology (τρόπος) applied was fallacious.[135] Scholarios refrains from explaining which *tropos* exactly is the legitimate one. His sympathy for Aquinas is adequate reason for his awkwardness. Scholarios was aware that apophaticism as understood in the Orthodox framework made the fewest concessions to Hellenic rationalism and was therefore best suited to radically opposing Plethon's Platonism – even if, admittedly, this was not a Thomist's favourite theological doctrine.

Spiritual illumination

The key difference between paganism and Christianity, wrote Maximus Confessor with reference to a discussion between some arrogant pagans and Clement's teacher Pantainus, is that god does not know beings through *nous* or sense perception. God knows beings as 'divine intentions (θελήματα)', namely as products of his will. Maximus essentially identifies *thelemata* with the Pseudo-Dionysian *logoi* of beings (λόγοι τῶν ὄντων) and predeterminations (προορισμοί).[136] Thus intellectual knowledge is by default excluded from any quest to reconnect with god: the world is the product of god's free will, not intellectual activity. Man is a part (μοῖρα) of god in so far as the *logoi* of being human exist within god. Further, man is said to be part of god owing to an innate tendency to ascend and assimilate to his primary cause.[137] But no

---

[134] Schol. *Ad exarchum Josephum, OC* 4.165.19–23.
[135] Schol. *Ad exarchum Josephum, OC* 4.164.3–5.
[136] Max. Conf. *Ambigua, PG* 91.1085B–C. Cf. Dion. Ar. *DN* 144.6–12; 188.6–10. On Maximus see Louth (1996) and on the doctrine of the *logoi* in Maximus, see also Cooper (2005) 92–5.
[137] Max. Conf. *Ambigua, PG* 91.1081C, 1084A.

ontological link or confusion exists between man and god in the Platonic, Plotinean and Plethonean sense. Human natural faculties (φυσικαὶ δυνάμεις) are not applicable in the quest for glorification. This is owing to the corruption of primordial human faculties that led to man's Fall. Man intentionally misused those powers that were originally devised to connect him to god if properly used.[138]

Orthodox mystics such as Maximus and Palamas believed that knowledge of god was possible through nature (κατὰ πνεῦμα φυσικὴ θεωρία).[139] *Theoria* does not mean that god is cognisable by human reason; it requires that the Holy Spirit injects itself into the human heart. Godlikeness consists in man's full communion in body and soul with the energy of god by divine grace. Physical senses as well as the faculties of the soul are purified and subsequently transmuted. This process is illustrated, according to Maximus, in Moses' and Elias' passing over (μετάβασις) from flesh to spirit during the transfiguration of Christ on Mount Thabor.[140]

Palamas compared faith to sense perception. Both are beyond discursive demonstration.[141] Spiritual illumination is not an intellectual or allegorical form of sight but a real, psychophysical visionary experience. In the funeral oration to his brother Basil, Gregory of Nyssa provides an example of this type of illumination that shows its deep roots in Greek patristics.[142] The only way to know god is as radiance and only on the part of those who are truly divinely enlightened; not by means of 'wisdom beyond the gates' but through supernatural vision:

Do you not see how superior is this light to the light of knowledge; I do not mean the knowledge of the Hellenic *mathemata* (for this does not even deserve to be called light, since the total sum of Hellenic knowledge is a lie or mixed with

---

[138] Max. Conf. *Ambigua, PG* 91.1097C.   [139] Max. Conf. *Ambigua, PG* 91.1128C–D.
[140] Max. Conf. *Ambigua, PG* 91.1127D.   [141] Sinkewicz (1982) 197.
[142] One night Basil was praying; suddenly, the whole building was illumined by a divine 'formless light', which did not flow out of any material source. And Basil was illumined. See Gr. Nyss. *In Bas. fratr.* 21.5–10. Even if we allow for the conventions of the genre, it is still clear that the type of illumination hailed here is by default incompatible with the Platonic-Aristotelian ideal of *theoretikos bios/theoretike zoe* that achieves enlightenment through dialectic and contemplation. Godlikeness is not a human accomplishment. Gr. Nyss. *De virgin.* 12.2.66–70 (cf. Nikolaou 1995: 153 n. 299).

lies, being closer to darkness than to light) but even to the knowledge of Holy scriptures. So much so that the one might be likened to a lamp shining in a dim place, whereas the light of mystical contemplation to the star shining at noonday, namely the sun. (Gr. Pal. *Triads* 2.3.18.36–42)

Illumination is restricted to an experience of divine energy – it does not extend to any knowledge of god's essence. God is unknowable in his essence but knowable in his energies. The divine light that the Hesychasts claimed to witness is an energy of god – not his essence, but the next best thing. This doctrine was ultimately founded upon the efforts of Pseudo- Dionysius and John of Damascus to enjoy all the merits of negative theology without sacrificing those of affirmative theology.[143] The Palamite position is essentially that of John: one cannot grasp god's essence, but only what may be said *about* essence (τὰ περὶ τὴν οὐσίαν), just as knowledge that soul is without a body, quantity or shape is knowledge *about* the soul, but not *of* the soul.[144] Palamas could also quote Basil, according to whom 'the operations of God descend towards us, *but his essence remains inaccessible*' and Maximus Confessor, who declares that 'all that God is, *save for an identity in essence*, we become when deified with grace'. It is impossible 'even for those who are deified by means of divine grace' to participate in divine essence, *but only in divine operations*.[145] The argument has deep roots in late antique apologetics. As Beck observes, John Chrysostom was fully persuaded that not even angels see the divine essence; and Theodoret of Cyrrhus tells us that the prophets who received divine revelation did not really see the essence of god, but only certain appearances of this essence according to their capacities.[146]

Orthodox mystics warned against expeditions of human intellect into the mysteries of divine essence – those conceptual expeditions that are motivated by philosophical curiosity: τῶν ἐννοιῶν τὰς περιέργους περὶ Θεοῦ ἐπιχειρήσεις.[147] We have seen that, since

---

[143] Gr. Pal. Διάλεξις μετὰ Γρηγ. 24 (PS 4.225.6–228.19).

[144] Joh. Dam. *Exp. fidei* 10.8–10.   [145] Gr. Pal. *Capita CL*, 111.7.

[146] Thdt. *Eranistes* 75.14–30; J. Chrys. *Hom. in Jo., PG* 59.98.6–10. Both examples in H. G. Beck (1979) 56.

[147] Neilos of Sinai, *E., PG* 79.161c. The favourite source of Gregory Palamas, Ps.-Dionysius Areopagita (*De mystica theologia* 142.12–16), was appalled by those who

the time of the Cappadocean Fathers, such endeavours counted as variants of conceptual idolatry (νοητὴ εἰδωλολατρεία) and self-idolatry (αὐτοείδωλον) *par excellence*.

Still, the unqualified transcendence of divine essence does not mean god is absent from this world. In the verses of Romanos Melodos, god is invisible above but became visible below: ἄνω ἀόρατος, γέγονας κάτω ὁρώμενος πᾶσι.[148] God is ἔξω and yet ἔσω to the extent that his essence is outside creation but his energies spiritualise and pertain matter. Platonists had no monopoly of epistemological optimism: Maximus, Palamas and the Hesychasts were deeply optimistic about man's potential to participate in the energy of god – in mind *and* body, too.

The revival of the Hellenic notion of intellectual illumination

Theodore Metochites unabashedly pronounced a maxim of Byzantine humanism that challenged the Orthodox notion of spiritual illumination: 'It is my position that rational enquiry is more important than anything else in the world.'[149] The advocacy of secular wisdom in the *Ethicus* portends an unconditional trust in the hidden recesses of human mind and soul that enable man to choose the right way of life (αἵρεσις βίου). This belief connects the first book of the *Nomoi* to the *Ethicus* and hints at a world-view enunciated and defended by both Plethon and Metochites:

Hence we are in a position not only to affirm Pythagoras' saying 'choose the best way of life (ὁ ἄριστος βίος) and habit will also render it the most pleasurable (ἡδύν)' but also this: 'choose the way of life that is really the best, namely the life of wisdom, which, I believe, Pythagoras too pursued, and you will find that this also happens to be the most pleasurable way of life'. For there can be no other thing more pleasurable to a really intelligent man (ὁ νοῦν ἔχων) than the devotion to and participation in intellectual endeavours (λόγοι). (*Eth.* 25)

---

purport to know God by means *of their own* knowledge (τῇ καθ᾽ αὑτοὺς γνώσει). Their godless and multifarious constructions have nothing to do with theology. The point is more pronounced in George Pachymeres' *Paraphrasis* of Ps.-Dionysius: pagan philosophers fail to understand that god is beyond their capacity to think; they still believe it is possible to know God on account of their own intellectual faculties (τῇ ἑαυτῶν γνώσει τὸ Θεῖον εἰδέναι).

[148] Rom. Mel. *Hymn.* 43.3.7.   [149] Thdr. Met. *Eth.* 61.

Inspired by Plato's belief in the possibility of comprehending true knowledge by means of education and intellectual purification, the *Ethicus* provides a fascinating account of how secular wisdom leads to *theoria*. Metochites' moral realism has at its centre the possibility of recovering by reason and following up 'traces of truth (τὸ ἀληθές)', just as Plethon's realism revolves around 'true doctrines' (τἀληθῆ δόγματα). Both reflect Plato's *aletheis phroneseis* and are equally elitist: pure intellectual pleasure relates to 'that part of man that is most divine' and should not be accessible to the profane (βέβηλοι).[150] Intellect is the 'most beautiful' and 'most precious' possession a man has – it is 'the rational divine spirit' (τὸ λογικὸν θεῖον πνεῦμα).[151] Uneducated and ignorant people can never be happier than those who utilise this gift and apply their judgement. By means of education and virtue, 'intellectual activity' evolves into self-reflection and culminates in 'the vision of beings (θεωρία τῶν ὄντων)'. Free from any distractions 'as in some sort of solitude' man entrusts his intellect with the task of parting from the world of phenomena into the infinity of essence, as if he were looking 'from some sort of a high outpost'. The intellect will thus be able progressively to comprehend 'the infinite harmonies of beings', participate in them and attain a 'most divine' contact without fear or pain. The intellect is the 'vessel of mind' led into the calm 'sea of the world's being', sailing by means of *theoria*. The infinite 'beauty of beings' infuses the intellect with the quality of beauty. Then man returns to his proper condition in order to enquire about and reflect on what he has seen. After retrieving the meaning behind every single thing and the reason for its existence, man is ultimately filled with surprise and admiration for the maker of everything. It is thus that 'the human soul may fly high in the sky with the wings of wisdom'.[152]

Essentially offering a secular version of the *Phaedrus* myth, Metochites goes on to repeat Plato's description of dialectic as a Promethean gift in the *Philebus*, and considers the intellect (*nous*) and reason (*logos*) to be divine dispensations,[153] legislators discerning what is best and resulting in a harmonious *politeia*.[154] We

---

[150] *Eth.* 26.   [151] *Eth.* 59.   [152] *Eth.* 32.   [153] *Eth.* 59.   [154] *Eth.* 61.

may begin to understand Plethon's appreciation for Metochites.[155] Both Plethon's epistemic optimism and political utopianism are steeped in this 'Hellenic' secular thought-world developed by Metochites and later humanists, which persisted as an undercurrent in Byzantine secular circles and literary salons (θέατρα).

What is most important for the present argument is that in the fourteenth century this outlook eventually managed to penetrate the Orthodox Church. From where Gregory Palamas was standing, this was the accomplishment of Barlaam of Calabria. Palamas' first epistle against Barlaam is entitled 'Against the Hellenic notion of illumination': *Καθ᾽ ἑλληνικῆς ἐποψίας.*[156] This is no rhetorical ornament. Barlaam introduced the 'wise men of old' favoured by Metochites into theological discourse. According to Philotheos Kokkinos, Barlaam 'called Aristotle and Plato and all the bunch that followed Plato *divine men* and *illumined* by god (πεφωτισμένοι)'.[157] He was then credited with applying the intellectualism of these Illuminati as a weapon against the Palamite mystical ideal of psychophysical illumination. In the final phase of his clash with Palamas he did not merely claim that the Hellenic philosophical approach to enlightenment was compatible with religious Orthodoxy, as Psellos did; nor that it complemented Christian piety in man's quest for godlikeness, as Metochites might have argued to defend himself. The surprising claim was that the route to illumination was better prescribed by the pagan Illuminati than by Palamas and the Hesychasts.

The conflict was occasioned by a misunderstanding of Barlaam's initial position. At first, the Calabrian appears to have been equally anti-Latin and anti-Hellenic in denying any possible knowledge of god by means of science. *Nous* cannot perceive god, hence there can be no scientific demonstration of divine essence or 'the realities surrounding supra-essential entity'. This did not necessarily lead to agnosticism, but rather to fideism. Barlaam backed up his position with reference to post-Iamblichean Neoplatonism and Syrianus. The 'ancients' excellently understood human weakness and divine transcendence, Barlaam wrote to Palamas, and 'they too were

---

[155] On Plethon and Metochites see above, pp. 108–9.   [156] Gr. Pal. *Ep.* 3.
[157] Phil. Cocc. *Enc. Greg. Pal.* 41.28–30.

sometimes illumined by god and surpassed ordinary men'. The Hellenic sages were not pagans (ἔξω) any longer but recategorised as 'the ancient' (παλαιοί). In another epistle to Palamas, Barlaam quoted the 'Pythagoreans Pantainetus, Brotinus, Philolaus', among others, as agreeing that the Good is supra-essential.[158] At this point the Calabrian appears to have still maintained that illumination is not attainable by human faculties.

Palamas proved far-sighted. Even if Barlaam's early views may be potentially interpreted in an 'orthodox' manner, his later correspondence shows a significant shift from the post-Iamblichean Platonic transcendentalism and fideism to the type of intellectual paganism that Palamas accused him of all along: 'The philosophical sciences lead naturally and of themselves to this truth given by God to the apostles and contribute to raising infallibly the greatest of the sacred symbols to their immaterial archetypes',[159] he wrote, and he advocated a type of asceticism in which there is nothing specifically Christian. According to Sinkewicz, 'it seems that Barlaam began to consider knowledge of God as an adjunct of purely natural philosophy. The character of gift or grace of God is absent. In his later writings any supernatural aspect has either disappeared or been severely compromised. Barlaam has thus taken the progression of his thought to its ultimate extreme.'[160]

Furthermore, Barlaam made again pertinent in the fourteenth century what Palamas christened 'the greatest of all Hellenic fallacies': the Platonic doctrine according to which *nous* is capable of separating from the body by means of intellectual *theoria*, a direct challenge to the Hesychast belief in man as psychosomatic unity. The proper method to approach god, says Palamas, is to force mind to return *within* body, that is, to recollect and enclose mind 'especially within *that body most interior to the body*, which we call the *heart*'.[161] On the other hand, says Palamas,

to make the mind 'go out', not only from fleshly thoughts, but out of the body itself, with the aim of contemplating intelligible visions – that is the greatest of the Hellenic errors, the root and source of all heresies, an invention of daemons,

[158] Barlaam, *Ep.* 1.826–45; *Ep.* 3.474–8; see here Sinkewicz (1982) 224–5; 233.
[159] Barlaam *ap.* Palamas *Triads* 2.1.5 quoted in Sinkewicz (1982) 237 n. 270.
[160] Sinkewicz (1982) 237.   [161] Gr. Pal. *Triads* 1.2.3.

a doctrine which engenders folly and is itself the product of madness. This is why those who speak by daemonic inspiration become beside themselves, not knowing what they are saying. *As for us, we recollect the mind not only within the body and heart, but also within itself.* (Gr. Pal. *Triads* 1.2.4.20–7)

Assuming a Platonist perspective, Barlaam launched his attack on Hesychast corporeal prayer. Sharing the same starting point as the notorious Plotinean 'flight of the alone to the Alone' (*Enn.* 6.9.11.51), the Barlaamite notion of 'prayer' constitutes a contemplative and intellectual activity that separates body and soul. On the grounds that the passions of the soul should be completely deadened, Barlaam saw physical stimuli and sentiments of pain or pleasure as an impediment. For his part, Palamas rightly observed that this notion of prayer removed abstinence from food, standing, bowing and anything causing physical distress or fatigue – essentially degenerating into pure intellectualism.[162] Barlaam revived the Pythagorean and Stoic position according to which pagan paideia (ἔξω παιδεία) leads to scientific knowledge (ἐπιστήμη) as the end of contemplation (θεωρία).[163] He is trying 'to persuade us to follow what are ostensibly Platonic and Socratic teachings (τάχα καὶ πλατώνεια καὶ σωκράτεια)', whereas in reality he revives Proclan mysticism. The path Barlaam was walking does not lead to light: it leads straight to darkness effected by Chaldean theurgy. Barlaam is seeking Apollonian illumination.[164] His aim is to mislead his contemporaries into substituting the pagan notion of enlightenment for the Orthodox one:

And now you were so arrogant as to write that we should consider the 'sages made foolish' as illumined (τοὺς μεμωραμένους σοφοὺς δεῖν οἴεσθαι πεφωτισμένους ἀναγράφειν ἐπήρθης) – those men who have degraded god below their intellect, arguing that it is difficult, but not impossible to conceive of (οἳ καὶ τὸν θεὸν ὑπὸ τὴν σφῶν αὐτῶν πεποίηνται νόησιν, χαλεπὸν εἶναι λέγοντες, ἀλλ' οὐκ ἀδύνατον, νοῆσαι θεόν). (Gr. Pal. *Ep.* 3.55.4–8)

Palamas was adamant. 'Have the Hellenes participated in the intelligible and divine light? Have they witnessed and *experienced* the majesty of god? Have they been summoned with god beyond wisdom, beyond reason, beyond intellect?' How could then Barlaam

---

[162] *Triads* 2.2.4.   [163] *Triads* 1.3.13.   [164] Gr. Pal. *Ep.* 3.22.4–5; 3.47.5–16.

come to praise those philosophers who have been demolished long ago! For they said that 'it is difficult to know god, but it is impossible to put his essence into words', which means that although they understood that god is beyond language, they still seriously considered the possibility that he does not transcend the human intellect. To be sure, they said that the divine is beyond proof; but they only meant that the divine transcends language, while maintaining that *the divine is knowable* by means of their innate vision (κατὰ δὲ τὴν ἐν ἑαυτοῖς θέαν) – thus considering themselves to be 'scientists of the divine (ἐπιστήμονας τῶν θείων ἑαυτούς)', as Barlaam too says![165] But 'this is what we are trying to put a stop to: the perverted application of and the abuse of the sciences, the exaggerated veneration accorded to them.'[166]

Palamas had every reason to see in this unconventional monk from Calabria the most serious threat to Christian Orthodoxy. Christians in late antiquity manipulated Plato to their ends; late Byzantine humanists appear to have paid them back in the same coin by appropriating Christian authorities of late antiquity as purportedly supporting their Platonising outlook.[167]

Infiltrated by means of 'heresy', core Hellenic views regarding assimilation to god, human nature and knowledge, penetrated the Church once again, now disguised as Platonically inspired Christian reformism. As Palamas saw it, when Orthodoxy begins dialogue on doctrinal matters with Hellenism it will sooner or later degenerate into Platonising heresy, even if Syrianus or Proclus occasionally appear conformable to Christian apophaticism.

There is a last aspect of Barlaam's contribution to the Hesychast controversy that is important and concerns the (re)application of a perilous vocabulary. Barlaam's reference to a perennial 'wisdom-in-itself' was readily identified by Palamas as marking a revival of Plato's metaphysics. Barlaam argued in favour of a unique idea of true knowledge (ἰδέα τῆς γνώσεως) or wisdom-in-itself (αὐτοσοφία), whose essence is not contained either in any of the

---

[165] Gr. Pal. *Ep.* 3.35.1–12.   [166] *Triads* 2.1.27.
[167] Thus Palamas (*Triads* 2.3.73) was naturally distressed to find Ps.-Dionysius quoted as supporting the view that 'our most excellent possession is the knowledge of beings, that is to say, philosophy'. See pp. 76–9 and 107–9 for examples from Psellos and Nikephoros Gregoras.

available 'philosophies', or in any of the 'philosophers'. In the same manner as men participate in the universal *genus* of man and are called men accordingly, so wisdom-in-itself offers the name of wisdom to its species. Palamas immediately exposed the anti-Christian implications of these philosophical experiments. If any direct revelation of god exists, then it is not exclusive to the apostles and the Fathers, but equally available to the ancient sages.[168] In fact, Barlaam appears to have announced a theme that runs through Plethon's proto-deism and conception of τἀληθῆ dogmata. As Palamas saw it, this leads to a 'revival of Plato':

> You stand up for philosophy: but if philosophy does not exist within god, nor among men, but nevertheless constitutes an idea, then are we to believe that philosophy exists in itself? This is how Plato is revived among us with all the accompanying fallacies! (Gr. Pal. *Triads* 2.1.22.18–23)

The condemnation of Plato's 'fallacies' in the *Synodicon of Ortho-doxy* reserves a prominent place for the belief in the existence of the realm of the Ideas. But anti-Palamite Byzantine humanism did not merely consider the possibility of an intelligible realm between the unqualified essence of god and the qualified creaturely substance. It also ventured to go beyond that. It considered the possibility that to know god's wisdom means to know his essence. This is, we shall see presently, a typically 'pagan' position featured in Plethon's reception of the *Chaldean Oracles*. Interestingly, one of the men accused of having argued in this direction is Prochoros Kydones, the last major representative of anti-Hesychasm and brother of Plethon's early instructor in Platonic philosophy.

Prochoros was condemned for arguing that the wisdom of god is the essence of god: 'he who comes to know the wisdom of god knows his essence, for the wisdom of god equals the seizure (κατάληψις) of his essence'. The 'science of the Good (ἡ τοῦ ἀγαθοῦ ἐπιστήμη)' is the same as the 'science of god's essence (ἡ ἐπιστήμη τῆς οὐσίας τοῦ Θεοῦ)'.[169] The reciprocity between the unknowability and supra-essentiality of god that John of Damascus captured and that runs through the whole of the Orthodox tradition

---

[168] Meyendorff (1959) 185.

[169] *Tomus II, PG* 151.699A: Ὁ γοῦν εἰδὼς τὴν σοφίαν αὐτοῦ, οἶδε τὴν οὐσίαν αὐτοῦ, ἐφόσον ἡ τοῦ Θεοῦ σοφία ἐστιν ἡ τῆς οὐσίας αὐτοῦ κατάληψις.

is reversed into one between secular epistemology and rational theology. Possibly elaborating on the Thomist reception of ancient philosophy, Prochoros was read as arguing that illumination is the product of the syllogistic method rather than of grace.[170]

The Hesychast controversy carried a rarely noted but crucial political dimension. The *Tomus* reporting on the assault of Prochoros Kydones on Palamism contains a note that nicely captures the reformist thrust unleashed by Byzantine humanism. 'In these times' (οἱ νῦν καιροί)' abandoned by god, says Prochoros, one has no other option but to turn to the syllogistic method 'as our sole assistant (ἐπικουρία) and light (φῶς)'. Right now, thought Prochoros, it is suicidal to 'drop from our hands the only tool left to uncover truth'. In Prochoros' description, blindness and deafness rule and 'devilish (διαβολιμαῖοι)' people claiming to be mystagogues are all over the place like beetles and ants coming out of their holes.[171] The pun is clear. Byzantium is in a lamentable and crumbling state. Philosophy provides the only *means of resistance*. Established religion will not do, for *this is*, as Prochoros had it, the cause of this ruin (ἀρά).

Around the same time, Nicholas Kabasilas reported and rebutted anonymous lay circles who went even further, announcing the death of Christianity. A few decades later Plethon applied the intellectual arsenal that led to the condemnation of secular cells to new polemical uses. He was making the same point in more radical terms: Orthodoxy was exhausted.[172]

The emperor John Kantakouzenos was Palamas' great supporter and the political catalyst of at least some of the latter's theological triumphs. Though the empire was decaying, John spent considerable time and effort in refuting Prochoros. Oddly, he either missed the political subtext – or, more likely, he chose to ignore it. In his text there is no anxiety as to why an intellectual like Prochoros was led to compare the ascendancy of Palamite theologians to an invasion of beetles and ants or how he came to think of the empire as sinking into obscurantism. Rather, John observes that according to Prochoros syllogism is the 'sole spark in the search of truth,

---

[170] *Tomus II, PG* 151.699B: τοῖς ἰδίοις λογισμοῖς.   [171] *Tomus II, PG* 151.701C–D.
[172] See below, Ch. 7, pp. 374–81.

as if truth had been extinguished'. Prochoros commits himself to a categorical mistake in so far as he does not acknowledge the right of theology to deal with the question of truth, 'as if one was to speak about politics through geometrical maxims or about the movement of the stars through strategy'. Intriguingly, John does not see in Prochoros the contamination of Orthodoxy by 'Latin' theology, but the revival of Hellenic pagan philosophy. He goes on to deal with the problem as an apologist, launching a typical attack on the diversification of opinion among pagan philosophers and the futility of any attempt by Hellenic philosophy to compete with Christian revelation.[173] All the apologetical clichés are here: Paul has shown that 'not only what you (Prochoros) call *light* (φῶς) was foolish but the whole of Hellenic wisdom'.[174] In 1368 Prochoros Kydones was anathematised, among other things, for propounding the view that faith is not founded upon revelation but on learning; further, for calling Aristotelian syllogisms *light* (φῶς).[175]

It will be objected that Prochoros' adversaries overread his arguments. The *Synodal Tome* explaining the reasons for his anathematisation hardly provides any opening to argue that this was the case. But quite apart from that, what matters here, as well as in the case of Barlaam, is not the question of Prochoros' Orthodoxy; rather, that the option of philosophical paganism was sufficiently plausible to be rejected. What matters is the discussion that took place concerning the right and capacity of Hellenic philosophy to claim its autonomy and evolve in unpredictable ways, that is, independently of the clerical and monastic tradition and free from hieratic constraints. Even if Barlaam and Prochoros were not consciously philosophical pagans, they stirred a debate involving ideas and tenets of philosophical paganism. These ideas were made available, remained in circulation and were constantly debated and reported, even if only to be rebutted. In this regard, dissenters such as Barlaam and Prochoros most clearly anticipate Plethon's radical redefinition of the interrelation between epistemology and ontology and announce its political implications.

---

173 Joh. Cant. *Refutationes duae Prochori Cydonii* 1.7.1–63.
174 Joh. Cant. *Ref.* 1.8.28–31.   175 *Tomus II, PG* 151.701D.

The political subtext of Prochoros' heresy that John left untouched was that the Byzantines were really experiencing an *Endzeit* – albeit not in the millenarian or apocalyptic sense that was current at the time but in the sense of an intellectual as well as political disintegration for which responsibility lies not with god, but with the people and their leaders.

The *Chaldean Oracles* reloaded

Plethon's recalibration of the *Chaldean Oracles* revives the debate between Byzantine humanism and Christian mysticism that appeared to have lost its impetus from the end of the fourteenth century. This edition and interpretation of a 'holy' text of Neoplatonic theurgy is a daring philosophical hermeneutical endeavour. It has been assumed that both *Logia* and *Nomoi* originally formed parts of a single manuscript that fell victim to Scholarios. Thus, in the Arabic translation the *Logia* assume the role of Plethon's 'Bible'.[176] This might be an exaggeration. Still, the intellectual connections between the two works prove beyond doubt that they were part of a single philosophical project.

Commenting on *Chaldean Oracle* fr. 101(des Places), Plethon launches a simultaneous attack on the theurgic as well as Palamite mystical belief in divine illumination. The oracle: 'do not evoke the image of nature that is directly visible', is interpreted thus:

Do not seek to see, with your physical eyes, an image of nature, that is to say, of the divine nature, for it is not possible to see this nature with human eyes. Hence, what appears to those initiated in the Mysteries, namely lightings, fire and anything of this sort are *symbols*, but not some sort of divine nature (*Orac. Chald.* fr. 24).

One target here is the Palamite belief that the light of Thabor is visible σωματικοῖς ὀφθαλμοῖς, that is to say, with physical eyes.[177] Though the anti-Hesychast faction was formally defeated, Plethon

---

[176] See the introduction by Tambrun to her edition of Plethon's *Oracles*, xiii. On Plethon's recension of the *Oracles*, his sources and the reattribution of the fragments to Zoroaster cf. Burns (2006); Tambrun (2006b) 961–2; Stausberg (1998) 57–69; Nikolaou (2004c) 51–63; Brisson (2006); Athanassiadi (2002).

[177] See Gr. Pal. *Triads* 3.3.9.25–7; *Homiliae* 34.8.1–14.

repeats its main argument that illumination cannot materialise.[178] Viewed against the background of the Hesychast controversy, the word 'symbols' is intriguing. Maximus Confessor used the word 'symbol' in a description of the light of Thabor. Barlaam thought to have found in Maximus a convenient declaration of the contingent and variable nature of psychophysical spiritual experience. Thus, he attacked the Hesychasts on the grounds that the light the apostles witnessed on Mount Thabor and which the Hesychasts claimed to experience as divine illumination was nothing but a 'symbol'. Palamas replied that when applying this term Maximus did not doubt the reality of the vision of the uncreated energy of god but rather intended to stress its esoteric and supra-rational dimension.[179] Plethon demystifies the term *symbol*, which is here redeployed against Christian illumination.

Intriguingly, Proclus too provides in his hymns a notion of illumination. His position claims an intermediate position between the notion of intellectual illumination according to the prePlotinean interpretation of Plato and Palamite mysticism. The soul prays to the gods in order to receive the 'pure light (φάος ἁγνόν)', the 'light of ascent (ἀναγώγιον φῶς)' and the 'valuable light (φάος ἐρίτιμον)'.[180] In accordance with the Iamblichean theurgic version of late antique Platonism, Proclus thinks of illumination as divine dispensation. This may be seen as a bridge between the pagan notion of enlightenment and the Palamite one. Yet Proclan illumination remains conceptual rather than experiential. The Muses are summoned to bring about a 'Bacchic' state of illumination through the 'noetic myths of wise men' rather than through any transformation of physical vision as is the case in the Hesychast tradition.[181] Once again, a tradition of 'old sages' or 'enlightened' philosophers holds the key to a conceptual vision of what ultimately *is*.

Plethon studied Proclus' hymns, took notes and is most probably responsible for the addition of their titles. Oddly, his own hymns

---

[178] Cf. the introduction by Tambrun to her edition of the Plethonean *Oracles*, 128–9; Tambrun (1992) 168–79.

[179] Cf. *Triads* 3.1.13 and Max. Conf. *Ambigua, PG* 91.1128A with the precious commentary of Staniloae ad loc. in the edition of Larchet *et al.*

[180] Procl. *Hymni* 1.40, 3.1, 3.15, 4.6, 6.9, 7.33.   [181] Procl. *Hymni* 3.11.

do not appear to bear traces of Proclan influence.[182] It would appear then that though Plethon was so heavily indebted to Proclus in philosophy, he was not at all in religious hymnography. This remarkable situation merits special attention. An explanation may lie in the absence from extant Plethonean hymns of that godsent 'pure' and 'valuable' φάος that so fascinated Proclus. Instead of spiritual illumination, Plethon introduces certain 'gods of learning (λόγιοι θεοί)', and they are the ones that he summons with his first prayer, 'whoever and however many ye may be'.[183] Given the implicit attack on Hesychast practices in the commentary on the *Chaldean Oracles* and on Orthodox mysticism in the *Nomoi*, we may plausibly surmise that Plethon consciously abandoned literary forms that were closely associated with Palamism or that could be read as potentially in accordance with Christian versions of experiential mysticism.

Plethon was not the only Platonising intellectual to move in this direction after Psellos and to fall under the spell of the *Oracles*. Nikephoros Gregoras was familiar with the collection, probably through Psellos. The 'oracles' served as a bridge between Gregoras' Neoplatonic tendencies and late antique pagan and hermetic theology.[184] Further, one might plausibly speculate that the oracles found their way into private discussions such as those held among elite intellectuals participating in those late Byzantine *theatra* or 'salons' beyond the control of the religious establishment. Still, Plethon is the first to deal critically with this mysterious collection. He appears to have complied happily with the imperative of his Platonic conscience by purifying the *Oracles* of Psellos' Christianising interpretation. This is an important move.

Commenting on Homer's 'golden chain', Psellos reports that the verses purportedly convey the replies given by the soul of Plato (dwelling in the world beyond in the company of Apollo and Hermes) to a certain Julian. This man enjoyed the rare privilege of knowing how to ascend to Plato's soul and ask whatever he wished by means of 'some sort of hieratic art'. Julian's son

---

[182] Van den Berg (2001) 5–6, 8.   [183] *Nomoi* 44 (1.4.1).
[184] Medvedev (1984) 130.

(curiously also called Julian) served as a medium or 'daemonic' in between.[185] Plethon either did not have access to this apocryphal story or consciously opted to suppress it. Though the idea of prophets revealing arcane knowledge is a commonplace in esoteric Neoplatonism, there is no sign of it in Plethon's commentary. The oracular verses are treated as philosophy of great antiquity. They are not messages from the world beyond or god (θεόθεν) any longer. They cease to be theurgic.

Plethon's selection is entitled Μαγικά λόγια τῶν ἀπό Ζωροάστρου Μάγων. We need not go as far as Tardieu does in assuming that Plethon's mentor Elissaios revealed to Plethon the supposedly deep connection between the Persian Magi and the Chaldeans.[186] Elissaios is as shadowy a figure as Julian the Medium. It appears that Plethon's direct source transmitting the *Oracles* is Psellos, who draws in his turn from Proclus' massive commentary on this work.[187] The expression οἱ ἀπό Ζωροάστρου μάγοι appears in Plutarch.[188] Moreover, Proclus' references to Zoroaster and his legendary antiquity suffice to render Zoroaster the ideal candidate for a reattribution of the fragments. The mythical veil surrounding Zoroaster and his authority function as warranty for the validity and truthfulness of the philosophy transmitted. In the *Nomoi* 'true doctrines' are attributed to Zoroaster and Plato not on the grounds that they originate with them, but because they were among the first to transmit them. Assuming that the word 'Chaldeans' signified at that time experts in magic and astrology,[189] Plethon's change in title is part of his attempt to redeem the philosophical core of the *logia* from specialists of this sort.

The Plethonean editorial work on the *Oracles* is a conscious move towards the secularisation of their contents. The reattribution

---

[185] Psell. *Opuscula logica, physica, allegopica, alia* 46.42–50 (ed. Duffy). Cf. *Suda*, iota 433–4.
[186] Tardieu (1987) 147.
[187] Cf. Stausberg (1998) 57; Brisson (2006) 140; Nikolaou (2004c) 53; Anastos (1948) 288. According to Marinus, *Procl.* 26, Proclus' commentary must have extended to some 1120 pages. See here Saffrey (1981) 218–19.
[188] Plut. *Quaestiones Convivales* 670D2; *De Iside et Osiride* 369D10: Ζωροάστρης ὁ μάγος. This link between Plutarch and Plethon is noted by Nikolaou (2004c) 35.
[189] Saffrey (1981) 216.

of the *Oracles* to Zoroaster is not the consequence of philological or comparative study on Plethon's part but a literary and ideological device designed to corroborate the archetypical value of the doctrines he stands for. In a sense, it is a hermeneutical version of a 'noble lie'.

The comparison with Psellos helps to uncover the intention behind Plethon's compilation and commentary on the 'oracles'. In fr. 110 the avid seeker of truth is advised to follow the 'channel of the soul': the route by which the soul descends to mortality. According to the oracle, the return of the soul to its heavenly seat is attainable by combining the 'sacred teaching (ἱερὸς λόγος)' with ritual (ἔργον). The 'sacred teaching', says Psellos, concerns the 'flower of the intellect'. This cannot of its own accord ascend to the highest point and thus embrace the divine. Just as the Chaldeans claimed to manipulate the human intellect towards god by means of theurgy, Christian piety does so by means of godsent illuminations. According to 'our theologian' Gregory of Nazianzus, the soul ascends through a combination of what is most intellectual and superior in us, that is reason (λόγος), with spiritual illumination (θεωρία).

Significantly, Psellos acknowledges that for Plato the 'ungenerated essence' is accessible to human reason and intellect – whereas for the 'Chaldean' the only route to ascend to god is by 'enhancing the vehicle of the soul by means of material rites: for he [the Chaldean] thinks that the soul is purified by stones, herbs and incantations and thus becomes well-wheeled for its ascent'.[190] It follows that 'the Chaldean' is closer to Gregory's perception of divine illumination (ἔλλαμψις) than Plato's rationalism could ever be. This is reason enough for Psellos to see Neoplatonic theurgy and Christianity as sharing common ground. It is also reason enough for Plethon to abandon both.

On a purely linguistic level Plethon agrees with Psellos that ascension of the soul is a question of reason (λόγος) and vision (θεωρία). Only now *theoria* does not come from without by means of illumination as in Gregory of Nazianzus. It may well come from within in the original Platonic sense of *theoria*. Hence,

---

[190] Ps. *Phil. minora* 131.15–132.15 O'Meara.

Plethon makes one concession in his commentary and observes that religious rites may complement the acquisition of the 'sacred teaching'. Still, philosophical discourse remains primary and non-negotiable.[191] There are problems with Plethon's fascinating attempt to secularise the *Oracles*. For example, fr. 107 (des Places) appears to point in the other direction:

> [T]*he plant of truth does not exist on earth*... Let be the rushing motion of the moon; she forever runs her course by the action of Necessity. The starry procession has not been brought forth for your sake. The wide-winged flight of birds is never true, nor the cuttings and entrails of sacrificial victims. All these are playthings, the props of commercial fraud. Flee these things, if you would open the sacred paradise of piety, where virtue, wisdom and good order are brought together. (trans. Majercik)

Psellos discovered in fr. 107 an apology for negative theology. Plethon prefers to exile the vexatious oracle from his collection without further ado. Tambrun and Athanassiadi have correctly noted that one might see in this 'oracle' a condemnation of 'Hellenic wisdom' in its entirety, but that this kind of 'cosmic pessimism' was in the eyes of Plethon wrong on philosophical grounds.[192] This begs the question: What are these grounds?

The key is provided by the notion of epistemic optimism in the *Nomoi*, which, we have seen, allows the faculty of the intellect to elevate man next to the gods in a communal expedition to intellectualise 'Zeus'. This renders cognisable what occurs necessarily as well as accidentally. While excluding fr. 107, Plethon reads fr. 1 (des Places) as confirming the kinship between human and divine nature and the potential knowability of the divine. The opening sentence of the 'oracle' is significant:

> So there is something intelligible, which you have to conceive by means of the 'flower of the intellect (ὃ χρή σε νοεῖν νόου ἄνθει)'. (*Orac.* Chald. fr. 1.1)

Plethon comments thus:

> One cannot conceive of the supreme god in the same manner as one conceives of the other intelligibles, but only by means of the 'flower of the intellect', that is

---

[191]   See the introduction by Tambrun to her edition of Plethon's *Oracles*, 63.
[192]   Athanassiadi (2002) 240; cf. the commentary of Tambrun to Plethon's recension of the *Oracles*, 155–6.

217

to say, the highest and simplest part of our intellect (τῷ τοῦ νοῦ ἄνθει, ἤτοι τῷ ἀκροτάτῳ καὶ ἑνιαίῳ τῆς ἡμετέρας νοήσεως). (Pleth. *Orac.* 28b)

In the *Nomoi* man possesses an 'essence similar to that of gods'. The most subtle of human tasks is to synchronise with the gods in a communal intellection of 'Zeus'.[193] In his commentary to the *Oracles* the 'flower of the intellect' stands for this irreducible 'essence'. The expression has a long history in Neoplatonism.[194] The conception of a highest point in our soul or *nous* that is able to connect man to the Soul or Intellect and god may be traced back to Plotinus' 'the Intellect within', as well as to Porphyry's primeval intellect (νοῦς προαιώνιος), and ultimately to Celsus, Numenius and to Plato's Seventh Epistle.[195] It echoes Plato's description in the *Timaeus* of the 'divine element' in human soul, also called a 'daemon', which is responsible for the divine rather than earthly origin of humanity.[196] Proclus speaks of the 'flower of the soul (τὸ ἄνθος τῆς ψυχῆς)', and 'the flower of our essence', according to which we assimilate to god.[197] Simplicius uses a similar expression: 'the summit of *nous* (ἀκρότατος νοῦς)'.[198] We may plausibly surmise that late Byzantine humanists were not unfamiliar with the philosophical consequences of this doctrine. In his crypto-paganising commentary on Synesius' *De insomniis*, Nikephoros Gregoras has this note on the use of the expression τὸ νοερὸν σπέρμα for the human soul: 'he [Synesius] calls the soul intelligible sperm, namely divine rather than human'.[199]

According to Plethon's interpretation of fr. 1.1 the supreme god is different from other intelligibles in so far as he is their summit, that is, in the same way that the Idea of the Good is different from other Ideas. Still, if god is intelligible, then god is comprehensible, which means god is not truly beyond Being. This is corroborated

[193] *Nomoi* 246 (3.43.75–7).

[194] See the commentary by Tambrun to her edition of Plethon's *Oracles*, 134.

[195] See Rist (1964): 213–25, who notes *Enn.* 5.3.14.15 and Porph. *ap.* Procl. *Theol. Plat.* 1.2.27. In *Philebus* 6a–29a, *nous* is the 'king of heaven and earth', responsible for ordering the whole revolving universe and controlling violence and 'universal wickedness' by means of law and order.

[196] *Ti.* 90a–d

[197] Procl. *In Prm.* 1071.30; *Eclogae* 4.51–8; *In Alc.* 247.11; 248.3; *In Ti.* 3.14.6–13; 212.9. But see also *Eph.* 1:17; Diadocus Photicensis, *Capita* 71.15.

[198] Simpl. *In de An.* 240.21–30, 245.8.   [199] Gregoras, *In Synes.* 43 Pietrosanti.

by Plethon's commentary on the last line of this notorious 'oracle', fr. 1.10:

Study the intelligible, for it exists beyond the intellect.

Which means study the intelligible because it exists *actually* outside *your* intellect. For even though the demiurge has sown *images of the intelligible entities* within you, they nevertheless reside *potentially* within your soul. Hence you have to participate actively in the knowledge of the intelligible. (Pleth. *Orac.* 28a)

Here too, it is worth making the comparison with Psellos. In the latter's Christianisation of the *Oracles* the meaning is that 'even though everything can be conceived of by the intellect, god, the primary Intelligible, exists beyond the intellect'. His caveat that god should not be conceived of in terms of any 'intelligible Otherness (ἑτερότητα νοεράν)' but rather in terms of intellectual excess (κατὰ μόνην τὴν νοητὴν ὑπερβολὴν) signifies a first daring break with Orthodox apophaticism and betrays the anxiety to align pagan intellectualism with Judaeo-Christian creationism.[200] For his part, Plethon makes no concessions. He openly affirms that the divine summit is conceivable by means of energising the summit of the human intellect.

This doctrine pushes the boundaries of Proclan epistemology. Plethon's images of 'intelligible entities' within us correspond to Proclus' 'essential reasons (οὐσιώδεις λόγοι)' of all things: 'every soul possesses in its own essence all the forms which the intellect possesses primitively'.[201] These are *a priori* cognitive and formative principles identical with the essence of the human soul that offer the route to knowledge by means of rational discourse. Intelligible entities transcend the human intellect only in so far as human beings fail to energise the kindred intelligible link within them. To this end theurgy is not necessary; what matters, is 'to participate actively in the knowledge of the intelligible'.

It might be objected that Plethon's Platonic, in reality secular, hermeneutical approach to a text traditionally considered as related

---

200 Psell. *Opuscula psychologica, theologica, daemonologica* 145.11–22 (ed. O'Meara).
201 *ET* 194. On 'essential reasons' see Steel (1997) 293–309.

to theurgy is odd. Things are more complicated than that. In the modern edition of the *Chaldean Oracles* a Proclan fragment transmits the pagan persuasion that intellectual mysticism and wisdom are the proper channels through which human beings participate among the ranks of gods. This confirms Plethon's approach:

And it is clear that the oracle teaches these things:

> 'A sweet desire takes hold of all (souls) to dwell forever on Olympus as companions of the immortal gods. But not all are permitted to set foot in these halls.'

When the person who had received the oracle, which had been delivered to him most fully, asked who it was, then, who achieved the ascent to the gods, and if it was the individual who especially preferred the life of the haruspex, the god added further:

> 'It is not whoever has thoughtfully placed his intention on the entrails (of sacrificial victims) who will immediately go to Olympus after the dissolution of the body, riding aloft on the light wings of the soul, but whoever is wise.'
> (Procl. *In Rempub.* 2.126.14–26 (*Or.* fr. 217 des Places); trans. Majercik)

Plethon and the Neoplatonists are not alone when talking of some sort of 'images of the intelligible entities' leading to divine knowledge. Expanding Maximus' doctrine of the *logoi* of beings, Gregory Palamas argued that man possesses *images* of those divine *logoi* that run through creation and reside in the creative intelligence. These images function as an esoteric mirror originally meant to give man the capacity to ascend to god through creation.[202] And yet Plethon and Palamas are poles apart.

The rift between, on the one hand, Proclan 'essential reasons (οὐσιώδεις λόγοι)' and Plethonean *images of the intelligible entities*, and, on the other hand, Palamas' *images of logoi* reflects that between Roman Orthodox mystical theology and Platonist epistemological optimism. According to Palamas, the images of the *logoi* are inactive as well as ineffective – for they were corrupted upon man's Fall. The human soul is totally deprived of divine life and incapable of energising on its own account these images to exit the default state of spiritual, but nonetheless very real

---

[202] Meyendorff (1959) 180. Cf. p. 291.

death. The primordial rupture with god accounts for the complete alienation of the soul from 'life within God'. This corresponds to a state of living death – a spiritual necrosis far worse than biological death.[203]

To the extent that Palamism considers Orthodoxy a mode of existence rather than a religious cult, the sentiments of Angst, despair and internal strife experienced by individuals are the product of a spiritual condition perpetuating a profound disharmony between human life and 'life within God'. Supernatural grace, experiential godlikeness and illumination promised to heal the whole of man as a psychophysical entity, even if this means reversing the popular notions of life and death. Symeon the New Theologian is here pertinent: 'Die and you shall live. You do not want to die? Well, then you are already dead.'[204]

Conversely, Proclan 'essential reasons' secretly operate as a form of internal 'breathing' or intellectual 'pulse' that may be fully awakened and stimulated by sense perception and rational discourse.[205] The essential reasons serve as the proper point of reference and scientific object of dialectical ascent. The philosopher comprehends intelligible realities by employing the techniques of dialectic, namely analytical reduction, discrimination, definition and deductive reasoning.[206] Human intellection is, as Proclus puts it in his *Commentary to Plato's Cratylus*, 'an idol (εἴδωλον) of the Intellect'. Its intellectual activity potentially manages to ascend to intelligible reality (τῆς ἀληθείας ἐφάπτεται), even if only partially.[207] It follows that the Palamite belief in the 'living death' of the soul's in this world is no more compatible with Proclus than it is with Plotinus. The post-Iamblichean tradition departed from Plotinus' belief in an undescended part of the soul remaining in a permanent state of intellectual activity. But in Proclus the descent of human soul hardly means that it resides in a condition of absolute inactivity and helplessness. The human condition as such does not equal spiritual death. The soul may on account of its own rational faculties energise the innate 'images of

[203] Meyendorff(1959) 179–82.   [204] Symeon, *Or. Eth.* 11.45 Darrouzès.
[205] Steel (1997) 297ff.   [206] Procl. *In Crat.* 3
[207] Procl. *In Crat.* 64.

intelligible entities' and recover firm knowledge necessary for its *eudaimonia*.

The underlying Platonic belief is that knowledge of god is tantamount to a humanly initiated ascent to self-knowledge and self-healing. From where Maximus and Palamas were standing, there could hardly be another doctrine as steeped in Hellenism as this one.

5

PAGAN ONTOLOGY

Towards a new ontology

The parallel reading of the *Nomoi* and the *Differences* reveals their author edging towards a reformation of ancient Greek ontology by advancing four theses that directly conflict with respective fundamental Christian distinctions. As if in a purposeful effort to corroborate the suspicions of Aquinas, Palamas, George of Trebizond and Scholarios that Platonism is the source of all things heretic, Plethon proceeds to a dechristianisation of Plato. Very disturbingly for his contemporary Christian theologians, he credits Plato with the following hallmarks of his pagan ontology:

1. Being *is* the supreme *genus*. Nothing exists outside Being – not even god. The pagan Platonic notion of *ousia* is substituted for the Judaeo-Christian belief in a transcendent personal divine agent. This challenges Palamas' distinction between supra-essential Being and categorical Being. According to Palamite Orthodoxy, the absolute transcendence and otherness of a personal agent is a ξένη φύσις, an 'alien nature' radically beyond and *essentially* different to the philosophical category of *ousia*.[1]
2. It is logically necessary to assume causes mediating between Being *qua* Being and the world of becoming and corruption. God is not beyond logical and ontological necessity. If the effects are analogous to causes, then the world of alteration cannot be the direct offspring of an immutable primary cause. By implication, god is *not* directly and immediately the productive cause of an ontologically distinct physical world.
3. A pagan theogony and cosmogony is substituted for Christian *ktisiology*. The world and intermediate orders of causes/gods represent aspects of a unified genealogy of Being, not an extra-deical construction (κτίσις). Rather than constructed, these causes/gods are

---

[1] Cf. Joh. Dam. *Exp. fidei* 13.58: πάντα ἀπέχει Θεοῦ, οὐ τόπῳ ἀλλὰ φύσει, and Gr. Pal. *Capita CL* 78.1.

THE ELEMENTS OF PAGAN PLATONISM

naturally born of 'Zeus' or each other, retaining a common biological-ontological link to Being *qua* Being. The orders of gods/causes intermediate between the world and god, as well as the world, fully qualify to the κατὰ φύσιν generation reserved in Christianity only for Christ/Logos. This cancels the distinction between creation according to god's free will (κατὰ βούλησιν) and the eternal generation (κατὰ φύσιν) of Christ/Logos in the Trinity. In other words, Plethon demolishes the exclusive distinction between *natura increata* and *natura creata*.

4. Multi-causalism carries a deterministic dimension, according to which freedom consists in discovering and aligning oneself to necessity/fate, rather than in escaping the compulsion of logical and ontological necessity through Christ/Logos. This means acquiring the knowledge of how causes interact, knowledge which, *contra Aristotelem*, is extended to cover what is considered 'accidental' too.

Chapters 5 and 6 focus on these four aspects of Plethon's cosmogony and ontology. But there is a significant contextual aspect of Plethon's re-sacralisation of *cosmos* and Being that needs to be taken into consideration. This concerns the mystical tradition of the Greek Orthodox East according to which the divine power/energy, sometimes seen as interchangeable with the all-presence of Christ/Logos, is transmitted to and runs through all parts of physical creation, spiritualising, energising and binding them together. Palamite theologians were always wary of avoiding pantheism or animism by means of their favourite motto that the essence of god is radically different from divine energy. Still, Palamite Orthodoxy made concessions to a belief of potentially panentheist consequences according to which god holds together and fills the world without being contained by it. Mere divine presence in matter is different to pagan gradations of ontological immanence: god 'fills everything and stays above every single thing', as Gregory of Nazianzus' verse goes: πάντα πληροῖ καὶ ἄνω παντὸς μένει.[2] Symeon the New Theologian put the relation between transcendence and divine presence in verses far superior to those of Gregory. Their aporetic nature fully transmits the

---

[2] Gr. Naz. *Carmina moralia* 749.10. Basil uses a similar expression: the Holy Spirit ἐπὶ πάντα διήκει. He then finds solid scriptural references: Πνεῦμα γάρ ἐστι τὸ πεπληρωκὸς τὰ σύμπαντα, κατὰ τὸ γεγραμμένον· Πνεῦμα γὰρ Κυρίου πεπλήρωκε τὴν οἰκουμένην, φησὶν ὁ Σολομών (*Eun.*, PG 29.741.25–37).

potential theological problems faced by Christian mystics and their opponents: How do the words *within* (ἔσω) and *without* (ἔξω) relate to god? 'I am *outside* everything because cut off from everything'; but then again, how could one assume that 'I, who carry everything within, for I hold together all creation, will not also be *within* my creations, though being their creator'?[3]

The tension of divine transcendence and divine immanence in the mystical tradition of Eastern Orthodoxy made itself fully felt during the iconoclastic controversy. Icon worship was authorised on the grounds that matter (to quote John of Damascus) is 'full of divine energy and grace' (θείας ἐνεργείας καὶ χάριτος ἔμπλεων).[4] This thesis demands considerable effort to avoid the hazardous confusion with its pagan counterpart, or rather, its blueprint: the belief that matter is not only divinely energised but actually participates (however imperfectly or remotely) in divine essence. The difference between pagan icon worship condemned by Christions and Roman Orthodox icon worship as defended by John of Damascus is ultimately one between unqualified ontological immanence and conditional divine presence. In the latter case the emphasis lies on a passive process, according to which the physical universe is filled by divine energy, whereas in the former case pagans insisted on an active process, according to which matter participates in a hierarchically ordered but unified Being.

My point here is that this difference came down to a careful choice of words and rendered the Eastern intellectual framework ideal for Plethon's project. I will be arguing that the fierce debates regarding the relation between essence and energies in god during the fourteenth-century Hesychast controversy fertilised and prepared the ground for Plethon's substitution of 'gods' for 'energies' and, *a fortiori*, for the conscious abolition of the distinction between uncreated essence and created substance. John of Damascus, Maximus Confessor and Gregory Palamas were determined

---

3 Symeon, *Hymni* 23.24–35: τίνος γὰρ ὁ κτίστης ἔσω, | ποίου δέ, εἰπέ μοι, ἔξω; | πάντα ἔνδον περιφέρω | ὡς συνέχων πᾶσαν κτίσιν, | πάντων ἔξω δὲ τυγχάνω | πάντων ὢν κεχωρισμένος· | ὁ γὰρ κτίστης τῶν κτισμάτων | πῶς οὐκ ἔσται πάντων ἔξω; | ὁ πρὸ πάντων δὲ ὑπάρχων | καὶ πληρῶν τὸ πᾶν ὡς πλήρης | πῶς οὐκ ἔσομαι καὶ κτίσας | ἐν τοῖς κτίσμασί μου πᾶσι;

4 Joh. Dam. *Πρὸς τοὺς διαβάλλοντας τὰς ἁγίας εἰκόνας*, PG 94.1245.

to maintain their fine and elaborate theological and philosophical distinctions at all costs. But Plethon was not.

Well versed in the theology of the Greek East, Plethon discerned echoes from a not so distant pagan past surviving within Eastern mysticism. Instead of shutting his ears to the evil sirens, he decided to pay attention to what they had to say – and set them free.

The threat of 'one *genus* of everything, Being'

For the whole Neoplatonic Christian tradition divine essence is trans-categorical. The One/god is outside the category of substance described by Aristotle or any set of categories. *Theologia* relates to what is beyond the reach of categorical being. Already Plotinus' reading of Aristotle revolved around the view that any category of Being is non-applicable to real Being.[5] The word *ousia* cannot be taken to refer univocally to both sensible being and supra-sensible being. This would render both species of a single *genus* that is neither sensible nor non-sensible.[6] Rather, the One is 'beyond' any possible category of Being and all *genera*.[7] The intelligible realm possesses no *ousia* predicated by categories of the sensible world. Finite beings are in the One, but the One is not in finite being.[8]

Aristotle's theory of the categories suits well two opposed views: the 'theistic' view that – after Porphyry – restricts their applicability to composite substances and kinds of sensible being, thus enjoying absolute freedom in introducing theological constructions in regard to the super-sensible realm of the One/god;[9] and the opposite secular or materialistic view that does not acknowledge any need to go beyond Aristotle's categorical *ousia* in any quest for what Plotinus calls the One and Palamas 'the supra-essential essence'. It is the former appropriation of Aristotle that prevailed. Notwithstanding that later Neoplatonists reconsidered the question whether Aristotle's categories may be applicable to

---

[5] *Enn.* 6.1.1.　　[6] *Enn.* 6.1.2.4–8.　　[7] *Enn.* 6.2.3.4–9.　　[8] *Enn.* 5.4.1.11–12.
[9] See for example the distinction between 'names relative to creation (ἐπὶ τῆς κτίσεως)' that are 'contingently applicable' to objects and the use of names 'in relation to divine nature (ἐπὶ τῆς θείας φύσεως)' in theology according to Gr. Nyssa, *Ad Ablabium* 43.3–44.6.

both the sensible and the intelligible realms, they all agreed that the One was beyond the category of Substance.[10]

Palamas' attack on fourteenth-century anti-mystical and secular tendencies utilises a variant of Plotinus' approach to Aristotle's categories that aims to show the limitations and restrictions of Greek ontology. Knowing god, he says, is different from knowing the laws of predication – different from human knowledge. Divine Being and divine knowledge are absolutely transcendent and not to be mingled with human apprehensions of Being and Knowledge. The category of substance is most remote from and radically, essentially different from divine nature, which is, as Palamas has it: a ξένη φύσις, an alien, personal nature.[11] His use of Exodus 3:14 is most instructive:

Perhaps he [Barlaam] will say that by the term 'essence' (οὐσία) he means this, that [God] possesses all these powers in Himself in a unique and unifying manner. *But, in the first place, it would be necessary to call this reality 'God', for such is the term for it, which we have received from the Church.* When God was conversing with Moses, He did not say, 'I am the essence (ἐγώ εἰμι ἡ οὐσία)', but 'I am He Who is (ἐγώ εἰμι ὁ ὤν)'. Thus it is not the One Who Is (ὁ ὤν) who derives from essence (ἡ οὐσία), but essence which derives from Him, for it is He who contains all being in Himself. (Gr. Pal. *Triads* 3.2.12.1–8; trans. Gendle with modifications)

This is no word-play between *on* and *ousia*. This is the whole clash between pagan ontological monism and Judaeo-Christian theism in a nutshell: namely, the opposition of *ousia* as a unified Being to the personhood of a supra-essential agent not only causally superior or ontologically pure and simple but *essentially* 'other' to creation.[12]

---

[10] Dillon (1997) 65–77.

[11] On the Eastern Orthodox notion of Personhood see Zizioulas (2006: *passim* and 165), on the clash between Cappadocian theology and ancient Greek ontology. Cf. John of Damascus on the Father as the cause of divine existence, *Exp. fidei* 25.

[12] See Zizioulas (2006) 164; (1985) 29–31: 'this ontological monism which characterizes Greek philosophy from its inception leads Greek thought to the concept of the cosmos, that is, of the harmonious relationship of existent things among themselves. Not even God can escape from this ontological unity and stand freely before the world, "face to face" in dialogue with it. He too is bound by ontological necessity to the world and the world to him, either through the creation of Plato's *Timaeus* or through the Logos of the Stoics or through the "emanations" of Plotinus' *Enneads* . . . However, in such a world it is impossible for the unforeseen to happen or for freedom to operate as an absolute and unrestricted claim to existence: whatever threatens cosmic harmony and is not explained by "reason" (*logos*), which draws all things together and leads them to this harmony

Elsewhere Palamas puts it in terms of a battle between the Hellenic conception of the first principle as ἕν and the Judaeo-Christian belief in God as εἷς: the pagan *One* versus *Him*. It is absurd to suppose that there exists 'one genus of everything, Being' and that He who is beyond everything is classified *within* Being – namely to suppose that Being is superior to One.[13] Palamas is elaborating on Aristotle's argument that it is impossible to include all things within a single *genus*.[14] Writing against Akindynos, he notes that it is demonstrated that god 'is a unique personal being and not a unique impersonal thing': εἷς καὶ οὐχ ἓν ἀποδείκνυται.[15]

And yet Palamas sees his contemporary experiments with pagan ontology as naturally leading to such an ontological subversion. He thus elucidates the word 'supra-essential' (ὑπερούσιος) by distinguishing between the category of substance and divine essence. The supra-essential is no species of substance: οὐδὲ τὸ ὑπερούσιον οὐσίας εἶδος.[16] Assuming that there are ten types of predication applicable to all beings, that is Aristotle's categories, then god is a super-essential essence (ὁ θεὸς οὐσία ὑπερούσιός ἐστιν) that acts as a creative agent without undergoing any synthesis or alteration.[17] Of Aristotle's categories only those of relation (πρός τι) and action (ποιεῖν) may be said of the super-essential essence, for god is related to the world through his energies and is a creative, hence active cause.[18] The quality of Being (ὀντότης) is only one 'unbegotten work' of god among others.[19] As Palamas put it, 'god is not Being (ὄν), if we think of everything else as beings (ὄντα);

---

and unity, is rejected and condemned.' Seen from this perspective, Plethon's ontology and notion of *heimarmene* are the epitome of pagan Hellenic world-view.

[13] Gr. Pal. *Triads* 2.3.34.23–5: ἓν ἁπάντων γένος, τὸ ὄν, καὶ ὁ ὑπὲρ πάντα ὢν εἷς ὑπ' αὐτό, καὶ τὸ ὂν τοῦ ἑνὸς τούτου κρεῖττον... In reality Barlaam too seems to have clarified, at least on one occasion, that god and beings are not paronymous. God is the One-in-itself (*hen*), not any other Being (*on*), free from the quality of Being (*ontotes*), unity, finitude or definition. God is *autoen*, One-in-itself and it is *atopon* to assume that there is anything in common (*koinon*) between the One and all beings (see Barlaam, *Ep.* 1.724–46). In other words: god is the radical *Other*, a personal agent. This comes close to the typically Orthodox notion of god's personhood.

[14] *Metaph.* 998b22–5: 'But it is impossible for either Unity or Being to be one genus of existing things. For there must *be differentiae* of each *genus*, and each *differentia* must be *one* ...'

[15] *Ep.* 1.9.2–3. On this passage see Sinkewicz (1982) 198.

[16] Gr. Pal. *Triads* 1.3.33.8.   [17] Gr. Pal. *Capita CL* 134.1–14.

[18] *Capita CL* 135.   [19] *Triads* 3.2.7.1–13.

and if he *is* Being, then nothing else qualifies as being'.[20] If the world is, then god *is not*; and if the world *is not*, then god *is*.

What Palamas opposed as an *ad absurdum* hypothesis within the Hesychast controversy, namely the assumption of 'one *genus* of everything, Being' becomes the axis of Plethon's radical Platonism in the next century. A common characteristic of both the *Differences* and the *Nomoi* is the non-distinction between ontology and theology. Scholarios was conscious of the threat posed by this move. *God is neither a genus nor classifiable within a genus*, he notes in a treatise 'On the distinction of divine energies among themselves and from the divine essence', concurring with Palamas.[21] Plethon's move in the *Differences* could not stay unnoticed.

In the *Differences* Being *is* a *genus*; further, Being is One. Plethon reverses both of Palamas' and John of Damascus' presuppositions of Orthodox faith, that God is beyond knowledge and beyond Being. The assumption of a common '*genus* of Being' in ontology counters the Eastern Orthodox theological notion of 'God' as a supra-essential agent beyond Being *and* non-Being, as well as Proclan Neoplatonism and appears to accord with the Thomist convertibility of Being and One.[22] The distinction between a fully transcendent uncreated essence and created substance is implicitly contested. The personhood of God recedes into the background giving place to a reborn monistic pagan philosophy preoccupied with maintaining at all cost the unity of Being.

---

[20] Gr. Pal. *Capita CL* 78.3–5: ὡς οὐδ᾽ ὄν ἐστιν, εἰ τἆλλα ὄντα ἐστίν· εἰ δ᾽ ἔστιν ἐκεῖνος ὤν, τἆλλα οὐκ ἔστιν ὄντα.

[21] Schol. *Distinctio essentiae divinae et operationum suarum*, *OC* 3.234.24–37; 3.236.34.

[22] *Diff.* 323.10–324.27. Plethon's break with the basic Neoplatonic position that the One *cannot* be Being has been shown by Tambrun (2003) 69–82; (2006a) 176; cf. Couloubaritsis (1997: 129 n. 55) for the Thomist parallels. Masai (1956: 213) correctly notes that Plethon sides with the Greek philosophical tradition in substituting Being for Judaeo-Christian 'creation', uniting all things into a common *genus*. In Masai's reading, though, the super-essential nature of the Plethonean supreme god is taken to mean that god is elevated above the *genus* of Being. In fact, in the *Differences* Plethon calls god *hyperousios* (*Diff.* 326.31–3; 337.19–21). Yet upon closer scrutiny we shall see that the word appears to carry a meaning very different to that of radical ontological differentiation between ucreated essence and created substance that Palamas read in Exodus 3:14. Rather, Plethon's 'hyperousios' marks a return to the original meaning of Plato's notorious expression *hepekeina tes ousias* (beyond Being) in *Republic* 509b in respect to the Idea of the Good. See pp. 243ff., 192–3, 218–19.

Divine Being and the world's Being are more than equivocal. Their difference is not really ontological, but one regarding the extent of participation within Being.

In Plethon ontological monism acquires its most militant version carrying resonances from a common Parmenidean-Platonic exemplar that was abandoned until his time by post-Plotinean Platonism: Οὐδὲν ἔστιν ἢ ἔσται ἄλλο πάρεξ τοῦ ἐόντος: there is nothing nor will be anything outside Being.[23] The best point of departure for exploring this thesis is a seemingly technical and ostensibly academic disagreement on Aristotle's theory of the equivocity of Being. In reality, this hides within one of the most fascinating clashes between Greek ontology and Christian theology in the history of philosophy.

Against the equivocity of Being

Aristotle's theory of the equivocity of Being is one of Plethon's primary targets in the *Differences*.[24] Why would the author of the *Nomoi* care to demolish Aristotle's theory? One of the few people – beside Scholarios – to have discerned the real significance and intentionality behind Plethon's move is Marsilio Ficino.

In his commentary on Pseudo-Dionysian *Divine Names* Ficino refers to Plethon as sharing the Platonist view that god *is not* beyond Being. According to Ficino, Dionysius sensibly considers god as super-essential, since god generates beings. Otherwise, says Ficino, the essence of god would be univocal with the essences of created beings, 'which is the opinion of certain famous metaphysicians *as well as that of Plethon the Platonic philosopher*'.[25]

---

[23] Parmenides 28 DK 8.36–7. Plethon's return to Parmenidean ontology is corroborated by the concomitant revival of the notions of Necessity and Fate (Ἀνάγκη, Μοῖρα) through his belief in *heimarmene*.

[24] See Aristotle's definition of equivocity in *Cat.* 1a1–3: 'Things are equivocally (*homonyma*) named, when they have the name only in common, the definition corresponding with the name being different. For instance, while a man and a portrait can properly both be called "animals", these are equivocally named. For they have the name only in common, the definitions corresponding with the name being different.' On univocity see *Cat.* 1a6–8: 'Things are univocally named, when not only they bear the same name, but the name means the same in each case – has the definition corresponding. Thus a man and an ox are called "animals"'.

[25] P. R. Blum (2006) xlv–xlvi; on Ficino and Plethon cf. Monfasani (2002) 198f.

Aristotle's theory of the equivocity of Being is here presupposed in order to maintain the distinction between created substance and god's essence. Without it nothing precludes the assumption that the essence of god and the essence of particular beings are somehow related, namely, that the word 'essence' is used in both cases to designate aspects of a single system.

The point Ficino makes is as pertinent to the Pseudo-Dionysian tradition as it was to the Neoplatonists. For example, according to Plotinus substance within the realm of becoming can only be called 'substance' equivocally: for it corresponds to coming into being rather than to Being properly so called.[26] It follows that any attack on Aristotle's theory of the equivocity of Being entails serious collateral damage. Its impact is not limited to Christian intellectuals but extends to all Neoplatonists making an implicit appeal to it. Though a Platonist, Plethon did launch the attack – the vision of a new and radical Platonism hardly required either the concordance of Plato and Aristotle or that among later Platonists. It relied on a modern interpretation of Plato's ontology.

Aristotle is 'certainly wrong if he supposes that two beings, one of them having a greater participation in being and the other less, are called *beings* equivocally'.[27] According to Aristotle, a pale thing is more pale than another, and a beautiful thing more beautiful than another.[28] Still, they *are* pale and beautiful respectively. A *genus* may be diversified into more perfect and less perfect forms. Hence, the white in wool is no less real white than is the white in snow.[29] By implication, Plethon argues that nothing forces us to accept the equivocity of Being. Even if one being *is* 'more' or 'less' than another, Being is still the *genus* of both this *and* the less perfect being.[30] In an epistle to Bessarion, Plethon makes the very same point: 'The fact that some beings participate in Being

[26] *Enn.* 6.3.2.1–4.   [27] *Diff.* 323.8–10.   [28] Cf. Arist. *Cat.* 5.4a1–2.

[29] *Sophista* may have provided Plethon's starting point here. See *Soph.* 237d: 'Visitor: It's obvious to us that we always apply this something to a being, since it is impossible to say it by itself, as if it were naked and isolated from all beings. Isn't that right? Theaetetus: Yes' (trans. White).

[30] On aspects of Plethon's attack on Aristotle see Evangeliou (2006) and Tavardon (1977). Cf. Pleth. *Contra Schol.* 23.39–40. Bessarion points out that according to one reading of Plato intelligible entities (*ta noeta*) may be taken to be equivocal to the first principle and sensible things equivocal to the intelligibles (Bess. *Ep.* 20, Mohler III 464.6–11).

more than others does not prevent us in the least from classifying all of them under a single *genus*.'[31] While in Aristotelian terms it is possible to argue that 'everything that is common' (τὰ κοινά) indicates not a 'this' (τόδε τι) but a 'such' (τοιόνδε), Plethon seeks to recover a universal and hence κοινόν *genus* of *what is* primarily.[32] Plethon shifts the focus from quantity and quality to substance.

He thus comes up with that 'one *genus* of everything, Being' (*Diff.* 323.21) that Palamas believed to have uncovered as the end of Barlaam's endeavours, and which was a plain absurdity for Aquinas and Scholarios too. All three (Palamas, Aquinas and Scholarios) had the same point of departure: Aristotle. The position of Aristotle is that the most universal of predicates, that is to say Being (ὄν) and One (ἕν), are coextensive but not *substances* or *genera*.[33] The 'One' is in every *genus* a definite entity, but in no case is its nature merely 'One'.[34] 'It is impossible', he argues, 'for anything predicated universally (τὰ καθόλου) to be a substance (οὐσία).'[35] The deeper significance of the Plethonean attempt to undercut Aristotle's case becomes apparent once we consider their respective theological applications.

The Aristotelean thesis that it is impossible for either Unity (ἕν) or Being (ὄν) to be one *genus* of existing things was taken up by Thomas Aquinas in the *Summa Theologiae* as well as in the *Summa contra Gentiles* in order to show 'that god is *not*

'Do not get upset', replied Plethon, 'if sensible things are said to be equivocal to the intelligibles.' This hardly affects the non-equivocity of Being. A particular man may be said to be equivocal with the intelligible man; but this does not necessarily mean that their *being* is also equivocal. We may say that a sea dog and an ordinary dog are dogs equivocally, in so far as we call them both 'dogs'. But this hardly means that their being is also meant equivocally: they both *are* in a non-equivocal sense (Pleth. *Ep. Bess.* 2, Mohler III 466.3–7). This is the same point made in *Contra Schol.* 23.26–35. I quote Woodhouse's paraphrase: 'The point which Aristotle failed to understand is that although every genus is shared equally in a verbal sense (λόγῳ) by all the species comprised in it, it is not shared equally in reality (τῷ δὲ πράγματι οὐκ ἐπίσης). "Being" is thus a univocal concept but unequally shared . . . Aristotle was mistaken in thinking that what is the case in verbal terms must also be the case in reality.'

[31] Pleth. *Ep. Bess.* 2, Mohler III 461.3–5.

[32] *Metaph.* 1003a8–9: οὐθὲν γὰρ τῶν κοινῶν τόδε τι σημαίνει ἀλλὰ τοιόνδε, ἡ δ' οὐσία τόδε τι.

[33] *Metaph.* 1053b17–24.   [34] *Metaph.* 1054a9–11.

[35] *Metaph.* 1038b8–9; 1038b34–5.

in some genus'.[36] Scholarios was familiar with Aquinas' use of Aristotle on this point, which he encountered as a translator.[37] Against the univocity of Being implied by pagan ontology, Aquinas argued that Being is *not* a *genus* but is said in different ways of diverse things (τὸ ὂν λέγεται πολλαχῶς).[38] This appropriation of Aristotle served ideally the case for the unqualifiable and non-negotiable transcendence of the Christian god, since, according to Aquinas, if god is *not* in a *genus* then neither can god be defined, nor demonstrated 'except through an effect'.[39] Conversely, if the first principle, namely Being-in-itself, *is* a *genus*, then, to paraphrase Aquinas, it is evident that god *can* be defined, for every definition is constituted from the *genus* and the differences.[40]

We have reached the crux of the matter, the heart of Plethon's paganism. *Mutatis mutandis* from a Thomist and Palamite perspective Plethon's recurrent affirmation against Aristotle's authority that Being *is* the universal *genus* implies that god *can* be seized insofar as extreme Being is still Being. To argue that Being *is* a *genus* is the necessary step towards the revival of monist ontology according to which there is no absolute ontological difference between supra-essential essence and 'created' substance, but only a diversification in regard to the extent according to which everything participates within the *genus* of Being.

Scholarios read between the lines of Plethon's *Differences* and grasped the deeper intentionality behind Plethon's refutation of Aristotle's theory of the equivocity of Being. God, protests Scholarios in *Against Plethon*, suffices as a cause. Why then linger on the question of any purportedly common ontological substratum that links god to creation?[41]

---

[36] Cf. *Metaph.* 998b22; Aquinas, *Summa contra Gentiles* 1.25.6; cf. *Summa Theologiae* 1.q3.a5.

[37] See Schol. *Epitome, OC* 5.1.25: ῞Οτι οὐκ ἔστιν (god) ἔν τινι γένει. Cf. Scholarios' translation of Aquinas' *De ente et essentiae OC* 6.6–11: Καὶ ἐκ τούτου ἔπεται μὴ εἶναι αὐτὸν (god) ἐν γένει . . .

[38] *Metaph.* 1003a33. See Tavardon (1977: 268–78) for the different understandings of *to on* by Plethon and Scholarios.

[39] Aquinas, *SCG* 1.25.7–8.

[40] Aquinas, *SCG* 1.25.7: 'From this [that God is not in some *genus*] it is evident that God *cannot* be defined, for every definition is constituted from the genus and the differences'.

[41] Schol. *Contra Pleth., OC* 4.49.9–11.

Plethon's point was that Aristotle introduced a form of ontological anarchy that cancelled the unity of Being by not allowing for that 'one thing in common between all things' and 'the relation *of all things* to the one source of their Being'. Interestingly, Plethon credited none other than Aristotle with the identification between substance (οὐσία) and Being *par excellence* (μάλιστα ὄν): 'If substance is that which most properly is (τὸ μάλιστα ὄν), as Aristotle himself says...'[42] Still, Aristotle disrupts ontological unity and prohibits the participation of everything *that is* in the One Being (ἓν ὄν):

> But we must further show that it is simply impossible for Being (ὄν) to be equivocal. For if *all things* derive from a single absolutely unique source (ἕν), numerous and indeed innumerable though they be, *they must still necessarily have one thing in common between them all.* So what else could that be other than Being, and that in no equivocal sense? For if it is to be equivocal, then it could not be One. Somewhere Aristotle himself says that 'beings abhor a state of disorder (*Metaph.* 1076a3–4)', and he quotes: 'The rule of many is not a good thing – let there be one ruler... (*Il.* 2.204)' His words are impressive in theory, but in practice *it is he himself who introduces the disorderly state of beings by refusing to allow the unity of Being.* (Pleth. *Diff.* 324.18–27)

At first sight this tantalising 'one thing in common' recalls the Stoic *koinon ti* opposed by Plotinus.[43] Stoic influences in Plethon's metaphysics should not be ruled out, even if according to the prologue of the *Nomoi* these are limited to moral philosophy. Yet before proceeding it is worth turning to the sibylline first proposition of the natural religion described in Plethon's *Memorandum to Theodore*, according to which there is 'one divine thing *within* all beings':

---

[42] *Diff.* 324.33; Plethon might be turning his opponent into an accomplice. Lagarde (1976: 60) suggested that Plethon has in mind *Metaph.* 1028b19; Chronis (1987: 58) correctly noted that this cannot be the case, since in that passage Aristotle is merely reporting Plato's opinion (among those of others) on substance. A more likely candidate is *Metaph.* 1028b3–4: 'Indeed, the question which was raised long ago, is still and always be, and which always baffles us –*What is Being?* – is in other words *What is substance?*' Be that as it may, Chronis notes that either way Plethon is misinterpreting Aristotle.

[43] Cf. *Enn.* 6.1.25, where Plotinus attacked the Stoic notion of 'common something' (*koinon ti*): 'And they have not left any room for differences with which they will be able to differentiate the *something.*'

ἓν μὲν εἶναί τι θεῖον ἐν τοῖς οὖσι, προὔχουσάν τινα τῶν ὅλων οὐσίαν.

there is one divine [thing] within all beings, an essence that surpasses all. (*Mem.* I 125.6–7)

It appears that in the *Memorandum to Theodore* Plethon has *Laws* Book 10 in mind when adding two further tenets of his unnamed, rational civic religion, which concern divine providence and justice.[44] Thus we may safely assume that the immanence of divine essence affirmed above is also taken to be a cornerstone of Platonic theology. Certainly the participle προὔχουσα implies the exceptional pre-eminence of this divine source and possibly its declining ontological presence within partial beings affirmed by similar forms of the same verb in the *Nomoi*.[45] Taken in itself there is nothing un-Christian in this expression. For example, a dogged Palamite, Philotheos Kokkinos, could approvingly cite a similar formulation by Pseudo-Dionysius Areopagita.[46] And yet in the context of Theodore's court Plethon's carefully calculated ambiguity and vagueness surrounding this 'divine something' (τι θεῖον) must have disturbed any theologian.[47] Not only because Plethon provocatively refrains from stating that it is exclusively from Orthodox Christianity that Theodore's subjects should seek religious guidance, as he was expected to do in a conventional Byzantine 'mirror for princes', but primarily because this unqualified *theion* appears to be immanent in the world of becoming. It is not truly beyond Being, for it is within beings (ἐν τοῖς οὖσι) and projects (another meaning of προέχω) Being – hence, it cannot but *be* Being.

Plethon circumvents the doctrinal *status quo* established after the Hesychast controversy. The Orthodox view was that it is not divine essence, but divine energies that are participated by created

---

[44] *Laws* 885b4–9.

[45] *Nomoi* 96 (3.15.74–7): προὔχον... ὁτιοῦν. Hence 'Poseidon' at *Nomoi* 204 (3.35,4.1–5), is superior in terms of power (προύχων σθένει).

[46] Phil. Cocc. *Contra Greg.* 10.1309–14: ἔστιν ὁ Θεὸς ὡς πᾶσαν δύναμιν ἐν ἑαυτῷ προέχων καὶ ὑπερέχων. Cf. Dion. Ar. *DN* 201.1–2.

[47] That the vague formulation is no random slip of the pen but the product of Plethon's tactic of dissimulation becomes apparent by the repetition of a similar expression in the beginning of another exposition of the principles of an unnamed religion in *Monodia in Helenam Palaeologinam*. See below, p. 302.

beings. According to the Orthodox doctrine that Plethon certainly was very conscious of, god's essence is totally absent from creation: it is only by will (κατὰ βούλησιν) and by his energies (κατ' ἐνέργειαν) that god relates to the world, not by his essence (κατ' οὐσίαν). Christian authors from the Cappadoceans to Palamas would only go as far as to attest that the divine energy runs *through* creation – but never that it resides *within* beings.[48] No such distinction appears either in the *Memorandum* or in the *Differences*. Already at such an early stage of his work Plethon defined god as constituting the predominant essence of beings, not as a supra-essential transcendent entity, but as a multi-centred radiant *ousia* diffusing and bestowing itself upon beings, rather than essentially residing outside (ἔξω, to recall John of Damascus) their Being.

It follows that there is more in the *Differences* passage defending the 'unity of Being' (324.18–27) quoted above than meets the eye. *Iliad* 2.204 has a long and illustrious history within Christian apologetics: this 'one ruler' was traditionally identified with the Judaeo-Christian god. Manuel Corinthios draws from this conventional application of the verse in his attack on Plethon, when describing 'a single essence that is eternal and immovable and separate from all sensible beings'.[49] In Plethon's case it is not god but *Being* that is equated with the single 'ruler'. Once again, the expected caveat that according to Roman Orthodoxy there is no community of essence or even *analogia entis* between God and Being is omitted.

By reverting to Aristotle's primary metaphysical application of the Homeric verse, while arguing that Being *is* a *genus* and nostalgically alluding to the 'unity of Being', Plethon wished at least some of his potential readers to consider the possibility that Being *qua* supreme *genus is* the sovereign-god. A similar use of the *Iliad* occurs in Julian's *Hymn to the King Helios*, Plethon's probable source, as we shall see presently.

In *Against Scholarios* the issue recurs in a passage full of carefully calculated ambiguities. Since all beings are produced by *one* god (εἷς θεός) it is necessary to assume that they are comprehended

---

[48] For references, see above, p. 98.
[49] Manuel Cor. *Adversus Gemistum et Bessarionem* 359.1–5.

by a single and common genus (ἓν κοινὸν γένος). The key clause is an allegedly Aristotelian axiom: 'one cause, one effect'.[50] This may be taken to mean two things: that god is 'one cause' and the *genus* of Being (or simply Being) a distinct 'effect';[51] or that god *qua* Being is one cause comprehending all beings within a single and common *genus*. The latter reading is supported by the Plethonean principle that there is no distinction between essence and energy in god.[52] Cause and effect coincide, which suggests that god is identifiable with Being. Plethon's reply to Bessarion's epistle *Concerning the Creator of the World* corroborates this interpretation.

This is a very bizarre exchange of letters. Manuel Corinthios is adamant that what we have here is abundant proof that Bessarion and Plethon 'were of one mind', an allusion to Bessarion's crypto-paganism.[53] According to Manuel, Bessarion's cover-up was to ask for 'solutions' to his queries regarding self-producing causes, whereas in reality these 'causes' stand for 'gods'.[54] Both Plethon and Bessarion 'feigned their participation in divine grace', while following Proclus in postulating a multitude of self-subsisting divinities.[55] Are these Manuel's calumnies?

No one likes religious persecutors in the hunt for ideological dissenters, and Manuel seems to have excelled in this, yet here he may well have been right when reading between the lines. Bessarion appears to have encoded queries on polytheism into queries on Neoplatonist causality. He opens his letter by noting that the potential reader of works by comrades of Plato such as Proclus, Hermeias and Damascius will hardly fail to notice that they all consider both the soul *and* 'the intellectual and intelligible gods' as self-substantial. Bessarion moves on to the discussion of

---

[50] *Contra Schol.* 23.8–13: ἡμεῖς δ' οἷς βεβαιότατα ἀφ' ἑνὸς θεοῦ τὰ ὄντα παρῆχθαι τὲ καὶ παράγεσθαι δοκεῖ, οὐδ' ἂν δυναίμεθα μὴ οὐ καὶ ἑνὶ αὐτὰ κοινῷ περιλαμβάνειν γένει, ἵνα δὴ καὶ ἓν μὲν ἑνὸς θεοῦ αἴτιον ᾖ.

[51] See Couloubaritsis (1997: 129), who sees Being *qua genus* in the *Differences* as different to god as the 'donator' of Being. Cf. above, n. 22 for Masai's similar reading. See below, pp. 243–50 for those reasons for considering Plethon's, as well as Plato's, first principle *within* Being.

[52] Pleth., *Diff.* 337.19–21.

[53] Manuel Cor. *Adv. Gem. et Bess.* 356.30–357.7; 366.28: συναποστάτης.

[54] Manuel Cor. *Adv. Gem. et Bess.* 356.20–5.

[55] Manuel Cor. *Adv. Gem. et Bess.* 360.26–361.1.

the self-substantiality of what he now calls 'beings *of this sort*' and successively to even more ambiguous language where the subject 'beings *of this sort*' is tacitly assumed and, like 'gods' in the beginning, does not resurface.[56] 'This is the overture to his work', remarks Manuel, and one may infer from it this man's solid faith to the pagan philosophers he cites! For, what sort of Christian would ever think that anything among beings could be self-subsistent and self-constituting?[57] Given the turmoil caused by the fourteenth-century Hesychast controversy one should give Manuel some credit here. This discussion on the 'self-substinence' of causes is odd, to say the least.

Bessarion makes of himself an easier target than Plethon does. The latter's reply is elusive and one wonders why, if this was really nothing but a purely academic discussion. There is no mention of 'gods' or 'beings of this sort' or, for that matter, of any other sort, something that must have disappointed Manuel. Yet in the section relevant to the question of 'equivocity versus univocity of beings' raised by Bessarion, Plethon cites two authorities: Proclus and Julian. The former identified the 'first cause (τὸ πρῶτον αἴτιον)' with 'One' and the 'Good'; the latter credited the 'first cause' with Being.[58] After all, asks Plethon, to what could Being be more appropriate than to what *is* in itself? Being is conferred on all beings from a single principle.[59]

Here the notion of Being *qua genus* is indistinguishable from the Julianic metaphysical notion of a first cause/One/Good *qua* Being. The Platonism and henotheism of Plethon's point of reference, Julian, are in perfect accord with the account of 'Zeus' in the *Nomoi*. Plethon seems to have taken note of a philosophical rather than a liturgical tenet of Julian's paganism: the identification of the One with Being.[60] It is worth following up Plethon's reference:

[56] Bess. *Ep.* 18, Mohler III 455.6–20.
[57] Manuel Cor. *Adv. Gem. et Bess.* 357.31–358.13.
[58] Pleth. *Ep. ad Bess.* 1, Mohler III 460.32–461.1.
[59] Pleth. *Ep. ad Bess.* 1, Mohler III 461.1.
[60] Raoul Kabakes, *heliolatres* and loyal student of Plethon, included Julian's *Hymn to the King Helios* in a manuscript containing works of his master. Kabakes quoted the first two verses of Plethon's ninth hymn to 'the celestial gods' that deal with the sun under the title of Julian's *Hymn*. As Bidez (1929: 76) observes, he was justified in relating this hymn to Julian's treatise. In another peculiar note in the margins of the manuscript, Raoul

[B]ut in a still loftier sense it [the universe] is guarded by the King, who is the centre of all things that exist. He, therefore, whether it is right to call him the Supra-Intelligible, or the Idea of Beings (ἰδέα τῶν ὄντων), and by Being I mean the whole intelligible region (τὸ νοητὸν σύμπαν), or the One (ἕν), since the One seems somehow to be prior to all the rest, or, to use Plato's name for him, the Good (τἀγαθόν); at any rate this uncompounded cause of the whole reveals to all existence beauty, and perfection, and oneness, and irresistible power; and in virtue of the primal creative substance that abides in it, produced, as middle among the middle and intellectual, creative causes, Helios the most mighty god, proceeding from itself and in all things like unto itself.[61]

In the *Nomoi* Plethon has 'Poseidon' for 'Helios' and 'Zeus' for One/Being/Good. Significantly, a little further down in his *Hymn to the King Helios* Julian too refers to Homer's familiar depiction of Zeus: 'For Zeus, as Homer says, since he is lord of all, constrains the other gods' (*Il.* 8.20–5). Plethon's use of *Iliad* 2.204 in the *Differences* hardly makes of him a monotheist in the Christian apologetical sense. He is following Julian, not Eusebius. Both Plethon and Julian are monists rather than monotheists: god/Being-in-itself as the supreme genus allows for all levels of the ontological hierarchy to participate in divine essence, even if to a different extent.

By contrast, Aristotle is thought to be persistently hostile to the One and to carve up Being. Aristotle is credited with inclining to 'atheism' – not with pure atheism, as Plethon clarifies in his *Reply to Scholarios*, but with a *tendency* to atheism.[62] Plethon reiterates the Proclan reception of Peripatetic philosophy, one formed by the

reproaches Plethon for not utilising Julian as much as he could have in regard to the mathematical interpretation of the universe. See Bidez (1929) 77, Grégoire (1929/30) 733: ὦ Πλήθων ἀγαθέ, ταύτην τὴν ἐξήγησιν (*sic*) τοῦ παρόντος λόγου παρέληπες, ἀξίαν καὶ ὀφέλημον (*sic*) οὖσαν, σοῦ ἀναλόγου καὶ ἀξίου ὄντος, καὶ μᾶλλον περὶ τῶν μαθειματικῶν (*sic*). That Plethon was versed in Julianic theology is now affirmed by contemporary scholarship. See Tambrun (2006a); Hladký (forthcoming). It should be noted that George of Trebizond's often quoted testimony (cf. Walker (2000) 61; Anastos (1948) 279ff.) that 'I have seen, I myself have seen and I have read prayers of his [Plethon] to the sun, hymns in which he extolled and adored the sun as creator of all things', does not render Plethon another worshipper of Kabakes' Sun god. Medvedev (1985: 739–47) has adequately shown that Plethon cannot be counted as reintroducing solar cult, though he copied Orphic and Proclan hymns dealing with the sun (contained in the *Marcianus graecus* 406). Besides, Julian's heliocentric theology does not appear to have influenced Plethon's hymns, in which the sun is a god among others 'fading in the light of the higher deities'.

[61] Jul. *Or.* 4.132C–D. The influence of this passage on Plethon is also noted by Tambrun (2006a) 131–2.

[62] Pleth. *Contra Schol.* 30.79–91.

interpretation of Alexander of Aphrodisias, according to which Aristotle's first principle is a principle of locomotion and a final cause, but *not* an efficient cause. Aristotle's prime mover moves the universe 'much like an ox moves a cart', it is an extra-mundane motive force that empties the universe of divine immanence and desacralises the perpetual divine productive process responsible for the precious unity inherent in all things.[63]

A return to Parmenides

Contrary to appearances then, the disagreement between Plethon and Scholarios regarding the merits of Plato and Aristotle was not part of any tedious 'academic' discussion between rival professors. Plethon's appeal to a unified ontology is a call for a 'closed' monistic ontology according to which *nothing exists outside Being* – not even god. By contrast, Scholarios' appeal to Aristotle safeguards the most fundamental Christian distinction: that between ontology and theology.

Plethon is trying to re-establish contact with an ancient tradition of conceptual paganism. Aquinas testifies to its antiquity when considering Parmenides as the founder of the univocal conception of Being.[64] Both the Plethonean critique of the equivocity of Being in Aristotle's *Categories* 5 and the notion of One Being as the highest One recall Parmenides' position as reported by Proclus in his commentary to Plato's *Parmenides:*

That the One Being must be prior to plurality you can grasp by a logical procedure, as follows. 'Being' is used either homonymously in all its applications, or synonymously, or as indicating predicates derived from and relative to one thing. But it is impossible that it is used homonymously, when we say that one thing 'is' more and another less; for *more* and *less* are not applicable to things that are named homonymously. And if 'One Being' is used synonymously of each of the things there are, or if it is used as derived from and relative to one thing, it *necessarily* follows that there is some Being (ἀνάγκη ἄρα εἶναί τι ὄν) prior to the many beings. (Procl. *In Prm.* 709.6–16; trans. Morrow and Dillon)

---

[63] *Contra Schol.* 15.1–16.7. Cf. Procl. *In Tim.* 1.266.28–30: οἱ δὲ Περιπατητικοὶ χωριστὸν μὲν εἶναί τι, ποιητικὸν δὲ οὐκ εἶναι, ἀλλὰ τελικόν. See also Simplicius' comments on Alexander's interpretation, Simpl. *In Phys.* 10.1362.11ff.

[64] On Aquinas on Parmenides and the univocity of Being see Wippel (2000) 70–1.

This is Plethon's point in the *Differences*. Eventually Proclus draws a distinction between 'Parmenides who speaks in the Poem' (τοῦ ἐν τοῖς ἔπεσιν), who identifies the One with Being (τὸ ἓν ὄν), and the 'Platonic Parmenides' (ὁ παρὰ Πλάτωνι Παρμενίδης), who presumably ascends from One Being to the One alone.[65] Thus, Proclus sides with those Neoplatonists who departed from the original pre-Plotinean interpretation of Plato, according to which the Idea of the Good is not really beyond Being. Since he acutely senses that *Republic* 509b is not enough to credit Plato with this belief, he strengthens this interpretation by falling on the Second Hypothesis of the *Parmenides* and concludes that 'the One is not the same as Being'.[66] In a manner presumably very unnerving for any carrier of 'pagan' and monist tendencies such as Plethon and Spinoza, the Proclan commentary on the *Parmenides* ends with a frustrating concession to *silence*.[67]

Still, the Parmenidean call for a unified onto-theology that is transmitted but not endorsed by Proclus (καὶ οὕτως ἓν ἀποκαλεῖ τὸ ὄν) and that restores the proposition 'Being is One' in its very centre may well be one of the immediate sources of Plethon's inspiration.[68] Plethon registers the message but disagrees with Proclus' preference for a 'Platonic Parmenides' allegedly departing from original Parmenidean monism. In the same vein as one of the immediate heirs of Socratic and Platonic teaching, Eucleides of Megara, and in full agreement with the pre-Plotinean interpretation of *Republic* 509b, Plethon brings Plato into agreement with Parmenides.[69] He thus reserves a prominent position for

---

[65] Procl. *In Prm.* 1240.29–37.

[66] Procl. *In Prm.* 1241.7–8: ἀλλ᾽ ὅτι μὲν τὸ ἓν οὐκ ἔστι ταὐτὸν καὶ τὸ ὄν.

[67] Procl. *In Prm.* 76κ; see above, Ch. 4, p. 191.

[68] Procl. *In Prm.* 708.35–709.6: 'So also Parmenides knows that intelligible plurality proceeds from the One Being, that prior to the many beings there is this fundamental One Being in which the plurality of the intelligibles has its unity. It is therefore far from true that he had to deny plurality because he posited the One Being – he who in the passages above supposes that beings are many; rather in saying that the many get their being, whatever it is, from the One Being, he rightly regards this cause as sufficient and so declares that Being is One.'

[69] According to Diogenes Laertius, Eucleides of Megara reverted to Parmenidean ontology and argued that the supreme Good is really one, though called by many names, 'sometimes wisdom, sometimes god, and again mind, and so forth. But all that is contradictory of the good he used to reject, declaring that it had no existence' (Diog. Laert. 2.106). By contrast, Maximus Confessor represents the Orthodox tradition when postulating

Parmenides in his golden chain of philosopher-guides who reveal the 'true doctrines' in the *Nomoi* and notes his connection to Plato, while criticising Simplicius in *Against Scholarios* for taking Aristotle to agree with 'Plato and Parmenides'.[70] The alliances are clear.

The Neoplatonic approach to *Parmenides* serves as the mine from which to draw material necessary for Plethon's type of Parmenidean-Platonic pagan ontology. Proclus credits Parmenides with a notorious analogy, one concerning the monad and its relation to numbers. Parmenides' One Being is seen as causally transcendent in the sense that the participated beings obtain Being from the One just as the monad transcends numbers while also being contained in them:

> Now Parmenides as I have often said before, seeing this monad of being transcending the plurality of being, calls being *one*, separating from it the plurality of things that proceed from it. (Procl. *In Prm.* 710.11–16)

This is the model of the *Nomoi* theogonic/cosmogonic pattern. Plethon uses the analogy of Monad/numbers in both the *Differences* and in the *Nomoi*, where it emerges as the most apt one for illustrating the relation between 'gods'/Forms and 'Zeus'/Being-in-itself.[71] The radical difference between One Being and Palamas' understanding of the essence of god as an alien *physis* is that according to Proclus' *Parmenides* (and Plethon's *Nomoi*) 'everything that comes *after* the One *participates* in the One, so that the dyad itself is also in a sense *one*, and therefore both unity and plurality'.[72]

This not to say that Plethon considers the world of becoming as univocal with the 'creator' in the sense that Ficino implied and Plotinus condemned. Plethon did not subscribe to the view that things receive an equal share of Being from the *genus* they belong to.[73] This type of crude pantheism is explicitly denied by Plethon,

---

that god 'has no contrary' and that non-Being is not a privation of 'Being properly so called', namely of divine essence, but only of qualified substance. Herein lies the important difference between Greek monism and Eastern Orthodox apophaticism. According to the latter, god is not only extra-mundane but in effect beyond Being *and* non-Being, that is to say, beyond the limits of ontology. See n. 98.

[70] Cf. *Nomoi* 32 (1.2.77); *Contra Schol.* 2.6.   [71] *Nomoi* 94 (3.15.24–35).
[72] Procl. *In Prm.* 712.   [73] *Enn.* 6.1.25.17–22.

who notes that the three species of substance (eternal, perpetual and temporal) are not equal in terms of ontological participation in 'Zeus', even though they form a unified ontological *systema*.[74] Plethon would unhesitatingly approve of Plotinus' example that one thing might have a larger share in fire, like a pot, and another less, so as not to become pot.[75] Rather like numbers, 'gods' and everything else *essentially* participate in the universal *genus* of Being, even if to a different extent and according to different modes. This qualification allows Plethon's radical Platonism to be as monistic as it gets – that is, in so far as it manages to escape the pantheism entailed by the position of an absolute univocity among all levels of Being.[76]

That 'Zeus' is not beyond Being

It will be objected that both Plethon and Scholarios apply the word *hyperousios* to describe god.[77] In what sense is Plethon's first principle transcendent? Recently, Tambrun noted the absence of negative theology from Plethon's theology. Hladký objected that this hardly means Plethon thought of the One in affirmative terms.[78] For his part, Couloubaritsis read Plethon as advocate of a *sui generis* type of theology that is neither polytheist in the Hellenic (pagan) sense nor monotheist in the Christian sense. According to this interpretation, god is both transcendent and immanent in the sense that god as a creative cause is separate from the emanating divine archetypes/Ideas.[79] The issue is crucial. In the late Byzantine context, any attempt to compromise the transcendence of a god commonly thought to be beyond Being and non-Being is abundant proof of a 'Hellenic' theology at work. Admittedly, it is true that

---

[74] *Nomoi* 96 (3.15.74–85).   [75] *Enn.* 6.3.7.30–5.

[76] Hence interpretations that see in Plethon an advocacy of the univocity of Being should be qualified. Certainly Plethon does not argue that the word 'Being' is applicable to both the divine and the universe in an unqualified sense – rather, his point is that there is no radical ontological difference or alterity in essence between diverse radiations and emanations of Being.

[77] *Diff.* 326.31; 337.7–28.

[78] See Tambrun (2006a), who points to Aelius Aristides as a possible source behind Plethon's shift from Neoplatonic and Christian negative theology to affirmative theology. Cf. Hladký (2009) 378–9.

[79] Couloubaritsis (2006) 155.

Plethon distinguishes between the One and gods/the world.[80] But the real question is: does Plethon mean this distinction in ontological terms, as Palamas and Scholarios do? Does he think that the essence of god is in itself radically disparate from the essence of everything else?

In a letter also exemplifying an interest in Plethon's calendar, Bessarion appears to presuppose that Plato's 'first principle' is 'Being in the proper sense': Plato's πρῶτον αἴτιον is κυρίως ὄν: Plato's Idea of the Good *is* Being – it is not beyond Being, that is transcendent, rather, Being properly speaking and understood. In this sense the Idea of the Good is different from anything else, in fact beyond anything else; nevertheless, it *is* Being.[81] It is significant that this approach to Plato's Idea of the Good was a defensible option in Plethon's context, moreover, one shared by both Bessarion and his teacher. As it happens, this has good chances of being the correct way to read the notorious passage in *Republic* 509b that appears to affirm that the Idea of Good is 'beyond being' (ἐπέκεινα τῆς οὐσίας). Bessarion and Plethon are in step with the original pre-Plotinean reception of Plato – one that modern scholarship has recently revisited. Though certain Neopythagoreans including Pseudo-Brotinus and Pseudo-Archytas appear to have thought that the first principle is superior to *ousia*,[82] the chief exponents of Middle Platonism identified god with the Idea of the Good and absolute Being.[83] As Baltes showed,

all Platonists before Plotinus confirm... that Plato's Idea of the Good is not ἐπέκεινα τοῦ ὄντος. For according to all these interpreters of Plato's philosophy, the Idea of the Good is something like the highest being, τὸ ὂν αὐτό, which bestows upon all other things their being.[84]

The expressions αὐτοόν and αὐτοαγαθός employed by Plethon were attributed to god by Numenius.[85] In both cases Numenius

---

[80] Hladký (2009) 379.   [81] Bess. *Ep.* 20, Mohler III 464.9.

[82] Baltes (1997) 17–19; Lilla (1997) 142.

[83] Even in the case of Celsus, who has been read as placing god above *nous* and *ousia* (cf. Cels. 7.45.11; Lilla 1997: 142), the Idea of the Good is still intelligible by an 'ineffable power' and hence not *really* beyond being (Baltes 1997: 13). In fact Celsus' god is closer to Julian's and Plethon's than to that of Christian apophaticism. For a different reading see Lilla (1997) 143 who brings attention to Cels. 6.65.

[84] Baltes (1997) 22.

[85] Num. fr. 20; fr. 17 des Places; *Nomoi* 132 (3.34,1.1); 168 (34,4.1).

interprets Plato as identifying divinity with Being-in-itself and the Good-in-itself. Numenius' god 'is at the same time περὶ τὰ νοητά σύμφυτος τῇ οὐσίᾳ, or even more than that, he is "being itself" (αὐτοόν) and as such he is even οὐσία'.[86] In other words, Numenius' first god is ousia, the principle of ousia and intelligence (νοῦς).[87]

The link between Numenius and Plethon is provided by Eusebius, who quotes the relevant fragments in his *Praeparatio evangelica*, a text with which Plethon was certainly familiar.[88] Plethon is also close to Plutarch's identification of true Being (ὄντως ὄν) with divinity in *De E apud Delphi*: ἀλλ' ἔστιν ὁ θεός.[89] The salutation *Thou art* (εἶ), according to Plutarch, denotes the eternity of Being, but at the same time the unity of Being. The use of εἶ ('you are') in both Plutarch and Plethon is tantalising: the former's εἶ ἕν (Thou art One) parallels the latter's ὄντως τε ὢν τῷ ὄντι εἶ, καὶ ἔτι εἰλικρινῶς ἕν (you are the one who really is and is simply One), especially since in the henotheist context of Plutarch's dialogue Apollo stands for the highest god.[90] This passage from *E apud Delphi* is reported by Eusebius in the same chapter of the *Praeparatio evangelica* as are Numenius' quotes.[91] It is noteworthy that Plethon excerpted passages from Plutarch's works and that according to Bessarion 'the most wise' Plutarch was one of Plethon's favourite points of reference.[92]

Besides, we have already seen that by rendering the Idea of the Good knowable, both Plato and Plethon compromise the transcendence of divine essence. Further, we shall see that the identification of 'Zeus' with fate divests god of his free will and hence

---

[86] Baltes (1997) 13–4 commenting on Num. fr. 15, 16, 17, all fragments transmitted by Eusebius in *PE* 11.

[87] Num. fr. 16 des Places; see here Lilla (1997) 142.

[88] Eus. *PE* 11.18, 22–3; 11, 22, 9–10. On Eusebius as a source of Plethon see Tambrun (2006a: 58 n.1) and Karamanolis (2002: 264–7) on the influence of Atticus fragments preserved by Eusebius upon Plethon's *Differences*.

[89] Plut. *E apud Delphi* 392E, 393A. On Plutarch's position cf. Lilla (1997) 142.

[90] Plut. *E apud Delphi* 393B (cf. Siniossoglou 2010a: 137 on Plutarch's henotheism); *Nomoi* 170 (3.34,4.2–3). The affinity between the language of Plutarch in *E apud Delphi* and Plethon's *Nomoi* is noted by Bargeliotes (1974) 131 n. 34; cf. Hladký (forthcoming).

[91] Eus. *PE* 11.10.16.5; 11.11.15.2.

[92] On the Plethonean *excerpta* from Plutarch's work see Manfredini (1972) 569–81. Cf. Bess. *Ep.* 20, Mohler III 464.14–19.

of his super-essentiality. Notwithstanding the linguistic affinities, the Platonic ἐπέκεινα τῆς οὐσίας and Plethon's description of the One as *hyperousion* are very different to the doctrinally Orthodox understanding of the Pseudo-Dionysian notion of the divine as ἐπέκεινα τῶν ὄντων and πάσης οὐσίας ἐπέκεινα.[93]

Against this background it is imperative to re-examine the question of god's super-essentiality according to Scholarios and Plethon. The word *hyperousios* in Plethon is not co-referential to the Roman Orthodox meaning attributed to the same word in Scholarios. This is a case of equivocity. The underlying conceptual opposition and tension is anticipated in Scholarios' treatise on the distinction between divine essence and divine operations. There the word is used in the Palamite sense.[94] All possible distinctions, says Scholarios, are either real (πραγματικήν) or conceptual devices (κατ᾽ ἐπίνοιαν). The distinctions between beings are real and not in thought only: for example this man cannot be united to that man and form a single individual, just as this man is not classifiable under the same kind as a horse. In what sense, then, is god's essence distinct from divine energies? Gregory Palamas, says Scholarios, examined the problem with the greatest scrutiny and concluded in accordance with the Fathers that the distinction is real – not a conceptual one, as Barlaam, Akindynos and their followers said.[95] Scholarios expressly clarifies in what regard is god 'beyond being', namely in the theistic sense of Palamite Orthodoxy that has at its centre the notion of a personal agent free of ontological necessity.

The essence of god is 'infinite times infinitely' beyond *any* essence.[96] The simplest unity (ἕν) is beyond any category of Being: *One* is beyond *Being*.[97] In the *Epistle to the Exarch Joseph* (*OC* 4.165.9–29) Scholarios argues against Plethon that god is *atomos*, indivisible – communal participation of other deities in god would inevitably render the godhead composite, which is one of

---

[93] Dion. Ar. *DN* 109.15–16, 163.20, 115.17–18: ἡ πάσης οὐσίας ἐπέκεινα καὶ πάσης γνώσεως.
[94] On Scholarios' treatment of Palamas see Guichardan (1933) 203–5.
[95] Schol. *Distinctio essentiae divinae et operationum suarum, OC* 3.228–39, here: 228.17–21.
[96] Schol. *Distinctio essentiae divinae, OC* 3.234.24–6.
[97] Schol. *Distinctio essentiae divinae, OC* 3.235.35–7.

his main arguments against Plethon's henotheism. For Scholarios god is *hyperousios* owing to his personal nature. He is *the Other* in reality, Palamas' *xene physis*. In the context of Eastern Orthodox apophaticism god is *hyperousios* not in so far as negative theology is applicable to describe what god is not (as is often the case with Neoplatonism and the *via negativa* in the Latin West) but in so far as god is beyond Being and non-Being at the same time.[98] It is one thing to say what god is not and another to say that god is beyond *what is* and *what is not*.

Conversely, for Plethon the One is *hyperousion* owing to its extreme position in the ontological ladder, one that does not allow any distinction between essence, energy and potentiality common to qualified essence.[99] Like Plato's Idea of the Good, Plethon's first principle is 'beyond being' only in regard to its unqualified modality of being and its causal priority over the intelligible realm of the Ideas. In the *Differences* Plethon credits Aristotle with the notion of essence (οὐσία) as proper Being (μάλιστα ὄν), hence essence is still Being. Analogously, the Platonists (οἱ περὶ Πλάτωνα) are said to understand the 'supra-essential one' as the 'extreme one' (τὸ ὑπερούσιον ἐν ἄκρως ἐν τίθενται),[100] that is, super-essentiality refers to the extremity of divine essence, not its ontological difference from anything else.[101] It is tantamount to the non-distinction between essence, power and energy – not to an ontological otherness of transcendent essence. Nothing suggests that the One is super-essential in the sense of being beyond Being and non-Being. The 'extreme one' is still One and thus not truly beyond Being.

---

[98] Arguing against 'the Greek philosophers' Maximus Confessor clarifies that 'the divine substance alone has no contrary' whereas 'non-being is the contrary of the substance of [created and qualified] beings' (*Capita de caritate* 2.28–9). Non-Being, he says, is the privation of Being – 'but not of Being properly so called, for it has no contrary; but of true Being by participation'. Hence, Being and non-Being depend upon the will of God as a transcendent personal agent.

[99] *Diff.* 337.19–21: Τοῦ μὲν γὰρ ὑπερουσίου ἑνός, ἅτε ἄκρως ἑνὸς ὄντος, οὔτε οὐσίαν οὔτε προσὸν οὔτε ἐνεργείαν οὔτε δύναμιν διακεκρίσθαι.

[100] *Diff.* 324.32; 326.30.2–4.

[101] See Plethon's commentary (Pleth. *Orac.* 3.1.31–2) on *Orac. Chald.* 3 des Places ('the Father snatched himself away, and did not enclose his own fire in his intellectual Power'), according to which the point is to signify what is exceptional in the Father's divinity (τὸ ἐξαίρετον αὐτοῦ τῆς θεότητος σημαίνει) as well as the fact 'that he cannot be counted within the sum of the other gods (καὶ θεοῖς σύμπασι τοῖς ἄλλοις οὐκ ἐνάριθμον)'. Brisson (2006: 140) notes the parting from Neoplatonism and the affinity with Middle Platonism that is implied here.

Reasonably in Plethon's *Prayer to the One God*, αὐτοαγαθότης and αὐτοαλήθεια are interchangeable with ἡ ὄντως ὀντότης, 'Being that properly is' and 'life of all Beings' (ἡ τῶν ὄντων ζωή).[102] In the *Nomoi* 'Zeus' is conceived of as proper Good (κυρίως ἀγαθός) and extreme Good (ἄκρως ἀγαθός), while in Bessarion's epistle to Plethon κυρίως ὄν is taken to designate Plato's Idea of the Good. By implication, 'Zeus' as Being-in-itself (αὐτοεόν) is analogous to the notion of essence (οὐσία) as proper Being (μάλιστα ὄν) in the *Differences*, and interchangeable with extreme Being (κυρίως ὄν), extreme Good (ἄκρως ἀγαθός) and 'Being that properly is' (ἡ ὄντως ὀντότης). In all cases, god/Zeus is still ὄν, ἕν and ἀγαθός, hence within Being, even if simply and principally so. Contrary to Palamite Orthodoxy, Plethon sees a single unified 'system' conditioned solely by the participation of each ontological level in Being. A participable being differs from Being *qua* Being because essence is conferred on it and emanates from the first principle in which it necessarily partakes, not because its essence is extra-deical (ἔξωθεν) or created *ex nihilo* according to divine will. The One *is* Being simply, whereas the other intelligibles only partake in its Being. As Alexandre put it, the principal position of Plethon's 'panthéisme rayonnant' is that god communicates his essence in various ways to a descending hierarchy that includes corporeal beings.[103]

The difference between the pagan Platonic and the Christian notions of the divine accounts for that between the prefixes *hyper-* and *auto-*.[104] Palamas turned against the use of the word *autoparaktos* in Christian theology, noting that the doctrine of a self-producing essence of god is typically 'Hellenic'.[105] No surprise then, if 'Zeus' in the *Nomoi* is self-engendered (αὐτοπάτωρ). Affirmative theology is pushed to the extreme, eliminating the possibility of a truly transcendent One. Rather, the One *is* Being without qualifications and conditions: 'Zeus' is self-engendered, Being *qua* Being, One in absolute simplicity (ὄντα τῷ ὄντι, καὶ εἰλικρινῶς ἕνα), the essence of the Good (αὐτό τε ὄντα, ὅ ἐστιν ἀγαθόν), 'being-in-itself', 'Good-in-itself' and one-in-itself

---

[102] Plethon, *Prayer*, 273 Alexandre.   [103] Alexandre (1858) lvi–lviii.
[104] See Zizioulas (1985) 89.   [105] Phil. Cocc. *Contra Greg.* 5.1050–5.

(αὐτοών, αὐτοέν, αὐτοαγαθός).[106] 'Zeus' is not *really* beyond Being (ὑπερούσιος) in the Christian sense of Pseudo-Dionysius and Palamas, for 'Zeus' is not beyond Being and Non-Being but Being-in-itself (αὐτοόν, αὐτοέν) that internally, necessarily and naturally confers Being to a hierarchically ordered and degrading yet organic system (σύστημα). To apply Scholarios' terms, the Hellenic notion of the One is beyond essence (ὑπερούσιος) in thought (κατ' ἐπίνοιαν), not in reality.

Similarly, in a liturgical hymn of the Plethonean neopagan religion, the 'One-in-Itself' (αὐτοέν) is also 'He-Who-is-in-Himself' (αὐτοών), a move that would appear to bring Plethon close to Palamas.[107] Still, the addendum that everything *emanates* (ἐκπροΐησι διακριδόν) from 'Zeus' makes clear that the presupposition of Palamas' theistic reading of ἐγώ εἰμι ὁ ὤν, namely the radical ontological distinction between uncreated Being and created Being, is absent from Plethon.[108]

By parting from Neoplatonic negative theology and returning to Parmenidean monism Plethon realised Palamas' nightmare. He has 'one *genus* of everything, Being' overthrow the One-Who-is. No Renaissance philosopher could possibly follow him through this dark path. In a work that has been rightly seen as a Neoplatonist's reaction to Plethon's *Differences*, the young Pico della Mirandola attempts to set things straight and notes that according to 'orthodox' Platonism god/the One is non-Being.[109] *Unum* is superior to *ens:* it is *prius*, namely *simplicius* and *communius*. Pico's nuanced approach contrasts sharply with Plethon's ontology. Plato, says Pico, may have believed that *unum et ens* are identical (*equalia*);

[106] *Nomoi* 46 (1.5.15–17), 132 (3.34,1.1), 150 (3.34,1.230). Cf. Plethon's commentary on the 'Oracles', 19.2. When Plethon considers 'Poseidon' as αὐτοείδος (*Nomoi* 158; 3.34,2.7) he does not mean that 'Poseidon' is really beyond (*hyper-*) all Ideas – for elsewhere 'Poseidon' is considered to be 'εἶδος ὤν' *par excellence*, namely the Idea of Ideas (*Nomoi* 104; 3.15.173). By analogy, 'Zeus' as αὐτοόν is not beyond Being, but Being in the most simple and pure sense.

[107] *Nomoi* 216 (3.34,1.1, 34,4.1).

[108] It is likely that Plethon allowed for some movements in the direction of the worship of a 'personal' god ('Zeus') within the framework of a mythologisation of pagan ontology, not least in order to meet practical religious needs of his potentially popular religion. Even in this case, though, 'Zeus' is naturally radiating Being, rather than fabricating or creating substance *ex nihilo* according to his will.

[109] Pico, *De ente et uno* 388 Garin (4 Blum); on Pico's attack on Plethon's Platonism see P. R. Blum (2006) xxv–lvii and (2010) 105–8.

but this equality only concerns Being as an absolutely simple essence opposed to 'non-Being', in which case 'one' and 'Being' coincide.[110] But in so far as the essence of beings is only derivative (*esse participatum*), Pico follows the standard Neoplatonic interpretation of the first hypothesis of the *Parmenides*: the One/god is superior to Being.[111] Obviously Plethon managed to stir the waters.

To see in Plethon a reformer of Platonism paving the way for Renaissance Platonism reveals only half the picture. To Renaissance eyes eager to see in Christianity the culmination of a *philosophia perennis*, the radicalism of Plethonean Platonism appears as incomprehensible as it appears horrifying to the heirs of Palamism. Proclan Neoplatonism, defended by Renaissance philosophers, saved Christian apophaticism from the resurgence of a pagan ontology that goes back to Plato himself, Julian and Parmenides.

Re-sacralising the physical world

Plethon's ontology has important consequences. Effectively sacralising and divinising the physical world, any notion of a necessary ontological conjunction between *cosmos* and the divine radically opposes the Judaeo-Christian belief in a single extramundane personal agent who freely creates material substance as a contingent product of his will (*creatio ex nihilo*). In the Roman Orthodox tradition the essence of god is *outside the All* (ἐκτὸς τοῦ παντὸς κατ᾽ οὐσίαν) and divine presence is confined to divine powers energising matter.[112] Conversely, the divine according to pagan philosophers has an intramundane aspect best represented by descriptions of an organic emanation and overflow of Being that naturally and essentially conjoins the first principle to the physical world. Plethon's ontology offers the presuppositions for a cosmogony that is also a theogony. In the *Nomoi* the narration of a series of biological births (γέννησις) expressly challenges the

---

[110] Pico, *De ente et uno* 390 Garin (6 Blum).
[111] Pico, *De ente et uno* 402 Garin (18 Blum).
[112] Ath. Alex. Presb. Περὶ τῆς ἐνανθρωπήσεως τοῦ Λόγου, 17; *PG* 25.125A–B.

Christian account of a creation (ποίησις) and fabrication (κτίσις) of the spatio-temporal order outside divine essence.[113] 'Zeus' is the primary originator: the *pangennetor* giving birth to all 'gods' either directly, or indirectly in the case of 'gods' and the world emanating from those first produced.[114] Using myth as his vehicle Plethon reiterates a central position in the *Timaeus*, namely the world-affirming belief in a perpetually renewed universe inhabited by inferior deities that have been ordained by a supreme cosmic principle:

> In regard to the universe, the first point is that this universe, *in which Zeus has placed those gods* that are second and third in the hierarchy, is perpetual – it has no beginning in time nor will it ever cease to exist. The second point is that this universe consists of many parts that are harmoniously arranged in order to form a unity. The third point is that it was arranged as perfectly as was possible to its maker, for he is the most perfect one, and he did not allow for anything unnecessary. Further, the universe is imperishable, remaining forever in its constitutional form. (*Recapitulation* 266 Alexandre)

Each of the gods of the second and third Plethonean order is responsible for an aspect of this world. They are 'captains' (ὕπαρχοι) or 'leaders' (ἡγεμόνες) operating *within* the universe, even if they transcend time and matter. The intra-celestial gods are inferior to these and are not only active within the world but conjoined to matter: these gods should be regarded as occupying a spatially determined place (τόπῳ θέσιν) for they are united with their material bodies.[115] Plethon's Platonic world is full of gods that are either enmattered, identical with heavenly bodies and hence intramundane, or operate within its realm while transcending matter. In either case the distinction between created nature and uncreated nature is diminished. The divine does not exist independently of the physical universe but is coextensive and partly resides within it.

As in the *Timaeus*, the emanation of the world in the *Nomoi* does not signify any passage from nothingness to Being but rather, as Masai observes, a ramification and diffusion of essence, not a

---

[113] See below pp. 252, 307 for the distinction between *ktisis* and *genesis* according to John of Damascus and its application in the case of the *Nomoi*.

[114] *Nomoi* 216 (3.35,16.3–6). Cf. *Nomoi* 206 (3.35,4.8); 220 (3.35,21.3): γεγάαμεν. The chapter on the 'birth of gods' is particularly pertinent here (*Nomoi* 92ff. (3.15)).

[115] *Nomoi* 56 (1.5.160–2).

synthesis, but an analysis and division.[116] Its generation is necessary, not a contingent or *ex nihilo* creation: as a product of 'Zeus's' absolute goodness it would be absurd to think that 'Zeus' could *not* be generating it. Similarly, 'Zeus' could not have made the universe inferior to what it is, since it is most beautiful and perfect.[117] In striking contrast to Christian creationism, Plethon follows the Platonic conception according to which the universe is an overflow of divine goodness rather than a production of god's free will. This stands for a natural process of generation coeval with the originator and both logically as well as ontologically necessary. Plethon succinctly reports how pagan is this notion of generation and underscores its opposition to creationism in the notorious treatise purportedly targeting Latin theology. Posing as a Christian, Plethon finds an all-too-convenient opening to present a summary of Hellenic popular religion:

> Pagan theology sets up one god, one indivisible (ἄτομον ἕν), above all things that exist and assigns him many children, some superior to others and some, in their turn, inferior to others... But it considers none worthy to be equal to or close to the father... In calling the children of god *gods* in their own right, and even calling them his products, it does not care to distinguish *creation* from *generation*, [divine] will from nature, or, to put it briefly, *energy* from *essence*. (*Contra Lat.* 302 Alexandre)[118]

The prominence of the language of nativity in the *Nomoi* merits some comment, for it is particularly significant for the opposition between Christian creationism and Hellenic theogony/cosmogony. John of Damascus explains the difference between γέννησις and κτίσις. *Birth* (γέννησις) means the procession of a being *from the essence* of the originator (ὁ γεννῶν). Thus, there is likeness and communion of essence between the originator and what is being generated (ὅμοιον κατ' οὐσίαν). By contrast, *creation* and *production* (κτίσις, ποίησις) designate what comes to be *outside* the creator (τὸ ἔξωθεν) consisting of an essence *different* to that of the creator or producer, in effect, what is 'totally dissimilar' to that essence.[119] From the Christian viewpoint Christ/Logos is naturally

---

[116] Masai (1957/8) 404.   [117] *Nomoi* 180 (3.34.4.156–63).
[118] On this passage and its connections to the *Nomoi* see Masai (1976) 34.
[119] Joh. Dam. *Exp. fidei* 8.60–2: οὐκ ἐκ τῆς οὐσίας τοῦ κτίζοντος καὶ ποιοῦντος γίνεσθαι τὸ κτιζόμενον καὶ ποιούμενον ἀνόμοιον παντελῶς.

(κατὰ φύσιν) born from God as *monogenes:* Christ/Logos is the 'Only-begotten' or 'Unique'. This is why, continues John, Logos is called *radiance (ἀπαύγασμα)*, namely because Logos is being born from the Father alone without the need of any combination of essences. There is no other process of natural generation or radiance similar to that of the Son.[120]

Judged from the Orthodox viewpoint of John of Damascus' distinction, the theogonic and cosmogonic process in the *Nomoi* disturbingly emerges in its totality as a natural (κατὰ φύσιν) radiance in the sense that Christ/Logos is in Christianity. In what is probably the most powerful covert assault on Christianity in the *Nomoi*, every single *eidos* is considered *monogenes* (unique), effectively subverting Christian theology.[121] Divested of its uniqueness, Christology is rendered obsolete. The privilege that Christian theology reserved only for Christ/Logos, namely kinship with the Father, is here offered to all levels of a matrix enabling the biological affiliation (συγγένεια) between its members – albeit each step of the ontological ladder enjoys this privilege to a different extent.

In modern terms, the Plethonean organic *systema* comprises beings that carry within them variations of one archetypical DNA code. This biological linkage accounts for that 'one thing in common' of the *Differences* and that 'one divine [thing] within all beings' in the *Memorandum to Theodore*.[122] The appropriation of the word *monogenes* and its application in an unabashedly pagan way is particularly intriguing. In the *Nomoi* Orthodox vocabulary is dechristianised, or, depending on one's perspective, re-paganised.[123] The restatement of the notion of κοινωνία is one further instance of the Plethonean attempt to redeploy Orthodox theological vocabulary. Basil sees the Father, Son and Holy Spirit as forming an indissoluble and continuous communion (κοινωνία).[124]

---

[120] Joh. Dam. *Exp. fidei* 8.108–13.

[121] *Nomoi* 100 (3.15.121–4): Καὶ ἕν τε δὴ καὶ μονογενὲς ἕκαστον ποιεῖν, ἵνα μηδὲ περίεργον ποιοῖ μηδὲν, καὶ τὸ ἐξ ἁπάντων αὖ ὅλον τέ τι καὶ ἕν, ᾗ ἐνεχώρει. Ἐνεχώρει δ᾽ οὐκ ἄλλῃ, ἢ τῇ κοινωνίᾳ. Cf. *Nomoi* 98 (3.15.81–3); 158 (3.34.2.12–20).

[122] See above, pp. 234–5.

[123] See *Nomoi* 198 (3.34.5.208–9) and below, Ch. 7, p. 390 for Plethon's use of τὸ ὁμόδοξον γένος to designate *homodoxia* not among Christians, but among pagans.

[124] Basil, *Ep.* 38.4. Cf. Collins (2001) 164–5.

253

Plethon turns the tables by extending this communion and differentiation of *ousia* to all levels of the ontological matrix. For Basil κοινωνία ensures the simultaneous effect of distinction and conjunction within the Trinity; for Plethon, κοινωνία means the same thing, only now for *all* levels of an organically understood and wholly vivified chain of intermediation. The Trinitarian notion of Christian god is rewritten with an unknown variant (x) abolishing the exclusivity of the Trinity. In place of the Christian οὗτοι οἱ τρεῖς ἕν εἰσι (1 John 5:8) Plethon has the notion of ἕν ἐκ πολλῶν, namely a multi-levelled *system* (σύστημα), according to which 'Zeus' diffuses his essence to orders and sub-orders of unique 'gods', thus forming an ontological community (κοινωνία).[125] There is still one communion, a single *ousia* and the person of the Father ('Zeus'-*propator*) as the ultimate cause, yet this pagan divine *koinonia* welcomes more than three contributions: gods of the first and second order, gods enmattered, in sum the whole 'bunch' (as Scholarios neatly put it in one of his epistles) enters into communion.

'Poseidon' and the first class of 'gods' have no mother, for 'Zeus' himself directly gives birth to them without the interference of a female principle.[126] The asexual birth of these gods, recalling that of Athena from Zeus's forehead, instigates a complicated process of successive births (γεννήσεις), and not κατὰ βούλησιν creation and fabrication (κτίσις) that leads to male causes/gods copulating with female causes under the supervision of 'Zeus'. As a result, whereas in the account of John of Damascus the world is by default outside God (ἔξωθεν) and god is absolutely κεχωρισμένος, there is nothing here outside the Being of 'Zeus' (οὐδέ τι χωρίς).[127] Moreover, whereas for John of Damascus divine Being is an 'infinite and indefinite sea of essence', the Plethonean 'Zeus' organises a multi-layered and well structured *systema* within this

---

[125] Cf. *Nomoi* 100 (3.15.123–8); 102 (3.15.157–9); 46 (1.5.36–41).

[126] *Nomoi* 92 (3.15.4–13). Here the feminine principle is seen as the cause of generated matter – a Neopythagorean echo.

[127] *Nomoi* 216 (3.35,16.3). Even the third species of substance that corresponds to temporal existence is 'born' from perpetual substance, which, in turn, emanates from eternal substance.

sea of essence in a constant state of mutual reciprocity and onto-logical dependence.[128] It has been said that with the Cappadocean notion of 'Being as communion' the ancient world 'heard for the first time that it is communion which makes beings "be": nothing exists without it, not even God'.[129] Plethon's restatement of ancient polytheism undercuts the surprise element in this otherwise promising thought. Divine κοινωνία is not an exclusively Christian privilege, he says. No other community is proper to beings but a community of Being regulated by the relation between species and *genera*. This leads to the production of 'a single system and one world that is as perfect as can be'.[130]

This sheds light on one of the few instances where Plethon appears to have really lost his patience with Scholarios while debating the differences between Plato and Aristotle. In *Against Scholarios* he appears particularly irritated by the suggestion that a mere similitude (ὁμοιότης) between god and created beings is adequate to sustain the unity of the world. For Plethon, as well as for Proclus, genuine ὁμοιότης presupposes *ontological* participation (κοινωνία). Here too Palamas is a useful resource, discerning the difficulties long before the Plethon–Scholarios debate. The hypostases of essence are analogous to what participates in essence, he says: 'the more candles one lights from one candle, the more hypostases of fire he gets'. Now, if the essence of god is participated 'by everything', then it follows that 'this essence has not three hypostases, but myriad hypostases'.[131] It is significant that these remarks target Byzantine humanists and anti-Palamites as committing or inclining to such errors. Using as a pretext the view that divine essence is everywhere present, says Palamas, Akindynos and his followers think that everything participates by

---

[128] Joh. Dam. *Exp. fidei* 9.12–13: πέλαγος οὐσίας ἄπειρον καὶ ἀόριστον.

[129] Zizioulas (1985) 17, quoted in Collins (2001) 178.

[130] *Nomoi* 102 (3.15.158–9): ἐς ἕν τι ἅπαντες σύστημα καὶ κόσμον ἕνα τὸν κάλλιστον ἐκ τῶν ἐνόντων συνεστᾶσι.

[131] Gr. Pal. *Capita CL* 109.1–6: Ἡ οὐσία, παρ' ὅσων ἐστὶ μετεχομένη, τοσαύτας καὶ τὰς ὑποστάσεις ἔχει· καὶ γὰρ ὁπόσας ἂν λαμπάδας ἀνάψοι τις ἀπὸ τῆς μιᾶς, τοσαύτας καὶ τὰς ὑποστάσεις τοῦ πυρὸς ἐποίησε. συμβαίνει τοίνυν, εἴπερ κατὰ τοὺς ἡμῖν ἀντικειμέ-νους ἡ οὐσία τοῦ θεοῦ μετέχεται καὶ ταῦτα παρὰ πάντων, μηκέτι τρισυπόστατον εἶναι ταύτην, ἀλλὰ μυριοϋπόστατον.

default (ἁπλῶς) in divine essence. In reality, god is present in all things without being participable. Plethon's polytheism was unconsciously yet potentially present within the humanist attack on Eastern Orthodox apophaticism.[132]

A hymn to 'Zeus' provides further insights into the nature of Plethonean theogony.[133] 'Zeus' did not produce anything spontaneously (ἐξ ὑπογυίου); rather, the process of generation is contemporaneous with the originator. The reminder that 'Zeus' could not possibly ever be ἄεργος is a restatement of the typical Neoplatonic and anti-Christian argument that it is impossible to think that god was ever inactive. The hymn is in tune with the doctrine of the eternity of the world expressly attested in Plethon's *Recapitulation*.[134] But here 'Zeus' is not bound by logical necessity alone; he is further confined by ontological necessity. 'Zeus' produces beings in his likeness, that is to say, 'nothing inferior to his power' because this accords to his nature, namely his being the Good in itself (αὐτὸ ὅ ἐστ' ἐσθλόν). The use of ἔδει in order to explain this necessary relation between generation of beings and Being-in-itself makes abundantly clear the difference from the Judaeo-Christian God, who creates freely according to his will. According to Plethon, there is no distinction between divine will and divine essence. Incessantly and from all eternity the Plethonean 'Zeus' gives birth to beings because it is the nature of his essence to do so. He is the Father of himself (αὐτοπάτωρ), 'truly Janus (ὄντως Ἰανός)' and the Father of all because the Good-in-itself cannot but be all that.

There is another way in which polarisation between intramundane and extra-mundane notions of divinity makes itself felt. This sees the physical universe as partly or wholly animate. The view is rudimentarily summarised in a passage concerning the origins of idolatry in Scholarios' translation of Aquinas' commentary to Aristotle's *De anima*. Aquinas' awareness was triggered by

[132] Gr. Pal. *Capita CL* 109.23–4, 109.12–13: ἀλλὰ καὶ ἁπλῶς ξύμπαντα τῆς θείας οὐσίας φασὶ μετέχειν ἀνουστάτῳ προφάσει τοῦ παρεῖναι ταύτην πανταχοῦ.

[133] *Nomoi* 202 (3.35,3.1–7): Οὐ μὴν ἐξ ὑπογυίου αὐτέων γ' οὐδὲν ἑοργώς, | Ἀλλ' ἐξ ὅσσου πέρ τε καὶ αὐτὸς ἔην, ἐκ τόσσου | Καὶ τάδ' ὁμοῖα ῥέζων, οὔποτ' ἐών γ' ἂν ἀεργός, | Οὐδέ κεν ἧσσον τῆς γε ἑῆς δυνάμεως εὖ ἔρδων | Ἦ, οἱ καὶ ἔδει, αὐτὸ ὅ ἐστ' ἐσθλὸν τελέθοντι.

[134] *Recapitulation* 266 Alexandre; cf. *Nomoi* 96 (3.15.54–6).

Aristotle's remark that 'some say that the soul is intermingled generally with the universe. That is perhaps why Thales thought that the whole world was full of divinities'.[135] According to Scholarios' version of Aquinas' commentary:

> There are, he [Aristotle] says, some who see a soul intermingled with the all, namely within the universe (τὴν ψυχὴν μεμίχθαι ἐν τῷ ὅλῳ ἤγουν ἐν τῷ παντί), thus placing soul within simple elements as well as within things composite. A philosopher called Thales was perhaps inspired by this opinion, when he said that *everything is full of gods* (πάντα πλήρη θεῶν εἶναι); perhaps he meant that the entire universe was animate (ἔμψυχον) and that its soul is god; that just as soul exists in all parts of each living thing in its totality, so were gods in every single part of the universe and everything thereof was 'full of divinities'. *And perhaps idolatry* (εἰδωλολατρεία) *evolved out of this doctrine.* (Schol. *Translatio commentarii Thomae Aquinae De anima Aristotelis OC* 6.1.13.8–15; Thales DK 11A22)

In this account the origins of idolatry effectively coincide with Ionian philosophy, with the nascence of Greek philosophy. Idolatry is traced back to Hellenic *cosmic piety*, the belief that the universe is animated, alive and divine. The 'world full of gods' in Plato's *Laws* Book 10 provides a classic example of the survival of pre-Platonic panpsychism and hylozoism that successively found their way into Proclan Platonism and Plethon's *Nomoi*.[136] *Laws* Book 10 aptly recapitulates the pagan belief in a cosmic soul vivifying the material universe and its relation to human rational discourse.[137]

Aquinas' correlation between panpsychism, polytheism, idolatry and the philosophical belief in a World-soul may be traced

---

[135] *De anima* 411a7–8.

[136] *Laws* 899b (trans. Saunders): 'Now consider all the stars and the moon and the years and the months and all the seasons: what can we do except repeat the same story? A soul or souls – and perfectly virtuous souls at that – have been shown to be the cause of these phenomena, and whether it is by their living presence in matter that they direct all the heavens, or by some other means, we shall insist that these souls are gods. Can anybody admit all this and still put up with people who deny that "everything is full of gods?"' See also Procl. *De sacrificia et magia* 149.29 Bidez: οὕτω μεστὰ πάντα θεῶν.

[137] *Laws* 967d–e (trans. Saunders): 'No mortal man can ever attain a truly religious outlook without risk of relapse unless he grasps the two doctrines we're now discussing: first, that the soul is far older than any created thing, and that it is immortal and controls the entire world of matter; and second (a doctrine we've expounded often enough before) that reason is the supreme power among the heavenly bodies. He also has to master the essential preliminary studies, survey with the eyes of a philosopher what they have in common, and use them to frame consistent rules of moral action.'

in another work translated by Scholarios into Greek, the *Epitome Summae contra gentiles Thomae Aquinae*. In a subsection entitled: 'That cultic veneration is due to god alone', we read that the Hellenes did not venerate the first principle alone, but 'a great many others too', such as intelligible essences (οἷον ταῖς νοεραῖς οὐσίαις), either taken in themselves or united with physical bodies. They also worshipped the souls of the stars and the daemons that followed – in sum, the whole of the world and its parts, 'which they consider animated' and 'certain icons', which is why they are called *idolaters*.[138] Plethon meets fully this first set of criteria for establishing paganism. *Nomoi* fully retains the echoes of archaic hylozoism and pagan animism, albeit transmitted by means of an intellectualised Platonic cosmogony/theogony.

In the *Nomoi* the mythologised *persona* called 'Poseidon' appears to correspond to Neoplatonic *nous*, the most common cause of the Platonist World-soul.[139] Eventually 'Poseidon' gives birth to gods/species (εἴδη) that are composed of soul *and* body and are responsible for rendering matter into a *cosmos*, that is, for its perpetual preservation or sustainment (σώζειν) and harmonious arrangement (κοσμεῖν).[140] They are divided into two further classes: those rooted within matter, and those presiding over matter, even if practically residing within it.[141] The first class comprises the non-rational corporeal nature, ultimately consisting of four principal species (εἴδη): fire, air, water and earth. Generated by 'Poseidon', the four basic elements are perpetually renewed and escape mortality, even if they are susceptible to change (ἔγχρονος) and deprived of reason.[142] The second class is tripartite and corresponds to *the rational soul* (ἡ λογικὴ ψυχή) of the universe, consisting of celestial gods (stars), daemons and the human soul.[143] The rational World-soul confirms the immanence of the divine within the world and excludes the possible intrusion of chance and accident.

---

[138] Schol. *Epitome, OC* 5.3.120.1–8.
[139] For the role of 'Poseidon' see below, Ch. 6, pp. 280–2.
[140] *Nomoi* 174 (3.34.3.68–73).   [141] *Nomoi* 174 (3.34.4.80–7).
[142] *Nomoi* 176 (3.34.4.97–9); 180 (3.34.4.148–9).
[143] *Nomoi* 176 (3.34.4.84–97); on the soul of the world see also *Nomoi* 80 (2.26.16–21): ἡ τοῦ οὐρανοῦ ψυχή, and 82 (2.16.30–4). On the stars as celestial gods see also *Nomoi* 138 (3.34.1.64–7).

As early as 1440/2 Plethon was asked to elaborate on his position that mortality differentiates man from the heavenly bodies. In the *Reply to Certain Questions* he maintains that the movement and perpetuity of the heavenly bodies proves that they possess a soul analogous to that of animals.[144] This satisfies Aquinas' and Scholarios' criteria of a *prima facie* idolatry, while compromising providence in the Christian theistic sense. In the *Nomoi* the Sun god is the link (κοινὸς ὅρος) between mundane gods and supermundane gods and the commander of this world. Followed by Selene, Lucifer (Heosphoros), Stilbon, Phaenon, Phaethon and Pyroeis go round the world, and in communion (κοινωνοῦντες) with Cronus and the other Titans they bring 'the whole of mortal nature to perfection'.[145] Here Plethon is drawing on the *Epinomis*.[146] But he is also echoing *Laws* Book 10: 'Presumably they [the gods] will necessarily be rulers, since they manage the entire heavens perfectly.'[147] Plethon contends that the universe (τὸ πᾶν) is not only perpetually renewed (ἀΐδιον) and imperishable – it also enjoys the privilege of contemplating (θεωρία) and cognising (ἔννοια) god by means of its rational nature/soul (τῇ λογικῇ φύσει).[148] Epistemological optimism meets ontological monism: it is not only man who strives to intellectual perfection and godlikeness but also the universe in its entirety, to the extent that both man and the universe are endowed with a rational soul; *a fortiori* so does the Platonic *polis* strive on the political level.

A case has been made that Plethon's assault on Aristotle's innovation regarding the Fifth Element in the *Differences* reintroduces

---

[144] Benakis (1986) 62.

[145] *Nomoi* 166 (3.34,3.26): τὴν θνητὴν σύμπασαν ἀποτελεῖτε φύσιν. In this regard Bessarion's comparison between Phaethon and Plethon perhaps hides within it more than poetic inspiration. In Bessarion's verses (Fabricius, *BG* 102) Γεμιστός ὅσον Φαέθων ἀστέρων παραλλάσσει, τόσον τῶν ἄλλων... κρατέει. This might well be a covert reference to the *Nomoi*.

[146] This has been shown by Fabio Pagani (2009: 183–4; 2008: 28), who notes that in his recension of Platonic texts Plethon tampered with *Epinomis* 986e3–987c7 and changed Aphrodite to Heosphoros, Hermes to Stilbon, the sun to Phainon, Zeus to Phaethon and Ares to Pyroeis.

[147] *Laws* 905e2–3: 'perfectly' (ἐντελεχῶς) or 'perpetually' (ἐνδελεχῶς), if one opts for Stobaeus' reading. For this problem see Mayhew (2006) 312–17. Plethon would have no difficulty in attributing both perfection and perpetuity to the gods.

[148] *Nomoi* 182 (3.34,4.163–6): Ἐν τούτῳ τῷ παντί, γέρας τι τοῦτο κάλλιστον τῇ λογικῇ φύσει συμπάσῃ, τὴν σεαυτοῦ ἔννοιάν τε καὶ θεωρίαν παρέσχες, ἧς καὶ ἡμεῖς τὸ ἔσχατόν σοι γεγόναμεν.

Plato's World-soul by the back door.[149] Aristotle's omission of a World-soul leads to the problematic assumption of the Fifth Element, a position dangerously bordering on materialism or, as Plethon has it, 'atheism'. Couloubaritsis observed that on this point Plethon performs a sharp anti-Aristotelean move by effectively arguing that Plato's self-moving World-soul is an idea at least as plausible as is Aristotle's unmoved mover.[150] On the other hand, the Aristotelian desacralisation of nature or 'atheism' suited Palamas and Scholarios well, for it showed precisely why the Stagirite needed to be complemented by Judaeo-Christian theism. The threat posed by Aristotle's physics and metaphysics to any attempt to maintain the Neoplatonic unity and subordinationism of Being re-emerges in chapter 9 of the *Differences*. There, Plethon attacks what he sees as a dichotomy introduced by Aristotle between the primary principle of locomotion and the 'passive' motion of the thing being moved.[151] This case of presumed homonymity leads to a division between essence and energy that intrigued Palamas and Scholarios but was hardly appealing to Plethon. Tellingly then, in *Against Scholarios* Aristotle is guilty of the same error as are the Christian 'sophists' in the *Nomoi*: of dangerous innovation, and further of introducing an idea that is not only *kainon* (new) but also *kenon* (nugatory).[152]

How was this revival of the Platonist World-soul in a philosophical context dominated by Aristotelianism possible? As usual with Plethon, the easy yet misleading way to interpret his philosophy is to explain the constitutive elements of his pagan outlook as a nostalgic act of reflection instigated by the study of dusty volumes of late antique Neoplatonic lore. But a closer look at the primary sources of late Byzantium shows that the pagan notion of a World-soul was still capable of resurfacing and triggering the awareness of Christian intellectuals, even if only to be rebutted.

---

[149] Couloubaritsis (2005) 73.

[150] See Couloubaritsis (2005: 74–5), who notes that had Plethon pursued more the consequences stemming from remarks of this sort he could easily claim the title of 'the first modern interpreter of Aristotelian thought'. Bargeliotes (1980) *passim* stresses the significance of Plethon's argument not only for a defence of Platonism but also for the disentanglement of Aristotle from the scholastic appropriations and misreadings.

[151] Pleth. *Diff.* 334.5–10.   [152] Pleth. *Contra Schol.* 29.51.

Constantly alert to prevent the resurgence of animism and pantheism, Gregory Palamas in his *Capita CL* refuted a contemporary preoccupation with precisely this idea of 'a cosmic soul'
(κοσμικὴ ψυχή) purportedly deriving from the Intellect (Plethon's
'Poseidon') and residing within the world. Interestingly, Palamas
indiscriminately classifies the doctrine as 'Hellenic', rather than
as specifically Platonic.[153] The 'Hellenic sages', says Palamas,
worshipped the world rather than its maker,

endowing the sense-perceptible and insensate stars with intelligence, in each case
proportionate in power and rank to its corporeal magnitude. And worshipping
these in their sorry manner, they address them as superior and inferior gods and
entrust them with dominion over the universe. On the basis of sensible things and
a corresponding philosophy have these men not inflicted shame, dishonour and
the ultimate penury on their own souls, and also the verily intelligible darkness
of punishment? (Gr. Pal. *Capita CL* 26.12–20 trans. Sinkewicz)

Notwithstanding that for obvious reasons it was highly unlikely
that anyone in late Byzantium would openly dare to endorse the
Hellenic belief in a 'cosmic soul', there is evidence that the notion
was of great 'academic' interest, casting its spell upon Palamas'
opponents. In the fourteenth century Pseudo-Aristotle's *De mundo*
was popular, providing insights into a sacralised universe more
aptly described as 'Hellenic' than 'Platonic'. It has also been
argued that Palamas felt compelled to refute the Platonic belief
regarding the World-soul because of the need to oppose its resurgence in the philosophical work of Nikephoros Gregoras, the most
illustrious lay scholar of his time.[154]

Commenting on Synesius' account of divination, Gregoras
explains how Synesius viewed the world as 'a living being, possessing a soul', since Synesius was a 'Hellene' tempted to compare
the world to a book: its parts are the letters of this book, namely
'the animals and plants and air and water and stones and everything else'. Just as information in different languages is read by
different peoples, in like manner, according to Synesius, prophets

---

[153] Gr. Pal. *Capita CL* 3.1–46. Cf. *Triads* 1.1.18.17–21. In a Platonic context the idea of
an *anima mundi* is clearly present in the *Epinomis*, though the *Timaeus'* conception of
the universe as a 'visible god' (34ab) certainly qualifies as 'idolatrous' and 'Hellenic'
from Aquinas', Palamas' and Scholarios' perspective.

[154] Kern (1947) 181–2. Cf. Guilland (1926) 202–4.

and oracles 'read' the material elements of this world and predict the future.[155] Plethon does not share the Neoplatonic fascination for theurgy, but he makes restricted concessions to divination. The art of predicting the future, he says, is proof that fate (*heimarmene*) is at work.

Plethon's cosmogonic ontology builds on the tenet of Hellenism reported and thus preserved by Gregoras that the world is ensouled and that its parts are unified by means of a reciprocal harmonious *koinonia* of its constitutive causes and powers – Plethon's 'gods'.[156] Whereas according to Christian apophaticism god creates *outside himself*,[157] Plethon returns to a pagan symbolic and mythologised ontology that is by necessity a theogony: 'Zeus', the gods/causes generated under his supervision and the rational soul are all parts of a unified and perfected *system* (ἕν τι παντελὲς σύστημα) and *cosmos* (κόσμος) consisting in the communion (κοινωνία) of 'a multitude of kinds (εἴδη): eternal, temporal, immortal and mortal'.[158] In this sense divine *ousia* is almost bound to the world by a typically Platonic rule of a compulsive ontological necessity that manifests itself on the moral level as *heimarmene*.

The notion of a unified ontological *systema* evolves out of Plethon's preoccupation in the *Differences* to show that causal generation does not equal temporal creation. Porphyry, Proclus and all advocates of the perpetuity of the world argued in this direction. Conversely, in *Against Plethon* Scholarios insists that Aristotle should be read as holding that temporal creation necessarily follows from causal generation.[159] According to appearances, the issue seems to be whether or not Aristotle agrees with Christian creationism. In *Against Scholarios* Plethon returns to the issue with a checkmate: equating temporal with causal generation, Scholarios may perhaps be able to 'save' Aristotle from the initial

---

[155] Synesius, *De insomniis* 2.2–17.   [156] *Recapitulation* 266 Alexandre.

[157] Zizioulas (1985) 91.

[158] *Nomoi* 102 (3.15.156–9). Cf. *Nomoi* 250 (3.43.113–17): ἐς ἕν τι τῷ ὄντι σύστημα συνεστήκῃ, 82 (2.27.4–8), 94 (3.15.40–45): ἕν ... σύστημα πάντων τε καὶ παντοίων εἰδῶν, 98 (3.15.82–3): τό τε αὖ σύστημα τὸ ἐξ ἁπάντων ὅλον τέ τι καὶ ἐν τῇ κοινωνίᾳ.

[159] Schol. *Contra Pleth.*, OC 4.11.1–4: δῆλός ἐστιν Ἀριστοτέλης, ὥσπερ καὶ ἄλλοι ἴσως τινές, τῇ κατ' αἰτίαν γενέσει καὶ τὴν χρονικὴν ἐξ ἀνάγκης ἕπεσθαι δοξάζων.

accusation of not sharing the belief in the creation of the world in time – yet only at the cost of proving himself a heretic:

> For if it were once granted that everything which owes its existence to a cause must also have had a beginning in time, then it would necessarily follow that the Son and the Spirit, having the Father as cause, must also have had a beginning in time. If you put forward this as your own assumption and that of the Church, then in addition to your general ignorance you would indeed appear to be a poor judge of the doctrines which are appropriate to the Church and those which are not. (Pleth. *Contra Schol.* 8.5–11)

Plethon was toying with Scholarios all along. In the *Differences*, at the very beginning of the whole controversy, Plethon claimed that his objective was to argue that Plato was more conformable to the doctrines of the Church regarding creation; but in *Against Scholarios* he appears to give himself away, declaring that, after all, both Plato and Aristotle shared the belief in the perpetuity of the world, only Plato argued 'much better and more divine-like' in this direction. Two nice quotations from the *Timaeus* show that Plethon was very conscious of the Proclan interpretation of the 'likely tale'.[160] The purported conformity between Plato and Christianity advocated in the opening of the *Differences* was only a contrivance to undermine Christian Aristotelianism, just as when he was attacking Christian theology *in toto* posing as a critic of Latin theology alone. The real target both in the *Differences* and even more pronounced in *Against Scholarios* is to undermine doctrinal Orthodoxy from within.

Unearthing the pagan *hereditas damnosa*

Recent interpretations of the *Nomoi* and the *Differences* have successfully compared Plethon's Platonism to Julianic and Middle Platonic Platonism, as well as to Proclan Neoplatonism.[161] Still, from the viewpoint of intellectual history Plethon's philosophy is no abstract trans-historical or ahistorical exercise. It is a reply to contemporary philosophical and theological issues. The *Nomoi*

---

[160] Pleth. *Contra Schol.* 10.47–65. On the perpetuity of the Platonic world according to pagan interpreters see Siniossoglou (2008a).

[161] Hladký (forthcoming); Tambrun (2006a).

and the *Differences* reflect unresolved problems that emerged in fourteenth-century Byzantium in a clash between opposed intellectual camps. These concern the resurfacing of diverging approaches to the relation between multiplicity and singularity in god, the definition of the categories 'monotheism' and 'polytheism', the tension between immanence and transcendence of the divine and the role of ancient philosophy in illumination. On a superficial level the anti-Hesychast assaults of the fourteenth century were continuously refuted and condemned for more than fifty years. Palamas was triumphing and Orthodoxy is usually said to have emerged as the clear winner. Yet upon closer scrutiny, Orthodoxy did not come alone out of this struggle.

From 1341 to 1368 the Hesychast controversy rudimentarily excavated three constitutive elements of the Plethonean project. These concern: (a) continuous reflections upon and experimentations with Platonic ontology; (b) successive attempts at relocating polytheism within a contemporary context and at defining the nature of polytheistic theology in theological terms; (c) the humanist call for the reappraisal of Aristotle's philosophy and its recalibration against the established interpretation.

The contributors to the 1368 *Tomus* seem to have appreciated the serious collateral damage for the Christian establishment. Clerical disquietude no more concerned particular assaults on Palamas, but 'new and bizarre' heresies constructed with raw material unearthed in the earliest phases of the controversy. This material was put to successive theological and philosophical experimentations, which did not fall short of reopening old and dangerous questions. Byzantine intellectuals in the fourteenth century moved towards the modern restitution of pagan ontology without actually reaching it. The honour was reserved for Plethon.

Whereas Barlaam, Akindynos, Gregoras, Prochoros and Demetrios Kydones constantly had to wave their Christian certificates in order to prove that they were less Platonist than Palamas was, Plethon consciously and actively took the tendencies that these men brought to the surface to their natural conclusion. Against the background of a disintegrating empire, the mutual intellectual exhaustion of Palamite theology and humanist approaches to ancient ontology gave birth to a radicalised upshot of Byzantine humanism that claimed to solve the theological and ontological problems addressed by Palamism in a more adequate way.

The return of the Hellenic 'unwilling and inefficacious essence'

Apophaticism and theism are intimately connected. A good statement of the reasoning behind this is provided, as so often, by John of Damascus: 'if types of knowledge concern beings, what is beyond knowledge in an absolute sense will also be beyond Being [in an absolute sense]; and, by implication, what is above Being will also be above knowledge'.[162] For Palamas union with divine reality takes place beyond knowledge, even though it may be metaphorically called 'knowledge', 'union', 'vision', 'sensation', 'intellection', 'illumination'.[163] On the contrary, Barlaam was accused of confounding 'divine knowledge' with knowledge in general, for he presumably allowed for a single *genus* of knowledge. This would render godlikeness a species, part and subject of the universal of knowledge (ἡ καθόλου γνῶσις). Palamas reasons that were knowledge of god a species of knowledge, then, *mutatis mutandis*, divine essence would have to be downgraded to a species of substance. For, to make 'divine knowledge' inferior to a unified generic knowledge,

this is the same as if one was to make of the unique supra-essential reality a part and species and subject of [the *genus* of] substance on the grounds of their equivocity, namely because it *is* and is called supra-essential *essence*, and then dared to mingle it with the universal *genus* of substance. (*Triads* 2.3.34.13–16)

It is on the grounds of this interweaving of epistemology and ontology, that Palamas accused Barlaam of confounding supra-essential essence with the *genus* of Being, postulating '*one genus of all, Being*', and classifying 'Him who is *One* above all' within this *genus*. To compromise divine knowledge effectively means that '*Being* is superior to the *One*'.[164] Thus, 'whoever mingles

---

[162] Joh. Dam. *Exp. Fid.* 4.28–31: Εἰ γὰρ τῶν ὄντων αἱ γνώσεις, τὸ ὑπὲρ γνῶσιν πάντως καὶ ὑπὲρ οὐσίαν ἔσται, καὶ τὸ ἀνάπαλιν τὸ ὑπὲρ οὐσίαν καὶ ὑπὲρ γνῶσιν ἔσται.

[163] Gr. Pal. *Triads* 2.3.33.1–27.

[164] *Triads* 2.3.34.21–26. See above, pp. 227–8.

what will not mingle and assimilates what is beyond knowledge with knowledge and who says that what is beyond intellection is cognisable' should readily realise that he is thus rendering what-is-beyond-knowledge superfluous: in other words, he is making *God* superfluous.[165] Belief in a transcendent agent is unnecessary; God is rendered an accidental or supplementary assumption. Being is substituted for God.

Plethon's revolutionary move to equate the One with Being and posit Being as a *genus* is potentially present as if in an eggshell about to break. In this conflict between Barlaam and Palamas it matters little whether Barlaam was philosophically a pagan, as Palamas accused him of being, a Christian deviating from the 'right' path, or a misunderstood Orthodox eagerly waiting to be 'rehabilitated' by modern research. Of importance is that in the particular context elaborate Hellenic notions of epistemology and ontology were in the air and were understood as a serious threat to Orthodoxy, while justly or not associated with 'heretical' members of the Church. The emergence of a distinctively pagan ontology was not only possible, but in practical terms only a question of time.

More evidence is apt here. According to Palamas, Akindynos taught that god possesses no energies but is pure divine essence. He merely *is* (*einai*), which means that god's will is indistinguishable from his real essence. The inescapable conclusion is that the Palamite distinction between energies and essence in god hopelessly compromised divine simplicity and purity. Akindynos argues that no distinction is proper to god and that the distinction between will and essence should be rejected as well. Palamas saw in Akindynos more than an intrusion of Augustinean and Thomist thought. The non-distinction of will and essence in god, he says, is a hallmark of paganism: 'let the martyr Justin be my witness! For he says [against the Hellenes] that god does not create through his essence, but through his will.' Justin was one of the first Christian apologists to deal with one of the principal differences between Hellenes and Christians. The Hellenes postulated that god creates by means of his Being, not by means of his will, 'as fire warms

---

[165] *Triads* 2.3.34.17–21.

thanks to its being'. According to the pagan position, *what god is, he wishes; and what he wishes, he is*. No distinction is proper to god and hence that between will and essence should be rejected as well.[166] The Hellenic contention is that there is no distinction between essence and energies in god, and this is precisely Akindynos' point.

Akindynos is read as substituting an 'unwilling and inefficacious essence' (ἀθέλητός τε καὶ ἀνενέργητος οὐσία),[167] a man-made notion of essence for God as a personal agent, that is, for God as beyond *both* Being and non-Being. The absolute identification of essence (οὐσία) and action (πρᾶξις) in Plethon's 'Zeus' in the *Nomoi* (clearly identifiable, as we have seen, with Plato's ἄκρως ἕν in the *Differences*, in which power, energy and essence are again indistinguishable) reinvigorates the anti-Palamite attack on the established Orthodox distinction between super-eminent divine essence and its energies.[168]

But this is not all. Akindynos is also credited with pantheistic and monist tendencies. If god has no will, then god did not *create* the world *ex nihilo*, which is to say that the spatio-temporal world is co-eternal with the divine essence and hence somehow conjoined to this essence.[169] The year is 1342 and the capital distinction between extra-mundane and intra-mundane notions of god is reported as seriously compromised by the return of the pagan belief in 'unwilling and inefficacious essence'. Regardless of what Akindynos (and some twenty years later Prochoros Kydones) really meant, Palamas testifies that a return to pagan ontology and cosmology was possible, if not already in full development, long before Plethon's *Differences* and the *Nomoi*. Disguised as philosophical discourse, Christian heresy provided a relatively safe vehicle for intellectual dissenters within the Church.

As in the case of Akindynos, Thomist influence on Plethon should not be excluded. Demetrios Kydones' translation of *Summa*

---

166 Ps.-Justin, *Quaest.*, PG 6.1428C–D.
167 Cf. Gr. Pal. *Contra Acind.* 2.20.97 (*PS* 3.154.5–155.7), 5.10.39 (*PS* 3.316.24–5); Ps.-Justin, *Quaest.*, PG 6.1433B.
168 *Nomoi* 54 (1.5.126–7); *Diff.* 326.30–7. Plethon assumes that according to 'the Platonists' such a distinction emerges at the level of *nous* – something that is not the case with Plotinus, *Enn.* 6.8.7.48: εἴ γε μηδὲ ἐπὶ τοῦ νοῦ τοῦτο.
169 Palamas, *Contra Acind.* 5.10.40 (*PS* 3.317.4–318.4).

contra gentiles and Prochoros Kydones' Περὶ οὐσίας καὶ ἐνεργείας may have served as channels communicating Latin speculations to the East.[170] Admittedly, the late Byzantine translation project of Aquinas is not unrelated to this attempt at reforming Orthodox theology from within. But it is remarkable that Palamas opposes Akindynos as a *homodoxon* of 'the Hellenes' and not as an agent of Latin theology. This was no rhetorical trope. Neither Palamas nor Justin was really erring when identifying a pagan doctrinal core. Rather, the Hellenic notion of the indistinguishability between energy and essence in god described by Plethon in his anti-Latin treatise[171] and opposed by Palamas comes markedly close to the Thomist conception of god as *actus purus*. Philosophically speaking the anti-Palamite and the Plethonean position (ostensibly denounced in the anti-Latin treatise, but endorsed in the *Nomoi*) corresponds to the Plotinean non-distinction between essence and energy in the One that resurfaces in Emperor Julian's pagan theology.[172] The testimony of two Orthodox theologians related to the Plethon affair is relevant here. Even Aristotle, who 'appears to have touched the surface of truth', says Manuel Corinthios, one of Plethon's dogged enemies, commits himself to the Hellenic error of identifying god's essence with his energy.[173] But more significant is the testimony of Mark Eugenikos, the student of Plethon who, we have seen, was very conscious of the differences between East and West. Mark certainly made the connection between Thomist thought and anti-Palamism in Byzantium.[174] But things are more complicated. Affirming the pagan intellectual roots of the identification between divine essence and energies, Mark testifies to their

---

[170] This was suggested by Demetracopoulos (2004: 35–8, and 2006), who points to the anti-Palamite John Kyparissiotes (ob. post 1377) as Plethon's probable source. John was a friend of Demetrios Kydones and made a strong case against the distinction between energy and essence in god.

[171] Plethon, *Contra Lat.* 302 Alexandre.

[172] *Enn.* 6.8.7.46–7: οὐ γὰρ ἡ μὲν ἕτερον, ἡ δ᾽ ἕτερόν ἐστιν. Cf. Jul. *Or.* 4.142D.

[173] Manuel Cor. *Adversus Gemistum et Bessarionem* 360.18–24.

[174] Mark Eugenikos credited Thomas and the 'Latins' with the same two major positions as advocated by the anti-Palamites: on the one hand the non-distinction between essence and divine will, and on the other, the view that divine energy is created, rather than uncreated. See Mark Eug. *Epist. encycl. contra Graeco-Latinos et decretum Synodi Florentinae* 6.45–7: οὗτοι δὲ μετὰ τῶν Λατίνων καὶ τοῦ Θωμᾶ τὴν μὲν θέλησιν ταὐτὸν τῇ οὐσίᾳ, τὴν δὲ θείαν ἐνέργειαν κτιστὴν εἶναι λέγουσι.

independent perseverance in the East from late antiquity to late Byzantium:

> We must not be surprised if *we do not find among the ancients any clear and defined distinction between the essence of God and His operation*. If, in our time, after the solemn confirmation of the truth and the universal recognition of the divine monarchy, *the partisans of profane wisdom* have created so much confusion in the Church over this question, and have even accused her of polytheism, what would not have been done in earlier times by those who, *puffed up with their own vain learning*, were seeking only an opportunity to confound our teachers?[175]

Corroboration comes from Plethon. In his treatise purportedly attacking Latin theology Plethon identifies the unity between energy and essence as a necessary condition of the pagan world-view, one abolishing the crucial distinction between *generation* and *creation*.[176] Plethon realised that this very Hellenic understanding of god as an 'unwilling and inefficacious' *ousia*, to recall Palamas, effectively compromises creation as an extra-deical event and opens the back door to Neoplatonist emanationism or 'generation'. His main point in the treatise is that Latin theology is (consciously or not) a paganising one. But then again Thomism was a dangerous competitor of Plethon's own application of Hellenic theology in the *Nomoi*, and hence worth Plethon's time and effort in rebutting, even if this meant a temporary alliance with Roman Orthodoxy. In the *Nomoi*, without a hidden agenda or any need to fall back on dissimulation, Plethon openly denies any distinction between the essence and energy of the supreme god, which is now defined as a self-producing Being naturally emanating a series of ontologically inferior deities: the *genera* of gods are 'constantly flowing' (ἀεὶ προϊόντες) at one with the perpetual activity of 'Zeus' (ἐνεργοῦ ἀεὶ ὄντος τοῦ Διός).[177] Obviously this is no *creation* but *generation*.

'Gods of Being' and 'created gods': polytheist notions within the Hesychast controversy

Between the condemnation of Barlaam in 1341 and that of Prochoros Kydones in 1368 the words πολυθεΐα and πολυαρχία

---

[175] Mark Eugenikos, quoted in Lossky (1976) 79; my emphasis.
[176] Pleth. *Contra Lat.* 302 Alexandre.   [177] *Nomoi* 52–4 (1.5.117–126).

appear to have enjoyed a popularity which had been unprecedented since late antiquity. The distinction between essence and
operations in god spurred a renewed interest in defining, understanding and clarifying the notions of monotheism and polytheism. Palamites and humanists were drawn more and more into a
bizarre discussion on the relation between unity and multiplicity in god and the world, even if primarily in order either to
substantiate, or to shake off mutual accusations of reverting and
degenerating into philosophical polytheism, that is to say, pagan
Platonism.

According to Palamas, divine operations correspond to a proliferation of divine energy (μερίζεται ἀμερίστως ἐν μεριστοῖς).[178]
They are uncreated and essential (οὐσιώδεις) but not identical with
god's supra-essential essence. The creation of the world *ex nihilo*,
its sustainment and procession, as well as man's glorification do
not compromise the immutability of a fully transcendent divine
essence. Thus Palamas hoped to avoid the charge of polytheism,
while also allowing for the experiential and spiritual illumination
promised by the Hesychast practices.

After years of dissimulation, Prochoros Kydones repeated a
variant of the argument of previous Byzantine humanists against
Palamas objecting that the distinction between essence and essential energies in god is pure sophistry.[179] Divine operations should
either be integrated within divine essence or downgraded to the
status of created beings. *Tertium non datur.* From a Palamite viewpoint neither is really an option: in the former case the Neoplatonists would be given in retrospection credit for objecting that
the Christian god shifts his essence in order to create and sustain
the universe. Moreover, this eventuality might be taken to mean a
proliferation of essences leading to polytheism: if the creative operation of god is seen as his essence, then the providential operation
should be made into another, his wisdom yet another, and so on.
Neither can the operations be equated with creation, for they stem

---

[178] Gr. Pal. *Capita CL* 74.1–15.

[179] This led to his condemnation in the *Tomus* of 1368. We shall see in the next chapter that
Prochoros' attack on Hesychasm was not unconnected with his perception of an urging
Zeitgeist – on the contrary, he appears to have argued that his theology is dictated by
the times he lived in.

from god and are by default uncreated rather than part and parcel of the extra-deical material universe. If the divine energies are created, then this means *mutatis mutandis* that the divine essence is created too. The thin line separating Palamas' persistence on the uncreated nature of divine operations and Hellenic polytheism occasionally appeared to evaporate, and Gregoras, among others, made a good case that Palamas had crossed it: Palamas' teachers, he avers, are Plato and Proclus: what else are these 'uncreated' energies but Platonic Forms, co-eternal and unbegotten like the Demiurge, that is to say, the 'gods' of the *Timaeus*?[180] Palamas was expressly accused of polytheism.

Neither was Demetrios Kydones ever persuaded that Prochoros had erred: 'is there any sensible man who would tolerate those men saying that the essence of the unique god is one thing, and another thing goodness, power, life and wisdom and everything else that Scripture and human common sense (οἱ κοινοὶ λογισμοὶ πάντων ἀνθρώπων) associate to god?' This leads to a division of essence, as if divine qualities had somehow fallen from Being properly understood (ἐκπεπτωκέναι τοῦ κυρίως ὄντος). There is no doubt for Demetrios that this multi-layered theology (πολυμερὴς θεολογία) comes dangerously close to Hellenic mythological construction of god as a multi-synthetical (πολυσύνθετον) being.[181]

Palamas' defence was that it is possible to call the energies 'god' while distinguishing them from divine essence without succumbing to ditheism or polytheism. 'One applies the word "sun" to the rays as well as to the source of the rays; yet it does not follow that there are *two* suns', he said.[182] Further: 'the fact of calling one ray "sun" in no way prevents us from thinking of a unique sun and a unique light.'[183] For all of Palamas' explicit and implicit references to Basil (who used the same metaphor to explain divine presence in 'earth, sea and air'),[184] the passionate and excellent

---

[180] Nik. Greg. *Antirrhetica priora* 213.1–17 Beyer (*Or.* 1.10).

[181] *Notizie* 434.77–435.14.

[182] Gr. Pal. *Triads* 3.3.11.7–8: ἥλιος γὰρ καὶ ἡ ἀκτὶς καὶ ὅθεν ἡ ἀκτὶς καλεῖται καὶ οὐ δύο παρὰ τοῦτο ἥλιοι.

[183] Gr. Pal. *Triads* 3.2.10.14–17: Ἀλλὰ τὰ τοιαῦτα Θεὸν ἕνα σέβειν καὶ θεότητα μίαν οὐδαμῶς προσίσταται, ἐπεὶ μηδ' ἥλιον ἕνα καὶ φῶς ἓν αὐτοῦ νομίζειν, τὸ καὶ τὴν ἀκτῖνα 'ἥλιον' καλεῖσθαι.

[184] Basil, *De spiritu sancto* 9.22.35–7.

efforts of Philotheos Kokkinos, not to mention the authority of John of Damascus, any student of philosophical paganism will find himself in familiar territory.

My point is that, consciously or not, Gregoras and Demetrios Kydones stumbled upon intellectual connections that Orthodox mystics from Pseudo-Dionysius to Maximus Confessor, Symeon the New Theologian and Gregory Palamas would rather have left in their well-deserved oblivion. For granted that, as Palamas has it, uncreated energies are manifestations of the natural energy *of* essence and that they are the essential energy of essence, in the sense that their existence derives from divine essence: how far is this really from the Proclan-Plethonean conception of a first principle conferring its Being to 'gods' which function as an executive board or sum of 'captains' or 'generals'? For the time being, let us bracket this question.

In the end it was the anti-Hesychast party of Barlaam and Akindynos that was condemned for reviving Plato's Forms owing to their teaching regarding the universals.[185] But a surprising new vocabulary made itself felt. Palamas' opponents went as far as to consider the uncreated energies of god as 'gods of beings' (θεοὶ τῶν ὄντων), 'created divinities' (κτισταὶ θεότητες) and 'creators' (δημιουργοί).[186] We shall see that the last term was applied by Plethon in the *Differences* in order to describe the Platonic Ideas. Caught in the same difficulties as Palamas, his critics appear to have provided dubious theological solutions and verbal experimentations that opened new fronts and made them vulnerable to the same accusation of polytheism as they made against the Hesychasts.

The *Tomus* of 1368 containing the anathematisation of Prochoros Kydones repeatedly stresses that Prochoros not only repeated earlier points by Barlaam and Akindynos but also 'gave birth to novel and bizarre heresies' that no previous heretic had ever dared to speak out. The reader is reminded at least three times that Prochoros was more blasphemous and dangerous than previous anti-Hesychasts.[187] In this connection it is important that the

---

[185] *Synodicon* 693–9.
[186] See e.g. Phil. Cocc. *Contra Greg.* 3.664–97.
[187] *Tomus II PG* 151.694B; 712C; 714A, 715A.

Tomus does not see in the anti-Palamist fraction an alliance of evil Latin agents eager to corrupt Orthodoxy by introducing Thomism. On the contrary, it contains a series of quotations attributed to Prochoros that purportedly back up the accusation of *polytheism*. Prochoros, we read, follows his 'mystagogues', namely Barlaam and Akindynos, in slandering the doctrine of the Church regarding divine energies as allegedly polytheistic; but it turns out that it is *he* who is the real ambassador of the belief 'in many divinities and in many created gods'.[188] The quotations attributed to Prochoros in the *Tomus* hide unexpected findings.

Prochoros appears to have twisted the distinction between uncreated energies and essence in god into a relation between 'created gods' and an 'uncreated god'. Clearly, this comes close to Neoplatonic henotheism.[189] The Synod pointed to the Devil as Prochoros' guide and mentor. But towards the end we find a more probable allusion to the source of his 'polytheism': 'he [Prochoros] says that many created divinities exist and slanders Saint Dionysius as allegedly testifying to this'. The Pseudo-Dionysian texts, then, were subjected to an unorthodox reading, producing the abominable blasphemies that shocked Philotheos and the Hesychasts participating in the Synod.[190]

By contrast, as Philotheos argued against Gregoras, 'we [the Palamite party] do not consider being, life, the good, wisdom, and such like either as essences or as creators of created beings, as polytheists do', or, of course, as mere creations, but rather as *powers* (δυνάμεις) dependent on a unique supra-essential first cause and principle. The unparticipable (ἀμέθεκτος) supra-essential essence of god may be said to be 'Being-in-itself', life-in-itself (αὐτοζωή) and divinity-in-itself (αὐτοθεότητα), whereas only god's providential, creative and other operations are participable (μεθεκτῶς) according to the capacity and constitution of each created being. All nature participates in the divine operation of creation, even though man alone potentially participates in that of glorification (θέωσις). It goes without saying that the legitimation of this distinction is ultimately seen as deriving from spiritual experience

---

[188] *Tomus II PG* 151.700A.   [189] *Tomus II PG* 151.700B–D.
[190] See for example *DN* 132.5–13; 137.1–8; *Cael. hier.* 43.12–13: Εὑρήσεις δὲ ὅτι καὶ θεοὺς ἡ θεολογία καλεῖ τάς τε οὐρανίας καὶ ὑπὲρ ἡμᾶς οὐσίας.

offered by divine grace – not upon philosophical discourse, which may be seen as a major discrepancy from, for example, Ockham's notion of divine *attributia*.

Philotheos launches a double accusation against Gregoras: first that he misappropriates the *lexis* and the meaning of Aristotle's category of state (ἔχειν) and second that he appeals to the authority of Aristotle with the intention of attacking Palamas' Orthodoxy. Gregoras takes the essence of a hand to be inseparable from the essence of a man and argues by analogy that the essence of divine energies cannot be different from the essence of God. Philotheos appeals to John of Damascus' commentary on Aristotle's categories to argue that 'man has a hand as part of the whole and not as his essence!'[191] But then follows the really interesting point: the category of *echein* is used equivocally in a number of ways relating to *created* beings only – its applicability does not extend to god's most simple nature, he says, extending John's point: τὸ ἔχειν τῶν ὁμωνύμων ἐστί.[192] Gregoras' unwillingness to comply with the established reading of Aristotle leads to blasphemous experimentations between Scylla and Charybdis, namely *polytheism* and *pantheism*:

When you say that God's creative operation, foreknowledge, providence and in sum every (divine) power and energy are God's essence, you commit yourself to one of two things: I mean either the position that God has many essences; or that his essence is not only compounded of many essences but even of unequal parts – which is precisely what our teachers of theology accused Eunomius of. But for your part you do not say that these (divine operations) partake in God's essence in the sense Eunomius did, but you claim that they are created (κτίσματα). *Which is the greatest of all blasphemies, I mean to pull down God to the level of creation due to his physical operations* (τὸ εἰς κτίσμα σπεύδειν συγκατασπᾶν τὸν Θεὸν διὰ τῶν αὐτοῦ φυσικῶν). (Phil. Cocc. *Contra Greg.* 3.370–9)

Philotheos cannot decide whether Gregoras is a polytheist or a monist. The same ambivalence is applicable to Plethon. What Philotheos *is* sure about is that Gregoras compromises the inalienable transcendence of God's essence. So does Plethon. Philotheos

---

[191] Phil. Cocc. *Contra Greg.* 3.349–60; Cf. Joh. Dam. *Dialectica sive Capita philosophica* 63.1–16.
[192] Joh. Dam. *Dialect.* 63.16–17.

is also sure that Gregoras does so by using Aristotle in 'unorthodox' ways. Gregoras is credited with endeavouring to reach god
by means of Aristotelian categories, manipulating the 'admirable
theologian' as his 'cover' for his assault on Orthodoxy.[193] Armed
with Aristotelian categories, the 'dialectician and philosopher'
Gregoras sails on a philosophical expedition essentially misunderstanding Aristotle. If your teacher Aristotle was present and
could hear you, says Philotheos to Gregoras, he would disapprove of the introduction of philosophical constructions in place
of the simple (ἁπλῶς) reception of truth. Those who have found
god have done so by means of experience (πεῖρα) and a habit
of mind (ἕξις), not merely by means of talks (λόγοι) and conjectures (στοχασμοί).[194] Though a Platonist scholar, Gregoras would
not leave the monopoly of interpreting Aristotle to the heirs of
John of Damascus. Interesting things could be done with revising
current understanding of ancient philosophy and even challenging the established reception of the number one θύραθεν ally of
Orthodoxy, Aristotle.

Who is theologically right in this debate between Palamites and
anti-Palamites is of little concern. Depending on one's theological
and political agenda it is possible to side with one party rather
than another. We have seen that in the seventeenth century the
Jesuits who tried to proselytise the Greek Orthodox population
in Santorini readily appropriated Nikephoros Gregoras and the
anti-Hesychasts as the ideal ally to strike Eastern Orthodoxy from
within its Greek-speaking intellectual context. What matters from
the viewpoint of the history of ideas is that the Hesychast controversy renewed interest in Plato's theory of the Forms, Aristotle and
Neoplatonic philosophical polytheism in a manner unimaginable
before. In its course the ablest fourteenth-century intellectuals persistently explored various ways in which one's understanding of
unity and multiplicity may be pagan Platonic rather than Christian.

---

[193] Phil. Cocc. *Contra Greg.* 3.285–7: Ἐκ γὰρ τῶν τοῦ σοῦ κατηγοριῶν Ἀριστοτέλους
τῶν κατὰ Θεοῦ λόγων ὁρμήσας ἅψασθαι, προκάλυμμα μὲν οἱονεὶ τῆς κατὰ τῶν ἱερῶν
ὕβρεως τὸν θαυμαστὸν τουτονὶ θεολόγον προάγεις.
[194] Phil. Cocc. *Contra Greg.* 8.723–9, 3.381–3, 6.830–1: Ἀλλ᾽ οἱ πείρᾳ καὶ ἕξει τὸν
ἀληθινὸν εὑρηκότες Θεόν. Cf. 10.459–60: Πείρᾳ γὰρ καὶ ἕξει μαθόντες οἱ θεοειδεῖς
οὗτοι θεολογοῦσι ταυτί, καὶ οὐ λόγοις ἁπλῶς οὐδὲ στοχασμοῖς.

Regardless of their primary concern, they unearthed and actively engaged with a Hellenic *hereditas damnosa*. Since Proclus' time there had been no such intensive theorising and reflection upon the notion of polytheism versus monotheism. This move had a profound impact that extended from the purely 'academic' level of theological disagreements to politics.

That the effects of this situation extended to and even influenced Plethon's time became apparent some seventy years after the condemnation of Prochoros' 'created gods'. Then, the issue resurfaced in a much more crucial Synod, now with added geopolitical and interreligious significance. In the 1438/9 Synod of Ferrara/Florence Mark Eugenikos credited the 'Latins' with the selfsame 'error' with which Philotheos burdened the Anti-Palamite party: 'The Latins', wrote Mark, consider divine energy in all its forms as created, hence 'holding the belief in a *created divinity* and created divine light and created Holy Spirit'.[195] Further, they introduce ὑποβάσεις and gradations (βαθμούς) within the Trinity thinking that the Father is greater than the Son and the Son greater than the Holy Spirit. 'These are Origenes' teachings' and Justinian rightly (εἰκότως) considered Origen a polytheist: πολύθεος.[196]

Juan de Torquemada, the Spanish ecclesiastic who carefully followed the proceedings of the Florence Synod, had another view of the matter. He interpreted the results of the Synod as an indirect condemnation of Palamite Orthodoxy, that is to say, of the very Platonic 'error' of postulating a second level of reality between divine substance and man.[197] As was the case with the Hesychast controversy, each side could plausibly condemn the other as guilty of paganism, either because of a proliferation of 'created' divinities reminiscent of the *Timaeus*' created gods, or because of reintroducing Plato's realm of the Ideas. Either way, the shadow of Plato's paganism fell upon both Palamite Orthodoxy and 'Latin' scholasticism. Of course, both Mark Eugenikos and Juan de Torquemada

---

[195] Mark Eug. *Epist. Encycl. Contra Graeco-Latinos et decretum Synodi Florentinae* 6.49–51: καὶ οὕτω κτιστὴν θεότητα καὶ κτιστὸν θεῖον φῶς καὶ κτιστὸν Πνεῦμα ἅγιον τὰ πονηρὰ πρεσβεύουσι κτίσματα.

[196] Mark Eug. *Capita syllogistica adversus Latinos* 43.1–20.

[197] See here Kuhlmann (1968) 108–9, but also the critical notes on Palamism from a Catholic viewpoint in 125, 135.

were perfectly capable of coming up with some exhaustive treatise on why one or the other side should readily be acquitted of such blasphemous suggestions.

The *Nomoi* intentionally bear no signposting as to the time and place they were compiled. I have argued that in reality they concern issues hotly debated and still open in Plethon's immediate intellectual context. Contrary to what Scholarios wants us to believe, Plethon did not need to consult any dusty volumes of Proclus in order to reopen the old case files regarding the relation between gods and god, the many and the One. Palamas' uncreated divine energies, like Gregoras' and Prochoros Kydones' 'created gods', are a reminder that the notion of polytheism, like the possibility of a distinctively pagan ontology sidestepping Orthodox theology, were seriously discussed before Plethon's *Nomoi* but much more recently than Proclus' lifetime, even if to be denounced rather than embraced. Plethon merely decided to cross the Rubicon.

6

SYMBOLIC THEOLOGY

The mythologisation of platonic ontology

Palamite 'energies' and Plethonean 'gods'

Plethon distinguishes three ways in which people think about the divine. Some believe in one unique god (monotheism). Others believe in many gods of about equal divinity (polytheism). Thirdly, there are those who believe in one superior god, who rules as an *archegetes* among lesser gods of varying divinity. Plethon favours the last view, namely henotheism, ultimately one deriving from Plotinus' exclamation that gods *are* god and amply represented by Proclus. Technically speaking, the religion of the *Nomoi* is henotheistic rather than 'polytheistic' or 'monotheistic', in so far as the first cause presides over lesser causes that proceed from it and are allotted with specific responsibilities and duties.[1]

Whereas Gregory Palamas distinguished between uncreated yet unqualified essence and uncreated but qualified energies in god and denied any allegiance to Hellenic philosophical doctrines, Plethon draws a seemingly similar distinction between the One ('Zeus') and the Many ('gods'), but claims to revive pagan Hellenism. Plethon and Palamas are concerned with the same problem: the relation between the transcendence and immanence of god, between his essence and activity or, to put it in terms of the *Nomoi*, between 'Zeus' and the gods. On a surface level Plethon's 'gods', Palamas' 'uncreated but participable divine energies' and the anti-Palamite experiments with notions such as 'created divinities' and 'gods of beings' provide alternative solutions to the question of how singularity relates to plurality. However, even though their starting point is the same, their replies are different.

---

[1] *Nomoi* 24 (1.1.108–13); Plot. *Enn.* 5.8.9.15–20; Siniossoglou (2010a) 127. See also Neri (2010) 113 and W. Blum (1988: 97), who rightly objects to Masai's and Woodhouse's monotheistic reading of Plethon.

Anti-Palamites from Barlaam to the Kydones brothers generally come down to two alternatives with regard to the relation between essence and energies in god. Either there is no such distinction but only a unique and simple divine essence; or divine operations should be recategorised as part of creation, rather than 'uncreated energies'. In his treatise against the Latins, Plethon reintroduces by the back door a third possibility. This is presented as an 'axiom' of 'Hellenic theology': the diversification of operations corresponds to the diversification of modes of subsistence (οὐσίαι). This 'axiom' is openly denounced as one 'most contrary to the Church'.[2] But this principle is presupposed and applied in the *Nomoi* in order to distinguish between three hypostases or species of substance (eternal, perpetual and temporal) conducive to the perfection of all parts of the Plethonean *system*. The species (εἶδος) of generated Being is triple, he says.[3] Because Being is diversified into three 'substances' (οὐσίαι) we should also assume three different modes of generation (γενέσεις).[4] Plethon reproduces the traditionally Neoplatonic tripartite distinction between *eternity* (attributed to 'Zeus'-absolute Being and the intelligible Ideas-gods), *perpetuity* (attributed to the perpetually renewed existence of the universe and the perpetual movement of intracelestial gods) and *time* (corresponding to the world of becoming and mortality. The word *ousiai* here does not signify the creation of ontologically disparate essences or essentially different substances but different modes of subsistence – what we might better describe as *hypostaseis* of a single essence.[5] This is the first step towards the Plethonean genealogy of Being that reintroduces the possibility of an intermediate multitude of substances *qua* hypostases of divine essence that administer respective powers.

The same principle is presupposed in the *Differences*. There, the creation of the material universe is not credited to god's immediate creative energy but distilled through a congenial *ousia* intermediate

---

[2] Plethon, *Contra Lat.* 300 Alexandre: ὧν μὲν αἱ δυνάμεις διάφοροι, καὶ αὐτὰ ἄν εἶναι ταῖς οὐσίαις διάφορα. Cf. *Nomoi* 242 (3.43.19–23).

[3] *Nomoi* 94–6 (3.15.49–50): Τριττὸν τὸ τῆς γενητῆς συμπάσης οὐσίας εἶναι εἶδος.

[4] *Nomoi* 96 (3.15.58–9): Τούτων τῶν οὐσιῶν τριῶν οὐσῶν, τρεῖς που δεῖ καὶ τὰς γενέσεις εἶναι. Though Plethon goes on to talk of these hypostases as three *ousiai* (*Nomoi* 96 (3.15.58)) he quickly returns to the generic notion of *ousia* at *Nomoi* 97–8 (3.15.74–85).

[5] For *ousia* as *hypostasis* in Platonism see Dörrie (1976).

between his extreme goodness and the material world.[6] According to the *Synodicon of Orthodoxy* this meant a clear reversion to pagan Platonism as condemned in the case of John Italos. Plethon's intermediate *ousia* is identifiable with the Platonist intellectual world (νοητὸς κόσμος) and Timaeus of Locri's 'ideal or eidetic (ἰδανικὸς, δηλαδὴ εἰδικός) world.[7] In a passage from the *Differences* that must have alarmed Scholarios and any recipient versed in both Christian and pagan theology, Plethon affirms that god is an *ousia*, which, however, is not the actual creative force; it is another *ousia*, or rather *hypostasis* congenial to the first principle, that is diversified into an intelligible paradigm:

> The proponents of the Forms do not suppose that god in his absolute perfection is the immediate creator of our universe but rather of *another* prior nature and substance, most akin to himself, eternal and incapable of change in perpetuity; and that he created the universe not directly by himself but through that substance. *Of that substance is composed, they say, an intelligible order* which Timaeus of Locri calls Ideal, meaning Formal. And they make an assemblage of these Forms of all kinds and their Intellects, and place a single perfect Intellect over the whole of the intelligible order, assigning to it the second place in the sovereignty of the universe after god in his absolute perfection. (*Diff.* 336.20–7)[8]

The pattern is reproduced in mythological terms in the *Nomoi*. 'Zeus' gives birth to 'Poseidon', the divine force responsible for the generation of beings intermediate between immortality and mortality.[9] 'Poseidon' is the most important active principle after 'Zeus'.[10] The correspondences between, on the one hand 'Poseidon' in the *Nomoi* and this eternal 'substance' in the *Differences* and, on the other hand, the realm of gods in the *Nomoi* and Plato's world of the Ideas defended in the *Differences* are unmistakable.

In creating 'Poseidon', 'Zeus' uses himself as an immediate paradigm.[11] Thus 'Poseidon' is the product of a self-reflection of the first principle which renders him analogous to the Plotinean *nous* and to 'Zeus' in Proclus' *Commentary on Cratylus*, who

---

[6] *Diff.* 336.20–5.   [7] *Diff.* 336.25–7.

[8] I follow Woodhouse's translation, though 'hypostasis' would be a more adequate rendering of *ousia* in the context of Plethon's ontology.

[9] *Nomoi* 180 (3.34,4.144–52).   [10] *Nomoi* 104 (3.15.172–6).

[11] *Nomoi* 92 (3.15.16–18).

proceeds as 'the creative Intellect' from the superior Intellect of 'Cronus'.[12] Plethon applies the Neoplatonic emanationist principle *ex uno non fit nisi unum* that was still preserved in the fourteenth century by Nikephoros Gregoras[13] but is also typical of the illuminationist philosophy of Suhrawardi, which is often related to Plethon's Neoplatonism. Regardless of the ancient and contemporary sources that Plethon might have consulted, it is telling that in the *Differences* he attributes the second position (τὰ δευτερεῖα) after the extreme Good (ὁ ἄκρως ἀγαθὸς θεός) to *nous*. This leaves little room for doubting that in the *Nomoi* Plethon is pursuing a mythologised version of beliefs that were credited in the former work to 'those who introduce Forms'.[14] Polytheism becomes once again the popular version of esoteric Platonism.

The theogony of the *Nomoi* appears to be in accord with Plethon's textual corrections to numerous works by Plato. Pagani showed that Plethon emendated and revised Platonic passages from the *Symposium*, the *Laws*, *Epinomis* and the *Gorgias* that were inconsistent with his version of philosophical Hellenism.[15] Plethon's aim was to restore an original mythological and philosophical pattern meant to be more ancient than that reported by Plato and morally as well as philosophically superior to the Homeric-Hesiodean one. Elsewhere, he suppressed the reference to the 'reign of Cronus' in *Gorgias* 523a–b, thus aligning Plato to his own pantheon, in which Cronus is not the father of Zeus

---

[12] Procl. *In Crat.* 104.20–3: κατὰ δὴ τούτους τοὺς προσδιορισμοὺς καὶ τὸν Δία τοῦ Κρόνου λέγεσθαι νομίσωμεν υἱόν· νοῦς γὰρ ὢν δημιουργικὸς ὁ Ζεὺς ἄλλου νοῦ πρόεισιν ὑπερτέρου καὶ ἑνοειδεστέρου.

[13] Always eager to understand ancient religion, Gregoras in his commentary on Synesius' *De insomniis* observed that for a Platonist like Synesius 'Zeus' corresponds to *nous* and wisdom (*sophia*) to its power. Thus he recalls the Anaxagorean doctrine that '*nous* orders (διακοσμεῖ) everything and is the cause of all' to back up the Platonic belief in the causal primacy of *nous*. Cf. Nik. Greg. *Expl. in Synesii De insomniis* 5.1–7 Guidorizzi; Plato, *Phd.* 97c. Much to Palamas' annoyance Gregoras also transmits in the fourteenth century the Plotinean version of Platonism, according to which *nous* stands intermediate between the pagan 'god' and anything else. In Plethon it is not Minerva that springs forth from 'Zeus', but 'Poseidon', chief among the 'Olympian' gods. It is 'Poseidon' who stands for *nous*, not 'Zeus'.

[14] *Diff.* 336.20–30: οἱ τὰ εἴδη τιθέμενοι.

[15] Pagani (2008) 38. Cf. Pagani (2006) 16–18 on the identification of Plethon's hand *in textu* in large parts of *Marcianus graecus* 188 (K) and Pagani (2009) for Plethon's recension of Plato's text.

but merely the primary divinity among the 'Titans'. In like manner, he removed from the discourse of Agathon in *Symposium* any references to Eros and Necessity being active before Zeus (*Symp.* 195b–c). As Pagani argued, this is a theological statement, meant to cleanse Plato's text of theological mistakes, regardless of whether in Plato's text it is only Agathon praising Eros, rather than Socrates philosophising. As Plethon saw it, no divinities could possibly have been active before Zeus, and the Platonic text should be rewritten accordingly regardless of literary context.[16] Pagani's interpretation is consistent with the fundamental position in the *Nomoi* that Plato and Zoroaster are messengers but not originators of true doctrines (*Nomoi* 252 (3.43.140ff.)). This authorised Plethon to intervene in the terminology applied to astral bodies in the *Epinomis* in order to bring it into accord with that used in the *Nomoi*. One is tempted to note here that Plethon's emendations provide us with a pagan equivalent to the Christian apologetical (mis)appropriation of Platonic texts that sought to render Plato conformable to Judaeo-Christianity by rewriting accordingly his *lexis*.[17]

The wordplay between *eidos* and Pos-*eidon* is obvious.[18] 'Poseidon' represents a form (εἶδος), but not '*this* or *that* form'; rather, 'Poseidon' is the *genus* of *all* forms and includes every single form in itself and all of them at once. Origen understood Christ/Logos in similar terms, namely as 'Idea of Ideas' and 'substance of substances'.[19] 'Poseidon' is also analogous to that 'unique separate Light', the first ontological principle to emanate from 'First Being' in Suhrawardi's *Hayakil-e Nur*.[20] The 'supermundane system (διάκοσμος)' consists of gods that are completely immaterial and exist beyond temporality. They are pure forms (εἴδη), immutable intelligible entities that remain in a permanent state of actuality. Their essence is indivisible.[21]

---

[16] Pagani (2009) 176–86; (2008) 31, 35.

[17] On the Christian appropriation of Plato see Siniossoglou (2008a) and (2010b).

[18] Masai (1956) 279.

[19] Orig. *Cels.* 6.64. Cf. Collins (2001) 163 n. 6, who notes the analogy to Plato's Idea of the Good.

[20] See Corbin's Prolegomena to Suhrawardi, *Œuvres Philosophiques*, vol. II, 28.

[21] *Nomoi* 46 (1.5.14–39).

The word εἶδος is something of a buzzword in Plethon's work and may alternately mean *form* or *species*. A significant passage from Proclus' *Commentary* on the *Parmenides* defining and elaborating on this term is particularly pertinent here:

In sum, then, the Idea in the truest sense is an incorporeal cause, transcending its participants, a motionless Being, exclusively and really a model, intelligible to souls through images, and intelligising causally the existents modelled upon it [3]. So that from all these problems we have ferreted out the single definition of an Idea in the true sense.

If, then, any wish to attack the concepts of Ideas, let them attack this definition, and not assume them to be either corporeal images (φαντασίαι) of their own minds, or coordinate with the things of this realm, *or devoid of Being*, or correspondent with our conceptions [2], or let them produce *some other sophistic definition* [4] such as these, and then fabricate their arguments on that basis; but let them bear in mind that *Parmenides declared the Ideas to be gods* [1], and that they subsist in god, as the Oracle also declares (fr. 37 des Places): 'The Intellect of the Father whirred, conceiving with his unwearying will/Ideas of every form' [5].

For the 'fount of the Ideas' is god, and the god in whom it is contained is the Demiurgic intellect; and if it is the primal Idea, then it is to this that the above definition, assembled from the problems posed by Parmenides, pertains. (Procl. *In Prm.* 934.38–935.21; trans. Morrow and Dillon; my emphasis)

Proclus offers a definition of *eidos* [3] and anticipates Plethon in two respects. First, in explictly following Parmenides (who, we may recall, has a prominent place in the list of sages in Book 1 of the *Nomoi*, just after Plato and before Timaeus)[22] and identifying Forms with gods, thus establishing the link between Parmenides, Platonic ontology and polytheism/henotheism; second, in launching an attack on Aristotle's theory of the equivocity of Being as well as on proto-nominalistic readings of Plato's theory of the Forms, thus providing a clear model for the Plethonean critique of Aristotle in the *Differences* [2]. In this passage we witness the intellectual ancestry of the late Byzantine conflict between Plethon and Scholarios regarding the primacy of Plato or Aristotle. Intriguingly, the enemies of Plato's genuine philosophy are accused of *sophistry* [4], as are the Christians in the *Nomoi*; and as in Plethon, the *Chaldean Oracles* are vehicles of those 'true doctrines' that

---

[22] *Nomoi* 32 (1.2.75–7).

Plato too tried to convey [5]. Proclus' opponents thought that the Ideas were 'devoid of Being'. They were guilty of the same error as was Scholarios, who appropriated Aristotle's theory of the equivocity of Being. This is the error of undermining the ontological unity of Plato's universe. The 'sophists' should 'bear in mind' that the Ideas are gods, and obviously gods possess Being. Clearly, the clash with the Aristotelean theologians in the *Differences* and in *Against Scholarios* regarding the exact nature of Plato's Forms concerns not only ontology but polytheism.

To return to the *Nomoi*, 'Zeus' creates a finite number of these εἴδη 'gods' by dichotomizing each in order to create the other and organising all into the first circle or level of the system.[23] The method of division employed by Plato in the *Sophist* might indeed have provided a pattern, and so does the dichotomic classification *per genus et differentiam* in the *arbor porphyriana*.[24] On the other hand, Hellenic mythology provides adequate inspiration in regard to similar ways of procession (Zeus/Athena). Plethon likens the procession of gods to the production of multiple images by means of mirrors. Gods as Ideas (εἴδη) are also idols (εἴδωλα), the outcome of a 'production of *idols*' (εἰδωλοποιία).[25] But it is the 'Parmenidean', according to Proclus, analogy between the Monad and numbers that Plethon acknowledges to be really a more apt one. As it happens, this corresponds to a shift in focus from mythology and popular religion to more philosophical considerations:

> If such a production of images requires the means of many mirrors, let us think of the Monad: namely how the Monad gives birth to all numbers by adding to itself each number in order to produce the next, without requiring the participation of any other cause. (*Nomoi* 94 (3.15.24–7))

---

[23] *Nomoi* 94 (3.15.35–45). I am not going to attempt any exhaustive account of the possible networks of references and fields of meaning connecting Plethon's mythological and symbolical system with Orphic and Hesiodean theogonies and/or Proclan, Plotinean and Plutarchean philosophy. To some extent, this has been achieved by others with good results. See the reconstruction of Plethonean pantheon in Alexandre (1858), Masai (1956), W. Blum (1988), Medvedev (1997), Bargeliotes (1980) and (1974) 130–5, Tambrun (2006a) and Hladký (forthcoming).

[24] Tambrun (2006a) 158; *Soph.* 219a–232b; Masai (1957/8) 404.

[25] *Nomoi* 93–4 (3.15.20–3).

This recalls Xenocrates' identification of Platonic Ideas with numbers and the Monad with divine Intellect.[26] The difference is that the Plethonean theogony is not a process of addition, but one of division. In the *Nomoi* 'Zeus' does not add the derived species to 'himself' but separates them from him. Hence, Plethon's παράγειν should be translated as *to confer* rather than *to produce*: 'Zeus' confers the essence as well as distinctive qualities proper to each of the gods (τὰ προσόντα).[27] The procession of divinities at *Nomoi* 158–68 follows a rational pattern according to which the more concrete, specific and material principles emanate deductively from the more abstract and generic ones. All gods participate in Zeus's essence, though to a different degree: gods are diversified with respect to their divinity, value (ἀξία), power (δύναμις) and properties.[28] In the same sense as the Idea of the Good unites Ideas in Plato, each god exists by himself/herself but simultaneously all gods constitute a single entity.

Supra-celestial gods are of two kinds: the 'Olympian' gods and the 'Titans'. The direct or legitimate children of 'Zeus' live in the 'superior part of the supra-celestial realm', Olympus. Each is created after the image of the god that precedes him and exercises authority over different areas. An important insight regarding Plethonean theogony is provided by W. Blum, who notes the role of dialectical transfer of essence in the whole process.[29] 'Poseidon', pure actuality, is paired with 'Hera', which stands for potentiality and matter. The symbolism carries Aristotelean overtones, though the coupling of 'Poseidon' and 'Hera', like that of the 'Helios' with 'Selene' later on, also recalls the Pythagorean indefinite dyad. 'Apollo' emanates from 'Hera' and controls identity; 'Artemis' controls difference; 'Hephaistus' stands for the state of rest and perseverance (Plethon possibly intended a wordplay between the

---

[26] Cf. Dam. *De princ.* 1.243.14–20. John Lydus (*Mens.* 2.6.1–6) transmits the interpretation according to which the Pythagorean Monad was called 'Hyperionis' because it surpasses all beings in terms of its unqualified Being (ὑπερεῖναι τῇ οὐσίᾳ). As in Plethon, this hardly means that the Monad is not-Being: it means that the essence of the Monad is simple and not composite, but as essence-in-itself it still *is* essence.

[27] Couloubaritsis (1997) 125 n. 41. Alexandre sees Zeus as 'communicating' his essence to all inferior deities. See above, p. 248.

[28] *Nomoi* 48 (1.5.36–54).   [29] W. Blum (1988) 64–7.

name *Hephaistos* and the verb ἐφίστημι);[30] 'Dionysus' stands for self-motion, improvement and perfection; 'Minerva' for motion that is externally caused, thrust and the obliteration of the superfluous. The *megista gene* of the *Sophist*, the '*genera* of being' of late antique commentators, namely being (ὄν), identity (ταυτότης), difference (ἑτερότης), movement (κίνησις) and rest (στάσις) are clearly discernible.[31] Other 'Olympian' gods take up specialist duties. 'Rhea' leads over primary bodies and elements; 'Pluto' rules over the immortal part of human beings; and so forth.

The indirect or 'illegitimate' children of 'Zeus', the 'Titans', stand for Ideas affecting the realm of mortality. A possible source is Proclus, who renders the 'Titans' and 'Cronus' responsible for division and differentiation.[32] In Plethon's Titanic realm, 'Cronus' presides over time – a clear reference to the alleged Orphic tradition reported by Proclus that merges Χρόνος (time) with Κρόνος;[33] 'Kore' (Persephone) rules over the human body.[34] Under the command of 'Zeus' and according to his legislation and allocution of appropriate 'situations' (καταστάσεις), these gods are responsible for the supervision of the whole of mutable nature,[35] 'which is, of course, generated in terms of its cause and in a perpetual state of becoming owing to motion but is uncreated in respect to time'.[36] Plethon is faithfully adhering to the allegorical interpretation of Plato's 'likely tale' as elaborated in late antique Neoplatonist cosmology. Intra-celestial gods form a lower circle or level of the system and are classifiable in two further categories as celestial and mundane gods. Intermediate between the realm of the Ideas and mortality is the degree of Helios, Selene, fixed stars and daemons. As already noted, the world of becoming is animated by a World-soul vivifying and sacralising a spatio-temporal realm dominated by deities intermingled with matter.[37] (See the table on p. 287.)

---

[30] Tambrun (2006a) 147.
[31] *Soph.* 254d–256d. Cf. Ammon. *In Porphyrii Eisagogen sive quinque voces, CAG* 4.3, 52.18–20. Cf. Tambrun (2006a) 159.
[32] Procl. *In Crat.* 106.15–30.   [33] Procl. *In Crat.* 109.1–9.
[34] For Plethon's identification of the Ideas with gods see Masai (1956) 220–5, Wokart (1986) 190–1.
[35] *Nomoi* 170 (3.34,4.18–20).   [36] *Nomoi* 160 (3.34,2.47–50).
[37] See above, Ch. 5, p. 258.

Ontological hierarchy according to Plethon

I	Being ('One-in-itself', 'Being-in-itself', 'Good-in-itself') = Zeus (god)					
Philosophical and cosmological categories	**Atemporal gods (Olympians)**	**II A** Actuality	= Poseidon (*nous*)	**Supra-celestial gods**	**Legitimate children of Zeus**	**Suprasensible-divine world**
		1. Power	= Hera			
		2. Identity	= Apollo			
		3. Difference	= Artemis			
		4. Rest	= Hephaistos			
		5. Motion				
		a. self-movement	= Dionysus			
		b. movement by external cause	= Minerva			
		B a) 1. Astral nature	= Atlas			
		2. Planets	= Tithonus			
		3. Fixed stars	= Dione			
		4. Daemonic nature	= Hermes			
		5. Human soul	= Pluto			
		b) 1. Corporeal nature	= Rhea			
		2. Ether and heat	= Leto			
		3. Air and cold	= Hecate			
		4. Water and flow	= Tethys			
		5. Earth and solidity	= Hestia			
	Temporal gods (Titans)	c) 1. Time	= Cronus		**Illegitimate children**	
		2. Reproduction	= Aphrodite			
		3. Animal nature	= Pan			
		4. Nature of plants	= Demeter			
		5. Human mortal nature	= Persephone			
	Immortal beings	**C** a) 1. Sun, moon, planets	= Helios, Selene, Eosphoros, Stilbon, ...	**Legitimate**	**Children of Poseidon**	**Intra-celestial, mundane world**
		2. Fixed stars	= unnamed divine stars			
		3. Daemonic nature	= daemons			
	Mortal beings	**III A** 1. Rational beings: humans		**Illegitimate**		
		2. Irrational beings: animals				
		3. Plants				
		4. Inorganic matter				

This table appears in Greek in Bargeliotes (1980) 49; it is here expanded and adapted with the permission of the author. See also Masai (1956) 224; Alexandre (1858) lix; Schultze (1874) 215.

Proclus' description of Olympian gods and the 'Titanic *genus*' in the commentary on Plato's *Cratylus* provides a good example of those Neoplatonic experimentations with mythological gods that anticipate Plethonean theogony.[38] Damascius' *De principiis* contains another interesting parallel to the procession of the 'Olympian' gods from 'Zeus', as well as to the paganising dimension of Plethon's attack on the equivocity of Being in the *Differences*. The question concerns the *homoeideia* of divinities: are they homogeneous, do they belong to the same *genus*, or not? Damascius replies that they do so in one sense, but not in another:

> If we assume that 'Eros' proceeded from 'Aphrodite' or that 'Minerva' proceeded from 'Zeus', then this procession is not homogeneous (ἀνομοειδὴς ἡ πρόοδος), for 'Eros' went out of the boundaries of 'Aphrodite' and 'Minerva' out of those of 'Zeus'; still, 'Minerva' possesses something 'of Zeus', and 'Eros' possesses something 'of Aphrodite', and to that extent they possess something of that *genus* to which belong their producers (καί τι ὁμοειδὲς ἔχουσι πρὸς τοὺς παράγοντας). (Dam. *De princ.* 1.247.3–6)

Damascius goes on to utilise the appellations of gods in order to clarify the ontological and logical status of homogeneous and non-homogeneous processions. Soon it turns out that the real object of discussion is not the Greek pantheon and the correspondences between 'Zeus' and 'Minerva' or 'Aphrodite' and 'Eros'. These have an explanatory or paradigmatic value. Rather, the real object is the very ancient problem regarding the relation between One and the Many.[39] Like Damascius, Plethon construed a symbolic ontology, which, though allowing polytheistic cult at a surface level, is primarily meant to organise all levels of Being into a rationally compiled finite community of Forms that also operate within the universe.

The word σύστημα constantly recurs in the *Nomoi*. It carries a meaning that directly challenges the Hesychasts' faith in the infinity and ultimately supra-rationality of divine will. Proclus is reported to have often recited the maxim that the duty of the true philosopher is not to adhere to the religious tradition of one city

---

[38] Procl. *In Crat.* 101.17–137.7.   [39] Dam. *De princ.* 1.248.28–249.1.

or one group of people, but rather to become 'hierophant of the whole *cosmos*'.[40] Plethon's *systema* signifies a universal, unified and common ontological network or pattern underlying Being that is encoded into a nexus of mythological correspondences.[41] As Plethon has it, mankind effectively participates in 'a *polis* of beings' (ἡ τῶν ὄντων παντελὴς πόλις). Within this *polis*, gods entrusted man with the task of harmonising the divine with the mortal element.[42] The notion of man as *methorion* authorises the application of the word *polis* in ontology and, *mutatis mutandis*, the political use of ontology. The 'system' of the *Nomoi* is meant to be a map of this *polis*.

By intellectualising mythology and corresponding 'gods' to Platonic *megista gene* and Aristotelean categories, Plethon endeavoured to construct a code for uncovering the blueprint of the world, or better, the blueprint of Being. The *Nomoi* is a *liber mundi* that seeks to render the system of the universe readable by promising to recover a long-forgotten Adamic language through the mythologisation of ontology. A more careful analysis confirms the impression that this system represents a radical turn from his contemporary doctrinal expositions of faith and theological treatises to religious-philosophical semiotics. As Medvedev observed, only a semantic analysis of the *Nomoi* pantheon can uncover its meaning: a nexus consisting of signs taken to represent the generic and essential relations, qualities and causes active within the system of the world.[43]

Similar endeavours flourished in Ottoman territory. In places like Adrianople and Bursa, where Plethon appears to have studied, syncretistic esoteric projects combined Hurufism and theosophic Kabbalah with angelology, Sufism and elements from the Abrahamic traditions. Two contemporary mystics, al-Bistami and Sheikh Bedreddin, sought a supra-confessional truth through 'the

---

[40] Marinus, *Procl.* 19.25–30: κοινῇ δὲ τοῦ ὅλου κόσμου ἱεροφάντης.

[41] Cf. *Nomoi* 102 (3.15.157–9); 82 (2.27.4–8): καὶ ἔτι Διΐ τῷ βασιλεῖ ἡ σύμπασα τοῦ ὄντος γένεσις ἐκ πάντων τε καὶ παντοίων εἰδῶν αἰωνίων, ἐγχρόνων, ἀθανάτων, θνητῶν, ἐς ἕν τι παντελὲς σύστημα, ἐς ὅσον οἷόν τ᾽ ἦν, κάλλιστά τε καὶ ἄριστα ἔχον, συγκεκροτημένη. Cf. *Nomoi* 94 (3.15.44–5): ἐς ἕν τι αὐτὸ σύστημα πάντων τε καὶ παντοίων εἰδῶν πλῆρες συστησάμενον. Cf. *Nomoi* 98 (3.15.82): τό τε αὖ σύστημα τὸ ἐξ ἁπάντων ὅλον τέ τι καὶ ἐν τῇ κοινωνίᾳ; *Nomoi* 172 (3.34,4.50).

[42] *Nomoi* 194 (3.34,5.146–54).   [43] Medvedev (1981) 545; (1984) 131.

science of letters and names' and religious sectarianism respectively. Given Plethon's sojourn in Ottoman land and his purported study by the shadowy Elissaios, the likelihood of contacts with Bedreddin, Muslim mystics or *Romaniotes* with an interest in the Kabbalah, Hurufism, and possibly the Platonising philosophy of Suhrawardi should by no means be excluded.[44]

Viewed from this angle the symbolic theology of the *Nomoi* is a type of Hellenic Kabbalah or pagan adaptation of the Hurufi 'science of names', in the sense that it represents a similar project utilising similar means to ascend to a supra-confessional truth, while tackling similar questions. For a Kabbalist in the tradition of Abraham Abulafia the Kabbalah primarily meant an incessant transmission of inalienable truths from antiquity up to his time, the recovery of which opened up the possibility of intellectual perfection and unity with the Active Intellect.[45] We have seen that Plethon's epistemology is based on a similar persuasion that the message will come across regardless of historical contingencies and that recipients capable of decoding it will always be there, either few or many. The relation between Plethonean gods and 'Zeus' recalls the hotly debated issue regarding the relation between the *sefirot* and *En Soph*: the *sefirot* could alternatively be viewed as instruments of god or the essence of god and various interpretative possibilities opened up depending on one's allegiance and attitude to Aristotelianism and Neoplatonism.[46] Further, the Plethonean intellectualisation of mythological *personae* is reminiscent of the kabbalistic approach to Jewish angelology. Another idea in the *Nomoi* consonant with medieval Kabbalism is that individual and national preservation (σωτηρία) are effectively conditioned by a determinist cosmic process, thus presupposing a proper understanding of the interaction between all levels of reality (or the *systema*, as Plethon calls it).[47]

---

[44] I discuss this possibility in Siniossoglou (2012).

[45] Tirosh-Samuelson (2006) 232. For Kabbalah in Byzantium see Idel (1998: 56, 192), who also locates an important Kabbalist text, in fact 'a vast compilation of various Kabbalistic sources' in late fourteenth- or early fifteenth-century Byzantium.

[46] Tirosh-Samuelson (2006) 233–4, 243.

[47] *Soteria* may refer to the preservation of a healthy bodily constitution (*Nomoi* 138 (3.34,1.76–8)); to the successful fulfilment of man's mission in this life (*Nomoi* 162 (3.34,2.67–9)): ἀλλ' ἄφθιτον καὶ ἀκέραιον ὑφ' ὑμῖν σωτῆρσι τὸ ἐν ἡμῖν θεῖον διασώζειν

The question posed by the relation between *sefirot* and *En Soph* in theosophic Kabbalah surfaced in the late Byzantine context in regard to the relation between divine energies and divine essence. What is, philosophically and theologically, the difference? Plethon's 'gods' subsist and operate in a manner radically different from that of Palamas' 'divine energies'. In Roman Orthodox mystical theology all existing beings participate in the most generic energy called the οὐσιοποιός energy; those that are alive also participate in the ζωοποιός energy that provides life; the ability to think and act wisely means participation in the σοφοποιός energy; ultimately, angels and men who have achieved illumination participate in the θεοποιός energy that grants godlikeness.[48] Creation may be described as either spiritualised by these divine energies or effectively emerging as a realisation of *logoi* of beings. In both cases these energies/*logoi* remain powers of a unique god. They do not carry individually diversified divine essence, as do gods in Plethon, nor are they identifiable with paradigmatic beings (ὄντα) of any kind.[49] Like 'reasons (λόγοι) of beings' in Maximus Confessor, the uncreated energies are a proliferation of god's energy and at the same time identical to god's will and wishes – hence not to be confused with either Platonic ideas, archetypes, *universalia* and *realia* upon which depend lower ontological strata, or with exemplary causes in the sense of Bonaventure's and Aquinas' divine ideas.[50] By contrast, we have seen that Plethon's declension of gods results from a diversification and distinction of divine essence rather than energy. Gods in the *Nomoi* enjoy a community of essence with 'Zeus', even if they do so diversely and to varying extents.[51]

Palamas was very conscious of the difference between his theology and pagan Platonism and defended himself against numerous accusations of polytheism by developing strong nominalist

---

πειρώμενοι); or, significantly, to the preservation of established political principles (*Nomoi* 198–200 (3.34,5.210–12): ἡ τῶν καθεστηκότων τε καὶ εὖ ἐχόντων σωτηρία). For a similar notion in Kabbalah see Idel (1998) 191. I deal with the political dimension of *soteria* according to Plethon in Ch. 7, pp. 345–6, 351.

[48] Gr. Pal. *Triads* 3.2.23.3–13; *Capita CL* 91.18–26.

[49] On Plethon's re-sacralisation of the world, see above, Ch. 5, pp. 224–5, 250ff.

[50] Gr. Pal. *Capita CL* 87.1–18.

[51] Cf. *Nomoi* 48 (1.5.36–41): ἡ ἑαυτοῦ [τοῦ Διὸς] κοινωνία, *Nomoi* 242 (3.43.32–4).

tendencies. Divine energies are 'formless', he says, because identical with divine wishes (θελήματα). Pythagoras and Plato are polytheists in so far as they postulate self-subsistent 'paradigms' and 'principles of being' intermediate between creation and divine supra-essentiality.[52] Plato's multi-causalism decreases the distance between created world and god and compromises the will and radical alterity of god as a personal agent. The significance of Palamas' and Maximus' position that the *logoi* of all beings do *not* correspond to concepts or ideas but to god's wishes (θελήματα) is that the world is conditioned as the contingent product of god's will and thus safeguarded from any interpretation that sees in it the necessary product of Platonic emanationism. This distinction between Christian *ktisis* and Plethon's pagan generation brings us to another pivotal disparity: contrary to the pagan Platonic paradigm to which Plethon reverts, the world according to Palamas and Maximus is not born *from within* god – it is extra-deical, namely created *by* god.

The identification of the supermundane gods with Forms and the insistence on their simultaneous transcendence and immanence point to a hierarchical ontology, rather than to the rigid religion of a theocratic polytheistic state.[53] On the other hand, in Plethon, no less than in Proclus and Damascius, gods are Ideas and not concepts. This means they are real. One wonders: what if we assume that Plethon's gods are not meant to be real entities anymore than is the Demiurge in the *Timaeus*? In other words: are Plethon's gods personal, or impersonal and abstract causes? Is it really a religion that Plethon describes in the *Nomoi*, or, as has been suggested, a 'religion'? The reply to these questions does not so much depend upon the larger or smaller concessions one is willing to make to allegory but rather on acknowledging the ability of Neoplatonism to serve well both esoteric and popular religion by means of the same structures.[54]

---

[52] Gr. Pal. *Triads* 3.3.9.17: ἀνείδεον εἶδος. Cf. 2.3.53.62; 3.2.26.

[53] So Codoñer (2005: 92 and n. 4) *contra* Monfasani (1992: 51), who argues that the 'titles of the remaining chapters give not the slightest hint that Pletho viewed any part of his doctrine as allegorical in nature'.

[54] See here Siniossoglou (2010a).

Paganism in the *Differences*: Forms as intellects, creators and originators

In the *Nomoi* Plethon follows Plato in so far as the essence of Ideas/gods is derived from the Idea of the Good/god. His 'gods' then claim their unique position within a hierarchical henotheistic genealogy and matrix of personifications. They may possess diversified essence conferred upon them from a first principle ('Zeus'), but they exist independently. They are 'Zeus's' children and offspring, hypostases individualised and self-subsistent in so far as they perform diverse tasks. Gods are given conventional names drawn from Greek mythology, personal names, and this should not be taken lightly.[55] In the *Differences* the divinities of the *Nomoi* correspond to certain unnamed 'producers', 'creators' and, significantly: *intellects*. It is worth insisting on this point, for it provides abundant proof of the underlying conceptual affinities between the two works.

Plethon notes that Aristotle 'has the least sympathy for eternal substances and Forms'.[56] By contrast, Scholarios and Aquinas credit Plato with the belief that 'the first god' ordains supervisors (προνοητάς) that are second and third in rank.[57] Following Aristotle, Scholarios objects that the Platonists unnecessarily assume the existence of a Being *qua genus* independently of particular beings. Evidently, Platonic multi-causalism bordered dangerously on polytheism, whereas Aristotle rendered the paradigmatic realm of the intelligible ideas/gods obsolete. According to Aristotle a principal difficulty with Plato's Ideas is that they are deemed incapable of introducing change. Thus they are considered unable to function as real causes within the world of generation and corruption (in the way that the Christian god does). If Aristotle's formal-paradigmatic cause (εἰδικὴ-παραδειγματικὴ αἰτία) functions by default as an efficient cause (ποιητικὴ αἰτία) too, as

---

[55] Seen in this light, Maximus' 'battle-arrays of angels' are closer to Plethon's gods than are his 'divine powers' (*Ambigua, PG* 91.1124C) or Palamas' uncreated energies, corresponding to distinct subjects with personal characteristics.

[56] Pleth. *Contra Schol.* 22.28–9: ὃ δὴ Ἀριστοτέλης ἐπὶ τῶν ἀιδίων οὐσιῶν τε καὶ εἰδῶν ἥκιστα προσίεται.

[57] Schol. *Epitome Summae contra gentiles, OC* 5.3.76.11–12.

Scholarios argued, then Aristotle's criticism of Plato's theory of the Forms may be conveniently appropriated as confirming the economy and sufficiency of Judaeo-Christian monotheism.[58] The absence of any reason to assume an active ontological hierarchy mediating between the Idea of the Good and the universe rendered Neoplatonist emanationism and *a fortiori* henotheism uneconomical and hence implausible. The Aristotelean criticism of Plato's ontology cancels out the dissemination of divine tasks to a plurality of intelligible agents, undermining the henotheist model of one sovereign presiding over many captains.

Scholarios' interpretation, according to which Aristotle's principle of locomotion (τὸ κινοῦν) is also an efficient cause, is basically that of Ammonius, son of Hermeias, and that of Simplicius.[59] But whereas Simplicius proceeded to this – in itself dubious – reading in order to align Aristotle's first principle with Plato's demiurge in the *Timaeus*, Scholarios opts for it in order to force the compatibility between Aristotle's first principle and the Judaeo-Christian god. The universe could thus be seen as the immediate product of an individual god's spontaneous decision rather than as necessarily emanating from a chain of intelligible productive causes.

In *Against Scholarios* Plethon fully realised that the Neoplatonic doctrine of a *symphonia* between Plato and Aristotle, once a serious rival to Christianity, was now providing Christian intellectuals such as Scholarios with first-class armoury.[60] This was reason enough for him to disagree with Simplicius, who now inadvertently served his opponent's aims. This said, Plethon does not abandon Aristotle too to Scholarios. In the *Differences* Plethon acknowledges the usefulness of Aristotle's criticism of Plato for Christian theism and goes on to claim him back to the pagan world-view:

[Aristotle] denies that objects of sense which are eternal owe their movement to the Forms (*Metaph.* 1071b12–16); and he does not believe that any cause whatever is necessary for their essence and being. So this is why he asks: what do

---

[58] Schol. *Contra Pleth., OC* 4.49.17–27.
[59] Simpl. *In Phys., CAG* 10.1363.8–10: γέγραπται δὲ βιβλίον ὅλον Ἀμμωνίῳ τῷ ἐμῷ καθηγεμόνι, πολλὰς πίστεις παρεχόμενον τοῦ καὶ ποιητικὸν αἴτιον ἡγεῖσθαι τὸν θεὸν τοῦ παντὸς κόσμου τὸν Ἀριστοτέλη... Cf. *In Phys., CAG* 10.1359.33–8; 1360.24–31.
[60] Cf. Schol. *Contra Pleth., OC* 4.3.11–13 and Pleth. *Contra Schol.* 2.1–2.

the Forms contribute to the objects of sense? Now, it might be said that he thinks the cause in this case must belong to the supreme god alone (ὁ πρεσβύτατος θεός). But although *anyone else* could say this, Aristotle could not. Why not? Because if he did he would be contradicting himself. (Pleth. *Diff.* 340.2–9; trans. Woodhouse; my emphasis)

The point is that Aristotle cannot pose as a monotheist as Jews and Christians can: did he not allow for different motive forces for each movement of the heavenly bodies?[61] Plethon shifts the focus of the discussion from the original criticism of Plato to the Christian use of Aristotle. Besides, Scholarios is wrong in assuming that Aristotle's god supports Christian creationism. Aristotle *conjoined* (συνηρτῆσθαι) the universe to the gods on account of their immortality. But this does not necessarily mean that he *subjoined* (ἐξηρτῆσθαι) the former to the latter, as Aristotle appears to do in Scholarios' *interpretatio Christiana*. Plethon is doing an excellent job of liberating Aristotle from a predetermined Christian interpretation. The difference between conjoining the divine to matter and subjoining matter to god accounts for that between the pagan notion of the sanctity of matter as depicted in, for example, Pseudo-Aristotle's *De mundo* and Judaeo-Christian theism.[62]

What Aristotle really meant is one technical aspect of the debate. There is also a latent theological and ideological one. By attacking the Christian appropriation of Aristotle the Platonic henotheist system of Forms/gods emerges as providing an explanation of locomotion and causation antagonistic to that of monotheism. Either

---

[61] *Diff.* 340.10–13.

[62] 'But you', he turns to Scholarios (*Contra Schol.* 13.1–11), 'do not seem to be in a position to comprehend how great is the difference between *conjoining* something to the divine and actually *subjoining* something to it.' In fact, in *De caelo* 270b9–11, which is here under discussion, Aristotle considers the 'highest place' to be *sunertemenon*. The Loeb translation by Guthrie preserves well the ambiguity of the word: 'All men have a conception of gods, and all assign the highest place to the divine, both Barbarians and Hellenes, as many as believe in gods, supposing, obviously, *that immortal is closely linked with immortal.*' Linked it may be, but is it also causally dependent? In *De caelo*, says Plethon, Aristotle did not say that gods are responsible for the immortality of the universe; he went only as far as affirming that the universe and the gods participate in a communal immortality. This hardly means that the divine is the *cause* of the universe, as Scholarios read him.

god is the prime mover and efficient cause of all kinds of movement; or Plato's theory of the Forms has to be brought into the
discussion in order to explain the movement of heavenly bodies.
'It might be said' that god is the only cause necessary to understand
the mechanics of the universe – but apparently this is not what the
'proponents of the Forms' (οἱ τὰ εἴδη τιθέμενοι) say, and Plethon
finds the perfect opening to transmit their view on the matter using
the first person plural.[63] Platonic Ideas are here called *originators*
(as are, we might recall, Damascius' 'gods') and *creators* securing, controlling and regulating the links of everything that is to the
universal sovereign:

> For is not Aristotle demonstrably ignorant of the most important matters in the
> light both of the numerous examples we have given and especially of the most
> important point – that *he denies the creation of eternal substances and the relation
> of all things to the one source of their being*; whereas Plato and the Platonists,
> on the contrary, place god as universal sovereign over all existing things, and
> assume him to be *the originator of originators, the creator of creators*, and refer
> everything without exception to him? (*Diff.* 342.28–34; trans. Woodhouse; my
> emphasis)

The shift from metaphysics to religion in the language of this passage happens so smoothly that it might well pass unnoticed. Aristotle's metaphysical fallacies are contrasted with Platonic henotheism. The former are an impediment to the rise of the latter. Aristotle
is accused of denying the 'creation of eternal substances', namely
Ideas that mediate between the Idea of the Good and the sensible
world. By contrast, the Platonists understand *god* as the *originator
of originators* and *creator of creators*. In *Against Scholarios* the
point is pursued further. The Forms/gods are not only thought-of
(νοούμεναι) by the divine Intellect; they are also *thinking principles* in their own right: they are intellects (νόες):

> By making of the Forms intellects (τὰ εἴδη νοῦς ποιῶν), Plato put them in charge
> of every single thing in realm of becoming. If Aristotle was unwilling to agree
> with this, he should have found some other way to make everything in nature
> subject to divine intellect. (Pleth. *Contra Schol.* 30.74–5)

The point recurs in the commentary on the *Chaldean Oracles*.
Intelligible Forms are 'thought-of' by the Father, yet at the same

---

[63] *Diff.* 341.16ff.

time they are capable of intellection.[64] The genuine pagan essence of these passages from the commentary to the *Chaldean Oracles* and *Against Scholarios* is revealed only when read parallel to *Nomoi* 46, 1.5.27–36. There, 'gods' immediately proceeding from Zeus are identified with pure forms and intellects (εἴδη δ᾽ ὄντα εἰλικρινῆ αὐτὰ καθ᾽ αὑτά, καὶ νοῦς ἀκινήτους) deriving their essence from 'Zeus'.[65] Here, the 'creator of creators', that is 'Zeus', is also significantly called 'King of kings (βασιλεῦ βασιλέων) and supreme among all sovereigns'. The Olympian gods are acknowledged as 'creators' working together in the production of the immortal universe.[66]

The defence of the integrity of Plato's theory of Ideas offers the metaphysical foundations for Plethon's henotheist religion. The need to maintain the thesis of a multitude of causes in the *Differences* and *Against Scholarios*, without succumbing to the 'thoughts of god' thesis, leads necessarily to the introduction of polytheism in the *Nomoi*. The first principle is the primary 'originator/creator' and the eternal substances are the secondary 'originators/creators', namely the *noes* we have already encountered. Plethon was ostensibly only trying to refute Aristotle – but as Scholarios reasonably complained, nowhere did he say that the *Differences* is an academic exercise (γυμνάσιον)![67] In fact, it was nothing of the sort. By explaining what 'the proponents of the Forms' think, Plethon was presenting an alternative to monotheism, a world of becoming presided over by distinct 'intellects', 'creators', 'originators'.[68] This alone was sufficient reason to justify the subtitle 'against polytheists' in Scholarios' *Against Plethon*.

The reidentification between Forms and Intellects is fully appreciated only in the light of earlier transformations of Platonic

---

[64] Pleth. *Orac.* 2.31: Νοούμεναι ἴυγγες…Ἴυγγας, τὰ νοητὰ εἴδη καλεῖ, νοούμενά τε πατρόθεν, καὶ αὐτὰ νοοῦντα· κινούμενά τε πρὸς τὰς νοήσεις βουλαῖς ἀφθέγκτοις, ἤτοι ἀκινήτοις κίνησιν.

[65] *Nomoi* 46 (1.5.27–36). Cf. below for a further correspondence with Plethon's *Monodia in Helenam Palaiologinam*.

[66] *Nomoi* 170 (3.34.4.15–16). Cf. *Diff.* 342.32: τὸν πάντων βασιλέα θεόν.

[67] Schol. *Contra Pleth.* 116.15–19.

[68] On the Neoplatonist equation between gods and *noes* see Procl. *ET* 160.1–2; Porph. *ap.* Iamb. *Myst.* 1.15.2–3; 15.20; Ammon. *In Aristotelis librum de interpretatione commentaries, CAG* 4.5, 132.8–15; here Aristotle too is read as equating gods with *noes*: 243.3. See also the procession of *noes* from *nous* in Dam. *De princ.* 1.243.28–32.

philosophy in the Byzantine context. Plotinus allowed for partial Intellects within *nous*, namely for a condition according to which '*nous* is not single, but one and many'.[69] According to Christianised versions of Platonism the divine Mind cannot be a synthesis of distinct partial intellects. It cannot be both single and multiple. This would mean that the divine is composite, a view dangerously close to Hellenic polytheism. The Byzantine reception of Platonism put emphasis on a single aspect of the Neoplatonic interpretation of Plato's theory of Forms, namely that they subsist in divinity and that 'Socrates defined the Forms as thoughts', as Proclus contends when commenting on *Parmenides* 132b.[70] This reading violates Plato's philosophy, for Plato does not really identify Ideas with thoughts of any supreme Intellect. Still, it had strong roots in Plotinus, Plutarch and Albinus. It potentially merges the demiurge of the *Timaeus* with the paradigm, possibly incorporating the Aristotelean conception of 'self-thought' into that of a 'First Mind' contemplating its Ideas/thoughts.[71] In Byzantium this interpretation of Plato tends to identify the '*genera* before the particulars' (πρὸ τῶν πολλῶν) with Ideas and god's thoughts.[72]

The question of whether Forms are sufficient entities or merely something like 'the thoughts of god' was resolved a long time before Plethon with a clear winner, the monotheist reading of Plato that made two claims: (1) The Forms are *ennoiai* and *enthymemata*, 'thoughts of god' (a notion in itself problematic for Palamite apophaticism), but not substances (οὐσίαι) as Plethon thought, nor intellects enjoying any sort of conditional independence; (2) by no means should the universals be considered as ontologically prior to the Demiurge; they exist neither before the Demiurge as a paradigm, nor with the Demiurge. Benakis has shown that all major Byzantine intellectuals held to this view: Photius, John Italos, Eustratios of Nikaia, Nikephoros Blemmydes, Nikephoros Choumnos and, significantly, Scholarios.[73] To give an example,

---

[69] *Enn.* 4.8.6–11: οὐ γὰρ εἷς μόνος, ἀλλ' εἷς καὶ πολλοί. Cf. *Enn.* 3.7.3.5ff.
[70] Procl. *In Prm.* 897.30–2.   [71] *Metaph.* 1074b33–5; Plut. *Quaest. Plat.* 1007C.
[72] Arethas, *Scholia in Porphyrii Isagogen* 21.22–4: ὅτι τὰ γένη καὶ τὰ εἴδη τριττά ἐστιν. ἢ γὰρ πρὸ τῶν πολλῶν εἰσιν, ἃ ἐν τῷ νῷ φαμεν τοῦ δημιουργοῦ (ἃ δὴ καὶ χωριστὰ νῦν καλεῖ).
[73] Benakis (1978/9) 326–37.

Psellos Christianised Plato by paraphrasing Plotinus' *Enneads* 5.9 and probably Proclus' commentary on the *Parmenides* quoted above. But like his Byzantine predecessors, Psellos appropriates that part of Plotinus and Proclus that suits best the monotheist cause: the idea of Forms as thoughts within god – without the complementary Proclan notion of these Forms *as* gods. Tellingly, Psellos' references show that he was conscious of the interpretation according to which Forms enjoy a conditional independence and subsist by themselves. Yet in the Byzantine context this would not hold: the Forms could not subsist outside the Demiurgic intellect.[74] As an anonymous Christian commentator on Porphyry's *Isagoge* put it, 'since the divine is by nature creative, it does not need any paradigm'.[75] Scholarios, we have seen, made the same point against Plethon.

In Plethon's immediate discursive context this type of Christian Platonism was conformable with late Byzantine translations of Aquinas. God thinks the Good and its Being; which means he is not *the* Good or Being.[76] On the other hand, the direct or indirect introduction of Platonic Forms in Christianity implied an *analogia entis* between uncreated archetypes and created beings that compromised the Orthodox doctrine that between god and creation does not exist community, similarity or analogy of any kind. Hence the doctrine of archetypical forms was condemned as heretical *par excellence* already by the Seventh Ecumenical Synod.

It might be argued that any reading of Plato that identifies Forms with intellects and implicitly with gods as Plethon does in the *Differences* is as biased as one that identifies Forms with god's 'thoughts'. This is formally speaking correct, but it ignores the significance of Plethon's move in the given intellectual context. His was a significant attempt at dechristianising Plato's theory of Forms that daringly parted from Psellos, Plotinus and Ammonius, in order to advance beyond the accumulation of

---

[74] Psell. *On Plato's doctrine of the Ideas* (Περὶ τῶν ἰδεῶν ἃς ὁ Πλάτων λέγει) 415–21 Benakis. See also the comments by Benakis in the introduction to his edition of the text, 395–7, and the review by Lagarde (1979).

[75] Benakis (1978/9) 337.

[76] Aquinas, *Summa contra gentiles* 1.72 as quoted in *Notizie* 17.

numerous hermeneutical strata conducive to the long-established *Plato Christianus* in Byzantium. Forms are restored as intellects and generators, in order for them *not* to be rendered obsolete by a monotheistic god, or downgraded to the status of 'thoughts of god', which essentially was, to Plethon's eyes, the same thing. To the extent that the interpretation of Forms as 'thoughts of god' was triggered by Aristotle's critique of Plato, it is intriguing that Plethon's reinterpretation and re-categorisation of Ideas as intellects occurs in a treatise against Aristoteleanism.

A tough question remains unanswered. Why is pagan Platonic multi-causalism and henotheism supposed to be philosophically preferable and more expedient than Palamite theism and apophaticism, namely more economical than assuming one single agent transcending both Being and non-Being and creating by his *will*, rather than owing to ontological necessity? This is, after all, Scholarios' main enquiry in *Against Plethon*. This question lies at the heart of the whole matter. I will deal with it after an *excursus* that summarises and systematises the main concepts introduced so far in this book (Chapter 2: ideological and religious dissimulation; Chapter 3: epistemological optimism; Chapter 4: pagan ontology; Chapter 5: henotheism) by addressing the case of a supposedly non-philosophical text that Plethon composed towards the end of his life. This concerns a monody.

The strange case of *Monodia in Helenam*

Plethon's *Monody for the Empress Helen* is dated to 1450.[77] The work was meant to be a lament. Strangely enough, it goes beyond the conventions of its genre in presenting a sketch of elementary theological propositions. As in *Memorandum to Theodore*, where Plethon experiments with the genre of *Fürstenspiegel* or 'mirrors for princes' in equally unorthodox ways, here too there is nothing even to imply that the author is Christian or that he belongs in a world marked by the intellectual war between Palamite Orthodoxy and the intrusion of Thomism. This is a bizarre fact,

---

[77] Lampros, *PP* 3.266–80; summary and partial translation in English in Woodhouse (1986) 310–12.

given the expectations from either a *Trostschrift* or a 'mirror for princes' in Byzantium. A third work purportedly targeting a non-philosophical audience written between the *Memorandum* and the *Monody* shows that this is no coincidence. The 1433 *Monodia in imperatricem Cleopam* contains a single sentence that pertains to Christianity and, for that matter, only indirectly so. Cleope's participation in 'our' mysteries has been read as certifying the author's ostensible adherence to Orthodoxy, though it is only the collective social identity of Byzantines as Christians that is really invoked here.[78]

Seventeen years later, in the *Monody for the Empress Helen* Plethon does not allow even that one concession to Christian religiosity. That Plethon did not deem it necessary to evoke the Judaeo-Christian tradition as the appropriate source (or, for that matter, not even as one probable source) for deriving comfort (or at least rhetorical embellishments) when coming to terms with death, loss and god, is in itself significant. It may well mean that at an advanced age and within the imperial court Plethon felt he could safely drop the mask of the pious Christian, even if a handful of references to the Bible or Gregory of Nazianzus would have taken him little effort to assemble.

On a first reading, the religious and philosophical ideas expressed in the *Monody* appear to expound an unnamed natural religion analogous to that prescribed in the *Memorandum to Theodore*. On a surface level Plethon conveys in abstract terms a universal religious sentiment that does not by default rule out Christianity. There is much to suggest that Plethon wanted at least some of the recipients of his *Monody* to see beneath this surface. To begin with, Plethon included in his monody key ideas and material featured in the *Nomoi*. When read in the light of the confessed paganism of the *Nomoi* and the professed Platonism of the

---

[78] Lampros, *PP* 4.167.13–14. Monfasani (1992: 49) preferred to emphasise this single and rather reluctant concession to Christianity, rather than the otherwise complete and provocative deviation from all Christian *topoi* and rhetorical ornaments that were, in Plethon's Byzantine context, expected to embellish a Byzantine lament. By contrast, Berger (2006: 86) correctly observed the questions arising with Plethon's two *Monodies*. See Tambrun (2006a: 49) and Masai (1956: 266–7) for the bizarre Plethonean idea of suicide in *Nomoi* 258 Alexandre, which is repeated in the *Monodia in Cleopam* 4.173.9–174.4.

Differences, the peculiar theological formulations in *Monody* emerge as a summary of the pagan Platonic ontology and epistemology advocated by Plethon in his philosophical pieces. Only here philosophical Hellenism is carefully disguised as a version of natural religion that fully exemplifies Plethon's talent in the exploitation of conceptual ambiguity:

That there is one certain god (Θεὸν μέν τινα) [1] presiding over all things and that he is creator and producer of all things and he is the extreme Good (ἄκρως ἀγαθόν) [2]: no one will doubt these propositions, provided that he considers them himself or that he comes to share them by hearing them from people who hold them to be true – that is to say, unless one is seriously out of his mind. Similarly, there is another proposition that all might hold: that between him [god] and us there is another nature [3], which may be a single *genus* or diversified into many *genera* [4], and which is superior to us, yet comes considerably short of god. For no one will make a case that we are the best of all of god's works [5]. Thus everybody will subscribe to the view that these species (φύσεις) superior to us are intellects [6] and souls which are superior to ours. And if these species are of this sort, what would their principal deed and exercise be, other than the contemplation of beings and even the intellection of the creator of everything [7]? Whoever is able to accomplish this intellection by means of his natural faculties shall never encounter an exercise that is superior or more blessed; and it is apparent that man is not only capable of achieving the contemplation of beings but also of furthering this intellection [8].

Consequently, man does not participate only in a community [9] of deeds with animals and does not act exclusively as animals do; he also participates in a community of deeds with those species that are superior to us, since he engages in the same contemplation as they do according to his power [10]. Further, it necessarily follows that those who participate in a community of deeds also participate in a community of their substances [11]. (*Monod. in Helenam* 275.10–277.1)

Already the first three words in this passage (Θεὸν μέν τινα) [1] cast serious doubts on the religious profession of this author. The abstract and neutral generic notion of a certain god undercuts Christian doctrinal exclusivity and scandalously compromises divine revelation.[79] The author then advances an understanding of divinity in exclusively affirmative terms, identifying god with the ἄκρως ἀγαθόν [2], the same Platonising formulation applied in

---

[79] We have seen that in *Mem. I* Plethon employed a similarly vague terminology when speaking of 'something divine' in all things. See above, Ch. 5, pp. 234–5.

the *Nomoi* to describe 'Zeus': ἄκρως ἀγαθός.[80] The author then postulates 'another nature' between god and 'us', compromising the Orthodox distinction between created substance and uncreated essence [3]. At one with the onto-theology of the *Nomoi* and the *Differences*, this intermediate *physis* interfering between divinity and 'creation' is unified and diversified: it is one *genus* multiplied into many *genera* [4]. As in the *Nomoi*, man is not god's masterpiece, but inferior to these *genera*, now identified with distinct natural constitutions (φύσεις) [5]. These *genera/physeis* are *intellects* (νοῦς) just as they are in the *Differences* and, significantly, in the *Nomoi*: εἴδη ... καὶ νοῦς [6].[81] What is more, like gods/species in the *Nomoi* and Platonic divinities in the *Phaedrus*, their task (ἔργον) is the contemplation of beings (ἡ τῶν ὄντων θεωρία) and the intellection of god (ἔννοια) [7].

This last capacity excludes the possibility that the 'intellects' in question are identifiable with Judaeo-Christian angels.[82] Any theologian as versed in Orthodox theology as Plethon was fully aware that the Eastern Fathers considered the angels incapable of knowing god, and scriptural authority was often quoted to this end.[83] In the Synod of Ferrara/Florence, Plethon's student Mark Eugenikos argued extensively in reply to a Latin query that 'not even the first among supermundane intellects (ὑπερκοσμίων νόων)' can see, comprehend or know divine essence. According to Mark, this

---

[80] *Nomoi* 242 (3.43.17). *Akros* is directly analogous to the *malista* used in the *Differences* for *on*, thus implying the equivalence between the *akros en* of the *Nomoi* and *malista on*.

[81] *Nomoi* 46 (1.5.27–32).

[82] Though Ps.-Dionysius uses the term *noes* to signify the angels (Dion Ar. *Cael. hier.* 34.11, 41.14, 42.1), his framework is always clearly conditioned by explicit references to Jewish prophets and Jewish angelology that are markedly absent in Plethon.

[83] Gr. Pal. *Ep.* 3.30.14–15. Joh. Dam. *Exp. fidei* 1.10–13: Μετὰ δὲ τὴν πρώτην καὶ μακαρίαν φύσιν οὐδεὶς ἔγνω ποτὲ τὸν θεόν, εἰ μὴ ᾧ αὐτὸς ἀπεκάλυψεν οὐκ ἀνθρώπων μόνον ἀλλ' οὐδὲ τῶν ὑπερκοσμίων δυνάμεων καὶ αὐτῶν φημι τῶν Χερουβὶμ καὶ Σεραφίμ. See above, p. 194 for scriptural references used by John of Damascus in precisely this context. This was also John of Chrysostom's position; see above, p. 202. Further, the concurrence between the commentary on the *Chaldean Oracles*, *Nomoi*, and the *Differences* in respect to these *intellects* makes it improbable that in the *Monodia* Plethon really meant *noes* to refer to Christian angelology, which does not appear to have ever attracted his interest. Of course, an audience unfamiliar with Plethonean philosophical works would hardly be in a position to immediately discern the paganism underlying the ambiguity of Plethon's theological remarks in the *Monodia* – which makes this text a unique exercise in philosophical dissimulation and misdirection.

would mean that divine essence is participable by agents other than Christ/Logos and the Holy Spirit (ἄπαγε!).[84] Here *noes* stand for 'angels' and Mark quotes John Chrysostom: pure divine essence (οὐσία ἀκραιφνής) cannot be the object of *theoria*; what may occur is a *condescension* (συγκατάβασις) according to the viewer's constitution, and no special privileges apply to the Seraphims.[85] The question was obviously closely knit to the Palamite distinction between essence and energy in god. The Greeks passionately defended their point of view until the last moment. Conversely, the view of Cardinal Cesarini and 'the Latins' was that the saints witness god's essence and not some bizarre reflection.[86] We may recall here that, as modern scholarship is always keen to underline, Plethon fully supported the Roman Orthodox dogma in Florence. Obviously, he did not intend nor had any reason to make concessions to Catholicism in his *Monodia*, when openly reintroducing the notion of a cognition of god's essence by an agency other than Christ/Logos.

Moreover, one wonders why a Christian author addressing a Christian audience within a Christian context would refrain from applying the standard vocabulary common to Judaeo-Christian angelology ('Seraphim', 'Cherubim') thus consciously decontextualising the Pseudo-Dionysian tradition while maintaining only a surface and faint association with it. The reply is that the Plethonean 'intellects' are not Judaeo-Christian angels but identifiable with the very pagan 'intellects' in *Nomoi* and the *Differences*.

Let us return to the text of the *Monody*. As in Book 1 of the *Nomoi*, these *genera*/intellects are not alone in their task (ἔργον). Man is 'by means of his natural faculties' able to join them [8], [10]. The absence of any notion of divine grace and supernatural illumination as well as of Christology is complemented by that of a communion (κοινωνία) that obviously does not refer to the

---

[84] Mark Eug. *Responsio ad Quaestiones Latinorum* 157.5–8; 159.24–34. A quotation from Maximus Confessor (*PG* 160.1–9) testifies to the typically Roman Orthodox roots of Markos' thinking. Cf. Kuhlmann (1968) 114–15.

[85] Joh. Chrys. *De incomprehensibili dei natura* 3.157–166; cf. Mark Eug. *Responsio ad quaestiones Latinorum* 154.8–10.

[86] See above, Ch. 2, p. 119; Kuhlmann (1968) 116.

relation between members of the Christian Trinity; it rather concerns the relation of man to these strange *physeis*/intellects, reverberating in the similar use of the word κοινωνία in the *Nomoi* [9]. Plethon expressly says that there is a κοινωνία of man and 'superior *genera*', for a community of deeds necessarily corresponds to a community of essence, or, as we read in the *Nomoi*, there is a necessary relation between effect and substance [11].[87] The shared *ergon* of the intellection of god (ἔννοια) not only elevates man to the level of god on account of his own natural powers but accounts for a congeniality and community of substance between man and divinity. Here, as in the *Nomoi*, the rupture between man and god is not diminished by the incarnation of Christ/Logos held as the one and only route to this end in the whole tradition of Greek Christianity, but by the natural faculty of contemplation and intellection. Plethon substitutes pagan epistemology for Christology. Further, he reverses once again the poles of John of Damascus' axiom regarding the interdependence between unknowability and supra-essentiality: because cognisable, the divine is not beyond being. Obviously, this precludes any Areopagitan reading of the passage.

Given the late date of composition we may plausibly surmise that the set of abstract theological theses in *Monody* are modelled upon the expressly pagan Platonic ones in the *Nomoi* and the *Differences*. Plethon chose to implement the pagan theology of the *Nomoi* in a supposedly non-academic piece without showing much concern for sustaining the image of a pious Orthodox delegate fighting for Orthodoxy in Florence. Plethon reversed the presuppositions of Orthodox religion, excluded Christology from his discussion of man and god, introduced a distinctively pagan epistemology and compromised the unknowability and supra-essentiality of the divine.

The presence of these hallmarks of a pagan Platonic world-view in theological sections of a monody that was widely circulated strengthens the suggestion that the theology of the *Nomoi* was not meant to remain 'esoteric'. As possibly when circulating *De fato*, Plethon was testing the waters: in the former case by excerpting a

---

[87] *Nomoi* 242 (3.43.19–23); Cf. W. Blum (1988) 111 n. 11.

whole chapter of the *Nomoi*, in the latter case by enticing certain members of the imperial court to explore his paganising ideas.

Polytheism, necessity and freedom

Intermediaries in the Pseudo-Dionysian tradition served as agents of communication between god and man; angels are god's handy tools of divine revelation and a considerable aid to prayer.[88] Creation is not their business. This capital distinction between Judaeo-Christian angelology and pagan multi-causality brings us back to Scholarios' principal objection that was left unanswered: what if the cause of generation 'belongs to the supreme god alone'? Why is pagan Platonism better equipped to explain the physical universe than theism – in other words, 'what do the Forms contribute to the objects of sense?' In Scholarios' reading Aristotle made god the principle of unity among all beings, 'responsible for every form and particular being'. By contrast, the Platonists' fallacy was to attribute to numbers and forms 'what is impossible', namely ontological independence, by rendering them the causes of beings. For how could it be that Forms are the cause of unity among created beings, since this is the responsibility of god?[89] In other words: why should the Forms/gods have to do god's job?

We have noted that Plethon qualified this attack on Platonist multi-causalism by exclaiming that 'anyone else' could launch it *but* Aristotle. Suppose then that, instead of hunting down Juvenalios and other pagans in the Peloponnese, Scholarios had pressed on and decided to return to 'what might be said', even if this meant making a concession to Plethon in leaving Aristotle out of the picture. Why should we go along with Platonic multi-causalism and not with the Judaeo-Christian assumption of a *single* providential cause? Taken in itself, Scholarios' set of related queries in *Against Plethon* appears reasonable enough. Is not the likeness (ὁμοιότης) of all things to god enough to ensure their unity? Why should one

---

[88] Arthur (2008) 87–93.   [89] Schol. *Contra Pleth., OC* 4.28.32–29.5.

assume that there is anything *more than likeness* between creation and god, namely a *community* of Being?[90]

These are not questions of a Peripatetic tediously finding ways to argue that *genera* do not exist apart from singulars. These are questions of a Christian preoccupied with maintaining the distinction between uncreated essence and created beings in order to prevent the re-emergence of Greek monism. They are also the questions of a translator of Aquinas, very conscious that Aristotle might be used to defend the distinction between the 'purity' of god's Being and that of any other being.[91] Like George of Trebizond, Scholarios noted that the subordinate gods effectively subvert the Christian radical distinction between creator and creation,[92] and he certainly did not fail to acknowledge the danger in Plethon's advocacy of the theory of Ideas in the *Differences*.

Later, when dealing with the pagan theology of the *Nomoi*, Scholarios used against polytheism an argument similar to that used against the introduction of Platonist Ideas in *Against Plethon*. If the first principle is supreme, then the other causes should not be called 'gods' in the first place. For they are creations (κτίσματα) of god; and if they are created, then they cannot be gods or *creators* of other gods: 'for these are contradictions caused by an improper use of the name god'.[93] God is the immediate and single creator of beings. The 'contradiction' and categorical mistake uncovered here may well be lifted from John of Damascus' attack on polytheism in his *Exposition of the Right Faith*.[94] As for the talk of gods in the Bible, Scholarios protests that one should correctly interpret the doctrinal meaning and allow for a metaphorical use of words that is unavoidable for reasons of 'economy, habit, or need', as when we call someone 'sun', or 'second sun', or 'another sun', because his virtue shines among people.[95] This is, we have seen, Palamas' and Philotheos' position, when explaining the distinction

---

90 Schol. *Contra Pleth.*, *OC* 4.49.7–16.
91 See Scholarios' translation of *De ente et essentia* 6.6.15–6:"Οθεν δι'αὐτῆς τῆς καθαρότη-τος αὐτοῦ ἐστιν εἶναι διακεκριμένον ἀπὸ παντὸς ἄλλου εἶναι.
92 Geo. Treb. *Comparatio* 2.2, 2.15; Schol. *Ad exarchum Josephum*, *OC* 4.166.2–4.
93 Schol. *Ad exarchum Josephum*, *OC* 4.166.4–5: Ἀντιφάσεις γὰρ ταῦτα, τῆς τοῦ Θεὸς ὀνόματος ἀκριβείας ὡς χρὴ τηρουμένης.
94 See Joh. Dam. *Exp. fidei* 14.   95 Schol. *Ad exarchum Josephum*, *OC* 4.167.7–21.

between essence and energy in god as one between the essence of the sun and sunrays.

Scholarios' argument against multi-causalism in *Against Plethon* as well as in his criticism of polytheism in the epistle to the Exarch Joseph concerns the necessity of assuming the very existence of numerous causes: the distinction, ordering and ruling of beings is fully accounted for by an individual primary cause, that renders uneconomical all talk regarding its immanence in a plurality of causes.[96]

On the other hand, for Plethon the introduction of Forms (and hence of polytheism) as distinct causes/intellects is both logically as well as ontologically necessary. The most succinct exposition of the pagan axiom luring Plethon to polytheism/henotheism is contained in the *Monody for the Empress Helen*: different substances (οὐσίαι) relate to different functions (ἔργα).[97] In the *Nomoi* too ontological diversity implies a difference in the modality of generation. This effectively means that all beings immediately participating in 'Zeus' are necessarily eternal, for they are modalities of simple and pure Being *qua* Being. By implication, it is logically impossible to credit 'Zeus' with the immediate production of a universe that is composite and perishable. Rather,

the pre-eternal (προαιώνιος) Zeus generates the whole 'eternal substance' (αἰώνιος οὐσία). He then confers the responsibility for the generation of temporal/perpetual substance to the eternal substance. Successively, he confers the responsibility for the generation of temporal/mortal substance to the temporal/perpetual substance. Hence each (kind of) substance takes up the generation that is appropriate and each is produced from its proper source, namely each comes forth from the substance that is its immediate superior. (*Nomoi* 96 (3.15.67–74))[98]

The necessary reciprocal relation between substances and modes of generation means that diversification among created beings is accounted for only by postulating diversification among respective

[96] Schol. *Ad exarchum Josephum*, OC 4.165.1–13.
[97] Pleth. *Monodia in Helenam* 277.2: Ἀνάλογον γὰρ δεῖ ἔχειν οὐσίας τε ἔργοις καὶ ἔργα οὐσίαις.
[98] *Nomoi* 96 (3.15.67–74); the process is also described in *Nomoi* 102 (3.15.141–51), where 'Zeus' uses his own essence as the first 'paradigm' and then the subsequent substances as 'paradigms' of those that follow – until the 'system' is complete.

causes. As Masai notes, from this viewpoint the Augustinean belief that diversification within creation may be explained by a *single* cause sounds like a straightforward perversion of Hellenic reason. Plethon's multi-causalism is intrinsically linked to polytheism, or, rather, the latter is founded upon the former.[99]

To the extent that Ideas are a diversification and differentiation of the essence of the Idea of the Good/'Zeus'/god and each Idea accounts for diverse modes of generation, Plethon assumes ideas/causes as gods necessarily different to god, even if cooperative. By contrast, Aristotle allowed for the *automaton* and thus avoided the compulsion of Platonist ontological multi-causalism. It appears then that any philosophy battling against chance and materialism in nature necessarily has to be a polytheistic one. In his comparison between Plato and Aristotle, George of Trebizond accused Plato of determinism and Bessarion had trouble in finding a way out of this criticism.[100] And yet in *Against Scholarios* it is Aristotle, Scholarios' main source against the necessity of committing oneself to the helplessly deterministic Platonic theory of Ideas, who is credited with the rule 'one effect, one cause'.[101] Plethon turns the tables on Scholarios: Aristotle misused the rule when multiplying the causes according to the multitude of movements of the heavenly bodies, thus rendering god one cause among others of the same rank and leading to every Christian's greatest fear: polyarchy. The contrast with what 'we hold' is devastating:

As far as *we* are concerned, *we* do of course hold that all beings have been produced and are being produced by one god. Hence *we* could not possibly deny that they are comprehended *by a single and common genus*, according to the rule 'one effect, one cause'. This does not mean that an indivisible thing derives from an indivisible cause, but that the One is indivisible on the one hand, and, on the other hand, it is the cause of one divisible Being. For Aristotle's axiom is not without merit, provided that one makes proper and knowledgeable use of it. (Pleth. *Contra Schol.* 23.8–13)

Does 'we' refer to 'us Christians', or 'us Platonists'? Is Plethon speaking here in his own person or is he posing as an Orthodox

---

[99] Masai (1957/8) 403, 405; Seitter (2005) 78.
[100] Cf. Bessarion, *In calumniatorem Platonis* 164ff.; Todt (2006) 162.
[101] Cf. *Gen et corr.* 336a27–8; *Diff.* 340.13; see Woodhouse (1986) 211 n. 97.

theologian, as in the *Reply to the Latin Treatise*? Scholarios must have wondered for a while, and so should we. The ambiguity of this passage is so tantalising it can only be intentional. Both Christians and pagan Platonists might subscribe to the thesis that 'all beings have been produced by one god', though παράγεσθαι is a first noticeable departure from ordinary creationist vocabulary relating to κτίσις that has god create the world rather than the world proceed from god. Moreover, the premise that One is the cause of Being hardly means that the world is the direct and extra-deical creation of a divine agent, which is what Scholarios was eager to hear.

There is a surreptitious sarcasm in Plethon's claim that he is merely showing the proper way to make use of an allegedly Aristotelean axiom that neither Aristotle nor Scholarios got right. As in the *Nomoi*, what Plethon really does is paganise Plato. When Aristotle's 'one effect, one cause' principle is applied to theology, it emerges that the *One* is the cause of *one* effect. This initiates a division (μερισμός) of Being to the end of allowing for a necessary ontological realm to mediate between the One as simple Being and the composite world of becoming. The word μεριστός (*Contra Schol.* 23.11) is significant: the connotations of distribution associated with μέρος in the sense of *allotment, lot* and *heritage* hint at the appointment of responsibilities to gods *qua* 'captains' in the *Nomoi*.[102] Μερισμός has a Neoplatonic theologico-philosophical signification of classification and declension according to which the distribution of divine essence to gods links the divine with matter. The inspiration is provided by *Laws* 903b, where Plato describes the ἔσχατος μερισμός, according to which god appoints rulers 'down to the smallest fraction' with a view to 'the preservation and excellence of the Whole'.

The *Laws* passage was adduced by Proclus in his commentary on the *Republic* as well as by Damascius in his commentary on the *Parmenides*. According to the former, Plato's 'ultimate division' means that divine providence (πρόνοια) subdivides itself giving birth to a multitude of *pronoiai* responsible for appropriate tasks of supervision. Each class of these *pronoiai* is derived from the

---

[102] LSJ s.v. μέρος.

preceding one, those that are less perfect from those that are more perfect, and those that are daemonic from those that are divine.[103] More than echoes of the passage are present in the *Nomoi*, where 'Zeus' is the cause for the distribution (μοῖρα) of Being to a finite number of beings (Forms) most congenial to divine nature and initiates a procession that ends with the 'last grade (ἔσχατον) in the hierarchy of rational nature' appropriate to mankind.[104]

These affinities with *Laws* 903b and the late antique Neoplatonic hierarchy of divine causes, when combined with the total absence of Pseudo-Dionysian negative theology and the advocacy of a supreme *genus* of Being, do not leave much room for doubt whether Plethon's 'we' in the *Reply to Scholarios* is meant to imply a pagan or Christian 'us'. As in the *Monody for the Empress Helen*, the possibility of reading between the lines a dechristianised Pseudo-Dionysius Areopagita, hence a genuinely pagan worldview, increases the potential ambiguity of the passage and showcases its circumlocution. Pseudo-Dionysius used the recognisably Proclan relation between indivisible One (ἀμερές) and divisible Beings (μεριστά) in order to explain how a multitude of 'gods' may proceed from god. But Plethon could not really claim to be as Orthodox as Pseudo-Dionysius. The latter's god is 'beyond the one in beings', 'is not one, does not partake in the one, and does not have the one'. We read nothing of the sort in Plethon. Negative theology is once again absent. Plethon agrees with Pseudo-Dionysius only in so far as both relate an *architheos* to 'many gods' who are, as Pseudo-Dionysius has it, 'divinely formed according to the power of each' and hence 'there seems to be and is and is said to be a multiplication and difference of the one God'.[105] Taken in itself, this notion might be part of an underlying pagan core in Pseudo-Dionysius, one liminised by his Christian reception but

---

[103] Cf. Procl. *In R.* 2.271.14–20; Dam. *In Prm.* 13.24–6: ὁ τῶν θεῶν ἔσχατος μερισμὸς ἄχρι τῆς ὕλης. Cf. Dam. *De princ.* 1.225.5–6; Procl. *In R.* 1.92.12–15.

[104] *Nomoi* 172 (3.34.4.30–1): οἱ συμπάσης τῆς λογικῆς φύσεως τὸ ἔσχατον εἰληχότες ἡμεῖς.

[105] Dion. Ar. *DN* 136.13–17: Πάλιν τῇ ἐξ αὐτοῦ θεώσει τῷ κατὰ δύναμιν ἑκάστου θεοειδεῖ θεῶν πολλῶν γιγνομένων δοκεῖ μὲν εἶναι καὶ λέγεται τοῦ ἑνὸς θεοῦ διάκρισις καὶ πολλαπλασιασμός, ἔστι δὲ οὐδὲν ἧττον ὁ ἀρχίθεος καὶ ὑπέρθεος ὑπερουσίως εἷς θεός, ἀμέριστος ἐν τοῖς μεριστοῖς, ἡνωμένος ἑαυτῷ καὶ τοῖς πολλοῖς ἀμιγὴς καὶ ἀπλήθυντος. Nikephoros Gregoras used the passage in *Hist. Rom.* 3.407.1–20.

which remains philosophically closer to Damascius than to Roman Orthodoxy.[106]

To readdress Scholarios' question, the procession of 'intellects', 'producers' and 'originators' in the *Differences* and *Against Scholarios* by means of a distribution of 'divisible' Being (Plato's ἔσχατος μερισμός) *is* necessary, for it accounts for the ultimate diversification inherent in the universe without qualifying the absolute and pure simplicity of Being *qua* Being ('Zeus'). The procession and declination of Being is a logical necessity in order to explain the diversification of Being among particular beings. By contrast, Scholarios' absolute dichotomy between god and creation failed to explain the alternation of locomotion and Being within the universe. A mere 'likeness' of the universe to god will not do in order to maintain its ultimate unity. 'In regard to that "similarity" between beings and the first cause', protests Plethon against Scholarios, 'which you take as conducive to their unity, it is obvious that you have no idea what you are talking about!'[107]

To Plethon's anger, Scholarios' suggestion of a mere 'similarity' between beings and a divine agent threatened the ontological unity of the whole *systema*, according to which any possible likeness must necessarily presuppose a real similarity *of* Being which is tantamount to a participation *in* Being.[108] The pattern is Proclan: the procession of gods in the *Commentary on the Cratylus* relies on likeness (ὁμοιότης) *and* community (κοινωνία) of Being attributed to gods and their children.[109] It is a relation of ontological necessity between Being in itself and all beings that Plethon is pursuing, not one safeguarding the non-negotiable freedom of god by means of *ex nihilo* creationism and divine will.[110]

---

[106] Mazzucchi (2006) identified Ps.-Dionysius with Damascius and read the Areopagitan corpus as a crypto-pagan counter-offensive.

[107] Pleth. *Contra Schol.* 23.12–5.   [108] *Nomoi* 96 (3.15.62–7).

[109] Procl. *In Crat.* 104.13–17: οὐδὲν γὰρ ἄλογον οὐδ' ἄμετρόν ἐστιν ἐν τοῖς κρείττοσιν ἡμῶν· ἀλλὰ τὰς προόδους ἡγείσθω δι' ὁμοιότητος γίνεσθαι καὶ μίαν κοινωνίαν τῆς οὐσίας εἶναι καὶ συνέχειαν τῶν δυνάμεων καὶ τῶν ἐνεργειῶν ἀδιαίρετον παρά τε τοῖς παισὶ καὶ τοῖς πατράσιν αὐτῶν.

[110] Of course, as we have seen one being may participate in Being more than another does; still, this hardly prevents us from classifying both under the single *genus* of Being. See *Contra Schol.* 23.18–22; 23.40–2: οὔκουν οὐδ' εἰ ἡ οὐσία τοῦ προσόντος μᾶλλον ὄν, κωλύσει τι τὸ ὄν μὴ οὐ καὶ γένος αὐτοῖν εἶναι ἀμφοῖν.

Fate

The Neoplatonic fixation with hierarchies is sometimes considered to be the source of the so-called 'fascistic' undertones of neopaganism.[111] One might be tempted to point out that the Plethonean nexus of gods leads to a closed multi-causalist model that hides within the most oppressive and remorseless type of determinism imaginable. This onto-theological system eliminates chance and randomness within creation, that is, the τύχη ἐξ ἀνάγκης, to recall Plato's attack on materialism in the *Laws*.[112] The Christian opponents of Plethon were quick to accuse him of sacrificing moral choice and the freedom of divine will on the altar of a deterministic and mechanistic theory of causality. Neither Nemesis nor Tyche appear in Plethon's pantheon. In their place Plethon put *heimarmene*: fate.

Plethon circulated the relevant chapter from the *Nomoi* focusing on fate (*heimarmene*) around 1439, apparently in order to test the waters.[113] It may well be that Scholarios launched an early attack (1444/53) on Plethon's *De fato* by compiling a *Florilegium Thomisticum* based on Demetrios Kydones' translation of Aquinas.[114] The three subsequent attacks on Plethon's views on fate by Matthew Kamariotes, Theodore of Gaza and Manuel Corinthios accentuate the impression that the notion of *fate* was seen as a dangerous competitor to Christian providence, to be taken at least as seriously as the mythologisation of Platonist Ideas and, according to Scholarios' orders, mercilessly combated. The

---

[111] Faber (1986) 15–16.

[112] *Laws* 889c. No surprise then that in a chapter on 'measure and symmetry' Plethon hails proportionality and definition as the proper qualifications for the manifestation of Being in its proper extremity, goodness and beauty. *Nomoi* 86 (3.11.19–21): Διὰ ταῦτα ἐν μέτρῳ τε ἀεὶ καὶ ὅρῳ τὸ μᾶλλόν τε ὂν καὶ ἅμα κάλλιόν τε καὶ ἄμεινον, οὐ τῷ ἀεί τε πλείονι καὶ ὅλως ἀορίστῳ. The Orthodox apophatic approach to the unqualified essence of god is implicitly discarded with a sharp condemnation of indefinite and indeterminate notions of Being: *Nomoi* 84 (3.11.2): Τὸ δὲ δὴ καλὸν τοῦτο ἐν μέτρῳ τε καὶ τοῖς συμμέτροις διωκτέον, καὶ ὅλως ὅρῳ, οὐκ ἐν ἀμετρίᾳ, οὐδέ γε τῷ ἀορίστῳ τε καὶ ἀεὶ πλείονι.

[113] Plethon's possible motive is noted by P. H. Beck (1937) 104. The alternative is that *Nomoi* 2.6 'somehow slipped out into other hands' (Woodhouse 1986: 318). On *De fato* cf. Masai (1956) 186–200.

[114] See Demetracopoulos (2007) 301–76, esp. 323–5 on the 'anti-Plethonic suitability of the anti-astrological arsenal' of the florilegium.

appalled and sarcastic rejection of Plethon's notion of fate by Marsilio Ficino contrasts with the radicalism of Plethonian paganism. The Christian orientation of Renaissance Platonism prevented the reconsideration of the established notion of personal freedom.[115]

The concept of fate was transported to Byzantium by Psellos, possibly one of Scholarios' targets when refuting *heimarmene* in a treatise devoted to predestination. In a typical example of his latent paganism, Psellos argued that the name (*onoma*) *fate* (*heimarmene*) 'is disgraced by the vulgar (*hoi polloi*) but is admired by those most wise'. Without naming Psellos, Scholarios put an abrupt end to these ambiguous games with 'names': 'to *us* the names 'providence' and 'destination (προορισμός)' are sufficient'.[116] Matthew Kamariotes was less diplomatic than his mentor when formulating in his refutation of Plethon's *De fato* a neat aphorism: whoever believes in fate *or even uses the very name 'fate'* ceases *ipso facto* to be Christian.[117] This means that alone the use of the term *fate* equals *apostasy*, a crime which inflicts the death penalty – as, we have seen, Scholarios made crystal clear by drawing on his legal knowledge when going after Juvenalios. Matthew was trying to take away from Plethon the alibi of merely conducting academic or encyclopaedic research, even if this meant authorising what appears today as Christian fundamentalism.

Though Psellos was particularly fond of ambiguities of the above sort, he also found another way to challenge the suppression of discussions on *heimarmene* in Byzantium. He re-formulated the original pagan notion of *heimarmene* in terms of a tool of divine providence responsible for the realm of generation alone. Now *heimarmene* became inferior to *pronoia* and was restricted to natural necessity. The Christian notion of freedom of will was not compromised. Psellos' moderate Platonism did not dare to contradict the tenet of Christian anthropology that man is superior to nature.[118] But Plethon's understanding of *heimarmene* does, amply exemplifying the difference between a helplessly servile

---

[115] On Ficino versus Plethon on fate, see Monfasani (2002) 185; Keller (1957) 363–70.
[116] Cf. Psell. *De omnifaria doctrina* 105.1–5; Schol. *Quaestiones theologicae de praedestinatione divina et de anima* 1.1.1ff.; Demetracopoulos (2007) 307.
[117] Cf. Matthew Kamariotes, *Contra Pleth.* 6.21–7 Astruc.
[118] See above, Ch. 4, pp. 187–9.

Platonism that tries to accommodate Christian concerns and an uncompromising pagan philosophy set loose with no concern for Christian anthropology.

In *De fato* the limited applicability that Psellos awkwardly ascribes to fate is alarmingly expanded in order to cover the whole *systema* of inferior and superior ontological classes. The pattern is familiar: before Plethon the category of substance was similarly constrained within the world of becoming with no possibility of a re-conceptualisation or applicability to the divine. In both cases Plethon extends Hellenic philosophy beyond ontology and physics to theology.

Orthodox writers in late Byzantium were well prepared to deal with the consequences of allowing fatalism into theology. Like other building blocks of Plethon's pagan philosophy, fate resurfaced during the Hesychast controversy. Demetrios Kydones attacked Palamas' distinction between god's essence and energies in god as introducing *heimarmene* in the sense that pagan Platonism did.[119] Given the association of divine energies with divine will the accusation did not hold long. Still, real doubts regarding the sufficiency of the Orthodox notion of providence were in the air. The most interesting case concerns the fatalistic outlook of Theodore Metochites. As Hunger perceptively noted, this casts serious shadows over Metochites' attempt to pose as a pious Orthodox Christian and avoid the harassment of those annoying informants eager at all times to turn in dissenting intellectuals.[120] Medvedev too observed that even in Metochites' overwhelmingly pessimistic version the Greek concept of fate was still such as to challenge and compromise Orthodox theology.[121]

In the particular fifteenth-century circumstances of an empire falling apart this version of fatalism was anything but useful to Plethon's reformist plans. Plethonean fatalism is Greek, as is that of Metochites, yet paradoxically enough it is an optimistic kind of fatalism. At one with Stoicism and Spinozism, Plethon predicates the word *fate* with a signification that claims to merge freedom

---

[119] *Notizie* 298–9; P. H. Beck (1937) 112.
[120] Hunger (1978) 52. See above, Ch. 2 on Metochites and dissimulation.
[121] Medvedev (1997) 127–45.

with necessity. In the introduction to the *Nomoi* the Stoics are cited as the model for moral philosophy and this reasonably suggests that Plethon's notion of *heimarmene* is of Stoic origin.[122] Clement of Alexandria and Plutarch served as further sources transmitting doctrines that are appropriated and re-calibrated, ensuing in what Scholarios understands as αὐτοματισμός, namely determinism: there are no occurrences without respective causes, says Plethon, just as there can be no unnecessary causes.[123] In the *Differences* Plethon has recourse to the same two theses: everything comes about (τὸ γιγνόμενον) by a necessary cause and every cause necessarily and definitely exercises its power.[124] A passage from Cicero's treatise *On Divination* introduces us to the meaning of *heimarmene* that Christians fiercely combated and Plethon reintroduced in late Byzantium:

> By 'fate', I mean what the Greeks call *heimarmene* – an ordering and sequence of causes, since it is the connection of cause to cause which out of itself produces anything. It is everlasting truth, flowing from all eternity. Consequently, nothing has happened which was not going to be, and likewise nothing is going to be of which nature does not contain causes working to bring that very thing about. This makes it intelligible that fate should be not the 'fate' of superstition, but that of physics, an everlasting cause of things – why past things happened, why present things are now happening and why future things will be. (LS 55L (Cic. *Div.* 1.125–6))

The vocabulary used by Plethon to describe *heimarmene* (ἀμετάστροφος, ἀπαράτρεπτος) recalls Stoic terminology while his conceptual understanding of necessity and fate appears decisively conditioned by Pseudo-Plutarch's notion of destiny as an energised (κατ' ἐνέργειαν) divine law that necessarily holds together and controls the world and the whole hierarchy of Being.[125] Whereas Plotinus exempted the One from the power of destiny, Plethon identifies 'Zeus' with *heimarmene*.[126] This is arguably the most striking Stoic tendency in Plethon's work. Like

---

[122] *Nomoi* 2 (proem. 1.8–9). On Plethon and Stoicism see Arabatzis (2008) 310; (2003) 230.

[123] *Nomoi* 64 (2.6.4–10); on Plutarch and Clement as Plethon's sources see Arabatzis (2008) 315–17 and (2003) 220–1.

[124] *Diff.* 332.30–2.   [125] Arabatzis (2005) 222, 226; cf. Ps.-Plut. *De fato* 568C–E.

[126] Arabatzis (2005) 232 notes the analogies with Ps.-Aristotle's *De mundo*, 401b8ff. and Chrysippus.

Chrysippus and Zeno, Plethon merges providence (*pronoia*) with fate (*heimarmene*), reviving a belief that was long dead in Byzantium and controversial even among pagan philosophers. For example, in Proclus' hymns, a source that Plethon knew well, necessity is subjugated to divine will.[127] By contrast, Plethon's *heimarmene* is unconstrained by anything like a superior and autonomous will of 'Zeus'. Rather, 'Zeus' *qua* fate necessarily confers being to all successive causes. The Plethonean *cosmos* resembles a clock tuned according to a preset pattern that precludes contingency as well as the eventuality of miraculous disruptions of its unity and *modus operandi*. Mechanistic theories of this kind are typical products of radical Enlightenment and modernity, yet they carry Stoic resonances.

The identification of 'Zeus' with *heimarmene* in the *Nomoi* is a logical consequence of the principle that necessity is superior to contingency. Assuming that a higher level of necessity implies a higher state of Being, then absolute necessity coincides with absolute goodness. Since 'Zeus' is the extreme Good (ἄκρως ἀγαθός), it follows that he is identifiable with extreme necessity (ἡ μεγίστη ἀναγκῶν).[128] A similar notion occurs in Avicenna, according to whom 'necessary Being is in itself pure Good' (*necesse esse per se est bonitas pura*).[129] It was observed that in this regard Plethon's conception of the first cause as the fountainhead of the Good comes markedly close to that of Avicenna. Two people personally involved with Plethon, Scholarios and Demetrios Kydones, testify to the popularity of Avicenna among Byzantine intellectuals; but it is also noteworthy that according to Scholarios, Avicenna falls within the field of expertise of Plethon's shadowy instructor, Elissaios.[130]

According to Plutarch's account of the doctrines of Chrysippus, 'no state or process is to the slightest degree other than in accordance with the rationale of Zeus, which he [Chrysippus] says is identical to fate'.[131] Alexander of Aphrodisias also testifies to the Stoic identification between the divine and fate:

---

[127] Procl. *Hymni* 1.16–17: ἅψ δὲ μεταστρωφῶσιν ἀναγκαίης λίνον αἴσης, εὖτε θέλεις.
[128] *Nomoi* 66 (2.6.26–35).
[129] Avicenna Latinus, *Liber de philosophia prima* 43 (van Riet).   [130] Akasoy (2008).
[131] LS 55R (Plut. *On Stoic Self-contradictions* 1056B–C).

Fate itself, Nature, and the reason according to which the whole is organised, they assert to be god; it is present in all that is and comes to be, and in this way employs the individual nature of every thing for the organisation of the whole. And such, to put it briefly, is the opinion they lay down concerning fate. (Alex. Aphrod. 192.27–193.2; trans. Sharples)

Unexploited by Christian apologetics and radically opposed to the Christian preoccupation with free will, Stoicism provided excellent raw material for Plethon's assault on the Christian world-view and its appropriation of Aristotle. Still, an epistle by Bessarion and Plethon's reply show that here too Plato is the man evoked as the *spiritus rector*. Bessarion wonders about the relation between Plethon's theory of fate and that of the 'most wise' Plutarch. The latter, we read, developed in his work on *heimarmene* a doctrine closely followed by the later Neoplatonists; and Alcinous in his *Epitome* seems to assert more or less the same doctrine. Bessarion takes advantage of the opportunity to ask for elucidations long overdue regarding *Republic* Book 8 and *Laws* Book 10: his discussion of these texts with Plethon was still open.[132] In reply Plethon does not deny the influence of Plutarch or Alcinous but points to the ultimate and common source: Plato. 'In regard to the doctrine of fate I will bring to your attention no other testimony but that of Plato in the *Epinomis*.' He goes on to quote *Epinomis* 982b5–c5:

The necessity of a soul that has acquired mind will prove itself by far the greatest of all necessities; *for it makes laws as ruler, not as ruled*: but this inalterable thing, when the soul has taken the best counsel in accord with the best mind, comes out as the perfect thing in truth and in accord with mind, and not even adamant could ever prove stronger than it or more inalterable; but in fact the three Fates have it in hold, and keep watch that what has been decided by each of the gods with the best counsel shall be perfect.

In Plethon's view Plato was misread by those who thought that the doctrine of fate was appropriate to an 'effeminate' soul. Plato understands fate as a supreme form of overruling power associated with the most wise type of soul, one, we may infer, 'that makes laws as ruler, not as ruled'.[133] This leads away from fatalism and credits Plato with a conception of fate usually associated with

---

[132] Bess. *Ep.* 20, Mohler III 464.12–25.
[133] Pleth. *Ep. Bess.* 2, Mohler III 466.7–17 (quotation from 466.7–8; my emphasis).

Stoicism, namely that the man who handles himself rightly cannot but necessarily triumph. Matthew Kamariotes did not miss the devastating consequences for the Christian perception of personal freedom implied by this aristocratic doctrine. Plethon makes freedom dependent upon the attainment of a theoretical ideal of virtue approximated through profane education and secular philosophy. By contrast, Christianity conditions freedom upon the autonomous and personal will common to all people alike.[134]

According to Cicero's defence of Stoic theory of divination, if we assume that all things happen by fate, then whoever could 'see with his mind the connection of all causes, he would certainly never be deceived'. Since, according to Cicero, only god is capable of this knowledge, men should be content with 'various signs that announce what is to come'.[135] In *Nomoi* 2.6 Plethon allows for divination. He thinks that this is abundant proof that fate is at work, essentially repeating Chrysippus's argument as reported by Diogenianus and reproduced by Eusebius, a source that Plethon was familiar with:

In the aforementioned book [i.e. Chrysippus, *On Fate*] he offers a further demonstration, along the following lines. The predictions of the soothsayers could not be true, he says, if all things were not embraced by fate. (LS 55P (Diogenianus *ap.* Eusebius *PE* 4.3.1))

Not least so, because heavenly bodies exercise power over man's life. In the *Nomoi* these bodies are 'temporal but perpetual' (ἔγχρονος μεν, ἀΐδιος δε [οὐσία]), hence superior to man's nature, which is 'temporal and mortal' (ἔγχρονος καὶ θνητή).[136] They are not *ktismata* as they are in Scholarios' theological system, where everything but the Trinitarian god falls into a single category, that of *ex nihilo* created beings. In this context the issue of whether corporeal bodies are animate or not, which occasioned Plethon's short *Reply to Certain Questions*, really concerns the position man occupies within nature. Presuming that heavenly bodies are animated and immortal, as Plethon publicly argued, they also exercise power over the sphere of mortality and human affairs; if they are

---

[134] Kamariotes, *Contra Pleth.* 194 Reimarus.   [135] LS 55O (Cicero, *Div.* 1.127).
[136] *Nomoi* 96 (3.15.54–8).

not, providence is an affair of god alone. The question is ultimately whether the universe comes before man or man before
the universe, a question that pagans like Plethon and Christians
like Scholarios and Matthew Kamariotes answer very differently.
The latter objects to Plethon that man is the only being that was
granted reason and soul: nature is not animated. Hence, man cannot
be said to be inferior to or ruled by nature; the human soul should
be placed above nature and is not influenced by corporeal bodies
or intermediaries – only by the creator-god.[137] Scholarios uses a
Thomist simile to carry the same point home: god immediately
controls human affairs like the archer who hits the target with an
arrow.[138]

Plethon's Forms/causes/*genera*/gods control the network of
fate/*heimarmene*. They causally possess future events. If everything subsists in appropriate causes, causes are gods, and by definition gods have foreknowledge, then everything is predetermined.
It is absurd to suppose that gods change their minds about the
future, or that they are influenced by inferior beings: this would
mean that one of their two decisions was erroneous. Future events
are 'written by fate'. The argument that the gods' foreknowledge
of all things means that all things occur necessarily is a typical
deterministic argument reported and refuted by the Aristotelian
Alexander of Aphrodisias.[139] Like Alexander, Psellos believed that
god's foreknowledge does not determine the course of what will
be: '[divine] foreknowledge is not the cause of what happens'.
By contrast, Plethon reiterates the argument that to reject gods
as necessary and determining causes of human affairs means to
deprive them of foreknowledge, thus of their divinity. In his mind
knowledge and action coincide, for so do energy and essence in
god.

We may recall that Plethon's epistemological optimism and
multi-causalism was extended to the point of postulating against
Aristotle the possibility of a science of the accidental. Aristotle's
position was that 'the cause of the accidental is matter, which

---

[137] Kamariotes, *Contra Pleth.* 134ff.
[138] Cf. Aquinas, *Quaestiones theologicae de praedestinatione divina et de anima* 1.2.4.8–
9; Demetracopoulos (2007) 319.
[139] Alex. Aphrod. *De fato, CAG* 2.2.200.12ff.

admits of variation from the usual'.[140] Plethon departs from this position by positing the causes of what occurs by accident *within* the world of Ideas. He thus allows to the human soul to conquer through intellectual illumination scientific knowledge even of what is said to happen accidentally. Theodore of Gaza put it thus:

> Taking necessity in nature to mean what cannot be otherwise, Plethon thinks that all things arise and pass away by an absolute necessity; and thereby he denies not only moral choice (προαίρεσις) and wish (βούλησις) but also nature (φύσις). For matter too is nature.[141]

Plethon's nexus of knowable causes/gods eliminates the contingent basis of Judaeo-Christian creationism and transcendentalism. The world is seen as necessarily *generated* but not freely *created*. But does it also eliminate man's freedom?

In a short treatise, *On the Definition of Death*, Psellos vaguely acknowledges that 'natural causes' as well as chance have an effect on human affairs. According to Psellos, 'we are governed by providence (*pronoia*), nature and freedom of will (*proairesis*)'.[142] This tripartite distinction recurs in Plethon's *De fato* confidently and straightforwardly. 'Men are free in one sense and not-free in another', for there are three factors determining their lives: external circumstances and things occurring or functioning by necessity; the peculiar quality of each man's *phronesis*, which depends upon the gods; and the exercise in wisdom, in which men differ owing to their diverse predispositions. Of these factors, only the latter can be controlled by us and is, as the Stoics have it, ἐφ' ἡμῖν. External circumstances and one's nature are beyond human power (οὐκ ἐφ' ἡμῖν) and largely responsible for what comes about.[143] According to Plethon, nature is superior to man, yet man's *phronesis* adapts itself and follows up external circumstances. The role of *phronesis* as a scientific *habitus* excludes fatalism. He thus sides with the view of Cicero and Seneca that understanding *heimarmene* is the key for an optimal life and thus for achieving freedom.

One is free when one is aligning one's actions to a secure knowledge of what is genuinely good. Freedom concurs with necessity.

---

[140] *Metaph.* 1027a14–15.   [141] Thdr. Gaz. *De fato* 15.1–4 (trans. Taylor).

[142] Psell. Περὶ ὁρισμοῦ τοῦ θανάτου 71. Cf. Benakis (2002b) 165–9.

[143] Cf. *Nomoi* 72–4 (2.6.85–110); Cic. *De fato* 7–8.

The man who acts prudently and wisely cannot lose his freedom. *Ducunt volentem fata nolentem trahunt:* fate leads the willing soul but drags along the unwilling one.[144] To Byzantine pessimism Plethon opposed the idea that everything has its proper place within a cosmic and mechanical hierarchy of Being. To understand the mechanics behind this chain of causality would be tantamount to knowledge and freedom. *Not the 'fate' of superstition, but that of physics:* contrary to Palamite apophaticism that elevates god as an agent beyond rationality, fate is perfectly and transparently rational.

At a time when the Ottoman siege guns were approaching the Byzantine outposts, Plethon replaced the 'democratic' Christian ideal of freedom as conscious affirmation of one's relation to god with an elite profane notion of freedom that promised to decode the secrets of necessity through virtuous statesmanship and handling. The Platonic-Stoic belief that nature is superior to man and that the matrix of natural causes exercises its power upon human affairs does not lead by default to Metochites' fatalism and devotion to an apolitical *otium cum dignitate*. The Plethonean concept of *heimarmene* serves optimism rather than pessimism, action rather than resentment. In this regard the Islamic understanding of predestination that provided the impetus behind the Turkish army may have exercised its influence upon Plethon's *heimarmene*. It is a plausible assumption that a substantial borrowing or at least inspiration that Plethon derived from Islam concerns the correlation between unconditional faith in predestination and political survival.[145] Whereas Scholarios popularised the apocalyptic scenarios regarding the imminent collapse of the disintegrating empire and the expiration of the mundane world as divine punishment for degenerated Byzantines living in sin and neopaganism, Plethon sees in the Ottoman advance the example of a people persuaded that they are destined to conquer rather than be enslaved. Echoes of this view are discernible in Plethon's pupil Laonikos Chalkokondyles, the historian of the fall of

---

[144] Seneca, *Ep.* 107.11.
[145] P. H. Beck (1937) 106. Cf. Hunger (1978) 24.

Constantinople. According to Laonikos, the Ottomans succeeded thanks to a combination of necessity and virtuous decision-making.[146]

With the Ottomans devouring the Byzantine Empire and with no substantial help expected from the West we may appreciate the contribution of Platonic-Stoic philosophy as the only serious competitor to the Islamic belief in predestination. Eventually Plethon applied Platonic-Stoic *heimarmene* as the metaphysical foundation to his notion of historical necessity. In the same sense that the bourgeois society was seen by Marx as necessarily meant to collapse and open up the way for socialism, Plethon saw in the crisis of Byzantium the realisation of a historically necessary transition to a new type of human being inscribed within a proto-nationalistic framework that was defined by an emerging notion of philosophical Hellenism. Scholarios too envisioned a new order of things – albeit one inscribed within an apocalyptic framework defined not by a political community but rather by religious ecumenism. Two competing and mutually exclusive notions of utopianism evolved. One was pagan, the other Christian.

---

[146] Harris (2003) 211–32.

PART III
MISTRA VERSUS ATHOS

7

INTELLECTUAL AND SPIRITUAL UTOPIAS

The birth of social engineering: the *Memoranda*

In 1953, while Europe was still in the process of recovering from the evils of the Second World War, Gilbert Murray published a little book on 'Hellenism and the Modern World'. His remarks on the origins of the Greek *polis* carried particular significance and relevance for an audience reconsidering its Western identity and seeking to understand the roots of European civilisation in search of hope and direction:

Early Greek origins are obscure; but the evidence seems to point to a period of great invasions, involving a break–up of settled society, in which populations fled here and there for refuge, tribes were scattered, the sacred graves of ancestors left behind, and old customs and conventions lost. There was danger all round; the only safety was within some πόλις, *some City or circuit Wall* [1]. Each group of refugees built its own *Polis* and became an organised body behind it – not of kinsmen, but of πολῖται – 'citizens'. There remained of their old life almost nothing, except what each man could carry with him, such things as he knew or remembered – what was called his σοφία, his Wisdom; and such personal qualities or abilities as made him definitely good for something – his virtue or ἀρετή [2]. The people who had taken refuge inside the *Polis* were mostly, as Strabo says, 'a mixed multitude', not uniform in their traditions or customs. *So they had to form new laws* [3] by agreement, often, no doubt, with a certain amount of compromise. That laid a heavy responsibility on the men themselves, *the responsibility of Freedom* [4]. They had no longer an unquestioned tradition to control or guide them: *they must fall back on what stores they had of active Sophia and Arete* [5]; they must control themselves, think for themselves [6]. They must remember not merely to be obedient to custom, which is easy, but to be really Just [7], which needs thought; to observe *Metron*, or Measure; to remember the rule of μηδὲν ἄγαν: Nothing Too Much; and to avoid above all things *Hubris*, Insolence or Excess, the deadly error to which all life is subject and which leads always to a fall [8].[1]

---

[1] Murray (1953) 24–5; my emphasis.

At the most precarious and crucial moment of the Byzantine Empire Plethon saw in the ideal of Greek *polis* precisely what Murray described as its very essence at a moment of intellectual crisis for the modern West: a safe harbour, and yet, beyond that, a principle of hope and a plan for salvation. The urgent measure towards the safety and the recovery of *politeia* in the Peloponnese concerns the fortification (διατείχισις, διατείχισμα) of the Isthmus by rebuilding the Hexamilion wall, intended to function as a 'circuit Wall' [1] and keep external danger out.[2] But beyond that Plethon reiterates in his advice to political authorities further characteristics of a Greek *polis* described above. These include the responsibility of the intellectual elite to ensure freedom and safety [4];[3] preparation to resist any attack using one's own resources, that is ἐκ τῶν ἐνόντων;[4] the need to choose the right way of life, called βίου προαίρεσις by Plethon;[5] the Platonic belief that justice means 'to do one's own job (τὰ αὑτοῦ πράττειν ἕκαστος)', develop personal skills as much as possible and avoid *polypragmosyne* [2];[6] the abolition of luxuries (τρυφή) and effeminacy (μαλακία), the avoidance of excess and the observance of *metron* [8];[7] the focus on those recesses of virtue (ἀρετή) that remained active [5];[8] the firm contention that the salvation of 'a *polis* or nation (ἔθνος)' depends upon the urgent recovery of the true contents of the notions of justice [7] and *politeia* and the development of corresponding new laws [3];[9] in a nutshell: philosophy and wisdom as means of resistance [6].

The *Memorandum* to the emperor Manuel II Palaiologos (*c.* 1418) and the *Memorandum* to the despot Theodore II (*c.* 1416) contain concrete suggestions and measures intended to effect two complementary ends: first, to reverse the 'illness of things (ἡ ἀσθένεια τῶν πραγμάτων)', and second, to pave the way for

---

[2] *Mem. II* 250.9–10; 252.6; 261.10–16; 262.8–9. See also Plethon's 1414 epistle to Manuel, *Or. Man., Lampros, PP,* 3.309.5–6, 311.4–15.

[3] *Mem. I* 128.18–21; *Mem. II* 247.8–9; 250.11; *Or. Man.* 312.3–5.

[4] *Mem. I* 130.15; 133.20; *Mem. II* 312.14–15.   [5] *Mem. I* 126.9.

[6] Cf. *Mem. I* 119.20–2, 121.1–5; *Resp.* 433a–b. See also *Mem. I* 132.7–10.

[7] *Mem. I* 133.5–18; 128.7–9

[8] Cf. *Mem. I* 116.21–2; 130.6–12; 129.10; *Or. Man.* 310.3–5.

[9] *Mem. I* 116.16–18; 118.12–14; 125.3–4. At *Mem. I* 116.10–11 the salvation of the Peloponnese is seen as an imperative of justice. See also *Mem. I* 118.17: τὴν πολιτείαν ἐπανορθωτέον.

the approximation of a σπουδαιοτάτη πολιτεία, a most virtu-ous constitution.[10] The *Memorandum to Manuel* is more urgent in tone and the ideas appear more fully developed. Perhaps this is because Manuel daringly clashed with the interests of the Moreote landlords,[11] thus boosting Plethon's confidence that the time was ripe for social transformation instigated by the man whom both he and Demetrios Kydones recognised as Plato's ideal philosopher-king.[12] Salvation will come about by necessity, provided that the despot and the emperor authorise a two-stage scheme claiming the right constitution as a vehicle to realise the perfectly just city-state. If the despot succeeds in achieving the *preservation* (σωτηρία) of the Peloponnese, he will then, Plethon thinks, easily 'discover everything else that is necessary to the virtue and embellishment of the *politeia*'. Consequently, the *Memoranda* do not contain a concrete utopia, but the guiding steps to come as close as possible to Plethon's political paradigm. These are clearly defined as 'not impossible, nor too difficult' steps towards the end of the perfect *politeia*, provided that people act collectively as if 'with one soul':

As we do not need – at least at present – anything else but salvation and to be saved, let's see what is left for us from the great Roman hegemony. Having lost everything, all that remains are two cities in Thrace, the Peloponnese (and even that not in its entirety) and perhaps some of the smallest islands, if any at all are left. Now, we have already shown that the salvation of cities comes about only by means of a great constitution (*politeia*). It follows that we have to reform the constitution by introducing the most just laws and the best rulers. Our situation is desperate and we are called to oppose most powerful opponents although we are most exhausted: so much more then is it necessary to fall back on a most just constitution that will rectify the weakness of our condition. We have mentioned how many and what sort of means are needed to render a constitution most just, having stated what is most essential to our present necessities, those that may be achieved without great difficulty. For surely these will be neither impossible nor too difficult for those capable of acting with one soul. (*Mem. I* 129.12–130.5)

[10] On Plethon's economic measures in the *Memoranda* cf. Garnsey (2009) and (2007); Matschke and Tinnefeld (2001) 358–65; Baloglou (2002) and (1998); W. Blum (1988); Peritore (1977); Tozer (1886); Nikolaou (2004b); Spentzas (1996). In 1852 the Scottish law maker and historian George Finley (1799–1875) produced a draft English translation of the *Memoranda* kept at the Archives of G. Finley at the British School of Athens and edited by Baloglou (2003). For summaries and partial translations of the *Memoranda* in English see Woodhouse (1986) 92–8 and 102–6. The *Memoranda* appear to have attracted the vivid interest of John Dee and Giacomo Leopardi. See here Neri (2010) 159–65, 283.

[11] Peritore (1977) 182.   [12] Zgoll (2005) 191–221.

It has been observed that 'the structure and ideology of his [Plethon's] reformed, model polity bear the clear imprint of Plato's Kallipolis'.[13] In fact, Plethon's *Memoranda* may be read in the same way as a mainstream – in my view correct – interpretation has dealt with Plato's utopianism. Kallipolis is a paradigm that may not be fully and immediately realisable in its totality but may be progressively and approximately approached.[14] Like Plato, Plethon thought that the ideal of a perfectly just *polis* was difficult to bring about; but he did not hold that it was impossible. The difference is that in Plethon's case immediate action was necessary. Plato's interlocutors in the *Republic* enjoyed the luxury of waiting for the right *kairos*. In the *Republic* the incentive to move in the direction of reifying the political paradigm is provided by the actual course of things. Manuel realised that 'the times and things are dire (χαλεπώτατοι οἱ καιροὶ καὶ τὰ πράγματα)'[15] and Plethon attempted to show that this most critical moment might also be most opportune for reforming existing society and approximating the 'most virtuous polity'.

Manuel's successful restoration of the Hexamilion wall in 1415 may have enhanced Plethon's confidence in the possibility of positively influencing the political authorities and approximating the σπουδαιοτάτη πολιτεία.[16] And yet the *Memoranda* are idiosyncratic 'mirrors for princes', or *Fürstenspiegeln*, that to all appearances failed to initiate change or attract followers.[17] The paganism

---

[13] Garnsey (2007) 55.   [14] See Burnyeat (1999) 297–308; Morrison (2007) 232–55.

[15] Manuel Pal. *Epitaphium in fratrem Theodorum* 113.19.

[16] The need to fortify the Peloponnese is affirmed by other contemporary sources: Mazaris, Chrysoloras and Chalkokondyles; on the restoration of the Hexamilion see Necipoğlu (2009) 259–63.

[17] A probable exception is the long epistle addressed to Constantine Palaiologos in 1444, in which Bessarion clearly echoes Plethonean reformism: the Peloponnese urgently needs a military reorganisation, he says; stupidity and inertia (μαλακία τε καὶ βλακεία) are destroying the nation. But not everything is lost (text in *Lampros, PP* 4.32–45). Stupefied by the technological marvels he had encountered in Rome, Bessarion suggests a new type of quasi-futuristic utopianism based on scientific-technological progress and mechanical production. The core is Plethonean – as the expression 'new Lacedaemonians' patently shows. (The epistle also in Mohler III: 439–49, here: 443.15. Cf. Necipoğlu (2009) 273–4; Baloglou 1998: 94–101; Matschke and Tinnefeld 2001: 362–5; Zakythinos 1975: 356–7; van Dieten 1979: 16). In 1471–2 Bessarion was involved in a plan for organising a colony consisting of Greek settlers in Sienese territory in Tuscany, which appears to be related to his epistle to Constantine Palaiologos. As Maltezou (2006: 104–5) notes, this ambitious plan for a settlement that could potentially evolve into a

of the *Nomoi*, a work unclassified in terms of genre that neither purports to persuade anyone nor invests hope in existing authorities, is a reaction to this failure.

On the other hand, Plethon never lost touch with reality, nor did he withdraw from political life. His last work, the Προσφωνημά-τιον πρὸς τὸν Δεσπότην Δημήτριον was written around 1451 in a brief intermission in the civil war in the Peloponnese between the two younger brothers of Constantine Palaiologos, Thomas and Demetrios.[18] The need to welcome peace and the advice to Demetrios to turn to the real problems of the Peloponnese show that Plethon was still involved in political life, capable of dealing pragmatically with historical circumstances and ready to provide his advice on the practical level. He died the next year. Thomas and Demetrios continued to fight each other. In 1459 Thomas led an insurrection against the Ottoman conquerors. In 1460 Demetrios submitted to Mehmed II.[19]

Social and political reform in the *Memoranda* consists of three strands: (a) the sharp division of the population into three classes; (b) the radical reconfiguration of the administration and military structure; and (c) the redistribution of land. Each of these measures was intended to remedy a chronic deficiency of Byzantine society and especially of the Peloponnese: (a) the disastrous interference in economical processes by noble landholders who put the interests of their inherited feuds above the collective well-being of the State and the Palaiologean imperial dynasty by involving themselves in the economic affairs of merchants and traders; (b) the oppression and exhaustion of peasants and labourers, who served simultaneously as producers of goods, taxpayers and defenders of the country; (c) the deficiencies of the Theme system in terms of agricultural productivity and the malfunction of basic economic functions during military campaigns. To these, one should add the separatism and isolationism of monasteries that possessed massive

Greek city-state in Italy proposed a new legal system based upon 'the laws of Justinian and the customs of the Byzantines' but allowing for modifications and amendments. Bessarion did not turn for inspiration to the past, but 'may well have been thinking along lines which became much more fully developed in the eighteenth and nineteenth centuries' (Harris 2006: 97).

[18] Pleth. *Prosphonematium ad Demetrium, Lampros, PP* 4.207–10.

[19] For the last days of Byzantine Morea see Necipoğlu (2009) 280–4.

amounts of land but showed little concern for the survival of the State.

In the *Memorandum to Theodore* Plethon suggests a tripartite division of the social body into three *genera* (γένη). The 'essential' (ἀναγκαιότατον) *genos* covers primary production processes and consists of farm labourers (αὐτουργικόν), land cultivators (γεωργικόν) and shepherds concerned with raw materials. In the *Memorandum to Manuel* this is the most valuable *genos* of the 'helots'. The reconceptualisation and redeployment of the word 'helot' may appear highly original, a product of a 'fine disregard of the associations of an opprobrious name'.[20] Inspiration behind this redescription of the helots was possibly drawn from Plato's comment in the *Laws* that no question caused more debates among the Greeks than whether the helot type of slavery should be admired or condemned.[21] Manufacturers (δημιουργικόν), merchants (ἐμπορικόν) and retailers (καπηλικόν) are classifiable within the second *genos*. In the *Memorandum to Manuel* Plethon is silent in regard to this second *genos* of retailers, traders and suppliers; instead, the spotlight is on the classes of farmers and soldiers.[22] Thirdly, the ruling class (ἀρχικὸν φῦλον) is concerned with the preservation of order, administration, justice and security of the State. The king is not above the law. He is a lawgiver assisted by a council with the sole concern of providing for the preservation of the *polis*-organism. The king, public officers, judges, government agents, intellectuals and consultants along with the military provide the armoury of the state.

In order to eliminate the clashes naturally occurring between economically prosperous and impoverished members of society, Plethon suggests that only men of middling economical status should participate as counsellors. They are more likely to avoid at once the greed typical of archontes and those relations of dependence often caused when people in despair strive to overcome poverty. It has been argued that this tripartite social model

---

[20] Tozer (1886) 372. Cf. *Mem. I* 119.5–28; *Mem. II* 255.18.

[21] *Laws* 776c; Ellissen (1860: 141) also notes Hdt. 9.28 and Thuc. 4.8.

[22] Smarnakis (2007: 107), observes that the absence of this second *genos* in *Mem. II* is complemented by the introduction of a new social group absent in *Mem. I*: the priests. On the role of these priests-cum-civil servants, see below pp. 372, 379, 381.

resembles the three-tiered feudal system of the medieval West.[23] One may recall that in the henotheist theology of the *Nomoi* Plethon works on the basis of a tripartite metaphysical structure in which divinities assume ambassadorial and intercessory positions, thus providing a pattern with definite political repercussions.[24]

The first novel reformist suggestion concerns the role of the ruling class. The ruling class is not allowed either to engage in commerce or to abuse its power by exploiting the other two political *genera*. The mixing of tradesmen with officials is an undesired result of bad government. One does not use donkeys for the work of horses of good breeding, nor horses for the work of donkeys. As a matter of fact, says Plethon, we do not even use the same horses for any type of work. There are horses more suitable for battle than for other labours: 'we should far more distinguish these things and not confound them in relation to man'.[25] Hence, the despot Theodore is asked to purify commerce from the officious interference of Peloponnesian archontes who, we are given to understand, are more than likely to impose 'unjust weights and every other means in their power' to ruin the interests of a miserable labouring class. The archontes should be transformed from greedy merchants exploiting the people of the Peloponnese into 'magistrates watching over the preservation and salvation of the people'. Plethon set the bar too high for Theodore. Even if the despot had had the means to impose his will upon the archontes, an aristocracy with little – if any – interest in the survival of collective entities or national security would not be transformed into Plato's guardians in the absence of a policy of social engineering.

The reconstruction and consolidation of society in the *Memoranda* presuppose the complete elimination of the old and the continuous inculcation of the principles of a new social morality. The archontes of Morea possessed inherited fiefdoms that remained uncultivated and held back the development of national economy.

---

[23] Smarnakis (2007) 108 and 112 n. 26.
[24] Bargeliotes (1974) 147: 'as his hierarchical world of Ideas was headed by the first Principle or Being in Itself, so his socio-political structure should be headed by a monarch, the king. The same is true of the rest of the classes, officers, servants and producers.' Of course, the pattern is typically Neoplatonic.
[25] *Mem. I* 132.7–12.

The wealth and well-being of this or that family was deemed more important than that of the people. To remedy this situation Plethonean reformism essentially demanded that family tradition and loyalty be thrown off together with all psychological and economical attachment to inherited fiefdoms and estates. Plethon elaborated and applied to his contemporary context Plato's call for the dissolution of family bonds among guardians in the *Republic*. The difference from Plato is that the transferability of this idea to the whole of the Peloponnese implied the collective abandonment of all domestic ties at all social levels. Intriguingly, small-scale sectarian movements on Ottoman ground such as the one initiated by Sheikh Bedreddin and his disciples struggled for a similar cause.[26]

In place of family and social ties Plethon introduces a notion of proto-national identity unprecedented in the history of Byzantium. This called for absolute ideological commitment and the subordination of all subjects to the single cause of *soteria*. The new morality entails the creation of a Hellenic nation-state in the ethnically riven fifteenth-century Peloponnese. According to the *Memoranda* the maintenance of the new *politeia* depends on the radical retuning of the relation between citizenry and army. The 'Helots' carry the fiscal burdens of the commonwealth by paying taxes. On the other hand, they are excused from military service and administrative duties. In its turn, the soldiery originates from the agricultural class but is exclusively concerned with guarding the country and is exempt from paying tax. The rationale behind this scheme is that the sentiment of honour in an army and its good disposition are not easily preserved once the soldiers are subjected to taxation. A rotation system ensures that citizens possessing military skills serve at one time as soldiers and at another as producers.[27] The two activities never concur. In the case of peasants unfit for military service Plethon suggests that they support soldiers economically. One helot is rendered responsible for sustaining one foot soldier and providing both his weapons and

---

[26] See Siniossoglou (2012).

[27] *Mem. II* 256.14–17. Ellissen observed that Plethon may have drawn inspiration from the Athenean στρατεία ἐν τοῖς μέρεσι mentioned by a scholiast of Aeschines (*Schol. gr. in Aeschin. et Isocrat.* 74 Dindorf).

provisions; two helots are made responsible for supporting one knight; and three helots for supporting an officer.

The agreement between peasants and professional soldiers has two significant results. First, it ensures the unity between social strata effecting distinct but mutually dependent operations: production and defence. Second, it fosters professionalism and specialisation conducive to the development of expertise in each of these operations. Anticipating *quattrocento* humanists, Plethon considers mercenary troops to be unreliable and potentially disastrous. Instead, Manuel is advised to build up a homogeneous national militia.[28] This is the very first thing Manuel has to take care of – everything else will follow. Clearly Plethon considered inefficient the traditional Byzantine *pronoia* system which awarded aristocrats with land grants in return for military service. This had to go, together with the archontes and their privileges. Plethon had a good case. The *pronoia* system only accelerated the demise of the State.[29] As for the urgent priority that Plethon ascribes to the organisation of a *homophulon* army, this resurfaces in a very interesting way in Machiavelli's *dictum* that 'where there are good arms, good laws follow'.[30] Plethon makes his point nicely in the *Memorandum to Manuel*: 'I think it is a joke to imagine that if we destroy our citizens financially we shall then be saved by hiring foreigners and strangers.'[31]

Four possible sources may have inspired Plethon. Nevra Necipoğlu has pointed out that the Plethonean division between professional army and taxpayers has a strong parallel in contemporary Ottoman practices. The Ottoman system distinguished between the 'askerî' military class that was exempted from taxes and the 'reaya' class of producers and taxpayers.[32] Given Plethon's interest and respect for the Ottoman *politeia* and laws, it is a defensible position that to some extent he hoped to hit the enemy with shafts made of his own wings.[33] The other three sources that may

---

[28] Cf. *Mem. I* 121.15; *Mem. II* 264.15: ἀκραιφνὴς στρατιά.

[29] See the remarks by Ostrogorsky (1954) 174.

[30] On Machiavelli on mercenaries see Skinner (1978) 130.

[31] *Mem. II* 252.18–20.   [32] Necipoğlu (2009) 275.

[33] See for example *Oratio ad Manuelem, Lampros, PP* 3.310.7–10: οἱ νῦν φοβερώτατοι οὗτοι ἡμῖν βάρβαροι, πολιτείᾳ κεχρημένοι . . .

have influenced Plethon are Plato's *Republic*, Sparta, and the constitution of the Pythagorean Hippodamus, whose ideas were transmitted by Aristotle. Ellissen noted the first.[34] In *Republic* 416d–e Plato says the following with regard to the guardians:

> Whatever sustenance moderate and courageous warrior-athletes require in order to have neither shortfall nor surplus in a given year they will receive by taxation on the other citizens as a salary for their guardianship.

Plato elaborates on variations of this idea in *Republic* 464b–c, 547d ('the fighting class will be prevented from taking part in farming, manual labour, or other ways of making money') and 543b–c: soldiers 'should receive their yearly upkeep from the other citizens as a wage for their guardianship and look after themselves and the rest of the city'. In Aristotle's *Politics* Plato's state requires a division of the social body similar to that pursued by the Spartans: 'So that in the end no other regulation will have been enacted except the exemption of the Guardians from the work of agriculture, which is a measure that even now the Spartans attempt to introduce.'[35] Plethon's two favourite points of reference, Plato and Sparta, appear in Aristotle pointing in the same direction. Besides, the principle of communality applied to the Guardians in Plato's *Kallipolis* is consonant with the rejection of private property among ancient Pythagorean circles as well as with Plethon's reformism.[36] Significantly, in the constitution of the Pythagorean Hippodamus reported by Aristotle the population is also divided into three classes: the artisans, the farmers and 'the third class that fought for the State in war and was the armed class'. Land was also separated into three categories ('sacred', 'private' and 'common'), of which the last 'provided the warrior class with food'. Hippodamus seems to have in mind a system according to which cultivators of this 'common land' are to be 'a different set of people from both those who cultivate the private farms and the

---

[34] Ellissen (1860: 140) notes that *Nomoi* 3.30, dealing with Περὶ τῶν εἰς τὸ κοινὸν ταμιεῖον εἰσφορῶν, may well have provided a fuller discussion or development of these measures. On Plethon and Sparta see Baloglou (2005).

[35] *Pol.* 1264a9–11.

[36] On Plato's concept of communality and the Pythagoras community within Croton, see Garnsey (2005) 83–7.

soldiers'.[37] Aristotle saw problems here, for this seems to create 'a fourth section of the state'. Plethon may have intended to produce a better version of Hippodamus' plan, retaining his idea of a clear distinction between peasants and soldiers but abolishing that between 'sacred', 'private' and 'common land'. Now *all* land is to be common.

Arguably the most radical measure that Plethon proposes concerns the confiscation of private holdings and their redistribution according to the capacity of inhabitants to cultivate soil. This plan for the abolition of private ownership is meant to ensure that no land remains neglected or idle and aims at an increase of production. The rule is simple enough. Private property is not an inalienable right; but labour is. By implication, labour should determine the right to occupy land and not the other way around. In practice, one may occupy parts of land wherever one chooses, provided that one is able to take full advantage of it and as long as it is not already occupied. If one fails in his duty as cultivator and producer, then the State redistributes the land to another occupier. The production of goods will be supervised, protected and regulated by the State with the clear objective of increasing primary production. Common utility determines the nature of communality:

All land is by nature common (κατὰ φύσιν κοινή) to all inhabitants and no one may claim any individual right to any part of it. Rather, it is permissible to everyone to plant wherever he wishes and build and plough as much of the land he desires and is able to. The condition is that each will become master of as much land and for as long as he will not neglect its cultivation while in his possession. No one will be paying money to anybody [as rent or taxes] nor be molested or impeded by anyone other than any person who might have previously taken the land through work according to the law regarding things that are in common and belong to no one more than another. (*Mem. II* 260.3–12)

The main effect of this plan is the unimpeded, continuous and self-regulating collaboration of producers (αὐτουργοί) that ensures immediate access to all parts of the Peloponnese suitable for cultivation. On the other hand, the insistence on priority means that Plethon must have also admitted, indirectly, that the 'right of use'

---

[37] *Pol.* 1267b22–38; 1268a33–41. The analogies between the constitution of Hippodamus and Plethon's *politeia* are noted by Baloglou (1998) 66–8; (2002) 199–200.

of land is transferable to the user's biological successors, provided that the latter showed a real interest in taking it up.[38]

Where does Plethon derive his idea of communality and community of property from? Peter Garnsey argued that Stoicising Golden Age primitivism might well be Plethon's source here.[39] As a jurist, Plethon must have surely known the long tradition of natural law theories, especially their widespread Christian versions. Gratian's motto that 'by the law of nature everything was in common' found its way into Thomas Aquinas. Further variants found their way into Gregory Palamas' *Homilies*. As the latter put it, everything is in common for it ultimately belongs to god – even if administered (here comes the decisive proviso) with god's permission, by humans. Plethon may have gone beyond such Christian advocacies of private ownership in attempting an unqualified retreat to the original core of natural law.

In the *Memoranda* property is a deviation from natural law just as atheism and superstition are considered deviations from an unnamed, Platonising natural religion. Plethon confidently transmits the essence of natural law and natural religion without integrating a single *topos* of the relevant literary symbolism: the Garden of Eden is absent and so are its pagan equivalents. Reason and utility suffice to evoke natural law without regressing either to Scripture or to quasi-mythical, quasi-philosophical accounts of the early state of humanity. Ellissen noted theoretical *Vergleichsmomente* with Rousseau's chapter *du domaine réel* in *Du Contrat Social* 1.9.[40] A more solid link with Plethon is provided by Thomas More, who also abandoned the notion of private property and turned against those who possessed land but did not increase production – including 'some abbots'. More may well have utilised Plethon; here, though, as Garnsey observed, he does not appear to have scored as well as Plethon did in his understanding of Platonic political thought. Contrary to Plethon, More perpetuated the common misunderstanding regarding Plato's alleged 'communism'.[41]

One of the major impediments to the recovery of late Byzantine economy was an absurdly vast number of tax burdens that crushed

[38] Spentzas (1996) 75.   [39] Garnsey (2007) 57.   [40] Ellissen (1860) 143.
[41] Garnsey (2007) 57.

the productive classes.[42] The immense number of tax burdens was more unbearable to the lower classes for it was complemented by exemptions from tax paying obtained by foreign merchants, monasteries, archontes and, predictably, their numerous friends known under the generic formulation οἱ οἰκεῖοι. Plethon himself profited from this policy of favouritism. By official decree 'Georgios Gemistos, his genuine sons and their male descendants' were released from paying the κεφαλιτίκιον tax 'for all eternity henceforth'.[43] Though profiting from this system, Plethon acknowledged its disastrous effects and suggested a reform of tax policy that aimed to liberate the productive forces of society and increase productivity.

The fiscal measures in Plethon's *Memorandum to Theodore* entail the abandonment of existing taxation systems. Fixed imposition in kind or money, says Plethon, has the disadvantage of ignoring the economic capacity of each taxpayer, while forced labour is too heavy and slavish. On the other hand, it is difficult to tax the body of citizens proportionately according to each citizen's means. Constant variations in one's income rendered precise calculation of taxes imprecise and complicated. The alternative of collecting taxes in small quantities many times each year raised the likelihood of corruption on the part of a large body of tax collectors. Plethon suggests a tripartite division of the annual produce of each piece of cultivated land enabling taxes to be regulated proportionately. This tripartite division of production recalling the one in Plato's *Laws*[44] is founded upon the following analysis of how taxation might best serve communal services:

Primary production requires three things: (a) labour, (b) the capital (τέλη) used by the labourers, be it oxen, vineyards, herds and the like, and (c) the protection of (a) and (b). Consequently, justice has it that production should come in the possession of three heads, namely of labourers, of those who provide the means for labour (τέλη) and of the guardians and saviours of all (by which we mean the emperors, rulers and other magistrates and the soldiers). These who belong in the *genus* of labourers and utilize their own capital (τέλη) – for they have permission (ἐξουσία) to work on any land and in any manner they like – must

---

[42] In fact Plethon reacts to this situation. See e.g. *Mem. I* 132.11–19.

[43] Yiannakopoulos (1990) 278–9.

[44] *Laws* 848a: ἐλευθέροις, οἰκέταις, δημιουργοῖς.

take two thirds of the produce, one for the labour invested and the other for the means they provide. The third portion they must bring to the community and to those who are charged with their protection (= the guardians), so that they may be exempt from any other tax or service. I consider this taxation as most just and a worthy reward and support to those who are entrusted with communal services. So much for taxes. (*Mem. I* 123.15–124.5)

With a self-sufficient Peloponnese in mind, Plethon called for the protection of domestic economy and measures against economic exploitation by the West. The continuous devaluation of Byzantine currency was one aspect of the monetary crisis that Plethon hoped to remedy by abolishing the circulation of foreign currency and those *falsae monetae* (πονηρὰ χαλκεῖα) that 'bring much profit to others while rendering us a proper object of ridicule'.[45] It was suggested that the foreign copper pieces that Plethon has in mind were the Venetian 'colonial' *tornesello*.[46] As in Plato's *Laws*, importation and exportation of goods is carefully regulated and a tax is imposed on articles not necessary to the social body at large. Luxuries are repeatedly condemned.[47] The distinction between merchants operating internationally and retailers operating domestically echoes *Republic* 371d4–7: 'Or is not "shopkeepers" the name we give to those who, planted in the agora, serve us in buying and selling, while we call those who roam from city to city "merchants"?' Public resources should not be pointlessly squandered but invested in security. An austere way of life echoing ancient Sparta is illustrated with an 'example from nature'. The eagle is a royal bird, though not at all as colourful as a peacock. Plethon's utopian scheme demands of citizens and soldiers the qualities of an eagle, not those of a peacock. From the viewpoint of economic history, Plethon's 'closed, self-sufficient, protectionist system' has been seen as 'an extreme reaction to the open, international markets of the period, and to the position that the Byzantine lands (much reduced by now) had in it'.[48]

Plethon insisted that the archontes of Morea should not compromise the economic activities of the lower classes in pursuit of their

---

[45] *Mem. II* 262.14–17; cf. Yiannakopoulos (1990) 298 n. 38.   [46] Laiou (2007) 223.

[47] *Laws* 847c; Cf. Xen. *Lac.* 7.3 for Lycurgus' plan to 'cut off the attraction of money for indulgence's sake'.

[48] Laiou (2007) 229.

own interests; he could not then possibly allow for a monastic system to lay claims on land, exploit peasants and undermine any State initiative to protect and regulate economy. Peritore observed that the monasteries that owned one-third to one-half of the total land of the empire and at least one-quarter in the Peloponnese, 'continued to confiscate peasant freehold through fraudulent litigation, corruption of officials, and economic pressure, but most often left the land uncultivated or tilled it in a most desultory fashion'.[49] This huge monastic network made impossible the redistribution of land and stood in the way of Plethon's concerns for the intensification of production.

Last but not least, monastic ideology was a serious obstacle to political mobilisation. Plethon submitted his two *Memoranda* against the background of the triumph of the Palamites, who established a new spiritual order with monasticism at its centre. With their alternative utopia based on supra-rational experience and propagating a profound distrust of secular concepts, monks and their spiritual leaders would be the first to boycott or sabotage any attempt at social transformation. While the state and its borders were disintegrating, Palamite patriarchs acquired more and more power. In the light of the Hesychast notion of salvation, Plethon's scheme of political rebirth was at best irrelevant and, at worst, yet another satanic opponent.

Plethon does not advise any direct and full confiscation of monastic properties. Perhaps because Manuel returned confiscated lands to monasteries in 1408 and again in 1414/15, for reasons we shall examine in due course, Plethon did not wish openly to contradict imperial authority. Instead, he suggests that monasteries should no longer receive economic support and donations. This meant the economical disempowerment of the monasteries.[50] The idea was not new. Psellos and Attaliates tell us that in order to meet military needs Isaac Comnenos (1057/9) confiscated monastic land and left the monks only with what was necessary for their subsistence. Like Attaliates, Plethon sarcastically observed that this was entirely compatible with the monastic denunciation of worldly goods.[51]

---

[49] Peritore (1977) 183. [50] Hunger (1978) 24. [51] Ševčenko (1957) 153–5.

This advice concerning the monasteries implied their isolation from the emerging collective identity of a political community (γένος) fighting for its survival. Monasteries would be left to die morally as well as economically. Whereas in the *Nomoi* monasticism is attacked on metaphysical and moral grounds, in the *Memorandum to Manuel* it is revealed to be a gargantuan internal enemy that obstructs common good. Monks intentionally or unintentionally serve the aims of the Turks: the enemy would especially wish that revenues that could be used for public security are spent uselessly, says Plethon, and this is what the monks shamelessly do. They undermine public good by being the recipients of improper donations and absorbing state revenues without producing anything.[52] How can one assume that the urgent expenses required to defend the country on top of those needed for public affairs may allow

for sustaining such a huge swarm of drones (σμῆνος κηφήνων), of which some say they are 'philosophising', the others that they are idle and still others request that they get their hands on much more than their services are worth? (*Mem. II* 259.17–19)

Clearly then the community cannot finance the 'idle and dronelike leisure' of monks.[53] The neat expression ἀργὴ καὶ κηφηνώδης ἕξις is lifted from *Laws* Book 10, where the Athenian stranger, quoting Hesiod, identifies 'neglect, idleness and indolence', the three qualities with which Plethon credits the monks, as vices of the soul (900e) concluding that:

In our view all idle and thoughtless bons vivants will be just the kind of people the poet said were 'like nothing so much as stingless drones'. (*Laws* 901a; trans. Saunders)[54]

Those who support monasticism appear to have lost touch with reality, says Plethon, for they do not realise 'that if the public (τὰ κοινά) is ruined, which god forbid, their own interest will likewise be destroyed'. This argument was common at the time. It is put

---

[52] *Mem. II* 258.5–259.6.   [53] *Mem. II* 259.12.

[54] Cf. Hes. *Opera et dies* 303–7: 'Both gods and men are angry with a man who lives idle, for in nature he is like the stingless drones who waste the labour of the bees, eating without working; but let it be your care to order your work properly, that in the right season your barns may be full of victual.'

forward by those anonymous laymen advocating the confiscation of monastic properties for defence needs portrayed in a treatise by Nicholas Kabasilas, to which I will return. Kabasilas' adversaries and Plethon seriously underestimated the monks' capacity to invest not only in their heavenly existence, but also in their more mundane interests. *Ta koina* were indeed ruined, but monasticism was not. Monasteries managed to survive under Turkish rule and many continued to be as well off as they were before, thanks to their skill in collaborating with political authorities. This was a development that secular officials could not predict at least at the time when Plethon was addressing Manuel II.

Plethon may have hoped that the majority of citizens of the *polis* would agree to his measures in all honesty without the need for dirigiste mechanisms. In Plato's *Laws* the legislator counts on εὐμένεια, the consent of citizens that facilitates the application of laws and enhances conformity to the established order.[55] Like Plato in the *Laws*, Plethon might have thought as optimal the willing and adamant commitment to common good. But like Plato, he also considered the possibility that certain stubborn people would obstruct the complete abolition of the distinction between the public and private spheres.[56] In that case the despot will have no difficulty in finding men who will cooperate with him. The choice of the word συγκαταπράξοντες is interesting: it means those who will *act* as if with one mind and in step with the ruler.

Aspiring to a *despotisme éclairé* full of Platonic resonances, Plethon advises the ruler to use the best men in establishing all necessary services and then 'correct the others by persuasion, benefits and punishments'. The recipe is a reasonable use of two things: on the one hand the desire for good (ἐπιθυμία), and, on the other, anger (θυμός) against those who commit crimes. Only the prefix ἐπι- seems to separate ἐπιθυμία from θυμός. There are resonances from Xenophon's account of Lycurgus' reform, according to which the key was to 'ensure that the good should have happiness

---

[55] *Laws* 723a.

[56] See *Laws* 853c–d (trans. Saunders): 'But we are human beings, legislating in the world today for the children of humankind, and we shall give no offense by our fear that one of our citizens will turn out to be, so to speak, a "tough egg", whose character will be so "hard boiled" as to resist softening; powerful as our laws are, they may not be able to tame such people, just as heat has no effect on tough beans.'

(εὐδαιμονίαν) and the wicked misery (κακοδαιμονίαν)'; in addition, Plethon is echoing Plato's distinction in the *Laws* between two methods in legislation, compulsion and persuasion (πειθοῖ καὶ βίᾳ).[57] The view that it is impossible to persuade everyone to abstain from greed closely follows Plato's belief that violence necessarily complements persuasion in the case of uneducated masses (ἐπὶ τὸν ἄπειρον παιδείας ὄχλον). Society cannot be remade without force, though, as in the case of Plato's εὐμένεια, force is ideally controlled by reason: 'it is impossible to obtain absent goods otherwise than by desiring and labouring for them; and it is impossible to preserve goods obtained otherwise than by making force obedient to reason'.[58]

One may distinguish between two types of social engineering: piecemeal and utopian. The former concerns small changes aimed to rectify specific deficiencies without radically reforming society; the latter corresponds to the blueprint of a holistic and large-scale social reconstruction.[59] In practice the engineering of Plethon's *politeia* required two things that render the *Memoranda* an excellent candidate for the first modern plan of utopian, rather than piecemeal social engineering. The first is that nothing will be spared for the common good. All means are perfectly justifiable in the light of the end of the common salvation (σωτηρία). The second is that the shift from a corrupted *politeia* to one mirroring the one in the *Memoranda* will succeed only if it takes place all at once without 'compromises and without taking into consideration whether things have appeared differently' to former rulers or even to this ruler in the past. Both points tacitly authorise forcible seizure and exercise of violence. The transition from a moribund empire to a healthy city-state will not be smooth.

If you desire to do what is most just and beneficial for you and for the people (*genos*), then apply yourself to the realisation of what I have suggested without compromises and without taking into consideration whether things have appeared differently to former emperors or princes or even whether you have thought about them differently in the past; do not consider whether you will be unpleasant to some either, but do everything and try everything that seems to be conducive

---

[57] Xen. *Lac.* 9.3; *Laws* 722b–c. Cf. *Resp.* 519e: ξυναρμόττων τοὺς πολίτας πειθοῖ τε καὶ ἀνάγκῃ.

[58] *Mem. I* 130.120–6; 120.14–16; *Laws* 722b.   [59] See Popper (1945) ch. 9.

to the common salvation. For you will do so in the knowledge that sometimes even physicians are obliged not to persist in the diagnoses made by others nor in what they themselves have thought proper, but strive in every way, sparing nothing which may seem useful in the present circumstances, sometimes cutting, sometimes burning and sometimes amputating a hand or foot to save the whole body (ὑπὲρ τῆς τοῦ ὅλου σώματος σωτηρίας). (*Mem. I* 134.17–135.7)

How much Plato is there in Plethon's plans of social reconstruction? And is it the *Republic*, the *Laws*, or both that he has in mind in the *Memoranda*? Like Plethon's 'common guardians' (*Mem. I* 120.12), Plato's Guardians in the *Republic* are the instruments of control employed by a protectionist state. The aim is the establishment of a security-focused society that abolishes corruption caused by consumption culture and the division into social classes in order to merge private life with common interest. But above all, it is Plato's correlation between preservation or σωτηρία, law, secular education and courage in the *Republic* that fertilises Plethon's thought. *Courage* ensures that the right conviction regarding danger will be conserved, a conviction dictated by *law* but mediated by *education*:

'The city is courageous, then, because of a part of itself that has the power to preserve through everything its belief about what things are to be feared, namely, that they are the things and kinds of things that the lawgiver declared to be such in the course of educating it. Or don't you call that courage?'

'I don't completely understand what you mean. Please, say it again.'

'I mean that courage is a kind of preservation.'

'What sort of preservation?'

'That preservation of the belief that has been inculcated by the law through education about what things and sorts of things are to be feared. And by preserving this belief 'through everything', I mean preserving it and not abandoning it because of pains, pleasures, desires, or fears.' (*Resp.* 429b–d; trans. Grube)

The most significant conceptual shift in the *Memoranda* consists in recovering this Platonic sense of the word σωτηρία as preservation of political entities and abandoning Christian *Heilsgeschichte*, which has salvation as redemption at its centre. The Platonic thesis in the *Republic* is that σωτηρία is the work of history and that it depends upon the resuscitation of the best constitution. Plethon opts for Plato's conception of 'what things are to be feared' and assumes the firm – Platonic – belief that the recovery (ἐπανόρθω-σις) of the *politeia* is humanly practicable: any *politeia* can be saved by means of virtue. Σωτηρία does not stand for spiritual salvation but for the preservation of the *polis*. It does not depend upon faith in a personal god and is not accomplished within either Church or monasticism, but through human intellectual and moral discourse deemed capable of acquiring the knowledge of 'the true doctrines': *talethe dogmata*.

It is thus that in Plethon's utopianism converge the epistemological and political variations of philosophical idolatry. The polarisation between Scholarios' and Plethon's notions of salvation, reflecting that between Platonism and Judaeo-Christianity, boils down to the possibility of such a secular and political ideology.

The motto of the first complete edition of the *Memoranda* published by Adolf Ellissen is Plato's famous premise that the way out of evils afflicting city-states is to turn either philosophers into kings or kings into philosophers (*Resp.* 473d).[60] The remark is not without merit if brought into relation with what we know about Manuel II Palaiologos. 'Statesman, soldier, diplomat, administrator, scholar, man of letters, theologian – a person of many talents and interests, excelling in all, Manuel Palaiologos would have been a man of extraordinary interest whenever he might have lived.'[61] Demetrios Kydones informs us that Manuel was a 'philosopher-king' of rare moral constitution and abilities. Manuel philosophised while a king, we read in an anonymous funeral oration drawing on *Republic* 473d, and while philosophising he continued to serve as an excellent general: 'and thus he managed to combine and harmonise these two things, philosophy and kingship'.[62] Plethon saw in Manuel those qualities that Plato looked for in Dionysius of Syracuse – and he asked for the same thing: a radical transformation of society initiated by a most virtuous philosopher-king. Further, he recognised the wise ruler who could manage to achieve something that most of his contemporaries deemed impossible: to resist Turkish invasion. Was Plethon

---

[60] Ellissen (1860) 2.   [61] Barker (1969) xxvii–xxviii.
[62] *Anonymous Funeral Oration on Manuel*, cited in J. Chrysostomides' introduction to his edition of Manuel's *Funeral Oration on his Brother Theodore*, 13 n. 36

losing touch with reality? There is a source pointing to the opposite conclusion.

In his account of Turkish military tactics in 1433, Bertrandon de la Broquière concluded that for all their bravery Turks were not invincible: 'I think I would dare to meet them with half as many, or even fewer, men as they are, as long as there was a strictly-obeyed prince who was willing to listen to the advice of people who know the ways of the Turks. I was told that had Emperor Sigismund listened, when he was fighting them, he would not have had to abandon his fortress.'[63] Plethon understood the ways of the Turks and the motive force behind their remarkable conquests. In Manuel he hoped to find an emperor who, unlike Sigismund, would really listen.

Three paths to salvation: Kydones, Scholarios, Plethon

In 1354 the Ottomans guided by Süleyman Bey had excellent reason to celebrate: they had made their first conquest in Europe. Ironically the name of the conquered city was *Kallipolis* (Gallipoli) – as is Plato's ideal city.

Byzantine intellectuals did not pay much attention to the intruders. They had been for years divided by the Hesychast controversy, soon to be revived, this time with the brothers Prochoros and Demetrios Kydones in the centre. The 'omphalopsychoi' Hesychasts were fully devoted to the pursuit of the Thaborine light and the excommunication of 'pagano-Latin' humanists. Preoccupied with *theoptia*, they did not have much interest in the fall of Kallipolis, even if they were remarkably skilled at making alliances, the most important of which was with John Kantakouzenos, and had successfully infused clerical as well as State institutions with their version of Orthodoxy. In theory Palamas' followers belonged to god, not to affairs of the world – something they put aside only in order to obstruct any possible secular reformation appearing over the horizon.

Upon the fall of Kallipolis, Demetrios Kydones, Plethon's early instructor in Platonic philosophy, wrote a *Memorandum* on the

---

[63] De la Broquière (1988) 146.

recent events. He suggested immediate action. To remain free the Byzantines should take back the city, which was of strategic importance for the defence of Constantinople. Of course, acknowledges Kydones, it is hardly a simple decision whether to go to war or to keep peace at all costs. People opt for one or the other depending on what furthers better their salvation (σωτηρία). Both options have their merits – it all depends on the circumstances. But one should be wary of equivocal uses of the word 'peace'. Moreover, one should not lose sight of *necessity*, the force innate in things (ἡ διὰ τῶν πραγμάτων ἀνάγκη):

> To maintain a form of peace under which we lose everything, this is no different from applying a pleasing word [i.e. *peace*] while suffering the worst of things. Hence, if by keeping silent we shall be able to enjoy what is dear to us, then I do agree with those who advise not to take any action; but if the comeliness of peace is restricted only in words (μέχρι ῥήματος μόνον), while the reality (τὰ ὄντα) proves to be a most difficult war indeed [i.e. in circumstances of nominal peace], then how could you possibly contradict those who urge you to fight, since necessity pushes us to do so even if we are reluctant? (Dem. Kyd. *Oratio de non reddenda Callipoli*, PG 154.1029D–1032A)

To interpret the *Memoranda* one needs to address this dire dilemma which the Byzantines still faced at the beginning of the fifteenth century: should they seek help from the Latins and resist the invasion or open the gates to the Turks? The former option meant the union of the two Churches, an option that clerical authorities and Plethon opposed in the Council of Ferrara/Florence.[64] The union of the Churches would eradicate not only the spiritual hegemony of the Orthodox Church, but also the assumptions behind Plethon's reformism.

For his part Kydones concluded that accepting the dominance of the Latins, though not the most attractive of solutions, was a lesser

---

[64] What if the Roman Orthodox Church had not clashed with the Latin Church and had decided to put Roman-ness above Orthodoxy? The issue remains hotly debated. Against Ahrweiler (1975: 126), who blamed the Byzantine anti-Latin passion for dragging Byzantium to its ruin, van Dieten (1979: 34) wrote the following, which, I think, fully (re)captures the ideology of Scholarios albeit without the Byzantine apocalypticism: 'Die Ablehnung der Kirchenunion war für die Byzantiner nicht nur ein Nein, sondern vor allem ein Ja, ein Ja zum Patroparadoton, zum religiösem Erbgut der Väter. Die Orthodoxie und in ihr das spätbyzantinische Griechentum überlebten, wenn auch sehr regenerationsbedürftig, die osmanische Expansion. Es erscheint fraglich, ob eine in Obödienz latinisierte, d.h. volksfremde Kirche, das erreicht hätte.'

evil than collaborating with the Turks. As a humanist and translator of Aquinas, Kydones believed that the political, philosophical and cultural bonds between Greeks and Latins were more important than the doctrinal rivalry of the Churches and the privileges of the post-Palamite clerical and monastic party in the East. As the main spokesman of unionist policy, Kydones played a major role in the relevant discussions. In 1369/70 Kydones was the man by the emperor's side when the latter personally submitted to Pope Urban V.[65] We may assume that his position remained the same towards the end of his life, when he instructed Plethon in Plato. In a 1366 memorandum entitled Ρωμαίοις συμβουλευτικός, Demetrios Kydones claimed that both Latins and Greeks were ultimately Romans bound by the relation between the empire and its colonies ('their city [Rome] is our metropolis'). Rome remained like a fortress in the West 'and sent us to rule over Asia; hence, one should think of both as a single people (δῆμος), us and them, and both cities [Rome and Constantinople] as one, arranged after the pattern of colony and metropolis'.[66] The Byzantines should reconnect themselves to a common and also ancient Roman identity by turning to the West and revitalising their common historical and cultural ties.[67]

Kydones was one of the first intellectuals to try to wake the Byzantines from their dormant state and make them aware that they were disarmed ideologically and facing their demise. His Ρωμαίοις συμβουλευτικός is a treatise that, like Plethon's later Memoranda, abandons the formula of Orthodox ecumenism. There is a tacit agreement between the two men that it is a grave mistake to turn in hope to Orthodoxy. Neither Kydones nor Plethon thought that any trans-national Orthodox coalition of the people in the Balkan peninsula was more important than ethnicity and political freedom, nor did they ever prepare themselves for that 'Byzantium after Byzantium' which, according to one debatable modern theory, presumably managed to survive under the Ottoman rule.[68]

---

[65] On Kydones and his circle of Latin sympathisers see Angold (2006) 65–9.
[66] Dem. Kyd. *Oratio pro subsidio Latinorum*, *PG* 154.977D.
[67] See here Medvedev (1984) 124.
[68] This is the thesis of Iorga (1935). Thus some maintain that the sultan ultimately sheltered his Roman Orthodox subjects by allowing them to preserve their identity in the

In this memorandum Kydones does not simply turn to his contemporary Latins. He *also* turns to antiquity in search of common ground between East and West. The vehicle of salvation lies neither in the present nor in antiquity *per se*, but in a modern reception of antiquity. Plethon's early mentor devised a political myth involving 'metropolis' and 'colonies' to support this reception. Before long the ensuing political ideology found fervent supporters. Cardinal Bessarion, one of Plethon's two most distinguished students, amply summed up the main point. In his eyes Italy was *quasi alterum Byzantium*.[69] Ironically, the other prodigious student, Mark Eugenikos, came to be the most important Greek Orthodox theologian of his time and *a fortiori* the most interesting opponent of Catholicism and the unionist policy of the Palaiologues.

Plethon went on to devise a political myth of different texture, with Lycurgus' Sparta rather than the metropolis of Rome at its centre. In this case the appeal to pagan antiquity does not serve to uncover any presumably common ground between East and West or to revive a long forgotten common Roman identity but to instigate the secular turn promised in the *Memoranda*. When this endeavour failed, the Plethonean appeal to antiquity remained the same, but its orientation and desideratum changed, shifting from the secularism of the *Memoranda* to the paganism of the *Nomoi*. To both ends the Christian history of Byzantium was totally irrelevant. This explains Plethon's complete silence in regard to the accomplishments of Christian emperors from Justinian to Manuel and his provocative insistence on classical antiquity alone.[70] Like Machiavelli's *Il principe*, Plethon's *Memoranda* apply a conceptual vocabulary that embodies a temporal and secular outlook on history, manifestly sidestepping Christian discourse. The appeal to virtue, political salvation, the recovery of the State, and the common good seek to supersede the Christian sacralised, hence non-historical and non-temporal notion of redemption and sovereignty.

---

framework of a *millet* (self-governing community). For a summary of the main positions see the careful and nuanced account of Bryer (2009) 865.

[69] Bessarion quoted in Irmscher (1994) 190 n. 18.

[70] On Plethon's approach to and interpretations of history see Smarnakis (2007) 105; (2005) 173–81.

Pocock's conjuring up of the 'Machiavellian moment' will help us elucidate this point.

With Machiavelli the republic confronts its temporal finitude in an attempt to 'remain morally and politically stable in a stream of irrational events conceived as essentially destructive of all systems of secular stability'.[71] The Plethonean moment is very similar to this. From where Plethon was standing it was not a republic or commonwealth, but a political community conceived as *genos* that faced its historical extinction and that sought to resist the tide of obscurantism valuing the Thaborine light more than mundane socio-political institutions. Plethon's historical rhetoric, namely his preoccupation with reconnecting the inhabitants of the Peloponnese with the illustrious past of Sparta even at the cost of constructing pseudo-historical accounts, is neither a mere rhetorical vehicle, nor a moralising tale to boost Manuel's and Theodore's confidence. It is an effort to bring to surface a historical consciousness capable of functioning as an antidote to millenarianism and apocalyptism.

Lycurgus and Sparta turned into symbolic parts of a proto-nationalistic, hence temporal, historical and man-made discourse intended to compete with Christian ecumenism.[72] Plethon is making a conceptual shift from one notion of redemption to another. Whereas Scholarios and Palamas conceptualise salvation as transcending history, Plethon intends to revert to the Platonic notion of σωτηρία as realisable within history by means of philosophy and virtue. The term σωτηρία regains its Platonic meaning of preservation and is freed of its Judaeo-Christian sense of spiritual redemption. Though salvation in the *Memoranda* appears defined by exclusively secular categories, the *Nomoi* provide a metaphysical and determinist framework that attributes to σωτηρία cosmic proportions well beyond the realm of individual and political decision-making. The shift from Byzantine to modern Greek identity and from the Christian globalised notion of spiritual identity to that of a nascent nationalism is epitomised in a famous quotation from Plethon's *Memorandum to Manuel*: 'We, whom you

---

[71] Pocock (1975) viii.
[72] On Plethon's Lycurgus and Sparta see Baloglou (2005) 141–8.

lead and over whom you reign, are Greek by descent (*genos*) and both the language and the paideia of our fathers testify to this.'[73] Manuel does not reign over Romans anymore, then; he reigns over Greeks.[74] Peritore has shown that the *Memoranda* 'demonstrate an early and visionary appreciation of the precondition of nationalism and national mobilisation' and observes that

his [Plethon's] nationalism, although quite modern in its denomination of the Hellenes as a genos united by language, ancestral culture, and common territory, is clearly a political myth designed to unify the court elites with the military, commercial and producing classes and to neutralize both Christian ideology, at once quietistic and divisive, and the 'feudalism' of the unruly landlords.[75]

Scholarios' call to welcome the Turks as divine agents may well appear as an option more expedient and pragmatist than those presented by Kydones and Plethon, owing to the fact that the empire was crumbling and on the verge of destruction. This said, Scholarios' primary motive force was not *Realpolitik*. The memory of the Latin occupation of Constantinople in 1204 still nourished a strong sentiment of anti-Latinism among the Byzantines that combined with Turco-Byzantine cultural exchanges in forming that powerful 'Turcophile' sentiment famously captured in Loukas Notaras' notorious cry that it is preferable to see in Contantinople the Turkish turban than the pontifical mitre.[76]

At one with the post-Palamite religious establishment, Scholarios speculated that the Orthodox Church would not survive under Latin domination whereas it might under Ottoman rule retain privileges and protect its interests. To a large extent this proved to be the case. A modern Orthodox theologian sympathetic to Orthodox hardliners such as Palamas and Mark Eugenikos put it thus: between a 'right disaster' and a 'false salvation', the anti-unionist

---

[73] *Mem. II* 247.14–15: Ἐσμὲν γὰρ οὖν ὧν ἡγεῖσθέ τε καὶ βασιλεύετε Ἕλληνες τὸ γένος, ὡς ἥ τε φωνὴ καὶ ἡ πάτριος παιδεία μαρτυρεῖ. On Plethon's notion of Hellenic identity see Bargeliotes (1974) 142. The Byzantines had already begun to designate themselves as *Hellenes* from the thirteenth century, a process coinciding with the rapid reduction of the territories of the Eastern Roman Empire and the collateral weakening of imperial identity and Byzantine self-consciousness. On Hellenic identity in this context see Kaldellis (2007a) and Harris (2000) 25–44.

[74] Vryonis (1991) 5–14.   [75] Peritore (1977) 172, 190. Cf. Neri (2010) 57.

[76] See here Balivet (2002) 526.

Byzantines chose the former.[77] Here the words *right* and *wrong* do not carry political or diplomatic weight but are primarily theological and existential in application. More than one transient worldview among others, Orthodoxy for Palamas and Mark Eugenikos stood for the right trope, existential position or mode of being (ὁ τρόπος τῆς ὑπάρξεως), one allegedly reflecting the right (Orthodox) understanding of the Trinitarian 'mode of being'. For these men Orthodoxy was more important than political community; religious, political and national identities were irrelevant outside the Orthodox way to be.

One finds a neat depiction of the situation and Scholarios' role in Doukas' account of the last efforts of the emperor to obtain help from the Latins in 1452, the year of Plethon's death. In the last days before the fall of the City, Constantine and 'several representatives of the Church assented to the union'. But 'the greater portion of the sacerdotal and monastic orders, abbots, archimandrites, nuns . . . not one among them assented to the union. Even the emperor only pretended to do so.' Then members of the antiunionist party,

coming to the cell of Gennadius, the former George Scholarios, in the Monastery of the Pantokrator, said to him 'And what shall we do?' He was in seclusion, but he took paper and set down his opinion in writing, thus making his counsel known. His message read as follows: 'Wretched Romans, how you have been deceived! Trusting in the might of the Franks you have removed yourselves from the hope of god. Together with the City which will soon be destroyed, you have lost your piety. Be Thou merciful to me, O Lord. I give witness before Thee that I am innocent of this offence. *You wretched citizens, have you any idea what you are doing? Captivity is about to befall you because you have lost the piety handed down to you by your fathers and you have confessed your impiety. Woe unto you in the judgement!*' Writing this and much more and nailing the document to the door of his cell, he shut himself in; and it was read. (Doukas, *Historia* 36.3; trans. Magoulias with modifications)[78]

Wretched citizens renders Scholarios' ἄθλιοι πολῖται. Roman citizenship had always been something to be proud of. Here it is

[77] Yannaras (1992) 76 (the English translation, p. 47, puts it more mildly by leaving out one word: 'They chose destruction rather than a false salvation').

[78] According to Doukas, *Hist.* 36.4, 'then those nuns, who considered themselves to be pure and dedicated to God in Orthodoxy, with common resolve and in accord with their teacher Gennadios, and with the abbots and the confessors and the remaining priests and laymen, cried aloud the anathema'.

declared morally and politically bankrupt. Judgement day is nigh and political institutions are of no use. The Byzantines betrayed Orthodoxy by considering union with the Latins. The Turkish conquest will come about by divine will as the penalty to be paid here on earth. Yet for Scholarios this hardly meant that Byzantines were really divested of hope. He went on to hail the superiority of a spiritual Christian identity irrelevant to mundane, political and historical conditions. If one aims to win the 'eternal home country' (ἡ ἀΐδιος πατρίς), he says, one should not shed many tears for the passions of a mundane sojourn (παροικία).[79] Plethon was spared the sight of Scholarios becoming patriarch under Turkish rule.

To a large extent the clash between Scholarios and Plethon comes down to conflicting estimations as to what is to be done with this *paroikia*, with the remnants of the Byzantine Empire, and, at a deeper level, with man's temporal existence as a whole. Scholarios sees in the attachment of his contemporaries to the Byzantine *paroikia* a potential obstacle to the quest for a quasi-Augustinean *civitas dei*; Plethon sees in it man's natural urge and capacity to realise the ideal state (σπουδαιοτάτη πολιτεία) sketched in the *Memoranda*. Scholarios invests hope in religious ecumenism and looks for his *patris* beyond temporality and history; Plethon identifies his home country with a modern nation-state that turns to history, mythology and paganism in order to construct its identity and self-consciousness. Like Scholarios and Kydones, Plethon abandoned Byzantine notions of Roman identity. He did so in order to mastermind a novel identity that is, at once, an ancient one: a Hellenic one. Paradoxically then, the first modern utopianist does not consider the past as an obstacle to reshaping human society, as communist utopianism did. On the contrary, Plethon seems to suggest that the real obstacle in pursuing the end of perfectibility is not the past, but the suppression of true knowledge regarding the intellectual ideal-type of this past. Scholarios' rage against Plethon's political utopianism stems from these radical discrepancies. There is a single perfect law, he says, addressing an imaginary Plethon, and only one *politeia* that is really the best of

---

[79] Schol. *Precationes diversae*, OC 4.355.28–30: Εἰ μέλλοιμεν τῆς πατρίδος ἐπιτυγχάνειν τῆς ἀϊδίου, οὐδὲν ἡμᾶς λυπήσει τὰ πάθη τῆς παροικίας.

all – you apostasise from the law and the heavenly *politeia* (σὺ δὲ αὐτῶν ἀποστάς) and on top of that you dare play the role of the lawgiver?[80]

Like Kydones and Plethon, Scholarios offered a competing alternative to the dying Roman identity of the Byzantines. Constantinople ceases to be a home country as one comes closer and closer to the eternal city of god. It is downgraded (or upgraded, depending on one's viewpoint) to a transit station possessing some symbolic or spiritual significance and able to survive even without national and political autonomy. Or is it rather the case that, in order for this path to eternity to surface, Byzantium as a political παροικία needs to pass away in the same sense that for Marx bourgeois society needs to be abolished for a socialist society to emerge? In any case, Constantinople was now seen as the capital of Orthodoxy, not of an empire.

Palamas would nod approvingly. An empire is not worth much in comparison with a spiritual home country which, once found, can neither be conquered nor compromised. Thus apostasy from this endeavour to reach the ἀΐδιος πατρίς is a graver crime than any other type of apostasy within a terrestrial polity. Regardless of issues of political expediency, Scholarios was popularising and emulating the Hesychast spiritual utopia, Palamas' conviction that salvation lies beyond human political constructions. The Hesychasts and Scholarios belong to a community without national ideology or geographical borders. In both cases spiritual identity eliminates national identity. Their *genos* is not Hellenic; it is Orthodox. The homeland of this Orthodox *genos* is invulnerable as long as Church and monasticism survive. This Christian utopia was not threatened by the Ottoman rule, for it was able to adapt to political authorities and function on a parallel rather than a confrontational level. Ottoman rule was an ideal host.

The majority of the population, including its religious leadership, was more keen, albeit for different reasons, to find refuge in old apocalyptic scenarios. The year 7000 after the creation of the world was traditionally regarded as the date the world would come

---

[80] Cf. Schol. *Ad exarchum Josephum*, OC 4.160.33–5; *Ad principessam Peloponnesi*, OC 4.153.16–17.

to an end.[81] Moreover, Byzantine Judaism represented by Graeco-phone (*Romaniotes*), Arabo-phone and Turco-phone Jews transmitted a fusion of apocalyptic and messianic traditions regarding the fall of Constantinople, the clash between Islam and Christianity and the end of time.[82] None other than Manuel II, Plethon's and Kydones' ideal Platonic philosopher-king, appears to have taken prophecies quite seriously, at least according to Athonite sources. In 1394 he purportedly enquired of a holy man whether the 'seventh age' would signal the end of the world, or time would be renewed.[83]

More often than not debates concerned the question whether one could know the precise date of the apocalypse, rather than whether the apocalypse was really about to take place. Plethon's contemporary, Joseph Bryennios, a native of Mistra and powerful figure in the Palaiologean circles announced the coming of the end of the world in front of the emperor. That the *synteleia* 'is nigh and just at the gates (ἐπὶ θύραις)' can be deduced from Christ's sayings but also 'from the nature of things (ἡ φύσις τῶν πραγμάτων)', he said. Just as a dying body (σῶμα ψυχορραγοῦν) suffers severe blows before its death, so the ecumene is afflicted by 'a thousand evils everywhere (τὰ μυρία παντοῦ διέσπαρται κακά)'.[84] A bizarre occult exposition involving the seven parts of the world, the seven key planets, the seven key metals, the seven key flowers, the seven outer parts of the human body, the seven inner parts of the body, the number seven in ecclesiastical life and so forth, leaves little doubt that the end of the seventh aeon coincides with the consummation of the world (συντέλεια).[85] One should await the *Endzeit* full of anticipation rather than with dread or anxiety: this will mark the end of a decadent and lamentable world, the passage from sin and corruption to immortality.[86]

---

[81] For those counting by *anno mundi* and taking as their starting point 1 September 5508 BCE it was transparently clear that (a) the world was made in six days, and (b) one day of the Lord corresponds to one thousand years (2 Peter 3:8; Ps. 89:4), hence the world will come to an end either around 500CE (for those writing before that date, like Irenaeus) or, according to an interpretation counting the seventh day, around 7000, namely 1500 CE. See here Congourdeau (1999) 55–97. Cf. Rigo (1992) 162–83 and Bryer (2009) 852.

[82] Gardette (2007b) 87–107, here: 88.   [83] Congourdeau (1999) 63.

[84] Bryennios, *On the End of the World (Λόγος Α' Περὶ συντελείας)* 1.191 Boulgaris.

[85] Bryennios, *On the End of the World* 1.192–201.

[86] Bryennios, *On the End of the World* 2.216–17.

Bryennios was no typical fatalist. In his view the graver the socio-political situation, the more crucial it is to prostrate oneself before god, repent and build a proper Christian profile useful on Judgement day. Filled with religious zeal, anxiety and worry, Bryennios sees in the coming end an *ultimatum* to submit oneself to divine authority by conforming to Christian ethics and exemplifying the piety necessary to obtain the ticket to individual salvation. Even so late in the day, he urges his flock to 'go after good deeds while you have feet; fill your eyes with tears while you have eyes, before they are covered with dirt; do good while you have hands . . . stand up, take action, hurry; my soul, let's prepare ourselves; the time to exit has come'.[87] Carrier of precisely this eschatological and apocalyptical tradition, Scholarios wrote a Χρονογραφία with the professed aim of calculating the precise date coinciding with the completion of 7,000 years of creation. He comes up with two alternative dates, 1 September 1492 or 1513. He opts for the former. As Congourdeau notes, Scholarios' death around 1472 prevented him from knowing, at least in this world, whether his mathematical calculations were correct.[88]

The Byzantine 'imperial eschatology' (*Reichseschatologie*) represented by Scholarios relies upon the Jewish Hellenistic view of kingship according to which a nation's fate is concordant with its religious piety.[89] We may recall here Scholarios' request to god to put an end 'as he thinks fit' to a Peloponnese sunk in paganism and redeem those few Christians left there suffering.[90] Like the Jews in the Old Testament, Palamas, Scholarios and Bryennios believed that piety guaranteed prosperity. Hence, occupation by foreign people is punishment for their loss of piety. It is thus that the end of the empire is equated with the end of the world, though Scholarios, after becoming patriarch under Turkish rule, was quick to distinguish between the two ends: apparently now there was, after all, time to repent and save the world.[91]

---

[87] Bryennios, *On the End of the World* 2.226; cf. Congourdeau (1999) 67.
[88] Congourdeau (1999) 70–3; cf. Bryer (2009) 852. The text of *Chronography* (Schol., *OC* 4.504–12) is corrected by Congourdeau (1999) 74–95.
[89] Podskalsky (1975) 79.   [90] See above, p. 151.
[91] But see van Dieten (1979: 26–9), who notes, that 'ein Einfluss dieser eschatologischen Ideen auf politische oder militärische Entscheidungen lässt sich nicht nachweisen'.

Even Hellenic astrology is appropriate to confirm the Byzantine apocalyptical tradition regarding the year 7000, and in this odd context Plethon's name pops up again. Today, thinks Scholarios, only a handful of degenerate Hellenes may possibly reinvigorate Plethon's fallacies, misled by the allure surrounding Plethon's reputation as a philosopher. But the astrological works of 'Hellenists that are more ancient' (παλαιότεροι Ἑλληνισταί) confirm that the consummation of everything is close.[92] This passage recalls Bryennios' καιρὸς ἐξόδου yet comes from a work compiled more than ten years after the fall of Constantinople, the *Refutatio erroris Judaeorum* (*c.* 1464). It testifies to the apocalyptic understanding of Scholarios' notion of καιρός, here significantly seen as potentially clashing with that of any 'Hellenists' still carrying on Plethon's legacy.

The Neoplatonic doctrine of an eternally generated world laid out in the *Nomoi* implies a perception of time as perpetual duration fiercely opposed to the Orthodox apocalyptical and eschatological understanding of history. Neoplatonic cosmology challenges Christian messianism and has important political consequences. Plethon's faith in a self-preserving nation-state countered Scholarios' welcome of the collapse of that empire as a fulfilment of divine will, as well as Christian scenarios regarding the imminent end of time.

In Scholarios *kairos* signifies the anticipated consummation of the world (προσδοκωμένην ἀλλοίωσιν).[93] In a pagan context the word has different associations. In Neoplatonist theurgy *kairos* coincided with the astrologically proper and favourable moment for performing hieratic rites that sought to exploit sympathetic interrelations between cosmos and the divine.[94] The *Memoranda* manifest the political significance of *kairos* as the opportune *momentum* to craft a new ideological, philosophical and political paradigm. The talk of the *present* (τὸ παρόν) towards the

---

[92] Schol. *Ref. erroris Judaeor. OC* 3.287.2–8: ἀλλὰ συγγράμμασι παλαιοτέρων Ἑλλ-ηνιστῶν ἐνετύχομεν εἰς ἀστρολογίαν ἀναγομένοις, ἐν οἷς ἔγγιστα τὴν τοιαύτην ἀλλοίωσιν ὁρίζονται καὶ αὐτοί.

[93] Schol. *Ref. erroris Judaeor. OC* 3.286.36–287.2.

[94] See for example Iamb. *Myst.* 267.12; Procl., *De sacrificia et magia* 149.5–9 Bidez: ὁ καιρὸς πρέπων.

end of the *Memorandum to Manuel* epitomises two aspects of Plethon's understanding of time (*kairos*). Manuel should not allow any longer for the perpetuation of 'the present state of things' (τὰ παρόντα): things are in a 'wretched and faulty' condition. And again: things cannot remain in their present state (τὸ παρὸν σχῆμα) 'without great danger and harm'.[95]

This is the Plethonean *kairos* or *momentum*: a moment in which a whole political and intellectual universe with its scale of values, tradition and history oscillates between existence and non-existence gazing at its demise and finitude, though still capable of ensuring its continuation through immediate reform. *Power is a near neighbour to necessity*, one reads in the *Golden Verses*, a piece Plethon had studied. His advice to political authorities stems from exactly this principle. In Plethon the word *kairos* does not merely convey the feeling of urgency but primarily refers to that auspicious opening for taking action. Manuel and Theodore were running out of time.

Ellissen suggested that Plethon's 'alarming frankness' with regard to monasticism may have provided an even worse service to his reformative aims than did his extravagant measures.[96] Plethon's radicalism may have compromised any chance for even a moderate reform. Just as his Platonism was too radical for the Italian humanists, who preferred the theory of a presumed *symphonia* between Plato and Aristotle, so his secularism in the *Memoranda* was too radical for the political authorities of Mistra. But Plethon's political extremism was not purely idiosyncratic. It was the product of pragmatic considerations.

Contrary to appearances, Plethon was not building a castle on sand. Nor was he a voice in the desert.

The secular turn

Plethon's reformism in the light of Nicolas Kabasilas' Discourse concerning Illegal Acts

Nicolas Kabasilas' 'Anti-Zealot' discourse is an invaluable source that testifies to large-scale attempts at the secularisation of the

---

[95] *Mem. II* 264.19–265.4.   [96] Ellissen (1860) 25–6.

State towards the end of the fourteenth century. The full title of Kabasilas' treatise is *Discourse concerning Illegal Acts of Officials Daringly Committed against Things Sacred* and it has been dated to *post* 1371.[97] The circumstances of the treatise are mysterious. Kabasilas was a prominent theologian of aristocratic origin who reported and inveighed against extensive plans for a radical socio-political reform.[98] In the past these plans have been associated with the revolt of the notorious anarcho-socialist 'Zealots' in Thessaloniki, of which Plethon surely must have heard, possibly through Kydones.[99] Kabasilas does not name the initiators and prefers to refer to them in abstract and legal terms, which may suggest

[97] See Ševčenko (1957), (1962); Barker (2003); Matschke and Tinnefeld (2001) 355.

[98] On Kabasilas see *HAB* 442–53 (Bibliogr.); Spiteris and Conticello (2002) 315–89; 389–95 (Bibliogr.).

[99] On the Zealots of Thessaloniki see Barker (2003); *ODB* III s.v. 'Zealots.' The editor of the *Discourse*, Ihor Ševčenko, argued that nothing in Kabasilas' treatise points to a specific Zealot programme. Following the example of the 1340 rebellion in Adrianople, the Zealots, a political party in Thessaloniki mainly representing impoverished social strata, took over the city and from 1342 to 1350 established a revolutionary regime of sheer licence that apparently performed atrocities and bloodbaths in order to achieve its reformist goals. 'The polity they sought to establish could not be regarded as an imitation of any other form', says Gregoras: it was not aristocratic, nor democratic, nor 'a modern and mixed type, composed of two or more constitutions.' The only name that seems appropriate to describe it, Gregoras continues, is *ochlokratia*: mob government. Demetrios Kydones and his family are one example of aristocrats forced by the new circumstances to abandon their properties and leave the city; others were massacred. For eight years the Zealots successfully kept Kantakouzenos out of Thessaloniki – as they also kept out Gregory Palamas. Sathas was the first to see in Zealots neither a reign of Terror nor a plundering and rabid mob, but freedom fighters and democratic patriots. Marxist historians discovered a popular movement that attempted to save Byzantium by means of communal reform. The evidence for this claim mainly comes from Kabasilas' *Discourse*, a fact that explains why Ševčenko's dissociation of this text from the Zealots stirred up a hornet's nest. As Ševčenko notes, according to a rival scholar 'my erroneous thesis followed the method of some of my American colleagues who attempt to minimize those movements in the life of mankind where the masses take destiny into their own hands and thereby inscribe glorious pages into the book of history' (Ševčenko, 1962: 404). However, it would be odd, to say the least, to argue that the anti-Palamite party did not sympathise with the efforts of the Zealots to keep Palamas out of the city. Moreover, a link must be assumed if we are to explain the political agenda of the Zealots: without support from intellectual circles it is inexplicable how a mob of rabid beggars managed to seize power for eight years, identify as its fatal enemies the Hesychasts and the ruling class and then present an agenda that somehow combined anti-monasticism with a programme for the redistribution of property. Plethon would hardly have any sympathy for anarcho-socialist upheavals of the Zealots' sort. As for Gregoras and, significantly, Kydones, their elitist humanism did not put any faith in popular movements. Social reform, we infer from the *Memoranda*, is from above, not below: it is a philosopher-king already at the top of the social pyramid that is urgently needed, not a revolting *demos*.

that he was still within their reach. Most probably Kabasilas' anonymous lay adversaries moved within circles of governmental officials close to Manuel II. Taking advantage of what appears to have been a breach in the influence exercised by the monastic party, these circles exerted considerable pressure in favour of social reform, the immediate recruitment of soldiers, the seizure of monastic property and its transfer to government-controlled landownership in order to meet immediate defence needs.

Most significantly, these unnamed lay adversaries of the clerical and monastic establishment justified their programme by openly announcing the spiritual and political death of Christianity:

> For there are some people who bring as an excuse [for their secularisation measures] the argument that in our times (τὸν καιρὸν ἤδη) God's laws have expired; that there were times when they were sovereign, but they are no longer. And that, it seems, just as the Saviour put an end to the old law by replacing it with his more superior law, so now it is their turn to substitute their laws for his. (Kabasilas, *Discourse* 31.1–4)

'Evil is so widespread', these anonymous reformers said, 'and virtue so scarce', that there can hardly be any doubt the time is ripe for the abolition of Christianity.[100] At the same time as Bryennios and Scholarios were interpreting the collapse of their world as a sign of the coming apocalypse, others saw in it a call to abandon a moribund religion and establish new *laws*. As in Plethon's *Memoranda*, the word *kairos* in the argument of Kabasilas' laymen signifies an opportune moment for radical change.

Kabasilas was witnessing the emergence of the modern conception of history according to which religion is not a question of revelation, but the product of social circumstances. His opponents appear persuaded that Christianity triumphed because of the exhaustion of previous intellectual and spiritual resources, not because it is the only true religion. By analogy, the late Byzantine circumstances called for the separation of legal and moral conduct from a moribund Christian world-view that was driving the empire to its demise.

This is a peculiarly modern conception of history able to distinguish keenly between the nascence and decay of historical circles.

---

[100] Kabasilas, *Discourse* 31.8–11.

The inference is that each circle requires appropriate *laws*. The *Nomoi* is a late reply to this call for a new set of laws based upon the diagnosis of a profound failure of Christianity that expressly links Kabasilas' secular interlocutors to Plethon. Intermediate between the plans reported by Kabasilas and the *Nomoi*, the quest for the *spoudaiotate politeia* in the *Memoranda* is another offspring of the selfsame conviction, albeit one investing hope in secularism rather than paganism. In any case, the real driving force behind Plethon's sibylline statement reported by George of Trebizond, according to which a new religion would be substituted for Christianity and Islam in the near future, was the pre-existing conviction that a new religious and intellectual paradigm or set of *laws* was about to surface.

For Kabasilas all legal issues were bound into Christian revelation. The wish to dissolve God's laws is a symptom of folly and excessive boldness.[101] Scholarios, we have seen, made the same point when contending that there is a single true law and *politeia*. This is not to say that Kabasilas held that everything was perfect. No skilled Christian rhetor of his quality would commit this error. His point is that the worse a disease, the more drastic the necessary cure, a principle with which both his interlocutors and Plethon might have agreed. But undoubtedly moral decadence was even worse in apostolic times when Christianity triumphed. It follows that it would be a grave mistake if people abandoned a cure that has already proven its efficacy.[102] This is a clear warning. It is aimed at those considering abandonment of an allegedly degenerated Orthodoxy and embarking on intellectual journeys in search of new laws or even religious reformism of the type that Prochoros Kydones was asking for at more or less the same time.[103]

The controversy between Kabasilas and his opponents is largely one regarding the competition between the state and the Church. After the defeat of the Serbs in the battle of Maritsa by the tactically superior Turkish forces (1371) the Byzantines authorised

---

[101] Kabasilas, *Discourse* 30.40–5. [102] Kabasilas, *Discourse* 31.11–24.
[103] We have seen (Ch. 4, p. 210) that without openly doubting Christianity, Prochoros Kydones was pointing to Palamite Orthodoxy as the curse (ἀρά) that ruined Byzantium and asked for a reform according to the 'only tool that is left to us', syllogistic philosophy.

the seizure of monastic properties. These were made into land grants (*pronoiai*) in order to meet defence needs.[104] Manuel later apologetically restored parts of these monastic properties (in 1408 and 1414/15), but these concessions hardly mean that discussions regarding the secularisation of monastic properties were brought to a halt.

What is particularly pertinent to the present investigation is the evidence confirming continuous attempts to urge the emperor to lay hands on Church property as late as 1383 or early 1384, much later than the revolt of the Zealots.[105] The State and even local magistrates proceeded to the alienation of monastic lands well into the eve of the fifteenth century in order to reward military nobility (the 'Soldiers' or *pronoiarioi*) with land (*pronoiai*). According to a law put into effect after 1371 and valid as late as 1420, the peasants cultivating monastic property were to pay seigniorial rent in the form of tax to the 'Soldiers'. The fact that around 1420 the monasteries appear to be in a situation much more lamentable than that of 1408 owing to the need to fund the *pronoiarioi* makes sufficiently clear, as Ostrogorsky notes, why the monasteries at the Holy Mountain were so eager to reconcile with the Turks. The latter guaranteed their internal autonomy and financial security and annihilated the armed aristocracy of the Byzantines.[106] We may add that the Turks also guaranteed to deliver Orthodoxy from secular projects such as those attacked in Kabasilas' *Discourse* and advanced in Plethon's *Memoranda*.

Not long before Plethon's *Memoranda* the anonymous officials in Kabasilas' *Discourse* raised the issue of the mismanagement of monastic and clerical property. The monks, they said, possess land that is not put to proper use. This has to be confiscated for the common good, in order to build walls, equip soldiers, build ships, feed the poor and support priests. The parallels with Plethon's *Memoranda* are intriguing. Like Plethon, these intellectual laymen pointed out that monastic ideology does not presuppose wealth; that the monks need protection from external threats too; that donations to monasteries should be controlled by the State; that

---

[104] Ostrogorsky (1954) 161.
[105] The evidence has been collected by Ševčenko (1962) 405–6.
[106] Ostrogorsky (1954) 172–3.

ecclesiastics should be separated from the monastic party; and that monks should be left to survive with only what is absolutely necessary. It is proper, they said, that whoever does not contribute to national safety should provide for those who do. The civil authorities have every right to intervene and put to good use property that is mismanaged. The relation of officials to their subjects, we read, is analogous to that of guardians to immature children. The former have the right to decide what is beneficial to their subjects, including the confiscation of mismanaged properties:

If, furthermore, these revenues are used to equip soldiers, who are going to die in defence of the sanctuaries, the laws, and the walls, is not that better than if the same revenues were used by the monks whose material needs are slight? The monks, more than anyone else, stand to benefit from the security of laws and walls; it is, therefore, proper that the monks should feed the soldiers, just as servants, peasants, bakers, and builders are fed by means provided by sacred property. (Kabasilas, *Discourse* 6.20–32; summary in Ševčenko 1957: 127).

Associated with or even operating from within the central imperial government, the men who argued thus, whether identifiable with consultants of Manuel II or not, present us with a consistent attempt at secularisation of which the measures in Plethon's *Memoranda* are a radicalisation. What is more, Kabasilas' legalistic counter-argumentation in defence of monastic and private property shows the obstacles that social reformism had to overcome and the type of opposition it encountered. Kabasilas developed a passionate advocacy of the inalienable right to private property that is summarised as follows:

The right of the authorities to supervise and dispose of a subject's property does not extend to private, but only to common property. Not even the emperor can ask for an account in case of wanton destruction of private property by its owner. No law is in existence which would enjoin the purposeful disposition of private property. It is considered by law as unconditionally held and inviolable. It follows that infringing upon the right of private property amounts to breaking the law . . . An official's right to interfere does not cover private property. It would be absurd to infer the official's right to that property from his function as a judge. (Kabasilas, *Discourse* 10.1–19; 14.11–18; summary in Ševčenko 1957: 128)

Kabasilas' point is tantamount to a man's reserving a seat in the theatre and obstructing others' access to it even if he is not going to attend the show. According to Aquinas, this man sins in so

364

far as he 'unreasonably prevents others from using the seat'.[107]
Plethon does not see in this man a sinner but an internal enemy
of the *politeia*. Kabasilas replies that, legally speaking, the man
is not obliged to be reasonable. He may do as he wishes with
the seat he has secured. Here Kabasilas appears more consistent
than Aquinas and Palamas. In his *Homilies* Palamas advocated a
Christian version of the Stoicising notion of natural law close to
that of earlier Christian intellectuals. In practice it is not property
owning as such, but its illicit seizure that goes against nature.[108] In
theory, natural resources like land and water and raw materials are
common property. Theologically speaking, everything is common
to all, because everything belongs to god. This said, humans are
the appointed managers of these treasures. Though god is the original proprietor of everything, the actual administration of property
is a question of human convention and legislation – a question of
politics, not theological or spiritual discourse. With such an appeal
to the spiritual character of his Church, Palamas could safely claim
at once that 'treasures are common to all as deriving from a common depository, namely god's creation'[109] while siding with the
usurper Kantakouzenos against the redistribution of land forcibly
seized by the Zealots of Thessaloniki. Understandably the former
was deemed a more suitable manager of god's property than the
latter.

In his *Homilies* Palamas does not inveigh against particular
social or political strata. The fault and error is always collective,
a 'common sin', which poor and rich alike are given to carry.[110]
The archontes of Morea are as guilty as is the exhausted peasantry.
Palamas is concerned with helping man to win the 'internal' or
'intellectual war' against sin and temptation, not with wars regarding external circumstances – which, we are given to understand,
are of a lesser significance.[111] As Byzantium was falling apart and
the Turks ascended to dominion, this deliberate focus on spiritual salvation sharply contrasts with Plethon's programme for the

[107] Garnsey (2007) 132.
[108] See Garnsey (2007) 127–8, 132 on Ambrose, and Aquinas.
[109] Gr. Pal. *Hom.* 13.10.12–13: κοινὰ γὰρ ἐκ κοινῶν ταμείων τῶν τοῦ Θεοῦ κτισμάτων
τὰ θησαυρίσματα.
[110] Gr. Pal. *Hom.* 1.6.   [111] Gr. Pal. *Hom.* 23.12.8–21

common preservation (κοινὴ σωτηρία) and recovery of σπουδαία πολιτεία that depends upon social, economic and religious reform.

Kabasilas assumed a legalistic stance when dealing with donations to monasteries too. Proprietors have the right to allow people administering their property to do so badly, if they so wish. No law controls the use of either property or donations. It follows that monks may manage their properties independently of what officials and advisors deem beneficial to the State. This argument counters Plethon's objection regarding monastic properties that remained in an idle state mismanaged and uncultivated. In this regard a slightly ironic observation by Kabasilas gains unexpected significance. The only way to change the current situation, he says, is to change the *law*:

> As it stands, the law prosecutes various kinds of thieves solely on the grounds that they take property unjustly. It does not ask the criminals whether they have put the stolen goods to proper use. *Should the 'good use' argument prevail, the laws would have to be revised and be made to concern themselves with the use of a thing, not the mode of its acquisition.* But then criminals would always be able to point to poor people whom they had provided with clothes and food, to churches which they had adorned, to lights which they had lit there, even to their contributions to the public treasury, *to the erection of walls*, and so forth. (Kabasilas, *Discourse* 20.1–19; summary in Ševčenko 1957: 130).

Mutatis mutandis the suggested seizure of private property for military ends would lead to a totalitarian form of government that is legally condemnable and financially a disaster. Kabasilas' point is summarised thus:

> If no one is free to dispose of his possessions, if officials wield unlimited power and the mere mention of the word State (τὸ κοινόν) brings fear of loss of private property, who will be interested in earning money, who will exercise any trade, profession or military art, knowing that all his earnings will go to others? From what source will taxes then be levied? That is why good officials have always striven to provide their subjects with liberty and internal security within the framework of justice. It is certainly unreasonable that those whose duty it is to prevent injustice and violence should acquire military strength by inflicting injustice and violence upon their subjects. (Kabasilas, *Discourse* 26.8–23; summary in Ševčenko 1957: 132)

This advocacy of a liberal economy coming from a mystic shows that the Hesychasts were not wholly devoted to their psychophysical techniques of prayer, but were able to appreciate the merits of *laissez-faire* strategies, especially when it came down to finding ways to protect their privileges. To this end, Kabasilas predictably advances arguments of a more 'spiritual' nature too. God preserves cities to which he is well disposed and destroys those which arouse his anger. By implication, a tax grudgingly paid would condemn the taxpayer's soul, which is much more important than the body.[112] Meaning: first save your soul, and then, if at all, the State. No ship, soldier or weapon is useful to a city, unless it has been acquired according to law; otherwise, this acquisition will bring harm to its users. The end does not sanction the means. Further: 'to be a ruler over one's compatriots is not an excuse for opposing god himself, and for removing him from the realm of human affairs'. This is a clear warning against any attempt to revise the conventional framework of existing 'mirrors for princes' according to which preservation of sovereignty relies upon the will of god, not the interest of the people. This is the theory that Demetrios Kydones and subsequently Plethon subverted. As they saw it, it does not take piety but virtue and excellence to truly make a ruler great.[113]

Kabasilas' main argument was that the secularisation of monastic property and state control of its management is legally unfounded; further, that it had to remain so, for a shift from a legal system that focuses on the mode of acquisition to one that puts first the use of that thing leads to logical fallacies. Anyone guilty of a crime could then argue that his cause was a 'good' one: 'even grave robbers would claim that they had fed their children and thus saved a household for the State'. Once the theoretical option of changing the legal system is ruled out, we are left with pragmatic considerations: how to conform with the existing law that protects private property, even if this means that defence needs of the State cannot be met.

The *Discourse* paves the way for Plethon's *Memoranda* by showing why imperial secularisation measures could not be consistently and efficiently applied without a groundbreaking reform instigated by a determined philosopher-king. Plethon was certainly

---

[112] *Discourse* 53.4–12; cf. Ševčenko (1957) 149.   [113] See below, pp. 369–74.

aware that any large-scale attempt to sustain an army by seizing private property would meet resistance based on legal arguments of the above type. Further, as a courtier and consultant within the imperial circles around Manuel II, Plethon was certainly aware of and possibly witnessed the failure of large-scale governmental secularisation plans described by Kabasilas. Whereas the latter was all too confident that such a reform was legally speaking absurd, for 'the laws would have to be revised and be made to concern themselves with the use of a thing, not the mode of its acquisition', Plethon argued that this shift was possible as part of a total regeneration of society affecting moral, political, military, religious and by default all legal parameters of social life. A tenet of the *Memoranda* is that in a just polity the use of land and production should condition ownership rather than vice versa.

Contrary to Kabasilas, Plethon believed that the *Zeitgeist* was not moving towards the abandonment of secularisation plans, but rather towards their radicalisation and intensification. And contrary to Scholarios, he did not consider occasional pagan-secular departures from Orthodoxy as signs of the coming end of the world, but as failed attempts to uncover the only escape route from an imminent destruction. Instead of considering confiscation of mismanaged monastic property against existing legislation, Plethon advises political authorities to pursue the change of all parameters of social life that rendered such legislation meaningful in the first place.

Kabasilas perceptively argued that secularisation measures justified by military necessity upset the established order. The same accusation of attempting to 'move the establishment' was addressed against Kydones, and Scholarios warned that 'this is not the time' to try new things.[114] In the *Memorandum to Manuel* this objection of advising 'views outside the established order (ἔξω τῶν καθεστηκότων γνῶμαι)' is unabashedly and unapologetically admitted. For the first time a late Byzantine intellectual daringly and openly asked for a complete, uncompromising and radical shift of the established order of things, rather than for its preservation at all costs, as Kabasilas and Scholarios

---

[114] See above, Ch. 2, p. 112.

did. The redistribution of property and the maximisation of production naturally follow from the rise of a new order of things that heralds the arrival of *spoudaiotate politeia*, the perfectly just polity. The catalyst to this process is the ruler's determination and wisdom.

Plethon and Kydones on sovereignty

Assuming that it was too late to save Kallipolis in 1354, as Demetrios Kydones found out when failing to arouse the awareness of his contemporaries with his *Memorandum*, one imagines how much more difficult it would have appeared to realise only a few years later a paradigmatic city-state echoing the Kallipolis of Plato's *Republic*. But there is more connecting than setting apart Kydones' political views and Plethon's *Memoranda*. The affinities between Plethon's ideal ruler and Demetrios Kydones' departure from late medieval conceptions of kingship show that in politics too his ideas are the organic outgrowth of secularist tendencies that were in full development since the fourteenth century. At one with Kydones, Plethon represents the last evolutionary stage of an emerging reconceptualisation of sovereignty that divests the ruler of his purported sanctity and puts in its stead the notion of *common interest*: τὸ συμφέρον.

In a recent study of sovereignty in Kydones, Christian Zgoll provided a useful hermeneutical model for understanding shifts in late Byzantine conceptions of sovereignty. Between the medieval sanctity of kingly rule and modern notions of political power Zgoll locates an intermediate or transient phase represented by Kydones. Royal absolutism makes the emperor unaccountable to the people and legislature by authorising his allegedly unconditional power as stemming from god. The sanctity of kingly rule in Byzantium derived from the Pauline tenet that authority is god-sent (Rom. 13:1–7). The latter view is present in Kydones but very vaguely and, significantly, without any distinctively Christian references.[115]

---

[115] Zgoll (2007) 55.

The novel understanding of sovereignty favoured by Kydones and Plethon revolves around the ruler's 'dignity' – not his sanctity. In the Byzantine context the attribution of ἁγιότης to the emperor was not only expected, but obligatory. To refuse or ignore this attribute of the emperor was tantamount to considering his rule illegitimate or in any case abandoned by god.[116] Breaking with this Byzantine tradition Kydones does not consider the emperor 'holy' (ἅγιος). Instead, he occasionally uses the adverb θεῖος, a move possibly associated with his love for antiquity. But in a total of 450 letters this happens around six times.[117] The essence of sovereignty ceases to be a *prima facie* divine gift unconditionally enjoyed by the ruler; it depends upon excellence, worthiness, and one's capacity to meet successfully the demands of kingship. With Kydones the unqualified Judaeo-Christian sanctity of sovereignty imperceptibly gives place to a demystified notion of kingship that is not fully secular yet, but clearly moves in this direction.

Whereas Byzantine imperial ideology in 'mirrors for princes' draws extensively on the Old Testament, Kydones purifies his conception of sovereignty of any biblical material. It appears that Kydones' fledgling notion of kingship is closer to that of *Il Principe* than to that of the Bible. Like Machiavelli, he suggests that the sovereign should seek inspiration in the study of Greek and Roman antiquity.[118] Moreover, there is little mention of specifically Christian virtues – and sovereignty is not founded upon them. Only once does Kydones mention Manuel's faith (πίστις): being an emperor does not automatically entail the traditionally quoted Christian virtues, just as the emperor's piety (εὐσέβεια) is not mentioned as the basis of sovereignty. Kydones' call to the emperor to elevate his dignity to Zeus's peak is a stepping stone between the ideal of King David and Machiavelli's *Il Principe*. One wonders whether a Greek deity still possessed any religious significance for a Christian scholar of the fourteenth century such as Kydones: rather, this appeal to Zeus is most probably part of a desacralisation process that substitutes a rhetorical figure for traditional Christian vocabulary.[119]

---

[116] Dagron (1996) 165; Zgoll (2007) 87.   [117] Zgoll (2007) 89.
[118] Zgoll (2007) 63.   [119] Zgoll (2007) 71–2.

The turn to secularism represented by Kydones utilises a pagan codex.

In Plethon's *Memoranda* the Pauline view of sovereignty is neither qualified nor marginal as it is in Kydones. It is completely absent. So is the notion of kingly sanctity held by Christian divine-right legitimists. In *Memorandum to Theodore* it is not Melchisedek or King David but Alexander the Great, Cyrrhus, Hercules and Lycurgus, to whom Plethon refers; in *Memorandum to Manuel* Plethon simply appeals to reason and argumentative force. As in Kydones, sovereignty ceases to be ecclesiastically or theologically sanctified. The address to Manuel opens with the formula 'most-divine Emperor (θειότατε αὐτοκράτωρ)' and ends with the wish that god may inspire Manuel to consider Plethon's measures. A passing note towards the middle of the address informs us that the divine ruler (ὁ θεῖος ἡγεμών) may have as many helots appointed to his service as he considers sufficient (but not as many as he likes). These expressions are the minimal saving clauses Plethon could possibly use in order to make the picture blurred. As in Kydones, the scarcity of religious attributes applicable to the emperor underlines the complete absence of any genuine theological foundation behind the emerging conceptualisation of imperial power. These are isolated rhetorical embellishments rather than carriers of the hyperbolic Byzantine glorifications of the presumably unimpeachable sacredness of imperial authority. Corroboration comes from the complete lack of composite adjectives beginning with θεο- in Kydones and Plethon. The adjective that appears to be most significant in the *Memorandum to Manuel* is κοινός: *public, common to all the people*, but also τὸ κοινόν: *the State*.

In a single paragraph 'common' or 'public interest(s)' and 'common' or 'public safety' occur seven times juxtaposed to three sarcastic references to what the monks consider 'sanctioned' by divine law: τὸ ὅσιον. The monks pretend to philosophise without contributing anything to public good. Now, says Plethon, what exactly is there to consider as 'sanctioned' in the case of some who, under the pretext of practising virtue, demand the right to lay their hands on wages necessary for public safety, or who take these wages away from those who are in need? These 'philosophers' do not deserve public support. It is neither proper, nor 'sanctioned' in any way that they should continue to receive money thus undermining public safety. The treatment that is really 'sanctioned' and proper to their profession (σχῆμα), says Plethon, is to allow them to enjoy untaxed what they produce, but divest them of any access to public resources. This means the monks should lose their privileges and work.[120]

By exposing the monks Plethon brings to the surface a clash between post-Palamite established notions of *to hosion* and a nascent modern understanding of public safety and prosperity (τὰ κοινά). The role of priests is further qualified as 'priests for the public' (τῷ κοινῷ ἱερωμένοι) and their needs specified as analogous 'to the lot of an officer of middling rank'.[121] We shall see that this effort to incorporate priesthood within the social system of civil servants is a direct challenge to the Hesychast takeover of clerical authority, ultimately targeting the capacity of Christianity to function antagonistically to political ideology. The aim is not limited to the secularisation of sovereignty but also to that of religious institutions. In Plethon's scheme priests do not serve god but primarily the public good. It is not the salvation of their soul that matters, but the salvation of *genos*. Their interest is identified with the interest of the State. Hence, in neither of his *Memoranda* does Plethon spare a word for the emperor's obligations to the Church or his religious duties as representative of Orthodoxy. The same remarkable phenomenon is observable in Kydones. And yet in Byzantium State and Church are usually assumed to be inseparable entities, with doctrinal disputes deemed *ipso facto* affairs of the State, and emperors such as Manuel and John Kantakouzenos expected to take action as pillars of Orthodoxy.

Kydones emphasised the ruler's compliance with *justice* and the *laws*.[122] The dignity (σχῆμα) of the king depends upon his attitude according to these civil virtues, rather than upon his religious Orthodoxy. It is not faith, but reason and action that matter. In Kydones as in Plethon, Manuel becomes the historical agent able to forge his own destiny as well as that of his people. Focusing on the emperor's σχῆμα and ignoring the presumed sacredness

---

[120] *Mem. II* 257.5–27.   [121] *Mem. II* 257.5–7.
[122] Zgoll (2007) 97; Dem. Kyd. *Ep.* 70 Loenertz.

of his imperial office, Kydones repeatedly pointed out that the emperor is bound to his people, as is soul to the body. This is a groundbreaking move, running contrary to the whole tradition of the Byzantine 'mirrors for princes' genre. The implication is that the source of kingship is not the emperor's relation to god, but his relation to the people. Like Plethon's call to authorities to stand up to the demands of the optimal *momentum* (καιρός), Kydones' emphasis on the ruler's dignity (σχῆμα) recalls a classic Stoic virtue associated with Roman republicanism: *magnitudo animae*, magnanimity, greatness of soul and mind, nobility of spirit that raises the ruler above all human vicissitudes.[123] These are qualities that the sovereign owes to nature and his own virtuous attitude. Before Plethon, Kydones locates the proper guide to political virtue in ideology and political philosophy rather than religious orthodoxy.[124] Interestingly, Kydones also uses the polarisation between philosophy and sophistry. He does not identify the Christians with sophists, as Plethon does in the *Nomoi*; but he does advise the emperor not to confuse Plato with Prodicus.[125]

Plethon and Kydones were bringing to its natural conclusion ideas on kingship that resurfaced within fourteenth-century Byzantine humanism: already in Theodore Metochites one finds a description of the sovereignty that departs from the hieratic type and is oriented towards a definition along personal qualities and individual virtues. The ideal of sovereignty in the *Memoranda* is moulded within this secular intellectual landscape of the Palaiologean Renaissance.

To the extent that Manuel is asked to take action according to the end of *to sympheron* and *ta koina*, Plethon not only divests imperial power of its sacredness but the emperor too of any *a priori* supremacy over the people. Manuel is not above the common good and conservation (σωτηρία) of *politeia*. He is their agent. Unlike Kydones, Plethon is not happy to give merely general advice regarding the positive qualities an emperor should exercise; he daringly points to precise measures. If no one else has the courage to enforce them, he says, he can do so himself. In

---

[123] See for example Cicero, *De finibus* 3.3.
[124] Beck (1952) 87; Medvedev (1984) 134.   [125] Dem. Kyd. *Ep.* 392.51–60 Loenertz.

the whole tradition of this most servile literary genre of 'mirrors for princes' there is no precedent of a statesman's going so far as to ask the prince to give him the formal permission to radically enforce whatever measures he deems necessary to the end of saving the *politeia* and reforming the whole socio-political system.[126] But then again, on this point Plethon certainly differs from Machiavelli too. It is not the security and safe distance of a consultant that he seeks but the adrenaline of action.

Disarming the religious establishment

Plethon's *Memorandum to Manuel* completes the secular turn exemplified in Kydones' letters to Manuel. Plethon openly replaces ecclesiastical and monastic definitions of virtue by political virtue. He does not go as far as to argue explicitly that the emperor's failure to provide for his subjects cancels his authority, but he comes remarkably close to this. Specific moral obligations and constraints are imposed on Manuel. Foremost among them are public safety (κοινὴ σωτηρία), the protection of healthy legal and political institutions and the responsibility to have able consultants in public affairs. Sovereignty is made conditional upon the successful recovery (ἐπανόρθωσις) of a seriously damaged *politeia*. God will neither renew nor safeguard Manuel's reign. Manuel has to do so by complying to *the sympheron*: the common interest, in this case the salvation of the Peloponnese.

Given the Byzantine conventions of the *Fürstenspiegel* genre this secular turn is almost as provocative as is the return to gods in the *Nomoi*. The dependency of sovereignty upon the emperor's ability to provide safety for his subjects meant that the will of the ruler and the instinct of self-preservation were placed higher

---

[126] *Mem. II* 265.8–12. Plethon does not go so far as to ask for the abolition of the monarchical system, partly because of his confidence in Manuel's ability to assume the role of Plato's philosopher-king, partly because in his mind only a thin line separates republicanism from anarchy. Like Kydones, he does not consider the possibility of popular sovereignty or revolutionary actions. The bloodshed and anarchy caused by the Zealots of Thessaloniki, of which Demetrios Kydones had first-hand experience, might have led to the belief that the monarch was still necessary to prevent total chaos and incite change. In this sense he is not a precursor of republicanism either: the real point of departure is the emperor's vertical power.

than any inexorable power of divine providence that Scholarios might evoke. Human values were deemed capable of transforming society and provided glory and dignity to the ruler.

This is a position diametrically opposed to the large tradition of Augustinean political theology according to which an ideal *civitas terrena* equals a *civitas diaboli*. Owing to man's fallen nature, divine providence has full control over human affairs and man is doomed never to achieve excellence by his own powers. Augustine's efforts to eradicate the pagan belief in man as potential author of his fate left a deep mark on medieval political thought visible, for example, in Aquinas and Dante.[127] According to Aquinas' very Augustinian belief, the sovereign should not act out of 'empty glory' but only out of 'love for eternal blessedness'.

Kydones is usually presented as a Thomist, yet in his letters to Manuel and John Kantakouzenos he moves in the opposite direction from Aquinas' *The Rule of Princes*. The primacy of the emperor's σχῆμα is a reminder that imperial action is bound by human concerns, not eternal blessedness. Kydones' anxiety regarding the Turkish presence in Europe led him in this direction, but his formation within the Greek Orthodox context might also have played a role. For all its mysticism, or rather because of its mysticism, Eastern Christianity provided a framework opposed to the Augustinean view on humanity, one in which Kydones' and Plethon's emphasis on man's ability to carve out his future contrasted less sharply than it would in the Thomist West.[128]

The importance of Plethon's notion of sovereignty extends beyond the Byzantine context. It is commonly affirmed that the Renaissance recovery of Ciceronian *virtus* and the emergence of the notion of *vir virtutis* provided man with the confidence to challenge Augustinian Christianity by emphasising man's capacity to be master of his own future.[129] And yet Plethon's secular notion

---

[127] Skinner (1978) 95–6; Pocock (1975) 38–41.

[128] The Orthodox view on primordial sin did not separate man from history and the world as radically as did Augustinian Christianity. Since Maximus Confessor's refutation of Origenes' pessimism it was possible to qualify (but never diminish) the distance between, on the one hand god's revelation through nature and history, and, on the other hand, god's revelation through Scripture. See here the commentary of Staniloae to Maximus' *Ambigua*, passim.

[129] Skinner (1978) 91, 100.

of kingship in the *Memoranda* comes before the Renaissance civic humanists, and, furthermore, in a manner more daring and explicit.

The absence of any concession to *fortune* in both *Memoranda* and the *Nomoi* is telling. Italian humanists opposed *virtus* to *fortuna* but they did not claim that *vir virtutis* is capable of completely eliminating the power of fortune, nor that one may ignore fortune. In other ways *Il Principe* comes close to Plethon's *Memoranda*, yet in his chapter on 'How far human affairs are governed by fortune' Machiavelli makes of fortune a goddess that is possibly 'the arbiter of half the things we do'. This leaves only the other half to be controlled and coerced by the prince's virtue.[130] Thus Cesare Borgia is reputed to have acquired his whole power thanks to good fortune – this is an example to be avoided but still one that underscores the power of that capricious goddess. Nothing of the sort comes up in Plethon's *Memoranda*.

Neither the wrath of God nor *fortuna* is mentioned as a possible limitation on the establishment of the ideal polity. Reason, history and the public good lead man on to mould his own destiny by accessing the code of Stoic-Platonic fate. Virtue is again the weapon of choice, but not against fortune, rather, against precise internal and external foes. God may inspire love (ἔρως) of great achievements in the despot Theodore. In that case the despot should know that salvation or disaster depends upon the exercise of virtue alone, and, so it seems, does 'everything' else: ἀλλ' ἐν τούτῳ τὸ ἄπαν ἐστί, καὶ τὸ σώζεσθαι ἢ ἀπολεῖσθαι τὰ ἡμέτερα ἐκ τούτου ἤρτηται.[131] In the *Nomoi* Plethon will once again neutralise the power of fortune when merging divine providence and fate into his notion of *heimarmene*.[132] As in the *Memoranda* the instinct of self-preservation triggered by the internal disintegration of the State and an imminent occupation generates a firm belief in man's innate power to control his destiny.

Petrarch and early *quattrocento* humanists invariably subjected virtue to the specific religious system of values prescribed by Christian religion, just as Ficino eventually subjugated his generic *philosophia perennis* to Judaeo-Christian revelation. When

---

[130] On Machiavelli and his predecessors on fortune see Skinner (1978) 120–1.
[131] *Mem. I* 130.6–12. [132] See above, Ch. 6, p. 317.

Petrarch equates wisdom with piety, he has the *Christian* notion of piety in mind.[133] Plethon too considers laws regarding religion as vital (κεφάλαιον) and piety is high on his list of virtues.[134] The crucial difference between Plethon and Italian humanists in this regard is that the former's notion of piety concerns a state religion that remains unnamed, undifferentiated, unspecified and eventually unidentifiable (*Memorandum to Theodore*) or is completely absent (*Memorandum to Manuel*).

In the case of the *Memorandum to Theodore* Judaeo-Christian piety and doctrinal exclusivity recede into the background to be replaced by three common notions of rational and natural religion that are familiar to readers of Plato's *Laws*: (a) that 'something divine' (τι θεῖον) exists; (b) that this shadowy 'divine' something (τὸ θεῖον αὐτό) takes care of things; and (c) that it is not tempted or manipulated by gifts 'and the like'. Contrary to the conventions of Byzantine *Fürstenspiegel* genre, there is not a single allusion to Judaeo-Christianity, Orthodoxy and the Fathers of the Church. For the first time the ideal of a *vir virtutis* is liberated from its Christian conceptual bondage, a radical move that until Machiavelli conventional Italian humanists did not dare to make in their 'mirrors for princes' theorising.

One might object that in the *Memorandum to Theodore* there is no reference to paganism either. Yet Plethon was expected to follow the Judaeo-Christian model of sovereignty in his *Fürstenspiegel*, whereas he was not expected to express any sympathy for paganism. His silence regarding both Christianity and paganism does not carry the same weight. His ignoring of Christianity is strong evidence of an already formed anti-Christian and non-Christian mindset, whereas the silence regarding paganism does not imply any sympathy for Christianity.

A contemporaneous Byzantine *memorandum* is helpful in estimating how provocative was Plethon's disentanglement of the question of political survival from Christian revelation. According to appearances, Joseph Bryennios' treatise *On the Fortification of Constantinople* (Περὶ τοῦ ἀνακτίσματος) had an aim similar to that of the addresses to Theodore and Manuel. Joseph delivered

---

[133] Skinner (1978) 92.   [134] *Mem. I* 125.3–5.

his talk in 1415 in Constantinople in order to mobilise the authorities to repair the walls of the city. Just as Plethon considered the
Hexamilion wall crucial for the defence of the Peloponnese, so
Bryennios considered the fortification of Constantinople vital for
the city. Both authors appear deeply concerned with the salvation
of the *genos*, yet the word is not employed co-referentially. Bryennios understands *genos* as essentially and necessarily Christian.
Whereas Plethon speaks of a Hellenic identity defined by the use
of the Greek language and paideia, Bryennios focuses on religious
orthodoxy. Plethon uses the antiquity of Sparta to illustrate the
significance of a Hellenic land (χώρα) inhibited by an ancient and
glorious autochthonous people: the Peloponnese is the 'mother'
and origin (ἀφορμή) of Greeks and Romans.[135] Identity formation is predicated on an ancient political community. Bryennios
too sees in Constantinople a mother (μητέρα), but he has no concern for either antiquity, or history and historical rhetoric. Rather,
Constantinople is the mother (μήτηρ), nurse (τροφός) and common home country (κοινὴ πατρίς) of all Orthodox Christians.[136]
Here identity is a question of religious faith and not ethnicity. In
Plethon's *Memoranda* the Turks pose an external threat yet their
military and moral qualities have to be carefully studied and even
emulated. They are βάρβαροι who 'are very formidable against
us' owing to their correct choice of legislature.[137] In Bryennios
the Turks are primarily infidels (ἀσεβεῖς). Where Bryennios sees
a clash of religions, Plethon sees a primarily political problem. It
goes without saying that the idea of confiscating monastic property to meet defence needs does not even cross the mind of pious
Bryennios. On the contrary, he points out that the abundance of
monasteries and churches in Constantinople is the chief reason to
defend the capital. This is a city set out and privileged by god.

Bryennios was not addressing monks or clerics, but a large lay
audience in order to organise a fund-raising campaign. The priority of religious Orthodoxy was not peculiar to Christian ingroups
but was expected to appeal to the whole population. Bryennios

---

[135] *Mem. II* 248.10–249.4.
[136] Joseph Bryennios, *Short Oration* (Δημηγορία Συντομωτάτη) 243–4.
[137] *Mem. I* 118.10–12.

was drawing from conventional *topoi* of Byzantine 'mirrors for princes', according to which the emperor's Orthodox piety was the guarantee for preserving the ecumenical nature of his kingship. The primary duty of the Byzantine emperor was to serve Orthodox faith and guide the world to god. And yet contrary to Scholarios' version of ecumenism Bryennios believes in the necessity of organising a defence against the Turkish invasion. At least on this occasion this native of Mistra has not delivered himself to apocalyptic numerology. But Plethon is unique in conceiving *genos* in secular terms, not sparing a word for what according to both Bryennios and Scholarios sets Manuel's subjects apart from Turks and Latins: Orthodoxy. What we have instead of religious Orthodoxy in the *Memorandum to Theodore* is a rational religion that remains purposefully unnamed, generic and unqualified.

In *Tractatus Politicus* (1677) Spinoza advances a plan for the official public religion of the State that is as intentionally vague as is the one here, allegedly founded upon common notions about the divine, justice and salvation. Spinoza's aim was to prevent public religion from growing in power by restricting its potential to function independently from and antagonistically to secular authority. As in Plethon's *Memorandum to Manuel* (257.6), priesthood is prefigured to serve the common good as set out by the ruling class. Unable to claim access to any exclusivist version of doctrinal orthodoxy, the clergy is disarmed. It can neither exploit credulity and superstition and thus exercise real power on the masses nor alienate itself from the secular elite and propound any alternative notion of authority. In the aftermath of the Palamite monastic 'takeover' of Church and State Plethon's scheme for a public state religion in the *Memorandum to Theodore* is suspiciously silent about Christian Orthodoxy and religious exclusivity. The aim was to neutralize Christian apocalypticism, ecumenism and fundamentalism by restraining the capacity of prominent spokesmen for the clerical and monastic establishment such as Scholarios and Bryennios to undermine or compete with secular political institutions. As in Spinoza, popular religion has an exclusively moral and political mission.

Plethon's 'divine something' hardly seems an appropriate recipient of ritual veneration. And yet in no case should the emperor generate the impression of inclining towards atheism and impiety. On the contrary, the people should perform ceremonies, *sacrifices* and offerings as 'symbols of confession'.[138] Such a religious policy, says Plethon, will undoubtedly foster virtue and eagerness to do good. On the contrary, atheism, failure to appreciate divine providence and superstition lead to the wrong 'choice of way of life': *hairesis biou*. Here lies the second important difference from the treatment of piety in the Byzantine and Italian 'mirrors for princes' genre. Not only does the religion of the State remain unnamed, but it is extolled for its commendable moral effect on people and sovereign; and not because it is the product of an allegedly exclusive and distinctively Christian revelation. The right doctrines regarding the divine are those that lead to a distinction between pleasure and the good.[139] For example, Nero and Sardanapalos are denounced for their indulgence in pleasure, which led to neglect of their country (πατρίδα).[140] Sovereigns go wrong when they scorn justice, truth and the common good, blinded by their love for gold and material wealth. Religion in the *Memorandum to Theodore* is above all a pedagogical tool guiding the prince to a modest and virtuous lifestyle. The model for Plethon's civil religion is contained in Plato's *Laws* Book 10. In both cases the absence of the notion of divine law from popular religion obstructs the development of religious fundamentalism that might potentially challenge the dominant political ideology and undercut its dissemination among the masses. Rather, religious faith is appreciated for its social function and utility, for the observance of civil rituals is conducive to civil justice and order, social stability and significantly, adherence to the rules of political authority.[141]

A comparison with the depiction of priesthood in earlier 'mirrors for princes' shows the radicalism of this move. According to a classic Byzantine 'mirror', the Κεφάλαια παραινετικά attributed to

---

[138] *Mem. I* 125.6; 126.6–7. The reference to *thusiai* by a man suspect of organising a pagan sect is intriguing, though it appears to have passed unnoticed by Plethon's contemporaries and modern scholarship, perhaps owing to the ambiguities of the word.

[139] *Mem. I* 126.7–11; 128.7. The word *eksamartanontes* used in this context does not mean that kings sin in the Christian sense of the word, but that they err and fail in their purpose.

[140] *Mem. I* 128.7–13.   [141] *Laws* 717a–718a, 885b.

Basil I the Macedonian (811–86) but most probably written by the patriarch Photius, priests are seen as 'spiritual fathers' exercising their power directly upon the emperor, thus circumventing the ordinary socio-political system. Given that the end of kingship is to realize god's will and become godlike, the ruler's success essentially depends upon his relation to the priesthood. The more the emperor acknowledges the Church, we read, the further he will ascend towards god; the more disrespect he shows to priests, the more angry he will make god.[142] Plethon puts an end to the dubious role of priests as mediators between the ruler and god. He makes of them civil servants. We shall see in a moment that he had good reasons to see this as a top priority of his reformative programme when addressing Manuel.

Manuel's mirror

Plethon's philosopher-king and Messiah of the Peloponnese, Manuel II, was not only the recipient of the famous Plethonean *Fürstenspiegel*, but also the author of an earlier 'mirror for princes'. Manuel's *Hypothekai* (*Testament of Kingly Education*; Ὑποθῆκαι βασιλικῆς ἀγωγῆς) is a 'mirror' intended for his son John and dated between 1399 and 1403. In the light of Manuel's *Hypothekai*, Plethon's *Memorandum to Manuel* conveys the impression of a consistent attempt to obliterate precisely that idea of kingship that was fervently defended and unreservedly shared by the actual recipient of the *Memorandum* a few years earlier.

For all his Platonic background and admirable political skills, in the *Hypothekai* Manuel appears in tune with previous Byzantine 'mirrors' in conditioning all aspects of statesmanship upon the exercise of that Christian piety, which allegedly guarantees god's protection and help. In the same vein as Photius' *Kephalaia*, Manuel has the ideal of the ruler's godlikeness depend upon his emulation of divine kingship and upon his relation to the Church. The relation between the Church and 'us', says Manuel, is one of a

---

[142] Ps.-Basil, *Kephalaia* 3.

mother (μήτηρ), nurse (τίτθη), teacher (διδάσκαλος), moulder (πλάστης), trainer (ἀλείπτης), route (ὁδός) and guide (ὁδηγός) – and of accomplice (συνεργός) and consolation (παράκλησις) in regard to what is best and most steadfast. (Manuel, *Hypothekai* 11)

In Manuel's *Hypothekai* kingship is conditioned within a framework well defined by doctrinal concerns. The religiosity of the emperor is no rhetorical ornament. The future ruler John is advised to show no mercy to heretics: in recompense for the preservation of doctrinal Orthodoxy god prolongs the ruler's stay in power and ensures his success.[143] This is the classic Jewish Hellenistic view on sovereignty that men like Kydones and Plethon opposed. Perhaps ironically, it is here voiced by the man who later urgently turned for help to the heretics *par excellence* (the Latins) in order to save his people, and who also saved Plethon, the most conspicuous apostate since Julian, from Scholarios' hands.

The advice in the *Hypothekai* was anything but wise given the circumstances. It meant throwing oil on the fire. During Manuel's reign the monastic party inspired by Palamism was still sabotaging the unionist project, taking over key clerical positions and claiming the role of genuine spokesmen of the people – at the same time as Manuel's political authority was disintegrating day by day. Corroboration comes from an external observer. The Spanish traveller Pero Tafur reported around 1437 that John VIII, Manuel's son, was 'like a Bishop without a See'.[144] Obviously the *Hypothekai* was not the best advice book for future princes.

Upon receiving Plethon's *Memorandum*, Manuel must have immediately observed in surprise that, properly speaking, this treatise was by no means classifiable as an ordinary 'mirror'. It was an attempt to regenerate the whole genre. But more than that, failure to put in a single word for Orthodoxy and for a close relation between the ruler and the Church made a strong statement that the Byzantine idea of kingship that Manuel had upheld for so long had come to its end and was unsuited to serve 'the common good' – and certainly this latter notion was meaningful to a ruler well versed in Plato as was Manuel. But would Manuel ever have considered the possibility that he had heretofore endorsed the wrong notion of

---

[143] *Hypothekai* 12.　　[144] Vasiliev (1932)112. Cf. Barker (1969) 294.

sovereignty, as Plethon's 'mirror' implied? It looks as if Plethon was addressing the wrong man. The *Memorandum* had no chance of success with the author of *Hypothekai*, either because Manuel sincerely viewed the Church as the 'mother' and 'nurse' of imperial authority, or, more likely, because political expediency did not leave him with any other option.

Manuel consistently ensured that his Christian piety would stay beyond doubt. A series of *prostagmata* issued in 1408 and in 1414–15 led to the alleviation of tax burdens previously imposed upon monasteries on the Holy Mountain. Barker saw here the result of 'certain economic conditions, if not pious aspirations'.[145] Yet the secularisation process was not completely reversed: it remained *en vigueur*, as Ostrogorsky noted.[146] The restoration of monastic property and the easing of taxes on monasteries did not come about by any naive and illusory belief that the Ottoman danger had disappeared. And certainly Manuel did not believe that paying due respect to the Orthodoxy of his time would ransom his empire. Were the heirs of Palamas or even Scholarios suitable guides for keeping the Turks out of Contantinople? Rather, Manuel needed the collaboration and appeasement of the Church in order to pursue the end of Church union, which was the only way he could hope to receive help from the Latins. This hardly meant that Plethon was wrong in investing all hopes for a secular turn in this man. A hitherto little noticed incident sheds light on the circumstances surrounding Plethon's *Memorandum* and the strong character of its recipient.

In 1416 Manuel seems to have expertly exploited circumstances to enhance the position of imperial authority in relation to the Church and thus hold the reins in ecclesiastical affairs. Manuel's non-conformity with the wishes of Patriarch Euthymios on a rather minor issue in 1415 led to the latter's attempt to completely liberate the Church from the emperor's control (μὴ κατάρχεσθαι ταύτην παρ' αὐτοῦ). In the event of failure, Euthymios threatened to go on 'strike' with the whole of the Church, which possibly meant a ceasing of all rituals (ἀργήσων ἑαυτὸν καὶ τὴν ἐκκλησίαν).[147]

---

[145] Barker (1969) 280 n. 141.
[146] Ostrogorsky (1954) 162–3; cf. Barker (1969) 297 n. 7, 301 n. 14.
[147] *Apomn.* 102.7–10.

The chasm between political and clerical authority was avoided owing to the death of the obstinate Euthymios in March 1416. The vacancy of the patriarchal throne provided the perfect opening for Manuel to make sure that the Church would not challenge his sovereignty again. Manuel threatened with a veto the appointment of a new patriarch unless the emperor's privileges and control over clerical matters was confirmed. The future patriarch should always keep in mind, as Manuel put it, 'what are his rights and what are those of the king'.[148]

This incident took place approximately two years before the circulation of the *Memorandum to Manuel*. In Plethon's eyes Manuel was clearly not afraid to subjugate the Church to political authority. Further, the construction of the Hexamilion wall might have strengthened his optimism about Manuel's ability to incite change. This optimism is reflected in the shift from the plans for a natural civic religion in the *Memorandum to Theodore* to the open polemic, in *Memorandum to Manuel*, against those exclusively concerned with the salvation of their soul and parasitically obstructing 'common preservation'. These are two parts of the same equation and have a complementary function. Similarly, though *Memorandum to Theodore* is an unequivocally anti-clerical work, it is only in the *Memorandum to Manuel* that we find a militant anti-monastic ideological agenda. This implies a familiarity with Manuel's inner persuasion and ideas that made Plethon confident that the emperor was beginning to see his point, namely that the conceptual shift from a sacralised to a demystified sovereignty that was urgently needed to save the Peloponnese could not be performed without clashing with the post-Palamite establishment and dealing with the consequences.

Paganism and totalitarianism: the *Memoranda* in their relation to the *Nomoi*

Both the community of Hesychast monks in Mount Athos and Plethon's *Memoranda* have been seen as the source of inspiration

---

[148] *Apomn.* 102.16–17: τίνα εἰσιν αὐτοῦ ἴδια καί τίνα τὰ τοῦ βασιλέως.

behind More's *Utopia*.[149] The latter possibility is more plausible, of course, since More might have been influenced by Plethon through the channel of Theodore of Gaza.[150] Still, the surmise that Hesychasm could have provided the basis for Thomas More's *Utopia*, though certainly odd and misleading, is philosophically intriguing. Erroneous theories may derive from valuable insights. The correct assumption behind this apparently absurd hypothesis is that Palamas and Plethon offer radically opposed versions of salvation and illumination that nevertheless qualify as utopian. Palamas represents a type of spiritual utopianism with latent apocalyptic tendencies fully exploited by Scholarios. In this case spiritual utopianism absorbs first the Church and then the State.

Plethon, however, is a precursor of a type of social utopianism that relies on political ideology. Political utopianism as laid out in the *Memoranda* prefigures modern nation-states. It envisages the separation of the State from the Church, depends upon national mobilisation and the securing of borders, and strives to achieve ideally just political institutions. It is the outgrowth of a humanist understanding of illumination that converts at the political level the cognitive process of grasping 'true doctrines' by human epistemic faculties into historical self-determination.

In this sense Plethon should be credited with a significant transformation in the history of utopian polities.[151] The firm belief that people are historical agents moulding their future and that the realisation of ideal society is a work of history, namely of appreciating the given cultural, intellectual and geographical circumstances, sharply contrasts with More's and Campanella's construction of ahistorical utopias in places unknown, unidentifiable or illusory,

---

[149] See Irmscher (1985) 261 for a brief discussion.

[150] For different attempts at a comparison between Plethon and More see Derrett (1965); Garnsey (2007) 57; Smarnakis (2007) 110. On More and Plato see Starnes (1990).

[151] Ahrweiler (1975) was right in assuming the existence of late Byzantine moves towards the emergence of competing versions of utopianism. But she does not consider Palamism to be a version of spiritual utopianism. On the other hand, van Dieten (1979) 12–13 argued against Ahrweiler that people like Plethon, Scholarios, Demetrios Kydones, Theodore Metochites, Manuel II Palaiologos and Joseph Bryennios did not flee from their political or clerical offices. In this sense, it is correct that they do not appear to oscillate between secular and theocratic utopias. Still, one recurring word confirms their intellectual utopianism: *soteria*. The conflicting meanings attributed to this word ('salvation' and 'preservation') are moulded by the clash between the Judaeo-Christian and the pagan-secular paradigms.

utopias that are not only u-topic but also 'a-chronic', that is, out-side history. In the two *Memoranda* Plethon does not distinguish between history and imagination: the call for an ideal state is indistinguishable from particular and urgent geopolitical considerations.

This concern with history brings Plethon closer to socialist utopias of the nineteenth century than to Thomas More. The two *Memoranda* on the salvation of the Peloponnese might be erroneously seen as hopelessly out of tune with the reality of a Byzantium eclipsed by the Ottoman Empire. In reality these relatively short treatises convey for the first time since the rise of Christian millenarianism in late antiquity the future tenet of secular utopianism and Marxist socialism: the conviction that social truths exist and that a just and perfect society based upon them will necessarily prevail and prosper. The same law of necessity (ἀνάγκη) that brings down a degenerate polity saves a right polity.

The *Memoranda* are more daring than the *Nomoi*. In the former case religion fulfils an urgent social need, separated from the State and controlled by it. Addressing political authorities, Plethon submitted a secular *politeia* close to that announced by Kabasilas' lay adversaries. Conversely, for all the experimentations with proto-deistic notions in the first book of the *Nomoi*, Plethon's *magnum opus* eventually departs from the *Memoranda* in falling back on and conforming to a tenet of the medieval world: that ideology, philosophy, economy and political institutions are hostages of religion in one form or another. In the *Nomoi* ideological and political reform presuppose religious reformism, the shift from Christianity to paganism. This accounts for the fact that liturgy and prayers take up whole chapters of the *Nomoi*.[152] To some this dependency of social change upon religion may be the most disappointing feature of Plethon's project. One might have wished to see the secularism of the *Memoranda* developed according to the guidelines set by Kydones and the mysterious lay circles that upset Kabasilas. Thus,

---

[152] On these cf. the classic paper by Anastos (1948); Schultze (1874) 311–18. O'Meara (2003: 203–4) sees in Plethon's insistence on the recitation of hymns a political significance and notes a parallel with al-Farabi's *Best State*. In both cases moral improvement and hence political regeneration rely on the 'correct' views about the divine. On the other hand, one might be tempted to see here a Neoplatonic theocracy.

it was recently argued that Plethon gives medieval replies to questions of a dawning age and that, contrary to More, he constructs his ideal polity from old materials.[153] While More escapes theocracy, Plethon does not. The *Nomoi* are less utopian than the *Memoranda* precisely because they allow for concessions to medieval theocracy in order to readdress the agenda of social change first developed in the *Memoranda*.

The principles of rational religion laid out in *Nomoi* Book I are compatible with the unnamed civic religion of the *Memorandum to Theodore*. And yet both are refuted by the development of the *Nomoi* project. The inescapable impression conveyed is that with the passage of time Plethon turned from the ideals of rational discourse and universally shared knowledge in *Nomoi* Book I to a totalitarian and theocratic plan. The latter prescribes the death penalty by fire in graveyards for anyone not sharing his opinions: 'whoever among the sophists (= Christians) devises doctrines contrary to ours, he too should be burned alive'.[154] If one rules out the possibility of grotesque irony (in the same sense as Plato's 'totalitarianism' appears in the light of a Straussian reading: as ironically pointing at the shortcomings of utopianism), then one is faced with a peculiar penal system marked by its fixation with the penalty of death by fire for deviation and ideological dissent. This might well be a darker offspring of that Platonic reasoning in the *Laws*, according to which in a nearly perfect *politeia* offences 'against the gods, one's parents or the state' naturally attract the death penalty. As the Athenian stranger has it, a man who enjoyed from his earliest years the best education but still does not abstain from 'acts of the greatest evil' such as religious and political subversion is 'beyond cure'.[155]

Plethon's penal system appears completely alien to Byzantine legislation in its priorities. Whereas the latter focused on the motive behind criminal acts in order to establish the extent of the accountability and responsibility of the defendant, in Plethon criminal acts

---

[153] Smarnakis (2007) 108, 110; (2005) 211.

[154] *Nomoi* 126 (3.31.83–5): καὶ σοφιστῶν, ἤν τις παρὰ τὰς ἡμετέρας ταύτας δόξας σοφιζόμενος ἀλῷ, ζῶν καὶ οὗτος κεκαύσεται. See above, p. 158.

[155] *Laws* 854e.

are uniformly punished regardless of whether they are the outcome of deliberation and planning or mere chance.[156]

Plethon's hegemony of Reason was meant to take the place of the Palamite hegemony of apophaticism: yet was it ultimately better equipped to protect human dignity? In 1877 the pioneer scholar of Plethon, George Finley, observed that Plethon would have rendered society more barbarous than he found it.[157] More recently, Donald Nicol noted that had Plethon's measures been implemented 'they would have produced an unpleasant mixture between a philosopher kingdom and a socialist military dictatorship'.[158] Plethon's penal system in the *Nomoi* has been seen as proof of the degeneration of rationalism into fanaticism, a painful reminder of how easily the pursuit of enlightenment shifts to barbarism. Plethon is a forerunner of both the Enlightenment and totalitarianism, we read.[159] Scholarios, we have seen, found here yet another excuse for consigning the whole work to the flames. In a sense he turned the tables on Plethon by using the totalitarianism of the *Nomoi* as the moral invoice for his own intolerance, and boosting those theological alibis that authorised the torture of Juvenalios and the persecutions of any evil 'pagans' purportedly active in the Peloponnese. Governors and civil authorities should maintain no scruples. Plethon would have done worse if he had been given the chance.

---

[156] Tourtoglou (1990) 45–53 provides an account of the Plethonean penal system in the light of Byzantine law. As a rule, Byzantine law presupposed that a murder or other crime had really taken place for it to be classifiable as a criminal act (cf. *Basilica* 2.2.217: οὐκ ἀπὸ τῆς προθέσεως, ἀλλὰ ἀπὸ τοῦ πρᾶξαι). By contrast, Plethon classifies attempted crimes and accomplished crimes within the same category: attempted murder is punished as if the murder actually happened. Thus, his view on adultery coincides with that in the Deuteronomy (5:21), making no distinction between adultery in thought and adultery in deed. Presumably on the same grounds accomplices to such acts are condemned to death. The penalty for homosexuality, rape and violation of animals is also death by fire (*Nomoi* 124–6). However, the jury has the right to change the penalty whereas any ambiguities in the laws call for interpretation by the judges (*Nomoi* 130), a practice that in the Byzantine context was usually to the benefit of the defendant. As Tourtoglou notes, the extreme severity of Plethon's penal system may be an attempt to establish the absolute equality of all citizens before the law. By contrast, the Byzantine law system allowed for numerous discriminations between penalties inflicted upon members of the privileged classes (εὔποροι) and those of impoverished social strata (ἄποροι).

[157] Finley (1877) 241. Cf. Tozer (1886) 378.

[158] Nicol (1993) 344; see also the discussion of Scholarios' and Plethon's theocratic plans in Demetracopoulos (2004).

[159] Wokart (1986) 196–7.

The tantalising question then is: why did Plethon move from the vision of a large-scale secularisation of the State described in the two *Memoranda* to one of a pagan utopia described in the concluding books of the *Nomoi*? How does the secular religion of the Address to Theodore relate to the pagan theocracy of the third book of the *Nomoi*? How is Plethon's move to be explained? One possibility is that the relation between the two parts of the *Nomoi* is analogous to that between the philosophical route that Plato describes in *Republic* Book 6 and his considerations regarding the inability of the masses to follow this route.[160] We need not see a contradiction here, but rather a complementary function recalling the relation between Plato's *Republic* and *Laws*.

A second possibility, in my view closer to truth, is to assume a developmentalist position. The paganism and the penal system of the *Nomoi* evolved out of the failure of the *Memoranda* to instigate a national awakening. The *Nomoi* is a reaction to the defeat of Byzantine humanism, just as political reformism in the *Memoranda* is a reaction to the bankruptcy of a pre-existing secular agenda and a radicalisation of earlier moderate and secular reformative projects. In the *Nomoi* Plethon shows himself to be fully persuaded of the failure of earlier secularisation plans, the *Memoranda* included. If popular religiosity cannot be neutralised, then it has to be redeployed as a weapon to the same greater end: the regeneration of the State. Islam and Palamism now become the model. The transformative project that evolves out of similar considerations asks for a holistic solution that would dispose of all ephemeral and transient experimentations with political authority.

The failure of both Byzantine humanism and the *Memoranda* were signs that the medieval world was not ready to change at the political and social level, even if intellectually it had entered the transitional phase to early modernity. Pragmatically speaking, Plethon had no alternative but to work with medieval notions of reform, though fully convinced that a new world was close. In his eyes, the pagan theocracy of the *Nomoi* was the only solution available after the defeat of secularism by the Hesychast 'Counter-Reformation' and the failure of the *Memoranda* to strike a chord.

[160] Cf. *Resp.* 428e5, 491b, 494a, 503d11; *Ti.* 51e.

Thus in the *Nomoi* Plethon addresses the same issue of nascent nationalism in different terms from those he employed in the *Memoranda*. The return to the ideal of the *polis* comes complete with a return to the old gods of the *polis*. This accounts for a relocalisation of the polytheistic cult that had died away with the ancient *polis*. It is not the ruler but gods as ministers of 'Zeus' who care for the 'common good', thus providing the precise example for the relation of the Hellenes with their *polis* and people (γένος).[161]

The passage that links the proto-nationalism of the *Memoranda* with the paganism of the *Nomoi* is contained in a hymn, where Plethon addresses not only gods, heroes and ancestors, but also his 'comrades (σύντροφοι)', 'companions (ἑταῖροι)' 'fellow-inhabitants', 'fellow-citizens (πολῖται)', 'friends' and, significantly, 'brothers (φράτορες)'. Among all these he has especially in mind 'those of you who have taken care of our common interests, above all you who have sacrificed your life for the freedom of your compatriots and that of a *genos* that thinks as you do'. These are the men who fought for ensuring the prosperity of the community and for 'rectifying what was not in the right condition'. The utopian, ideally just *polis* of the *Nomoi* is meant to connect with the long history of a 'like-minded' community: a ὁμόδοξον γένος.[162] Masai saw a connection between the use of φράτορες and Scholarios' condemnation of Plethon's φρατρία, namely the religious guild operating in Mistra.[163] This is very probable. But the meaning of φράτορες is not exhausted in that of a secret brotherhood, as Scholarios' contemptuous use of φρατρία implies. In the context of the *Nomoi* and in the light of the re-conceptualisation of γένος in the *Memoranda* Plethon attempts a return to the original meaning of the word, which designates members of a clan tied by strong bonds, a tribe of kindred race – a πάτρα (Dor. for φράτρα).[164] The earlier quest for communal self-determination in the *Memoranda* is present in the *Nomoi*, albeit in pagan rather than secular terms.

It is politically significant that in the *Nomoi* the *sancti loci* of traditional paganism are extended so as to cover the soil of a

---

[161] *Nomoi* 150 (3.34,1.227–40).   [162] *Nomoi* 198 (3.34,5.203–15).
[163] Masai (1956) 306.   [164] See LSJ s.v. φράτρα.

ritually purified and re-sacralised home country (τόπος).[165] The original account of an ancient indigenous Peloponnesian community (γένος) in the *Memoranda* issues in an enhanced notion of communality (τὸ κοινόν) predicated on a quasi-religious bond between land and its inhabitants. More than citizens (πολῖται) of a *spoudaiotate politeia*, those who acknowledge this communal bond become *phratores*, members of a secret *homodoxon* guild. In this context the words σωτηρία and ἐπανόρθωσις used in the *Memoranda* are also redeployed in the *Nomoi*: the members of Plethon's guild are devoted to freedom, to the preservation (σωτηρία) of the established order (τὰ καθεστηκότα) and the restitution (ἐπανόρθωσις) of what was incorrectly altered.[166]

Consequently the admission of popular polytheist religion, the ritual liturgies and the cultic henotheism of the *Nomoi* are more than a consequence of assuming Plato's multi-causalism. They also signify a reconnection between cult and land that ensues from the return to *polis*. Just as the introduction of a new calendar signifies an attempt to reclaim time or the right relation to time, the introduction of popular 'national' deities reclaim the *locus* of ancestral religiosity and announces the departure from the religious ecumenism represented by the Orthodox Church. In Plethon's eyes, religious ecumenism developed when the old city–states became obsolete; thus, a return to *polis* is tantamount to a rebirth of local cult. Ecumenism is concomitant with monotheism. The reversal of this evolution from *polis* to ecumene necessarily implies the reversal of the process leading from polytheism to monotheism. The reinstitution of gods was meant to meet the need for a local cult within the state of the Peloponnese but also to signpost its nascence. The Plethonean 'national' gods are a by-product of the unresolved conceptual polarity between *polis* and *ecumene*.

In the *Memoranda* Plethon invested hope in the public call for a mass campaign for political mobilisation instigated and led by the emperor Manuel and despot Theodore. In the *Nomoi* this belief in official channels and established political authorities is replaced by plans for an underground cell that cuts off any contact with

---

[165] See *Nomoi* 230 (3.36.11–13) on the ritual purification of land (topos).
[166] *Nomoi* 198 (3.34,5.207–11).

secular as well as religious structures and moves independently of its contemporary socio-political framework, migrating deep within its own vision of resistance. Given the polytheist focus and the appropriation and re-conceptualisation of a distinctively Christian vocabulary in the *Nomoi*, the expression ὁμόδοξον γένος acquires new meaning. Whereas in the *Memorandum* to Manuel Plethon closely defined the Hellenic political community according to language and paideia, he now does so by an appeal to *homodoxia* that involves religious 'orthodoxy' – not Christian, but pagan.[167]

---

[167] The contrast with Scholarios' use of the ὁμόδοξος is telling of Plethon's tactic to paganise Christian vocabulary. Cf. Schol. *Adnotatio ad Eccl. Adv.*, *OC* 3.167.25–6: ἡ πνευματικὴ τῶν ὁμοδόξων κοινωνία καὶ ἡ τελεία ὑποταγὴ πρὸς τοὺς γνησίους ποιμένας. See above, Ch. 5, p. 253.

PART IV

THE PATH OF ULYSSES AND THE PATH OF ABRAHAM

8

CONCLUSION

The origins of Plethon's pagan Platonism: the developmentalist thesis

The fall of Kallipolis in 1354 had certain unexpected consequences for Archbishop Gregory Palamas. On board a ship forced to halt off the coast of Kallipolis to avoid shipwreck, Palamas and the other passengers observed the movements of the Turks on the European shore. Before long the ship was captured and all prisoners, including the illustrious archbishop, were taken to Lampsacus. In an epistle 'to his Church, while being a prisoner in Asia', which nicely contrasts with Kydones' *Memorandum* urging the Byzantines to take back Kallipolis, Palamas interprets the events along the lines of divine economy thus: 'we have been delivered into their hands [i.e. of those 'most barbarian of all barbarians'] as a minor punishment for our many sins in the face of God'.[1] The 'calamities' that befall Constantinople are 'sent from above' and the archbishop is unsure whether to see in them divine 'disciplining' or God's 'abandonment'.

But what is really of interest in this epistle comes next. Palamas tells us that the vast majority of Christians he met in Bithynia were asking why God had 'abandoned our people (γένος) in this way'.[2] The Turks who captured Palamas appear to have offered a straightforward reply. The conquest is abundant proof of the

---

[1] Gr. Pal. 'Epistle to his Church' 3 (*PS* 4.121.4–14). For this fascinating document, in which the Turks are called by the archaic name *Achaimenidae* see Georgiades Arnakis (1951) 104–18. Orhan Gazi arranged for Palamas to discuss theology with a mysterious group of people called Chionai. Palamas' *dialexis* is edited in vol. IV of *PS* (pp. 148–65). For the question of the identity of the shadowy sages and this inter-religious encounter, which cannot be dealt with here, see Georgiades Arnakis (1951) 107–9; Balivet (1999a) 151–80 and (1993) 2–4; Miller (2007) 28: 'at the end of the debate everyone seems satisfied, except for one of the Chionai, who punches Palamas in the eye'.

[2] Gr. Pal. 'Epistle to his Church' 9 (*PS* 4.125.20–3): τῶν δε πλειόνων τὴν αἰτίαν ἀπαιτούντων τῆς περὶ τὸ ἡμέτερον γένος παρὰ Θεοῦ τοσαύτης ἐγκαταλείψεως.

failure of the Christian religion: 'This impious, hated by God and all-abominable people', writes the Hesychast, 'boast that they have conquered the Romans because they are favoured by God.'[3]

That this view was widespread finds corroboration in a notorious dialogue written by Manuel II on the difference between Islam and Christianity.[4] While in Turkish captivity in 1390/1 in Ankara, Manuel appears to have conversed 'for endless winter nights' with a wise and influential old man from Babylon. Reflecting on the presuppositions of this dialogue, Manuel finds fault with the 'fixed idea' of his interlocutor that his people are prospering whereas the Romans are sunk in despair. The Muslim philosopher, so thought Manuel, was *parti pris* and misled by historical contingencies.[5]

Plethon would fully agree with the first clause laid out by Palamas' capturers and Manuel's interlocutor. Christianity could not guarantee the liberty and prosperity of the Byzantine citizens any longer. The impression that Christianity was a moribund religion responsible for the lamentable state of the empire was taking shape long before Plethon. So was the implication that the time was ripe and possibly opportune for radical changes. The testimony of Nicholas Kabasilas regarding those shadowy yet powerful lay circles in late fourteenth-century Constantinople testifies to both claims.[6]

It is in this intellectual context that we should revisit the testimony of George of Trebizond. When Plethon announced in Florence that 'within a few years the entire world, with one mind and one preaching' would adopt a new religion, he was not unique in considering Christianity to be morally and philosophically bankrupt. Nor was he alone in looking for a novel religious paradigm beyond the rivalry between Christianity and Islam. So did Sheikh Bedreddin, Plethon's contemporary Ottoman utopian reformer, who appears to have studied at the same place at the

---

[3] Gr. Pal. 'Epistle to his Church' 8 (*PS* 4.124.7–9): Μεγαλαυχοῦσι γαρ τὸ δυσσεβὲς καὶ θεομισὲς καὶ παμμίαρον τοῦτο γένος, ὡς ὑπὸ τῆς σφῶν θεοφιλίας ἐπικρατοῦντες Ρωμαίων.

[4] Recently the dialogue between Manuel and the Persian wise man achieved notoriety owing to an important albeit controversial lecture delivered by Pope Benedict XVI on 12 September 2006 at the University of Regensburg. See here Demetracopoulos (2008).

[5] Manuel Pal. *Dial.*, PG 156.128–9.

[6] See above, pp. 359–69.

same time. Both men shared the belief that a *phratria* or sect, namely a small, dynamic movement destined to grow up in an alien environment, may actually succeed in instigating a radical socio-political reform.[7] But only in Plethon's case did the need to adapt to a changing world mean falling back on philosophical Hellenism.

Plethon and Byzantine humanism

How was it possible for such a radical form of Hellenism to emerge in the fifteenth century after ten centuries of clerical indoctrination? I have argued that secular and pagan Platonic tendencies latently persisted through Byzantine intellectual history. They were either parasitically attached to Orthodox Christianity as heresy, or transmitted through the channel of religious and intellectual dissimulation.

Plethon's philosophical paganism and utopianism correspond to the third phase in a tripartite transformative process of Platonism. The first phase of this process took place in late antiquity when pagan Platonism clashed with Christianity at the intellectual level. The completion of the second phase marks the adaptation of Platonism to a Christian world by means of its transformation into humanism during the first and second Byzantine Renaissances. In the fifteenth century the failure of Byzantine humanism to reform Roman Orthodoxy from within and overthrow Palamism led Plethon to a radicalised pagan version of Platonism. Plethon's project was both philosophically and politically a profound reaction to the prevalence of Palamite Orthodoxy, a response to the Palamite counter-offensive to those humanist tendencies that made a gesture towards ancient philosophy. Seen in this light, the *Memoranda* are part of a progressive evolution of Platonism into a political religion that was aborted by doctrinal Orthodoxy and the post-Palamite clerical establishment. The *Nomoi* project is a reaction to the violent interruption of this evolutionary process.

Palamite sources affirm that in the late fourteenth century pagan philosophers, Plato foremost among them, were still seen as

---

[7] Siniossoglou (2012).

mystagogues by a certain branch of Byzantine 'enlightened' intellectuals. There is a thin yet fine line connecting Plato's ideal of
πεφιλοσοφηκότες ὀρθῶς in the *Phaedrus*, the mystics and thyrsus-
bearers whom Plato identifies with the true philosophers, the
philosophers whom Barlaam the Calabrian venerated as some
sort of Illuminati (οἱ πεφωτισμένοι, οἱ θεόπται), and Plethon's
σοφοί in the *Nomoi*.[8] The Byzantine intellectuals responsible for
the reinvigoration of these 'Enlightened-ones' were, in the eyes
of their opponents, anything but Orthodox Christians, even if they
were persistently self-defined as such. As Palamas saw it, Hellenism was working from within Christian heresy, or rather, Hellenism was using Christian heresy as its vehicle and means of
expression.

At the same time as a reaction to the ultimate prevalence of
Palamism, Plethon's paganism is a radicalisation of pagan Hellenic tendencies let loose in the course of the Hesychast controversy. These did not disappear upon the formal defeat of the
humanist movement in the decades following the Synod of 1368.
The Orthodox establishment had greater difficulty in suppres-
sing the pagan core of the humanist world-view than in combating the intrusion of 'Latinising' tendencies. The intellectual
roots of this world-view were too deep. Philosophical Hellenism
was not a force newly introduced by means of translations, as was
Thomism.

Anti-Palamite discourse created a new, raw framework that still
claimed to be Christian yet facilitated, if not encouraged, the
potential emergence of intellectual converts to Hellenism. The
pagan Platonic intellectual forces that Palamas combated found
in Plethon a new host willing to take them to their most radicalised position, beyond that reached by Barlaam and the brothers
Kydones. Plethon disagreed with fourteenth-century Byzantine
humanists on this crucial point: the possibility of subjugating
pagan philosophy to Judaeo-Christianity. Oddly at first sight,
he was here in full agreement with Gregory Palamas. The aim
was no longer a Christian reformation derived from the moderate experimentation with secularism and the thought of ancient

---

[8] Cf. *Phaedrus* 69c–d; *Nomoi* 252 (3.43.137); see also above, pp. 205–7.

Illuminati. Rather, Plethon brought these pre-existing tendencies towards a distinctive anti-Christian and pagan outlook to their conclusion.

The need to be radical was one-way, given the context. Not only did Palamism triumph, but Platonists like Theodore Metochites, whom Plethon greatly esteemed, for all their contribution to a revival of secularism, mitigated radicalism and adopted a defeatist, pessimistic world-view that made too many concessions to authority and bordered dangerously on the idea of man as a helpless puppet of cosmic powers. To some extent, these transparently non-Christian tendencies helped to challenge the Christian idea of divine providence and announce the need for a strong ideological substitute: Plethon's *heimarmene*. In the meantime they weakened the will and capacity of the Byzantines to resist the devastating attacks of the Turks.[9]

Metochites' ideal of θεωρητικὸς βίος is, indeed, a revival of Plato, albeit an apolitical and introvert one that did not ask for collective action any more than did the Hesychasts' prayers. The moderate and compromising Platonism of the fourteenth century offered the foundations for Plethon's radical reform; but taken in itself, this type of Platonism mollified and smoothed over the need for action. In the last analysis it prevented the crystallisation of any real alternative to Scholarios' view that the fall of Byzantium and Hellenism was 'God's will'. It facilitated and preserved, rather than opposed the political theology of the religious establishment.

This said, the anti-Hesychast party was not defeated before removing chunks out of the Orthodox armour. Ironically, it was Plethon, a man apparently much closer to Eastern Christianity than to the Latin West, who took up the task of continuing the humanist endeavour. Viewed from this angle, Plethon's Platonism was above all else a unique attempt to reverse and trace back the evolution of Byzantine humanism to its historical and religious origins: philosophical paganism. Building on the rational perception of knowledge that was fully developed in the fourteenth century, the *Nomoi* merge the secular Plato of Byzantine humanism with the archetypical Plato of late antique pagan Neoplatonism.

---

9 Beck (1952) 126ff.; Klein-Franke (1972) 2.

The question of Plethon's anti-unionist agenda

The fourteenth-century intellectual clash between Palamism and humanism over the definition of Roman Orthodoxy provided Plethon with raw material and direct links to Hellenising streams that he could not possibly fit into a Roman Catholic framework, let alone foster and develop. Even before the Hesychast controversy, a long series of Byzantine humanists from Psellos to Nikephoros Gregoras by way of Theodore Metochites constantly experimented with Platonist epistemology and ontology, creating a chain that provided the theoretical presuppositions for re-establishing a genuine Platonist political and metaphysical paradigm within a kindred geographical, linguistic and intellectual context.

I have argued that this provides the key to explain Plethon's role at the Ferrara/Florence Synod of 1438/9. Syropoulos' chronicle reflects the priorities of an apologetical and political agenda.[10] But even if we assume that his portrait of Plethon is accurate, this hardly means that Plethon supported Orthodoxy for the same reasons as his student Mark Eugenikos did. Rather, Plethon supported Orthodox Christianity because in his eyes Latin Christianity fell short of providing the conceptual building blocks and intellectual connections necessary for his Platonic reformation.

The Greek Catholic George of Trebizond was certainly right in one thing: Hellenism in the East had always been so strong that even though Palamite theology fiercely combated philosophical paganism, it was itself liable to the accusation of sheltering paganising and Platonising tendencies – at least from a 'Latin' viewpoint. Roman Orthodox mysticism could only with great effort escape the recurrent accusation of engulfing and nourishing two doctrines that, since the time of the Cappadoceans, Maximus Confessor and Symeon the New Theologian, were subject to interpretations that carried the evil seed of pre-Christian religiosity. I mean the distinction between essence and energies in god and the interrelated doctrine of divine immanence, according to which divine energy pertains, connects and energises the whole of creation. The principal objection of all major anti-Palamite intellectuals was that

---

[10] Pagani (2008) 14–16; see above, pp. 125–7.

a plurality of divine energies comes dangerously close to Proclan henotheism while in a sense re-sacralising the physical world.[11] With one possible exception, Celtic Christianity, this Hellenic connection was atrophic in the Latin West.[12]

This rendered Plethon's endeavour purposeful in the Greek context. Paradoxical as it may appear at first sight, in the Roman East the theology of the Orthodox religious establishment that Plethon endeavoured to subvert shared common intellectual roots with the henotheist and panentheist paradigm that he was promoting.

Plethon supported the Orthodox delegation because in his eyes the religious imperialism of the Catholics was far more of an obstacle than the introvert Palamite mysticism of the East. The tottering Byzantium was more likely to revert to its ancient philosophical roots, which were absent from or inactive in the West. The streams of ancient wisdom, to paraphrase Psellos, might surface in a Peloponnese about to collapse – but they were more than likely to be suppressed under the hegemony of Thomism. If anything like a pagan Platonic revival was ever to take place, it could do so only within the intellectual context of Roman East. This was enough reason for Plethon to be more anti-Latin than was Scholarios.

This thesis finds corroboration in the failure of Plethon's radical Platonism to strike a chord among Renaissance Platonists. Ultimately, Plethon's Platonism was meaningful in Byzantium, not in the Latin Renaissance. Outside the late Byzantine framework Plethon's philosophical paganism was divested of its *raison d'être*.

Beyond Orthodox and Latin Christianity:
a call for reformation

Hellenism as a self-sufficient intellectual paradigm was despised by the Palamites but never openly or unconditionally embraced by their humanist opponents. The mutual exhaustion of the two

[11] The concession to modern terminology implied by the term *henotheism* is made here for heuristic reasons. See Chapters 5 and 6 for a full discussion of the relation between Palamism and philosophical paganism.

[12] Eastern mystical theology appears to have affinities with Celtic Christianity, one version of Christianity that also assimilated pagan religiosity, possessed strong monastic roots and challenged the legalism of Roman Christianity and Latin scholasticism. On Celtic Christianity and the East see Chrysostomos Koutloumousianos (2008) 62, 95, 143.

intellectual camps left two alternatives for escaping from political and theological dead-ends: either Thomism, which emerged in the early fifteenth century as the new force challenging the authority of Palamas, or Hellenism. The controversy between George the Philosopher, the hardline Platonist who found refuge in Mistra around 1360, and Demetrios Kydones that took place around 1365–9 is telling of the dilemmas that anti-Palamites faced on the aftermath of their defeat. Both men had done their service to the cause of Byzantine humanism and fourteenth-century anti-Palamism. Their philosophical ways parted with the ascendancy of Palamism to intellectual hegemony when the ex-comrades had to choose between Thomism and complying with the Orthodox establishment. George's criticism of Kydones' fondness for Aquinas makes sufficiently clear that not all anti-Palamites were eventually absorbed by Thomism and that philhellenism presented an alternative even if that meant 'parting from one's friends full of joy'.[13]

In Kydones' full support for scholasticism, George appears to have recognised some sort of apostasy from the legacy of ancient Greece. For his part, Kydones did not fail to observe that George's overzealous admiration for and belief in the superiority of ancient philosophy potentially bordered on paganism: 'My dearest friend', Kydones begins one of his epistles, 'you are so dependent upon Plato's doctrines that you put everything second to his Muse . . . '[14] Kydones' epistles make clear that in his eyes allegiance to the West was politically the most expedient and prudent choice. But he is on less solid ground in trying to persuade George the Philosopher that Aquinas would make even Plato and Aristotle join the Church and abandon the Academy and Peripatos.[15] Byzantine theologians such as Kydones' student John Kyparissiotes, Plethon's students Bessarion and John Argyropoulos recognised Thomism as the only option. The early Scholarios, too, considered the possibility of a dialogue between East and West. Plethon is one of those few men who, like George the Philosopher, did not follow Kydones in his Thomist and unionist ideas. On the one hand, Plethon's

---

[13] Dem. Kyd. *Ep.* 32.16–22.   [14] Dem. Kyd. *Ep.* 33.4–5.
[15] Dem. Kyd. *Ep.* 33.72–6.

anti-Aristotelianism is a reply to the ascendance of Thomism.[16] It is also a rejection of Eastern Orthodoxy. In his eyes pagan Platonism emerged naturally as the only force not in fact worn out but on the contrary strengthened by the intellectual civil war of the fourteenth century.

Seen in this light Plethon is a forerunner of the Reformation rather than the Renaissance. The Plethonean attempt to steer a course between Orthodox Christianity as represented by the heirs of Palamas and Kydones' Thomism anticipates Luther's belief in the exhaustion of Christian theological discourse and the reformative call to subvert the hegemony of clericalism.

Plethon's anti-Latin treatise, ostensibly rebutting John Argyropoulos' pro-Latin sentiments, is particularly significant in this regard. One of Plethon's dogged enemies, the acute Orthodox theologian Manuel Corinthios, was at one with Scholarios in holding that Plethon's anti-unionist and anti-Latin convictions by no means dictated that his profession of Orthodoxy was sincere. Manuel appears to have been the first to discern behind Plethon's little treatise the seed of a new theology that belonged neither to the Western nor to the Eastern Church. Plethon's treatise against the Latins did not intend to refute Argyropoulos and bring him back onto the right track of Orthodoxy but rather suggested that beyond Eastern and Western Christianity a third option was always possible.[17] Certainly, in the *Differences*, the *Nomoi* and other works, the urge to open a third way leads to philosophical paganism. But in a sense the anti-Latin treatise stands out in the Plethonean corpus for suggesting that this selfsame subversive thrust could potentially lead to a reformation of Christianity rather than Hellenism.

The essence of pagan Platonism

Plethon was a pagan on philosophical rather than ritual grounds. There are four constitutive conceptual elements of his radical interpretation of Plato that clash with Roman Orthodoxy: a distinctively

---

[16] See Couloubaritsis (2006) 145; already Alexandre (1858: lxxvii) had interpreted the Neoplatonism of the *Nomoi* as a reaction to scholasticism.

[17] As Manuel has it (*BG* 100) Plethon κριτὴν καθεστῶτα ἑαυτὸν ἐν τοῖς πράγμασιν.

pagan ontology; epistemic optimism; multi-causalism or 'poly-theism'; and political utopianism. This type of Platonism sub-merges the Judaeo-Christian notion of an ineffable divine Being within the human apprehension and cognition of Being; it ren-ders illumination dependent upon intellectual ascent; it advances a multi-causalist metaphysical model that substitutes the deter-minist notion of *heimarmene* or fate for Christian free will and allows for an intermediate realm of Ideas/gods that compromises the Orthodox dichotomy between uncreated/unqualified essence and created/qualified substance; and it redefines salvation as the humanly realisable approximation of an ideally just polity. These are manifestations of a self-sufficient Platonic Ideal-type. For the first time since late antiquity Plato's philosophy was reac-tivated in order to launch an assault on Christian theology and refocus on political rather than spiritual utopianism.

Plethon is also a Platonist in so far as he develops the notion that approximation to divine truths and approximation to socio-political truths are strands of one and the same project. In the *Timaeus* knowledge of god is difficult but not impossible and in the *Republic* Socrates declares that 'the things we have said about the city and its constitution' are hard to come about 'but not impossible'.[18] Significantly, the *Timaeus* begins with a summary of the *Republic*. Political reformism is intrinsically linked to tough epistemological, physical and cosmological endeavours. After all, in the *Republic* politicians are philosophers 'who are able to grasp what is always the same in all respects'. To really *know* 'each thing that is' means to comprehend the ontological paradigm of the Forms – a prerequisite for establishing Kallipolis: 'there is no way the city can be happy until it is designed by artists using the divine pattern'.[19] The quest for Being results in the quest for an ideal State.

I have argued that Plethon offers a radicalised variant of this thesis. The return to One *qua* Being in the *Differences* and in the *Nomoi* corresponds to a return to the ideal of the 'most vir-tuous polity' (σπουδαιοτάτη πολιτεία)' in the two *Memoranda*. Ontological *nostos* and political *utopia* come together.

---

[18] *Ti.* 28c3–5; *Resp.* 540d.   [19] *Resp.* 484b–d, 500d.

Plethon found in Plato's closely defined and ordered *polis* a pattern suitable for the conservation of a utopian *politeia*. This model sharply contrasts with the openness of religious ecumenism. So does the Plethonean wish to comprehend Being contrast with apophaticism. Since late antiquity the Fathers of the Church branded any attempt at an intellectual circumspection (περιγραφή) of the divine as idolatrous.[20] Plethon abandoned the openness of theological apophaticism, which transcends both Being *and* non-Being, and opted for a 'closed' Platonic ontology that strives to apprehend the One *qua* Being within the limits of human reason. Plethonean ontology is tantamount to a self-sufficient *systema* hierarchically and rationally organised, thus humanly cognisable and finite that excludes Christian negative theology.

In other words, Plethon was aiming at a philosophical relocalisation of the notion of Being within exclusively ontological categories that mirrored the political relocalisation of Hellenism within the Peloponnesian framework. This disjunction between a distinctively pagan Platonic ontology and Orthodox theology translated into an ideological polarity between Plethon's emerging proto-nationalism and the dominant trans-nationalism favoured by the Eastern Church.

Plethon's works reflect this tension diversely. The technical philosophical vocabulary and the form of a public lecture assumed in the *Differences between Plato and Aristotle* kept well hidden the actual polemical core of this seemingly academic work. Similarly, the esoteric character and the mythological façade of *Nomoi* have perplexed modern scholarship with regard to Plethon's intentions. In the *Differences* as well as in the *Nomoi* Plethon challenged apophaticism and the major proposition shared by Palamas and Aquinas that god is *not* in a *genus*, that the essence of god is ultimately inaccessible to the human intellect. By subverting this central maxim of Christianity, Plethon advanced a world-view founded upon a distinctively pagan ontology. If god is cognisable, then he is not really beyond Being. By implication, there is no need to maintain belief either in an exclusive divine revelation or in a complementary soteriology.

[20] For περιγραφή as generating conceptual idolatry see above, pp. 31–6.

The philosophical paganism in the *Nomoi* does not stand alone. Rather, the doctrinal affinities between the *Nomoi*, the *Differences*, the commentary to the *Chaldean Oracles* and the *Monodia in Helenam Palaeologinam* point to a consistent philosophical and theological paradigm that Plethon pursued by employing different literary vehicles depending on context and audience. The distribution of *De fato* independently of the rest of the *Nomoi* implies that Plethon did not intend to confine his philosophical paganism to some sort of an unpublished literary exercise. He was testing the waters.

It might be objected that Plethon's *Memoranda* are utterly different from Plethon's philosophical paganism as crystallised in the *Nomoi* project. The former are addressed to the political authorities and meant as a political-social intervention; by contrast, the *Nomoi* are an introvert work in progress that appears to aim at a pagan secret society. The relation between the *Memoranda* and the *Nomoi* is more complicated than that.

The two are connected by their anti-Christian intentionality. The *Memoranda*, I argued in Part III, are as provocative and anti-Christian as is the *Nomoi* – provided one looks at them in their proper literary and historical context. Plethon's proto-nationalism in the *Memoranda* is the reaction to the evolution of Palamism from mystical theology to political ideology. They constitute a call to the secularisation of the state based on the imperatives of natural religion. They have nothing specifically or expressly Christian about them. Rather, the theological principles in the *Memorandum to Theodore* are abstract and dechristianised. They sharply contrast with the confessed and genuinely Judaeo-Christian view on man, history and the state that was expected from and is prevalent in all Byzantine 'mirrors for princes', including the 'mirror' written by Manuel II, the addressee of one of the *Memoranda*.

Taken together with the large-scale secularisation plans reported by Kabasilas in his 'Anti-Zealot' treatise, and when opposed to the conventions of the 'mirrors for princes' genre as exemplified in Manuel's own 'mirror', the *Memoranda* convey a daring secular and humanist reformist ideal that is anticipated only by Demetrios Kydones. Its complete suppression by the monastic takeover of

Church and State led naturally to a more radical reply: the philosophical paganism of the *Nomoi*.

The failure of the secular reformism of the *Memoranda* instigated the pagan utopianism of the *Nomoi*. Natural religion and secularism in the former case and philosophical Hellenism in the latter are two sides of the same coin. One side is primarily exemplified in the *Memoranda* and is largely compatible with the humanist outlook of Demetrios Kydones; the other is openly pagan, primarily exemplified in the *Nomoi* and the *Differences between Plato and Aristotle*. In the *Memoranda* Plethon suggests the reorganisation of *politeia* according to rational and secular categories while excluding a gargantuan monastic movement on the grounds that, as in Plato, man may achieve individual and collective salvation by means of his moral and intellectual qualities, rather than by psychophysical exercise. In the *Nomoi* though, Plethon moves from this secular type of Platonism to pagan religion as the motive force for socio-political reformation. Both projects are consequences and ramifications of a single diehard Platonic intellectual paradigm.

My contention is that the *Nomoi* project is not only a reaction to the defeat of an emerging humanist philosophical paradigm but also one to aborted attempts at large-scale secularisation of the State to which Plethon personally contributed with the two *Memoranda*. The paganism of the *Nomoi* is the product of Plethon's coming to terms with reality rather than the opposite. The cold reception of the secular measures contained in the *Memoranda* made abundantly clear that appeals to political authority and plans for extended secularisation of the State were condemned to failure. And yet in Plethon's case the source that provided inspiration for the *Memoranda*, that is Platonism, was also capable of generating more extreme and idiosyncratic versions of utopianism.

In this regard it is instructive to read the *Memoranda* alongside the *Monody for the Empress Helen*.[21] Possibly like the distribution of *De fato*, the *Monody* confirms that Plethon expected some, at least, among the recipients of his popular works to become

---

[21] *Lampros, PP* 3.275.10–277.1; *Mem. I* 125.3–22.

acquainted with his pagan philosophy, even if this meant employing considerable skill in calculated obscurity. Purportedly reporting fundamental theological propositions, but in reality subverting all Byzantine genre conventions, the *Monody* recalls the *Memoranda* in persistently refraining from admitting even a single reference to Christianity. When read parallel to the *Nomoi* and the *Differences*, the theological propositions of the *Monody* cease to appear to relate to an abstract monotheistic religion (a notion which was scandalous enough in itself), and are shown to be consistent with epistemological and ontological premises that are fundamentally incompatible with Judaeo-Christianity, yet fully compatible with the pagan Platonic framework of the *Nomoi*.[22] This reading of the *Monody* makes abundantly clear that the *Nomoi* was not a product of any purely literary, 'esoteric' experimentations with paganism.

Philosophical implications of the Plato–Aristotle controversy

Plethon's Platonism signifies a return to what the Cappadoceans defined as 'conceptual idolatry', that is, the merging of God with human concepts about god. Maximus Confessor appears to have recognised in Hellenism an intellectual thrust that threatened to subvert the super-essentiality and ineffability of the Judaeo-Christian God and turn man into an 'assassin of Logos'.[23] To some extent, the anxiety of Maximus explains why, from an Orthodox perspective, there has been a tendency to see in Plethon a forerunner of Nietzsche.[24] Still, it is Plethon's reception of Plato that poses more questions.

Augustine is often quoted as affirming that of all philosophers Platonists are closer to Christianity. Augustine seems to have overlooked the fact that sometimes the most dangerous opponent is the one standing closest to you. In the *Differences* Plethon had no difficulty in maintaining the Augustinean theory of a proximity

---

[22] On this reading of *Monody* see Ch. 6, pp. 300–6. Cf. Masai (1956) 267.

[23] Max. Conf. *Ambigua*, PG 91.1129C: φονευταὶ τοῦ Λόγου.

[24] Sherrard (1974) 123. But see the introduction, p. 36 for Nietzsche as forerunner of the post-modern relativist trend that liquidates the difference between Platonism and Christianity by downgrading both to the status of idolatry.

between Platonism and Christianity in a calculated move to undermine the philosophical foundations of Eastern Orthodoxy from within. Throughout his life Plethon posed as a 'ritual Christian'. Ideologically and philosophically he belonged to an underground tradition of philosophical Hellenism that goes back to Plato. To the extent that one is sympathetic to the Plethonean interpretation of Plato's epistemology, ontology and political philosophy, one may identify in Plato, rather than in Plethon alone, a genuinely pagan core that undermines the philosophical viability of any possible Platonic-Christian synthesis.

These days the question regarding the differences between Plato and Aristotle is irrelevant to one's religious identity. Contemporary scholarship might be unwilling to admit any necessary link between Platonism and paganism. And yet when Scholarios and George of Trebizond first crossed swords with Plethon they had no doubt that in the *Differences* Plethon was manipulating Plato as a vehicle to convey pagan philosophical notions. Of course, Scholarios claimed that he was equally well disposed towards Plato and Aristotle.[25] We should do well to treat this statement with the same circumspection as Plethon's declaration in the *Differences* that his assault on Aristotle stems from an interest in showing that Plato serves the Church better than Aristotle does. In the former case Scholarios puts forward the traditional view of agreement between Plato and Aristotle as an alibi for neutralising the threat presented by Plethon's radical Platonism. In the latter case, Plethon undermines the philosopher who appeared to the Church as an authority, Aristotle, while pretending to serve the Church. Both are expressions of dissimulation.

Besides a deeply rooted Christian suspicion that Plato was the host of all things heretical that was newly confirmed by Thomas,[26] Scholarios and George of Trebizond had further reasons to contend that Plato offered the ideal opening for experiments with paganism. In the course of the Hesychast controversy the discussion regarding the universals (τὰ καθόλου) was again made relevant and was reconnected with the fallacies of 'Hellenic theology'.[27]

---

[25] Schol. *Contra Pleth., OC* 4.26–9. [26] See above, introduction, pp. 16–17.

[27] Gr. Pal. *Ep.* 1.9.10–21.

In Chapter 5 I argued that in the second half of the fourteenth century Palamites and anti-Hesychasts continuously exchanged mutual accusations of pagan Platonism and, significantly, polytheism. Each side accused the other of resurrecting Plato's Forms and reintroducing to theology self-subsistent entities that compromised the transcendence of god. One thing is certain: by the end of the century Platonism was again in vogue, this time as the seedbed of paganising Christian heresy.

But is this the only reason why Plethon opts for Plato rather than Aristotle for developing his pagan ontology and epistemology? Why do Christians from Hippolytus to Aquinas, Palamas and Scholarios associate Plato with heresy? What is in Plato's philosophy that invites ideological and religious dissent and doctrinal disestablishment? The reply, I have suggested, is to be found in the Plotinean reception of Aristotle's categories. These were arguably suitable for understanding the world of becoming, but not for approaching intellectually the divine realm. From early on, Aristotelianism was felt to have had a restricted scope posing as the ideal curriculum for an easily supervised *Schulphilosophie* and a useful tool of theological indoctrination. Aristotle's conceptual apparatus was treated as if it was incapable of functioning on the religious level without its host: Christian Orthodoxy. The critique of Plato's realm of Ideas/gods could be readily appropriated as purportedly supporting the radical ontological difference between a qualifiable sphere of creation and a super-essential unqualifiable godhead. Further, Aristotle's deliberate focus on the empirical realm ostensibly complemented rather than competed with supernatural revelation and Palamite notions of illumination.[28] Aristotelian empiricism was potentially conformable to the mystical end of psychophysical experience of divine energies, thus leading away from intellectual illumination of the Platonic type. Man may indeed strive to acquire a firm knowledge of the particular manifestation of beings in this world, even of the energies of god – but not of divine Being-in-itself.

By contrast, Platonists never ceased to claim openly or covertly access to a supra-sensible world for which Aristotelians had little

---

[28] See above p. 275 for Philotheos' use of Aristotle.

understanding or interest. The shifts and transformations of Platonism had always been less predictable. Platonism was a slippery and ambitious philosophy, hard to fit into particular boxes. Theologians like Scholarios were always aware of the fact that revivals of Plato's philosophy might at any time claim to address religious questions officially monopolised by Orthodox theology. At the level of ideas Platonism was the only antagonist of the Christian religion.

In Scholarios' eyes Plato was potentially dangerous precisely because he could be read in unpredictable ways owing to his tendency to argue confusingly (συγκεχυμένως) rather than clearly as Aristotle does (διωρισμένως καὶ σαφῶς).[29] The late Plato 'obscured the glory of philosophy by mathematics', he says, to the extent that his audience either pays attention to the surface literary qualities of his work or is diverted into a futile search for its concealed meaning. This is the problem with devout followers of Plato, continues Scholarios, namely that each one makes a different guess as to the meaning of his philosophy and disagrees about what is supposedly crystal clear.[30] And yet 'these men around Plethon (οἱ περὶ Πλήθωνα)' unabashedly scorn Aristotle's attention to detail and precision as πολυπραγμοσύνην καὶ μικρολογίαν.[31] Posing as Christian in the *Differences* and in *Reply to Scholarios*, Plethon claimed to use Aristotle to refute the standard Christian deductions from Aristotelian premises. The Plethonean attack on Aristotle is in reality a counter-attack on Roman Orthodoxy as defended by Aristotelians including Palamas and Scholarios. By crediting Aristotle, the Christians' privileged authority, with atheistic tendencies, Plethon undermined the solidarity of Orthodox theology while introducing pagan Platonism by the back door. The discussion regarding the superiority of Plato or Aristotle initiated by the *Differences* was a Trojan horse.

---

[29] Schol. *Contra Pleth.*, OC 4.108.20–6.   [30] Schol. *Contra Pleth.*, OC 4.15.33–16.1.
[31] Schol. *Contra Pleth.*, OC 4.17.36–7. Similarly, in an attempt to explain why the early Fathers of the Church preferred Plato to Aristotle, George of Trebizond (*Comparatio* 2.1.1.4–5) argued that Aristotle was not well known in late antiquity, but also that Plato's obscure style functions more or less as a verbal trap. For George of Trebizond against Plato see Hankins (1990: 236–45), who notes that this treatise 'has an excellent claim to rank among the most remarkable mixtures of learning and lunacy ever penned'.

By undermining the alleged compatibility between Aristotle and Christianity Plethon was doing more than stand up for pagan Platonism or deprive Christian rhetoric of its favourite point of reference. He was also paving the way for a liberation of Aristotle from successive Christian misreadings. For example, in *Against Plethon* Scholarios, following Palamas and Philotheos, praises Aristotle to some extent for his adherence to metaphysical doctrines that are traditionally held (ἡ πάτριος δόξα), while bringing to the foreground Aristotle's respect for 'those most competent' in regard to doctrines divinely inspired.[32] In *Against Scholarios* Plethon exposes Scholarios' use of Aristotle as manipulation. There is nothing in the passages from *Metaphysics* that Scholarios quotes confirming faith in any 'holy and revealed necessity'.[33] The clear inference is that Aristotle was misleadingly quoted as allowing for a divine power in the Christian sense. Plethon reports Scholarios' other misuses of Aristotle too, for example when observing that Aristotle was not an advocate of a creation *ex nihilo* any more than Plato was; and that Aristotle also believed in the immortality and transmigration of the soul, though at times he was uncertain and, in contrast to Plato, did not make the point forthrightly.[34] Scholarios would do well then, we read, to cast into the flames the commentaries on Aristotle that he says he is working on.[35] Scholarios' destruction of the *Nomoi* by fire might be seen as a reply to Plethon's sarcasms here.

Plethon was deeply interested in reorienting Aristotle to a non-Christian world-view, and he worked to this end both in the

---

[32] Cf. Schol. *Contra Pleth., OC* 4.16.17–26 (and 4.22.10–13); *Metaph.* 1074a16–17, 1074b12–14.

[33] Cf. Pleth. *Contra Schol.* 10.65–11.1; Schol. *Contra Pleth., OC* 4.16.17–26. In fact, Scholarios decontextualises and manipulates *Metaph.* 1074a16–17: 'And thus it is reasonable to suppose that there are as many immovable principles – *the statement of logical necessity may be left to more competent thinkers*', as well as *Metaph.* 1074b12–14, a passage that concerns ancient beliefs regarding the divinity of heavenly bodies: 'To this extent only, then, are the views of our forefathers and of earliest thinkers intelligible to us.' Plethon objects that Scholarios misappropriates *Metaph.* 1074a16–17. The 'more competent thinkers' Aristotle refers to are those more expert than himself in astronomy, not any affirming the Christian 'holy and revealed' power/necessity. Aristotle was unsure in a specialised scientific question and he left it to those expert in astronomy to give a definite reply: 'That is Aristotle's point in this passage; but to judge from your own use of it, you have not the slightest idea of what he means.'

[34] Pleth. *Contra Schol.* 10.42–6; 25.38–44.   [35] Pleth. *Contra Schol.* 19.14–19.

Differences and in *Against Scholarios*. At the outset he appears to be in accord with Simplicius' and Proclus' aim, namely to uncover the essence of ancient philosophy. He then breaks with a very important aspect of their endeavour: the belief that Plato and Aristotle were in agreement. On the other hand, it is noticeable that Plethon's adversaries, namely Scholarios and Theodore of Gaza, argue in favour of such agreement. Why would Scholarios take up the Neoplatonic line of argument and why would Plethon depart from a long-established tradition that tried to harmonise the two most important philosophers?

A close reading of the Plethon–Scholarios conflict reveals that the *symphonia* theory gradually became a serious obstacle to any potential regeneration of philosophical Hellenism. Admittedly, observes Plethon, in late antiquity Simplicius used the *symphonia* theory as part of his anti-clerical rhetoric (κατὰ τῆς ἐκκλησίας), that is to say, in order to promote a unified Hellenic worldview. Simplicius was targeting those members of the Church who slandered Hellenic philosophers for being divided and holding conflicting views. He did his best to return the accusation by aligning Aristotle with Plato and Parmenides. The implicit point was that it was Christian theologians who lacked doctrinal unity, not the Hellenes. Scholarios appropriates Simplicius' anti-Christian argument, unaware that it best exposes his own condition, 'for you are often in a state of schism within yourself'.[36]

In the Byzantine context the *symphonia* theory and late antique pagan hermeneutics could hardly function any longer as a weapon of anti-Christian discourse, as Simplicius initially intended. Aristotelianism had long been used as a tool of doctrinal exposition. The admission of the *symphonia* theory meant that Plato could hardly threaten the Church more than Aristotle did. It effectively neutralised Plato. Claiming that Plato and Aristotle were fundamentally in agreement, while also advancing a predetermined and utilitarian reading of Aristotle, Christian intellectuals such as Scholarios and Theodore of Gaza hoped to dictate how Plato was to be read, appropriated and applied. Plato could not be put to any

---

[36] Pleth. *Contra Schol.* 2.1–13.

reformatory cause for as long as he was read as agreeing with a badly digested Aristotle.

Political implications of the Plato–Aristotle controversy

The clash between competing understandings of Platonism and Aristotelianism in the East carries with it religious and philosophical significance but also political implications. It is remarkable that Aristotelians like Scholarios were keen to compromise with the conquerors, whereas Byzantine humanists of Neoplatonic tendencies turned to the West to mould a novel philosophical as well as religious identity. Is it therefore the case that in the late Byzantine context Aristotelianism was particularly embraced by those promoting collaboration with the Ottomans, whereas Platonism provided the philosophical incentive not only for religious but also for ideological and political resistance? As Balivet notes in an article provocatively entitled 'Aristote au service du sultan!', this might be a simplistic way of understanding the problem. This said, the fact remains that 'those who stayed in Byzantium under the Turkish regime were more often pupils of the Lyceum than of the Academy'.[37] Aristotelians such as George Amiroutzes and George of Trebizond were eager to claim the role of a 'new Aristotle' for 'the new Alexander' – namely the sultan.[38] Scholarios took the role of the new patriarch under Turkish rule. No known Platonist seems to have applied for either of these positions.

Meanwhile, the cases of Greek *émigrés* in the second half of the fifteenth century and the early sixteenth appear to corroborate Plethon's connection between Platonism and proto-nationalism. A few examples will illustrate the point. Like Bessarion, another devoted pupil of Plethon, Michael Apostoles, worked from Italy for the cause of liberating Greece from Ottoman occupation in a desperate attempt to persuade the Latins to intervene. The liberation of Greece was of primary concern to Marullus Tarcaniota too, whose neopagan *hymni naturales* are most probably

---

[37] Balivet (1999a) 150.
[38] Balivet (1999b) 148–9. As Balivet notes the anti-Plethonist and Aristotelian Matthew Kamariotes also assumed an important role under Turkish rule.

influenced by Plethon. Arsenios Apostoles (1465–1535) continued the philological work of his father Michael and edited Alci-
nous/Albinus' introduction to Plato and Psellos' scientific works.
Like his father, Arsenios appears to have thought that the ideological preparation necessary to liberate the 'Hellenes' and establish
a neo-Hellenic state begins with the dissemination and study of
Platonic philosophy. Perhaps the most prominent exponent of this
circle is Markos Musuros (1470–1517), editor of the complete
works of Plato and author of an *Ode to Plato* prefixed to his *editio
princeps*.[39] In these cases the link between Platonism and proto-
nationalism first revived by Plethon finds new forms of expression
and sharply contrasts with both the explicit preference for Aristotle and the policy followed by the Eastern Church in the Ottoman
Empire.

What attracted Plethon to Plato's political philosophy in the
first place? The reply is to be found in Plato's notion of *politeia*
as a closed, organic political entity that the governors 'should let
grow so long as in its growth it consents to remain a unity, but
no further'.[40] This ideal was irreconcilable with Orthodox religious trans-national ecumenism. The idea of political community
present within the Platonic understanding of *politeia* as an organic,
finite and ordered system clashed with the potential universalism
that philosophers such as Palamas and Scholarios recognised in
Aristotle.

The case of Averroes shows that this reading of Aristotle had
deep roots. Averroes sensed the tension between the ecumenism of
the *shari' a*, which aimed at a universal society encompassing all
mankind, and Plato's belief in the organisation of a large number of
virtuous communities of limited size defined by the antiquity and
nature of the inhabitants, their neighbours and geography. Thus
Averroes points at the 'indubitable truth' of the possibility of a
universal society, presumably favoured by Aristotle.[41] Aristotle
served the universalism of Averroes. He could be re-calibrated
to serve the Orthodox universalism represented by Palamas and

---

[39] On national awakening and Platonism in Michael and Arsenios Apostoles, Markos
Musuros and Marullus Tarcaniota see the remarks of Bargeliotes (2009) 51–2. See also
Geanakoplos (1962) 290.
[40] *Resp.* 423b9–10. [41] Cf. Averroes, *On Plato's* Republic 44.20–46.26; *Resp.* 423a–e.

Scholarios, and thus implicitly the sultan and the Ottoman imperial ideology.

It might be objected that Aristotle too is an advocate of the ideal of the city-state. He is in agreement with Plato in so far as he postulates that 'experience also shows that it is difficult and perhaps impossible for a state with too large a population to have good legal government'.[42] And yet Aristotle is easy prey to a convenient misappropriation when he observes that the potential ordering of an excessively large number of people 'would surely be a task for divine power, which holds even this universe together'.[43] The political Darwinism of Aristotle that begins with the household, passes on to the 'village' and then to the 'city-state' may be extended in the framework of a political but messianic teleology that added a divinely ordered *ecumene* as the real end of this evolutionary process.[44]

We have seen that apophaticism in theology appeared compatible with Aristotle's metaphysics and categories by claiming to carry on from where the latter ostensibly stopped. In the same way, Aristotelean political philosophy appeared conformable to an understanding of *politeia* that claimed to complement his *Politics* and advance beyond Plato's 'closed' and finite Kallipolis. This led to Scholarios' 'heavenly *politeia*'.

In Plethon's epistemology illumination (ἔλλαμψις) stands for the highest level of a *religio mentis*, that is the culmination of a human initiated intellectual endeavour, as opposed to spiritual illumination; in like manner, in his political thought Plethon makes a daring conceptual shift with regard to the meaning of the word σωτηρία. In the *Memoranda* Plethon shifts the focus from the Christian understanding of σωτηρία as salvation to that of σωτηρία as the safekeeping of man-made political entities. This is Plato's understanding of σωτηρία as the preservation of a terrestrial *politeia*.[45] Scholarios' anticipation of redemption (σωτηρία) in a heavenly *politeia* was a severe disincentive for the preservation of any terrestrial polity. According to Scholarios, the obliteration of the latter is the stepping stone to attaining the former. His call to approach this

---

[42] *Pol.* 1326a24–8, 1326b.   [43] *Pol.* 1326a30–5.   [44] *Pol.* 1252a–b.
[45] *Resp.* 429c, 465d.

'eternal home country' effectively presupposed opening the gates of Constantinople to the conquering Turks in order to advance beyond transient and mundane notions of political ideology. The gap between Plethon's and Scholarios' conceptualisation of the word σωτηρία is as irrevocable and absolute as is that between Plato's and Christ's understanding of the same word.

In the last analysis the πατρίς of Plethon is different from that of Scholarios. Lévinas made a comparison that captures well this difference between Jewish-Christian ecumenism as advocated by Scholarios and the Plethonean attempt to reinvigorate Platonic utopianism. This concerns two archetypical figures whose shadow hangs over the clash between Plethon and Scholarios, as much as it does over that between Lévinas and Heidegger:

> To the myth of Ulysses returning to Ithaca, we wish to oppose the story of Abraham who leaves his fatherland forever for a yet unknown land and forbids his servant to even bring back his son to the point of departure.[46]

Plethon tells a narrative of return, Scholarios one of departure. The former is Ulysses' path, one of homecoming to the Greek *polis*, ancient onto-theology and the gods that died away when the ancient ideal of *polis* was abandoned. Plethon's Ithaca is Mistra and the Peloponnese – that is, what was left of Greece. Scholarios opts for Abraham's path and tells the story of a journey that has different points of departure and arrival. Like Palamas, he turns his back for ever on the remnants of the Byzantine Empire and departs from the whole Hellenic tradition of τὰ πάτρια. Salvation is meta-historical. It is apocalyptic, millenarian and messianic. Zion is beyond history, a fatherland represented by the unity of the Church, not by that of the ontological ladder or 'system' as circumscribed in the *Nomoi*, nor by the restoration of any 'most-virtuous polity' as envisaged in the *Memoranda*. Plethon sought his utopia within history, Scholarios placed redemption in the world beyond.

---

[46] Lévinas (1986) 348.

9

EPILOGUE

'Spinozism before Spinoza', or the pagan roots of modernity

Plethon has been considered the *spiritus rector* of the Florentine Academy, or at any rate as a Byzantine forerunner of Renaissance Platonism announcing the end of medieval ways to do philosophy and the dawn of a new era. Conversely, he has been held to have had limited influence among Italian humanists.[1] But philosophically the decisive issue lies elsewhere: in the difference between the version of Platonism developed by the Italian humanists and the essence of Platonism as recaptured by Plethon. It is because of this hermeneutical disparity that the alleged connection between Plethon's Platonism and Renaissance Platonism is a misleading preconception in need of revision.

It was recently suggested that the significance of Plethon lies in the field of 'cultural mnemonics', in his 'symbolic status as the "second Plato" from the East' carrying esoteric knowledge to the West.[2] This is correct. However, there are other ways to think

---

[1] Masai (1953: 83–8) was one of the first to deal critically with the problem of Byzantine influences in Renaissance Platonism, though seeing Plethon's *Differences* as a 'genuine manifestation of Renaissance Platonism'. Monfasani (1992: 52–3) – reverting to the 1902 thesis of Della Torre – argued against Masai that Plethon's *Differences* inaugurated a long and international debate regarding the relation between Plato and Aristotle but did not cause any significant involvement with Plethon's Platonism nor substantially influence the philosophy of its recipients. Hankins (1990: 436–40) also argued that Plethon's influence was 'much slighter than has often been assumed'. See also Tambrun (2010) on the reasons for not overestimating the influence of Plethon's *Differences* upon his Italian contemporaries. On the other hand, Blum has noted that Pico's *De ente et uno* (1491) may be read as a reply to Plethon's distinction between the Platonic and the Aristotelean views on the One and Being (P. R. Blum 2010: 106) and that Cusanus' *De docta ignorantia* can also be seen as a reaction to Plethon's provocative views (P. R. Blum 2004: 168). Further, as Beyer has observed, Lauro Quirini followed closely Plethon's argument in a short dialogue that presents Aristotle's spirit giving its replies to Plethon's attack. But apart from that, Beyer (1994: 4) is right that the survival of plenty of manuscripts from the fifteenth century is abundant proof that Plethon's work aroused continued interest even if, as Masai assumed, the work caused bewilderment. Admittedly, the existence of these manuscripts contrasts sharply with the limited appeal exercised by the ideas of their author upon the philosophical formation of their recipients.

[2] Hanegraaff (2009) 41; Neri (2010) 288–91.

about Plethon's significance. In this epilogue I will make a case that the discontinuity between Plethon's philosophical paganism and Renaissance Platonism is an indication for the deeper philosophical significance of his project. Plethon's ideas might have been unique in the Renaissance context. But they may not be so from the viewpoint of a history of ideas that focuses on intellectual connections that transcend strict periodisation. Plethon bears a more concrete significance because of the underlying conceptual affinity between his philosophical paganism and early modern secular philosophical notions. Plethon is primarily significant because he announces hallmarks of modernity.

The Plethonean effort to reform the way in which Plato and Aristotle were thought of by Palamites in the East and Thomists in the West was fuelled by the firm belief that Platonism was possible only as paganism. Plethon signals the first consistent dechristianisation of Platonic ontology, one that was subsequently suppressed by Ficino and Renaissance philosophers. It is not a *Plato Christianus* but a *Plato Paganus* that he is echoing. Plethon's interpretation of Plato mirrored the pagan Platonism of Celsus and Julian and broke with moderate or mainstream Platonism as introduced by Plotinus and late Neoplatonists. Still, it was the latter type of Platonism that defined the intellectual identity of Renaissance Platonists. Holding to the theory of a concordance or *symphonia* between Plato and Aristotle, the Renaissance Platonists effectively derailed the Plethonean project of dechristianising Plato.

Whereas Palamas and Plethon were conscious of the irreducible difference between Hellenism and Judaeo-Christianity as conflicting world-views, Ficino and Pico perpetuated the comfortable theory of their harmonious cohabitation. For example, in his treatment of the *Chaldean Oracles*, Ficino parts from Plethon's paganism and commentary by amalgamating the Persian Magi with the New Testament Magi.[3] Obviously, Renaissance Platonists did not want to follow Plethon down the dark alley of Platonism *qua* paganism, nor did they even consider this option. Their Platonism has an apologetical aspect.[4] But most importantly, during the

---

[3] Tambrun (2010).   [4] Masai (1953) 89; Hanegraaff (2009) 41.

Italian Renaissance the possibility of a monistic (i.e. pagan) Platonic ontology was ignored.

The situation changed on the eve of modernity when philosophers and textual critics including Gundling and Bayle called for a reinvestigation of Renaissance certainties regarding Plato, Aristotle, Hellenism and Christianity. The case for a new reception of ancient philosophy that Plethon made in his *Differences* was not restated until Spinoza, whose 'paganising' philosophy cast its shadow over a Europe still nourished by the Renaissance myth of an alleged compatibility between natural theology and Judaeo-Christian exclusivity. Pierre Bayle and Jean Le Clerc and their like daringly exposed the fallacious basis of the Renaissance *prisca theologia*. This presumably aligned Plato with Judaeo-Christianity, while in reality subsuming the former to the ultimate truth of the latter. Le Clerc objected that both Renaissance humanism and Latin scholasticism prioritised an approach to ancient philosophy that was manipulative and rhetorical. In order to subjugate Plato to religious orthodoxy, scholastics as well as Renaissance humanists did not hesitate to gloss over essential differences between the Hellenic and the Judaeo-Christian outlooks. Further, the attempts of Vico, Doria, Conti and Gundling to define the relation between Platonism, Spinozism and Christianity led to the growing realisation that the quest for establishing what Plato really thought and meant required an autonomous study of his philosophy. Modernity overthrew the Renaissance hermeneutical model by exposing the precious *prisca theologia* of Renaissance humanists as a rhetorical device put to the service of Christian doctrine. As Jonathan Israel put it, pagan philosophers had begun to speak for themselves again.[5]

The early modern approach to ancient philosophy was a reaction to Renaissance philosophy, rather than its continuation. Plethon anticipates not Renaissance Platonism, but the modern call for a novel reception of ancient philosophy. The hermeneutical endeavour in the *Differences* qualifies as the first modern reading of Plato and Aristotle, in as much as, long before Bayle and Le Clerc, it calls for a study of Plato and Aristotle independently of a long

[5] Israel (2006) 537–42.

established Christian hegemony of interpretation and ideological manipulation. The early modern intellectuals reached their ground-breaking conclusions in the last quarter of the seventeenth century thanks to the newly developed tools of textual criticism. Plethon was already there in the middle of the fifteenth century through philosophical hermeneutics.

Plethon's Platonism confirms a now largely forgotten thesis developed in the first years of the seventeenth century by Bayle, the German textual critic Niklaus Hieronymus Gundling and Lutheran scholarship. This is that Platonism and Spinozism share a common monist basis, one that, from a Christian position, is 'atheistic'. In the following pages I will restate Gundling's and Bayle's thesis according to which a *Spinozismus ante Spinozam* is responsible for the survival and transmission of pagan Platonic monism to early modernity. In my version of this thesis, Plethon's radical rehabil-itation of Plato is the philosophical mid-point between Platonism and the notorious proto-Spinozist spirit.

In 1701 Buddeus believed he had uncovered and traced the development of 'Spinozism before Spinoza' (*Spinozismus ante Spinozam*) to its origins. Machiavelli (whose secular tendencies in *Il Principe* are anticipated, we have seen, by those in Plethon's *Memoranda*) was classed in the company of early Enlightenment thinkers such as Pomponazzi in a category of *athei speculativi*. This 'philosophical atheism' ostensibly planted the seed for the philosophy of the chief modern exponent of atheism, pantheism and of all sorts of heresy: Baruch de Spinoza. In like manner, Pierre Bayle and Diderot considered Cesalpino to be another proto-Spinozist who allowed only one unified reality, thus challenging the supra-essential nature of God. Giordano Bruno was also seen as a precursor of Spinozism owing to his perception of the whole universe as 'one being'.

Gundling took a step further in locating the intellectual roots of this early modern movement of proto-Spinozism in Plato. Redeem-ing Platonism from successive Christian dualistic misreadings and particularly from Renaissance syncretistic contortions, Gundling published an article with the catchy title 'Plato atheos'. He pointed out – against Buddeus – that the Platonic god is immanent in the world of becoming, not transcendent in the Christian sense of the word, and acts out of necessity, not out of free will. According to Gundling, for all their obvious differences, Plato and Spinoza make remarkably similar claims: Plato postulates that *unum omnia et omnia unum*, Spinoza believed in *unam substantiam*. Both positions challenge the Judaeo-Christian doctrine of providential creation *ex nihilo* asserting a world emanating from and participating in a primary cause.[6]

Predictably, Gundling's thesis stirred the waters. His approach ruled out an accommodation of Plato within the tradition of a Christian *prisca theologia* of the Ficino type. If Gundling was right, Renaissance Platonists were misled in their belief that Plato prefigured Judaeo-Christianity. But beyond that, the roots of Spinozism should be looked for in a generic Platonic paradigm.

The philosophical affinities between Plethon's reception of Plato and 'Spinozism' makes this a defensible assumption. To begin with, the comprehensibility of god as the *ultimum* of human intellection is a particularly modern premise, typical of the Father of Enlightenment, Spinoza. Much like Plethon, Spinoza believed that the intellect stands for an eternal part of our mind that is naturally fitted to acquire and possess knowledge of god. Intellectual perfectibility is natural to man. But most importantly, Spinoza opposes the equivocal use of the word 'substance' more daringly than Descartes had ever done.

Challenging the scholastic position that derives its inspiration from Aristotle's theory of the equivocity of Being, Spinoza advanced a one-substance monistic theory according to which all things proportionally express the essence of god. The more we know their essence, the more we know divine essence.

This reciprocity between monistic ontology and epistemic optimism is a tenet of the philosophical paradigm that vitalises Plethon's pagan Platonism. Long before Spinoza, Plethon turned against the equivocity of Being and established a unified ontology that challenged the most fundamental Christian Orthodox doctrine: that there is no community, nor similarity, nor even anything resembling a possible ontological analogy between created

---

[6] On the controversy regarding Plato as founder of proto-Spinozism, Gundling and the reaction of men like Fabricius, Brucker and Zimmermann see Israel (2006) 483, 486–91.

substance and the uncreated essence of god. In both cases the transcendence of the Judaeo-Christian godhead is abolished and nature is rendered ontologically connected to god. Thirdly, much like Plethon, Spinoza develops an essentially Stoic deterministic world-view according to which to be free means to synchronise with necessity. Moreover, we have also seen that, like Plethon, Spinoza advances a political religion that seeks to disarm clericalism in markedly similar ways.[7]

Whereas Spinoza mainly conversed with ancient philosophy indirectly through a critical assessment of Descartes' philosophy, Plethon did so by reverting to the primary sources: Plato, Aristotle and their appropriation by the Christian theological authorities. The pagan-secular reformation envisaged in the *Memoranda*, the *Differences* and the *Nomoi* is ultimately the product of an original and extended hermeneutical exercise that is, in its own right, unprecedented.

This represents a significant shift from one tradition or way of doing philosophy to another. It marks a departure from the Proclan commentary tradition, which aimed at preserving Platonism under circumstances conditioned by the Christian hegemony of discourse. Ancient philosophy was not seen as capable of providing an alternative to the political, ideological and religious crisis of late Byzantium. H. D. Saffrey noted that with Proclus the philosophy of Plato becomes a *mystagogia*: it acquires a sacred value – and in this sense Proclus' spiritualism prefigures medieval philosophy.[8] Plethon struggled to move away from precisely this medieval Christian reading of Plato. Though well versed in Proclus, Plethon is pursuing a modern Plato, not a mystical medieval one. Plethon's Platonism was not another heresy of humanist tendencies inspired by Plato; rather, it pressed for its philosophical and doctrinal autonomy. For the first time since Julian, Platonism seemed capable of abandoning its parasitical life within Christian heresy –one that had provided pagan Platonism with the means to survive for centuries – and claim its self-sufficiency as a consistent philosophical and religious world-view that had its own answers on offer.

---

[7] See Ch. 7, p. 379.   [8] Saffrey (1984) 182.

This explains why Proclan hierarchies are subverted, theurgy abandoned, the *Chaldean Oracles* amended and secularised, but above all, why there is a break with the Neoplatonic commentary tradition in both its aims and form. Tellingly, in the *Nomoi* Plato is neither quoted nor commented on. The essence of Platonic philosophy is extracted and reformulated according to new philosophical concerns, just as in the *Memoranda* Plato is utilised in order to meet immediate reformatory needs. Plethon's express interest was in modernising the Platonist world-view, not in producing introverted commentaries after the example of Proclus and Simplicius. He consciously abandons the safe yet tired constructs of Neoplatonist commentary, instead advancing a reading of ancient philosophy that is definitely modern.

A century before Luther, Plethon employed hermeneutics as the main means for providing an alternative to Orthodox and Latin Christianity. The upshot we might well describe today as *modern* in so far as Plethon claimed that justice, moral philosophy, as well as knowledge and truthfulness depend upon a universally valid rational discourse rather than upon the authority of inherited religious institutions. In particular the first book of the *Nomoi* qualifies as a manifesto of modernity owing to its (re)introduction of common notions and rational discourse as sufficient criteria for choosing correctly from among a variety of possible *haireseis biou*. By making an appeal to a *consensus gentium*, this move anticipates one of the greatest achievements of modern Enlightenment rationalists.

Voltaire's *Le philosophe ignorante* (1766) features a chain of ancient sages as exponents of a trans-historical moral principle that is very similar to the one in the *Nomoi* (Zoroaster, Pythagoras, Plato). Modern deism is associated with classicism, free-thought, moral realism, political reformism and natural religion that culminated in the Enlightenment. Plethon testifies to its pagan Platonic roots. The driving intention of the *Nomoi* to fashion ideology and utopianism into a science, a systematic and applicable science that fully exploits the intellectual capacity of man, became the tenet of nineteenth-century ultra-radical heirs of the Enlightenment as well as of utopian socialism. One of the first scholars to focus on Plethon's political reformism, H. F. Tozer, wrote at a time when the cult of progress and the utopianism of Saint-Simonist cells still exercised fascination among European intellectuals. Tozer noted a parallel between Plethon's scheme and the reformist plans of Saint-Simon 'in our century, which in several points it resembles'.[9] This was the view of Charles Alexandre, too.[10] They were right. Like Plethon, Saint-Simonists attempted to reintroduce an archetypical religion founded upon positivism, radical reformism, the re-sacralisation of the physical universe and human *ratio*, eventually resulting in an imaginary institution of society or 'social imaginary'.[11]

It is no coincidence then that the first consistent attempt to revive polytheism on Greek soil after Plethon took place in the aftermath of 1789, when utopian circles continued to experiment with variations of the revolutionary Cult of the Highest Being. Around 1797/9 Jacobins in Kephalonia combined their plans for the redistribution of land, direct democracy, communality and abolition of all debts with a call for the overthrow of the Christian religion and a return to the 'national' polytheist religion of the Greeks.[12] Once again, utopianism and paganism combined to subvert the political and clerical establishment and initiate the regeneration of mankind.[13] Anticipating Enlightenment *philosophes*, Saint-Simonist intellectuals, ultra-radical Jacobins and quixotic heretics, Plethon oscillates between the ancient, medieval and

---

[9] Tozer (1886) 378–9. Hence, 'we may admire Plethon for his determination, in spite of all discouragements, not to despair of the state. But his scheme, like that of Saint-Simon in our own century, which in several points it resembles, must be reckoned among those which could not have taken a practical form.'

[10] Alexandre (1858) lxxxiv.

[11] On the social imaginary and utopianism in Saint-Simonism see Picon (2002).

[12] For the sources reporting on this virtually unknown utopian endeavour see Siniossoglou (2008b) 46 and n. 63.

[13] Within the same context, the intellectual ramifications of Plethon's Platonist-deist virtue of *theosebeia* are discernible in the cult of Theosebeia founded by Theophilos Kaires, the radical philosopher and heretic who reacted to anti-Enlightenment conservatism by attempting to reinstitute a 'sacred philosophy'. Like Plethon, Kaires turned back to antiquity in order to retrieve the essence of what Proclus christened 'Greek Theosophy' (Procl. *Plat. Theol.* 5.127.16: Ἑλληνικὴ θεοσοφία) and establish with old materials a modern rational religion, eventually clashing with the clerical establishment. On Plethon and Kaires see Argyropoulos (1987/8) 391–5; (1982) 207–12; Siniossoglou (2008b) 81–2. Podskalsky (1977: 38 n. 125) correctly recognised in Plethon a theosophist, though without noting the parallels with Neoplatonic and modern versions of philosophical theosophy.

modern intellectual paradigms. To some extent oxymoronic, the Plethonean project appears to promise a return to Plato and paganism; and yet, consciously or not, Plethon was pointing forward towards the ambiguities of modernity. After all, one of the major modernist poets, Ezra Pound, was deeply fascinated by Plethon.[14]

In a nutshell: Plethon discerned the connection between secularism and paganism that lies at the centre of the project of modernity. His version of philosophical Hellenism anticipates modernity by separating Church and monasticism from the affairs of the State; by posing the crucial question regarding the relation between *genos* and State and prioritising a proto-national mobilisation; by opposing to religious messianism and mysticism a rational notion of godlikeness and political/natural religion that runs through the Enlightenment ideal of incessant scientific and political progress; and finally by advancing from Platonism those deist and monist tendencies that became dominant in modern religious experimentations from Spinozist pantheism to the 'religion of humanity' of Auguste Comte and the cult of progress of Saint-Simon.

---

[14] On Plethon's influence on Pound's occult interests and poetry see Tryphonopoulos (1992) 127, 138–42.

BIBLIOGRAPHY

Primary sources

This list mainly contains (a) editions of Plethon's works, (b) editions of other primary sources used in this book that are either not included in the *TLG* or are different from those included in the *TLG*.

Anonymous, *Prolegomena Philosophiae Platonicae*, ed. L. G. Westerink; French trans. J. Trouillard. Paris 1990.

Averroes, *On Plato's* Republic, ed. and Eng. trans. R. Lerner. London 1974.

Avicenna Latinus, *Liber de philosophia prima sive scientia divina*, ed. S. van Riet, vol. I. Louvain and Leiden 1977.

Gregory Palamas, *The One Hundred and Fifty Chapters*, ed. and trans. R. E. Sinkewicz. Rome 1988.

Triads, ed. J. Meyendorff, *Grégoire Palamas. Défense des saints hésychastes* (Spicilegium Sacrum Lovaniense. Études et documents 30). Louvain 1973; Eng. trans. N. Gendle. New York 1992.

John Italos, *Quaestiones quodlibetales* (ἀπορίαι καὶ λύσεις), ed. P. Joannou. Ettal 1956.

Joseph Bryennios, 'On the end of the world (περὶ συντελείας λόγοι I–II)', in *Τὰ εὑρεθέντα*, ed. E. Boulgaris, vol. II. Leipzig 1784: 190–207 and 208–26.

'On the fortification of Constantinople (Περὶ τοῦ τῆς Πόλεως ἀνακτίσματος)', in N. Tomadakes (ed.), *Περὶ Ἁλώσεως τῆς Κωνσταντινουπόλεως*. Thessaloniki 1993: 243–52.

Leon Choirosphaktes, *Chiliostichos theologia*, ed. and German trans. I. Vassis. Berlin 2002.

Manuel Corinthios (The Grand Rhetor), *Liber de Marco Sanctissimo Metropolitano Ephesi et de Florentina Synodo, nec non Adversus Gemistum et Bessarionem, impiorumque eorum librorum refutatio*, ed. L. Petit, *PO* 17 (1923): 354–84.

Manuel Palaiologos, *Funeral Oration on his Brother Theodore*, ed. J. Chrysostomides. Thessaloniki 1985.

Hypothekai ('Υποθῆκαι βασιλικῆς ἀγωγῆς), *PG* 156.313–84.

Letters, text, trans. and notes by G. T. Dennis. Washington 1977.

Mark Eugenikos, *Anti-unionist Works*, in Petit, *Documents*: 198–253.

Matthew Kamariotes, *Orationes duae contra Plethonem De fato* (Λόγοι δύο πρὸς Πλήθωνα περὶ εἱμαρμένης), ed. Reimarus. Leipzig 1721; 'La fin inédite du

Contra Plethonem de Matthieu Camariotes', ed. C. Astruc, *Scriptorium* 9 (1955): 246–62.

Maximus Confessor, *Ambigua*, ed. Larchet *et al.*, commentary by D. Staniloae. Paris 1994.

Nikephoros Gregoras, *Historia Romana*, German trans. J. van Dieten, vol. IV. Stuttgart 1994.

Explicatio in librum Synesii De insomniis, ed. P. Pietrosanti. Bari 1999.

Nikolaos Kabasilas, *Discourse concerning Illegal Acts of Officials Daringly Committed against Things Sacred* ('Sermo contra zelatores'), ed. I. Ševčenko, *DOP* 11 (1957): 91–125.

Oracula Chaldaica, ed., Eng. trans. and commentary R. Majercik. Leiden 1989; ed. and French trans. E. des Places. Paris 1971.

Pico della Mirandola, G. (1956) *De dignitate hominis*, ed. and German trans. E. Garin. Berlin 1968; Eng. trans. A. R. Caponigri. Washington 1956.

De ente et uno, Über das Seiende und das Eine, ed. and German trans. P. R. Blum *et al.* Hamburg 2006.

Plethon (Georgios Gemistos), *Consilium ad despotam Theodorum de Peloponneso* (Συμβουλευτικὸς πρὸς τὸν Δεσπότην Θεόδωρον περὶ τῆς Πελοποννήσου), ed. Sp. Lampros, *PP* 4.113–35; draft Eng. trans. by G. Finley in Baloglou (2003): 26–35; German trans. W. Blum (1988): 151–72; Ellissen (1860): 105–30; Spanish trans. F. L. Lisi and J. Signes. Salamanca 1995; Modern Greek trans. Baloglou (2002).

Contra De dogmate Latino librum, ed. C. Alexandre, in Alexandre: 300–11.

Contra Scholarii pro Aristotele obiectiones (Πρὸς τὰς Σχολαρίου ὑπὲρ Ἀριστοτέλους ἀντιλήψεις), ed. E. V. Maltese. Leipzig 1988; partial Eng. trans. and summary in Woodhouse (1986): 283–307.

De differentiis (Περὶ ὧν Ἀριστοτέλης πρὸς Πλάτωνα διαφέρεται), ed. B. Lagarde, *Byzantion* 43 (1973): 321–43; Eng. trans. in Woodhouse (1986): 192–214; German trans. W. Blum (1988): 112–50; Italian trans. M. Neri. Rimini 2001.

De virtutibus (Περὶ ἀρετῶν), ed., French trans., intro. and commentary by B. Tambrun (Corpus Philosophorum Medii Aevi 7). Athens and Leiden 1987; German trans. G. Schandl in Blum and Seitter (2005): 25–34; Russian trans. in Medvedev (1997): 291–300; Italian trans. in Neri (2010): 422–53.

Manuel d'astronomie, ed. A. Tihon and R. Mercier. Louvain-la-Neuve 1997.

Monodia in Helenam Palaeologinam, ed. Sp. Lampros, *PP* 3.266–80.

Nomoi (Νόμων συγγραφή), ed. C. Alexandre, French trans. A. Pellisier. Paris 1858; repr. Amsterdam 1966; partial repr. with an introduction by R. Brague, Paris 1982; partial Eng. trans. in Woodhouse (1986): 322–56; Spanish trans. F. L. Lisi and J. Signes. Salamanca 1995; Russian trans. in Medvedev (1997): 220–90; partial German trans. W. Blum in Blum and Seitter (2005): 7–23; Modern Greek trans. D. K. Chatzemichael. Athens 2005.

Oracles chaldaïques. Recension de Georges Gémiste Pléthon (Μαγικὰ λόγια τῶν ἀπὸ Ζωροάστρου Μάγων. Γεωργίου Γεμιστοῦ Πλήθωνος ἐξήγησις εἰς τὰ αὐτὰ λόγια), ed., French trans. intro., and commentary by B. Tambrun (Corpus Philosophorum Medii Aevi 3). Athens, Paris and Brussels 1995.

Oratio ad Manuelem (Πρὸς τὸν βασιλέα [Μανουὴλ]), ed. Sp. Lampros *PP* 3.309–12.

Oratio ad Manuelem Palaeologum de rebus in Peloponneso (εἰς Μανουὴλ Παλαιολόγον περὶ τῶν ἐν Πελοποννήσῳ πραγμάτων), ed. Sp. Lampros, *PP* 3.246–65; draft Eng. trans. by G. Finley in Baloglou (2003): 36–42; German trans. W. Blum (1988): 173–87; Ellissen (1860): 85–104; Modern Greek trans. Baloglou (2002).

Recapitulation of Zoroastrian and Platonic Doctrines (Ζωροαστρείων τε καὶ Πλατωνικῶν δογμάτων συγκεφαλαίωσις), ed. C. Alexandre, in Alexandre: 262–8; German trans. W. Blum (1988): 94–6.

Reply to Certain Questions (Πρὸς ἠρωτημένα ἄττα ἀπόκρισις), ed. L. Benakis, in Benakis (1974): 349–59.

Plotinus, *Enneads*, Modern Greek trans. and commentary by P. Kalligas, 4 vols. Athens. 2004–.

Porphyry, *Lettera a Marcella*, Italian trans., intro. and notes by R. Sodano. Milan 2006.

Proclus, *Proklos: Kommentar zu Hesiods Werken und Tagen*, ed. and German trans. P. Marzillo. Munich 2010.

Commentary on Plato's Parmenides; Eng. trans. G. Morrow and J. Dillon. Princeton, NJ 1987.

Psellos, *On Plato's Doctrine of the Ideas* (Περὶ τῶν ἰδεῶν ἃς ὁ Πλάτων λέγει), ed. L. Benakis, Φιλοσοφία 5–6 (1975/6): 393–23.

Pseudo-Basil, Κεφάλαια παραινετικά, ed. K. Emminger, *Studien zu den griechischen Fürstenspiegeln III*. Munich 1913.

Suhrawardi, *The Philosophy of Illumination* (Hikmat al-ishraq), ed. and Eng. trans. J. Walbridge and H. Ziai. Provo, Utah 1999.

Œuvres philosophiques et mystiques, vol. II, ed. and prolegomena H. Corbin. Teheran 1970.

Theodore of Gaza, *De fato*, ed. and Eng. trans. J. W. Taylor. Toronto 1925; cf. Mohler III: 239–46.

Theodore Metochites, *Ethicus*, ed. J. D. Polemes. Athens 1995.

Modern works

Ahrweiler, H. (1975) *L'idéologie politique de l'empire byzantine*. Paris.

Akasoy, A. (2008) 'Plethons *Nomoi*. Ein Beitrag zum Polytheismus in spätbyzantinischer Zeit und seiner Rezeption in der islamischen Welt', *Revista Mirabilia*, http://www.revistamirabilia.com/Numeros/Num2/akasoy.html.

Alexandre, C. (1858) 'Notice historique et critique', in C. Alexandre (ed.) *Pléthon: Traité des lois*. Paris: i–c.

Anastos, M. V. (1952) 'Pletho, Strabo and Columbus', *AIPhO* 12: 1–18.

(1948) 'Pletho's calendar and liturgy,' *DOP* 4: 183–305.

Angold, M. (2006) 'Byzantium and the West 1204–1453', in *CHC*: 53–78.

Arabatzis, G. (2008) 'Pléthon et les stoïciens. Système et fragment', *Archiv für mittelalterliche Philosophie und Kultur* 14: 305–32.

(2005) 'Le système de Pléthon et la nécessité,' in *Hasard et nécessité dans la philosophie Grecque*. Athens: 215–36.

(2003) 'Πλήθωνος Περὶ Ἀρετῶν καὶ στωικὴ ἠθική. Ἔρευνες γιὰ τὶς πηγὲς καὶ τὴν χρονολόγηση τοῦ ἔργου', *Φιλοσοφία* 33: 218–31.

Argyropoulos, R. (1987/8) 'Theosebeia in Plethon's work', *Φιλοσοφία* 17–18: 391–5.

(1982) 'Georges Gémistos Pléthon et la pensée néohellénique du 18e siècle', *JÖByz* 32.2: 207–12.

Arthur, R. A. (2008) *Pseudo-Dionysius as Polemicist: the Development and Purpose of the Angelic Hierarchy in Sixth Century Syria*. Burlington.

Athanassiadi, P. (2002) 'Byzantine commentators on the *Chaldaean Oracles*: Psellos and Plethon', in Ierodiakonou (2002): 237–52.

Aubenque, P. (1962) *Le problème de l'être*. Paris.

Balivet, M. (2007) 'Église et clercs byzantins dans l'épopée turque', *Byz F* 39: 49–78.

(2002) 'Les contacts byzantino-turcs entre rapprochement politique et échanges culturels (milieu XIIe–milieu XVe s.)', in M. Bernardini, C. Borelli *et al.* (eds.), *Europa e Islam tra i secoli XIV e XVI*, vol. II. Napoli: 525–47.

(1999a) *Byzantins et Ottomans: relations, interaction, succession*. Istanbul.

(1999b) 'Aristote au service du Sultan! Ouverture aux Turcs et Aristotélisme chez quelques penseurs byzantins du quinzième siècle', in Balivet (1999a): 139–50.

(1999c) 'Byzantins judaïsants et Juifs islamisés: Kâhin-χιόνες', in Balivet (1999a): 151–80.

(1999d) 'Textes de fin d'empire, récits de fin du monde: à propos de quelques thèmes communs aux groupes de la zone byzantino-turque', in Balivet (1999a): 181–96.

(1997) *Pour une concorde islamo-chrétienne: démarches byzantines et latines à la fin du Moyen-Age (de Nicolas de Cues à Georges de Trébizonde)*. Rome.

(1995) *Islam, mystique et révolution armée dans les Balkans ottomans: vie de Cheikh Bedreddin le 'Hallaj des Turcs' (1358/59–1416)*. Istanbul.

(1993) 'Culture ouverte et échanges inter-religieux dans les villes ottomanes du XIVe siècle', in E. Zachariadou (ed.), *The Ottoman Emirate (1300–1389)*. Rethymnon: 1–6 (reprinted in Balivet 1999a: 13–20).

Baloglou, Chr. (2005) 'The institutions of Ancient Sparta in the works of Pletho', *A&A* 51: 137–50.

(2003) 'George Finlay and Georgios Gemistos Plethon. New evidence from Finley's records', *MEG* 3: 23–42.

(2002) Γεώργιος Γεμιστός Πλήθων ἐπὶ τῶν Πελοποννησιακῶν πραγμάτων (Βυζαντινὸ κείμενο, μετάφρασις, σχόλια). Athens 2002.

(1998) *Georgios Gemistos Plethon: ökonomisches Denken in der spätbyzantinischen Geisteswelt*, preface by B. Schefold. Athens.

Baltes, M. (1997) 'Is the Idea of the Good in Plato's *Republic* beyond Being?', in Joyal (1997): 3–23.

Bargeliotes, L. (2009) 'The Enlightenment and the Hellenic "genos": From Plethon to Vulgaris', *Skepsis* 20: 44–61.

(1990) 'Plotinus and Plethon as defenders of the Hellenic logos', Ἐπετηρὶς Ἑταιρείας Βυζαντινῶν Σπουδῶν 48: 377–96.

(1980) Ἡ κριτικὴ τοῦ Ἀριστοτέλους παρὰ Πλήθωνι ὡς ἔκφρασις τοῦ ἀντιαριστοτελισμοῦ κατὰ τὸν ΙΕ΄ αἰῶνα. Athens.

(1979) 'Man as *methorion* according to Pletho', *Diotima* 7: 14–20.

(1974) 'Pletho's philosophy of religion and ethics', *Diotima* 2: 125–49.

Bargeliotes, L. and Moutsopoulos, E. (1987) Πλατωνισμὸς καὶ Ἀριστοτελισμὸς κατὰ τὸν Πλήθωνα. Athens.

Barker, J. W. (2003) 'Late Byzantine Thessaloniki: a second city's challenges and responses', *DOP* 57: 5–33.

(1969) *Manuel II Palaeologus (1391–1425): a Study in Late Byzantine Statesmanship*. New York.

Baudrillard, J. (1975) *Le miroir de la production, ou, l'illusion critique du matérialisme historique*. Paris.

Beck, H. G. (1963) 'Humanismus und Palamismus', *XIIe Congrès International d' Études Byzantines*, vol. I, ed. Comité Yugoslave des études byzantines. Belgrade: 63–82 (reprinted in H. G. Beck, *Ideen und Realitäten in Byzanz: Gesammelte Aufsätze*, London 1972: ch. V).

(1952) *Theodoros Metochites: Die Krise des byzantinischen Weltbildes in 14. Jahrhundert*. Munich.

Beck, P. H. (1937) *Vorsehung und Vorherbestimmung in der theologischen Literatur der Byzantiner* (Orientalia christiana analecta 114). Rome.

Benakis, L. (2002a) *Texts and Studies on Byzantine Philosophy* (Βυζαντινὴ Φιλοσοφία: Κείμενα καὶ μελέτες). Athens.

(2002b) Ἐλευθερία καὶ ἀναγκαιότητα στὴν Βυζαντινὴ Φιλοσοφία', in Benakis (2002a): 159–76.

(1986) 'Die Stellung des Menschen im Kosmos in der byzantinischen Philosophie', in C. Wenin (ed.), *L'homme et son univers au Moyen Age*. Louvain-La-Neuve: 56–76 (reprinted in Benakis 2002a: 137–57).

(1978/9) 'Το πρόβλημα τῶν γενικῶν ἐννοιῶν καὶ ὁ ἐννοιολογικὸς ρεαλισμὸς τῶν Βυζαντινῶν', *Φιλοσοφία* 8–9: 311–40 (reprinted in Benakis 2002a: 107–36).

(1974) 'Γεωργίου Γεμιστοῦ Πλήθωνος, *Πρὸς ἠρωτημένα ἅττα ἀπόκρισις*. Γιὰ τὸ ἀριστοτελικὸ ἀξίωμα τῆς ἀντιφάσεως καὶ γιὰ τὴ σύνθετη φύση τοῦ ἀνθρώπου', *Φιλοσοφία* 4: 330–76 (reprinted in Benakis 2002a: 585–632).

Benakis, L. and Baloglou, Chr. (eds.) (2003) *Proceedings of the International Congress on Plethon and his Time*. Athens and Mystras.

Benoist, A. de (1990) 'Sacré païen et désacralisation judéo-chrétienne', in D. Théraios (ed.), *Quelle religion pour l'Europe?* Geneva.

Benson, B. E. (2002) *Graven Ideologies: Nietzsche, Derrida & Marion on Modern Idolatry.* Illinois.

Berger, A. (2006) 'Plethon in Italien', in Konstantinou (2006): 79–89.

Beyer, H.-V. (1994) 'Lauro Quirini, ein Venezianer unter dem Einfluss Plethons', *JÖByz* 44: 1–19.

(1989) 'Demetrios Kabasilas, Freund und späterer Gegner des Gregoras', *JÖByz* 39: 135–77.

(1976) 'Ideengeschichtliche Vorbemerkungen zum Inhalt der ersten "Antirrhetika" des Gregoras', in H.-V. Beyer (ed. and German trans.) *Nikephoros Gregoras, Antirrhetika I.* Vienna: 17–118.

Bidez, J. (1929) *La tradition manuscrite et les éditions des discours de l'Empereur Julien.* Paris.

Billig, M., Condor, S., Edwards, D. *et al.* (eds.) (1988) *Ideological Dilemmas: a Social Psychology of Everyday Thinking.* London.

Blanchet, M. H. (2008) *Georges-Gennadios Scholarios (vers 1400-vers 1472): un intellectuel orthodoxe face à la disparition de l'empire byzantin.* Paris.

(2007) 'L'église byzantine à la suite de l'union de Florence (1439–1445): de la contestation à la scission', *ByzF* 39: 79–123.

Blockley, R. C. (1983) *The Fragmentary Classicising Historians of the Later Roman Empire*, vol. II. Liverpool.

(1981) *The Fragmentary Classicising Historians of the Later Roman Empire*, vol. I. Liverpool.

Blum, P. R. (2010) *Philosophy of Religion in the Renaissance*, Burlington, VT.

(2006) introduction to P. R. Blum *et al.*, *Pico della Mirandola, Über das Seiende und das Eine.* Hamburg: ix–lxxiv.

(2005) 'Die graue Eminenz des Renaissance-Platonismus: Georgios Gemistos Plethon', in Blum and Seitter (2005): 119–30.

(2004) *Philosophieren in der Renaissance*, Stuttgart.

Blum, W. (2005) 'Die Anerkennung Plethons in der Nachwelt', in Blum and Seitter (2005): 45–59.

(1988) *Georgios Gemistos Plethon. Politik, Philosophie und Rhetorik im spätbyzantinischen Reich (1355–1452).* Stuttgart.

Blum, W. and Seitter, W. (eds.) (2005) *Georgios Gemistos Plethon (1355–1452): Reformpolitiker, Philosoph, Verehrer der alten Götter* (Tumult 29). Zurich.

Brisson, L. (2006) 'Pléthon et les *Oracles Chaldaïques*', in Cacouros and Congourdeau (2006): 127–42.

Bryer, A. (2009) 'The Roman Orthodox World (1393–1492)', in J. Shepard (ed.), *The Cambridge History of The Byzantine Empire (c. 500–1492).* Cambridge: 852–80.

Burger, T. (1987) *Max Weber's Theory of Concept Formation: History, Laws, and Ideal Types.* Durham, NC.

Burns, D. (2006) 'The Chaldean Oracles of Zoroaster, Hekate's couch, and Platonic orientalism in Psellos and Plethon', Aries 6.2: 158–79.

Burnyeat, M. (1999) 'Utopia and fantasy: the practicability of Plato's ideally just city', in G. Fine (ed.), Plato, vol II: Ethics, Politics, Religion and the Soul. Oxford: 297–308.

Cacouros, M. and Congourdeau, M.-H. (eds.) (2006) Philosophie et sciences à Byzance de 1204 à 1453: les textes, les doctrines et leur transmission, Leuven.

Cañellas, N. (2002) 'Gregorio Akíndinos', TBT, vol. II: 189–256.

Cholij, R. (2002) Theodore the Stoudite: the Ordering of Holiness. Oxford.

Chronis, N. (1987) Ἡ κριτικὴ τοῦ Πλήθωνος ἐπὶ τῆς διδασκαλίας τοῦ Ἀριστοτέλη γιὰ τὰ καθόλου', in Bargeliotes and Moutsopoulos (1987): 57–64.

Chrysostomos Koutloumousianos (2008) Ὁ Θεὸς τῶν Μυστηρίων. Ἡ Θεολογία τῶν Κελτῶν στὸ Φῶς τῆς Ἑλληνικῆς Ἀνατολῆς. Mount Athos.

Cleary, J. J. (ed.) (1997) The Perennial Tradition of Neoplatonism. Leuven.

Codoñer, J. S. (2005) 'Die plethonische "Religion"', in Blum and Seitter (2005): 91–100.

Cohen, R. A. (1994) Elevations: the Height of the Good in Rosenzweig and Lévinas. Chicago.

Collins, P. (2001) Trinitarian Theology: West and East. Karl Barth, the Cappadocian Fathers, and John Zizioulas. Oxford.

Congourdeau, M.-H. (1999) 'Byzance et la fin du monde. Courants de pensée apocalyptiques sous les Paléologues', in B. Lellouch and S. Yerasimos (eds.), Les traditions apocalyptiques au tournant de la chute de Constantinople (Varia Turcica 33). Paris: 55–97.

Constantelos, D. J. (1998) 'A conflict between ancient Greek philosophy and Christian Orthodoxy in the Late Greek Middle Ages', in D. J. Constantelos, Christian Hellenism: Essays and Studies in Continuity and Change. New York: 67–73.

Cooper, A. G. (2005) The Body in St Maximus the Confessor: Holy Flesh, Wholly Deified. Oxford.

Constas, N. (2002) 'Mark Eugenikos', TBT, vol. II: 411–75.

Copleston, F. (1999) A History of Philosophy: Hobbes to Hume. London.

Couloubaritsis, L. (2006) 'Platonismes et aristotélismes à Byzance dans l'empire de Nicée et sous les Paléologues', in Cacouros and Congourdeau (2006): 143–56.

(2005) 'Prolegomena zur Kosmologie Plethons', in Blum and Seitter (2005): 69–76 (= Cahiers du groupe de recherche sur la philosophie et le langage. Grenoble 1991: 135–43).

(1997) 'La métaphysique de Pléthon: ontologie, théologie et pratique du mythe', in Images de Platon et lectures de ses œuvres: les interprétations de Platon à travers les siècles, ed. A. Neschke-Hentschke. Louvain and Paris: 117–52.

433

(1986) 'Physis et techne dans le *De differentiis* de Plethon', in *L'homme et son univers au Moyen Age I*. Louvain-la-Neuve: 333–40 (German trans. 'Physis und techne in den *Unterschieden* von Plethon', in Blum and Seitter (2005): 63–8).

Cumont, F. (1911) *The Oriental Religions in Roman Paganism*. Chicago.

Dabrowska, M. (1991) 'Hellenism at the court of Despots of Mistra in the first half of the fifteenth century', in Salamon (1991): 157–67.

Dagron, G. (1996) *Empereur et prêtre. Etude sur le 'césaropapisme' byzantin*. Paris.

Dain, A. (1942) 'Sur un manuscrit grec de Salamanque', *Emerita* 10: 1–12.

Darko, E. (1930) 'Wirkungen des Platonismus im griechischen Mittelalter', *ByzZ* 30: 13–18.

Dedes, D. (1985) 'Die wichtigsten Gründe der Apostasie des Georgios Gemistos (Plethon)', *Φιλοσοφία* 15/16: 352–75.

De la Broquière, B. (1988) *The Voyage d'Outremer by Bertrandon*, ed. and trans. G. R. Kline. New York.

Demetracopoulos, J. (2008) 'Pope Benedict XVI's use of the Byzantine Emperor Manuel II Palaiologos' *Dialogue with a Muslim Muterizes*: the scholarly background', *Archiv für mittelalterliche Philosophie und Kultur* 15: 264–303.

(2007) 'Georgios Scholarios – Gennadios II's *Florilegium Thomisticum II (De fato)* and its anti-Plethonic Tenor', *RecTh* 74.2: 301–76.

(2006) 'Georgios Gemistos-Plethon's dependence on Thomas Aquinas' *Summa contra gentiles* and *Summa theologiae*', *Archiv für mittelalterliche Philosophie und Kultur* 12: 276–341.

(2004) *Πλήθων καὶ Θωμᾶς Ἀκυινάτης. Ἀπό τὴν ἱστορία τοῦ Βυζαντινοῦ θωμισμοῦ*. Athens.

Dennis, G. T. (1960) *The Reign of Manuel II Palaeologus in Thessalonica, 1382–1387*. Rome.

Derrett, J. D. M. (1965) 'Gemistos Plethon, the Essenes and More's Utopia', *H&R* 27: 579–603.

Derrida, J. (1978) *Writing and Difference*, trans. A. Bass. Chicago.

Dillon, J. M. (1997) 'Iamblichus' *noera theoria* of Aristotle's *Categories*', in H. J. Blumenthal and J. F. Finamore (eds.), *Iamblichus: the Philosopher*. Iowa City: 65–77.

(2002) 'Die Vita Pythagorica – ein Evangelium?', in M. Von Albrecht, J. Dillon *et al.* (eds.), *Jamblich Peri tou Pythagoreiou Biou; Pythagoras: Legende-Lehre – Lebensgestaltung*. Darmstadt: 295–302.

Dörrie, H. (1976) 'Hypostasis. Wirt- und Bedeutungsgeschichte', in H. Dörrie, *Platonica Minora*. Munich: 13–69.

Dörrie, H. and Baltes, M. (1996) *Der Platonismus in der Antike*, vol. IV. Stuttgart and Bad Canstatt.

Ellissen, A. (1860) *Georgius Gemistus Plethon's Denkschriften über die Angelegenheiten des Peloponnes*. Leipzig.

Evangeliou, Chr. (2006) 'Pletho's critique of Aristotelian novelties', in Chr. Evangeliou, *Hellenic Philosophy: Origin and Character*. Aldershot: 153–70.

Faber, R. (1986) 'Pagan und Neo-paganismus. Versuch einer Begriffserklärung', in Faber and Schlesier (1986): 10–25.

Faber, R. and R. Schlesier (eds.) (1986) *Die Restauration der Götter*. Würzburg.

Finley, G. (1877) *A History of Greece: From its Conquest by the Romans to the Present Time, B.C. 146 to A.D. 1864*, vol. IV: *Mediaeval Greece and the Empire of Trebizond, A.D. 1204–1461*, ed. H. F. Tozer. London.

Fleischer, C. H. (2010) 'Ancient wisdom and new sciences: prophecies at the Ottoman court in the fifteenth and early sixteenth centuries', in M. Farhad and S. Bagci (eds.), *Falnama: the Book of Omens*. London: 232–43.

Gardette, Ph. (2007a) *Etudes imagologiques et relations interconfessionnelles en zone byzantino-ottomane*. Istanbul.

(2007b) 'Croyances apocalyptiques au moment de la prise de Constantinople: rencontres entre traditions judéo-byzantines et turques', in Gardette (2007a): 87–107.

(2007c) 'Pour en finir avec Pléthon et son maître juif Elisée', in Gardette (2007a): 147–64.

(2002) *Djalal-od-Din Rumi, Raymond Lulle, Rabbi Abraham Aboulafia ou l'amour du dialogue interconfessionel*. Istanbul.

Garnsey, P. (2009) 'Gemistus Plethon and Platonic political philosophy', in Ph. Rousseau and E. Papoutsakis (eds.), *Transformations of Late Antiquity: Essays for Peter Brown*. Aldershot: 327–40.

(2007) *Thinking about Property: From Antiquity to the Age of Revolution*. Cambridge.

(2005) 'Pythagoras, Plato and communality: a note', *Hermathena* 179: 77–87.

Gass, W. (1844) *Gennadius und Pletho. Aristotelismus und Platonismus in der griechischen Kirche*. Breslau.

Gay, P. (1966) *The Enlightenment: an Interpretation. The Rise of Modern Paganism*. London.

Geanakoplos, D. J. (1962) *Greek Scholars in Venice: Studies in the Dissemination of Greek Learning from Byzantium to Western Europe*. New York.

Gentile, S. (1994) 'Giorgio Gemisto Pletone e la sua influenza sull'umanesimo Fiorentino', in Viti (1994): 813–32.

Georgiades Arnakis, G. (1951) 'Gregory Palamas among the Turks and documents of his captivity as historical sources', *Speculum* 26: 104–18.

Gill, J. (1961) *The Council of Florence*. Cambridge.

Gouillard, J. (1981) *La vie religieuse à Byzance*. London.

(1965) 'L'hérésie dans l'empire byzantine des origines au XIIe siècle', *T&MByz* 1: 299–324 (reprinted in Gouillard 1981: ch. 1).

Grégoire, H. (1929/30) 'Les manuscrits de Julien et le mouvement néopaien de Mistra: Démétrius Rhallis et Gémiste Pléthon', *Byzantion* 5: 730–6.

Guichardan, P. S. (1933) *Le problème de la simplicité divine en Orient et en Occident aux XIVe et XVe siècles: Grégoire Palamas, Duns Scot, Georges Scholarios; étude de théologie comparée.* Lyon.

Guilland, R. (1926) *Essai sur Nicéphore Grégoras: l'homme et l'œuvre.* Paris.

Hanegraaff, W. J. (2009) 'The pagan who came from the East: George Gemistos Plethon and Platonic Orientalism', in W. J. Hanegraaff and J. Pijnenburg (eds.), *Hermes in the Academy: Ten Years' Study of Western Esotericism at the University of Amsterdam.* Amsterdam: 33–50.

(ed.) (2006a) *Dictionary of Gnosis and Western Esotericism.* Leiden.

(2006b) 'Tradition', in Hanegraaff (2006a): 1125–35.

Hankins, J. (1990) *Plato in the Italian Renaissance*, 2 vols. (Columbia Studies in the Classical Tradition 17). Leiden.

Hardt, I. (1812) *Catalogus codicum manuscriptorum Graecorum Bibliothecae Regiae Bavaricae*, vol. v. Munich.

Harris, J. (2006) 'Cardinal Bessarion and the Ideal State', in Konstantinou (2006): 91–7.

(2003) 'The influence of Plethon's idea of fate on the historian Laonikos Chalkokondyles', in Benakis and Baloglou (2003): 211–32.

(2000) 'Being a Byzantine after Byzantium: Hellenic identity in Renaissance Italy', *Kambos: Cambridge Papers in Modern Greek* 8: 25–44.

Hausherr, I. (1978) *The Name of Jesus.* Kalamazoo.

(1927) 'La méthode d'oraison hésychaste', *OCP* 9.2: 100–209.

Hladký. V. (forthcoming) *Plato's Second Coming: an Outline of the Philosophy of George Gemistos Plethon* (PhD dissertation, Prague 2007).

(2009) review of Tambrun (2006a), *Byzantinoslavica* 67: 372–80.

Horujy, S. S. (2004) *Hesychasm: an Annotated Bibliography.* Moscow.

Hunger, H. (1978) *Die hochsprachliche profane Literatur der Byzantiner*, vol. I. Munich.

Idel, M. (1998) *Messianic Mystics.* Yale University Press.

Ierodiakonou, K. (ed.) (2002) *Byzantine Philosophy and its Ancient Sources.* Oxford.

Iorga, N. (1935) *Byzance après Byzance: continuation de l'histoire de la vie byzantine.* Bucarest.

Irmscher, J. (1994) 'Die Epitaphe auf Georgios Gemistos Plethon', *JÖByz* 44: 187–91.

(1985) 'Die christliche und die byzantinische Utopie', *SIFC* 3.2: 250–66.

Israel, J. (2006) *Enlightenment Contested: Philosophy, Modernity, and the Emancipation of Man 1670–1752.* Oxford.

Jerphagnon, L. (1990) 'Les sous-entendus anti-chrétiens de la *Vita Plotini* ou l'évangile de Plotin selon Porphyre', *MH* 47: 41–52.

Joannou, P. (1956) *Christliche Metaphysik in Byzanz*, vol. I: *Die Illuminationslehre des Michael Psellos und John Italos.* Ettal.

Jonas, H. (1966) *The Phenomenon of Life: Toward a Philosophical Biology.* New York.

Joyal, M. (ed.) (1997) *Studies in Plato and the Platonic Tradition: Essays presented to John Whittaker.* Aldershot and Hampshire.

Jugie, M. (1912) 'Barlaam de Seminaria', *DHGE* 6, cols. 817–34.

Kaldellis, A. (forthcoming) 'Byzantine philosophy inside and out: orthodoxy and dissidence in counterpoint', in K. Ierodiakonou (ed.), *The Many Faces of Byzantine Philosophy.* Athens.

(2007a) *Hellenism in Byzantium: the Transformations of Greek Identity and the Reception of the Classical Tradition.* Cambridge.

(2007b) 'A Byzantine argument for the equivalence of all religions: Michael Attaleiates on ancient and modern Romans', *IJCT* 14: 1–22.

(2005) 'Republican theory and political dissidence in Ioannes Lydos', *BMGS* 29: 1–16.

(2004) *Procopius of Caesarea: Tyranny, History, and Philosophy at the End of Antiquity.* Philadelphia.

(2003) 'The religion of Ioannes Lydos', *Phoenix* 57.3/4: 300–16.

(1999a) *The Argument of Psellos'* Chronographia. Leiden and Boston.

(1999b) 'The historical and religious views of Agathias: a reinterpretation', *Byzantion* 69: 206–52.

Karamanolis, G. (2002) 'Plethon and Scholarios on Aristotle', in Ierodiakonou (2002): 253–82.

Karlin-Hayter, P. (1965), 'Arethas, Choirosphactes and the Saracen Vizir', in *Byzantion* 35: 455–81 (reprinted in *Studies in Byzantine Political History*, London 1981, ch. IX).

Keller, A. (1957) 'Marsiglio Ficino and Gemistos Plethon on fate and free will', *Journal of the Warburg and Courtauld Institutes* 20/3–4: 363–70.

Kenny, A. (1989) 'Review of Woodhouse, *George Gemistos Plethon. The Last of the Hellenes'*, *The EHR* 104: 727.

Kern, C. (1947) 'La théologie de Grégoire Palamas', *Irénikon* 20: 6–33, 164–93.

Kidwell, C. (1989) *Marullus: Soldier Poet of the Renaissance.* London.

Klein-Franke, F. (1972) 'Die Geschichte des frühen Islam in einer Schrift des Georgios Gemistos Pletho', *ByzZ* 65: 1–8.

Knös, B. (1950) 'Gémiste Pléthon et son souvenir', *Bulletin de l'Association Guillaume Budé. Supplément Lettres d'Humanité* 9: 97–185.

Kolditz, S. and Müller, R. S. (eds.) (2005) *Geschehenes und Geschriebenes: Studien zu Ehren von Günther S. Henrich und Klaus-Peter Matschke.* Leipzig.

Kolias, G. T. (1939) *Léon Choerosphactès, magistre, proconsul et patrice: biographie, correspondance.* Athens.

Konstantinou, E. (ed.) (2006) *Der Beitrag der byzantinischen Gelehrten zur abendländischen Renaissance des 14. und 15. Jahrhunderts.* Frankfurt.

Krausmüller, D. (2006) 'The rise of Hesychasm', in *CHC*: 101–26.

Kristeller, P. O. (1972) 'Byzantine and Western Platonism in the fifteenth century', in P. O. Kristeller, *Renaissance Concepts of Man.* New York: 86–109.

Kuhlmann, J. (1968) *Die Taten des einfachen Gottes.* Würzburg.

Lagarde, B. (1979) Review of 'Michel Psellos, Περὶ τῶν ἰδεῶν ἃς ὁ Πλάτων λέγει. Introduction, ed. et traduction en grec moderne par Linos G. Benakis', *Byzantion* 49: 566–71.

(1976) 'Georges Gémiste Pléthon, *Des Différences entre Platon et Aristote*, edition, traduction et commentaire', 2 vols. unpublished PhD dissertation, Université Paris IV, Sorbonne.

Laiou, A. (2007) *The Byzantine Economy*. Cambridge.

Lauritzen, F. (2006/7) 'Psellos and the Nazireans', *REByz* 64/65: 359–64.

Lemerle, P. (1971) *Le premier humanisme byzantin: notes et remarques sur enseignement et culture à Byzance des origines au Xe siècle*. Paris.

Lévinas, E. (1994) *In the Time of the Nations*, trans. M. B. Smith. London.

(1986) 'The Trace of the Other', in M. C. Taylor (ed.), *Deconstruction in Context*. Chicago.

Lilla, R. C. (1997) 'Neoplatonic hypostases and Christian Trinity', in Joyal (1997): 127–89.

Livanos, Chr. (2010) 'Monotheists, dualists and pagans', in P. Stephenson (ed.), *The Byzantine World*. London and New York: 103–13.

(2006) *Greek Tradition and Latin Influence in the Work of George Scholarios: Alone against All of Europe*. Piscaway, NJ.

(2003) 'The conflict between Scholarios and Plethon: religion and communal identity in early modern Greece', in G. Nagy and A. Stavrakopoulou (eds.), *Modern Greek Literature: Critical Essays*. New York: 24–41.

Lossky, V. (1976) *The Mystical Theology of the Eastern Church*. London.

Louth, A. (2002) *St. John Damascene: Tradition and Originality in Byzantine Theology*. Oxford.

(1996) *Maximus the Confessor*. Oxford.

Magdalino, P. (1997) 'In search of the Byzantine courtier: Leo Choirosphaktes and Constantine Manasses', in H. Maguire (ed.), *Byzantine Court Culture from 829 to 1204*. Washington, DC: 141–65.

Maillard, J.-F. (2008) 'Réflexions sur une légende: Pléthon, Cosme de Médicis et l'hermétisme ficinien', in J. Dupèbe (ed.), *Esculape et Dionysos: mélanges en l'honneur de Jean Céard*. Paris: 67–85.

Maltese, E. V. (1990) 'Pletone nell' Utopia di Thomas More?', *Res Publica Litterarum* 13: 147–54.

Maltezou, Chr. (2006) 'Still more on the political views of Bessarion', in Konstantinou (2006): 99–105.

Mamone, K. (1990) Ὀρθόδοξη ἀντιρρητικὴ κατὰ Πλήθωνος', in Πρακτικὰ τοῦ Συμποσίου Ἀπὸ τὴν φωτεινὴ κληρονομιὰ τοῦ Μυστρᾶ στὴν Τουρκοκρατία (Πελοποννησιακά, Παράρτημα 16). Athens: 209–24.

Manfredini, M. (1972) 'Giorgio Gemisto Pletone e la tradizione manoscritta di Plutarco', *ASNP* 3.2.2: 569–81.

Mannheim, K. (1997) *Ideology and Utopia*, preface by Louis Wirth; with a new introduction by Bryan S. Turner. London.

Marion, J.-L. (1991) *Dieu sans l'être*. Paris.

Masai, F. (1976) 'Renaissance platonicienne et controverses trinitaires à Byzance au XVe siècle', in *XVIe Colloque International de Tours. Platon et Aristote à la Renaissance*: 25–43.

—— (1965) 'La notion de Renaissance, equivoques et malentendus', *Revue belge d'archéologie et d'histoire de l'art* 34: 137–66.

—— (1958) 'La restauration du paganisme par Georges Gemiste Pléthon', in *Il mondo antico nel rinascimento*. Florence: 55–63.

—— (1957/8) 'Platonisme et christianisme au XVe siècle', *Revue de l'Université de Bruxelles* 10: 392–412.

—— (1956) *Pléthon et le Platonisme de Mistra*. Paris.

—— (1953) 'Le problème des influences byzantins sur le platonisme italien de la Renaissance', *Bulletin de l'Association Guillaume Budé*, serie 3.4, *Supplément Lettres d'Humanité* 12: 82–90.

Matschke, K.-P. and Tinnefeld, F. (2001) *Die Gesellschaft im späten Byzanz: Gruppen, Strukturen und Lebensformen*. Cologne.

Matula, J. (2009) 'Science and religion in Byzantine thought: skepsis and paganism', in G. Borbély and G. Geréby (eds.), *Religio Academici: Essays on Scepticism, Religion, and the Pursuit of Knowledge*. Budapest: 54–64.

—— (2008) 'Od jednoty k mnohosti v diele Georgia Gemistha Plethona', in M. Jaburek (ed.), *Jednota a Mnohost*. (Summary in English.) Olomouc: 99–109.

—— (2003) 'Georgios Gemistos Pletho and the idea of universal harmony', in Benakis and Baloglou (2003): 161–70.

Mayhew, R. (2006) 'Plato, *Laws* X, 905E3: *entelechos* or *endelechos*', *CQ* 56.1: 312–17.

Mazzucchi, C. M. (2006) 'Damascio, Autore del Corpus Dionysiacum, e il dialogo περὶ πολιτικῆς ἐπιστήμης, *Aevum: Rassegna di scienze storiche linguistiche e filologiche* 80.2: 299–334.

Medvedev, I. P. (1997) Византийский гуманизм XIV-XV вв. Saint Petersburg.

—— (1993) 'The so-called ΘΕΑΤΡΑ as a form of communication of the Byzantine Intellectuals in the 14th and 15th centuries', in N. G. Moschonas (ed.), Πρακτικὰ τοῦ Β' διεθνοῦς συμποσίου: Ἡ ἐπικοινωνία στὸ Βυζάντιο. Athens: 227–35.

—— (1991) 'Ἡ ὑπόθεση τοῦ ἀποστάτη Ἰουβεναλίου ἀπὸ τὴν ἄποψη τοῦ δικαίου', Βυζαντιναὶ Μελέται 3: 152–73 (Russian version in *The 17th International Byzantine Congress: Major Papers*. Moscow 1986: 31–44).

—— (1985) 'Solar cult in Plethon's philosophy', Βυζαντινά 13: 739–47.

—— (1984) 'Tendances vers une renaissance dans la culture byzantine tardive', Βυζαντιακά 4: 113–36.

—— (1981) 'Neue philosophische Ansätze im späten Byzanz', *JÖByz* 31.1: 529–48.

Mergiale-Falaga, S. (1991) 'Γύρω ἀπὸ τὴν πνευματικὴ ζωὴ στὸ Δεσποτᾶτο τοῦ Μυστρᾶ κατὰ τὸν 14° αἰῶνα', Βυζαντιναὶ Μελέται 3: 241–60.

Meyendorff, J. (1982) *The Byzantine Legacy in the Orthodox Church*. New York.

(1974) *Byzantine Hesychasm: Historical, Theological and Social Problems.* London.

(1971) 'Society and culture in the fourteenth century: religious problems', *XIV Congrès international des études byzantines, Rapports 1.* Moscow: 51–65 (reprinted in Meyendorff 1974: ch. VIII).

(1962) 'Palamismus und Humanismus', *XIIe Congrès international des études byzantines* vol. I, ed. Comité Yugoslave des études byzantines. Belgrade: 329–30.

(1959) *Introduction à l'étude de Gregoire Palamas.* Paris.

(1955) 'Un mauvais théologien de l'unité: Barlaam le Calabrais', in *L'église et les églises. Études et travaux offerts à Dom Lambert Baudouin*, vol. II: 47–64 (reprinted in Meyendorff 1974: ch. V).

(1953) 'Les débuts de la controverse hésychaste', *Byzantion* 23: 87–120 (reprinted in Meyendorff 1974: ch. I).

Miller, R. A. (2007) 'Religious versus ethnic identity in fourteenth-century Bithynia: Gregory Palamas and the case of the Chionai', in B. Tezcan and K. K. Barbir (eds.), *Identity and Identity Formation in the Ottoman World: a Volume of Essays in Honour of Norman Itzkowitz.* Madison, WI: 27–42.

Mohler, L. (1923) *Kardinal Bessarion als Theologe, Humanist und Staatsmann: Funde und Forschungen*, vol. I: *Darstellung.* Paderborn.

Monfasani, J. (2005) 'Pletho's date of death and the burning of his *Laws*', *ByzZ* 98.2: 459–63.

(2002) 'Marsilio Ficino and the Plato–Aristotle Controversy', in M. J. B. Allen, V. Rees and M. Davies (eds.), *Marsilio Ficino: His Theology, his Philosophy, his Legacy*, Leiden: 179–202.

(1994) 'Pletone, Bessarione e la processione dello Spirito Santo', in Viti (1994): 833–59.

(1992) 'Platonic paganism in the fifteenth century', in M. A. Di Cesare (ed.), *Reconsidering the Renaissance.* Binghampton, NY: 45–61 (reprinted in *Byzantine Scholars in Renaissance Italy.* Aldershot 1995: ch. X).

(1976) *George of Trebizond: a Biography and a Study of his Rhetoric and Logic.* Leiden.

Morrison, D. R. (2007) 'The utopian character of Plato's Ideal City', in G. R. F. Ferrari (ed.), *The Cambridge Companion to Plato's Republic.* Cambridge: 232–55.

Moschos, D. (1998) Πλατωνισμός ἢ χριστιανισμός; Οἱ φιλοσοφικὲς προϋποθέσεις τοῦ ἀντιησυχασμοῦ τοῦ Νικηφόρου Γρηγορᾶ. Athens.

Mulsow, M. and Stamm, M. (eds.) (2005) *Konstellationsforschung.* Frankfurt.

Murray, G. (1953) *Hellenism and the Modern World.* London.

Nicol, D. (1993) *The Last Centuries of Byzantium, 1261–1453*, 2nd edition. Cambridge.

Necipoğlu, N. (2009) *Byzantium between the Ottomans and the Latins: Politics and Society in the Late Empire.* Cambridge.

Neri, M. (ed.) (2010) *Pletone: trattato delle virtù*. Introduction and text. Milan.

Nietzsche, F. (2005) *The Anti-Christ, Ecce homo, Twilight of the Idols, and Other Writings*, ed. A. Ridley, J. Norman. Cambridge.

(2001) *The Gay Science*, ed. B. Williams, trans. J. Nauckhoff and A. Del Caro. Cambridge.

Nikolaou, Th. (2004a) *Πληθωνικά*. Thessaloniki.

(2004b) 'Αἱ περὶ Πολιτείας καὶ Δικαίου Ἰδέαι τοῦ Γ. Γεμιστοῦ- Πλήθωνος', in Nikolaou (2004a): 90–191 (first published as a monograph, Thessaloniki 1974).

(2004c) 'Ὁ Ζωροάστρης εἰς τὸ φιλοσοφικὸν σύστημα τοῦ Γ. Γεμιστοῦ Πλήθωνος', in Nikolaou (2004a): 19–66.

(1995) *Askese, Mönchtum und Mystik in der Orthodoxen Kirche*. St Ottilien.

(1982) 'Gemistos Plethon und Proklos. Plethon's Neuplatonismus am Beispiel seiner Psychologie', *JÖByz* 32.4: 387–99 (Greek translation in Nikolaou 2004a: 67–82).

Obolensky, D. (2007) 'Late Byzantine culture and the Slavs: a study in acculturation', in J. Shepard (ed.), *The Expansion of Orthodox Europe: Byzantium, the Balkans and Russia*. Aldershot: 473–96.

O'Meara, D. J. (2003) *Platonopolis. Platonic Political Philosophy in Late Antiquity*. Oxford.

Ostrogorsky, G. (1954) *Pour l'histoire de la féodalité byzantine*. Brussels.

Pagani, F. (2009) '*Damnata verba:* censure di Pletone in alcuni codici platonici', *ByzZ* 102.1: 167–202.

(2008) 'Filosofia e teologia in Giorgio Gemisto Pletone: la testimonianza dei codici Platonici', *Rinascimento* 49: 3–45.

(2006) 'Un nuovo testimone della *recensio* pletoniana al testo di Platone: il Marc. Gr. 188 (K)', *Res Publica Litterarum* 29: 5–20.

Paschoud, F. (2006) 'A propos des *Fragments* 8–61 de l'ouvrage historique d'Eunape correspondant aux livres 3 et 4 de l'*Histoire nouvelle* de Zosime', in F. Paschoud, *Eunape, Olympiodore, Zosime: Scripta minora*. Bari: 473–97.

Pearson, J. E. (2006) 'Neopaganism', in Hanegraaff (2006a): 828–33.

Pépin, J. (1986) 'Cosmic Piety', in A. H. Armstrong (ed.) *Classical Mediterranean Spirituality: Egyptian, Greek, Roman*. London: 408–35.

Peritore, N. P. (1977) 'The political thought of Gemistos Plethon: a Renaissance Byzantine reformer', *Polity* 10.2: 168–91.

Picon, A. (2002) *Les Saint-Simoniens, raison, imaginaire et utopie*. Paris.

Pocock, J. G. A. (1975) *The Machiavellian Moment: Florentine Political Thought and the Atlantic Republican Tradition*. Princeton and London.

Podskalsky, G. (2003) *Von Photios zu Bessarion: der Vorrang humanistisch geprägter Theologie in Byzanz und deren bleibende Bedeutung*. Wiesbaden.

(1977) *Theologie und Philosophie in Byzanz*. Munich.

(1976) 'Nikolaos von Methone und die Proklosrenaissance in Byzanz', in *OCP* 42: 509–23.

(1975) 'Der Fall Konstantinopels in der Sicht der Reichseschatologie und der Klagelieder. Vorahnungen und Reaktionen', *AKG* 57: 71–86.

Popper, K. (1996) 'Epistemology and industrialization', in M. A. Notturno (ed.) *The Myth of the Framework: In Defence of Science and Rationality*. London.

(1945) *The Open Society and its Enemies*, vol. 1. London.

Raszewsky, J. (forthcoming) *Jerzy Gemistos Plethon i jego helleńskie państwo*, PhD dissertation. University of Warsaw.

Renard, J. (ed.)(2004) *Knowledge of God in Classical Sufism: Foundations of Islamic Mystical Theology*. New Jersey.

Ricci, C. (1924) *Il Tempio Malatestiano*. Rome.

Rigo, A. (1992) 'L'anno 7000, la fine del mondo e l'Impero cristiano. Nota su alcuni passi di Giuseppe Briennio, Simeone de Tessalonica et Gennadio Scolario', in G. Ruggieri (ed.), *La cattura della fine. Variazioni dell' escatologia in regime di Cristianità*. Genova: 162–83.

Rist, J. M. (1964) 'Mysticism and transcendence in later Neoplatonism', *Hermes* 92: 213–25.

Rochow, I. (1991) 'Der Vorwurf des Heidentums als Mittel der innenpolitischen Polemik in Byzanz', in Salamon (1991): 133–56.

Ronchey, S. (2006) *L'enigma di Piero. L'ultimo bizantino e la crociata fantasma nella rivelazione di un grande quadro*. Milan.

(2003) 'Giorgio Gemisto Pletone e i Malatesta', in *Sul Ritorno di Pletone. Un filosofo a Rimini*. Rimini: 11–24.

Russell, N. (2006) 'Prochoros Cydones and the fourteenth-century understanding of Orthodoxy', in A. Louth and A. Casiday (eds.), *Byzantine Orthodoxies: Papers from the Thirty-sixth Spring Symposium of Byzantine Studies*. Aldershot: 75–91.

Ryder, J. R. (2010) *The Career and Writings of Demetrius Kydones: a Study of Fourteenth-century Byzantine Politics, Religion and Society*. Leiden and Boston.

Sacks, K. S. (1986) 'The meaning of Eunapius' *History*', in *History and Theory* 25.1: 52–67.

Salamon, M. (ed.) (1991) *Paganism in the Later Roman Empire and in Byzantium*. Cracow.

Saffrey, H. D. (1996) 'Florence, 1492: the reappearance of Plotinus', *Renaissance Quarterly* 49.3: 488–508.

(1984) 'Quelques aspects de la spiritualité des philosophes néoplatoniciens de Jamblique à Proclus et Damascius', *Revue des sciences philosophiques et idéologiques* 68: 169–82.

(1981) 'Les Néoplatoniciens et les oracles chaldaïques', *Revue des études Augustiniennes* 27: 209–25.

Schultze, F. (1874) *Georgios Gemistos Plethon und seine reformatorischen Bestrebungen*. Jena 1874 (reprinted in Subsidia Byzantina 9, Leipzig 1975).

Schulz, P. (1999) 'Georgios Gemistos Plethon, Georgios Trapezuntios, Kardinal Bessarion. Die Kontroverse zwischen Platonikern und Aristotelikern im

15. Jahrhundert', in P. R. Blum (ed.), *Philosophen der Renaissance. Eine Einführung*. Darmstadt: 22–32.

Sedley, D. (1999) 'The ideal of godlikeness', in G. Fine (ed.), *Plato 2: Ethics, Politics, Religion, and the Soul*. Oxford: 309–28.

Seitter, W. (2005) 'Gibt es ein Bild von Plethon?', in Blum and Seitter (2005): 131–42.

Ševčenko, I. (1984) 'The Palaeologan Renaissance', in W. Treadgold (ed.), *Renaissances before the Renaissance, Cultural Revivals of Late Antiquity and the Middle Ages*. Stanford: 144–71.

(1981) *Society and Intellectual Life in Late Byzantium*. London.

(1962) 'A postscript on Nicolas Cabasilas "Anti-Zealot" Discourse', *DOP* 16: 403–8.

(1957) 'Nicolas Cabasilas' "Anti-Zealot" Discourse: a reinterpretation', *DOP* 11: 79–171 (reprinted in Ševčenko 1981, ch. IV).

Shawcross, T. (2008) '"Do thou nothing without counsel": political assemblies and the ideal of good government in the thought of Theodore Palaeologus and Theodore Metochites', *Al-Masaq* 20.1: 89–118.

Sherrard, Ph. (1974) 'The symbolical career of Georgios Gemistos Plethon', in *Studies in Comparative Religion* 8.2: 112–27 (Greek version: Ἡ συμβολικὴ σταδιοδρομία τοῦ Γεωργίου Γεμιστοῦ Πλήθωνος', *Δευκαλίων* 14 (1974): 129–45.

Siniossoglou, N. (forthcoming) 'The difference between Platonic intellectual mysticism and Christian mysticism: a typology of mystical discourse', in C. Macris (ed.), *La mystique païenne: entre theôria et theourgia*, Paris.

(2012) 'Sect and utopia in shifting empires: Plethon, Elissaeus, Bedreddin', *BMGS* 36.2.

(2010a) 'From philosophic monotheism to imperial henotheism: esoteric and popular religion in late antique Platonism', in S. Mitchell and P. van Nuffelen (eds.), *Monotheism between Pagans and Christians in Late Antiquity*. Leuven: 127–48.

(2010b) 'Plato Christianus: the colonisation of Plato and identity formation in Late Antiquity', in P. Hummel (ed.), *Pseudologie: études sur la fausseté dans la langue et dans la pensée*, Paris: 145–76.

(2008a) *Plato and Theodoret: the Christian Appropriation of Platonic Philosophy and the Hellenic Intellectual Resistance*. Cambridge.

(ed.) (2008b) Θεόφιλος Καΐρης, '*Γνωστική*' – '*Στοιχεῖα Φιλοσοφίας*', text, introduction and appendices. Athens and Andros.

Sinkewicz, R. E. (2002) 'Gregory Palamas', *TBT* vol. II: 131–88.

(1982) 'The doctrine of the knowledge of God in the early writings of Barlaam the Calabrian', *Mediaeval Studies* 44: 196–242.

(1980) 'A new interpretation for the first episode in the controversy between Barlaam the Calabrian and Gregory Palamas', *JThS* 31: 489–500.

Skaltsas, G. (1998) *La dynamique de la transformation éschatologique chez Grégoire de Nysse: étude sur les rapports de la pensée patristique à la philosophie grecque ancienne*, PhD dissertation. Paris.

Skinner, Q. (1978) *The Foundations of Modern Political Thought*, vol. I. Cambridge.

Smarnakis, Y. (forthcoming) Ἀναγέννηση καὶ Βυζάντιο. Τὸ παράδειγμα τοῦ Πλήθωνα. Athens (PhD dissertation, University of Athens 2005).

(2007) 'A contribution to the archaeology of modern utopian thought: history and utopia in Plethon's œuvre', *Historein* 7: 103–13.

(2005) 'Ἀρχαία ἱστορία καὶ ἑρμηνευτικὲς στρατηγικὲς στὸν Πλήθωνα', in T. Kiousopoulou (ed.), Ἡ ἅλωση τῆς Κωνσταντινούπολης καὶ ἡ μετάβαση ἀπὸ τοὺς μεσαιωνικοὺς στοὺς νεώτερους χρόνους. Heracleion: 173–81.

Spentzas, S. (1996) Γεμιστὸς Πλήθων, ὁ φιλόσοφος τοῦ Μιστρᾶ. Οἱ οἰκονομικές, κοινωνικὲς καὶ δημοσιονομικὲς του ἀπόψεις, 4th edition with a preface by C. M. Woodhouse. Athens.

Spiteris, Y. and Conticello, C. G. (2002) 'Nicola Cabasilas Chamaetos', *TBT* vol. II: 315–410.

Starnes, C. (1990) *The New Republic: a Commentary on Book I of More's Utopia Showing its Relation to Plato's Republic*. Ontario.

Stausberg, M. (1998) *Faszination Zarathustra*, vol. I. Berlin.

Steel, C. (1997) 'Breathing thought: Proclus on the innate knowledge of the soul', in Cleary (1997): 293–309.

Tambrun, B. (2010) 'Pourquoi Cosme de Médicis a fait traduire Platon', in M. A. Amir-Moezzi and J.-D. Dubois (eds.), *Pensée grecque et sagesse orientale: hommage à Michel Tardieu*. Turnhout: 635–49.

(2006a) *Pléthon. Le retour de Platon*. Paris.

(2006b) 'Plethon, Georgios Gemistos', in Hanegraaff (2006a): 961–3.

(2003) 'L'être, l'un et la pensée politique de Pléthon', in Benakis and Baloglou (2003): 67–93.

(1992) 'Allusions antipalamites dans le *Commentaire* de Pléthon sur les *Oracles chaldaïques*', *RE Aug* 38: 168–79.

Tardieu, M. (1987) 'Pléthon lecteur des Oracles', *Mêtis* 2: 141–64.

(1980) 'Pletho arabicus. Identification et contenu du manuscrit arabe d'Istanbul, Topkapi Serai, Ahmet III 1896', *JA* 268: 35–57.

Täschner, F. (1929) 'Georgios Gemistos Plethon. Ein Beitrag zur Frage der Übertragung von islamischem Geistesgut nach dem Abendlande', *Der Islam* 18: 236–43.

Tavardon, P. (1977) 'Le conflit de Georges Gémiste Pléthon et de Georges Scholarios au sujet de l'expression *tò on légetai pollachos*', *Byzantion* 47: 268–78.

Taylor, J. W. (1921) *Georgios Gemistos Pletho's criticism of Plato and Aristotle*. Menasha.

Taylor, T. (2004 [1812]) *A Dissertation on the Philosophy of Aristotle*. Frome.

Tinnefeld, F. (2002) 'Georgios Gennadios Scholarios', *TBT* vol. II: 477–541.

(1981) Introduction to *Demetrios Kydones: Briefe I.1*. Stuttgart: 4–74.

Tirosh-Samuelson, H. (2006) 'Philosophy and Kabbalah: 1200–1600', in D. H. Frank and O. Leaman (eds.), *The Cambridge Companion to Medieval Jewish Philosophy*. Cambridge: 218–57.

Todt, K. P. (2006) 'In Calumniatorem Platonis: Kardinal Johannes Bessarion (ca. 1403–1472) als Vermittler und Verteidiger der Philosophie Platons', in Konstantinou (2006): 149–68.

Toland, J. (1997) Christianity Not Mysterious, text, associated works and critical essays, ed. P. McGuinness, A. Harrison and R. Kearney. Dublin.

Tourtoglou, M. A. (1990) 'Ποινικὲς ἀντιλήψεις τοῦ Γ. Γ. Πλήθωνος στοὺς Νόμους', Πρακτικὰ τοῦ Συμποσίου Ἀπὸ τὴν φωτεινὴ κληρονομιὰ τοῦ Μυστρᾶ στὴ Τουρκοκρατία (Πελοποννησιακά, Παράρτημα 16): 45–53.

Toynbee, A. (1981) The Greeks and their Heritages. Oxford.

Tozer, H. F. (1886) 'A Byzantine reformer', JHS 7: 353–80.

Tryphonopoulos, D. (1992) The Celestial Tradition: a Study of Ezra Pound's The Cantos. Waterloo, Ontario.

Tsirpanlis, C. N. (1993) 'Byzantine humanism and Hesychasm in the thirteenth and fourteenth centuries: synthesis or antithesis, reformation or revolution?', The Patristic and Byzantine Review 12: 13–24.

Van den Berg, R. M. (2001) Proclus' Hymns: Essays, Translations, Commentary. Leiden.

Van Dieten, J.-L. (1979) 'Politische Ideologie und Niedergang im Byzanz der Palaiologen', Zeitschrift für Historische Forschung 6: 1–35.

Van Dijk, T. A. (2008) Discourse and Context: a Sociocognitive Approach. Cambridge.

Vasiliev, A. A. (1932) 'Pero Tafur, a Spanish traveller of the fifteenth century and his visit to Constantinople, Trebizond and Italy', Byzantion 7: 75–122.

Versnel, H. S. (1987) 'What did ancient man see when he saw a god? Some reflections on Greco-Roman epiphany', in D. van der Plas (ed.), Effigies Dei: Essays on the History of Religions. Leiden: 42–55.

Viti, P. (ed.) (1994) Firenze e il Concilio del 1439 (Biblioteca Storica Toscana 29.2). Florence.

Vryonis, S. (1991) 'Byzantine cultural self-consciousness in the fifteenth century', in S. Curcic and D. Mouriki (eds.), The Twilight of Byzantium: Aspects of Cultural and Religious History in the Late Byzantine Empire. Princeton, NJ: 5–14.

Walker, D. P. (2000) Spiritual and Demonic Magic from Ficino to Campanella. Stroud.

Ware, K. (1995) 'Act out of Stillness': the Influence of Fourteenth-century Hesychasm on Byzantine and Slav Civilization. Toronto.

Webb, R. (1989) 'The Nomoi of Gemistos Plethon in the light of Plato's Laws', Journal of the Warburg and Courtauld Institutes 52: 214–19.

Weber, M. (1949) The Methodology of the Social Sciences, ed. and trans. by E. A. Shils and H. A. Finch. Illinois.

Westerink, L. G. (1990) 'Das Rätsel des untergründigen Neuplatonismus', in D. Harlfinger (ed.), ΦΙΛΟΦΡΟΝΗΜΑ: Festschrift für Martin Sicherl zum 75. Geburtstag, von Textkritik bis Humanismusforschung. Paderborn: 105–23.

Wilson, N. G. (1983) Scholars of Byzantium. Rev. edition 1996. London.

Wind, E. (1968) *Pagan Mysteries in the Renaissance*. New York.

Wippel, J. F. (2000) *The Metaphysical Thought of Thomas Aquinas*. Washington.

Woodhouse, C. M. (1986) *Georgios Gemistos Plethon. The Last of the Hellenes*. Oxford.

Wokart, N. (1986) 'Hellenische Theologie. Die Religionsreform des Georgios Gemistos Plethon', in Faber and Schlesier (1986): 183–97.

Yannaras, Chr. (1992), Ὀρθοδοξία καὶ Δύση στὴ Νεώτερη Ἑλλάδα. Athens (*Orthodoxy and the West: Hellenic Self-identity in the Modern Age*, Eng. trans. P. Chamberas and N. Russell. Brookline, MA 2006).

Yiannakopoulos T. D. (1990) 'Δημοσιονομικαὶ θεωρίαι Πλήθωνος', in Πρακτικὰ τοῦ Συμποσίου Ἀπὸ τὴν φωτεινὴ κληρονομιὰ τοῦ Μυστρᾶ στὴ Τουρκοκρατία (Πελοποννησιακά, Παράρτημα 16): 273–359.

Zachariadou, E. A. (2006) 'Mount Athos and the Ottomans c. 1350–1550', in *CHC*: 154–68.

Zagorin, P. (1990) *Ways of Lying: Dissimulation, Persecution and Conformity in Early Modern Europe*. Cambridge, MA.

Zakythinos, D. A. (1975) *Le Despotat grec de Morée II*, ed., rev. and expanded by Chryssa Maltézou. London.

(1952) 'Mouvement intellectuel dans le Despotat de Morée', *L'hellénisme contemporain* 2.4–5: 339–66.

Zervos, Chr. (1973) *Un philosophe néoplatonicien du XIe siècle: Michel Psellos, sa vie, son oeuvre, ses luttes philosophiques, son influence*. Paris.

Zeses, Th. (1988) Γεννάδιος Β' Σχολάριος. Βίος, συγγράμματα, διδασκαλία, 2nd edition. Athens.

Zintzen, C. (1983) 'Bemerkungen zum Aufstiegsweg der Seele in Jamblichs *De mysteriis*', in H. D. Blume and F. Mann (eds.), *Platonismus und Christentum, Festschrift für Heinrich Dörrie* (*JAChr*. Ergänzungsband 10). Münster: 312–28.

Zizioulas, J. (2006) *Communion and Otherness: Further Studies in Personhood and the Church*. London.

(1985) *Being as Communion: Studies in Personhood and the Church*. London.

Zgoll, C. (2005) 'Geschichtsdeutung und Herrscherbild in Zeiten des Niedergangs. Demetrios Kydones über die Not des byzantinischen Reiches und Manuel II. Palaiologos', in Kolditz and Müller (2005): 191–221.

(2007) *Heiligkeit, Ehre, Macht: Ein Modell für den Wandel der Herrschaftskonzeption im Spätmittelalter am Beispiel der byzantinischen Kydonesbriefe*. Cologne.

INDEX

447

67031288R00263

Made in the USA
Middletown, DE
17 March 2018